EIGHTH EDITION

STORY
AND
STRUCTURE

EIGHTH EDITION

STORY
AND
STRUCTURE

LAURENCE PERRINE

THOMAS R. ARP
Southern Methodist University

HARCOURT BRACE JOVANOVICH COLLEGE PUBLISHERS

Fort Worth Philadelphia San Diego New York Orlando Austin San Antonio
Toronto Montreal London Sydney Tokyo

Publisher: Ted Buchholz
Acquisitions Editor: Stephen T. Jordan
Developmental Editor: Helen Triller
Senior Project Editor: Steve Welch
Senior Production Manager: Annette Dudley Wiggins
Book Designer: Carol Kincaid
Permissions Editor: Eleanor Garner

Address for Editorial Correspondence: Harcourt Brace Jovanovich College Publishers, 301 Commerce Street, Suite 3700, Fort Worth, TX 76102.

Address for Orders: Harcourt Brace Jovanovich, Inc., 6277 Sea Harbor Drive, Orlando, FL 32887. 1-800-782-4479, or 1-800-433-0001 (in Florida).

Copyrights and Acknowledgements appear on pages 557–559, which constitute a continuation of the copyright page.

Printed in the United States of America
Library of Congress Catalog Card Number: 92-71194
ISBN: 0-15-583792-3
2 3 4 5 6 7 8 9 0 1   016   9 8 7 6 5 4 3 2 1

Preface

Story and Structure is designed for the college student who is beginning a serious study of fiction. Our initial assumption is that some stories repay more richly than others the time and effort expended in reading them, and our objective is to help the student identify, understand, enjoy, and prefer such stories. To this end we examine the major elements of fiction and suggest some criteria for judgment.

A short story is "a short fiction." Attempts to define it more narrowly prove unsuccessful, for exceptions always exist that escape the definer's net. No such attempt is made here. Our interest is in the art of fiction, in understanding and enjoying and making judgments about it. Though short stories (and one short novel) are used for illustration, the elements discussed are elements to be found in all fiction.

The eighth edition of *Story and Structure* contains forty-six stories, a slight increase over the seventh edition. Fourteen stories are new to this edition. Seventeen of the stories are by women. Five stories were written by members of racial or ethnic minorities, three of them occupying key positions in Part One of this book. The range of experiences presented is diverse in terms of geography, time period, and human concerns, so that a reader will share vicariously in many of the joys and sorrows of our time and the recent past.

New to this edition are unobtrusive paragraph numbers (every fifth paragraph) and a section on "Writing about Fiction," both added at the request of readers of the seventh edition.

For assistance and advice in the making and remaking of this book I am indebted to many persons, and I have expressed my gratitude to them by name in earlier editions. Thomas R. Arp, who assisted me in preparing the sixth and seventh editions of *Story and Structure*, has played the major role in selecting the stories for this edition and in revising its text. I warmly welcome Tom to his new role as coauthor.

L. P.

Professional Acknowledgments

The following instructors have offered helpful reactions and suggestions for this eighth edition of *Story and Structure*.

Mary K. Allen
Cameron University

Irene A. Bania
Erie Community College

Craig Barrow
University of Tennessee, Chattanooga

Louise D. Bentley
Union University

Dee Bielecki
North Greenville College

Don Blankenship
West Valley College

Edith C. Blankenship
Central Alabama Community College

Charles Bordogna
Bergen Community College

Gail Bounds
Chesapeake College

Susan McCann Butler
Thomas Nelson Community College

Randall Calhoun
Ball State University

Catherine Calloway
Arkansas State University

Warren J. Carson
University of South Carolina,
Spartanburg

Sophie H. Cashdollar
Dyersburg State Community College

Ruth M. Cimperman
Milwaukee Area Technical College

Betty Cochran
Beaufort County Community College

Elizabeth T. Coffman
Faulkner State Community College

Sue Coody
Weatherford College

Matthew Cooney, Jr.
Salem State College

Ruth L. Couch
Arkansas State University, Beebe

Carol Couthen
Jacksonville State University

Charlotte C. Crittenden
Georgia Southern University

Diane Crotty
University of Wisconsin, Oshkosh

Brenda Crowe
Gadsden State Community College

Elizabeth H. Davis
Southern Arkansas University

Jerome S. Dees
Kansas State University

Charles DeMatteo
Sage Evening College

Marvin Diogenes
University of Arizona

Robert Douglas
University of Alaska, Anchorage

Richard Downing
Pasco-Hernando Community College

Marianne R. B. Duty
John Tyler Community College

Nancy M. Fabisinski
Calhoun Community College

James E. Fitzmaurice
St. Mary's College

Anne Ruffin Folsom
New River Community College

Charles H. Glendinning
Edinboro University of Pennsylvania

Alice Griffin
Lehman College, CUNY

John D. Hain
Tennessee Temple University

Minon A. Hamm
Union College

John K. Hanes
Duquesne University

Ruth M. Harrison
Arkansas Tech University

Patty Ray Hawkins
Tennessee Temple University

Jane N. Heymann
Mitchell Community College

Lynn G. Hildenbrand
Chesapeake College

Robert M. Hogge
Weber State University

Ruby T. Johnson
Wallace State Community College

James L. Jolly, Jr.
Shelton State Community College

Joyce Jolly
Shelton State Community College

Harvey Kassebaum
Cuyahoga Community College

David Kelly
Dyersburg State Community College

Marilyn King
Northeast Alabama State Junior College

Mary Kramer
University of Lowell

Val Larsen
Virginia Polytechnic Institute

William Lawlor
University of Wisconsin, Stevens Point

Glenn Lewis
York College, CUNY

Howard F. Livingston
Pace University

Gary W. Longrie
Milwaukee Area Technical College

Vincent Lopresti
University of Wisconsin, Oshkosh

Edgar J. Lovelady
Grace College

Gerald F. Luboff
County College of Morris

John R. McCarthy
Franklin Pierce College

Mary McCauley
Dyersburg State Community College

Alexander J. Maxwell
Shoreline Community College

Terry Miller
Indian River Community College

Virginia Ramey Mollenkott
William Paterson College of New Jersey

Jan Park Moore
Frank Phillips College

Nancy Moore
University of Wisconsin, Stevens Point

Walter E. Mullen
Mississippi Gulf Coast Community
College

Margaret H. Murphy
Patrick Henry College

David M. Packard
John A. Logan College

Barbara L. Parker
William Paterson College

Daniel D. Peterson
Southern University, Baton Rouge

Ernest R. Pinson
Union University

Ernest M. Rosenthal
Salem State College

Mariann Russell
Sacred Heart University

Charles J. Ryan
University of Lowell, North Campus

Donald N. Schweda
Quincy College

Philip D. Segal
Queensborough Community College,
CUNY

Craig L. Shurtleff
Illinois Central College

Keith Slocum
Montclair State College

LeNita Beetem Smith
Northwestern Oklahoma State
University

Fiona I. Sohns
West Valley College

John P. Steele
Salem State College

Mitchell E. Summerlin
Calhoun Community College

Charles J. Thomas
Bergen Community College

Victor H. Thompson
Thomas Nelson Community College

E. Guy Turcotte
Mount Wachusett Community College

L. M. Vause
Weber State University

Robert Weathersby
Dalton College

John P. Weber
Cypress College

Judith A. Weise
SUNY, Potsdam

Glenn E. Whitesides
Newberry College

David W. Wickham
Mountain View College

CONTENTS

Preface

PART 1   The Elements of Fiction   1

CHAPTER ONE   *Escape and Interpretation*   3

Richard Connell   The Most Dangerous Game   8
Thomas Wolfe   The Child by Tiger   24

CHAPTER TWO   *Plot*   41

Graham Greene   The Destructors   49
Alice Munro   Prue   61

CHAPTER THREE   *Character*   66

Sherwood Anderson   I'm a Fool   71
Alice Walker   Everyday Use   80
Katherine Mansfield   Miss Brill   88

CHAPTER FOUR   *Theme*   92

Isaac Bashevis Singer   The Son from America   99
    Translated by the author and Dorothea Straus
Neil Bissoondath   There Are a Lot of Ways to Die   105
Philip Roth   Defender of the Faith   117

CHAPTER FIVE   *Point of View*   142

Willa Cather   Paul's Case   148
Margaret Atwood   Rape Fantasies   163
Ernest Hemingway   Hills Like White Elephants   171
Ernest J. Gaines   Just Like a Tree   175

CHAPTER SIX   *Symbol and Irony*   194

Albert Camus   The Guest   202
Flannery O'Connor   Greenleaf   212
Anton Chekhov   Gooseberries   229
   Translated by Avrahm Yarmolinsky

CHAPTER SEVEN   *Emotion and Humor*   239

EXERCISE   243

McKnight Malmar   The Storm   243
Nadine Gordimer   Once Upon a Time   253

James Thurber   The Catbird Seat   258
Frank O'Connor   The Drunkard   265

Truman Capote   A Christmas Memory   273
Benjamin Capps   The Night Old Santa Claus Came   282

CHAPTER EIGHT   *Fantasy*   289

D. H. Lawrence   The Rocking-Horse Winner   291
Nathaniel Hawthorne   Young Goodman Brown   303

CHAPTER NINE   *The Scale of Value*   315

GENERAL QUESTIONS FOR ANALYSIS AND EVALUATION   318

EXERCISE   320

O. Henry   A Municipal Report   320
Susan Glaspell   A Jury of Her Peers   332

EXERCISE   349

William Faulkner   *Spotted Horses*   349
William Faulkner   *Mule in the Yard*   363

PART 2　Stories for Further Reading　375

Alice Adams　Fog　376
Raymond Carver　The Bridle　385
John Cheever　The Swimmer　398
Stephen Crane　The Bride Comes to Yellow Sky　407
Louise Erdrich　A Wedge of Shade　416
Richard Ford　Great Falls　424
Shirley Jackson　The Lottery　436
James Joyce　Eveline　443
Walter McDonald　The Track　447
Bobbie Ann Mason　Wish　450
Herman Melville　Bartleby the Scrivener　456
Edgar Allan Poe　The Cask of Amontillado　484
Katherine Anne Porter　The Jilting of Granny Weatherall　489
Jean Rhys　Pioneers, Oh, Pioneers　496
Leslie Marmon Silko　Private Property　503
Eudora Welty　A Worn Path　510
Tobias Wolff　Say Yes　517

Appendix　*Writing about Fiction*　521

Glossary of Fictional Terms　551

Index of Authors and Titles　561

PART 1

The Elements of Fiction

CHAPTER ONE

Escape and Interpretation

The first question to ask about fiction is, Why bother to read it? With life as short as it is, with so many pressing demands on our time, with books of information, instruction, and discussion waiting to be read, why should we spend precious time on works of imagination? The eternal answers to this question are two: enjoyment and understanding.

Since the invention of language, people have taken pleasure in following and participating in the imaginary adventures and imaginary experiences of imaginary men and women. Whatever — without causing harm — serves to make life less tedious, to make the hours pass more quickly and pleasurably, surely needs nothing else to recommend it. Enjoyment — and ever more enjoyment — is the first aim and justification of reading fiction.

But, unless fiction gives something more than pleasure, it hardly justifies itself as a subject of serious study. Unless it expands or refines our minds or quickens our sense of life, its value is not appreciably greater than that of video games, bridge, or ping-pong. To have a compelling claim on our attention, it must yield not only enjoyment but understanding.

The experience of humankind through the ages is that literature may furnish such understanding and do so effectively — that the depiction of imagined experiences can provide authentic insights. "The truest history," said Diderot of the novels of Samuel Richardson, "is full of falsehoods, and your romance is full of truths." But the bulk of fiction does not present such insights. Only some does. Initially, therefore, fiction may be classified into two broad categories: literature of escape and literature of interpretation.

Escape literature is that written purely for entertainment — to help us pass the time agreeably. **Interpretive literature** is written to broaden and deepen and sharpen our awareness of life. Escape literature takes us *away* from the real world: it enables us temporarily to forget our troubles. Interpretive literature takes us, through the imagination, deeper *into* the real world: it enables us to understand our troubles. Escape literature has as its only object pleasure. Interpretive literature has as its object pleasure *plus* understanding.

Having established a distinction, however, we must not exaggerate or oversimplify it. Escape and interpretation are not two great bins, into one or the other of which we can toss any given story. Rather, they are opposite ends of a scale — the two poles between which the world of fiction spins. The difference between them does not lie in the absence or presence of a "moral." The story that in all of its incidents and characters is shallow may have an unimpeachable moral, while the interpretive story may have no moral at all in any conventional sense. The difference does not lie in the absence or presence of "facts." The historical romance may be full of historical information and yet be pure escape in its depiction of human behavior. The difference does not lie in the presence or absence of an element of fantasy. The escape story may have a surface appearance of everyday reality, while the tale of seeming wildest fancy may press home on us some sudden truth. The difference between the two kinds of literature is deeper and more subtle than any of these distinctions. A story becomes interpretive as it illuminates some aspect of human life or behavior. An interpretive story presents us with an insight — large or small — into the nature and conditions of our existence. It gives us a keener awareness of what it is to be a human being in a universe sometimes friendly, sometimes hostile. It helps us to understand our world, our neighbors, and ourselves.

Perhaps we can clarify the difference by suggestion. Escape writers are like inventors who devise a contrivance for our diversion. When we push the button, lights flash, bells ring, and cardboard figures move jerkily across a painted horizon. Interpretive writers are discoverers: they take us out into the midst of life and say, "Look, here is the world!" Escape writers are full of tricks and surprises: they pull rabbits out of hats, saw beautiful women in two, and snatch brightly colored balls out of the air. Interpretive writers take us behind the scenes, where they show us the props and mirrors and seek to make clear the illusions. This is not to say that interpretive writers are merely reporters. More surely than escape writers they shape and give form to their materials. But they shape and form them always with the intent that we may see, feel, and understand them better, not for the primary purpose of furnishing entertainment.

Now, just as there are two kinds of fiction, there are also two kinds of readers. Immature readers seek only escape.* Even when they think they are reading for interpretation or some useful moral, they insist that what they read return them always some pleasant or exciting image of the world or some flattering image of themselves. We all begin with fairy tales. Our early reading experiences are likely to be with stories such as that of Cinderella, whose fairy godmother transforms a pumpkin and mice into a coach-and-four, whose slim foot is the only one that fits the crystal slipper, who rises superior to her cruel stepmother and taunting stepsisters to marry and "live happily ever after" with the charming prince, and who—never for a moment anything but sweet and virtuous—forgives her former tormenters.

Though most people move on from fairy tales into a seemingly more adult kind of reading, they may well be mistaken in thinking that they have progressed. The element of unreality in fiction does not lie primarily in magic wands and fairy godmothers but in a superficial treatment of life. The story of a shopgirl who is lifted from the painful conditions of her work and home life by a handsome young suitor from the upper classes may be as truly a Cinderella story as the one we read in childhood, though its setting is Hoboken rather than a kingdom by the sea. Unfortunately, many readers never grow beyond the fairy tale except in the most elementary of senses. In some ways, perhaps, their movement is backward, for it involves a loss of that sense of wonder that marks the child's vision.

There are many signs of immature readers. They make fixed demands of every story and feel frustrated and disappointed unless these demands are satisfied. Often they stick to one type of subject matter. Instead of being receptive to any story that puts human beings in human situations, they read only sports stories, western stories, love stories, crime stories, or science fiction. If they are willing to accept a wider

*The distinction made in this book between "mature" and "immature" readers is based not on age or status, but only on the possession of literary perception, judgment, and taste. Young people may often be more "mature" in this respect than their elders, and students sometimes more so than their teachers. Like the distinction between escape literature and interpretive literature, that between "mature" and "immature" readers is relative, not absolute. The terms do not represent two categories into which all readers may be classified, but simply the opposed ends of a graduated scale. No sharp line divides one class from the other: some students may be more mature than others in one aspect of their reading and less mature in another. Nor should the distinction between "mature" and "immature" *readers* be taken to refer to any category other than *literary* experience; it does not imply moral, ethical, or social values—an "immature" reader may be wholly admirable as a person, while a "mature" reader may display serious defects of character or behavior.

range of experience, they nevertheless still want every story to conform to several strict though perhaps unconsciously formulated expectations. Among the most common of these expectations are (1) a sympathetic hero or heroine—one with whom the reader can identify and whose adventures and triumphs the reader can share; (2) a plot in which something exciting is always happening and in which there is a strong element of suspense; (3) a happy outcome that sends the reader away undisturbed and optimistic about the world; (4) a theme—if the story has a theme—that confirms the reader's already-held opinions of the world.

There is nothing wrong with any of these characteristics as story elements. Significant fiction has been written having all of them. The error lies in elevating these characteristics to form a set of rigid requirements that a story must meet to be enjoyed. Such limitations restrict drastically the opportunity for expanding one's experience or broadening one's insights. They reduce one's demands on literature to a formula.*

Immature readers want the essentially familiar combined with superficial novelty. Each story must have a slightly new setting or twist or "gimmick," though the fundamental features of the characters and situations remain the same. These readers evaluate a story not by its truth but by its twists, turns, and surprises, by its suspense or its love interest. They want stories to be mainly pleasant. Evil, danger, and misery may appear in them, but not in such a way that they need really be taken seriously or are felt to be oppressive or permanent. Immature readers

---

*Fiction is sometimes roughly divided into **commercial** fiction—that written for wide popular consumption—and **quality** fiction—that written with a more serious artistic intent. In commercial fiction, the most general formula has a sympathetic hero faced with obstacles that he finally overcomes to achieve his goal. Most frequently, the hero's goal is to win the hand of the heroine; therefore, the most common subtype of the formula is boy meets girl, boy loses girl, boy wins girl. The hero is usually ruggedly handsome, and the heroine is beautiful or at least winsomely attractive. Even when the hero's primary objective is something other than love, commercial writers usually toss in a beautiful girl in order to supply their stories with some element of "love interest." The cheaper types of commercial fiction are generally characterized by a good deal of physical conflict—fistfights and gunfights—and by crude contrasts between good and evil. Although its more sophisticated forms use less obvious contrasts between good and evil and put less emphasis on physical conflict, they still cling to the happy ending. These forms are often concerned with marital problems that find a happy solution or with sentimental treatments of children or old people, in which the "innocent wisdom" of childhood or the "mellow wisdom" of old age is shown to be superior to the "practical wisdom" of the years between. In contrast, quality fiction does not rely upon tested formulas. It is more original—sometimes experimental—and seeks to be interpretive. All of the classifications made in this chapter are meant to be suggestive rather than rigid: absolute distinctions between commercial and quality fiction, between escape and interpretation, or between immature and mature readers cannot be made. One blends into the other.

want reading that slips easily and smoothly through the mind, requiring little mental effort. Most of all, they want something that helps sustain their fantasy life, providing ready-made daydreams in which they overcome their limitations, thwart their enemies, and win success or fame or the desired mate.

Discriminating readers, in contrast, take deeper pleasure in fiction that deals significantly with life than in fiction based on the formulations of escape. They do not reject escape literature, for escape literature need not be cheap or trite. It may be original, witty, absorbing, beautifully written, and artistically constructed. Some of literature's most enduring masterpieces are essentially escape — Barrie's *Peter Pan* and Stevenson's *Treasure Island*, for instance. Such reading may be a refreshment for the mind and spirit. For a steady diet, however, discriminating readers prefer interpretive literature. They know, moreover, that an exclusive diet of escape, especially of the cruder sorts, has two dangers: (1) it may leave us with merely superficial attitudes toward life; (2) it may actually distort our view of reality and give us false concepts and false expectations.

Fiction, like food, is of different nutritive values. Some is rich in protein and vitamins; it builds bone and sinew. Some is highly agreeable to the taste but not permanently sustaining. Some may be adulterated and actually harmful to our health. Escape fiction is of the latter two sorts. The harmless kind bears frankly on the face of it what it is. It pretends to be nothing other than pleasant diversion and never asks to be taken seriously. The second kind masquerades under the appearance of interpretation. It pretends to give a faithful treatment of life as it is — perhaps even thinks that it does so — but through its shallowness it subtly falsifies life in every line. Such fiction, taken seriously and without corrective, may give us false notions of reality and lead us to expect from experience what experience does not provide.

When we enter a library and glance at the books on the shelves, we are at first likely to be bewildered by their variety and profusion. Thousands of books sit there, each making its claim on us, each seeming to cry out "Read me! Read me! Read me!" or "No, read *me!*" We have time to read only a fraction of them. If we are wise, we shall read as many as we can without neglecting the other claims of life. Our problem is how to get the most out of what time we have. To make the richest use of our portion, we need to know two things: (1) how to get the most out of any book we read and (2) how to choose the books that will best repay the time and attention we devote to them. The assumption of this book is that a proper selection will include both fiction and nonfiction — nonfiction as an indispensable fund of information and ideas, of one kind of knowledge of the world; fiction as an equally indispensable source of a different kind of knowledge, a knowledge of experience, felt in the emotions as well as apprehended by the mind. The aim of this book is to aid in the growth of understanding and judgment.

Richard Connell
The Most Dangerous Game

"Off there to the right — somewhere — is a large island," said Whitney. "It's rather a mystery — "

"What island is it?" Rainsford asked.

"The old charts call it 'Ship-Trap Island,'" Whitney replied. "A suggestive name, isn't it? Sailors have a curious dread of the place. I don't know why. Some superstition — "

"Can't see it," remarked Rainsford, trying to peer through the dank tropical night that was palpable as it pressed its thick warm blackness in upon the yacht.

5 "You've good eyes," said Whitney, with a laugh, "and I've seen you pick off a moose moving in the brown fall bush at four hundred yards, but even you can't see four miles or so through a moonless Caribbean night."

"Nor four yards," admitted Rainsford. "Ugh! It's like moist black velvet."

"It will be light in Rio," promised Whitney. "We should make it in a few days. I hope the jaguar guns have come from Purdey's. We should have some good hunting up the Amazon. Great sport, hunting."

"The best sport in the world," agreed Rainsford.

"For the hunter," amended Whitney. "Not for the jaguar."

10 "Don't talk rot, Whitney," said Rainsford. "You're a big-game hunter, not a philosopher. Who cares how a jaguar feels?"

"Perhaps the jaguar does," observed Whitney.

"Bah! They've no understanding."

"Even so, I rather think they understand one thing — fear. The fear of pain and the fear of death."

"Nonsense," laughed Rainsford. "This hot weather is making you soft, Whitney. Be a realist. The world is made up of two classes — the hunters and the huntees. Luckily, you and I are the hunters. Do you think we've passed that island yet?"

15 "I can't tell in the dark. I hope so."

"Why?" asked Rainsford.

THE MOST DANGEROUS GAME   First published in 1924. Richard Connell (1893–1949) was a native of New York state, graduated from Harvard, and served a year in France with the United States Army during World War I.

"The place has a reputation — a bad one."

"Cannibals?" suggested Rainsford.

"Hardly. Even cannibals wouldn't live in such a God-forsaken place. But it's gotten into sailor lore, somehow. Didn't you notice that the crew's nerves seemed a bit jumpy to-day?"

"They were a bit strange, now you mention it. Even Captain Nielsen — " 20

"Yes, even that tough-minded old Swede, who'd go up to the devil himself and ask him for a light. Those fishy blue eyes held a look I never saw there before. All I could get out of him was: 'This place has an evil name among seafaring men, sir.' Then he said to me, very gravely: 'Don't you feel anything?' — as if the air about us was actually poisonous. Now, you mustn't laugh when I tell you this — I did feel something like a sudden chill.

"There was no breeze. The sea was as flat as a plate-glass window. We were drawing near the island then. What I felt was a — a mental chill; a sort of sudden dread."

"Pure imagination," said Rainsford. "One superstitious sailor can taint the whole ship's company with his fear."

"Maybe. But sometimes I think sailors have an extra sense that tells them when they are in danger. Sometimes I think evil is a tangible thing — with wave lengths, just as sound and light have. An evil place can, so to speak, broadcast vibrations of evil. Anyhow, I'm glad we're getting out of this zone. Well, I think I'll turn in now, Rainsford."

"I'm not sleepy," said Rainsford. "I'm going to smoke another pipe on 25 the after deck."

"Good night, then, Rainsford. See you at breakfast."

"Right. Good night, Whitney."

There was no sound in the night as Rainsford sat there, but the muffled throb of the engine that drove the yacht swiftly through the darkness, and the swish and ripple of the wash of the propeller.

Rainsford, reclining in a steamer chair, indolently puffed on his favorite brier. The sensuous drowsiness of the night was on him. "It's so dark," he thought, "that I could sleep without closing my eyes; the night would be my eyelids — "

An abrupt sound startled him. Off to the right he heard it, and his ears, 30 expert in such matters, could not be mistaken. Again he heard the sound, and again. Somewhere, off in the blackness, some one had fired a gun three times.

Rainsford sprang up and moved quickly to the rail, mystified. He strained his eyes in the direction from which the reports had come, but it was like trying to see through a blanket. He leaped upon the rail and balanced himself there, to get greater elevation; his pipe, striking a rope, was knocked from his mouth. He lunged for it; a short, hoarse cry came from his lips as he realized he had reached too far and had lost his balance. The cry was pinched off short as the blood-warm waters of the Caribbean Sea closed over his head.

He struggled up to the surface and tried to cry out, but the wash from the speeding yacht slapped him in the face and the salt water in his open mouth made him gag and strangle. Desperately he struck out with strong strokes after the receding lights of the yacht, but he stopped before he had swum fifty feet. A certain cool-headedness had come to him; it was not the first time he had been in a tight place. There was a chance that his cries could be heard by some one aboard the yacht, but that chance was slender, and grew more slender as the yacht raced on. He wrestled himself out of his clothes, and shouted with all his power. The lights of the yacht became faint and ever-vanishing fireflies; then they were blotted out entirely by the night.

Rainsford remembered the shots. They had come from the right, and doggedly he swam in that direction, swimming with slow, deliberate strokes, conserving his strength. For a seemingly endless time he fought the sea. He began to count his strokes; he could do possibly a hundred more and then —

Rainsford heard a sound. It came out of the darkness, a high screaming sound, the sound of an animal in an extremity of anguish and terror.

He did not recognize the animal that made the sound; he did not try to; with fresh vitality he swam toward the sound. He heard it again; then it was cut short by another noise, crisp, staccato.

"Pistol shot," muttered Rainsford, swimming on.

Ten minutes of determined effort brought another sound to his ears — the most welcome he had ever heard — the muttering and growling of the sea breaking on a rocky shore. He was almost on the rocks before he saw them; on a night less calm he would have been shattered against them. With his remaining strength he dragged himself from the swirling waters. Jagged crags appeared to jut into the opaqueness, he forced himself upward, hand over hand. Gasping, his hands raw, he reached a flat place at the top. Dense jungle came down to the very edge of the cliffs. What perils that tangle of trees and underbrush might hold for him did not concern Rainsford just then. All he knew was that he was safe from his enemy, the sea, and that utter weariness was on him. He flung himself down at the jungle edge and tumbled headlong into the deepest sleep of his life.

When he opened his eyes he knew from the position of the sun that it was late in the afternoon. Sleep had given him new vigor; a sharp hunger was picking at him. He looked about him, almost cheerfully.

"Where there are pistol shots, there are men. Where there are men, there is food," he thought. But what kind of men, he wondered, in so forbidding a place? An unbroken front of snarled and ragged jungle fringed the shore.

He saw no sign of a trail through the closely knit web of weeds and trees; it was easier to go along the shore, and Rainsford floundered along by the water. Not far from where he had landed, he stopped.

Some wounded thing, by the evidence a large animal, had thrashed about in the underbrush; the jungle weeds were crushed down and the moss was lacerated; one patch of weeds was stained crimson. A small, glittering object not far away caught Rainsford's eye and he picked it up. It was an empty cartridge.

"A twenty-two," he remarked. "That's odd. It must have been a fairly large animal too. The hunter had his nerve with him to tackle it with a light gun. It's clear that the brute put up a fight. I suppose the first three shots I heard was when the hunter flushed his quarry and wounded it. The last shot was when he trailed it here and finished it."

He examined the ground closely and found what he had hoped to find — the print of hunting boots. They pointed along the cliff in the direction he had been going. Eagerly he hurried along, now slipping on a rotten log or a loose stone, but making headway; night was beginning to settle down on the island.

Bleak darkness was blacking out the sea and jungle when Rainsford sighted the lights. He came upon them as he turned a crook in the coast line, and his first thought was that he had come upon a village, for there were many lights. But as he forged along he saw to his great astonishment that all the lights were in one enormous building — a lofty structure with pointed towers plunging upward into the gloom. His eyes made out the shadowy outlines of a palatial château; it was set on a high bluff, and on three sides of it cliffs dived down to where the sea licked greedy lips in the shadows.

"Mirage," thought Rainsford. But it was no mirage, he found, when he 45 opened the tall spiked iron gate. The stone steps were real enough; the massive door with a leering gargoyle for a knocker was real enough; yet about it all hung an air of unreality.

He lifted the knocker, and it creaked up stiffly, as if it had never before been used. He let it fall, and it startled him with its booming loudness. He thought he heard steps within; the door remained closed. Again Rainsford lifted the heavy knocker, and let it fall. The door opened then, opened as suddenly as if it were on a spring, and Rainsford stood blinking in the river of glaring gold light that poured out. The first thing Rainsford's eyes discerned was the largest man Rainsford had ever seen — a gigantic creature, solidly made and black-bearded to the waist. In his hand the man held a long-barreled revolver, and he was pointing it straight at Rainsford's heart.

Out of the snarl of beard two small eyes regarded Rainsford.

"Don't be alarmed," said Rainsford, with a smile which he hoped was disarming. "I'm no robber. I fell off a yacht. My name is Sanger Rainsford of New York City."

The menacing look in the eyes did not change. The revolver pointed as rigidly as if the giant were a statue. He gave no sign that he understood Rainsford's words, or that he had even heard them. He was dressed in uniform, a black uniform trimmed with gray astrakhan.

"I'm Sanger Rainsford of New York," Rainsford began again. "I fell off a 50 yacht. I am hungry."

The man's only answer was to raise with his thumb the hammer of his revolver. Then Rainsford saw the man's free hand go to his forehead in a military salute, and he saw him click his heels together and stand at attention. Another man was coming down the broad marble steps, an erect, slender man in evening clothes. He advanced to Rainsford and held out his hand.

In a cultivated voice marked by a slight accent that gave it added precision and deliberateness, he said: "It is a very great pleasure and honor to welcome Mr. Sanger Rainsford, the celebrated hunter, to my home."

Automatically Rainsford shook the man's hand.

"I've read your book about hunting snow leopards in Tibet, you see," explained the man. "I am General Zaroff."

55 Rainsford's first impression was that the man was singularly handsome; his second was that there was an original, almost bizarre quality about the general's face. He was a tall man past middle age, for his hair was a vivid white; but his thick eyebrows and pointed military mustache were as black as the night from which Rainsford had come. His eyes, too, were black and very bright. He had high cheek bones, a sharp-cut nose, a spare, dark face, the face of a man used to giving orders, the face of an aristocrat. Turning to the giant in uniform, the general made a sign. The giant put away his pistol, saluted, withdrew.

"Ivan is an incredibly strong fellow," remarked the general, "but he has the misfortune to be deaf and dumb. A simple fellow, but, I'm afraid, like all his race, a bit of a savage."

"Is he Russian?"

"He is a Cossack," said the general, and his smile showed red lips and pointed teeth. "So am I."

"Come," he said, "we shouldn't be chatting here. We can talk later. Now you want clothes, food, rest. You shall have them. This is a most restful spot."

60 Ivan had reappeared, and the general spoke to him with lips that moved but gave forth no sound.

"Follow Ivan, if you please, Mr. Rainsford," said the general. "I was about to have my dinner when you came. I'll wait for you. You'll find that my clothes will fit you, I think."

It was to a huge, beam-ceilinged bedroom with a canopied bed big enough for six men that Rainsford followed the silent giant. Ivan laid out an evening suit, and Rainsford, as he put it on, noticed that it came from a London tailor who ordinarily cut and sewed for none below the rank of duke.

The dining room to which Ivan conducted him was in many ways remarkable. There was a medieval magnificence about it; it suggested a baronial hall of feudal times with its oaken panels, its high ceiling, its vast refectory table where twoscore men could sit down to eat. About the hall were the mounted heads of many animals — lions, tigers, elephants, moose, bears; larger or more perfect specimens Rainsford had never seen. At the great table the general was sitting, alone.

"You'll have a cocktail, Mr. Rainsford," he suggested. The cocktail was surpassingly good; and, Rainsford noted, the table appointments were of the finest — the linen, the crystal, the silver, the china.

65 They were eating *borsch*, the rich, red soup with whipped cream so dear to Russian palates. Half apologetically General Zaroff said: "We do our best

to preserve the amenities of civilization here. Please forgive any lapses. We are well off the beaten track, you know. Do you think the champagne has suffered from its long ocean trip?"

"Not in the least," declared Rainsford. He was finding the general a most thoughtful and affable host, a true cosmopolite. But there was one small trait of the general's that made Rainsford uncomfortable. Whenever he looked up from his plate he found the general studying him, appraising him narrowly.

"Perhaps," said General Zaroff, "you were surprised that I recognized your name. You see, I read all books on hunting published in English, French, and Russian. I have but one passion in my life, Mr. Rainsford, and it is the hunt."

"You have some wonderful heads here," said Rainsford as he ate a particularly well cooked filet mignon. "That Cape buffalo is the largest I ever saw."

"Oh, that fellow. Yes, he was a monster."

"Did he charge you?"

"Hurled me against a tree," said the general. "Fractured my skull. But I got the brute."

"I've always thought," said Rainsford, "that the Cape buffalo is the most dangerous of all big game."

For a moment the general did not reply; he was smiling his curious red-lipped smile. Then he said slowly: "No. You are wrong, sir. The Cape buffalo is not the most dangerous big game." He sipped his wine. "Here in my preserve on this island," he said in the same slow tone, "I hunt more dangerous game."

Rainsford expressed his surprise. "Is there big game on this island?"

The general nodded. "The biggest."

"Really?"

"Oh, it isn't here naturally, of course. I have to stock the island."

"What have you imported, general?" Rainsford asked. "Tigers?"

The general smiled. "No," he said. "Hunting tigers ceased to interest me some years ago. I exhausted their possibilities, you see. No thrill left in tigers, no real danger. I live for danger, Mr. Rainsford."

The general took from his pocket a gold cigaret case and offered his guest a long black cigaret with a silver tip; it was perfumed and gave off a smell like incense.

"We will have some capital hunting, you and I," said the general. "I shall be most glad to have your society."

"But what game — " began Rainsford.

"I'll tell you," said the general. "You will be amused, I know. I think I may say, in all modesty, that I have done a rare thing. I have invented a new sensation. May I pour you another glass of port, Mr. Rainsford?"

"Thank you, general."

The general filled both glasses, and said: "God makes some men poets. Some He makes kings, some beggars. Me He made a hunter. My hand was made for the trigger, my father said. He was a very rich man with a quarter of a million acres in the Crimea, and he was an ardent sportsman. When I was

70

75

80

85

only five years old he gave me a little gun, specially made in Moscow for me, to shoot sparrows with. When I shot some of his prize turkeys with it, he did not punish me; he complimented me on my marksmanship. I killed my first bear in the Caucasus when I was ten. My whole life has been one prolonged hunt. I went into the army — it was expected of noblemen's sons — and for a time commanded a division of Cossack cavalry, but my real interest was always the hunt. I have hunted every kind of game in every land. It would be impossible for me to tell you how many animals I have killed."

The general puffed at his cigaret.

"After the debacle in Russia I left the country, for it was imprudent for an officer of the Czar to stay there. Many noble Russians lost everything. I, luckily, had invested heavily in American securities, so I shall never have to open a tea room in Monte Carlo or drive a taxi in Paris. Naturally, I continued to hunt — grizzlies in your Rockies, crocodiles in the Ganges, rhinoceroses in East Africa. It was in Africa that the Cape buffalo hit me and laid me up for six months. As soon as I recovered I started for the Amazon to hunt jaguars, for I had heard they were unusually cunning. They weren't." The Cossack sighed. "They were no match at all for a hunter with his wits about him, and a high-powered rifle. I was bitterly disappointed. I was lying in my tent with a splitting headache one night when a terrible thought pushed its way into my mind. Hunting was beginning to bore me! And hunting, remember, had been my life. I have heard that in America business men often go to pieces when they give up the business that has been their life."

"Yes, that's so," said Rainsford.

The general smiled. "I had no wish to go to pieces," he said. "I must do something. Now, mine is an analytical mind, Mr. Rainsford. Doubtless that is why I enjoy the problems of the chase."

90   "No doubt, General Zaroff."

"So," continued the general, "I asked myself why the hunt no longer fascinated me. You are much younger than I am, Mr. Rainsford, and have not hunted as much, but you perhaps can guess the answer."

"What was it?"

"Simply this: hunting had ceased to be what you call 'a sporting proposition.' It had become too easy. I always got my quarry. Always. There is no greater bore than perfection."

The general lit a fresh cigaret.

95   "No animal had a chance with me any more. That is no boast; it is a mathematical certainty. The animal had nothing but his legs and his instinct. Instinct is no match for reason. When I thought of this it was a tragic moment for me, I can tell you."

Rainsford leaned across the table, absorbed in what his host was saying.

"It came to me as an inspiration what I must do," the general went on.

"And that was?"

The general smiled the quiet smile of one who has faced an obstacle and surmounted it with success. "I had to invent a new animal to hunt," he said.

"A new animal? You're joking."

"Not at all," said the general. "I never joke about hunting. I needed a new animal. I found one. So I bought this island, built this house, and here I do my hunting. The island is perfect for my purposes — there are jungles with a maze of trails in them, hills, swamps — "

"But the animal, General Zaroff?"

"Oh," said the general, "it supplies me with the most exciting hunting in the world. No other hunting compares with it for an instant. Every day I hunt, and I never grow bored now, for I have a quarry with which I can match my wits."

Rainsford's bewilderment showed in his face.

"I wanted the ideal animal to hunt," explained the general. "So I said:
'What are the attributes of an ideal quarry?' And the answer was, of course: 'it must have courage, cunning, and, above all, it must be able to reason.'"

"But no animal can reason," objected Rainsford.

"My dear fellow," said the general, "there is one that can."

"But you can't mean — " gasped Rainsford.

"And why not?"

"I can't believe you are serious, General Zaroff. This is a grisly joke."

"Why should I not be serious? I am speaking of hunting."

"Hunting? Good God, General Zaroff, what you speak of is murder."

The general laughed with entire good nature. He regarded Rainsford quizzically. "I refuse to believe that so modern and civilized a young man as you seem to be harbors romantic ideas about the value of human life. Surely your experiences in the war — "

"Did not make me condone cold-blooded murder," finished Rainsford stiffly.

Laughter shook the general. "How extraordinarily droll you are!" he
said. "One does not expect nowadays to find a young man of the educated class, even in America, with such a naive, and, if I may say so, mid-Victorian point of view. It's like finding a snuff-box in a limousine. Ah, well, doubtless you had Puritan ancestors. So many Americans appear to have had. I'll wager you'll forget your notions when you go hunting with me. You've a genuine new thrill in store for you, Mr. Rainsford."

"Thank you, I'm a hunter, not a murderer."

"Dear me," said the general, quite unruffled, "again that unpleasant word. But I think I can show you that your scruples are quite ill founded."

"Yes?"

"Life is for the strong, to be lived by the strong, and, if need be, taken by the strong. The weak of the world were put here to give the strong pleasure. I am strong. Why should I not use my gift? If I wish to hunt, why should I not? I hunt the scum of the earth — sailors from tramp ships — lascars, blacks, Chinese, whites, mongrels — a thoroughbred horse or hound is worth more than a score of them."

"But they are men," said Rainsford hotly.

"Precisely," said the general. "That is why I use them. It gives me plea-sure. They can reason, after a fashion. So they are dangerous."

"But where do you get them?"

The general's left eyelid fluttered down in a wink. "This island is called Ship-Trap," he answered. "Sometimes an angry god of the high seas sends them to me. Sometimes, when Providence is not so kind, I help Providence a bit. Come to the window with me."

Rainsford went to the window and looked out toward the sea.

"Watch! Out there!" exclaimed the general, pointing into the night. Rainsford's eyes saw only blackness, and then, as the general pressed a but-ton, far out to sea Rainsford saw the flash of lights.

The general chuckled. "They indicate a channel," he said, "where there's none: giant rocks with razor edges crouch like a sea monster with wide-open jaws. They can crush a ship as easily as I crush this nut." He dropped a walnut on the hardwood floor and brought his heel grinding down on it. "Oh, yes," he said, casually, as if in answer to a question, "I have electricity. We try to be civilized here."

"Civilized? And you shoot down men?"

A trace of anger was in the general's black eyes, but it was there for but a second, and he said, in his most pleasant manner: "Dear me, what a righ-teous young man you are! I assure you I do not do the thing you suggest. That would be barbarous. I treat these visitors with every consideration. They get plenty of good food and exercise. They get into splendid physical condition. You shall see for yourself to-morrow."

"What do you mean?"

"We'll visit my training school," smiled the general. "It's in the cellar. I have about a dozen pupils down there now. They're from the Spanish bark San Lucar that had the bad luck to go on the rocks out there. A very inferior lot, I regret to say. Poor specimens and more accustomed to the deck than to the jungle."

He raised his hand, and Ivan, who served as waiter, brought thick Turk-ish coffee. Rainsford, with an effort, held his tongue in check.

"It's a game, you see," pursued the general blandly. "I suggest to one of them that we go hunting. I give him a supply of food and an excellent hunt-ing knife. I give him three hours' start. I am to follow, armed only with a pistol of the smallest caliber and range. If my quarry eludes me for three whole days, he wins the game. If I find him" — the general smiled — "he loses."

"Suppose he refuses to be hunted?"

"Oh," said the general, "I give him his option, of course. He need not play that game if he doesn't wish to. If he does not wish to hunt, I turn him over to Ivan. Ivan once had the honor of serving as official knouter to the Great White Czar, and he has his own ideas of sport. Invariably, Mr. Rains-ford, invariably they choose the hunt."

"And if they win?"

The smile on the general's face widened. "To date I have not lost," he said.

Then he added, hastily: "I don't wish you to think me a braggart, Mr. Rainsford. Many of them afford only the most elementary sort of problem. Occasionally I strike a tartar. One almost did win. I eventually had to use the dogs."

"The dogs?"

"This way, please. I'll show you."

The general steered Rainsford to a window. The lights from the windows sent a flickering illumination that made grotesque patterns on the courtyard below, and Rainsford could see moving about there a dozen or so huge black shapes; as they turned toward him, their eyes glittered greenly.

"A rather good lot, I think," observed the general. "They are let out at seven every night. If anyone should try to get into my house — or out of it — something extremely regrettable would occur to him." He hummed a snatch of song from the Folies Bergère.

"And now," said the general, "I want to show you my new collection of heads. Will you come with me to the library?"

"I hope," said Rainsford, "that you will excuse me tonight, General Zaroff. I'm really not feeling at all well."

"Ah, indeed?" the general inquired solicitously. "Well, I suppose that's only natural, after your long swim. You need a good, restful night's sleep. Tomorrow you'll feel like a new man, I'll wager. Then we'll hunt, eh? I've one rather promising prospect — "

Rainsford was hurrying from the room.

"Sorry you can't go with me tonight," called the general. "I expect rather fair sport — a big, strong black. He looks resourceful — Well, good night, Mr. Rainsford; I hope you have a good night's rest."

The bed was good, and the pajamas of the softest silk, and he was tired in every fiber of his being, but nevertheless Rainsford could not quiet his brain with the opiate of sleep. He lay, eyes wide open. Once he thought he heard stealthy steps in the corridor outside his room. He sought to throw open the door; it would not open. He went to the window and looked out. His room was high up in one of the towers. The lights of the château were out now, and it was dark and silent, but there was a fragment of sallow moon, and by its wan light he could see, dimly, the courtyard; there, weaving in and out in the pattern of shadow, were black, noiseless forms; the hounds heard him at the window and looked up, expectantly, with their green eyes. Rainsford went back to the bed and lay down. By many methods he tried to put himself to sleep. He had achieved a doze when, just as morning began to come, he heard, far off in the jungle, the faint report of a pistol.

General Zaroff did not appear until luncheon. He was dressed faultlessly in the tweeds of a country squire. He was solicitous about the state of Rainsford's health.

"As for me," sighed the general, "I do not feel so well. I am worried, Mr. Rainsford. Last night I detected traces of my old complaint."

150 To Rainsford's questioning glance the general said: "Ennui. Boredom."

Then, taking a second helping of Crêpes Suzette, the general explained: "The hunting was not good last night. The fellow lost his head. He made a straight trail that offered no problems at all. That's the trouble with these sailors; they have dull brains to begin with, and they do not know how to get about in the woods. They do excessively stupid and obvious things. It's most annoying. Will you have another glass of Chablis, Mr. Rainsford?"

"General," said Rainsford firmly, "I wish to leave this island at once."

The general raised his thickets of eyebrows; he seemed hurt. "But, my dear fellow," the general protested, "you've only just come. You've had no hunting—"

"I wish to go to-day," said Rainsford. He saw the dead black eyes of the general on him, studying him. General Zaroff's face suddenly brightened.

155 He filled Rainsford's glass with venerable Chablis from a dusty bottle.

"Tonight," said the general, "we will hunt—you and I."

Rainsford shook his head. "No, general," he said. "I will not hunt."

The general shrugged his shoulders and delicately ate a hothouse grape. "As you wish, my friend," he said. "The choice rests entirely with you. But may I not venture to suggest that you will find my idea of sport more diverting than Ivan's?"

He nodded toward the corner to where the giant stood, scowling, his thick arms crossed on his hogshead of chest.

160 "You don't mean—" cried Rainsford.

"My dear fellow," said the general, "have I not told you I always mean what I say about hunting? This is really an inspiration. I drink to a foeman worthy of my steel—at last."

The general raised his glass, but Rainsford sat staring at him.

"You'll find this game worth playing," the general said enthusiastically. "Your brain against mine. Your woodcraft against mine. Your strength and stamina against mine. Outdoor chess! And the stake is not without value, eh?"

"And if I win—" began Rainsford huskily.

165 "I'll cheerfully acknowledge myself defeated if I do not find you by midnight of the third day," said General Zaroff. "My sloop will place you on the mainland near a town."

The general read what Rainsford was thinking.

"Oh, you can trust me," said the Cossack. "I will give you my word as a gentleman and a sportsman. Of course you, in turn, must agree to say nothing of your visit here."

"I'll agree to nothing of the kind," said Rainsford.

"Oh," said the general, "in that case—But why discuss that now? Three days hence we can discuss it over a bottle of Veuve Cliquot, unless—"

170 The general sipped his wine.

Then a businesslike air animated him. "Ivan," he said to Rainsford, "will supply you with hunting clothes, food, a knife. I suggest you wear moccasins; they leave a poorer trail. I suggest too that you avoid the big swamp in the southeast corner of the island. We call it Death Swamp. There's quicksand there. One foolish fellow tried it. The deplorable part of it was that Lazarus followed him. You can imagine my feelings, Mr. Rainsford. I loved Lazarus; he was the finest hound in my pack. Well, I must beg you to excuse me now. I always take a siesta after lunch. You'll hardly have time for a nap, I fear. You'll want to start, no doubt. I shall not follow till dusk. Hunting at night is so much more exciting than by day, don't you think? Au revoir, Mr. Rainsford, au revoir."

General Zaroff, with a deep, courtly bow, strolled from the room.

From another door came Ivan. Under one arm he carried khaki hunting clothes, a haversack of food, a leather sheath containing a long-bladed hunting knife; his right hand rested on a cocked revolver thrust in the crimson sash about his waist. . . .

Rainsford had fought his way through the bush for two hours. "I must keep my nerve. I must keep my nerve," he said through tight teeth.

He had not been entirely clear-headed when the château gates snapped shut behind him. His whole idea at first was to put distance between himself and General Zaroff, and, to this end, he had plunged along, spurred on by the sharp rowels of something very like panic. Now he had got a grip on himself, had stopped, and was taking stock of himself and the situation.

He saw that straight flight was futile; inevitably it would bring him face to face with the sea. He was in a picture with a frame of water, and his operations, clearly, must take place within that frame.

"I'll give him a trail to follow," muttered Rainsford, and he struck off from the rude paths he had been following into the trackless wilderness. He executed a series of intricate loops; he doubled on his trail again and again, recalling all the lore of the fox hunt, and all the dodges of the fox. Night found him leg-weary, with hands and face lashed by the branches, on a thickly wooded ridge. He knew it would be insane to blunder on through the dark, even if he had the strength. His need for rest was imperative and he thought: "I have played the fox, now I must play the cat of the fable." A big tree with a thick trunk and outspread branches was nearby, and, taking care to leave not the slightest mark, he climbed up into the crotch, and stretching out on one of the broad limbs, after a fashion, rested. Rest brought him new confidence and almost a feeling of security. Even so zealous a hunter as General Zaroff could not trace him there, he told himself; only the devil himself could follow that complicated trail through the jungle after dark. But, perhaps, the general was a devil —

An apprehensive night crawled slowly by like a wounded snake, and sleep did not visit Rainsford, although the silence of a dead world was on the jungle. Toward morning when a dingy gray was varnishing the sky, the cry of some startled bird focused Rainsford's attention in that direction. Something was coming through the bush, coming slowly, carefully, coming by the same winding way Rainsford had come. He flattened himself down on the limb, and through a screen of leaves almost as thick as tapestry, he watched. The thing that was approaching was a man.

It was General Zaroff. He made his way along with his eyes fixed in utmost concentration on the ground before him. He paused, almost beneath the tree, dropped to his knees and studied the ground. Rainsford's impulse was to hurl himself down like a panther, but he saw the general's right hand held something metallic — a small automatic pistol.

180   The hunter shook his head several times, as if he were puzzled. Then he straightened up and took from his case one of his black cigarets; its pungent incense-like smoke floated up to Rainsford's nostrils.

Rainsford held his breath. The general's eyes had left the ground and were traveling inch by inch up the tree. Rainsford froze there, every muscle tensed for a spring. But the sharp eyes of the hunter stopped before they reached the limb where Rainsford lay; a smile spread over his brown face. Very deliberately he blew a smoke ring into the air; then he turned his back on the tree and walked carelessly away, back along the trail he had come. The swish of the underbrush against his hunting boots grew fainter and fainter.

The pent-up air burst hotly from Rainsford's lungs. His first thought made him feel sick and numb. The general could follow a trail through the woods at night; he could follow an extremely difficult trail; he must have uncanny powers; only by the merest chance had the Cossack failed to see his quarry.

Rainsford's second thought was even more terrible. It sent a shudder of cold horror through his whole being. Why had the general smiled? Why had he turned back?

Rainsford did not want to believe what his reason told him was true, but the truth was as evident as the sun that had by now pushed through the morning mists. The general was playing with him! The general was saving him for another day's sport! The Cossack was the cat; he was the mouse. Then it was that Rainsford knew the full meaning of terror.

185   "I will not lose my nerve. I will not."

He slid down from the tree, and struck off again into the woods. His face was set and he forced the machinery of his mind to function. Three hundred yards from his hiding place he stopped where a huge dead tree leaned precariously on a smaller, living one. Throwing off his sack of food, Rainsford took his knife from its sheath and began to work with all his energy.

The job was finished at last, and he threw himself down behind a fallen log a hundred feet away. He did not have to wait long. The cat was coming again to play with the mouse.

Following the trail with the sureness of a bloodhound, came General Zaroff. Nothing escaped those searching black eyes, no crushed blade of grass, no bent twig, no mark, no matter how faint, in the moss. So intent was the Cossack on his stalking that he was upon the thing Rainsford had made before he saw it. His foot touched the protruding bough that was the trigger. Even as he touched it, the general sensed his danger and leaped back with the agility of an ape. But he was not quick enough; the dead tree, delicately adjusted to rest on the cut living one, crashed down and struck the general a glancing blow on the shoulder as it fell; but for his alertness, he must have been smashed beneath it. He staggered, but he did not fall; nor did he drop his revolver. He stood there, rubbing his injured shoulder, and Rainsford, with fear again gripping his heart, heard the general's mocking laugh ring through the jungle.

"Rainsford," called the general, "if you are within the sound of my voice, as I suppose you are, let me congratulate you. Not many men know how to make a Malay man-catcher. Luckily, for me, I too have hunted in Malacca. You are proving interesting, Mr. Rainsford. I am going now to have my wound dressed; it's only a slight one. But I shall be back. I shall be back."

When the general, nursing his bruised shoulder, had gone, Rainsford took up his flight again. It was flight now, a desperate, hopeless flight, that carried him on for some hours. Dusk came, then darkness, and still he pressed on. The ground grew softer under his moccasins; the vegetation grew ranker, denser; insects bit him savagely. Then, as he stepped forward, his foot sank in the ooze. He tried to wrench it back, but the muck sucked viciously at his foot as if it were a giant leech. With a violent effort, he tore loose. He knew where he was now. Death Swamp and its quicksand.

His hands were tight closed as if his nerve were something tangible that some one in the darkness was trying to tear from his grip. The softness of the earth had given him an idea. He stepped back from the quicksand a dozen feet or so, and, like some huge prehistoric beaver, he began to dig.

Rainsford had dug himself in in France when a second's delay meant death. That had been a placid pastime compared to his digging now. The pit grew deeper; when it was above his shoulders, he climbed out and from some hard saplings cut stakes and sharpened them to a fine point. These stakes he planted in the bottom of the pit with the points sticking up. With flying fingers he wove a rough carpet of weeds and branches and with it he covered the mouth of the pit. Then, wet with sweat and aching with tiredness, he crouched behind the stump of a lightning-charred tree.

He knew his pursuer was coming; he heard the padding sound of feet on the soft earth, and the night breeze brought him the perfume of the general's cigaret. It seemed to Rainsford that the general was coming with unusual swiftness; he was not feeling his way along, foot by foot. Rainsford, crouching there, could not see the general, nor could he see the pit. He lived a year in a minute. Then he felt an impulse to cry aloud with joy, for he heard the sharp crackle of the breaking branches as the cover of the pit gave way; he heard the sharp scream of pain as the pointed stakes found their mark. He leaped up from his place of concealment. Then he cowered back. Three feet from the pit a man was standing, with an electric torch in his hand.

190

"You've done well, Rainsford," the voice of the general called. "Your Burmese tiger pit has claimed one of my best dogs. Again you score. I think, Mr. Rainsford, I'll see what you can do against my whole pack. I'm going home for a rest now. Thank you for a most amusing evening."

195   At daybreak Rainsford, lying near the swamp, was awakened by the sound that made him know that he had new things to learn about fear. It was a distant sound, faint and wavering, but he knew it. It was the baying of a pack of hounds.

Rainsford knew he could do one of two things. He could stay where he was and wait. That was suicide. He could flee. That was postponing the inevitable. For a moment he stood there, thinking. An idea that held a wild chance came to him, and, tightening his belt, he headed away from the swamp.

The baying of the hounds drew nearer, then still nearer, nearer, ever nearer. On a ridge Rainsford climbed a tree. Down a watercourse, not a quarter of a mile away, he could see the bush moving. Straining his eyes, he saw the lean figure of General Zaroff; just ahead of him Rainsford made out another figure whose wide shoulders surged through the tall jungle weeds; it was the giant Ivan, and he seemed pulled forward by some unseen force; Rainsford knew that Ivan must be holding the pack in leash.

They would be on him any minute now. His mind worked frantically. He thought of a native trick he had learned in Uganda. He slid down the tree. He caught hold of a springy young sapling and to it he fastened his hunting knife, with the blade pointing down the trail; with a bit of wild grapevine he tied back the sapling. Then he ran for his life. The hounds raised their voices as they hit the fresh scent. Rainsford knew now how an animal at bay feels.

He had to stop to get his breath. The baying of the hounds stopped abruptly, and Rainsford's heart stopped too. They must have reached the knife.

200   He shinnied excitedly up a tree and looked back. His pursuers had stopped. But the hope that was in Rainsford's brain when he climbed died, for he saw in the shallow valley that General Zaroff was still on his feet. But Ivan was not. The knife, driven by the recoil of the springing tree, had not wholly failed.

"Nerve, nerve, nerve!" he panted, as he dashed along. A blue gap showed between the trees dead ahead. Ever nearer drew the hounds. Rainsford forced himself on toward that gap. He reached it. It was the shore of the sea. Across a cove he could see the gloomy gray stone of the château. Twenty feet below him the sea rumbled and hissed. Rainsford hesitated. He heard the hounds. Then he leaped far out into the sea. . . .

When the general and his pack reached the place by the sea, the Cossack stopped. For some minutes he stood regarding the blue-green expanse of water. He shrugged his shoulders. Then he sat down, took a drink of brandy from a silver flask, lit a perfumed cigaret, and hummed a bit from *Madame Butterfly*.

General Zaroff had an exceedingly good dinner in his great paneled dining hall that evening. With it he had a bottle of Pol Roger and half a bottle of Chambertin. Two slight annoyances kept him from perfect enjoyment. One was the thought that it would be difficult to replace Ivan; the other was that his quarry had escaped him; of course the American hadn't played the game — so thought the general as he tasted his after-dinner liqueur. In his library he read, to soothe himself, from the works of Marcus Aurelius. At ten he went up to his bedroom. He was deliciously tired, he said to himself, as he locked himself in. There was a little moonlight, so, before turning on his light, he went to the window and looked down at the courtyard. He could see the great hounds, and he called: "Better luck another time," to them. Then he switched on the light.

A man, who had been hiding in the curtains of the bed, was standing there.

"Rainsford!" screamed the general. "How in God's name did you get here?"

"Swam," said Rainsford. "I found it quicker than walking through the jungle."

The general sucked in his breath and smiled. "I congratulate you," he said. "You have won the game."

Rainsford did not smile. "I am still a beast at bay," he said, in a low, hoarse voice. "Get ready, General Zaroff."

The general made one of his deepest bows. "I see," he said. "Splendid! One of us is to furnish a repast for the hounds. The other will sleep in this very excellent bed. On guard, Rainsford. . . ."

He had never slept in a better bed, Rainsford decided.

QUESTIONS

1. On what simple ironic reversal is the plot of the story based? What two meanings has the title?
2. How important is suspense in the story? In what ways is it aroused and sustained? What part do chance and coincidence play in the story?
3. Discuss the characterizations of Rainsford and General Zaroff. Which one is more fully characterized? Are both characters plausible?
4. What purpose is served by the "philosophical" discussion between Whitney and Rainsford at the beginning of the story (paragraphs 7–24)? What limitation does it show Rainsford to have? To what extent is his character illuminated during the course of the story? Does he change his ideas?
5. In what ways is the discussion between Whitney and Rainsford paralleled by the after-dinner discussion between Rainsford and Zaroff (paragraphs

68–130)? In these discussions, is Rainsford more like Whitney or Zaroff? How does he differ from Zaroff? Does the end of the story resolve that difference?

6. Is the principal emphasis of the story on plot, character, or theme? On escape or interpretation? Support your answer.

Thomas Wolfe
The Child by Tiger

> Tiger, tiger, burning bright
> In the forests of the night,
> What immortal hand or eye
> Could frame thy fearful symmetry?

One day after school, twenty-five years ago, several of us were playing with a football in the yard at Randy Shepperton's. Randy was calling signals and handling the ball. Nebraska Crane was kicking it. Augustus Potterham was too clumsy to run or kick or pass, so we put him at center, where all he'd have to do would be to pass the ball back to Randy when he got the signal.

It was late in October and there was a smell of smoke, of leaves, of burning in the air. Nebraska had just kicked to us. It was a good kick, too — a high, soaring punt that spiraled out above my head, behind me. I ran back and tried to get it, but it was far and away "over the goal line" — that is to say, out in the street. It hit the street and bounded back and forth with that peculiarly erratic bounce a football has.

The ball rolled away from me down toward the corner. I was running out to get it when Dick Prosser, Shepperton's new Negro man, came along, gathered it up neatly in his great black paw and tossed it to me. He turned in then, and came on down the alleyway, greeting us as he did. He called all of us "Mister" except Randy, and Randy was always "Cap'n" — "Cap'n Shepperton." This formal address — "Mr." Crane, "Mr." Potterham, "Mr." Spangler, "Cap'n" Shepperton — pleased us immensely, gave us a feeling of mature importance and authority.

"Cap'n Shepperton" was splendid! It had a delightful military association, particularly when Dick Prosser said it. Dick had served a long enlistment in the United States Army. He had been a member of a regiment of crack Negro troops upon the Texas border, and the stamp of the military man was evident in everything he did. It was a joy, for example, just to watch him split up kindling. He did it with a power, a kind of military order, that was astounding. Every stick he cut seemed to be exactly the same length and

THE CHILD BY TIGER First published in 1937. Thomas Wolfe (1900–1938) was born and grew up in Asheville, North Carolina. An altered, expanded version of this story was included in Chapter 8 of his novel *The Web and the Rock* (1939).

shape as every other one. He had all of them neatly stacked against the walls of the Shepperton basement with such regimented faultlessness that it almost seemed a pity to disturb their symmetry for the use for which they were intended.

It was the same with everything else he did. His little whitewashed base- 5 ment room was as spotless as a barracks room. The bare board floor was always cleanly swept, a plain bare table and a plain straight chair were stationed exactly in the center of the room. On the table there was always just one object: an old Bible almost worn out by constant use, for Dick was a deeply religious man. There was a little cast-iron stove and a little wooden box with a few lumps of coal and a neat stack of kindling in it. And against the wall, to the left, there was an iron cot, always precisely made and covered cleanly with a coarse gray blanket.

The Sheppertons were delighted with him. He had come there looking for work just a month or two before, and modestly presented his qualifications. He had, he said, only recently received his discharge from the Army and was eager to get employment, at no matter what wage. He could cook, he could tend the furnace, he knew how to drive a car — in fact, it seemed to us boys that there was very little that Dick Prosser could not do. He could certainly shoot. He gave a modest demonstration of his prowess one afternoon, with Randy's .22, that left us gasping. He just lifted that little rifle in his powerful black hands as if it were a toy, without seeming to take aim, pointed it toward a strip of tin on which we had crudely marked out some bull's-eye circles, and he simply peppered the center of the bull's-eye, putting twelve holes through a space one inch square, so fast we could not even count the shots.

He knew how to box too. I think he had been a regimental champion. At any rate, he was as cunning and crafty as a cat. He never boxed with us, of course, but Randy had two sets of gloves, and Dick used to coach us while we sparred. There was something amazingly tender and watchful about him. He taught us many things — how to lead, to hook, to counter and to block — but he was careful to see that we did not hurt each other.

He knew about football, too, and today he paused, a powerful, respectable-looking Negro man of thirty years or more, and watched us for a moment as we played.

Randy took the ball and went up to him. "How do you hold it, Dick?" he said. "Is this right?"

Dick watched him attentively as he gripped the ball, and held it back 10 above his shoulder. The Negro nodded approvingly and said, "That's right, Cap'n Shepperton. You've got it. Only," he said gently, and now took the ball in his own powerful hand, "when you gits a little oldah yo' handses gits biggah and you gits a bettah grip."

His own great hand, in fact, seemed to hold the ball as easily as if it were an apple. And, holding it so a moment, he brought it back, aimed over his outstretched left hand as if he were pointing a gun, and rifled it in a beautiful, whizzing spiral thirty yards or more to Gus. He then showed us how to kick, how to get the ball off of the toe in such a way that it would rise and spiral cleanly. He knew how to do this too. He must have got off kicks there, in the yard at Shepperton's, that traveled fifty yards.

He showed us how to make a fire, how to pile the kindling so that the flames shot up cone-wise, cleanly, without smoke or waste. He showed us how to strike a match with the thumbnail of one hand and keep and hold the flame in the strongest wind. He showed us how to lift a weight, how to tote a burden on our shoulders in the easiest way. There was nothing that he did not know. We were all so proud of him. Mr. Shepperton himself declared that Dick was the best man he'd ever had, the smartest darky that he'd ever known.

And yet? He went too softly, at too swift a pace. He was there upon you sometimes like a cat. Looking before us, sometimes, seeing nothing but the world before us, suddenly we felt a shadow at our backs and, looking up, would find that Dick was there. And there was something moving in the night. We never saw him come or go. Sometimes we would waken, startled, and feel that we had heard a board creak, and the soft clicking of a latch, a shadow passing swiftly. All was still.

"Young white fokes, oh, young white gent'mun," — his soft voice ending in a moan, a kind of rhythm in his hips — "oh, young white fokes, Ise tellin' you" — that soft low moan again — "you gotta love each othah like a brothah." He was deeply religious and went to church three times a week. He read his Bible every night. It was the only object on his square board table.

15   Sometimes Dick would come out of his little basement room, and his eyes would be red, as if he had been weeping. We would know, then, that he had been reading his Bible. There would be times when he would almost moan when he talked to us, a kind of hymnal chant that came from some deep and fathomless intoxication of the spirit, and that transported him. For us, it was a troubling and bewildering experience. We tried to laugh it off and make jokes about it. But there was something in it so dark and strange and full of a feeling that we could not fathom that our jokes were hollow, and the trouble in our minds and in our hearts remained.

Sometimes on these occasions his speech would be made up of some weird jargon of Biblical phrases, of which he seemed to have hundreds, and which he wove together in this strange pattern of his emotion in a sequence that was meaningless to us, but to which he himself had the coherent clue. "Oh, young white fokes," he would begin, moaning gently, "de dry bones in de valley. I tell you, white fokes, de day is comin' when He's comin' on dis earth again to sit in judgment. He'll put de sheep upon de right hand and de goats upon de left. Oh, white fokes, white fokes, de Armageddon day's a-comin', white fokes, an' de dry bones in de valley."

Or again, we could hear him singing as he went about his work, in his deep rich voice, so full of warmth and strength, so full of Africa, singing hymns that were not only of his own race but familiar to us all. I don't know where he learned them. Perhaps they were remembered from his Army days. Perhaps he had learned them in the service of former masters. He drove the Sheppertons to church on Sunday morning, and would wait for them throughout the morning service. He would come up to the side door of the church while the service was going on, neatly dressed in his good dark suit, holding his chauffeur's hat respectfully in his hand, and stand there humbly and listen during the course of the entire sermon.

And then, when the hymns were sung and the great rich sound would swell and roll out into the quiet air of Sunday, Dick would stand and listen, and sometimes he would join in quietly in the song. A number of these favorite Presbyterian hymns we heard him singing many times in a low rich voice as he went about his work around the house. He would sing Who Follows in His Train? or Alexander's Glory Song, or Rock of Ages, or Onward, Christian Soldiers!

And yet? Well, nothing happened — there was just "a flying hint from here and there," and the sense of something passing in the night. Turning into the square one day as Dick was driving Mr. Shepperton to town, Lon Everett skidded murderously around the corner, sideswiped Dick and took the fender off. The Negro was out of the car like a cat and got his master out. Shepperton was unhurt. Lon Everett climbed out and reeled across the street, drunk as a sot at three o'clock. He swung viciously, clumsily, at the Negro, smashed him in the face. Blood trickled from the flat black nostrils and from the thick liver-colored lips. Dick did not move. But suddenly the whites of his eyes were shot with red, his bleeding lips bared for a moment over the white ivory of his teeth. Lon smashed at him again. The Negro took it full in the face again; his hands twitched slightly, but he did not move. They collared the drunken sot and hauled him off and locked him up. Dick stood there for a moment, then he wiped his face and turned to see what damage had been done to the car. No more now, but there were those who saw it who remembered later how the eyes went red.

Another thing: Sheppertons had a cook named Pansy Harris. She was a comely Negro wench, young, plump, black as the ace of spades, a good-hearted girl with a deep dimple in her cheeks and faultless teeth, bared in the most engaging smile. No one ever saw Dick speak to her. No one ever saw her glance at him, or him at her, and yet that smilingly good-natured wench became as mournful-silent and as silent-sullen as midnight pitch. She went about her work as mournfully as if she were going to a funeral. The gloom deepened all about her. She answered sullenly now when spoken to.

One night toward Christmas she announced that she was leaving. In response to all entreaties, all efforts to find the reason for her sudden and unreasonable decision, she had no answer except a sullen repetition of the assertion that she had to leave. Repeated questionings did finally wring from her a sullen statement that her husband needed her at home. More than this she would not say, and even this excuse was highly suspect, because her husband was a Pullman porter, only home two days a week and well accustomed to do himself such housekeeping tasks as she might do for him.

The Sheppertons were fond of her. They tried again to find the reason for her leaving. Was she dissatisfied? "No'm" — an implacable monosyllable, mournful, unrevealing as the night. Had she been offered a better job elsewhere? "No'm" — as untelling as before. If they offered her more wages, would she stay with them? "No'm," again and again, sullen and unyielding, until finally the exasperated mistress threw her hands up in a gesture of defeat and said, "All right then, Pansy. Have it your own way, if that's the way you feel. Only for heaven's sake don't leave us in the lurch until we get another cook."

This, at length, with obvious reluctance, the girl agreed to. Then, putting on her hat and coat and taking the paper bag of "leavings" she was allowed to take home with her at night, she went out the kitchen door and made her sullen and morose departure.

This was on Saturday night, a little after eight o'clock. That afternoon Randy and I had been fooling around the basement and, seeing that Dick's door was slightly ajar, we looked in to see if he was there. The little room was empty, swept and spotless, as it had always been.

25 But we did not notice that! We saw it! At the same moment, our breaths caught sharply in a gasp of startled wonderment. Randy was the first to speak. "Look!" he whispered. "Do you see it?"

See it! My eyes were glued upon it. Squarely across the bare board table, blue-dull, deadly in its murderous efficiency, lay a modern repeating rifle. Beside it was a box containing one hundred rounds of ammunition, and behind it, squarely in the center, face downward on the table, was the familiar cover of Dick's worn old Bible.

Then he was on us like a cat. He was there like a great dark shadow before we knew it. We turned, terrified. He was there above us, his thick lips bared above his gums, his eyes gone small and red as rodents'.

"Dick!" Randy gasped, and moistened his dry lips. "Dick!" he fairly cried now.

It was all over like a flash. Dick's mouth closed. We could see the whites of his eyes again. He smiled and said softly, affably, "Yes, suh, Cap'n Shepperton. Yes, suh! You gent'mun lookin' at my rifle?" he said, and moved into the room.

30 I gulped and nodded my head and couldn't say a word, and Randy whispered, "Yes." And both of us still stared at him, with an expression of appalled and fascinated interest.

Dick shook his head and chuckled. "Can't do without my rifle, white fokes. No, suh!" he shook his head good-naturedly again. "Ole Dick, he's — he's — he's an ole Ahmy man, you know. If they take his rifle away from him, why, that's jest lak takin' candy from a little baby. Yes, suh!" he chuckled, and picked the weapon up affectionately. "Ole Dick felt Christmas comin' on — he-he — I reckon he must have felt it in his bones" — he chuckled — "so I been savin' up my money. I just thought I'd hide this heah and keep it as a big supprise fo' the young white fokes untwil Christmas morning. Then I was gonna take the young white fokes out and show 'em how to shoot."

We had begun to breathe more easily now and, almost as if we had been under the spell of the Pied Piper of Hamelin, we had followed him, step by step, into the room.

"Yes, suh," Dick chuckled, "I was just fixin' to hide this gun away twill Christmas Day, but Cap'n Shepperton — hee!" He chuckled heartily and slapped his thigh. "You can't fool ole Cap'n Shepperton. He just must've smelled this ole gun right out. He comes right in and sees it befo' I has a chance to tu'n around. . . . Now, white fokes" — Dick's voice fell to a tone of low and winning confidence — "now that you's found out, I'll tell you what I'll do. If you'll just keep it a supprise from the other white fokes twill Christmas Day, I'll take all you gent'mun out and let you shoot it. Now, cose," he went on quietly, with a shade of resignation, "if you want to tell on me, you can, but" — here his voice fell again, with just the faintest, yet most eloquent shade of sorrowful regret — "old Dick was looking fahwad to this; hopin' to give all the white fokes a supprise Christmas Day."

We promised earnestly that we would keep his secret as if it were our own. We fairly whispered our solemn vow. We tiptoed away out of the little basement room as if we were afraid our very footsteps might betray the partner of our confidence.

This was four o'clock on Saturday afternoon. Already, there was a somber moaning of the wind, gray storm clouds sweeping over. The threat of snow was in the air. 35

Snow fell that night. It came howling down across the hills. It swept in on us from the Smokies. By seven o'clock the air was blind with sweeping snow, the earth was carpeted, the streets were numb. The storm howled on, around houses warm with crackling fires and shaded light. All life seemed to have withdrawn into thrilling isolation. A horse went by upon the streets with muffled hoofs. Storm shook the houses. The world was numb. I went to sleep upon this mystery, lying in the darkness, listening to that exultancy of storm, to that dumb wonder, that enormous and attentive quietness of snow, with something dark and jubilant in my soul I could not utter.

A little after one o'clock that morning I was awakened by the ringing of a bell. It was the fire bell of the city hall, and it was beating an alarm — a hard fast stroke that I had never heard before. Bronze with peril, clangorous through the snow-numbed silence of the air, it had a quality of instance and menace I had never known before. I leaped up and ran to the window to look for the telltale glow against the sky. But almost before I looked, those deadly strokes beat in upon my brain the message that this was no alarm for fire. It was a savage clangorous alarm to the whole town, a brazen tongue to warn mankind against the menace of some peril, secret, dark, unknown, greater than fire or flood could ever be.

I got instantly, in the most overwhelming and electric way, the sense that the whole town had come to life. All up and down the street the houses were beginning to light up. Next door, the Shepperton house was ablaze with light from top to bottom. Even as I looked, Mr. Shepperton, wearing an overcoat over his pajamas, ran down the snow-covered steps and padded out across the snow-covered walk toward the street.

People were beginning to run out of doors. I heard excited shouts and questions everywhere. I saw Nebraska Crane come pounding down the middle of the street. I knew that he was coming for me and Randy. As he ran by Shepperton's, he put his fingers to his mouth and whistled piercingly. It was a signal we all knew.

I was all ready by the time he came running down the alley toward our cottage. He hammered at the door; I was already there.

"Come on!" he said, panting with excitement, his black eyes burning with an intensity I'd never seen before. "Come on!" he cried. We were half-way out across the yard by now. "It's that nigger. He's gone crazy and is running wild."

"Wh-wh-what nigger?" I gasped, pounding at his heels.

Even before he spoke, I had the answer. Mr. Crane had already come out of his house, buttoning his heavy policeman's overcoat as he came. He had paused to speak for a moment to Mr. Shepperton, and I heard Shepperton say quickly, in a low voice, "Which way did he go?"

Then I heard somebody cry, "It's that nigger of Shepperton's!"

Mr. Shepperton turned and went quickly back across his yard toward the house. His wife and two girls stood huddled in the open doorway, white, trembling, holding themselves together, their arms thrust into the wide sleeves of their kimonos.

The telephone in Shepperton's house was ringing like mad, but no one was paying any attention to it. I heard Mrs. Shepperton say quickly, as he ran up the steps, "Is it Dick?" He nodded and passed her brusquely, going toward the phone.

At this moment, Nebraska whistled piercingly again upon his fingers and Randy Shepperton ran past his mother and down the steps. She called sharply to him. He paid no attention to her. When he came up, I saw that his fine thin face was white as a sheet. He looked at me and whispered, "It's — it's Dick!" And in a moment, "They say he's killed four people."

"With — " I couldn't finish.

Randy nodded dumbly, and we both stared there for a minute, aware now of the murderous significance of the secret we had kept, with a sudden sense of guilt and fear, as if somehow the crime lay on our shoulders.

Across the street a window banged up in the parlor of Suggs's house, and Old Man Suggs appeared in the window, clad only in his nightgown, his brutal old face inflamed with excitement, his shock of silvery white hair awry, his powerful shoulders, and his thick hands gripping his crutches.

"He's coming this way!" he bawled to the world in general. "They say he lit out across the square! He's heading out in this direction!"

Mr. Crane paused to yell back impatiently over his shoulder, "No, he went down South Dean Street! He's heading for Wilton and the river! I've already heard from headquarters!"

Automobiles were beginning to roar and sputter all along the street. Across the street I could hear Mr. Potterham sweating over his. He would whirl the crank a dozen times or more; the engine would catch for a moment, cough and sputter, and then die again. Gus ran out-of-doors with a kettle of boiling water and began to pour it feverishly down the radiator spout.

Mr. Shepperton was already dressed. We saw him run down the back steps toward the carriage house. All three of us, Randy, Nebraska, and myself, streaked down the alleyway to help him. We got the old wooden doors open. He went in and cranked the car. It was a new one, and started up at once. Mr. Shepperton backed out into the snowy drive. We all clambered up on the running board. He spoke absently, saying, "You boys stay here. . . . Randy, your mother's calling you," but we all tumbled in and he didn't say a word.

He came backing down the alleyway at top speed. We turned into the street and picked up Mr. Crane at the corner. We lit out for town, going at top speed. Cars were coming out of alleys everywhere. We could hear people shouting questions and replies at one another. I heard one man shout, "He's killed six men!"

I don't think it took us over five minutes to reach the square, but when we got there, it seemed as if the whole town was there ahead of us. Mr. Shepperton pulled the car up and parked in front of the city hall. Mr. Crane leaped out and went pounding away across the square without another word to us.

From every corner, every street that led into the square, people were streaking in. One could see the dark figures of running men across the white carpet of the square. They were all rushing in to one focal point.

The southwest corner of the square where South Dean Street came into it was like a dog fight. Those running figures streaking toward that dense crowd gathered there made me think of nothing else so much as a fight between two boys upon the playgrounds of the school at recess time. The way the crowd was swarming in was just the same.

But then I *heard* a difference. From that crowd came a low and growing mutter, an ugly and insistent growl, of a tone and quality I had never heard before. But I knew instantly what it meant. There was no mistaking the blood note in that foggy growl. And we looked at one another with the same question in the eyes of all.

Only Nebraska's coal-black eyes were shining now with a savage sparkle even they had never had before. "Come on," he said in a low tone, exultantly.

"They mean business this time, sure. Let's go." And he darted away toward the dense and sinister darkness of the crowd.

Even as we followed him we heard coming toward us now, growing, swelling at every instant, one of the most savagely mournful and terrifying sounds that night can know. It was the baying of the hounds as they came up upon the leash from Niggertown. Full-throated, howling deep, the savagery of blood was in it, and the savagery of man's guilty doom was in it too.

They came up swiftly, fairly baying at our heels as we sped across the snow-white darkness of the square. As we got up to the crowd, we saw that it had gathered at the corner where my uncle's hardware store stood. Cash Eager had not yet arrived, but, facing the crowd which pressed in on them so close and menacing that they were almost flattened out against the glass, three or four men were standing with arms stretched out in a kind of chain, as if trying to protect with the last resistance of their strength and eloquence the sanctity of private property.

Will Hendershot was mayor at that time, and he was standing there, arm to arm with Hugh McNair. I could see Hugh, taller by half a foot than anyone around him, his long gaunt figure, the gaunt passion of his face, even the attitude of his outstretched bony arms, strangely, movingly Lincoln-esque, his one good eye blazing in the cold glare of the corner lamp with a kind of cold inspired Scotch passion.

"Wait a minute! You men wait a minute!" he cried. His words cut out above the clamor of the mob like an electric spark. "You'll gain nothing, you'll help nothing if you do this thing!"

They tried to drown him out with an angry and derisive roar. He shot his big fist up into the air and shouted at them, blazed at them with that cold single eye, until they had to hear. "Listen to me!" he cried. "This is no time for mob law! This is no case for lynch law! This is a time for law and order! Wait till the sheriff swears you in! Wait until Cash Eager comes! Wait—"

He got no farther. "Wait, hell!" cried someone. "We've waited long enough! We're going to get that nigger!"

The mob took up the cry. The whole crowd was writhing angrily now, like a tormented snake. Suddenly there was a flurry in the crowd, a scatter-ing. Somebody yelled a warning at Hugh McNair. He ducked quickly, just in time. A brick whizzed past him, smashing the plate-glass window into fragments.

And instantly a bloody roar went up. The crowd surged forward, kicked the fragments of jagged glass away. In a moment the whole mob was storm-ing into the dark store. Cash Eager got there just too late. He arrived in time to take out his keys and open the front doors, but as he grimly remarked it was like closing the barn doors after the horse had been stolen.

The mob was in and helped themselves to every rifle they could find. They smashed open cartridge boxes and filled their pockets with the loose cartridges. Within ten minutes they had looted the store of every rifle, every cartridge in the stock. The whole place looked as if a hurricane had hit it. The mob was streaming out into the street, was already gathering round the dogs a hundred feet or so away, who were picking up the scent at that point, the place where Dick had halted last before he had turned and headed south, downhill along South Dean Street toward the river.

The hounds were scampering about, tugging at the leash, moaning softly with their noses pointed to the snow, their long ears flattened down. But in that light and in that snow it almost seemed no hounds were needed to follow Dick. Straight as a string right down the center of the sheeted car tracks, the Negro's footsteps led away until they vanished downhill in the darkness. 70

But now, although the snow had stopped, the wind was swirling through the street and making drifts and eddies in the snow. The footprints were fading rapidly. Soon they would be gone.

The dogs were given their head. They went straining on softly, sniffing at the snow; behind them the dark masses of the mob closed in and followed. We stood there watching while they went. We saw them go on down the street and vanish. But from below, over the snow-numbed stillness of the air, the vast low mutter of the mob came back to us.

Men were clustered now in groups. Cash Eager stood before his shattered window, ruefully surveying the ruin. Other men were gathered around the big telephone pole at the corner, pointing out two bullet holes that had been drilled cleanly through it.

And swiftly, like a flash, running from group to group, like a powder train of fire, the full detail of that bloody chronicle of night was pieced together.

This was what had happened. Somewhere between nine and ten o'clock that night, Dick Prosser had gone to Pansy Harris's shack in Niggertown. Some said he had been drinking when he went there. At any rate, the police had later found the remnants of a gallon jug of raw corn whisky in the room. What happened, what passed between them, was never known. And, besides, no one was greatly interested. It was a crazy nigger with "another nigger's woman." 75

Shortly after ten o'clock that night, the woman's husband appeared upon the scene. The fight did not start then. According to the woman, the real trouble did not come until an hour or more after his return.

The men drank together. Each was in an ugly temper. Shortly before midnight, they got into a fight. Harris slashed at Dick with a razor. In a second they were locked together, rolling about and fighting like two madmen on the floor. Pansy Harris went screaming out-of-doors and across the street into a dingy little grocery store.

A riot call was telephoned at once to police headquarters on the public square. The news came in that a crazy nigger had broken loose on Gulley Street in Niggertown, and to send help at once. Pansy Harris ran back across the street toward her little shack.

As she got there, her husband, with blood streaming from his face, staggered out into the street, with his hands held up protectively behind his head in a gesture of instinctive terror. At the same moment, Dick Prosser appeared in the doorway of the shack, deliberately took aim with his rifle and shot the fleeing Negro squarely through the back of the head. Harris dropped forward on his face into the snow. He was dead before he hit the ground. A huge dark stain of blood-soaked snow widened out around him. Dick Prosser seized the terrified Negress by the arm, hurled her into the shack, bolted the door, pulled down the shades, blew out the lamp and waited.

80 A few minutes later, two policemen arrived from town. They were a young constable named Willis, and John Grady, a lieutenant of police. The policemen took one look at the bloody figure in the snow, questioned the frightened keeper of the grocery store and, after consulting briefly, produced their weapons and walked out into the street.

Young Willis stepped softly down on to the snow-covered porch of the shack, flattened himself against the wall between the window and the door, and waited. Grady went around to the side and flashed his light through the window, which, on this side, was shadeless. Grady said in a loud tone: "Come out of there!"

Dick's answer was to shoot him cleanly through the wrist. At the same moment Willis kicked the door in and, without waiting, started in with pointed revolver. Dick shot him just above the eyes. The policeman fell forward on his face.

Grady came running out around the house, rushed into the grocery store, pulled the receiver of the old-fashioned telephone off the hook, rang frantically for headquarters and yelled out across the wire that a crazy nigger had killed Sam Willis and a Negro man, and to send help.

At this moment Dick stepped out across the porch into the street, aimed swiftly through the dirty window of the little store and shot John Grady as he stood there at the phone. Grady fell dead with a bullet that entered just below his left temple and went out on the other side.

85 Dick, now moving in a long, unhurried stride that covered the ground with catlike speed, turned up the long snow-covered slope of Gulley Street and began his march toward town. He moved right up the center of the street, shooting cleanly from left to right as he went. Halfway up the hill, the second-story window of a two-story Negro tenement flew open. An old Negro man stuck out his ancient head of cotton wool. Dick swiveled and shot casually from his hip. The shot tore the top of the old Negro's head off.

By the time Dick reached the head of Gulley Street, they knew he was coming. He moved steadily along, leaving his big tread cleanly in the middle of the sheeted street, shifting a little as he walked, swinging his gun cross-wise before him. This was the Negro Broadway of the town, but where those poolrooms, barbershops, drugstores and fried-fish places had been loud with dusky life ten minutes before, they were now silent as the ruins of Egypt. The word was flaming through the town that a crazy nigger was on the way. No one showed his head.

Dick moved on steadily, always in the middle of the street, reached the end of Gulley Street and turned into South Dean — turned right, uphill, in the middle of the car tracks, and started toward the square. As he passed the lunchroom on the left, he took a swift shot through the window at the counter man. The fellow ducked behind the counter. The bullet crashed into the wall above his head.

Meanwhile, at police headquarters, the sergeant had sent John Chapman out across the square to head Dick off. Mr. Chapman was perhaps the best-liked man upon the force. He was a pleasant florid-faced man of forty-five, with curling brown mustaches, congenial and good-humored, devoted to his family, courageous, but perhaps too kindly and too gentle for a good policeman.

John Chapman heard the shots and ran. He came up to the corner by Eager's hardware store just as Dick's last shot went crashing through the lunchroom window. Mr. Chapman took up his post there at the corner behind the telephone post that stood there at that time. Mr. Chapman, from his vantage point behind this post, took out his revolver and shot directly at Dick Prosser as he came up the street.

By this time Dick was not more than thirty yards away. He dropped quietly upon one knee and aimed. Mr. Chapman shot again and missed. Dick fired. The high-velocity bullet bored through the post a little to one side. It grazed the shoulder of John Chapman's uniform and knocked a chip out of the monument sixty yards or more behind him in the center of the square. **90**

Mr. Chapman fired again and missed. And Dick, still coolly poised upon his knee, as calm and steady as if he were engaging in a rifle practice, fired again, drilled squarely through the center of the post and shot John Chapman through the heart. Then Dick rose, pivoted like a soldier in his tracks and started down the street, straight as a string, right out of town.

This was the story as we got it, pieced together like a train of fire among the excited groups of men that clustered there in trampled snow before the shattered glass of Eager's store.

But now, save for these groups of talking men, the town again was silent. Far off in the direction of the river, we could hear the mournful baying of the hounds. There was nothing more to see or do. Cash Eager stopped, picked up some fragments of the shattered glass and threw them in the window. A policeman was left on guard, and presently all five of us — Mr. Shepperton, Cash Eager and we three boys — walked back across the square and got into the car and drove home again.

But there was no more sleep, I think, for anyone that night. Black Dick had murdered sleep. Toward daybreak, snow began to fall again. The snow continued through the morning. It was piled deep in gusting drifts by noon. All footprints were obliterated; the town waited, eager, tense, wondering if the man could get away.

They did not capture him that day, but they were on his trail. From time to time throughout the day, news would drift back to us. Dick had turned east along the river and gone out for some miles along the Fairchilds road. **95**

There, a mile or two from Fairchilds, he crossed the river at the Rocky Shallows.

Shortly after daybreak, a farmer from the Fairchilds section had seen him cross a field. They picked the trail up there again and followed it across the field and through a wood. He had come out on the other side and got down into the Cane Creek section, and there, for several hours, they lost him. Dick had gone right down into the icy water of the creek and walked upstream a mile or so. They brought the dogs down to the creek, to where he broke the trail, took them over to the other side and scented up and down.

Toward five o'clock that afternoon they picked the trail up on the other side, a mile or more upstream. From that point on, they began to close in on him. The dogs followed him across the fields, across the Lester road, into a wood. One arm of the posse swept around the wood to head him off. They knew they had him. Dick, freezing, hungry and unsheltered, was hiding in that wood. They knew he couldn't get away. The posse ringed the wood and waited until morning.

At 7:30 the next morning he made a break for it. He got through the line without being seen, crossed the Lester road and headed back across the field in the direction of Cane Creek. And there they caught him. They saw him plunging through the snowdrift of a field. A cry went up. The posse started after him.

Part of the posse were on horseback. The men rode in across the field. Dick halted at the edge of the wood, dropped deliberately upon one knee and for some minutes held them off with rapid fire. At two hundred yards he dropped Doc Lavender, a deputy, with a bullet through the throat.

The posse came in slowly, in an encircling, flankwise movement. Dick got two more of them as they closed in, and then, as deliberately as a trained soldier retreating in good order, still firing as he went, he fell back through the wood. At the other side he turned and ran down through a sloping field that bordered on Cane Creek. At the creek edge, he turned again, knelt once more in the snow and aimed.

It was Dick's last shot. He didn't miss. The bullet struck Wayne Foraker, a deputy, dead center in the forehead and killed him in his saddle. Then the posse saw the Negro aim again, and nothing happened. Dick snapped the breech open savagely, then hurled the gun away. A cheer went up. The posse came charging forward. Dick turned, stumblingly, and ran the few remaining yards that separated him from the cold and rock-bright waters of the creek.

And here he did a curious thing — a thing that no one ever wholly understood. It was thought that he would make one final break for freedom, that he would wade the creek and try to get away before they got to him. Instead, he sat down calmly on the bank and, as quietly as if he were seated on his cot in an Army barracks, he unlaced his shoes, took them off, placed them together neatly at his side, and then stood up like a soldier, erect, in his bare bleeding feet, and faced the mob.

The men on horseback reached him first. They rode up around him and discharged their guns into him. He fell forward in the snow, riddled with bullets. The men dismounted, turned him over on his back, and all the other men came in and riddled him. They took his lifeless body, put a rope around his neck and hung him to a tree. Then the mob exhausted all their ammunition on the riddled carcass.

By nine o'clock that morning the news had reached town. Around eleven o'clock, the mob came back along the river road. A good crowd had gone out to meet it at the Wilton Bottoms. The sheriff rode ahead. Dick's body had been thrown like a sack and tied across the saddle of the horse of one of the deputies he had killed.

It was in this way, bullet-riddled, shot to pieces, open to the vengeful and the morbid gaze of all, that Dick came back to town. The mob came back right to its starting point in South Dean Street. They halted there before an undertaking parlor, not twenty yards away from where Dick knelt to kill John Chapman. They took that ghastly mutilated thing and hung it in the window of the undertaker's place, for every woman, man, and child in town to see.

And it was so we saw him last. We said we wouldn't look. But in the end we went. And I think it has always been the same with people. They protest. They shudder. And they say they will not go. But in the end they always have their look.

At length we went. We saw it, tried wretchedly to make ourselves believe that once this thing had spoken to us gently, had been partner to our confidence, object of our affection and respect. And we were sick with nausea and fear, for something had come into our lives we could not understand.

We looked and whitened to the lips, craned our necks and looked away, and brought unwilling, fascinated eyes back to the horror once again, and craned and turned again, and shuffled in the slush uneasily, but could not go. And we looked up at the leaden reek of day, the dreary vapor of the sky, and, bleakly, at these forms and faces all around us — the people come to gape and stare, the poolroom loafers, the town toughs, the mongrel conquerors of earth — and yet, familiar to our lives and to the body of our whole experience, all known to our landscape, all living men.

And something had come into life — into our lives — that we had never known about before. It was a kind of shadow, a poisonous blackness filled with bewildered loathing. The snow would go, we knew; the reeking vapors of the sky would clear away. The leaf, the blade, the bud, the bird, then April, would come back again, and all of this would be as it had ever been. The homely light of day would shine again familiarly. And all of this would vanish as an evil dream. And yet not wholly so. For we would still remember the old dark doubt and loathing of our kind, of something hateful and unspeakable in the souls of men. We knew that we should not forget.

Beside us, a man was telling the story of his own heroic accomplishments to a little group of fascinated listeners. I turned and looked at him. It was

Ben Pounders of the ferret face, the furtive and uneasy eye, Ben Pounders of the mongrel mouth, the wiry muscles of the jaw, Ben Pounders, the collector of usurious lendings to the blacks, the nigger hunter. And now Ben Pounders boasted of another triumph. He was the proud possessor of another scalp.

"I was the first one to git in a shot," he said. "You see that hole there?" He pointed with a dirty finger. "That big hole right above the eye?" They turned and goggled with a drugged and feeding stare.

"That's mine," the hero said, turned briefly to the side and spat tobacco juice into the slush. "That's where I got him. Hell, after that he didn't know what hit him. He was dead before he hit the ground. We all shot him full of holes then. We sure did fill him full of lead. Why, hell, yes," he declared, with a decisive movement of his head, "we counted up to two hundred and eighty-seven. We must have put three hundred holes in him."

And Nebraska, fearless, blunt, outspoken as he always was, turned abruptly, put two fingers to his lips and spat between them, widely and contemptuously.

"Yeah — *we!*" he grunted. "*We* killed a big one! We — we killed a b'ar, we did! . . . Come on, boys," he said gruffly. "Let's be on our way!"

And, fearless and unshaken, untouched by any terror or any doubt, he moved away. And two white-faced, nauseated boys went with him.

A day or two went by before anyone could go into Dick's room again. I went in with Randy and his father. The little room was spotless, bare and tidy as it had always been. But even the very austerity of that little room now seemed terribly alive with the presence of its black tenant. It was Dick's room. We all knew that. And somehow we all knew that no one else could ever live there again.

Mr. Shepperton went over to the table, picked up Dick's old Bible that still lay there, open and face downward, held it up to the light and looked at it, at the place that Dick had marked when he last read in it. And in a moment, without speaking to us, he began to read in a quiet voice:

"The Lord is my shepherd; I shall not want.

"2. He maketh me to lie down in green pastures: he leadeth me beside the still waters.

"3. He restoreth my soul: he leadeth me in the paths of righteousness for his name's sake.

"4. Yea, though I walk through the valley of the shadow of death, I will fear no evil: for thou art with me — "

Then Mr. Shepperton closed the book and put it down upon the table, the place where Dick had left it. And we went out the door, he locked it, and we went back into that room no more forever.

The years passed, and all of us were given unto time. We went our ways. But often they would turn and come again, these faces and these voices of the past, and burn there in my memory again, upon the muted and immortal geography of time.

And all would come again — the shout of the young voices, the hard thud of the kicked ball, and Dick moving, moving steadily, Dick moving, moving silently, a storm-white world and silence, and something moving, moving in the night. Then I would hear the furious bell, the crowd a-clamor and the baying of the dogs, and feel the shadow coming that would never disappear. Then I would see again the little room that we would see no more, the table and the book. And the pastoral holiness of that old psalm came back to me and my heart would wonder with perplexity and doubt.

For I had heard another song since then, and one that Dick, I know, had 125 never heard, and one perhaps he might not have understood, but one whose phrases and whose imagery it seemed to me would suit him better:

> What the hammer? What the chain?
> In what furnace was thy brain?
> What the anvil? What dread grasp
> Dare its deadly terrors clasp?
>
> When the stars threw down their spears,
> And water'd heaven with their tears,
> Did He smile His work to see?
> Did He who made the lamb make thee?

"*What* the hammer? *What* the chain?" No one ever knew. It was a mystery and a wonder. There were a dozen stories, a hundred clues and rumors; all came to nothing in the end. Some said that Dick had come from Texas, others that his home had been in Georgia. Some said that it was true that he had been enlisted in the Army, but that he had killed a man while there and served a term at Leavenworth. Some said he had served in the Army and had received an honorable discharge, but had later killed a man and had served a term in a state prison in Louisiana. Others said that he had been an Army man, but that he had gone crazy, that he had served a period in an asylum, that he had escaped from prison, that he was a fugitive from justice at the time he came to us.

But all these stories came to nothing. Nothing was ever proved. Men debated and discussed these things a thousand times — who and what he had been, what he had done, where he had come from — and all of it came to nothing. No one knew the answer. But I think that I have found the answer. I think I know from where he came.

He came from darkness. He came out of the heart of darkness, from the dark heart of the secret and undiscovered South. He came by night, just as he passed by night. He was night's child and partner, a token of the other side of man's dark soul, a symbol of those things that pass by darkness and that still remain, a symbol of man's evil innocence, and the token of his mystery, a projection of his own unfathomed quality, a friend, a brother and a mortal enemy, an unknown demon, two worlds together — a tiger and a child.

QUESTIONS

1. Discuss the setting of the story. How important is it? How much do we learn about the town and its people? On what implicit premise are the black-white relationships in this town based?
2. The story begins and ends with stanzas from William Blake's poem, "The Tiger." How does this poem relate to the theme of the story? If you are not familiar with it, look it up and read the whole poem. How is it related to the passage in the Bible to which Dick's Bible was left open (paragraphs 118–21)?
3. The second sentence in "The Most Dangerous Game" is, "It's rather a mystery." Are there any "mysteries" in this story? With what kind of mystery is each story concerned? To what extent is the mystery in each resolved?
4. Dick Prosser's character, like that of General Zaroff, consists of many contradictions. Discuss. In his contradictions, is Dick completely unlike the people of the white community? Why does he "go crazy"? Is his character more or less plausible than General Zaroff's?
5. Compare the manhunt in this story with that in "The Most Dangerous Game." How is it similar? How is it different?
6. What feelings and considerations motivate the whites in tracking Dick down? What meaning has Dick's final gesture of removing his shoes and awaiting the posse (paragraph 102)? How does this action contrast with the way his body is treated by the whites?
7. "The Most Dangerous Game" ends with General Zaroff's death. "The Child by Tiger" continues for several pages after Dick Prosser's death. Why? In what element of the story is each author most interested?
8. The narrator tells this story twenty-five years after its events took place. What importance does this removal in time have for the meaning of the story?
9. Discuss the conflict of good and evil as it is presented in this story and in "The Most Dangerous Game." Which story has greater moral significance? Why?

CHAPTER TWO
Plot

Plot is the sequence of incidents or events of which a story is composed, presented in a significant order. When recounted by itself, it bears about the same relationship to a story that a map does to a journey. Just as a map may be drawn on a finer or grosser scale, so may a plot be recounted with lesser or greater detail. It may include what characters say or think, as well as what they do, but it leaves out description and analysis and concentrates ordinarily on major happenings.

Because plot is the easiest element in fiction to comprehend and put into words, less-experienced readers tend to equate it with the content of the work. When asked what a story is about, they may say that it is about a person who does certain things, or to whom certain things happen — not that it is about a certain kind of person or that it presents a particular insight into life. Immature readers read chiefly for plot; mature readers read for whatever revelations of character or life may be presented by means of plot. Because they read chiefly for plot, immature readers may put a high valuation on intricacy of plot or on violent physical action. On the one hand, they may want schemes and intrigues, mixed identities, disguises, secret letters, hidden passages, and similar paraphernalia. On the other, they may demand fights by land and sea, dangerous missions, hazardous journeys, hair-breadth escapes. There is nothing improper in liking such things, of course, and sometimes the greatest fiction provides them. But if readers can be satisfied *only* with stories having these elements, they are like persons who can enjoy only highly spiced foods. Physical action by itself, after all, is meaningless. In a good story a minimum of physical action may be used to yield a maximum of insight. Every story has *some* action, but for a worthwhile story it must be *significant* action. For a superior writer there may be as much significant action in the way a man greets a friend as in how he handles a sword.

Conceivably a plot might consist merely of a sequence of related actions. Ordinarily, however, both the excitement craved by immature readers and the meaningfulness demanded by mature readers arise out of some sort of **conflict** — a clash of actions, ideas, desires, or wills. Characters may be pitted against some other person or group of persons (conflict of person against person); they may be in conflict with some external force — physical nature, society, or "fate" (conflict of person against environment); or they may be in conflict with some elements in their own natures (conflict of person against himself or herself). The conflict may be physical, mental, emotional, or moral. There is conflict in a chess game, where the competitors sit quite still for hours, as surely as in a wrestling match; emotional conflict may be raging within a person sitting quietly in an empty room.

The central characters in a conflict, whether sympathetic or unsympathetic as persons, are referred to as **protagonists***; the forces arrayed against them, whether persons, things, conventions of society, or traits of their own characters, are the **antagonists**. In some stories the conflict is single, clear-cut, and easily identifiable. In others it is multiple, various, and subtle. A person may be in conflict with other persons, with social norms or nature, and with herself or himself, all at the same time, and sometimes may be involved in conflict without being aware of it.

"The Most Dangerous Game" illustrates most of these kinds of conflict. Rainsford, the protagonist, is pitted first against other men — against General Zaroff and Whitney in the discussions preceding the manhunt and against Zaroff and Ivan during the manhunt. Early in the story he is pitted against nature when he falls into the sea and is unable to get back to the yacht. At the beginning of the manhunt, he is in conflict with himself when he tries to fight off his panic by saying to himself, over and over, "I must keep my nerve. I must keep my nerve." The various conflicts illuminated in this story are physical (Rainsford against the sea and Zaroff), mental (Rainsford's initial conflict of ideas with Whitney and his battle of wits with Zaroff during the manhunt, which Zaroff refers to as "outdoor chess"), emotional (Rainsford's efforts to control his terror), and moral (Rainsford's refusal to "condone cold-blooded murder" in contrast with Zaroff's contempt for "romantic ideas about the value of human life").

Excellent interpretive fiction has been written utilizing all four of these major kinds of conflict. The cheaper varieties of commercial fic-

---

*The technical term **protagonist** is preferable to the popular terms "hero" or "heroine" because it is less ambiguous. The protagonist is simply the central character, the one whose struggles we follow with interest, whether he or she be good or bad, sympathetic or repulsive. A "hero" or "heroine" may be *either* a person of heroic qualities *or* simply the main character, heroic or unheroic.

tion, however, emphasize the conflict between man and man, depending on the element of physical conflict to supply the main part of their excitement. It is hard to conceive of a western story without a fistfight or a gunfight. Even in the crudest kinds of fiction, however, something more will be found than mere physical combat. Good men will be arrayed against bad men, and thus the conflict will also be between moral values. In cheap fiction this conflict is usually clearly defined in terms of moral absolutes, hero versus villain. In interpretive fiction, the contrasts are likely to be less marked. Good may be opposed to good or half-truth to half-truth. There may be difficulty in determining what *is* the good, and internal conflict tends therefore to be more frequent than physical conflict. In the world in which we live, significant moral issues are seldom sharply defined — judgments are difficult, and choices are complex rather than simple. Interpretive writers are aware of this complexity and are more concerned with displaying its various shadings of moral values than with presenting glaring contrasts of good and evil, right and wrong.

Suspense is the quality in a story that makes readers ask "What's going to happen next?" or "How will this turn out?" and impels them to read on to find the answers to these questions. Suspense is greatest when the readers' curiosity is combined with anxiety about the fate of some sympathetic character. Thus in the old serial movies — often appropriately called "cliffhangers" — a strong element of suspense was created at the end of each episode by leaving the hero hanging from the edge of a cliff or the heroine tied to the railroad tracks with the express train rapidly approaching. In murder mysteries — often called "who-dun-its" — suspense is created by the question of who committed the murder. In love stories it is created by the question "Will the boy win the girl?" or "Will the lovers be reunited, and how?" In more sophisticated forms of fiction the suspense often involves not so much the question *what* as the question *why* — not "What will happen next?" but "How is the protagonist's behavior to be explained in terms of human personality and character?" The forms of suspense range from crude to subtle and may concern not only actions but psychological considerations and moral issues. Two common devices for achieving suspense are to introduce an element of **mystery** (an unusual set of circumstances for which the readers crave an explanation), or to place the protagonist in a **dilemma** (a position in which he or she must choose between two courses of action, both undesirable). But suspense can be readily created for most readers by placing *anybody* on a seventeenth-story window ledge or simply by bringing together two physically attractive young people.

In "The Most Dangerous Game," suspense is initiated in the opening sentences with Whitney's account of the mystery of "Ship-Trap Island," of which sailors "have a curious dread" — a place that seems to emanate evil. The mystery grows when, in this out-of-the-way spot, Rainsford discovers an enormous château with a leering gargoyle knocker on its massive door and is confronted by a bearded giant pointing a long-barreled revolver straight at his heart. A second mystery is introduced when General Zaroff tells Rainsford that he hunts "more dangerous game" on this island than the Cape buffalo. He then puts off Rainsford's (and the reader's) curiosity for some thirty-six paragraphs before revealing what the game is. Meanwhile, by placing the hero in physical danger, a second kind of suspense is introduced. Initiated by Rainsford's fall into the sea and his confrontation with Ivan, this kind of suspense becomes the principal suspense device in the second half of the story. Will Rainsford escape — and how? — are the questions that keep the reader going. The manhunt itself begins with a dilemma. Rainsford must choose between three undesirable courses of action: he can hunt men with Zaroff; he can let himself be hunted; or he can submit to being tortured by Ivan. During the hunt, he is faced with other lesser dilemmas. For instance, on the third day, pursued by Zaroff's hounds, "Rainsford knew he could do one of two things. He could stay where he was and wait. That was suicide. He could flee. That was postponing the inevitable."

Suspense is usually the first quality mentioned by immature readers when asked what makes a good story — and, indeed, unless a story makes us eager to keep on reading it, it can have little merit at all. Nevertheless, the importance of suspense is often overrated. After all, we don't listen to a Beethoven symphony to discover how it will turn out. A good story, like a good dinner, should furnish its pleasure as it goes, because it is amusing or well written or morally penetrating or because the characters are interesting to live with. One test of a story is whether it creates a desire to read it again. Like a Beethoven symphony, a good story should be as good or better on a second or third encounter — when we already know what is going to happen — as on the first. Discriminating readers, therefore, while they do not *disvalue* suspense, may be suspicious of stories in which suspense is artificially created — by the simple withholding of vital information, for instance — or in which suspense is all there is. They will ask whether the author's purpose has been merely to keep them guessing what will happen next or to reveal something about experience. They will be less interested in whether the man on the seventeenth-story window ledge will jump than in the reasons for his being on the ledge. When the readers' primary interest is shifted from

"What happens next?" to "*Why* do things happen as they do?" or "What is the significance of this series of events?" they have taken their most important step forward.

Closely connected with the element of suspense in a short story is the element of **surprise**. If we know ahead of time exactly what is going to happen in a story and why, there can be no suspense; as long as we do not know, whatever happens comes with an element of surprise. The surprise is proportional to the unexpectedness of what happens; it becomes pronounced when the story departs radically from our expectation. In the short story such radical departure is most often found in a **surprise ending:** one that reveals a sudden new turn or twist.

As with physical action and suspense, less-experienced readers make a heavier demand for surprise than do experienced readers. The escape story supplies a surprise ending more frequently than does the interpretive. There are two ways by which the legitimacy and value of a surprise ending may be judged: (1) by the fairness with which it is achieved and (2) by the purpose that it serves. If the surprise is brought about as a result of an improbable coincidence or an unlikely series of small coincidences, or by the planting of false clues (details whose only purpose is to mislead the readers), or through the withholding of information that the readers ought to have been given earlier in the story, or by manipulation of the point of view (see Chapter 5), then we may well dismiss it as a cheap trick. If, on the other hand, the ending that comes at first as a surprise seems perfectly logical and natural as we look back over the story, we may grant it as fairly achieved. Again, a surprise ending may be judged as trivial if it exists simply for its own sake — to shock or to titillate the reader. We may judge it as a fraud if it serves, as it does in much routine commercial fiction, to conceal earlier weaknesses in the story by giving the readers a shiny bauble at the end to absorb and concentrate their attention. Its justification comes when it serves to open up or to reinforce the meaning of the story. The worthwhile surprise is one that furnishes illumination, not just a reversal of expectation.

Whether or not a story has a surprise ending, immature readers often demand that it have a **happy ending:** the protagonist must solve his problems, defeat the villain, win the girl, "live happily ever after." A common obstacle confronting readers who are making their first attempts to enjoy interpretive fiction is that such fiction often, though by no means always, ends unhappily. They are likely to label such stories as "depressing" and to complain that "real life has troubles enough of its own" or, conversely, that "real life is seldom as unhappy as all that."

Two justifications may be made for the **unhappy ending**. First, many situations in real life have unhappy endings; therefore, if fiction is to illuminate life, it must present defeat as well as triumph. Commercial sports-story writers usually write of how an individual or a team achieves victory against odds. Yet, if one team wins the pennant, thirteen others must lose it, and if a golfer wins a tournament, fifty or a hundred others must fail to win it. In situations like these, at least, success is much less frequent than failure. Sometimes sports writers, for a variant, will tell how an individual lost the game but learned some important moral lesson — good sportsmanship, perhaps, or the importance of fair play. But here again, in real life, such compensations are gained only occasionally. Defeat, in fact, sometimes embitters people and makes them less able to cope with life than before. Thus we need to understand and perhaps expect defeat as well as victory.

Second, the unhappy ending has a peculiar value for writers who wish us to ponder life. The story with a happy ending has been "wrapped up" for us: readers are sent away feeling pleasantly if vaguely satisfied with the world and cease to think about the story searchingly. The unhappy ending, on the other hand, may cause them to brood over the results, to go over the story in their minds, and thus by searching out its implications to get more from it. Just as we can judge individuals better when we see how they behave in times of trouble, so we can see deeper into life when it is pried open for inspection. The unhappy endings are more likely to raise significant issues. Shakespeare's tragedies reverberate longer and more resonantly than his comedies. The ending of "The Most Dangerous Game" is designed to resolve all our anxieties. The ending of "The Child by Tiger" is designed to make us brood over the mysteries and contradictions of human nature — that is, of our own natures.

Discriminating readers evaluate an ending not by whether it is happy or unhappy but by whether it is logical in terms of what precedes it* and by the fullness of revelation it affords. They have learned that an ending that meets these tests can be profoundly satisfying, whether happy or unhappy. They have learned also that a story, to be artistically satisfying, need have no ending at all in the sense that its central conflict is resolved in favor of protagonist or antagonist. In real life some problems are never solved and some contests never permanently won. A story, therefore,

---

*The movies or television sometimes make a book with an unhappy ending into a film with a happy ending. Such an operation, if the book was artistically successful, sets aside the laws of logic and the expectations we naturally build on them.

may have an **indeterminate ending**, one in which no definitive conclusion is reached. Conclusion of some kind there must of course be: the story, if it is to be an artistic unit, cannot simply stop. But the conclusion need not be in terms of a resolved conflict. We cannot be sure whether Miss Brill in Mansfield's story (page 88) consciously realizes that she has created a fantasy life for herself, nor whether such a realization (if it occurs) will permanently change her life. But the story is more effective without a resolution, for it leaves us pondering the question: is it always better to face reality, or may a life based on fantasy be preferable?

Artistic unity is essential to a good plot. There must be nothing in the story that is irrelevant, that does not contribute to the total meaning, nothing that is there only for its own sake or its own excitement. Good writers exercise rigorous selection: they include nothing that does not advance the central intention of the story. But they not only select; they also arrange. The incidents and episodes are placed in the most effective order, which is not necessarily the chronological order, and when rearranged in chronological order by the reader, make a logical progression. In a highly unified story each event grows out of the preceding one in time and leads logically to the next. The various stages of the story are linked together in a chain of cause and effect. With such a story one seldom feels that events might as easily have taken one turn as another. One feels not that the author is managing the plot but rather that the plot has a quality of inevitability, given a certain set of characters and an initial situation.

An author who gives a story a turn unjustified by the situation or the characters involved is guilty of **plot manipulation**. Any unmotivated action furnishes an instance of plot manipulation. We suspect authors of plot manipulation also if they rely too heavily on chance or on coincidence to bring about a solution to a story. In Poe's famous story "The Pit and the Pendulum," when the victim of the Spanish Inquisition is rescued by the outstretched arm of the commanding general of the invading French army just at the moment when the converging fiery walls of his torture chamber have caused him to fall fainting into the abyss, we have a notorious example of such a contrived or manipulated ending.*

Chance cannot be barred from fiction, of course, any more than it can be barred from life. But if an author uses an improbable chance to effect

---

*This kind of coincidental resolution is sometimes referred to as *deus ex machina* ("god from the machine") after the practice of some ancient Greek dramatists in having a god descend from heaven at the last minute (in the theater by means of a stage machine) to rescue the protagonist from some impossible situation. The general in Poe's story is clearly the modern counterpart of such a supernatural deliverer.

a resolution to a story, the story loses its sense of conviction and inevitability. The objections to such a use of coincidence* are even more forcible, for coincidence is chance compounded. Coincidence may be justifiably used to initiate a story, and occasionally to complicate it, but not to resolve it. It is objectionable in proportion to its improbability, its importance to the story, and its nearness to the end. If two characters in a story both start talking of the same topic at once, it may be a coincidence but hardly an objectionable one. If they both decide suddenly to kill their mothers at the same time, we may find the coincidence less acceptable. But the use of even a highly improbable coincidence may be perfectly appropriate at the start of a story. Just as a chemist may wonder what will happen if certain chemical elements are placed together in a test tube, an author may wonder what will happen if two former lovers accidentally meet in Majorca, where they longed as young lovers to go, long after they have each married someone else. The improbable initial situation is justified because it offers a chance to observe human nature in conditions that may be particularly revealing, and mature readers demand only that the author develop a story logically from that initial situation. But the writer who uses a similar coincidence to resolve a story is avoiding the logic of life rather than revealing it. It is often said that fact is stranger than fiction: it *should* be stranger than fiction. In life almost any concatenation of events is possible; in a story the sequence of events should be probable.

There are various approaches to the analysis of plot. We may, if we wish, draw diagrams of different kinds of plots or trace the development of rising action, climax, and falling action. Such procedures, however, if they are concerned with the examination of plot *per se*, are not likely to take us far into the story. Better questions will concern themselves with the *function* of plot — with the relationship of each incident to the total meaning of the story. Plot is important, in interpretive fiction, for what it reveals. The analysis of a story through its central conflict is likely to be especially fruitful, for it rapidly takes us to what is truly at issue in the story. In testing a story for quality, it is useful to examine how the incidents and episodes are connected, for such an examination is a test of the story's probability and unity. We can never get very far, however, by

***Chance** is the occurrence of an event that has no apparent cause in antecedent events or in predisposition of character. In an automobile accident in which a drunk, coming home from a party, crashes into a sober driver from behind, we say that the accident was a chance event in the life of the sober driver but that it was a logical consequence in the life of the drunk. **Coincidence** is the chance concurrence of *two* events that have a peculiar correspondence. If the two drivers involved in the accident had been brothers and were coming from different places, it would be coincidence.

analysis of plot alone. In any good story, plot is inextricable from character and total meaning. Plot by itself gives little more indication of the total story than a map gives of the quality of a journey.

Graham Greene
The Destructors

1

It was the eve of August Bank Holiday that the latest recruit became the leader of the Wormsley Common Gang. No one was surprised except Mike, but Mike at the age of nine was surprised by everything. "If you don't shut your mouth," somebody once said to him, "you'll get a frog down it." After that Mike had kept his teeth tightly clamped except when the surprise was too great.

The new recruit had been with the gang since the beginning of the summer holidays, and there were possibilities about his brooding silence that all recognized. He never wasted a word even to tell his name until that was required of him by the rules. When he said "Trevor" it was a statement of fact, not as it would have been with the others a statement of shame or defiance. Nor did anyone laugh except Mike, who finding himself without support and meeting the dark gaze of the newcomer opened his mouth and was quiet again. There was every reason why T., as he was afterwards referred to, should have been an object of mockery — there was his name (and they substituted the initial because otherwise they had no excuse not to laugh at it), the fact that his father, a former architect and present clerk, had "come down in the world" and that his mother considered herself better than the neighbors. What but an odd quality of danger, of the unpredictable, established him in the gang without any ignoble ceremony of initiation?

The gang met every morning in an impromptu car-park, the site of the last bomb of the first blitz. The leader, who was known as Blackie, claimed to have heard it fall, and no one was precise enough in his dates to point out that he would have been one year old and fast asleep on the down platform

THE DESTRUCTORS   First published in 1954. The setting is London nine years after the conclusion of World War II (1939–1945). During the first sustained bombing attacks on London ("the first blitz") from September 1940 to May 1941, many families slept in the Underground (i.e., subway) stations, which were used as bomb shelters. "Trevor" was typically an upper-class English name. Sir Christopher Wren (1632–1723), England's most famous architect, designed St. Paul's Cathedral and many other late seventeenth- and early eighteenth-century buildings. Graham Greene (1904–1991), who was born just outside London, lived in that city at various stages of his life.

of Wormsley Common Underground Station. On one side of the car-park leant the first occupied house, No. 3, of the shattered Northwood Terrace — literally leant, for it had suffered from the blast of the bomb and the side walls were supported on wooden struts. A smaller bomb and some incendiaries had fallen beyond, so that the house stuck up like a jagged tooth and carried on the further wall relics of its neighbor, a dado, the remains of a fireplace. T., whose words were almost confined to voting "Yes" or "No" to the plan of operations proposed each day by Blackie, once startled the whole gang by saying broodingly, "Wren built that house, father says."

"Who's Wren?"

5   "The man who built St. Paul's."

"Who cares?" Blackie said. "It's only Old Misery's."

Old Misery — whose real name was Thomas — had once been a builder and decorator. He lived alone in the crippled house, doing for himself: once a week you could see him coming back across the common with bread and vegetables, and once as the boys played in the car-park he put his head over the smashed wall of his garden and looked at them.

"Been to the lav," one of the boys said, for it was common knowledge that since the bombs fell something had gone wrong with the pipes of the house and Old Misery was too mean to spend money on the property. He could do the redecorating himself at cost price, but he had never learnt plumbing. The lav was a wooden shed at the bottom of the narrow garden with a star-shaped hole in the door: it had escaped the blast which had smashed the house next door and sucked out the window-frames of No. 3.

The next time the gang became aware of Mr. Thomas was more surprising. Blackie, Mike and a thin yellow boy, who for some reason was called by his surname Summers, met him on the common coming back from the market. Mr. Thomas stopped them. He said glumly, "You belong to the lot that play in the car-park?"

10   Mike was about to answer when Blackie stopped him. As the leader he had responsibilities. "Suppose we are?" he said ambiguously.

"I got some chocolates," Mr. Thomas said. "Don't like 'em myself. Here you are. Not enough to go round, I don't suppose. There never is," he added with somber conviction. He handed over three packets of Smarties.

The gang were puzzled and perturbed by this action and tried to explain it away. "Bet someone dropped them and he picked 'em up," somebody suggested.

"Pinched 'em and then got in a bleeding funk," another thought aloud.

"It's a bribe," Summers said. "He wants us to stop bouncing balls on his wall."

15   "We'll show him we don't take bribes," Blackie said, and they sacrificed the whole morning to the game of bouncing that only Mike was young enough to enjoy. There was no sign from Mr. Thomas.

Next day T. astonished them all. He was late at the rendezvous, and the voting for the day's exploit took place without him. At Blackie's suggestion the gang was to disperse in pairs, take buses at random and see how many free rides could be snatched from unwary conductors (the operation was to be carried out in pairs to avoid cheating). They were drawing lots for their companions when T. arrived.

"Where you been, T.?" Blackie asked. "You can't vote now. You know the rules."

"I've been *there*," T. said. He looked at the ground, as though he had thoughts to hide.

"Where?"

"At Old Misery's." Mike's mouth opened and then hurriedly closed again with a click. He had remembered the frog.

"At Old Misery's?" Blackie said. There was nothing in the rules against it, but he had a sensation that T. was treading on dangerous ground. He asked hopefully, "Did you break in?"

"No. I rang the bell."

"And what did you say?"

"I said I wanted to see his house."

"What did he do?"

"He showed it to me."

"Pinch anything?"

"No."

"What did you do it for then?"

The gang had gathered round: it was as though an impromptu court were about to form and to try some case of deviation. T. said, "It's a beautiful house," and still watching the ground, meeting no one's eyes, he licked his lips first one way, then the other.

"What do you mean, a beautiful house?" Blackie asked with scorn.

"It's got a staircase two hundred years old like a corkscrew. Nothing holds it up."

"What do you mean, nothing holds it up. Does it float?"

"It's to do with opposite forces, Old Misery said."

"What else?"

"There's paneling."

"Like in the Blue Boar?"

"Two hundred years old."

"Is Old Misery two hundred years old?"

Mike laughed suddenly and then was quiet again. The meeting was in a serious mood. For the first time since T. had strolled into the car-park on the first day of the holidays his position was in danger. It only needed a single use of his real name and the gang would be at his heels.

"What did you do it for?" Blackie asked. He was just, he had no jealousy, he was anxious to retain T. in the gang if he could. It was the word "beautiful" that worried him — that belonged to a class world that you could still see parodied at the Wormsley Common Empire° by a man wearing a top

Wormsley Common Empire: a music hall for revues and popular entertainments

hat and a monocle, with a haw-haw accent. He was tempted to say, "My dear Trevor, old chap," and unleash his hell hounds. "If you'd broken in," he said sadly — that indeed would have been an exploit worthy of the gang.

"This was better," T. said. "I found out things." He continued to stare at his feet, not meeting anybody's eye, as though he were absorbed in some dream he was unwilling — or ashamed — to share.

"What things?"

"Old Misery's going to be away all tomorrow and Bank Holiday."

Blackie said with relief, "You mean we could break in?"

"And pinch things?" somebody asked.

Blackie said, "Nobody's going to pinch things. Breaking in — that's good enough, isn't it? We don't want any court stuff."

"I don't want to pinch anything," T. said. "I've got a better idea."

"What is it?"

T. raised his eyes, as grey and disturbed as the drab August day. "We'll pull it down," he said. "We'll destroy it."

Blackie gave a single hoot of laughter and then, like Mike, fell quiet, daunted by the serious implacable gaze. "What'd the police be doing all the time?" he asked.

"They'd never know. We'd do it from inside. I've found a way in." He said with a sort of intensity, "We'd be like worms, don't you see, in an apple. When we came out again there'd be nothing there, no staircase, no panels, nothing but just walls, and then we'd make the walls fall down — somehow."

"We'd go to jug," Blackie said.

"Who's to prove? And anyway we wouldn't have pinched anything." He added without the smallest flicker of glee, "There wouldn't be anything to pinch after we'd finished."

"I've never heard of going to prison for breaking things," Summers said.

"There wouldn't be time," Blackie said. "I've seen housebreakers at work."

"There are twelve of us," T. said. "We'd organize."

"None of us know how . . ."

"I know," T. said. He looked across at Blackie, "Have you got a better plan?"

"Today," Mike said tactlessly, "we're pinching free rides . . ."

"Free rides," T. said. "You can stand down, Blackie, if you'd rather . . ."

"The gang's got to vote."

"Put it up then."

Blackie said uneasily, "It's proposed that tomorrow and Monday we destroy Old Misery's house."

"Here, here," said a fat boy called Joe.

"Who's in favor?"

T. said, "It's carried."

"How do we start?" Summers asked.

"He'll tell you," Blackie said. It was the end of his leadership. He went away to the back of the car-park and began to kick a stone, dribbling it this way and that. There was only one old Morris in the park, for few cars were left there except lorries: without an attendant there was no safety. He took a flying kick at the car and scraped a little paint off the rear mudguard. Beyond, paying no more attention to him than to a stranger, the gang had gathered round T.; Blackie was dimly aware of the fickleness of favor. He thought of going home, of never returning, of letting them all discover the hollowness of T.'s leadership, but suppose after all what T. proposed was possible — nothing like it had ever been done before. The fame of the Wormsley Common car-park gang would surely reach around London. There would be headlines in the papers. Even the grown-up gangs who ran the betting at the all-in wrestling and the barrow-boys would hear with respect of how Old Misery's house had been destroyed. Driven by the pure, simple and altruistic ambition of fame for the gang, Blackie came back to where T. stood in the shadow of Misery's wall.

T. was giving his orders with decision: it was as though this plan had 70 been with him all his life, pondered through the seasons, now in his fifteenth year crystalized with the pain of puberty. "You," he said to Mike, "bring some big nails, the biggest you can find, and a hammer. Anyone else who can better bring a hammer and a screwdriver. We'll need plenty of them. Chisels too. We can't have too many chisels. Can anybody bring a saw?"

"I can," Mike said.

"Not a child's saw," T. said. "A real saw."

Blackie realized he had raised his hand like any ordinary member of the gang.

"Right, you bring one, Blackie. But now there's a difficulty. We want a hacksaw."

"What's a hacksaw?" someone asked. 75

"You can get 'em at Woolworth's," Summers said.

The fat boy called Joe said gloomily, "I knew it would end in a collection."

"I'll get one myself," T. said. "I don't want your money. But I can't buy a sledge-hammer."

Blackie said, "They are working on No. 15. I know where they'll leave their stuff for Bank Holiday."

"Then that's all," T. said. "We meet here at nine sharp." 80

"I've got to go to church," Mike said.

"Come over the wall and whistle. We'll let you in."

2

On Sunday morning all were punctual except Blackie, even Mike. Mike had had a stroke of luck. His mother felt ill, his father was tired after Saturday night, and he was told to go to church alone with many warnings of what would happen if he strayed. Blackie had had difficulty in smuggling out the saw, and then in finding the sledge-hammer at the back of No. 15. He approached the house from a lane at the rear of the garden, for fear of the policeman's beat along the main road. The tired evergreens kept off a stormy sun: another wet Bank Holiday was being prepared over the Atlantic, beginning in swirls of dust under the trees. Blackie climbed the wall into Misery's garden.

There was no sign of anybody anywhere. The lav stood like a tomb in a neglected graveyard. The curtains were drawn. The house slept. Blackie lumbered nearer with the saw and the sledge-hammer. Perhaps after all nobody had turned up: the plan had been a wild invention: they had woken wiser. But when he came close to the back door he could hear a confusion of sound hardly louder than a hive in swarm: a clickety-clack, a bang bang, a scraping, a creaking, a sudden painful crack. He thought: it's true, and whistled.

85   They opened the back door to him and he came in. He had at once the impression of organization, very different from the old happy-go-lucky ways under his leadership. For a while he wandered up and down stairs looking for T. Nobody addressed him: he had a sense of great urgency, and already he could begin to see the plan. The interior of the house was being carefully demolished without touching the outer walls. Summers with hammer and chisel was ripping out the skirting-boards in the ground floor dining-room: he had already smashed the panels of the door. In the same room Joe was heaving up the parquet blocks, exposing the soft wood floor-boards over the cellar. Coils of wire came out of the damaged skirting and Mike sat happily on the floor clipping the wires.

On the curved stairs two of the gang were working hard with an inadequate child's saw on the banisters — when they saw Blackie's big saw they signaled for it wordlessly. When he next saw them a quarter of the banisters had been dropped into the hall. He found T. at last in the bathroom — he sat moodily in the least cared-for room in the house, listening to the sounds coming up from below.

"You've really done it," Blackie said with awe. "What's going to happen?"

"We've only just begun," T. said. He looked at the sledge-hammer and gave his instructions. "You stay here and break the bath and the wash-basin. Don't bother about the pipes. They come later."

Mike appeared at the door. "I've finished the wires, T.," he said.

90   "Good. You've just got to go wandering round now. The kitchen's in the basement. Smash all the china and glass and bottles you can lay hold of. Don't turn on the taps — we don't want a flood — yet. Then go into all the rooms and turn out drawers. If they are locked get one of the others to break them open. Tear up any papers you find and smash all the ornaments. Better take a carving-knife with you from the kitchen. The bedroom's opposite here. Open the pillows and tear up the sheets. That's enough for the moment. And you, Blackie, when you've finished in here crack the plaster in the passage up with your sledge-hammer."

"What are you going to do?" Blackie asked.

"I'm looking for something special," T. said.

It was nearly lunch-time before Blackie had finished and went in search of T. Chaos had advanced. The kitchen was a shambles of broken glass and china. The dining-room was stripped of parquet, the skirting was up, the door had been taken off its hinges, and the destroyers had moved up a floor. Streaks of light came in through the closed shutters where they worked with the seriousness of creators — and destruction after all is a form of creation. A kind of imagination had seen this house as it had now become.

Mike said, "I've got to go home for dinner."

"Who else?" T. asked, but all the others on one excuse or another had brought provisions with them. 95

They squatted in the ruins of the room and swapped unwanted sandwiches. Half an hour for lunch and they were at work again. By the time Mike returned, they were on the top floor, and by six the superficial damage was completed. The doors were all off, all the skirtings raised, the furniture pillaged and ripped and smashed — no one could have slept in the house except on a bed of broken plaster. T. gave his orders — eight o'clock next morning, and to escape notice they climbed singly over the garden wall, into the car-park. Only Blackie and T. were left: the light had nearly gone, and when they touched a switch, nothing worked — Mike had done his job thoroughly.

"Did you find anything special?" Blackie asked.

T. nodded. "Come over here," he said, "and look." Out of both pockets he drew bundles of pound notes. "Old Misery's savings," he said. "Mike ripped out the mattress, but he missed them."

"What are you going to do? Share them?"

"We aren't thieves," T. said. "Nobody's going to steal anything from this house. I kept these for you and me — a celebration." He knelt down on the floor and counted them out — there were seventy in all. "We'll burn them," he said, "one by one," and taking it in turns they held a note upwards and lit the top corner, so that the flame burnt slowly towards their fingers. The grey ash floated above them and fell on their heads like age. "I'd like to see Old Misery's face when we are through," T. said. 100

"You hate him a lot?" Blackie asked.

"Of course I don't hate him," T. said. "There'd be no fun if I hated him." The last burning note illuminated his brooding face. "All this hate and love," he said, "it's soft, it's hooey. There's only things, Blackie," and he looked round the room crowded with the unfamiliar shadows of half things, broken things, former things. "I'll race you home, Blackie," he said.

3

Next morning the serious destruction started. Two were missing — Mike and another boy whose parents were off to Southend and Brighton in spite of the slow warm drops that had begun to fall and the rumble of thunder in the estuary like the first guns of the old blitz. "We've got to hurry," T. said.

Summers was restive. "Haven't we done enough?" he said. "I've been given a bob for slot machines. This is like work."

105 "We've hardly started," T. said. "Why, there's all the floor left, and the stairs. We haven't taken out a single window. You voted like the others. We are going to *destroy* this house. There won't be anything left when we've finished."

They began again on the first floor picking up the top floor-boards next to the outer wall, leaving the joists exposed. Then they sawed through the joists and retreated into the hall, as what was left of the floor heeled and sank. They had learnt with practice, and the second floor collapsed more easily. By the evening an odd exhilaration seized them as they looked down the great hollow of the house. They ran risks and made mistakes: when they thought of the windows it was too late to reach them. "Cor," Joe said, and dropped a penny down in the dry rubble-filled well. It cracked and span among the broken glass.

"Why did we start this?" Summers asked with astonishment; T. was already on the ground, digging at the rubble, clearing a space along the outer wall. "Turn on the taps," he said. "It's too dark for anyone to see now, and in the morning it won't matter." The water overtook them on the stairs and fell through the floorless rooms.

It was then they heard Mike's whistle at the back. "Something's wrong," Blackie said. They could hear his urgent breathing as they unlocked the door.

"The bogies?"° Summers asked.

110 "Old Misery," Mike said. "He's on his way." He put his head between his knees and retched. "Ran all the way," he said with pride.

"But why?" T. said. "He told me . . ." He protested with the fury of the child he had never been, "It isn't fair."

"He was down at Southend," Mike said, "and he was on the train coming back. Said it was too cold and wet." He paused and gazed at the water. "My, you've had a storm here. Is the roof leaking?"

"How long will he be?"

"Five minutes. I gave Ma the slip and ran."

115 "We better clear," Summers said. "We've done enough, anyway."

"Oh, no, we haven't. Anybody could do this—" "This" was the shattered hollowed house with nothing left but the walls. Yet the walls could be preserved. Façades were valuable. They could build inside again more beautifully than before. This could again be a home. He said angrily, "We've got to finish. Don't move. Let me think."

"There's no time," a boy said.

bogies: police

"There's got to be a way," T. said. "We couldn't have got this far . . ."

"We've done a lot," Blackie said.

"No. No, we haven't. Somebody watch the front." 120

"We can't do any more."

"He may come in at the back."

"Watch the back too." T. began to plead. "Just give me a minute and I'll fix it. I swear I'll fix it." But his authority had gone with his ambiguity. He was only one of the gang. "Please," he said.

"Please," Summers mimicked him, and then suddenly struck home with the fatal name. "Run along home, Trevor."

T. stood with his back to the rubble like a boxer knocked groggy against 125 the ropes. He had no words as his dreams shook and slid. Then Blackie acted before the gang had time to laugh, pushing Summers backward. "I'll watch the front, T.," he said, and cautiously he opened the shutters of the hall. The grey wet common stretched ahead, and the lamps gleamed in the puddles. "Someone's coming, T. No, it's not him. What's your plan, T.?"

"Tell Mike to go out to the lav and hide close beside it. When he hears me whistle he's got to count ten and start to shout."

"Shout what?"

"Oh, 'Help,' anything."

"You hear, Mike," Blackie said. He was the leader again. He took a quick look between the shutters. "He's coming, T."

"Quick, Mike. The lav. Stay here, Blackie, all of you till I yell." 130

"Where are you going, T.?"

"Don't worry. I'll see to this. I said I would, didn't I?"

Old Misery came limping off the common. He had mud on his shoes and he stopped to scrape them on the pavement's edge. He didn't want to soil his house, which stood jagged and dark between the bomb-sites, saved so narrowly, as he believed, from destruction. Even the fanlight had been left unbroken by the bomb's blast. Somewhere somebody whistled. Old Misery looked sharply round. He didn't trust whistles. A child was shouting: it seemed to come from his own garden. Then a boy ran into the road from the car-park. "Mr. Thomas," he called. "Mr. Thomas."

"What is it?"

"I'm terribly sorry, Mr. Thomas. One of us got taken short, and we 135 thought you wouldn't mind, and now he can't get out."

"What do you mean, boy?"

"He's got stuck in your lav."

"He'd no business . . . Haven't I seen you before?"

"You showed me your house."

"So I did. So I did. That doesn't give you the right to . . ." 140

"Do hurry, Mr. Thomas. He'll suffocate."

"Nonsense. He can't suffocate. Wait till I put my bag in."

"I'll carry your bag."

"Oh no, you don't. I carry my own."

"This way, Mr. Thomas."

"I can't get in the garden that way. I've got to go through the house."

"But you *can* get in the garden this way, Mr. Thomas. We often do."

"You often do?" He followed the boy with a scandalized fascination. "When? What right? . . ."

"Do you see . . . ? The wall's low."

"I'm not going to climb walls into my own garden. It's absurd."

"This is how we do it. One foot here, one foot there, and over." The boy's face peered down, an arm shot out, and Mr. Thomas found his bag taken and deposited on the other side of the wall.

"Give me back my bag," Mr. Thomas said. From the loo° a boy yelled and yelled. "I'll call the police."

"Your bag's all right, Mr. Thomas. Look. One foot there. On your right. Now just above. To your left." Mr. Thomas climbed over his own garden wall. "Here's your bag, Mr. Thomas."

"I'll have the wall built up," Mr. Thomas said. "I'll not have you boys coming over here, using my loo." He stumbled on the path, but the boy caught his elbow and supported him. "Thank you, thank you, my boy," he murmured automatically. Somebody shouted again through the dark. "I'm coming, I'm coming," Mr. Thomas called. He said to the boy beside him, "I'm not unreasonable. Been a boy myself. As long as things are done regular. I don't mind you playing round the place Saturday mornings. Sometimes I like company. Only it's got to be regular. One of you asks leave and I say Yes. Sometimes I'll say No. Won't feel like it. And you come in at the front door and out at the back. No garden walls."

"Do get him out, Mr. Thomas."

"He won't come to any harm in my loo," Mr. Thomas said, stumbling slowly down the garden. "Oh, my rheumatics," he said. "Always get 'em on Bank Holiday. I've got to go careful. There's loose stones here. Give me your hand. Do you know what my horoscope said yesterday? 'Abstain from any dealings in first half of week. Danger of serious crash.' That might be on this path," Mr. Thomas said. "They speak in parables and double meanings." He paused at the door of the loo. "What's the matter in there?" he called. There was no reply.

"Perhaps he's fainted," the boy said.

"Not in my loo. Here, you come out," Mr. Thomas said, and giving a great jerk at the door he nearly fell on his back when it swung easily open. A hand first supported him and then pushed him hard. His head hit the opposite wall and he sat heavily down. His bag hit his feet. A hand whipped the key out of the lock and the door slammed. "Let me out," he called, and heard the key turn in the lock. "A serious crash," he thought, and felt dithery and confused and old.

A voice spoke to him softly through the star-shaped hole in the door.

loo: outdoor toilet (an older term for "lav")

"Don't worry, Mr. Thomas," it said, "we won't hurt you, not if you stay quiet."

Mr. Thomas put his head between his hands and pondered. He had noticed that there was only one lorry in the car-park, and he felt certain that the driver would not come for it before the morning. Nobody could hear him from the road in front, and the lane at the back was seldom used. Anyone who passed there would be hurrying home and would not pause for what they would certainly take to be drunken cries. And if he did call "Help," who, on a lonely Bank Holiday evening, would have the courage to investigate? Mr. Thomas sat on the loo and pondered with the wisdom of age.

After a while it seemed to him that there were sounds in the silence — they were faint and came from the direction of his house. He stood up and peered through the ventilation-hole — between the cracks in one of the shutters he saw a light, not the light of a lamp, but the wavering light that a candle might give. Then he thought he heard the sound of hammering and scraping and chipping. He thought of burglars — perhaps they had employed the boy as a scout, but why should burglars engage in what sounded more and more like a stealthy form of carpentry? Mr. Thomas let out an experimental yell, but nobody answered. The noise could not even have reached his enemies.

4

Mike had gone home to bed, but the rest stayed. The question of leadership no longer concerned the gang. With nails, chisels, screwdrivers, anything that was sharp and penetrating, they moved around the inner walls worrying at the mortar between the bricks. They started too high, and it was Blackie who hit on the damp course and realized the work could be halved if they weakened the joints immediately above. It was a long, tiring, unamusing job, but at last it was finished. The gutted house stood there balanced on a few inches of mortar between the damp course and the bricks.

There remained the most dangerous task of all, out in the open at the edge of the bomb-site. Summers was sent to watch the road for passers-by, and Mr. Thomas, sitting on the loo, heard clearly now the sound of sawing. It no longer came from his house, and that a little reassured him. He felt less concerned. Perhaps the other noises too had no significance.

A voice spoke to him through the hole. "Mr. Thomas."

"Let me out," Mr. Thomas said sternly.

"Here's a blanket," the voice said, and a long grey sausage was worked through the hole and fell in swathes over Mr. Thomas's head.

"There's nothing personal," the voice said. "We want you to be comfortable tonight."

"Tonight," Mr. Thomas repeated incredulously.

"Catch," the voice said. "Penny buns — we've buttered them, and sausage-rolls. We don't want you to starve, Mr. Thomas."

Mr. Thomas pleaded desperately. "A joke's a joke, boy. Let me out and I won't say a thing. I've got rheumatics. I got to sleep comfortable."

"You wouldn't be comfortable, not in your house, you wouldn't. Not now."

"What do you mean, boy?" but the footsteps receded. There was only the silence of night: no sound of sawing. Mr. Thomas tried one more yell, but he was daunted and rebuked by the silence — a long way off an owl hooted and made away again on its muffled flight through the soundless world.

At seven next morning the driver came to fetch his lorry. He climbed into the seat and tried to start the engine. He was vaguely aware of a voice shouting, but it didn't concern him. At last the engine responded and he backed the lorry until it touched the great wooden shore that supported Mr. Thomas's house. That way he could drive right out and down the street without reversing. The lorry moved forward, was momentarily checked as though something were pulling it from behind, and then went on to the sound of a long rumbling crash. The driver was astonished to see bricks bouncing ahead of him, while stones hit the roof of his cab. He put on his brakes. When he climbed out the whole landscape had suddenly altered. There was no house beside the car-park, only a hill of rubble. He went round and examined the back of his car for damage, and found a rope tied there that was still twisted at the other end round part of a wooden strut.

The driver again became aware of somebody shouting. It came from the wooden erection which was the nearest thing to a house in that desolation of broken brick. The driver climbed the smashed wall and unlocked the door. Mr. Thomas came out of the loo. He was wearing a grey blanket to which flakes of pastry adhered. He gave a sobbing cry. "My house," he said. "Where's my house?"

"Search me," the driver said. His eye lit on the remains of a bath and what had once been a dresser and he began to laugh. There wasn't anything left anywhere.

"How dare you laugh," Mr. Thomas said. "It was my house. My house."

"I'm sorry," the driver said, making heroic efforts, but when he remembered the sudden check to his lorry, the crash of bricks falling, he became convulsed again. One moment the house had stood there with such dignity between the bomb-sites like a man in a top hat, and then, bang, crash, there wasn't anything left — not anything. He said, "I'm sorry. I can't help it, Mr. Thomas. There's nothing personal, but you got to admit it's funny."

QUESTIONS

1. Who is the protagonist in this story — Trevor, Blackie, or the gang? Who or what is the antagonist? Identify the conflicts of the story.
2. How is suspense created?
3. This story uses the most common basic formula of commercial fiction: protagonist aims at a goal, is confronted with various obstacles between himself

and his goal, overcomes the obstacles and achieves his goal. How does this story differ from commercial fiction in its use of this formula? Does the story have a happy ending?

4. Discuss the gang's motivations, taking into account (a) the age and beauty of the house, (b) Blackie's reasons for not going home after losing his position of leadership, (c) the seriousness with which the boys work at their task, and their loss of concern over their leadership, (d) the burning of the banknotes, (e) their consideration for Old Misery, (f) the lorry driver's reaction. What characteristics do the gang's two named exploits — pinching free rides and destroying the house — have in common?

5. Of what significance, if any, is the setting of this story in blitzed London? Does the story have anything to say about the consequences of war? About the causes of war?

6. Explain as fully as you can the causes of the gang's delinquency, taking into account (a) their reaction to the name Trevor, (b) their reaction to Old Misery's gift of chocolates, (c) Blackie's reaction to the word "beautiful," (d) Trevor's comments on "hate and love," (e) Summers's reaction to the word "Please," (f) the setting.

7. What good qualities do the delinquents in this story have? Do they differ as a group from other delinquent gangs you have read or know about? If so, account for the differences.

8. On the surface this is a story of action, suspense, and adventure. At a deeper level it is about delinquency, war, and human nature. Try to sum up what the story says about human nature in general.

Alice Munro
Prue

Prue used to live with Gordon. This was after Gordon had left his wife and before he went back to her — a year and four months in all. Some time later, he and his wife were divorced. After that came a period of indecision, of living together off and on; then the wife went away to New Zealand, most likely for good.

Prue did not go back to Vancouver Island, where Gordon had met her when she was working as a dining-room hostess in a resort hotel. She got a job in Toronto, working in a plant shop. She had many friends in Toronto by that time, most of them Gordon's friends and his wife's friends. They liked Prue and were ready to feel sorry for her, but she laughed them out of it. She is very likable. She has what eastern Canadians call an English accent, though she was born in Canada — in Duncan, on Vancouver Island. This

PRUE First published in 1981. Alice Munro was born in 1931 and grew up in the rural town of Wingham, Ontario. She attended the University of Western Ontario for two years, was married in 1951, and moved with her husband to British Columbia, where she continued to write while raising a family of three daughters. She divorced and returned to Ontario in 1972, where she remarried, and now lives in Clinton. She has published one novel and six books of short stories.

accent helps her to say the most cynical things in a winning and lighthearted way. She presents her life in anecdotes, and though it is the point of most of her anecdotes that hopes are dashed, dreams ridiculed, things never turn out as expected, everything is altered in a bizarre way and there is no explanation ever, people always feel cheered up after listening to her; they say of her that it is a relief to meet somebody who doesn't take herself too seriously, who is so unintense, and civilized, and never makes any real demands or complaints.

The only thing she complains about readily is her name. Prue is a school-girl, she says, and Prudence is an old virgin; the parents who gave her that name must have been too shortsighted even to take account of puberty. What if she had grown a great bosom, she says, or developed a sultry look? Or was the name itself a guarantee that she wouldn't? In her late forties now, slight and fair, attending to customers with a dutiful vivacity, giving pleasure to dinner guests, she might not be far from what those parents had in mind: bright and thoughtful, a cheerful spectator. It is hard to grant her maturity, maternity, real troubles.

Her grownup children, the products of an early Vancouver Island mar-riage she calls a cosmic disaster, come to see her, and instead of wanting money, like other people's children, they bring presents, try to do her ac-counts, arrange to have her house insulated. She is delighted with their pre-sents, listens to their advice, and, like a flighty daughter, neglects to answer their letters.

5   Her children hope she is not staying on in Toronto because of Gordon. Everybody hopes that. She would laugh at the idea. She gives parties and goes to parties; she goes out sometimes with other men. Her attitude toward sex is very comforting to those of her friends who get into terrible states of passion and jealousy, and feel cut loose from their moorings. She seems to regard sex as a wholesome, slightly silly indulgence, like dancing and nice dinners — something that shouldn't interfere with people's being kind and cheerful to each other.

Now that his wife is gone for good, Gordon comes to see Prue occa-sionally, and sometimes asks her out for dinner. They may not go to a restau-rant; they may go to his house. Gordon is a good cook. When Prue or his wife lived with him he couldn't cook at all, but as soon as he put his mind to it he became — he says truthfully — better than either of them.

Recently he and Prue were having dinner at his house. He had made Chicken Kiev, and crème brûlée for dessert. Like most new, serious cooks, he talked about food.

Gordon is rich, by Prue's — and most people's — standards. He is a neur-ologist. His house is new, built on a hillside north of the city, where there used to be picturesque, unprofitable farms. Now there are one-of-a-kind, architect-designed, very expensive houses on half-acre lots. Prue, describing Gordon's house, will say, "Do you know there are four bathrooms? So that if four people want to have baths at the same time there's no problem. It seems a bit much, but it's very nice, really, and you'd never have to go through the hall."

Gordon's house has a raised dining area — a sort of platform, surrounded by a conversation pit, a music pit, and a bank of heavy greenery under sloping glass. You can't see the entrance area from the dining area, but there are no intervening walls, so that from one area you can hear something of what is going on in the other.

During dinner the doorbell rang. Gordon excused himself and went down the steps. Prue heard a female voice. The person it belonged to was still outside, so she could not hear the words. She heard Gordon's voice, pitched low, cautioning. The door didn't close — it seemed the person had not been invited in — but the voices went on, muted and angry. Suddenly there was a cry from Gordon, and he appeared halfway up the steps, waving his arms. 10

"The crème brûlée," he said. "Could you?" He ran back down as Prue got up and went into the kitchen to save the dessert. When she returned he was climbing the stairs more slowly, looking both agitated and tired.

"A friend," he said gloomily. "Was it all right?"

Prue realized he was speaking of the crème brûlée, and she said yes, it was perfect, she had got it just in time. He thanked her but did not cheer up. It seemed it was not the dessert he was troubled over but whatever had happened at the door. To take his mind off it, Prue started asking him professional questions about the plants.

"I don't know a thing about them," he said. "You know that."

"I thought you might have picked it up. Like the cooking." 15

"She takes care of them."

"Mrs. Carr?" said Prue, naming his housekeeper.

"Who did you think?"

Prue blushed. She hated to be thought suspicious.

"The problem is that I think I would like to marry you," said Gordon, with no noticeable lightening of his spirits. Gordon is a large man, with heavy features. He likes to wear thick clothing, bulky sweaters. His blue eyes are often bloodshot, and their expression indicates that there is a helpless, baffled soul squirming around inside this doughty fortress. 20

"What a problem," said Prue lightly, though she knew Gordon well enough to know that it was.

The doorbell rang again, rang twice, three times, before Gordon could get to it. This time there was a crash, as of something flung and landing hard. The door slammed and Gordon was immediately back in view. He staggered on the steps and held his hand to his head, meanwhile making a gesture with the other hand to signify that nothing serious had happened, Prue was to sit down.

"Bloody overnight bag," he said. "She threw it at me."

"Did it hit you?"

"Glancing." 25

"It made a hard sound for an overnight bag. Were there rocks in it?"

"Probably cans. Her deodorant and so forth."

"Oh."

Prue watched him pour himself a drink. "I'd like some coffee, if I might," she said. She went to the kitchen to put the water on, and Gordon followed her.

30 "I think I'm in love with this person," he said.

"Who is she?"

"You don't know her. She's quite young."

"Oh."

"But I do think I want to marry you, in a few years' time."

35 "After you get over being in love?"

"Yes."

"Well. I guess nobody knows what can happen in a few years' time."

When Prue tells about this, she says, "I think he was afraid I was going to laugh. He doesn't know why people laugh or throw their overnight bags at him, but he's noticed they do. He's such a proper person, really. The lovely dinner. Then she comes and throws her overnight bag. And it's quite reasonable to think of marrying me in a few years' time, when he gets over being in love. I think he first thought of telling me to sort of put my mind at rest."

She doesn't mention that the next morning she picked up one of Gordon's cufflinks from his dresser. The cufflinks are made of amber and he bought them in Russia, on the holiday he and the wife took when they got back together again. They look like squares of candy, golden, translucent, and this one warms quickly in her hand. She drops it into the pocket of her jacket. Taking one is not a real theft. It could be a reminder, an intimate prank, a piece of nonsense.

40 She is alone in Gordon's house; he has gone off early, as he always does. The housekeeper does not come till nine. Prue doesn't have to be at the shop until ten; she could make herself breakfast, stay and have coffee with the housekeeper, who is her friend from olden times. But once she has the cufflink in her pocket she doesn't linger. The house seems too bleak a place to spend an extra moment in. It was Prue, actually, who helped choose the building lot. But she's not responsible for approving the plans — the wife was back by that time.

When she gets home she puts the cufflink in an old tobacco tin. The children bought this tobacco tin in a junk shop years ago, and gave it to her for a present. She used to smoke, in those days, and the children were worried about her, so they gave her this tin full of toffees, jelly beans, and gumdrops, with a note saying, "Please get fat instead." That was for her birthday. Now the tin has in it several things besides the cufflink — all small things, not of great value but not worthless, either. A little enamelled dish, a sterling-silver spoon for salt, a crystal fish. These are not sentimental keepsakes. She never looks at them, and often forgets what she has there. They are not booty, they don't have ritualistic significance. She does not take something every time she goes to Gordon's house, or every time she stays over, or to mark what she might call memorable visits. She doesn't do it in a daze and she doesn't seem to be under a compulsion. She just takes something, every now and then, and puts it away in the dark of the old tobacco tin, and more or less forgets about it.

QUESTIONS

1. Notice that the story moves back and forth between past tense and present tense. What is the purpose of these shifts? Can you infer how much time has elapsed in Prue's life between the dinner at Gordon's and the present?
2. The story explicitly defines the characteristics of Gordon. What are they, and what incidents support those definitions? Are there aspects of his personality that are not explained by the given definitions?
3. Prue is presented both directly (as in paragraph 2) and indirectly, through her actions. Are there any mysteries that surround her? What is the importance of the discussion of her name (paragraph 3)?
4. Identify the conflicts between Prue and Gordon. Does Prue display any conflicts with herself, or with her environment?
5. Is the ending of the story determinate or indeterminate? Give evidence for your choice.

CHAPTER THREE

Character

In the preceding chapter plot was considered apart from character, as if the two were separable. Actually, like the ends of a seesaw, the two are one substance; there can be no movement at one end without movement at the other. The two ends of the seesaw may be talked about separately, however, and we can determine which element in any story is being emphasized — which end is up and which is down. As fiction passes from escape to interpretive, the character end is likely to go up. Experienced readers are less interested in actions done by characters than in characters doing actions.

Reading for character is more difficult than reading for plot, for character is much more complex, variable, and ambiguous. Anyone can repeat what a person has done in a story, but considerable skill may be needed to describe what a person *is*. Even the puzzles posed by the detective story are less complex and put less strain on comprehension than does human nature. Hence, escape fiction tends to emphasize plot and to present characters that are relatively simple and easy to understand. Less-experienced readers demand that the characters be easily identifiable and clearly labeled as good or bad; they must not be so complex as to tax the readers' understanding.

Immature readers also demand that the main character always be an attractive one. If the main character is male, he need not be perfect, but he must ordinarily be fundamentally decent — honest, good-hearted, and preferably good looking. If he is not virtuous, he must have strong compensatory qualities — he must be daring, dashing, or gallant. He may defy law and order only if he has a tender heart, a great love, or a gentleman's code. Readers who make these demands do so because for them the story is not a vehicle for understanding but material for a daydream. Identifying with the main character as they read, they vicariously share that character's adventures, escapes, and triumphs. The main character must therefore return them a pleasing image of self, must be someone such as they imagine themselves to be or such as they would like to be. In this way the story subtly flatters its readers, who forget their own inadequacies and satisfy their egos. If the hero or heroine has vices, these vices must be such as the readers themselves would not mind or would enjoy having. Some escape fiction has been about the man or woman who is appealing but sexually promiscuous. Readers have thus been able to indulge imaginatively in forbidden pleasures without losing a flattering self-image.

Interpretive fiction does not necessarily renounce the attractive central character. It simply furnishes a greater variety of central characters, characters that are less easily labeled and pigeonholed, characters that are sometimes unsympathetic. Human nature is not often entirely bad or perfectly good, and interpretive fiction deals usually with characters that are neither.

Once we get past the need of a mechanical opposition between hero and villain, we discover that fiction offers an unparalleled opportunity to observe human nature in all its complexity and multiplicity. It enables us to know people, to understand them, and to learn compassion for them, as we might not otherwise do. In some respects we can know fictional characters even better than we know real people. For one thing, we observe them in situations that are always significant and that serve to bring forth their character as the ordinary situations of life only occasionally do. For another, we can view their inner life in a way that is impossible to us in ordinary life. Authors can tell us, if they wish, exactly what is going on in a character's mind and exactly what the character feels. In real life we can only guess at these inner thoughts and feelings from a person's external behavior, which may be designed to conceal what is going on inside. In limited ways, therefore, we can know people in fiction more thoroughly than we can know them in real life. And by knowing fictional characters we can also understand people in real life better than we otherwise could.

Authors present their characters either directly or indirectly. In **direct presentation** they tell us straight out, by exposition or analysis, what the characters are like, or have someone else in the story tell us what they are like. In **indirect presentation** the authors *show* us the characters in action; we infer what they are like from what they think or say or do. Graham Greene uses direct presentation when he tells us about Blackie: "He was just, he had no jealousy." He uses indirect presentation when he shows Blackie allowing the gang to vote on Trevor's project, accepting the end of his leadership fairly calmly, taking orders from Trevor without resentment, burning banknotes with Trevor, and racing him home. In this story, of course, the word "just" has a slight ironic twist — it applies only to behavior within the gang — and Greene presents this indirectly. Margaret Atwood (page 163) relies entirely on indirect presentation to show us that her narrator Estelle is shrewd, commonsensical, and good humored.

The method of direct presentation has the advantages of being clear and economical, but it can scarcely ever be used alone. The characters must act, if there is to be a story; when they do not act, the story approaches the condition of an essay. The direct method, moreover, unless supported by the indirect, may not be emotionally convincing. It will give us not a character but an explanation. Readers want to be shown as well as told. They need to see and hear and overhear. A story is successful when the characters are **dramatized** — shown speaking and acting, as in a drama. If we are really to believe in the selfishness of a character, we must see the character acting selfishly. Successful writers therefore rely mainly on indirect presentation and may use it entirely.

When most convincing, characterization also observes three other principles. First, the characters are **consistent** in their behavior: they do not behave one way on one occasion and a different way on another unless there is clearly a sufficient reason for the change. Second, the characters are **motivated** in whatever they do, especially when there is any change in their behavior: we must be able to understand the reasons for what they do, if not immediately, at least by the end of the story. Third, the characters are **plausible** or lifelike. They must be neither paragons of virtue nor monsters of evil nor an impossible combination of contradictory traits. Whether we have observed anyone like them in our own experience or not, we must feel that they have come from the author's experience — that they could appear somewhere in the normal course of events.

In proportion to the fullness of their development, the characters in a story are relatively flat or round.* **Flat characters** are characterized by one or two traits; they can be summed up in a sentence. **Round characters** are complex and many sided; they might require an essay for full analysis. Both types of character can have the vitality that good fiction demands. Round characters live by their very roundness, by the many

---

*These terms were originated by the novelist E. M. Forster, who discussed them in *Aspects of the Novel* (New York: Harcourt, 1927), 103–18.

points at which they touch life. Huck Finn, in all respects an individual, lives vigorously in the imagination of the reader, while scholars and critics debate his moral development. Flat characters, though they touch life at only one or two points, may be made memorable in the hands of an expert author through some individualizing detail of appearance, gesture, or speech. Ebenezer Scrooge, in Dickens's *A Christmas Carol*, can be summed up and fully expressed in the two words "miserly misanthropy," but his "Bah! Humbug!" makes him live vividly in every reader's memory.

In good fiction all characters are characterized fully enough to justify their roles in the story and make them convincing. Most short stories will hardly have room for more than one or two very fully developed characters. Minor characters must necessarily remain flat. If the primary intention of a story is something other than the exhibition of character, none of the characters may be fully developed. Inferior fiction, however, is often built around characters who are insufficiently characterized to justify their roles. The essential nature and motivations of the protagonist may be so vaguely indicated that we are neither shocked nor convinced by any unusual action he performs or change of nature he undergoes. If a thief suddenly reforms and becomes an honest man, we must obviously know a great deal about him if the change is to be truly convincing. It is easier, of course, for writers to leave the characterization shadowy and hope that this weakness will slip by their readers unnoticed — as with inexperienced readers it very well may.

A special kind of flat character is the **stock character** — stereotyped figures who have occurred so often in fiction that their nature is immediately known: the strong silent sheriff, the brilliant detective of eccentric habits, the mad scientist who performs fiendish experiments on living human beings, the beautiful international spy of mysterious background, the comic Englishman with a monocle and an exaggerated Oxford accent, the handsome brave hero, the beautiful modest heroine, the cruel stepmother, the sinister villain with a waxed black mustache. Such stock characters are found very often in inferior fiction since they require neither imagination nor observation on the part of the writer and are instantly recognizable to the reader. Like interchangeable parts, they might be transferred from one story to another with little loss of efficacy. Really good writers, however, may take a conventional type and by individualizing touches create a new and memorable figure. Conan Doyle's Sherlock Holmes is constructed on a pattern often imitated since, but he outlives the imitations and remains in our imaginations long after we have forgotten the details of his adventures. To the degree that characters have such individualizing touches, they become less flat and accordingly less stock.

All fictional characters may be classified as static or developing. The **static character** is the same sort of person at the end of the story as at the beginning. The **developing** (or dynamic) **character** undergoes a permanent change in some aspect of character, personality, or outlook. The change may be a large or a small one; it may be for better or for worse; but it is something important and basic: it is more than a change in condition or a minor change in opinion. Cinderella is a static character, though she rises from cinder girl to princess. Dick Prosser in "The Child by Tiger" is a dynamic character, for he changes from a gentle, "amazingly tender," "deeply religious" man (who tells the white boys, "you gotta love each othah like a brothah") into a "crazy" killer. Paul in "Paul's Case" (page 148) is likewise dynamic, for his need to escape from everyday reality grows progressively stronger.

Obviously, we must not expect many developing characters in *any* piece of fiction: in a short story there is not usually room for more than one. A not-infrequent basic plan of short stories is to show change in the protagonist as the result of a crucial situation in his life. When this is done in an interpretive story, the change is likely to be the surest clue to the story's meaning. To state and explain the change will be the best way to get at the point of the story. In escape fiction, changes in character are likely to be more superficial, intended merely to ensure a happy ending. Such changes are necessarily less believable. A convincing change usually meets three conditions: (1) it is within the possibilities of the character who makes it, (2) it is sufficiently motivated by the circumstances in which the character is placed, and (3) it is allowed sufficient time for a change of its magnitude believably to take place. Basic changes in human character seldom occur suddenly. Interpretive writers do not present bad people who suddenly reform at the end of the story and become good, or drunkards who jump on the wagon at a moment's notice. They are satisfied with smaller changes that are carefully prepared.

Human life began, we are told, when God breathed life into a handful of dust and created Adam. Fictional life begins when an author breathes life into characters and convinces us of their reality. Though fullness of characterization need not be the ultimate aim, soundness of characterization is a test by which an author stands or falls. The reader of good fiction lives in a world where the initial act of creation is repeated again and again by the miracle of imagination.

Sherwood Anderson
I'm a Fool

It was a hard jolt for me, one of the most bitterest I ever had to face. And it all came about through my own foolishness, too. Even yet sometimes, when I think of it, I want to cry or swear or kick myself. Perhaps, even now, after all this time, there will be a kind of satisfaction in making myself look cheap by telling of it.

It began at three o'clock one October afternoon as I sat in the grandstand at the fall trotting and pacing meet at Sandusky, Ohio.

To tell the truth, I felt a little foolish that I should be sitting in the grandstand at all. During the summer before, I had left my hometown with Harry Whitehead and, with a nigger named Burt, had taken a job as swipe with one of the two horses Harry was campaigning through the fall race meets that year. Mother cried and my sister Mildred, who wanted to get a job as a schoolteacher in our town that fall, stormed and scolded about the house all during the week before I left. They both thought it something disgraceful that one of our family should take a place as a swipe with race horses. I've an idea Mildred thought my taking the place would stand in the way of her getting the job she'd been working so long for.

But after all I had to work, and there was no other work to be got. A big lumbering fellow of nineteen couldn't just hang around the house and I had got too big to mow people's lawns and sell newspapers. Little chaps who could get next to people's sympathies by their sizes were always getting jobs away from me. There was one fellow who kept saying to everyone who wanted a lawn mowed or a cistern cleaned that he was saving money to work his way through college, and I used to lay awake nights thinking up ways to injure him without being found out. I kept thinking of wagons running over him and bricks falling on his head as he walked along the street. But never mind him.

I got the place with Harry and I liked Burt fine. We got along splendid together. He was a big nigger with a lazy sprawling body and soft, kind eyes, and when it came to a fight he could hit like Jack Johnson.° He had Bucephalus, a big black pacing stallion that could do 2.09 or 2.10 if he had to, and I had a little gelding named Doctor Fritz that never lost a race all fall when Harry wanted him to win.

5

I'M A FOOL   First published in 1922. The time of the story ("before prohibition") is probably well before 1919, when the Eighteenth Amendment was passed. The racing in the story is harness racing, in which the horse draws a light two-wheeled vehicle seating the driver. *Swipe* is a slang term for one who rubs down horses. Sherwood Anderson (1876–1941) grew up in northern Ohio near Sandusky.

Jack Johnson: world heavyweight boxing champion, 1908–1915, black

We set out from home late in July, in a box car with the two horses and after that, until late November, we kept moving along to the race meets and the fairs. It was a peachy time for me, I'll say that. Sometimes now I think that boys who are raised regular in houses, and never have a fine nigger like Burt for best friend, and go to high schools and college, and never steal anything, or get drunk a little, or learn to swear from fellows who know how, or come walking up in front of a grandstand in their shirt sleeves and with dirty horsy pants on when the races are going on and the grandstand is full of people all dressed up — What's the use of talking about it? Such fellows don't know nothing at all. They've never had no opportunity.

But I did. Burt taught me how to rub down a horse and put the bandages on after a race and steam a horse out and a lot of valuable things for any man to know. He could wrap a bandage on a horse's leg so smooth that if it had been the same color you would think it was his skin, and I guess he'd have been a big driver, too, and got to the top like Murphy and Walter Cox and the others if he hadn't been black.

Gee whizz! it was fun. You got to a county-seat town, maybe say on a Saturday or Sunday, and the fair began the next Tuesday and lasted until Friday afternoon. Doctor Fritz would be, say, in the 2.25 trot on Tuesday afternoon and on Thursday afternoon Bucephalus would knock 'em cold in the "free-for-all" pace. It left you a lot of time to hang around and listen to horse talk, and see Burt knock some yap cold that got too gay, and you'd find out about horses and men and pick up a lot of stuff you could use all the rest of your life, if you had some sense and salted down what you heard and felt and saw.

And then at the end of the week when the race meet was over, and Harry had run home to tend up to his livery-stable business, you and Burt hitched the two horses to carts and drove slow and steady across country, to the place for the next meeting, so as to not overheat the horses, etc., etc., you know.

Gee whizz! Gosh amighty! the nice hickory-nut and beechnut and oaks and other kinds of trees along the roads, all brown and red, and the good smells, and Burt singing a song called "Deep River," and the country girls at the windows of houses and everything. You can stick your colleges up your nose for all me. I guess I know where I got my education.

Why, one of those little burgs of towns you came to on the way, say now on a Saturday afternoon, and Burt says, "Let's lay up here." And you did.

And you took the horses to a livery stable and fed them, and you got your good clothes out of a box and put them on.

And the town was full of farmers gaping, because they could see you were racehorse people, and the kids maybe never see a nigger before and was afraid and run away when the two of us walked down their main street.

And that was before prohibition and all that foolishness, and so you went into a saloon, the two of you, and all the yaps come and stood around, and there was always some one pretended he was horsy and knew things and spoke up and began asking questions, and all you did was to lie and lie all you could about what horses you had, and I said I owned them, and then some fellow said, "Will you have a drink of whiskey?" and Burt knocked his eye out the way he could say, offhand like, "Oh, well, all right, I'm agreeable to a little nip. I'll split a quart with you." Gee whizz!

But that isn't what I want to tell my story about. We got home late in November and I promised mother I'd quit the race horses for good. There's a lot of things you've got to promise a mother because she don't know any better.

And so, there not being any work in our town any more than when I left there to go to the races, I went off to Sandusky and got a pretty good place taking care of horses for a man who owned a teaming and delivery and storage and coal and real-estate business there. It was a pretty good place with good eats, and a day off each week, and sleeping on a cot in a big barn, and mostly just shoveling in hay and oats to a lot of big good-enough skates of horses that couldn't have trotted a race with a toad. I wasn't dissatisfied and I could send money home.

And then, as I started to tell you, the fall races come to Sandusky and I got the day off and I went. I left the job at noon and had on my good clothes and my new brown derby hat I'd bought the Saturday before, and a stand-up collar.

First of all I went downtown and walked about with the dudes. I've always thought to myself, "Put up a good front," and so I did it. I had forty dollars in my pockets and so I went into the West House, a big hotel, and walked up to the cigar stand. "Give me three twenty-five cent cigars," I said. There was a lot of horsemen and strangers and dressed-up people from other towns standing around in the lobby and in the bar, and I mingled amongst them. In the bar there was a fellow with a cane and a Windsor tie on, that it made me sick to look at him. I like a man to be a man and dressed up, but not to go put on that kind of airs. So I pushed him aside, kind of rough, and had me a drink of whiskey. And then he looked at me, as though he thought maybe he'd get gay, but he changed his mind and didn't say anything. And then I had another drink of whiskey, just to show him something, and went out and had a hack out to the races, all to myself, and when I got there I bought myself the best seat I could get up in the grandstand, but didn't go in for any of these boxes. That's putting on too many airs.

And so there I was, sitting up in the grandstand as gay as you please and looking down on the swipes coming out with their horses, and with their dirty horsy pants on and the horseblankets swung over their shoulders, same as I had been doing all the year before. I liked one thing about the same as the other, sitting up there and feeling grand and being down there and looking up at the yaps and feeling grander and more important, too.

One thing's about as good as another, if you take it just right. I've often said that.

Well, right in front of me, in the grandstand that day, there was a fellow with a couple of girls and they was about my age. The young fellow was a nice guy, all right. He was the kind maybe that goes to college and then comes to be a lawyer or maybe a newspaper editor or something like that, but he wasn't stuck on himself. There are some of that kind are all right and he was one of the ones.

He had his sister with him and another girl and the sister looked around over his shoulder, accidental at first, not intending to start anything — she wasn't that kind — and her eyes and mine happened to meet.

You know how it is. Gee, she was a peach! She had on a soft dress, kind of a blue stuff and it looked carelessly made, but was well sewed and made and everything. I knew that much. I blushed when she looked right at me and so did she. She was the nicest girl I've ever seen in my life. She wasn't stuck on herself and she could talk proper grammar without being like a school-teacher or something like that. What I mean is, she was O.K. I think maybe her father was well-to-do, but not rich to make her chesty because she was his daughter, as some are. Maybe he owned a drug store or a dry-goods store in their home town, or something like that. She never told me and I never asked.

My own people are all O.K. too, when you come to that. My grandfather was Welsh and over in the old country, in Wales he was — But never mind that.

The first heat of the first race come off and the young fellow setting there with the two girls left them and went down to make a bet. I knew what he was up to, but he didn't talk big and noisy and let everyone around know he was a sport, as some do. He wasn't that kind. Well, he come back and I heard him tell the two girls what horse he'd bet on, and when the heat trotted they all half got to their feet and acted in the excited, sweaty way people do when they've got money down on a race, and the horse they bet on is up there pretty close at the end, and they think maybe he'll come on with a rush, but he never does because he hasn't got the old juice in him, come right down to it.

And then, pretty soon, the horses came out for the 2.18 pace and there was a horse in it I knew. He was a horse Bob French had in his string but Bob didn't own him. He was a horse owned by a Mr. Mathers down at Marietta, Ohio.

This Mr. Mathers had a lot of money and owned some coal mines or something and he had a swell place out in the country, and he was stuck on race horses, but was a Presbyterian or something, and I think more than likely his wife was one, too, maybe a stiffer one than himself. So he never raced his horses hisself, and the story round the Ohio race tracks was that when one of his horses got ready to go to the races he turned him over to Bob French and pretended to his wife he was sold.

So Bob had the horses and he did pretty much as he pleased and you can't blame Bob, at least, I never did. Sometimes he was out to win and sometimes he wasn't. I never cared much about that when I was swiping a horse. What I did want to know was that my horse had the speed and could go out in front, if you wanted him to.

And, as I'm telling you, there was Bob in this race with one of Mr. Mathers's horses, was named "About Ben Ahem"° or something like that, and was fast as a streak. He was a gelding and had a mark of 2.21, but could step in .08 or .09.

Because when Burt and I were out, as I've told you, the year before, there was a nigger Burt knew, worked for Mr. Mathers and we went out there one day when we didn't have no race on at the Marietta Fair and our boss Harry was gone home.

And so everyone was gone to the fair but just this one nigger and he took us all through Mr. Mathers's swell house and he and Burt tapped a bottle of wine Mr. Mathers had hid in his bedroom, back in a closet, without his wife knowing, and he showed us this Ahem horse. Burt was always stuck on being a driver but didn't have much chance to get to the top, being a nigger, and he and the other nigger gulped the whole bottle of wine and Burt got a little lit up.

So the nigger let Burt take this About Ben Ahem and step him a mile in a track Mr. Mathers had all to himself, right there on the farm. And Mr. Mathers had one child, a daughter, kinda sick and not very good looking, and she came home and we had to hustle to get About Ben Ahem stuck back in the barn.

I'm only telling you to get everything straight. At Sandusky, that afternoon I was at the fair, this young fellow with the two girls was fussed, being with the girls and losing his bet. You know how a fellow is that way. One of them was his girl and the other his sister. I had figured that out.

"Gee whizz," I says to myself, "I'm going to give him the dope."

He was mighty nice when I touched him on the shoulder. He and the girls were nice to me right from the start and clear to the end. I'm not blaming them.

And so he leaned back and I give him the dope on About Ben Ahem. "Don't bet a cent on this first heat because he'll go like an oxen hitched to a plow, but when the first heat is over go right down and lay on your pile." That's what I told him.

Well, I never saw a fellow treat any one sweller. There was a fat man sitting beside the little girl, that had looked at me twice by this time, and I at her, and both blushing, and what did he do but have the nerve to turn and ask the fat man to get up and change places with me so I could set with his crowd.

Gee whizz, craps amighty. There I was. What a chump I was to go and

°**"About Ben Ahem":** Abou Ben Adhem is the title character of a well-known poem by Leigh Hunt.

get gay up there in the West House bar, and just because that dude was standing there with a cane and that kind of a necktie on, to go and get all balled up and drink that whiskey, just to show off.

Of course she would know, me setting right beside her and letting her smell of my breath. I could have kicked myself right down out of that grandstand and all around that race track and made a faster record than most of the skates of horses they had there that year.

Because that girl wasn't any mutt of a girl. What wouldn't I have give right then for a stick of chewing gum to chew, or a lozenger, or some licorice, or most anything. I was glad I had those twenty-five cent cigars in my pocket and right away I gave that fellow one and lit one myself. Then that fat man got up and we changed places and there I was, plunked right down beside her.

They introduced themselves and the fellow's best girl, he had with him, was named Miss Elinor Woodbury, and her father was a manufacturer of barrels from a place called Tiffin, Ohio. And the fellow himself was named Wilbur Wessen and his sister was Miss Lucy Wessen.

I suppose it was their having such swell names that got me off my trolley. A fellow, just because he has been a swipe with a race horse, and works taking care of horses for a man in the teaming, delivery, and storage business isn't any better or worse than any one else. I've often thought that, and said it too.

But you know how a fellow is. There's something in that kind of nice clothes, and the kind of nice eyes she had, and the way she had looked at me, awhile before, over her brother's shoulder, and me looking back at her, and both of us blushing.

I couldn't show her up for a boob, could I?

I made a fool of myself, that's what I did. I said my name was Walter Mathers from Marietta, Ohio, and then I told all three of them the smashingest lie you ever heard. What I said was that my father owned the horse About Ben Ahem and that he had let him out to this Bob French for racing purposes, because our family was proud and had never gone into racing that way, in our own name, I mean, and Miss Lucy Wessen's eyes were shining, and I went the whole hog.

I told her about our place down at Marietta, and about the big stables and the grand brick house we had on a hill, up above the Ohio River, but I knew enough not to do it in no bragging way. What I did was to start things and then let them drag the rest out of me. I acted just as reluctant to tell as I could. Our family hasn't got any barrel factory, and since I've known us, we've always been pretty poor, but not asking anything of any one at that, and my grandfather, over in Wales — but never mind that.

We sat there talking like we had known each other for years and years, and I went and told them that my father had been expecting maybe this Bob French wasn't on the square, and had sent me up to Sandusky on the sly to find out what I could.

And I bluffed it through I had found out all about the 2.18 pace, in which About Ben Ahem was to start.

I said he would lose the first heat by pacing like a lame cow and then he would come back and skin 'em alive after that. And to back up what I said I took thirty dollars out of my pocket and handed it to Mr. Wilbur Wessen and asked him, would he mind, after the first heat, to go down and place it on About Ben Ahem for whatever odds he could get. What I said was that I didn't want Bob French to see me and none of the swipes.

Sure enough the first heat come off and Abut Ben Ahem went off his stride, up the back stretch, and looked like a wooden horse or a sick one, and come in to be last. Then this Wilbur Wessen went down to the betting place under the grandstand and there I was with the two girls, and when that Miss Woodbury was looking the other way once, Lucy Wessen kinda, with her shoulder you know, kinda touched me. Not just tucking down, I don't mean. You know how a woman can do. They get close, but not getting gay either. You know what they do. Gee whizz. 50

And then they give me a jolt. What they had done, when I didn't know, was to get together, and they had decided Wilbur Wessen would bet fifty dollars, and the two girls had gone and put in ten dollars each, of their own money, too. I was sick then, but I was sicker later.

About the gelding, About Ben Ahem, and their winning their money, I wasn't worried a lot about that. It came out O.K. Ahem stepped the next three heats like a bushel of spoiled eggs going to market before they could be found out, and Wilbur Wessen had got nine to two for the money. There was something else eating at me.

Because Wilbur come back, after he had bet the money, and after that he spent most of his time talking to that Miss Woodbury, and Lucy Wessen and I was left alone together like on a desert island. Gee, if I'd only been on the square or if there had been any way of getting myself on the square. There ain't any Walter Mathers, like I said to her and them, and there hasn't ever been one, but if there was, I bet I'd go to Marietta, Ohio, and shoot him tomorrow.

There I was, big boob that I am. Pretty soon the race was over, and Wilbur had gone down and collected our money, and we had a hack downtown, and he stood us a swell supper at the West House, and a bottle of champagne beside.

And I was with the girl and she wasn't saying much, and I wasn't saying much either. One thing I know. She wasn't stuck on me because of the lie about my father being rich and all that. There's a way you know . . . Craps amighty. There's a kind of girl you see just once in your life, and if you don't get busy and make hay, then you're gone for good and all, and might as well go jump off a bridge. They give you a look from inside of them somewhere, and it ain't no vamping, and what it means is — you want that girl to be your wife, and you want nice things around her like flowers and swell clothes, and 55 you want her to have the kids you're going to have, and you want good music played and no ragtime. Gee whizz.

There's a place over near Sandusky, across a kind of bay, and it's called Cedar Point. And after we had supper we went over to it in a launch, all by ourselves. Wilbur and Miss Lucy and that Miss Woodbury had to catch a ten o'clock train back to Tiffin, Ohio, because, when you're out with girls like that you can't get careless and miss any trains and stay out all night, like you can with some kinds of Janes.

And Wilbur blowed himself to the launch and it cost him fifteen cold plunks, but I wouldn't never have knew if I hadn't listened. He wasn't no tin horn kind of a sport.

Over at the Cedar Point place, we didn't stay around where there was a gang of common kind of cattle at all.

There was big dance halls and dining places for yaps, and there was a beach you could walk along and get where it was dark, and we went there.

60 She didn't talk hardly at all and neither did I, and I was thinking how glad I was my mother was all right, and always made us kids learn to eat with a fork at the table, and not swill soup, and not be noisy and rough like a gang you see around a race track that way.

Then Wilbur and his girl went away up the beach and Lucy and I sat down in a dark place, where there was some roots of old trees the water had washed up, and after that the time, till we had to go back in the launch and they had to catch their trains, wasn't nothing at all. It went like winking your eye.

Here's how it was. The place we were setting in was dark, like I said, and there was the roots from that old stump sticking up like arms, and there was a watery smell, and the night was like — as if you could put your hand out and feel it — so warm and soft and dark and sweet like an orange.

I most cried and I most swore and I most jumped up and danced, I was so mad and happy and sad.

When Wilbur come back from being alone with his girl, and she saw him coming, Lucy she says, "We got to go to the train now," and she was most crying too, but she never knew nothing I knew, and she couldn't be so all busted up. And then, before Wilbur and Miss Woodbury got up to where we was, she put her face up and kissed me quick and put her head up against me and she was all quivering and — Gee whizz.

65 Sometimes I hope I have cancer and die. I guess you know what I mean. We went in the launch across the bay to the train like that, and it was dark, too. She whispered and said it was like she and I could get out of the boat and walk on water, and it sounded foolish, but I knew what she meant.

And then quick we were right at the depot, and there was a big gang of yaps, the kind that goes to the fairs, and crowded and milling around like cattle, and how could I tell her? "It won't be long because you'll write and I'll write to you." That's all she said.

I got a chance like a hay barn afire. A swell chance I got.

And maybe she would write me, down at Marietta that way, and the letter would come back, and stamped on the front of it by the U.S.A. "there ain't any such guy," or something like that, whatever they stamp on a letter that way.

And me trying to pass myself off for a big-bug and a swell—to her, as decent a little body as God ever made. Craps amighty—swell chance I got!

And then the train come in, and she got on it, and Wilbur Wessen, he come and shook hands with me, and that Miss Woodbury was nice too and bowed to me, and I at her, and the train went and I busted out and cried like a kid.

Gee, I could have run after the train and made Dan Patch° look like a freight train after a wreck but, socks amighty, what was the use? Did you ever see such a fool?

I'll bet you what—if I had an arm broke right now or a train had run over my foot—I wouldn't go to no doctor at all. I'd go set down and let her hurt and hurt—that's what I'd do.

I'll bet you what—if I hadn't a drunk that booze I'd never been such a boob as to go tell such a lie—that couldn't never be made straight to a lady like her.

I wish I had that fellow right here that had on a Windsor tie and carried a cane. I'd smash him for fair. Gosh darn his eyes. He's a big fool—that's what he is.

And if I'm not another you just go find me one and I'll quit working and be a bum and give him my job. I don't care nothing for working, and earning money, and saving it for no such boob as myself.

QUESTIONS

1. This story is told by an uneducated young man who is handicapped in the telling by bad grammar, an inadequate vocabulary, ignorance, and a digressive story-telling method. Find a good exemplification of each. Why do these handicaps advance rather than hinder the story? What is the story's main purpose?

2. What kind of moral standards does the swipe have? Is he mean? Where does he get his moral standards?

3. What is the swipe's attitude toward education? Can you reconcile "You can stick your colleges up your nose for all me" (paragraph 10) with "The young fellow was a nice guy, all right. He was the kind maybe that goes to college and then comes to be a lawyer . . ." (paragraph 21)? What is an *ambivalent* attitude? What is *rationalization*? Explain the swipe's attitude.

4. The main tenet of the swipe's rather rudimentary philosophy of life is "Put up a good front." On what occasions in the story does the swipe put up a

Dan Patch: one of the fastest harness horses in history

good front? Is this the philosophy of a mature individual? What is the difference between "putting up a good front" and "putting on airs"?

5. Another tenet of the swipe's philosophy is that "A fellow, just because he has
been a swipe with a race horse, and works taking care of horses for a man in
the teaming, delivery, and storage business isn't any better or worse than any
one else" (paragraph 42). Why has the swipe "often thought that, and said it
too"? Why is he so impressed by the "swell names" and good clothes of the
Wessens and Miss Woodbury? What is his attitude toward being a swipe?
What does he like about being a swipe?

6. Why does the swipe resent the man in the Windsor tie? Why does he like
Burt and the Wessens and Miss Woodbury? Why does he refer to most people as "yaps"?

7. Evaluate the swipe's emotional maturity in the light of his reactions to the
little chap who got jobs away from him, what he would do to the real Walter
Mathers if there were one, his behavior toward the man in the Windsor tie,
what he would like to happen to himself at the end of the story.

8. What psychological term might be used to explain the swipe? Account for
his behavior in terms of his size, his social and economic background, his
success in school, his earning ability.

9. The swipe blames his whopper at the race track on the whiskey, and he
blames the whiskey on the man in the Windsor tie. What is the real reason
for his behavior?

10. How is your attitude toward the swipe affected by the fact that you hear his
story from himself? How would it be different if you had heard it from, say, a
high-school counselor?

Alice Walker
Everyday Use

for your grandmama

I will wait for her in the yard that Maggie and I made so clean and wavy
yesterday afternoon. A yard like this is more comfortable than most people
know. It is not just a yard. It is like an extended living room. When the hard
clay is swept clean as a floor and the fine sand around the edges lined with
tiny, irregular grooves, anyone can come and sit and look up into the elm tree
and wait for the breezes that never come inside the house.

EVERYDAY USE   First published in 1973. Alice Walker was born in Georgia in 1944, attended Spelman College for two years, earned her B.A. from Sarah Lawrence, and was
active in the civil rights movement. She has taught and been writer-in-residence at various
colleges including Jackson State, Tougaloo, Wellesley, the University of California at
Berkeley, and Brandeis. The names adopted by two of the characters in the story reflect the
practice among some members of the black community of rejecting names inherited from
the period of slavery and selecting others more in keeping with their African heritage. The
greetings used by Hakim and Wangero ("Asalamalakim" and "Wa-su-zo-Tean-o") are apparently adaptations of Arabic and African languages.

Maggie will be nervous until after her sister goes: she will stand hopelessly in corners, homely and ashamed of the burn scars down her arms and legs, eying her sister with a mixture of envy and awe. She thinks her sister has held life always in the palm of one hand, that "no" is a word the world never learned to say to her.

You've no doubt seen those TV shows where the child who has "made it" is confronted, as a surprise, by her own mother and father, tottering in weakly from backstage. (A pleasant surprise, of course: What would they do if parent and child came on the show only to curse out and insult each other?) On TV mother and child embrace and smile into each other's faces. Sometimes the mother and father weep, the child wraps them in her arms and leans across the table to tell how she would not have made it without their help. I have seen these programs.
Sometimes I dream a dream in which Dee and I are suddenly brought together on a TV program of this sort. Out of a dark and soft-seated limousine I am ushered into a bright room filled with many people. There I meet a smiling, gray, sporty man like Johnny Carson who shakes my hand and tells me what a fine girl I have. Then we are on the stage and Dee is embracing me with tears in her eyes. She pins on my dress a large orchid, even though she had told me once that she thinks orchids are tacky flowers.
In real life I am a large, big-boned woman with rough, man-working   5
hands. In the winter I wear flannel nightgowns to bed and overalls during the day. I can kill and clean a hog as mercilessly as a man. My fat keeps me hot in zero weather. I can work outside all day, breaking ice to get water for washing; I can eat pork liver cooked over the open fire minutes after it comes steaming from the hog. One winter I knocked a bull calf straight in the brain between the eyes with a sledge hammer and had the meat hung up to chill before nightfall. But of course all this does not show on television. I am the way my daughter would want me to be: a hundred pounds lighter, my skin like an uncooked barley pancake. My hair glistens in the hot bright lights. Johnny Carson has much to do to keep up with my quick and witty tongue.
But that is a mistake. I know even before I wake up. Who ever knew a Johnson with a quick tongue? Who can even imagine me looking a strange white man in the eye? It seems to me I have talked to them always with one foot raised in flight, with my head turned in whichever way is farthest from them. Dee, though. She would always look anyone in the eye. Hesitation was no part of her nature.

"How do I look, Mama?" Maggie says, showing just enough of her thin body enveloped in pink skirt and red blouse for me to know she's there, almost hidden by the door.
"Come out into the yard," I say.
Have you ever seen a lame animal, perhaps a dog run over by some careless person rich enough to own a car, sidle up to someone who is ignorant

enough to be kind to him? That is the way my Maggie walks. She has been like this, chin on chest, eyes on ground, feet in shuffle, ever since the fire that burned the other house to the ground.

Dee is lighter than Maggie, with nicer hair and a fuller figure. She's a woman now, though sometimes I forget. How long ago was it that the other house burned? Ten, twelve years? Sometimes I can still hear the flames and feel Maggie's arms sticking to me, her hair smoking and her dress falling off her in little black papery flakes. Her eyes seemed stretched open, blazed open by the flames reflected in them. And Dee. I see her standing off under the sweet gum tree she used to dig gum out of; a look of concentration on her face as she watched the last dingy gray board of the house fall in toward the red-hot brick chimney. Why don't you do a dance around the ashes? I'd wanted to ask her. She had hated the house that much.

I used to think she hated Maggie, too. But that was before we raised the money, the church and me, to send her to Augusta to school. She used to read to us without pity; forcing words, lies, other folks' habits, whole lives upon us two, sitting trapped and ignorant underneath her voice. She washed us in a river of make-believe, burned us with a lot of knowledge we didn't necessarily need to know. Pressed us to her with the serious way she read, to shove us away at just the moment, like dimwits, we seemed about to understand.

Dee wanted nice things. A yellow organdy dress to wear to her graduation from high school; black pumps to match a green suit she'd made from an old suit somebody gave me. She was determined to stare down any disaster in her efforts. Her eyelids would not flicker for minutes at a time. Often I fought off the temptation to shake her. At sixteen she had a style of her own: and knew what style was.

I never had an education myself. After second grade the school was closed down. Don't ask me why: in 1927 colored asked fewer questions than they do now. Sometimes Maggie reads to me. She stumbles along good-naturedly but can't see well. She knows she is not bright. Like good looks and money, quickness passed her by. She will marry John Thomas (who has mossy teeth in an earnest face) and then I'll be free to sit here and I guess just sing church songs to myself. Although I never was a good singer. Never could carry a tune. I was always better at a man's job. I used to love to milk till I was hooked in the side in '49. Cows are soothing and slow and don't bother you, unless you try to milk them the wrong way.

I have deliberately turned my back on the house. It is three rooms, just like the one that burned, except the roof is tin; they don't make shingle roofs any more. There are no real windows, just some holes cut in the sides, like the portholes in a ship, but not round and not square, with rawhide holding the shutters up on the outside. This house is in a pasture, too, like the other one. No doubt when Dee sees it she will want to tear it down. She wrote me once that no matter where we "choose" to live, she will manage to come see us. But she will never bring her friends. Maggie and I thought about this and Maggie asked me, "Mama, when did Dee ever *have* any friends?"

She had a few. Furtive boys in pink shirts hanging about on washday after school. Nervous girls who never laughed. Impressed with her, they worshipped the well-turned phrase, the cute shape, the scalding humor that erupted like bubbles in lye. She read to them.

When she was courting Jimmy T she didn't have much time to pay to us, but turned all her faultfinding power on him. He *flew* to marry a cheap city girl from a family of ignorant flashy people. She hardly had time to recompose herself.

When she comes I will meet — but there they are!

Maggie attempts to make a dash for the house, in her shuffling way, but I stay her with my hand. "Come back here," I say. And she stops and tries to dig a well in the sand with her toe.

It is hard to see them clearly through the strong sun. But even the first glimpse of leg out of the car tells me it is Dee. Her feet were always neat-looking, as if God himself had shaped them with a certain style. From the other side of the car comes a short, stocky man. Hair is all over his head a foot long and hanging from his chin like a kinky mule tail. I hear Maggie suck in her breath. "Uhnnnh," is what it sounds like. Like when you see the wriggling end of a snake just in front of your foot on the road. "Uhnnnh."

Dee next. A dress down to the ground, in this hot weather. A dress so loud it hurts my eyes. There are yellows and oranges enough to throw back the light of the sun. I feel my whole face warming from the heat waves it throws out. Earrings gold, too, and hanging down to her shoulders. Bracelets dangling and making noises when she moves her arm up to shake the folds of the dress out of her armpits. The dress is loose and flows, and as she walks closer, I like it. I hear Maggie go "Uhnnnh" again. It is her sister's hair. It stands straight up like the wool on a sheep. It is black as night and around the edges are two long pigtails that rope about like small lizards disappearing behind her ears.

"Wa-su-zo-Tean-o!" she says, coming on in that gliding way the dress makes her move. The short stocky fellow with the hair to his navel is all grinning and he follows up with "Asalamalakim, my mother and sister!" He moves to hug Maggie but she falls back, right up against the back of my chair. I feel her trembling there and when I look up I see the perspiration falling off her chin.

"Don't get up," says Dee. Since I am stout it takes something of a push. You can see me trying to move a second or two before I make it. She turns, showing white heels through her sandals, and goes back to the car. Out she peeks next with a Polaroid. She stoops down quickly and lines up picture after picture of me sitting there in front of the house with Maggie cowering behind me. She never takes a shot without making sure the house is included. When a cow comes nibbling around the edge of the yard she snaps it and me and Maggie *and* the house. Then she puts the Polaroid in the back seat of the car, and comes up and kisses me on the forehead.

Meanwhile Asalamalakim is going through motions with Maggie's hand. Maggie's hand is as limp as a fish, and probably as cold, despite the sweat, and she keeps trying to pull it back. It looks like Asalamalakim wants to shake hands but wants to do it fancy. Or maybe he don't know how people shake hands. Anyhow, he soon gives up on Maggie.

"Well," I say. "Dee."

25   "No, Mama," she says. "Not 'Dee,' Wangero Leewanika Kemanjo!"

"What happened to 'Dee'?" I wanted to know.

"She's dead," Wangero said. "I couldn't bear it any longer, being named after the people who oppress me."

"You know as well as me you was named after your aunt Dicie," I said. Dicie is my sister. She named Dee. We called her "Big Dee" after Dee was born.

"But who was *she* named after?" asked Wangero.

30   "I guess after Grandma Dee," I said.

"And who was she named after?" asked Wangero.

"Her mother," I said, and saw Wangero was getting tired. "That's about as far back as I can trace it," I said. Though, in fact, I probably could have carried it back beyond the Civil War through the branches.

"Well," said Asalamalakim, "there you are."

"Uhnnnh," I heard Maggie say.

35   "There I was not," I said, "before 'Dicie' cropped up in our family, so why should I try to trace it that far back?"

He just stood there grinning, looking down on me like somebody inspecting a Model A car. Every once in a while he and Wangero sent eye signals over my head.

"How do you pronounce this name?" I asked.

"You don't have to call me by it if you don't want to," said Wangero.

"Why shouldn't I?" I asked. "If that's what you want us to call you, we'll call you."

40   "I know it might sound awkward at first," said Wangero.

"I'll get used to it," I said. "Ream it out again."

Well, soon we got the name out of the way. Asalamalakim had a name twice as long and three times as hard. After I tripped over it two or three times he told me to just call him Hakim-a-barber. I wanted to ask him was he a barber, but I didn't really think he was, so I didn't ask.

"You must belong to those beef-cattle peoples down the road," I said. They said "Asalamalakim" when they met you, too, but they didn't shake hands. Always too busy: feeding the cattle, fixing the fences, putting up salt-lick shelters, throwing down hay. When the white folks poisoned some of the herd the men stayed up all night with rifles in their hands. I walked a mile and a half just to see the sight.

Hakim-a-barber said, "I accept some of their doctrines, but farming and raising cattle is not my style." (They didn't tell me, and I didn't ask, whether Wangero [Dee] had really gone and married him.)

We sat down to eat and right away he said he didn't eat collards and pork was unclean. Wangero, though, went on through the chitlins and corn bread, the greens and everything else. She talked a blue streak over the sweet potatoes. Everything delighted her. Even the fact that we still used the benches her daddy made for the table when we couldn't afford to buy chairs.

"Oh, Mama!" she cried. Then turned to Hakim-a-barber. "I never knew how lovely these benches are. You can feel the rump prints," she said, running her hands underneath her and along the bench. Then she gave a sigh and her hand closed over Grandma Dee's butter dish. "That's it!" she said. "I knew there was something I wanted to ask you if I could have." She jumped up from the table and went over in the corner where the churn stood, the milk in it clabber by now. She looked at the churn and looked at it.

"This churn top is what I need," she said. "Didn't Uncle Buddy whittle it out of a tree you all used to have?"

"Yes," I said.

"Uh huh," she said happily. "And I want the dasher, too."

"Uncle Buddy whittle that, too?" asked the barber.

Dee (Wangero) looked up at me.

"Aunt Dee's first husband whittled the dash," said Maggie so low you almost couldn't hear her. "His name was Henry, but they called him Stash."

"Maggie's brain is like an elephant's," Wangero said, laughing. "I can use the churn top as a centerpiece for the alcove table," she said, sliding a plate over the churn, "and I'll think of something artistic to do with the dasher."

When she finished wrapping the dasher the handle stuck out. I took it for a moment in my hands. You didn't even have to look close to see where hands pushing the dasher up and down to make butter had left a kind of sink in the wood. In fact, there were a lot of small sinks; you could see where thumbs and fingers had sunk into the wood. It was beautiful light yellow wood, from a tree that grew in the yard where Big Dee and Stash had lived.

After dinner Dee (Wangero) went to the trunk at the foot of my bed and started rifling through it. Maggie hung back in the kitchen over the dishpan. Out came Wangero with two quilts. They had been pieced by Grandma Dee and then Big Dee and me had hung them on the quilt frames on the front porch and quilted them. One was in the Lone Star pattern. The other was Walk Around the Mountain. In both of them were scraps of dresses Grandma Dee had worn fifty and more years ago. Bits and pieces of Grandpa Jarrell's Paisley shirts. And one teeny faded blue piece, about the size of a penny matchbox, that was from Great Grandpa Ezra's uniform that he wore in the Civil War.

"Mama," Wangero said sweet as a bird. "Can I have these old quilts?"

I heard something fall in the kitchen, and a minute later the kitchen door slammed.

"Why don't you take one or two of the others?" I asked. "These old things was just done by me and Big Dee from some tops your grandma pieced before she died."

"No," said Wangero. "I don't want those. They are stitched around the borders by machine."

60 "That'll make them last better," I said.

"That's not the point," said Wangero. "These are all pieces of dresses Grandma used to wear. She did all this stitching by hand. Imagine!" She held the quilts securely in her arms, stroking them.

"Some of the pieces, like those lavender ones, come from old clothes her mother handed down to her," I said, moving up to touch the quilts. Dee (Wangero) moved back just enough so that I couldn't reach the quilts. They already belonged to her.

"Imagine!" she breathed again, clutching them closely to her bosom.

"The truth is," I said, "I promised to give them quilts to Maggie, for when she marries John Thomas."

65 She gasped like a bee had stung her.

"Maggie can't appreciate these quilts!" she said. "She'd probably be backward enough to put them to everyday use."

"I reckon she would," I said. "God knows I been saving 'em for long enough with nobody using 'em. I hope she will!" I didn't want to bring up how I had offered Dee (Wangero) a quilt when she went away to college. Then she had told me they were old-fashioned, out of style.

"But they're *priceless!*" she was saying now, furiously; for she has a temper. "Maggie would put them on the bed and in five years they'd be in rags. Less than that!"

"She can always make some more," I said. "Maggie knows how to quilt."

70 Dee (Wangero) looked at me with hatred. "You just will not understand. The point is these quilts, *these* quilts!"

"Well," I said, stumped. "What would *you* do with them?"

"Hang them," she said. As if that was the only thing you *could* do with quilts.

Maggie by now was standing in the door. I could almost hear the sound her feet made as they scraped over each other.

"She can have them, Mama," she said, like somebody used to never winning anything, or having anything reserved for her. "I can 'member Grandma Dee without the quilts."

75 I looked at her hard. She had filled her bottom lip with checkerberry snuff and it gave her face a kind of dopey, hangdog look. It was Grandma Dee and Big Dee who taught her how to quilt herself. She stood there with her scarred hands hidden in the folds of her skirt. She looked at her sister with something like fear but she wasn't mad at her. This was Maggie's portion. This was the way she knew God to work.

When I looked at her like that something hit me in the top of my head and ran down to the soles of my feet. Just like when I'm in church and the spirit of God touches me and I get happy and shout. I did something I never had done before: hugged Maggie to me, then dragged her on into the room, snatched the quilts out of Miss Wangero's hands and dumped them into Maggie's lap. Maggie just sat there on my bed with her mouth open.

"Take one or two of the others," I said to Dee.

But she turned without a word and went out to Hakim-a-barber.

"You just don't understand," she said, as Maggie and I came out to the car.

"What don't I understand?" I wanted to know.   80

"Your heritage," she said. And then she turned to Maggie, kissed her, and said, "You ought to try to make something of yourself, too, Maggie. It's really a new day for us. But from the way you and Mama still live you'd never know it."

She put on some sunglasses that hid everything above the tip of her nose and her chin.

Maggie smiled; maybe at the sunglasses. But a real smile, not scared. After we watched the car dust settle I asked Maggie to bring me a dip of snuff. And then the two of us sat there just enjoying, until it was time to go in the house and go to bed.

QUESTIONS

1. Characterize the speaker and evaluate her reliability as a reporter and interpreter of events. Where does she refrain from making judgments? Where does she present less than the full truth? Do these examples of reticence undercut her reliability?

2. Describe as fully as possible the lives of the mother, Dee, and Maggie prior to the events of the story. How are the following incidents from the past also reflected in the present actions: (a) Dee's hatred of the old house; (b) Dee's ability "to stare down any disaster"; (c) Maggie's burns from the fire; (d) the mother's having been "hooked in the side while milking a cow"; (e) Dee's refusal to accept a quilt when she went away to college?

3. As evidence of current social movements and as innovations that the mother responds to, what do the following have in common: (a) Dee's new name and costume; (b) Hakim's behavior and attitudes; (c) the "beef-cattle peoples down the road"; (d) Dee's concern for her "heritage"?

4. Does the mother's refusal to let Dee have the quilts indicate a permanent or temporary change of character? Why has she never done anything like it before? Why does she do it now? What details in the story prepare for and foreshadow that refusal?

5. How does the physical setting give support to the contrasting attitudes of both the mother and Dee? Does the author indicate that one or the other of them is entirely correct in her feelings about the house and yard?

6. Is Dee wholly unsympathetic? Is the mother's victory over her altogether positive? What emotional ambivalence is there in the final scene between Maggie and her mother in the yard?

Katherine Mansfield
Miss Brill

Although it was so brilliantly fine — the blue sky powdered with gold and great spots of light like white wine splashed over the Jardins Publiques — Miss Brill was glad that she had decided on her fur. The air was motionless, but when you opened your mouth there was just a faint chill, like a chill from a glass of iced water before you sip, and now and again a leaf came drifting — from nowhere, from the sky. Miss Brill put up her hand and touched her fur. Dear little thing! It was nice to feel it again. She had taken it out of its box that afternoon, shaken out the moth powder, given it a good brush, and rubbed the life back into the dim little eyes. "What has been happening to me?" said the sad little eyes. Oh, how sweet it was to see them snap at her again from the red eiderdown! . . . But the nose, which was of some black composition, wasn't at all firm. It must have had a knock, somehow. Never mind — a little dab of black sealing-wax when the time came — when it was absolutely necessary . . . Little rogue! Yes, she really felt like that about it. Little rogue biting its tail just by her left ear. She could have taken it off and laid it on her lap and stroked it. She felt a tingling in her hands and arms, but that came from walking, she supposed. And when she breathed, something light and sad — no, not sad, exactly — something gentle seemed to move in her bosom.

There were a number of people out this afternoon, far more than last Sunday. And the band sounded louder and gayer. That was because the Season had begun. For although the band played all the year round on Sundays, out of season it was never the same. It was like some one playing with only the family to listen; it didn't care how it played if there weren't any strangers present. Wasn't the conductor wearing a new coat, too? She was sure it was new. He scraped with his foot and flapped his arms like a rooster about to crow, and the bandsmen sitting in the green rotunda blew out their cheeks and glared at the music. Now there came a little "flutey" bit — very pretty! — a little chain of bright drops. She was sure it would be repeated. It was; she lifted her head and smiled.

Only two people shared her "special" seat: a fine old man in a velvet coat, his hands clasped over a huge carved walking-stick, and a big old woman, sitting upright, with a roll of knitting on her embroidered apron. They did not speak. This was disappointing, for Miss Brill always looked forward to the conversation. She had become really quite expert, she thought, at listening as though she didn't listen, at sitting in other people's lives just for a minute while they talked round her.

MISS BRILL   Written in 1921; first published in 1922. "Jardins Publiques" is French for Public Gardens. Katherine Mansfield (1888–1923) was born and grew up in New Zealand, but lived her adult life in London with various sojourns on the Continent.

She glanced, sideways, at the old couple. Perhaps they would go soon. Last Sunday, too, hadn't been as interesting as usual. An Englishman and his wife, he wearing a dreadful Panama hat and she button boots. And she'd gone on the whole time about how she ought to wear spectacles; she knew she needed them; but that it was no good getting any; they'd be sure to break and they'd never keep on. And he'd been so patient. He'd suggested everything — gold rims, the kind that curve round your ears, little pads inside the bridge. No, nothing would please her. "They'll always be sliding down my nose!" Miss Brill had wanted to shake her.

The old people sat on the bench, still as statues. Never mind, there was always the crowd to watch. To and fro, in front of the flower beds and the band rotunda, the couples and groups paraded, stopped to talk, to greet, to buy a handful of flowers from the old beggar who had his tray fixed to the railings. Little children ran among them, swooping and laughing; little boys with big white silk bows under their chins, little girls, little French dolls, dressed up in velvet and lace. And sometimes a tiny staggerer came suddenly rocking into the open from under the trees, stopped, stared, as suddenly sat down "flop," until its small high-stepping mother, like a young hen, rushed scolding to its rescue. Other people sat on the benches and green chairs, but they were nearly always the same, Sunday after Sunday, and — Miss Brill had often noticed — there was something funny about nearly all of them. They were odd, silent, nearly all old, and from the way they stared they looked as though they'd just come from dark little rooms or even — even cupboards!

Behind the rotunda the slender trees with yellow leaves down drooping, and through them just a line of sea, and beyond the blue sky with gold-veined clouds.

Tum-tum-tum tiddle-um! tiddle-um! tum tiddley-um tum ta! blew the band.

Two young girls in red came by and two young soldiers in blue met them, and they laughed and paired and went off arm-in-arm. Two peasant women with funny straw hats passed, gravely, leading beautiful smoke-colored donkeys. A cold, pale nun hurried by. A beautiful woman came along and dropped her bunch of violets, and a little boy ran after to hand them to her, and she took them and threw them away as if they'd been poisoned. Dear me! Miss Brill didn't know whether to admire that or not! And now an ermine toque and a gentleman in gray met just in front of her. He was tall, stiff, dignified, and she was wearing the ermine toque she'd bought when her hair was yellow. Now everything, her hair, her face, even her eyes, was the same color as the shabby ermine, and her hand, in its cleaned glove, lifted to dab her lips, was a tiny yellowish paw. Oh, she was so pleased to see him — delighted! She rather thought they were going to meet that afternoon. She described where she'd been — everywhere, here, there, along by the sea. The day was so charming — didn't he agree? And wouldn't he, perhaps? . . . But he shook his head, lighted a cigarette, slowly breathed a great deep puff into her face, and, even while she was still talking and laughing, flicked the match away and walked on. The ermine toque was alone; she smiled more brightly than ever. But even the band seemed to know what she was feeling and played more softly, played tenderly, and the drum beat, "The Brute! The Brute!" over and over. What would she do? What was going to happen now? But as Miss Brill wondered, the ermine toque turned, raised her hand as though she'd seen some one else, much nicer, just over there, and pattered away. And the band changed again and played more quickly, more gayly than ever, and the old couple on Miss Brill's seat got up and marched away, and such a funny old man with long whiskers hobbled along in time to the music and was nearly knocked over by four girls walking abreast.

Oh, how fascinating it was! How she enjoyed it! How she loved sitting here, watching it all! It was like a play. It was exactly like a play. Who could believe the sky at the back wasn't painted? But it wasn't till a little brown dog trotted on solemn and then slowly trotted off, like a little "theater" dog, a little dog that had been drugged, that Miss Brill discovered what it was that made it so exciting. They were all on stage. They weren't only the audience, not only looking on; they were acting. Even she had a part and came every Sunday. No doubt somebody would have noticed if she hadn't been there; she was part of the performance after all. How strange she'd never thought of it like that before! And yet it explained why she made such a point of start-ing from home at just the same time each week — so as not to be late for the performance — and it also explained why she had quite a queer, shy feeling at telling her English pupils how she spent her Sunday afternoons. No wonder! Miss Brill nearly laughed out loud. She was on the stage. She thought of the old invalid gentleman to whom she read the newspaper four afternoons a week while he slept in the garden. She had got quite used to the frail head on the cotton pillow, the hollowed eyes, the open mouth and the high pinched nose. If he'd been dead she mightn't have noticed for weeks; she wouldn't have minded. But suddenly he knew he was having the paper read to him by an actress! "An actress!" The old head lifted; two points of light quivered in the old eyes. "An actress — are ye?" And Miss Brill smoothed the newspaper as though it were the manuscript of her part and said gently: "Yes, I have been an actress for a long time."

10   The band had been having a rest. Now they started again. And what they played was warm, sunny, yet there was just a faint chill — a something, what was it? — not sadness — no, not sadness — a something that made you want to sing. The tune lifted, lifted, the light shone; and it seemed to Miss Brill that in another moment all of them, all the whole company, would begin singing. The young ones, the laughing ones who were moving together, they would begin, and the men's voices, very resolute and brave, would join them. And then she too, she too, and the others on the benches — they would come in with a kind of accompaniment — something low, that scarcely rose or fell, something so beautiful — moving . . . And Miss Brill's eyes filled with tears and she looked smiling at all the other members of the company. Yes, we

understand, we understand, she thought — though what they understood she didn't know.

Just at that moment a boy and girl came and sat down where the old couple had been. They were beautifully dressed; they were in love. The hero and heroine, of course, just arrived from his father's yacht. And still soundlessly singing, still with that trembling smile, Miss Brill prepared to listen.

"No, not now," said the girl. "Not here, I can't."

"But why? Because of that stupid old thing at the end there?" asked the boy. "Why does she come here at all — who wants her? Why doesn't she keep her silly old mug at home?"

"It's her fu-fur which is so funny," giggled the girl. "It's exactly like a fried whiting."

"Ah, be off with you!" said the boy in an angry whisper. Then: "Tell me, ma petite chère — " 15

"No, not here," said the girl. "Not *yet*."

On her way home she usually bought a slice of honeycake at the baker's. It was her Sunday treat. Sometimes there was an almond in her slice, sometimes not. It made a great difference. If there was an almond it was like carrying home a tiny present — a surprise — something that might very well not have been there. She hurried on the almond Sundays and struck the match for the kettle in quite a dashing way.

But today she passed the baker's by, climbed the stairs, went into the little dark room — her room like a cupboard — and sat down on the red eiderdown. She sat there for a long time. The box that the fur came out of was on the bed. She unclasped the necklet quickly; quickly, without looking, laid it inside. But when she put the lid on she thought she heard something crying.

QUESTIONS

1. We view the people and events of this story almost entirely through the eyes and feelings of its protagonist. The author relies upon indirect presentation for her characterization of Miss Brill. After answering the following questions, write as full an account as you can of the nature and temperament of the story's main character.
2. What nationality is Miss Brill? What is the story's setting? Why is it important?
3. How old is Miss Brill? What are her circumstances? Why does she listen in on conversations?
4. Why does Miss Brill enjoy her Sundays in the park? Why especially this Sunday?
5. Of what importance to the story is the woman in the ermine toque?
6. What is Miss Brill's mood at the beginning of the story? What is it at the end? Why? Is she a static or a developing character?
7. What function does Miss Brill's fur serve in the story? What is the meaning of the final sentence?

CHAPTER FOUR

Theme

"Daddy, the man next door kisses his wife every morning when he leaves for work. Why don't you do that?"

"Gracious, little one, I don't even know the woman."

"Daughter, your young man stays until a very late hour. Hasn't your mother said anything to you about this habit of his?"

"Yes, father. Mother says men haven't altered a bit."

For readers who contemplate the two jokes above, a significant difference emerges between them. The first joke depends only upon a reversal of expectation. We expect the man to explain why he doesn't kiss his wife; instead he explains why he doesn't kiss his neighbor's wife. The second joke, though it contains a reversal of expectation, depends as much or more for its effectiveness on a truth about human life; namely, that *people tend to grow more conservative as they grow older*, or that *parents often scold their children for doing exactly what they did themselves when young*. This truth, which might be stated in different ways, is the *theme* of the joke.

The **theme** of a piece of fiction is its controlling idea or its central insight. It is the unifying generalization about life stated or implied by the story. To derive the theme of a story, we must determine what its central *purpose* is: what view of life it supports or what insight into life it reveals.

Not all stories have theme. The purpose of a horror story may be simply to scare readers, to give them gooseflesh. The purpose of an adventure story may be simply to carry readers through a series of exciting escapades. The purpose of a murder mystery may be simply to pose a problem for readers to try to solve (and to prevent them from solving it, if possible, until the last paragraph). The purpose of some stories may be simply to provide suspense or to make readers laugh or to surprise them with a sudden twist at the end. Theme exists only (1) when an author has seriously attempted to record life accurately or to reveal some truth about it or (2) when an author has deliberately introduced as a unifying element some concept or theory of life that the story illustrates. Theme exists in all interpretive fiction but only in some escape fiction. In interpretive fiction it is the purpose of the story; in escape fiction, when it exists, it is merely an excuse, a peg to hang the story from.

In many stories the theme may be equivalent to the revelation of human character. If a story has as its central purpose to exhibit a certain kind of human being, our statement of theme may be no more than a concentrated description of the person revealed, with the addition, "Some people are like this." Frequently, however, a story through its portrayal of specific persons in specific situations will have something to say about the nature of all human beings or about their relationship to each other or to the universe. Whatever central generalization about life arises from the specifics of the story constitutes theme.

The theme of a story, like its plot, may be stated very briefly or at greater length. With a simple or very brief story, we may be satisfied to sum up the theme in a single sentence. With a more complex story, if it is successfully unified, we can still state the theme in a single sentence, but we may feel that a paragraph — or occasionally even an essay — is needed to state it adequately. A rich story will give us many and complex insights into life. In stating the theme in a sentence, we must pick the *central* insight, the one that explains the greatest number of elements in the story and relates them to each other. For theme is what gives a story its unity. In any story at all complex, however, we are likely to feel that a one-sentence statement of theme leaves out a great part of the story's meaning. Though the theme of *Othello* may be expressed as "Jealousy exacts a terrible cost," such a statement does not begin to suggest the range and depth of Shakespeare's play. Any successful story is a good deal more and means a good deal more than any one-sentence statement of theme that we may extract from it, for the story will modify and expand this statement in various and subtle ways.

We must never think, once we have stated the theme of a story, that the whole purpose of the story has been to yield up this abstract statement. If this were so, there would be no reason for the story: we could stop with the abstract statement. The function of interpretive writers is not to state a theme but to vivify it. They wish to deliver it not simply to our intellects but to our emotions, our senses, and our imaginations.

The theme of a story may be little or nothing except as it is embodied and vitalized by the story. Unembodied, it is a dry backbone, without flesh or life.

Sometimes the theme of a story is explicitly stated somewhere in the story, either by the author or by one of the characters. More often, however, the theme is implied. Story writers, after all, are story writers, not essayists or philosophers. Their first business is to reveal life, not to comment on it. They may well feel that unless the story somehow expresses its own meaning, without their having to point it out, they have not told the story well. Or they may feel that if the story is to have its maximum emotional effect, they must refrain from interrupting it or making remarks about it. They are also wary of spoiling a story for perceptive readers by "explaining" it as some people ruin jokes by explaining them. For these reasons theme is more often left implicit than stated explicitly. Good writers do not ordinarily write a story for the sole purpose of "illustrating" a theme, as do the writers of parables or fables. They write stories to bring alive some segment of human existence. When they do so searchingly and coherently, theme arises naturally out of what they have written. Good readers may state the generalizations for themselves.

Some readers—especially inexperienced readers—look for a "moral" in everything they read—some rule of conduct that they regard as applicable to their lives. They consider the words "theme" and "moral" to be interchangeable. Sometimes the words are interchangeable. Occasionally the theme of a story may be expressed as a moral principle without doing violence to the story. More frequently, however, the word "moral" is too narrow to fit the kind of illumination provided by a first-rate story. It is hardly suitable, for instance, for the kind of story that simply displays human character. Such nouns as "moral" and "lesson" and "message" are therefore best avoided in the discussion of fiction. The critical term **theme** is preferable for several reasons. First, it is less likely to obscure the fact that a story is not a preachment or a sermon: a story's *first* object is enjoyment. Second, it should keep us from trying to wring from every story a didactic pronouncement about life. The person who seeks a moral in every story is likely to oversimplify and conventionalize it—to reduce it to some dusty platitude like "Be kind to animals" or "Look before you leap" or "Crime does not pay." The purpose of interpretive story writers is to give us a greater awareness and a greater understanding of life, not to inculcate a code of moral rules for regulating daily conduct. In getting at the theme of the story it is better to ask not *What does this story teach?* but *What does this story reveal?* Readers who interpret Anderson's "I'm a Fool" as being merely a warning against lying have missed nine-tenths of the story. It is really a marvelously penetrating exploration of a complex personality. The theme is *not* "Honesty is the best policy" but something more like this: "A young man of decent background who fails in various enterprises may develop ambivalent or contradictory values as well as feelings of inferiority. Consciously or unconsciously he will adopt various stratagems to compensate for these feelings by magnifying his importance both in his own eyes and in the eyes of others. If these stratagems backfire, he may recognize his folly but not the underlying reasons for it." Obviously, this dry statement is a poor thing beside the living reality of the story. But it is a more faithful abstracting of the content of the story than any "moral."

The revelation offered by a good story may be something fresh or something old. The story may bring us some insight into life that we had not had before, and thus expand our horizons, or it may make us *feel* or *feel again* some truth of which we have long been merely intellectually aware. We may know in our minds, for instance, that "War is horrible" or that "Old age is often pathetic and in need of understanding," but these are insights that need to be periodically renewed. *Emotionally* we may forget them, and if we do, we are less alive and complete as human beings. Story writers perform a service for us — interpret life for us — whether they give us new insights or refresh and extend old ones.

The themes of commercial and quality stories may be identical, but frequently they are different. Commercial stories, for the most part, confirm their readers' prejudices, endorse their opinions, ratify their feelings, and satisfy their wishes. Usually, therefore, the themes of such stories are widely accepted platitudes of experience that may or may not be supported by the life around us. They represent life as we would like it to be, not always as it is. We should certainly like to believe, for instance, that "Motherhood is sacred," that "True love always wins through," that "Virtue and hard work are rewarded in the end," that "Cheaters never win," that "Old age brings a mellow wisdom that compensates for its infirmity," and that "Every human being has a soft spot in him somewhere." Interpretive writers, however, being thoughtful observers of life, are likely to question these beliefs and often to challenge them. Their ideas about life are not simply taken over ready-made from what they were taught in Sunday school or from the books they read as children; they are the formulations of sensitive and independent observers who have collated all that they have read and been taught with life itself. The themes of their stories therefore do not often correspond to the pretty little sentiments we find inscribed on candy valentines. They may sometimes represent rather somber truths. Much of the process of maturing as a reader lies in the discovery that there may be more nourishment and deeper enjoyment in assimilating these somber truths than in licking the sugar off of candy valentines.

We do not, however, have to accept the theme of an interpretive story any more than we do that of a commercial story. Though we should never summarily dismiss it without reflection, we may find that the theme of a story represents a judgment on life with which, on examination, we cannot agree. If it is the reasoned view of a seasoned and serious artist, nevertheless, it cannot be without value to us. There is value in knowing what the world looks like to others, and we can thus use a judgment to expand our knowledge of human experience even though we cannot ourselves accept it. Genuine artists and thoughtful observers, moreover, can hardly fail to present us with partial insights along the way although we disagree with the total view. Good readers, therefore, will not reject a story because they reject its theme. They can enjoy any story that arises from sufficient depth of observation and reflection and is artistically composed, though they disagree with its theme; and they will prefer it to a shallower, less thoughtful, or less successfully integrated story that presents a theme they endorse.

Discovering and stating the theme of a story is often a delicate task. Sometimes we will *feel* what the story is about strongly enough and yet find it difficult to put this feeling into words. If we are skilled readers, it is perhaps unnecessary that we do so. The bare statement of the theme, so lifeless and impoverished when abstracted from the story, may seem to diminish the story to something less than it is. Often, however, the attempt to state a theme will reveal to us aspects of a story that we should otherwise not have noticed and will thereby lead to more thorough understanding. The ability to state theme, moreover, is a test of our understanding of a story. Inexperienced readers often think they understand a story when in actuality they have misunderstood it. They understand the events but not what the events add up to. Or, in adding up the events, they arrive at an erroneous total. People sometimes miss the point of a joke. It is not surprising that they should frequently miss the point of a good piece of fiction, which is many times more complex than a joke.

There is no prescribed method for discovering theme. Sometimes we can best get at it by asking in what way the main character has changed in the course of the story and what, if anything, the character has learned before its end. Sometimes the best approach is to explore the nature of the central conflict and its outcome. Sometimes the title will provide an important clue. At all times we should keep in mind the following principles:

1. Theme should be expressible in the form of a statement with a subject and a predicate. It is insufficient to say that the theme of a story is motherhood or loyalty to country. Motherhood and loyalty are simply subjects. Theme must be a statement *about* the subject. For instance, "Motherhood sometimes has more frustrations than rewards" or "Loyalty to country often inspires heroic self-sacrifice." If we express the theme in the form of a phrase, the phrase must be convertible to sentence form. A phrase such as "the futility of envy," for instance, may be converted to the statement "Envy is futile": it may therefore serve as a statement of theme.

2. The theme should be stated as a *generalization* about life. In stating theme we do not use the names of the characters or refer to precise places or events, for to do so is to make a specific rather than a general statement. The theme of "The Destructors" is not that "The Wormsley Common Gang of London, in the aftermath of World War II, found a creative outlet in destroying a beautiful two-hundred-year-old house designed by Sir Christopher Wren." Rather, it is something like this: "The dislocations caused by a devastating war may produce among the young a conscious or unconscious rebellion against all the values of the reigning society — a rebellion in which the creative instincts are channeled into destructive enterprises."

3. We must be careful not to make the generalization larger than is justified by the terms of the story. Terms like *every, all, always* should be used very cautiously; terms like *some, sometimes, may* are often more accurate. The theme of "Everyday Use" is not that "Habitually compliant and tolerant mothers will eventually stand up to their bullying children," for we have only one instance of such behavior in the story. But the story does sufficiently present this event as a climactic change in a developing character. Because the story's narrator recalls precise details of her previous behavior that she brings to bear on her present decision, we can safely infer that this decision will be meaningful and lasting, and should feel we can generalize beyond the specific situation. The theme might be expressed thus: "A person whose honesty and tolerance have long made her susceptible to the strong will of another may reach a point where she will exert her own will for the sake of justice," or more generally, "Ingrained habits can be given up if justice makes a greater

demand." Notice that we have said *may* and *can*, not *will* and *must*. Only occasionally will the theme of a story be expressible as a universal generalization. In "The Child by Tiger" we know from Wolfe's use of Blake's poem and from his concluding paragraphs that the author considers Dick Prosser not as a special case but as a symbol of something present in us all. The soul of every man (so the story seems to say) is mysterious in its origins and contains unfathomed possibilities for evil and violence as well as for innocence and love.

4. Theme is the *central* and *unifying* concept of a story. Therefore (a) it accounts for all the major details of the story. If we cannot explain the bearing of an important incident or character on the theme, either in exemplifying it or modifying it in some way, it is probable that our interpretation is partial and incomplete, that at best we have got hold only of a subtheme. Another alternative, though it must be used with caution, is that the story itself is imperfectly constructed and lacks entire unity. (b) The theme is not contradicted by any detail of the story. If we have to overlook or blink at or "force" the meaning of some significant detail in order to frame our statement, we may be sure that our statement is defective. (c) The theme cannot rely upon supposed facts — facts not actually stated or clearly implied by the story. The theme exists *inside*, not *outside*, the story. The statement of it must be based on the data of the story itself, not on assumptions supplied from our own experience.

5. There is no *one* way of stating the theme of a story. The story is not a guessing game or an acrostic that is supposed to yield some magic verbal formula that won't work if a syllable is changed. It merely presents a view of life, and, as long as the above conditions are fulfilled, that view may surely be stated in more than one way. Here, for instance, are three possible ways of stating the theme of "Miss Brill": (a) A person living alone may create a protective fantasy life by dramatizing insignificant activities, but such a life can be jeopardized when she is forced to see herself as others see her. (b) Isolated elderly people, unsupported by a network of family and friends, may make a satisfying adjustment through a pleasant fantasy life, but when their fantasy is punctured by the cold claw of reality, the effect can be devastating. (c) Loneliness is a pitiable emotional state that may be avoided by refusing to acknowledge that one feels lonely, though such an avoidance may also require one to create unrealistic fantasies about oneself.

6. We should avoid any statement that reduces the theme to some familiar saying that we have heard all our lives, such as "You can't judge a book by its cover" or "A stitch in time saves nine." Although such a statement *may* express the theme accurately, too often it is simply a lazy

shortcut that impoverishes the essential meaning of the story in order to save mental effort. When readers force every new experience into an old formula, they lose the chance for a fresh perception. Instead of letting the story expand their knowledge and awareness of the world, they fall back dully on a cliché. To come out with "Honesty is the best policy" as the theme of "I'm a Fool" is almost to lose the whole value of the story. If the impulse arises to express the meaning of a story in a ready-made phrase, it should be suppressed.

Isaac Bashevis Singer
The Son from America

The village of Lentshin was tiny — a sandy marketplace where the peasants of the area met once a week. It was surrounded by little huts with thatched roofs or shingles green with moss. The chimneys looked like pots. Between the huts there were fields, where the owners planted vegetables or pastured their goats.

In the smallest of these huts lived old Berl, a man in his eighties, and his wife, who was called Berlcha (wife of Berl). Old Berl was one of the Jews who had been driven from their villages in Russia and had settled in Poland. In Lentshin, they mocked the mistakes he made while praying aloud. He spoke with a sharp "r." He was short, broad-shouldered, and had a small white beard, and summer and winter he wore a sheepskin hat, a padded cotton jacket, and stout boots. He walked slowly, shuffling his feet. He had a half acre of field, a cow, a goat, and chickens.

The couple had a son, Samuel, who had gone to America forty years ago. It was said in Lentshin that he became a millionaire there. Every month, the Lentshin letter carrier brought old Berl a money order and a letter that no one could read because many of the words were English. How much money Samuel sent his parents remained a secret. Three times a year, Berl and his wife went on foot to Zakroczym and cashed the money orders there. But they never seemed to use the money. What for? The garden, the cow, and the goat provided most of their needs. Besides, Berlcha sold chickens and eggs, and from these there was enough to buy flour for bread.

THE SON FROM AMERICA   First published in 1973. The story makes use of the two environments most familiar to its author. Isaac Bashevis Singer (1904–1991), who was awarded the Nobel Prize for Literature in 1978, was born in Poland and educated in a rabbinical seminary in Warsaw. He worked as a translator and editor in Poland until his emigration to the United States in 1935. His first work here was for a Yiddish paper in New York City, where he began publishing sketches and stories. He continued to write in Yiddish, and then translated his work into English, usually with the help of an assistant. This story was translated by the author and Dorothea Straus.

No one cared to know where Berl kept the money that his son sent him. There were no thieves in Lentshin. The hut consisted of one room, which contained all their belongings: the table, the shelf for meat, the shelf for milk foods, the two beds, and the clay oven. Sometimes the chickens roosted in the woodshed and sometimes, when it was cold, in a coop near the oven. The goat, too, found shelter inside when the weather was bad. The more prosperous villagers had kerosene lamps, but Berl and his wife did not believe in newfangled gadgets. What was wrong with a wick in a dish of oil? Only for the Sabbath would Berlcha buy three tallow candles at the store. In summer, the couple got up at sunrise and retired with the chickens. In the long winter evenings, Berlcha spun flax at her spinning wheel and Berl sat beside her in the silence of those who enjoy their rest.

5   Once in a while when Berl came home from the synagogue after evening prayers, he brought news to his wife. In Warsaw there were strikers who demanded that the czar abdicate. A heretic by the name of Dr. Herzl° had come up with the idea that Jews should settle again in Palestine. Berlcha listened and shook her bonneted head. Her face was yellowish and wrinkled like a cabbage leaf. There were bluish sacks under her eyes. She was half deaf. Berl had to repeat each word he said to her. She would say, "The things that happen in the big cities!"

Here in Lentshin nothing happened except usual events: a cow gave birth to a calf, a young couple had a circumcision party, or a girl was born and there was no party. Occasionally, someone died. Lentshin had no cemetery, and the corpse had to be taken to Zakroczym. Actually, Lentshin had become a village with few young people. The young men left for Zakroczym, for Nowy Dwor, for Warsaw, and sometimes for the United States. Like Samuel's, their letters were illegible, the Yiddish mixed with the languages of the countries where they were now living. They sent photographs in which the men wore top hats and the women fancy dresses like squiresses.

Berl and Berlcha also received such photographs. But their eyes were failing and neither he nor she had glasses. They could barely make out the pictures. Samuel had sons and daughters with gentile names — and grandchildren who had married and had their own offspring. Their names were so strange that Berl and Berlcha could never remember them. But what difference do names make? America was far, far away on the other side of the ocean, at the edge of the world. A Talmud teacher who came to Lentshin had said that Americans walked with their heads down and their feet up. Berl and Berlcha could not grasp this. How was it possible? But since the teacher said so it must be true. Berlcha pondered for some time and then she said, "One can get accustomed to everything."

And so it remained. From too much thinking — God forbid — one may lose one's wits.

Dr. Herzl: Theodore Herzl (1869–1904), the founder of Zionism. In 1896 he won worldwide notice for his book *The Jewish State*, and in 1897 he organized the first Zionist World Conference.

One Friday morning, when Berlcha was kneading the dough for the Sabbath° loaves, the door opened and a nobleman entered. He was so tall that he had to bend down to get through the door. He wore a beaver hat and a cloak bordered with fur. He was followed by Chazkel, the coachman from Zakroczym, who carried two leather valises with brass locks. In astonishment Berlcha raised her eyes.

The nobleman looked around and said to the coachman in Yiddish, 10 "Here it is." He took out a silver ruble and paid him. The coachman tried to hand him change but he said, "You can go now."

When the coachman closed the door, the nobleman said, "Mother, it's me, your son Samuel — Sam."

Berlcha heard the words and her legs grew numb. Her hands, to which pieces of dough were sticking, lost their power. The nobleman hugged her, kissed her forehead, both her cheeks. Berlcha began to cackle like a hen, "My son!" At that moment Berl came in from the woodshed, his arms piled with logs. The goat followed him. When he saw a nobleman kissing his wife, Berl dropped the wood and exclaimed, "What is this?"

The nobleman let go of Berlcha and embraced Berl. "Father!"

For a long time Berl was unable to utter a sound. He wanted to recite holy words that he had read in the Yiddish Bible, but he could remember nothing. Then he asked, "Are you Samuel?"

"Yes, Father, I am Samuel." 15

"Well, peace be with you." Berl grasped his son's hand. He was still not sure that he was not being fooled. Samuel wasn't as tall and heavy as this man, but then Berl reminded himself that Samuel was only fifteen years old when he had left home. He must have grown in that faraway country. Berl asked, "Why didn't you let us know that you were coming?"

"Didn't you receive my cable?" Samuel asked.

Berl did not know what a cable was.

Berlcha had scraped the dough from her hands and enfolded her son. He kissed her again and asked, "Mother, didn't you receive a cable?"

"What? If I lived to see this, I am happy to die," Berlcha said, amazed by 20 her own words. Berl, too, was amazed. These were just the words he would have said earlier if he had been able to remember. After a while Berl came to himself and said, "Pescha, you will have to make a double Sabbath pudding in addition to the stew."

It was years since Berl had called Berlcha by her given name. When he wanted to address her, he would say, "Listen," or "Say." It is the young or those from the big cities who call a wife by her name. Only now did Berlcha begin to cry. Yellow tears ran from her eyes, and everything became dim. Then she called out, "It's Friday — I have to prepare for the Sabbath." Yes, she had to knead the dough and braid the loaves. With such a guest, she had to make a larger Sabbath stew. The winter day is short and she must hurry.

Sabbath: Saturday for Jews

Her son understood what was worrying her, because he said, "Mother, I will help you."

Berlcha wanted to laugh, but a choked sob came out. "What are you saying? God forbid."

The nobleman took off his cloak and jacket and remained in his vest, on which hung a solid-gold watch chain. He rolled up his sleeves and came to the trough. "Mother, I was a baker for many years in New York," he said, and he began to knead the dough.

25 "What! You are my darling son who will say Kaddish° for me." She wept raspingly. Her strength left her, and she slumped onto the bed.

Berl said, "Women will always be women." And he went to the shed to get more wood. The goat sat down near the oven; she gazed with surprise at this strange man — his height and his bizarre clothes.

The neighbors had heard the good news that Berl's son had arrived from America and they came to greet him. The women began to help Berlcha prepare for the Sabbath. Some laughed, some cried. The room was full of people, as at a wedding. They asked Berl's son, "What is new in America?" And Berl's son answered, "America is all right."

"Do Jews make a living?"

"One eats white bread there on weekdays."

30 "Do they remain Jews?"

"I am not a gentile."

After Berlcha blessed the candles, father and son went to the little synagogue across the street. A new snow had fallen. The son took large steps, but Berl warned him, "Slow down."

In the synagogue the Jews recited "Let Us Exult" and "Come, My Groom." All the time, the snow outside kept falling. After prayers, when Berl and Samuel left the Holy Place, the village was unrecognizable. Everything was covered in snow. One could see only the contours of the roofs and the candles in the windows. Samuel said, "Nothing has changed here."

Berlcha had prepared gefilte fish, chicken soup with rice, meat, carrot stew. Berl recited the benediction over a glass of ritual wine. The family ate and drank, and when it grew quiet for a while one could hear the chirping of the house cricket. The son talked a lot, but Berl and Berlcha understood little. His Yiddish was different and contained foreign words.

35 After the final blessing Samuel asked, "Father, what did you do with all the money I sent you?"

Berl raised his white brows. "It's here."

"Didn't you put it in a bank?"

"There is no bank in Lentshin."

"Where do you keep it?"

Kaddish: a prayer of mourning for the dead

Berl hesitated. "One is not allowed to touch money on the Sabbath but I will show you." He crouched beside the bed and began to shove something heavy. A boot appeared. Its top was stuffed with straw. Berl removed the straw and the son saw that the boot was full of gold coins. He lifted it.

"Father, this is a treasure!" he called out.

"Well."

"Why didn't you spend it?"

"On what? Thank God, we have everything."

"Why didn't you travel somewhere?"

"Where to? This is our home."

The son asked one question after the other, but Berl's answer was always the same: they wanted for nothing. The garden, the cow, the goat, the chickens provided them with all they needed. The son said, "If thieves knew about this, your lives wouldn't be safe."

"There are no thieves here."

"What will happen to the money?"

"You take it."

Slowly, Berl and Berlcha grew accustomed to their son and his American Yiddish. Berlcha could hear him better now. She even recognized his voice. He was saying, "Perhaps we should build a larger synagogue."

"The synagogue is big enough," Berl replied.

"Perhaps a home for old people."

"No one sleeps in the street."

The next day after the Sabbath meal was eaten, a gentile from Zakro- czym brought a paper — it was the cable. Berl and Berlcha lay down for a nap. They soon began to snore. The goat, too, dozed off. The son put on his cloak and his hat and went for a walk. He strode with his long legs across the marketplace. He stretched out a hand and touched a roof. He wanted to smoke a cigar, but he remembered it was forbidden on the Sabbath. He had a desire to talk to someone, but it seemed that the whole of Lentshin was asleep. He entered the synagogue. An old man was sitting there, reciting psalms. Samuel asked, "Are you praying?"

"What else is there to do when one gets old?"

"Do you make a living?"

The old man did not understand the meaning of these words. He smiled, showing his empty gums, and then he said, "If God gives health, one keeps on living."

Samuel returned home. Dusk had fallen. Berl went to the synagogue for the evening prayers and the son remained with his mother. The room was filled with shadows.

Berlcha began to recite in a solemn singsong, "God of Abraham, Isaac, and Jacob, defend the poor people of Israel and Thy name. The Holy Sabbath is departing; the welcome week is coming to us. Let it be one of health, wealth, and good deeds."

"Mother, you don't need to pray for wealth," Samuel said. "You are wealthy already."

Berlcha did not hear — or pretended not to. Her face had turned into a cluster of shadows.

In the twilight Samuel put his hand into his jacket pocket and touched his passport, his checkbook, his letters of credit. He had come here with big plans. He had a valise filled with presents for his parents. He wanted to bestow gifts on the village. He brought not only his own money but funds from the Lentshin Society in New York, which had organized a ball for the benefit of the village. But this village in the hinterland needed nothing. From the synagogue one could hear hoarse chanting. The cricket, silent all day, started again its chirping. Berlcha began to sway and utter holy rhymes inherited from mothers and grandmothers.

> The holy sheep
> In mercy keep,
> In Torah and good deeds;
> Provide for all their needs,
> Shoes, clothes, and bread
> And the Messiah's tread.

QUESTIONS

1. Characterize Berl and Berlcha. How well educated are they? How intelligent? How imaginative? How sensible? What is the chief source of stability in their lives? Are they meant to be taken as unusual or as typical characters of the village and region where they live? Does the storyteller view them with scorn, pity, humor, respect, or admiration? (More than one of these may be a correct answer.)
2. How *might* or *could* Berl and Berlcha have well spent Samuel's monthly remittances if they had had more imagination or knowledge?
3. Characterize Samuel. In what ways are his values different from those of his parents? In what ways are they the same? Can Samuel be regarded as the antagonist of the story? Why or why not?
4. Comment on each of the following in its relationship to characterization or theme in the story: (a) Berlcha's reaction to the Talmud teacher's saying that Americans walked with their heads down and their feet up, (b) Berlcha's remark that "One can get accustomed to everything," (c) the storyteller's comment that "From too much thinking — God forbid — one may lose one's wits," (d) the narrative statement that "the door opened and a nobleman entered," (e) the coachman's trying to give the "nobleman" change for his silver ruble, (f) Berlcha's response to Samuel's declaration that he will help her with the baking, (g) Berl's saying of Berlcha's weeping, "Women will always be women," (h) Berl's answer to Samuel's question about why he didn't spend the money.
5. Frame a statement of theme for the story.

Neil Bissoondath

There Are a Lot of Ways to Die

It was still drizzling when Joseph clicked the final padlocks on the door. The name-plate, home-painted with squared gold letters on a black background and glazed all over with transparent varnish to lend a professional tint, was flecked with water and dirt. He took a crumpled handkerchief from his back pocket and carefully wiped the lettering clean: JOSEPH HEAVEN: CARPET AND RUG INSTALLATIONS. The colon had been his idea and he had put it in over his wife's objections. He felt that it provided a natural flow from his name, that it showed a certain reliability. His wife, in the scornful voice she reserved for piercing his pretensions, had said, "That's all very well and good for Toronto, but you think people here care about that kind of thing?" But she was the one people accused of having airs, not him. As far as he was concerned, the colon was merely good business; and as the main beneficiary of the profits, she should learn to keep her mouth shut.

He had forgotten to pick up his umbrella from just inside the door where he had put it that morning. Gingerly, he extended his upturned palm, feeling the droplets, warm and wet, like newly spilled blood. He decided they were too light to justify reopening the shop, always something of an event because of the many locks and chains. This was another thing she didn't like, his obsession, as she called it, with security. She wanted a more open storefront, with windows and showcases and well-dressed mannequins smiling blankly at the street. She said, "It look just like every other store around here, just a wall and a door. It have nothing to catch the eye." He replied, "You want windows and showcases? What we going to show? My tools? The tacks? The cutter?" Besides, the locks were good for business, not a week went by without a robbery in the area. Displaying the tools would be a blatant invitation, and a recurrent nightmare had developed in which one of his cutters was stolen and used in a murder.

Across the glistening street, so narrow after the generosity of those he had known for six years, the clothes merchants were standing disconsolately in front of their darkened stores, hands in pockets, whistling and occasionally examining the grey skies for the brightening that would signal the

THERE ARE A LOT OF WAYS TO DIE   Published in 1985 in Neil Bissoondath's collection *Digging Up the Mountains*. The author was born in 1955 in Sangre Grande, a small market town in Trinidad. In 1973 he went to Toronto to study at York University, and he has since made Canada his permanent home. He studied French at the university, and for eight years taught English to immigrants and French-speaking Canadians while writing at night, then began writing full time. This story is presumably set in Port of Spain, the capital of Trinidad, the island nation off the coast of Venezuela that was a Spanish and then English colony before achieving independence in 1964.

end of the rain and the appearance of shoppers. They stared blankly at him. One halfheartedly jabbed his finger at a stalactitic line of umbrellas and dusty raincoats, inviting a purchase. Joseph showed no interest. The merchant shrugged and resumed his tuneless whistling, a plaintive sound from between clenched front teeth.

Joseph had forgotten how sticky the island could be when it rained. The heat, it seemed, never really disappeared during the night. Instead, it retreated just a few inches underground, only to emerge with the morning rain, condensing, filling the atmosphere with steam. It put the lie to so much he had told his Canadian friends about the island. The morning rain wasn't as refreshing as he'd recalled it and the steam had left his memory altogether. How could he have sworn that the island experienced no humidity? Why had he, in all honesty, recalled tender tropical breezes when the truth, as it now enveloped him, was the exact, stifling opposite? Climate was not so drastically altered, only memory.

5   He walked to the end of the street, his shirt now clinging to his shoulders. The sidewalk, dark and pitted, seemed to glide by under his feet, as if it were itself moving. He squinted, feeling the folds of flesh bunching up at the corner of his eyes, and found he could fuzzily picture himself on Bloor Street, walking past the stores and the bakeries and the delicatessens pungent with Eastern European flavors, the hazy tops of buildings at Bloor and Yonge far away in the distance. He could even conjure up the sounds of a Toronto summer: the cars, the voices, the rumble of the subway under the feet as it swiftly glided towards downtown.

Joseph shook himself and opened his eyes, not without disappointment. He was having this hallucination too often, for too long. He was ashamed of it and couldn't confess it even to his wife. And he mistrusted it, too: might not even this more recent memory also be fooling him, as the other had done? Was it really possible to see the tops of buildings at Yonge from Bathurst? He wanted to ask his wife, pretending it was merely a matter of memory, but she would see through this to his longing and puncture him once more with that voice. She would call him a fool and not be far wrong. Were not two dislocations enough in one man's lifetime? Would not yet a third prove him a fool?

Their return had been jubilant. Friends and relatives treated it as a victory, seeking affirmation of the correctness of their cloistered life on the island, the return a defeat for life abroad. The first weeks were hectic, parties, dinners, get-togethers. Joseph felt like a curiosity, an object not of reverence but of silent ridicule, his the defeat, theirs the victory. The island seemed to close in around him.

They bought a house in the island's capital. The town was not large. Located at the extreme north-western edge of the island, having hardly expanded from the settlement originally established by Spanish adventurers as a depot in their quest for mythic gold, the town looked forever to the sea, preserving its aura of a way-station, a point at which to pause in brief respite from the larger search.

At first, Joseph had tried to deny this aspect of the town, for the town was the island and, if the island were no more than a way-station, a stopover from which nothing important ever emerged, then to accept this life was to accept second place. A man who had tasted of first could accept second only with delusion: his wife had taken on airs, he had painted his black-and-gold sign.

Then the hallucination started, recreating Bloor Street, vividly recalling the minute details of daily life. He caught himself reliving the simple things: buying milk, removing a newspaper from the box, slipping a subway token into the slot, sitting in a park. A chill would run through him when he realized they were remembrances of things past, possibly lost forever. The recollected civility of life in Toronto disturbed him, it seemed so distant. He remembered what a curious feeling of well-being had surged through him whenever he'd given directions to a stranger. Each time was like an affirmation of stability. Here, in an island so small that two leisurely hours in a car would reveal all, no one asked for directions, no one was a stranger. You couldn't claim the island: it claimed you.

The street on which their house stood used to be known all over the island. It was viewed with a twinge of admired notoriety and was thought of with the same fondness with which the islanders regarded the government ministers and civil servants who had fled the island with pilfered cash: an awed admiration, a flawed love. The cause of this attention was a house, a mansion in those days, erected, in the popular lore, by a Venezuelan general who, for reasons unknown, had exiled himself to a life of darkly rumored obscurity on the island. As far as Joseph knew, no one had ever actually seen the general: even his name, Pacheco, had been assumed. Or so it was claimed; no one had ever bothered to check.

Eventually the house became known as Pacheco House, and the street as Pacheco Street. It was said that the house, deserted for as long as anyone could remember and now falling into neglect, had been mentioned passingly in a book by an Englishman who had been looking into famous houses of the region. It was the island's first mention in a book other than a history text, the island's first mention outside the context of slavery.

The house had become the butt of schoolboys' frustration. On their way home after school, Joseph and his friends would detour to throw stones at the windows. In his memory, the spitting clank of shattering glass sounded distant and opaque. They had named each window for a teacher, thus adding thrust and enthusiasm to their aim. The largest window, high on the third floor — the attic, he now knew, in an island which had no attics — they named LeNoir, after the priest who was the terror of all students unblessed by fair skin or athletic ability. They were more disturbed by the fact that the priest himself was black; this seemed a greater sin than his choice of vocation. They had never succeeded in breaking the LeNoir window. Joseph might have put this down to divine protection had he not lost his sense of religion early on. It was a simple event: the priest at his last try at communion had showered him with sour breath the moment the flesh of Christ slipped onto Joseph's tongue. Joseph, from then on, equated the wafer with decaying flesh.

The LeNoir window went unscathed for many years and was still intact when, after the final exams, Joseph left the island for what he believed to be forever.

15   The raindrops grew larger, making a plopping sound on the sidewalk. A drop landed on his temple and cascaded down his cheek. He rubbed at it, feeling the prickly stubble he hadn't bothered to shave that morning.

Pacheco House was just up ahead, the lower floors obscured by a jungle of trees and bush, the garden overgrown and thickening to impenetrability. Above the treeline, the walls — a faded pink, pockmarked by the assault of stones and mangoes — had begun disintegrating, the thin plaster falling away in massive chunks to reveal ordinary grey brick underneath. The remaining plaster was criss-crossed by cracks and fissures created by age and humidity.

During his schooldays, the grounds had been maintained by the government. The house had been considered a tourist attraction and was displayed in brochures and on posters. An island-wide essay competition had been held, "The Mystery of Pacheco House," and the winning essay, of breathless prose linked by words like *tropical* and *verdant* and *lush* and *exotic*, was used as the text of a special brochure. But no tourists came. The mystery withered away to embarrassment. The government quietly gave the house up. The Jaycees, young businessmen who bustled about in the heat with the added burden of jackets and ties, offered to provide funds for the upkeep. The offer was refused with a shrug by the Ministry of Tourism, with inexplicable murmurings of "colonial horrors" by the Ministry of Culture. The house was left to its ghosts.

From the street Joseph could see the LeNoir window, still intact and dirt-streaked. He was surprised that it still seemed to mock him.

Joseph had asked his nephew, a precocious boy who enjoyed exhibiting his scattered knowledge of French and Spanish and who laughed at Joseph's clumsy attempts to resurrect the bits of language he had learnt in the same classes, often from the same teachers, if the boys still threw stones at Pacheco House. No, his nephew had informed him, after school they went to the sex movies or, in the case of the older boys, to the whorehouses. Joseph, stunned, had asked no more questions.

20   The rain turned perceptibly to a deluge, the thick, warm drops penetrating his clothes and running in rivulets down his back and face. The wild trees and plants of the Pacheco garden nodded and drooped, leaves glistening dully in the half-light. The pink walls darkened as the water socked into them, eating at the plaster. The LeNoir window was black; he remembered some claimed to have seen a white-faced figure in army uniform standing there at night. The story had provided mystery back then, a real haunted house, and on a rainy afternoon schoolboys could feel their spines tingle as they aimed their stones.

On impulse Joseph searched the ground for a stone. He saw only pebbles; the gravel verge had long been paved over. Already the sidewalk had cracked in spots and little shoots of grass had fought their way out, like wedges splitting a boulder.

He continued walking, oblivious of the rain.

Several cars were parked in the driveway of his house. His wife's friends were visiting. They were probably in the living room drinking coffee and eating pastries from Marcel's and looking through *Vogue* pattern books. Joseph made for the garage so he could enter, unnoticed, through the kitchen door. Then he thought, "Why the hell?" He put his hands into his pockets — his money was soaked and the movement of his fingers ripped the edge off a bill — and calmly walked in through the open front door.

His wife was standing in front of the fake fireplace she had insisted on bringing from Toronto. The dancing lights cast multicolored hues on her caftan. She almost dropped her coffee cup when she saw him. Her friends, perturbed, stared at him from their chairs which they had had grouped around the fireplace.

His wife said impatiently, "Joseph, what are you doing here?"   25

He said, "I live here."

She said, "And work?"

He said, "None of the boys show up this morning."

"So you just drop everything?"

"I postponed today's jobs. I couldn't do all the work by myself."   30

She put her cup down on the mantelpiece. "Go dry yourself off. You wetting the floor."

Her friend Arlene said, "Better than the bed."

They all laughed. His wife said, "He used to do that when he was a little boy, not so, Joseph?"

She looked at her friends and said, "You know, we having so much trouble finding good workers. Joseph already fire three men. Looks like we're going to have to fire all these now."

Arlene said, "Good help so hard to find these days."   35

His wife said, "These people like that, you know, girl. Work is the last thing they want to do."

Arlene said, "They 'fraid they going to melt if rain touch their skin."

His wife turned to him. "You mean not one out of twelve turned up this morning?"

"Not one."

Arlene, dark and plump, sucked her teeth and moved her tongue   40
around, pushing at her cheeks and making a plopping sound.

Joseph said, "Stop that. You look like a monkey."

His wife and Arlene stared at him in amazement. The others sipped their coffee or gazed blankly at the fireplace.

Arlene said witheringly, "I don't suffer fools gladly, Joseph."

He said, "Too bad. You must hate being alone."

His wife said, "Joseph!"   45

He said, "I better go dry off." Still dripping, he headed for the bedroom. At the door he paused and added, "People should be careful when they talking about other people. You know, glass houses . . ." He was suddenly exhausted: what was the point? They all knew Arlene's story. She had once been a maid whose career was rendered transient by rain and imagined illness; she had been no different from his employees. Her fortune had improved only because her husband — who was referred to behind his back as a "sometimes worker" because sometimes he worked and sometimes he didn't — had been appointed a minister without portfolio in the government. He had lost the nickname because now he never worked, but he had gained a regular check, a car and a chauffeur, and the tainted respectability of political appointment.

Joseph slammed the bedroom door and put his ear to the keyhole: there was a lot of throat-clearing; pages of a *Vogue* pattern book rustled. Finally, his wife said, "Come look at this pattern." Voices oohed and ahhed and cooed. Arlene said, "Look at this one." He kicked the door and threw his wet shirt on the bed.

The rain had stopped and the sky had cleared a little. His wife and her friends were still in the living room. It was not yet midday. His clothes had left a damp patch on the bed, on his side, and he knew it would still be wet at bedtime. He put on a clean set of clothes and sat on the bed, rubbing the dampness, as if this would make it disappear. He reached up and drew the curtains open; gray, drifting sky, vegetation drooping and wet, like wash on a line; the very top of Pacheco House, galvanized iron rusted through, so thin in parts that a single drop of rain might cause a great chunk to go crashing into the silence of the house. Except maybe for the bats, disintegration was probably the only sound now to be heard in Pacheco House. The house was like a dying man who could hear his heart ticking to a stop.

Joseph sensed that something was missing. The rainflies, delicate antlike creatures with brown wings but no sting. Defenseless, wings attached to their bodies by the most fragile of links, they fell apart at the merest touch. After a particularly heavy rainfall, detached wings, almost transparent, would litter the ground and cling to moist feet like lint to wool. As a child, he used to pull the wings off and place the crippled insect on a table, where he could observe it crawling desperately around, trying to gain the air. Sometimes he would gingerly tie the insect to one end of a length of thread, release it, and control its flight. In all this he saw no cruelty. His friends enjoyed crushing them, or setting them on fire, or sizzling them with the burning end of a cigarette. Joseph had only toyed with the insects; he could never bring himself to kill one.

There was not a rainfly in sight. The only movement was that of the clouds and dripping water. In the town, the insects had long, and casually, been eradicated. He felt the loss.

He heard his wife call her friends to lunch. He half expected to hear his name but she ignored him: he might have not been there. He waited a few more minutes until he was sure they had all gone into the dining room, then slipped out the front door.

Water was gurgling in the drains, rushing furiously through the iron gratings into the sewers. In the street, belly up, fur wet and clinging, lay a dead dog, a common sight. Drivers no longer even bothered to squeal their tires.

Joseph walked without direction, across streets and through different neighborhoods, passing people and being passed by cars. He took in none of it. His thoughts were thousands of miles away, on Bloor Street, on Yonge Street, among the stalls of Kensington Market.

He was at National Square when the rain once more began to pound down. He found a dry spot under the eaves of a store and stood, arms folded, watching the rain and the umbrellas and the raincoats. A man hurried past him, a handkerchief tied securely to his head the only protection from the rain. It was a useless gesture, and reminded Joseph of his grandmother's warnings to him never to go out at night without a hat to cover his head, "because of the dew."

National Square was the busiest part of town. Cars constantly sped by, 55 horns blaring, water splashing. After a few minutes a donkey cart loaded with fresh coconuts trundled by on its way to the Savannah, a wide, flat park just north of the town where the horse races were held at Christmas. A line of impatient cars crept along behind the donkey cart, the leaders bobbing in and out of line in search of an opportunity to pass.

Joseph glanced at his watch. It was almost twelve-thirty. He decided to have something to eat. Just around the corner was a cheap restaurant frequented by office workers from the government buildings and foreign banks which enclosed the square. Holding his hands over his head, Joseph dashed through the rain to the restaurant.

Inside was shadowed, despite the cobwebby fluorescent lighting. The walls were lined with soft-drink advertisements and travel posters. One of the posters showed an interminable stretch of bleached beach overhung with languid coconut-tree branches. Large, cursive letters read: Welcome To The Sunny Caribbean. The words were like a blow to the nerves. Joseph felt like ripping the poster up.

A row of green metal tables stretched along one wall of the rectangular room. A few customers sat in loosened ties and shirt-sleeves, sipping beer and smoking and conversing in low tones. At the far end, at a table crowded with empty bottles and an overflowing ashtray, Joseph noticed a familiar face. It was lined and more drawn than when he'd known it, and the eyes had lost their sparkle of intelligence; but he was certain he was not mistaken. He went up to the man. He said, "Frankie?"

Frankie looked up slowly, unwillingly, emerging from a daydream. He said, "Yes?" Then he brightened. "Joseph? Joseph!" He sprang to his feet, knocking his chair back. He grasped Joseph's hand. "How you doing, man? It's been years and years. How you doing?" He pushed Joseph into a chair and loudly ordered two beers. He lit a cigarette. His hand shook.

Joseph said, "You smoking now, Frankie?"

"For years, man. You?"

Joseph shook his head.

Frankie said, "But you didn't go to Canada? I thought somebody tell me . . ."

"Went and came back. One of those things. How about you? How the years treat you?"

"I work in a bank. Loan officer."

"Good job?"

"Not bad."

Joseph sipped his beer. The situation wasn't right. There should have been so much to say, so much to hear. Frankie used to be his best friend. He was the most intelligent person Joseph had ever known. This was the last place he would have expected to find him. Frankie had dreamt of university and professorship, and it had seemed, back then, that university and professorship awaited him.

Frankie took a long pull on his cigarette, causing the tube to crinkle and flatten. He said, "What was Canada like?" Before Joseph could answer, he added, "You shouldn't have come back. Why did you come back? A big mistake." He considered the cigarette.

The lack of emotion in Frankie's voice distressed Joseph. It was the voice of a depleted man. He said, "It was time."

Frankie leaned back in his chair and slowly blew smoke rings at Joseph. He seemed to be contemplating the answer. He said, "What were you doing up there?"

"I had a business. Installing carpets and rugs. Is a good little business. My partner looking after it now."

Frankie looked away, towards the door. He said nothing.

Joseph said, "You ever see anybody from school?"

Frankie waved his cigarette. "Here and there. You know, Raffique dead. And Jonesy and Dell."

Joseph recalled the faces: boys, in school uniform. Death was not an event he could associate with them. "How?"

"Raffique in a car accident. Jonesy slit his wrists over a woman. Dell . . . who knows? There are a lot of ways to die. They found him dead in the washroom of a cinema. A girl was with him. Naked. She wasn't dead. She's in the madhouse now."

"And the others?" Joseph couldn't contemplate the death roll. It seemed to snuff out a little bit of his own life.

"The others? Some doing something, some doing nothing. It don't matter."

Joseph said, "You didn't go to university?"

Frankie laughed. "No, I didn't."

Joseph waited for an explanation. Frankie offered none.

Frankie said, "Why the hell you come back from Canada? And none of this 'It was time' crap."

Joseph rubbed his face, feeling the stubble, tracing the fullness of his chin. "I had some kind of crazy idea about starting a business, creating jobs, helping my people."

Frankie laughed mockingly.

Joseph said, "I should have known better. We had a party before we left. A friend asked me the same question, why go back. I told him the same thing. He said it was bullshit and that I just wanted to make a lot of money and live life like a holiday. We quarreled and I threw him out. The next morning he called to apologize. He was crying. He said he was just jealous." Joseph sipped the beer, lukewarm and sweating. "Damn fool."

Frankie laughed again. "I don't believe this. You mean to tell me you had the courage to leave *and* the stupidity to come back?" He slapped the table, rocking it and causing an empty beer bottle to fall over. "You always used to be the idealist, Joseph. I was more realistic. And less courageous. That's why I never left."

"Nobody's called me an idealist for years." The word seemed more mocking than Frankie's laugh.

Frankie said, "And now you're stuck back here for good." He shook his head vigorously, drunkenly. "A big, idealistic mistake, Joseph."

"I'm not stuck here." He was surprised at how much relief the thought brought him. "I can go back any time I want."

"Well, go then." Frankie's voice was slurred, and it held more than a hint of aggressiveness.

Joseph shook his head. He glanced at his watch. He said, "It's almost one. Don't you have to get back to work?"

Frankie called for another beer. "The bank won't fall down if I'm not there."

"We used to think the world would fall down if not for us."

"That was a long time ago. We were stupid." Frankie lit another cigarette. His hand shook badly. "In this place, is nonsense to think the world, the world out there, have room for you."

Joseph said, "You could have been a historian. History was your best subject, not so?"

"Yeah."

"You still interested in history?"

"Off and on. I tried to write a book. Nobody wanted to publish it."

"Why not?"

"Because our history doesn't lead anywhere. It's just a big, black hole. Nobody's interested in a book about a hole."

"You know anything about Pacheco House?"

"Pacheco House? A little."

"What?"

"The man wasn't a Venezuelan general. He was just a crazy old man from Argentina. He was rich. I don't know why he came here. He lived in the house for a short time and then he died there, alone. They found his body about two weeks later, rotting and stinking. They say he covered himself with old cocoa bags, even his head. I think he knew he was going to die and after all that time alone he couldn't stand the thought of anyone seeing him. Crazy, probably. They buried him in the garden and put up a little sign. And his name wasn't really Pacheco either, people just called him that. They got it from a cowboy film. I've forgot what his real name was but it don't matter. Pacheco's as good as any other."

"That's all? What about the house itself?"

"That's all. The house is just a house. Nothing special." Frankie popped the half-finished cigarette into his beer bottle, it sizzled briefly. He added, "R.I.P. Pacheco, his house and every damn thing else." He put another cigarette between his lips, allowing it to droop to his chin, pushing his upper lip up and out, as if his teeth were deformed. His hands shook so badly he couldn't strike the match. His eyes met Joseph's.

Joseph couldn't hold the gaze. He was chilled. He said, "I have to go."

Frankie waved him away.

110   Joseph pushed back his chair. Frankie looked past him with bloodshot eyes, already lost in the confusion of his mind.

Joseph, indicating the travel poster, offered the barman five dollars for it. The man, fat, with an unhealthy greasiness, said, "No way."

Joseph offered ten dollars.

The barman refused.

Joseph understood: it was part of the necessary lie.

115   Gray clouds hung low and heavy in the sky. The hills to the north, their lower half crowded with the multicolored roofs of shacks, poverty plain from even so great a distance, were shrouded in mist, as if an inferno had recently burned out and the smoke not yet cleared away.

Some of his workers lived there, in tiny, crowded one-room shacks, with water sometimes a quarter-mile away at a mossy stand-pipe. There was a time when the sight of these shacks could move Joseph to pity. They were, he believed, his main reason for returning to the island. He really had said, "I want to help my people." Now the sentence, with its pomposity, its naivety, was just an embarrassing memory, like the early life of the minister's wife.

But he knew that wasn't all. He had expected a kind of fame, a continual welcome, the prodigal son having made good, having acquired skills, returning home to share the wealth, to spread the knowledge. He had anticipated a certain uniqueness but this had been thwarted. Everyone knew someone else who had returned from abroad — from England, from Canada, from the States. He grew to hate the stock phrases people dragged out: "No place like home, this island is a true Paradise, life's best here." The little lies of self-doubt and fear.

The gate to Pacheco House was chained but there was no lock: a casual locking-up, an abandonment. The chain, thick and rusted, slipped easily to the ground, leaving a trace of gritty oxide on his fingertips. He couldn't push the gate far; clumps of grass, stems long and tapering to a lancet point, blocked it at the base. He squeezed through the narrow opening, the concrete pillar rough and tight on his back, the iron gate leaving a slash of rust on his shirt. Inside, wild grass, wet and glistening, enveloped his legs up to his knees. The trees were further back, thick and ponderous, unmoving, lending the garden the heavy stillness of jungle.

Walking, pushing through the grass, took a little effort. The vegetation sought not so much to prevent intrusion as to hinder it, to encumber it with a kind of tropical lassitude. Joseph raised his legs high, free of the tangle of vines and roots and thorns, and brought his boots crashing down with each step, crushing leaves into juicy blobs of green and brown, startling underground colonies of ants into frenzied scrambling. Ahead of him, butterflies, looking like edges of an artist's canvas, fluttered away, and crickets, their wings beating like pieces of stiff silk one against the other, buzzed from tall stalk to tall stalk, narrowly avoiding the grasshoppers which also sought escape. A locust, as long as his hand and as fat, sank its claws into his shirt, just grazing the surface of his skin. He flicked a finger powerfully at it, knocking off its head; the rest of the body simply relaxed and fell off.

Once past the trees, Joseph found himself at the house. The stone foundation, he noticed, was covered in green slime and the wall, the monotony of which was broken only by a large cavity which must once have been a window, stripped of all color. He made his way to the cavity and peered through it into the half-darkness of a large room. He carefully put one leg through, feeling for the floor. The boards creaked badly but held. 120

The room was a disappointment. He didn't know what he had expected — he hadn't really thought about it — but its emptiness engendered an atmosphere of uncommon despair. He felt it was a room that had always been empty, a room that had never been peopled with emotion or sound, like a dried-up old spinster abandoned at the edge of life. He could smell the pungency of recently disturbed vegetation but he didn't know whether it came from him or through the gaping window.

He made his way to another room, the floorboards creaking under the wary tread of his feet; just another empty space, characterless, almost shapeless in its desertion. A flight of stairs led upwards, to the second floor and yet another empty room, massive, dusty, cobwebs tracing crazy geometric patterns on the walls and the ceiling. In the corners the floorboards had begun to warp. He wondered why all the doors had been removed and by whom. Or had the house ever had doors? Might it not have been always a big, open, empty house, with rooms destined to no purpose, with a façade that promised mystery but an interior that took away all hope?

He had hoped to find something of Pacheco's, the merest testament to his having existed, a bed maybe, or a portrait, or even one line of graffiti. But were it not for the structure itself, a vacuous shell falling steadily to ruin, and the smudges of erroneous public fantasy fading like the outer edges of a dream, Pacheco might never have existed. Whatever relics might have been preserved by the government had long been carted away, probably by the last workmen, those who had so cavalierly slipped the chain around the gate, putting a period to a life.

Joseph walked around the room, his footsteps echoing like drumbeats. Each wall had a window of shattered glass and he examined the view from each. Jumbled vegetation, the jungle taking hold in this one plot of earth in the middle of the town: it was the kind of view that would have been described in the travel brochures as *lush* and *tropical*, two words he had grown to hate. Looking through the windows, recalling the manicured grounds of his youth, he felt confined, isolated, a man in an island on an island. He wondered why anyone would pay a lot of money to visit such a place. The answer came to him: for the tourist, a life was not to be constructed here. The tourist sought no more than an approximation of adventure; there was safety in a return ticket and foreign passport.

125 There was no way to get to the attic, where the LeNoir window was. Another disappointment: the object of all that youthful energy was nothing more than an aperture to a boxed-in room, airless and musty with age and probably dank with bat mess.

He made his way back down the stairs and out the gaping front door. The air was hot and sticky and the smell of vegetation, acrid in the humidity, was almost overpowering.

Frankie had said that Pacheco was buried in the garden and that a marker had been erected. Joseph knew there was no hope of finding it. Everything was overgrown: the garden, the flowers, the driveway that had once existed, Pacheco's grave, Pacheco himself, the mysterious South American whose last act was to lose his name and his life in sterile isolation.

Joseph began making his way back to the gate. Over to the left he could see the path he had made when going in, the grass flat and twisted, twigs broken and limp, still dripping from the morning rain. He felt clammy, and steamy perspiration broke out on his skin.

At the gate, he stopped and turned around for a last look at the house: he saw it for what it was, a deceptive shell that played on the mind. He looked around for something to throw. The base of the gate-pillars was cracked and broken and moss had begun eating its way to the centre. He broke off a piece of the concrete and flung it at the LeNoir window. The glass shattered, scattering thousands of slivers into the attic and onto the ground below.

130 His wife wasn't home when he returned. The house was dark and silent. Coffee cups and plates with half-eaten pastries lay on the side-tables. The false fireplace had been switched off. On the mantelpiece, propped against his wife's lipstick-stained cup, was a notepad with a message: "Have gone out for the evening with Arlene. We have the chauffeur and the limo coz Brian's busy in a cabinet meeting. Don't know what time I'll be back." She hadn't bothered to sign it.

He ripped the page from the notepad: he hated the word "coz" and the word "limo" and he felt a special revulsion for "Arlene" and "Brian," fictitious names assumed with the mantle of social status. As a transient domestic, Arlene had been called Thelma, the name scribbled on her birth certificate, and Brian's real name was Balthazar. Joseph avoided the entire issue by simply referring to them as the Minister and the Minister's Wife. The sarcasm was never noticed.

He took the notepad and a pencil and sat down. He wrote *Dear* then crossed it out. He threw the page away and started again. He drew a circle, then a triangle, then a square: the last disappointment, it was the most difficult act. Finally, in big square letters, he wrote, *I am going back*. He put the pad back on the mantelpiece, switched on the fireplace lights, and sat staring into their synchronized dance.

QUESTIONS

1. Construct the chronology of Joseph's life, from his school days to the present, identifying motives he had for the major decisions he has made.
2. Account for Joseph's distaste for his wife's friends Arlene and Brian. To what extent do the reasons for his distaste also account for his attitude toward his wife?
3. What has been the importance of Pacheco House to Joseph in his past and what is it in the present?
4. What does the encounter with Frankie reveal to Joseph? Why does it end with his wanting to buy the travel poster?
5. The title of the story explicitly states its theme. How many events, incidents, and observations can be related to it? Include in your survey not only persons who are literally dead (the man called Pacheco), but the deaths of other forms of life, and of customs and manners, ideas, and values. For example, what kind of loss is implied by the contrast between schoolboy activities in the past and present (paragraph 19)?
6. What in Joseph seems to have died? Does his decision to go "back" in the last paragraph imply that he will be able to recover it? What do the geometric drawings he makes on the pad suggest about his decision?

Philip Roth
Defender of the Faith

In May of 1945, only a few weeks after the fighting had ended in Europe, I was rotated back to the States, where I spent the remainder of the war with a training company at Camp Crowder, Missouri. Along with the rest of the Ninth Army, I had been racing across Germany so swiftly during the late

DEFENDER OF THE FAITH First published in 1959. World War II officially ended in Europe with the surrender of Germany on May 7, 1945; it ended in the Pacific with the surrender of Japan on September 2, 1945. The action of the story occurs within that interval. Philip Roth, of Jewish parentage, was born (1933) and grew up in Newark, New Jersey, and was educated at Rutgers, Bucknell, and the University of Chicago. He enlisted in the army in 1955 after receiving his M.A. in English but was discharged within a year due to a back injury suffered during basic training.

winter and spring that when I boarded the plane, I couldn't believe its destination lay to the west. My mind might inform me otherwise, but there was an inertia of the spirit that told me we were flying to a new front, where we would disembark and continue our push eastward — eastward until we'd circled the globe, marching through villages along whose twisting, cobbled streets crowds of the enemy would watch us take possession of what, up till then, they'd considered their own. I had changed enough in two years not to mind the trembling of old people, the crying of the very young, the uncertainty and fear in the eyes of the once arrogant. I had been fortunate enough to develop an infantryman's heart, which, like his feet, at first aches and swells but finally grows horny enough for him to travel the weirdest paths without feeling a thing.

Captain Paul Barrett was my C.O. in Camp Crowder. The day I reported for duty, he came out of his office to shake my hand. He was short, gruff, and fiery, and — indoors or out — he wore his polished helmet liner pulled down to his little eyes. In Europe, he had received a battlefield commission and a serious chest wound, and he'd been returned to the States only a few months before. He spoke easily to me, and at the evening formation he introduced me to the troops. "Gentlemen," he said. "Sergeant Thurston, as you know, is no longer with this company. Your new first sergeant is Sergeant Nathan Marx, here. He is a veteran of the European theater, and consequently will expect to find a company of soldiers here, and not a company of *boys*."

I sat up late in the orderly room that evening, trying half-heartedly to solve the riddle of duty rosters, personnel forms, and morning reports. The Charge of Quarters slept with his mouth open on a mattress on the floor. A trainee stood reading the next day's duty roster, which was posted on the bulletin board just inside the screen door. It was a warm evening, and I could hear radios playing dance music over in the barracks. The trainee, who had been staring at me whenever he thought I wouldn't notice, finally took a step in my direction.

"Hey, Sarge — we having a G.I. party tomorrow night?" he asked. A G.I. party is a barracks cleaning.

"You usually have them on Friday nights?" I asked him.

"Yes," he said, and then he added, mysteriously, "that's the whole thing."

"Then you'll have a G.I. party."

He turned away, and I heard him mumbling. His shoulders were moving and I wondered if he was crying.

"What's your name, soldier?" I asked.

He turned, not crying at all. Instead, his green-speckled eyes, long and narrow, flashed like fish in the sun. He walked over to me and sat on the edge of my desk. He reached out a hand. "Sheldon," he said.

"Stand on your feet, Sheldon."

Getting off the desk, he said, "Sheldon Grossbart." He smiled at the familiarity into which he'd led me.

"You against cleaning the barracks Friday night, Grossbart?" I said. "Maybe we shouldn't have G.I. parties. Maybe we should get a maid." My tone startled me. I felt I sounded like every top sergeant I had ever known.

"No, Sergeant." He grew serious, but with a seriousness that seemed to be only the stifling of a smile. "It's just — G.I. parties on Friday night, of all nights."

He slipped up onto the corner of the desk again — not quite sitting, but not quite standing, either. He looked at me with those speckled eyes flashing, and then made a gesture with his hands. It was very slight — no more than a movement back and forth of the wrist — and yet it managed to exclude from our affairs everything else in the orderly room, to make the two of us the center of the world. It seemed, in fact, to exclude everything even about the two of us except our hearts.

"Sergeant Thurston was one thing," he whispered, glancing at the sleeping C.Q., "but we thought that with you here things might be a little different."

"We?"

"The Jewish personnel."

"Why?" I asked, harshly. "What's on your mind?" Whether I was still angry at the "Sheldon" business, or now at something else, I hadn't time to tell, but clearly I was angry.

"We thought you — Marx, you know, like Karl Marx. The Marx Brothers. Those guys are all — M-a-r-x. Isn't that how *you* spell it, Sergeant?"

"M-a-r-x."

"Fishbein said — " He stopped. "What I mean to say, Sergeant — " His face and neck were red, and his mouth moved but no words came out. In a moment, he raised himself to attention, gazing down at me. It was as though he had suddenly decided he could expect no more sympathy from me than from Thurston, the reason being that I was of Thurston's faith, and not his. The young man had managed to confuse himself as to what my faith really was, but I felt no desire to straighten him out. Very simply, I didn't like him.

When I did nothing but return his gaze, he spoke, in an altered tone. "You see, Sergeant," he explained to me, "Friday nights, Jews are supposed to go to services."

"Did Sergeant Thurston tell you you couldn't go to them when there was a G.I. party?"

"No."

"Did he say you had to stay and scrub the floors?"

"No, Sergeant."

"Did the Captain say you had to stay and scrub the floors?"

"That isn't it, Sergeant. It's the other guys in the barracks." He leaned toward me. "They think we're goofing off. But we're not. That's when Jews go to services, Friday night. We have to."

"Then go."

"But the other guys make accusations. They have no right."

"That's not the Army's problem, Grossbart. It's a personal problem you'll have to work out yourself."

"But it's un*fair*."

I got up to leave. "There's nothing I can do about it," I said.

Grossbart stiffened and stood in front of me. "But this is a matter of *religion*, sir."

"Sergeant," I said.

"I mean 'Sergeant,'" he said, almost snarling.

"Look, go see the chaplain. You want to see Captain Barrett, I'll arrange an appointment."

"No, no. I don't want to make trouble, Sergeant. That's the first thing they throw up to you. I just want my rights!"

"Damn it, Grossbart, stop whining. You have your rights. You can stay and scrub floors or you can go to shul — "°

The smile swam in again. Spittle gleamed at the corners of his mouth. "You mean church, Sergeant."

"I mean shul, Grossbart!"

I walked past him and went outside. Near me, I heard the scrunching of the guard's boots on gravel. Beyond the lighted windows of the barracks, young men in T shirts and fatigue pants were sitting on their bunks, polishing their rifles. Suddenly there was a light rustling behind me. I turned and saw Grossbart's dark frame fleeing back to the barracks, racing to tell his Jewish friends that they were right — that, like Karl and Harpo, I was one of them.

The next morning, while chatting with Captain Barrett, I recounted the incident of the previous evening. Somehow, in the telling, it must have seemed to the Captain that I was not so much explaining Grossbart's position as defending it. "Marx, I'd fight side by side with a nigger if the fella proved to me he was a man. I pride myself," he said, looking out the window, "that I've got an open mind. Consequently, Sergeant, nobody gets special treatment here, for the good *or* the bad. All a man's got to do is prove himself. A man fires well on the range, I give him a weekend pass. He scores high in P.T., he gets a weekend pass. He *earns* it." He turned from the window and pointed a finger at me. "You're a Jewish fella, am I right, Marx?"

"Yes, sir."

"And I admire you. I admire you because of the ribbons on your chest. I judge a man by what he shows me on the field of battle, Sergeant. It's what he's got *here*," he said, and then, though I expected he would point to his chest, he jerked a thumb toward the buttons straining to hold his blouse across his belly. "Guts," he said.

"O.K., sir. I only wanted to pass on to you how the men felt."

shul: synagogue

"Mr. Marx, you're going to be old before your time if you worry about how the men feel. Leave that stuff to the chaplain — that's his business, not yours. Let's us train these fellas to shoot straight. If the Jewish personnel feels the other men are accusing them of goldbricking — well, I just don't know. Seems awful funny that suddenly the Lord is calling so loud in Private Grossman's ear he's just got to run to church."

"Synagogue," I said.

"Synagogue is right, Sergeant. I'll write that down for handy reference. Thank you for stopping by." 50

That evening, a few minutes before the company gathered outside the orderly room for the chow formation, I called the C.Q., Corporal Robert LaHill, in to see me. LaHill was a dark, burly fellow whose hair curled out of his clothes wherever it could. He had a glaze in his eyes that made one think of caves and dinosaurs. "LaHill," I said, "when you take the formation, remind the men that they're free to attend church services *whenever* they are held, provided they report to the orderly room before they leave the area."

LaHill scratched his wrist, but gave no indication that he'd heard or understood.

"LaHill," I said, "*church*. You remember? Church, priest, Mass, confession."

He curled one lip into a kind of smile; I took it for a signal that for a second he had flickered back up into the human race.

"Jewish personnel who want to attend services this evening are to fall out 55 in front of the orderly room at 1900," I said. Then, as an afterthought, I added, "By order of Captain Barrett."

A little while later, as the day's last light — softer than any I had seen that year — began to drop over Camp Crowder, I heard LaHill's thick, inflectionless voice outside my window: "Give me your ears, troopers. Toppie says for me to tell you that at 1900 hours all Jewish personnel is to fall out in front, here, if they want to attend the Jewish Mass."

At seven o'clock, I looked out the orderly-room window and saw three soldiers in starched khakis standing on the dusty quadrangle. They looked at their watches and fidgeted while they whispered back and forth. It was getting dimmer, and, alone on the otherwise deserted field, they looked tiny. When I opened the door, I heard the noises of the G.I. party coming from the surrounding barracks — bunks being pushed to the walls, faucets pounding water into buckets, brooms whisking at the wooden floors, cleaning the dirt away for Saturday's inspection. Big puffs of cloth moved round and round on the windowpanes. I walked outside, and the moment my foot hit the ground I thought I heard Grossbart call to the others "'Ten-*hut!*'" Or maybe, when they all three jumped to attention, I imagined I heard the command.

Grossbart stepped forward, "Thank you, sir," he said.

"'Sergeant,' Grossbart," I reminded him. "You call officers 'sir.' I'm not an officer. You've been in the Army three weeks — you know that."

He turned his palms out at his sides to indicate that, in truth, he and I 60 lived beyond convention. "Thank you anyway," he said.

"Yes," a tall boy behind him said. "Thanks a lot."

And the third boy whispered, "Thank you," but his mouth barely fluttered, so that he did not alter by more than a lip's movement his posture of attention.

"For what?" I asked.

Grossbart snorted happily. "For the announcement. The Corporal's announcement. It helped. It made it — "

"Fancier." The tall boy finished Grossbart's sentence.

Grossbart smiled. "He means formal, sir. Public," he said to me. "Now it won't seem as though we're just taking off — goldbricking because the work has begun."

"It was by order of Captain Barrett," I said.

"Aaah, but you pull a little weight," Grossbart said. "So we thank you." Then he turned to his companions. "Sergeant Marx, I want you to meet Larry Fishbein."

The tall boy stepped forward and extended his hand. I shook it. "You from New York?" he asked.

"Yes."

"Me too." He had a cadaverous face that collapsed inward from his cheekbone to his jaw, and when he smiled — as he did at the news of our communal attachment — revealed a mouthful of bad teeth. He was blinking his eyes a good deal, as though he were fighting back tears. "What borough?" he asked.

I turned to Grossbart. "It's five after seven. What time are services?"

"Shul," he said, smiling, "is in ten minutes. I want you to meet Mickey Halpern. This is Nathan Marx, our sergeant."

The third boy hopped forward. "Private Michael Halpern." He saluted.

"Salute officers, Halpern," I said. The boy dropped his hand, and, on its way down, in his nervousness, checked to see if his shirt pockets were buttoned.

"Shall I march them over, sir?" Grossbart asked. "Or are you coming along?"

From behind Grossbart, Fishbein piped up. "Afterward, they're having refreshments. A ladies auxiliary from St. Louis, the rabbi told us last week."

"The chaplain," Halpern whispered.

"You're welcome to come along," Grossbart said.

To avoid his plea, I looked away, and saw, in the windows of the barracks, a cloud of faces staring out at the four of us. "Hurry along, Grossbart," I said.

"O.K., then," he said. He turned to the others. "Double time, *march!*"

They started off, but ten feet away Grossbart spun around and, running backward, called to me "Good *shabbus,*° sir!" And then the three of them were swallowed into the alien Missouri dusk.

shabbus: Sabbath

Even after they had disappeared over the parade ground, whose green was now a deep blue, I could hear Grossbart singing the double-time cadence, and as it grew dimmer and dimmer, it suddenly touched a deep memory — as did the slant of the light — and I was remembering the shrill sounds of a Bronx playground where, years ago, beside the Grand Concourse, I had played on long spring evenings such as this. It was a pleasant memory for a young man so far from peace and home, and it brought so many recollections with it that I began to grow exceedingly tender about myself. In fact, I indulged myself in a reverie so strong that I felt as though a hand were reaching down inside me. It had to reach so very far to touch me! It had to reach past those days in the forests of Belgium, and past the dying I'd refused to weep over; past the nights in German farmhouses whose books we'd burned to warm us; past endless stretches when I had shut off all softness I might feel for my fellows, and had managed even to deny myself the posture of a conqueror — the swagger that I, as a Jew, might well have worn as my boots whacked against the rubble of Wesel, Münster, and Braunschweig.

But now one night noise, one rumor of home and time past, and memory plunged down through all I had anesthetized, and came to what I suddenly remembered was myself. So it was not altogether curious that, in search of more of me, I found myself following Grossbart's tracks to Chapel No. 3, where the Jewish services were being held.

I took a seat in the last row, which was empty. Two rows in front of me sat Grossbart, Fishbein, and Halpern, holding little white Dixie cups. Each row of seats was raised higher than the one in front of it, and I could see clearly what was going on. Fishbein was pouring the contents of his cup into Grossbart's, and Grossbart looked mirthful as the liquid made a purple arc between Fishbein's hand and his. In the glaring yellow light, I saw the chaplain standing on the platform at the front; he was chanting the first line of the responsive reading. Grossbart's prayer book remained closed on his lap; he was swishing the cup around. Only Halpern responded to the chant by praying. The fingers of his right hand were spread wide across the cover of his open book. His cap was pulled down low onto his brow, which made it round, like a yarmulke.° From time to time, Grossbart wet his lips at the cup's edge; Fishbein, his long yellow face a dying light bulb, looked from here to there, craning forward to catch sight of the faces down the row, then of those in front of him, then behind. He saw me, and his eyelids beat a tattoo. His elbow slid into Grossbart's side, his neck inclined toward his friend, he whispered something, and then, when the congregation next responded to the chant, Grossbart's voice was among the others. Fishbein looked into his book now, too; his lips, however, didn't move.

Finally, it was time to drink the wine. The chaplain smiled down at them as Grossbart swigged his in one long gulp, Halpern sipped, meditating, and Fishbein faked devotion with an empty cup. "As I look down amongst the

yarmulke: skull cap

congregation" — the chaplain grinned at the word — "this night, I see many new faces, and I want to welcome you to Friday-night services here at Camp Crowder. I am Major Leo Ben Ezra, your chaplain." Though an American, the chaplain spoke deliberately — syllable by syllable, almost — as though to communicate, above all, with the lip readers in his audience. "I have only a few words to say before we adjourn to the refreshment room, where the kind ladies of the Temple Sinai, St. Louis, Missouri, have a nice setting for you."

Applause and whistling broke out. After another momentary grin, the chaplain raised his hands, palms out, his eyes flicking upward a moment, as if to remind the troops where they were and Who Else might be in attendance. In the sudden silence that followed, I thought I heard Grossbart cackle, "Let the goyim° clean the floors!" Were those the words? I wasn't sure, but Fishbein, grinning, nudged Halpern. Halpern looked dumbly at him, then went back to his prayer book, which had been occupying him all through the rabbi's talk. One hand tugged at the black kinky hair that stuck out under his cap. His lips moved.

The rabbi continued. "It is about the food that I want to speak to you for a moment. I know, I know, I know," he intoned, wearily, "how in the mouths of most of you the *trafe*° food tastes like ashes. I know how you gag, some of you, and how your parents suffer to think of their children eating foods unclean and offensive to the palate. What can I tell you? I can only say, close your eyes and swallow as best you can. Eat what you must to live, and throw away the rest. I wish I could help more. For those of you who find this impossible, may I ask that you try and try, but then come to see me in private. If your revulsion is so great, we will have to seek aid from those higher up."

A round of chatter rose and subsided. Then everyone sang "Ain Kelohainu"°; after all those years, I discovered I still knew the words. Then, suddenly, the service over, Grossbart was upon me. "Higher up? He means the General?"

90   "Hey, Shelly," Fishbein said, "he means God." He smacked his face and looked at Halpern. "How high can you go!"

"Sh-h-h!" Grossbart said. "What do you think, Sergeant?"

"I don't know," I said. "You better ask the chaplain."

"I'm going to. I'm making an appointment to see him in private. So is Mickey."

Halpern shook his head. "No, no, Sheldon — "

95   "You have rights, Mickey," Grossbart said. "They can't push us around."

"It's O.K.," said Halpern. "It bothers my mother, not me."

Grossbart looked at me. "Yesterday he threw up. From the hash. It was all ham and God knows what else."

"I have a cold — that was why," Halpern said. He pushed his yarmulke back into a cap.

---

goyim: gentiles   *trafe:* nonkosher   **"Ain Kelohainu":** "There's no God like our God"

"What about you, Fishbein?" I asked. "You kosher, too?"

He flushed. "A little. But I'll let it ride. I have a very strong stomach, and I don't eat a lot anyway." I continued to look at him, and he held up his wrist to reinforce what he'd just said; his watch strap was tightened to the last hole, and he pointed that out to me.

"But services are important to you?" I asked him.

He looked at Grossbart. "Sure, sir."

" 'Sergeant.' "

"Not so much at home," said Grossbart, stepping between us, "but away from home it gives one a sense of his Jewishness."

"We have to stick together," Fishbein said.

I started to walk toward the door; Halpern stepped back to make way for me.

"That's what happened in Germany," Grossbart was saying, loud enough for me to hear. "They didn't stick together. They let themselves get pushed around."

I turned. "Look, Grossbart. This is the Army, not summer camp."

He smiled. "So?"

Halpern tried to sneak off, but Grossbart held his arm.

"Grossbart, how old are you?" I asked.

"Nineteen."

"And you?" I said to Fishbein.

"The same. The same month, even."

"And what about him?" I pointed to Halpern, who had by now made it safely to the door.

"Eighteen," Grossbart whispered. "But like he can't tie his shoes or brush his teeth himself. I feel sorry for him."

"I feel sorry for all of us, Grossbart," I said, "but just act like a man. Just don't overdo it."

"Overdo what, sir?"

"The 'sir' business, for one thing. Don't overdo that," I said.

I left him standing there. I passed by Halpern, but he did not look at me. Then I was outside, but, behind, I heard Grossbart call, "Hey, Mickey, my *leben*,° come on back. Refreshments!"

"*Leben!*" My grandmother's word for me!

One morning a week later, while I was working at my desk, Captain Barrett shouted for me to come into his office. When I entered, he had his helmet liner squashed down so far on his head that I couldn't even see his eyes. He was on the phone, and when he spoke to me, he cupped one hand over the mouthpiece. "Who the hell is Grossbart?"

"Third platoon, Captain," I said. "A trainee."

"What's all this stink about food? His mother called a goddam congressman about the food." He uncovered the mouthpiece and slid his helmet up

leben: darling

until I could see his bottom eyelashes. "Yes, sir," he said into the phone. "Yes, sir. I'm still here, sir. I'm asking Marx, here, right now — "

125 He covered the mouthpiece again and turned his head back toward me. "Lightfoot Harry's on the phone," he said, between his teeth. "This congressman calls General Lyman, who calls Colonel Sousa, who calls the Major, who calls me. They're just dying to stick this thing on me. Whatsa matter?" He shook the phone at me. "I don't feed the troops? What is this?"

"Sir, Grossbart is strange — " Barrett greeted that with a mockingly indulgent smile. I altered my approach. "Captain, he's a very orthodox Jew, and so he's only allowed to eat certain foods."

"He throws up, the congressman said. Every time he eats something, his mother says, he throws up!"

"He's accustomed to observing the dietary laws, Captain."

"So why's his old lady have to call the White House?"

130 "Jewish parents, sir — they're apt to be more protective than you expect. I mean, Jews have a very close family life. A boy goes away from home, sometimes the mother is liable to get very upset. Probably the boy mentioned something in a letter, and his mother misinterpreted."

"I'd like to punch him one right in the mouth," the Captain said. "There's a war on, and he wants a silver platter!"

"I don't think the boy's to blame, sir. I'm sure we can straighten it out by just asking him. Jewish parents worry — "

"*All* parents worry, for Christ's sake. But they don't get on their high horse and start pulling strings — "

I interrupted, my voice higher, tighter than before. "The home life, Captain, is very important — but you're right, it may sometimes get out of hand. It's a very wonderful thing, Captain, but because it's so close, this kind of thing . . ."

135 He didn't listen any longer to my attempt to present both myself and Lightfoot Harry with an explanation for the letter. He turned back to the phone. "Sir?" he said. "Sir — Marx, here, tells me Jews have a tendency to be pushy. He says he thinks we can settle it right here in the company . . . Yes, sir . . . I *will* call back, sir, soon as I can." He hung up. "Where are the men, Sergeant?"

"On the range."

With a whack on the top of his helmet, he crushed it down over his eyes again, and charged out of his chair. "We're going for a ride," he said.

The Captain drove, and I sat beside him. It was a hot spring day, and under my newly starched fatigues I felt as though my armpits were melting down into my sides and chest. The roads were dry, and by the time we reached the firing range, my teeth felt gritty with dust, though my mouth had been shut the whole trip. The Captain slammed the brakes on and told me to get the hell out and find Grossbart.

I found him on his belly, firing wildly at the five-hundred-feet target. Waiting their turns behind him were Halpern and Fishbein. Fishbein, wear-

ing a pair of steel-rimmed G.I. glasses I hadn't seen on him before, had the
appearance of an old peddler who would gladly have sold you his rifle and the
cartridges that were slung all over him. I stood back by the ammo boxes,
waiting for Grossbart to finish spraying the distant target. Fishbein straggled
back to stand near me.

"Hello, Sergeant Marx," he said. 140

"How are you?" I mumbled.

"Fine, thank you. Sheldon's really a good shot."

"I didn't notice."

"I'm not so good, but I think I'm getting the hang of it now. Sergeant, I
don't mean to, you know, ask what I shouldn't — " The boy stopped. He was
trying to speak intimately, but the noise of the shooting forced him to shout
at me.

"What is it?" I asked. Down the range, I saw Captain Barrett standing 145
up in the jeep, scanning the line for me and Grossbart.

"My parents keep asking and asking where we're going," Fishbein said.
"Everybody says the Pacific. I don't care, but my parents — if I could relieve
their minds, I think I could concentrate more on my shooting."

"I don't know where, Fishbein. Try to concentrate anyway."

"Sheldon says you might be able to find out."

"I don't know a thing, Fishbein. You just take it easy, and don't let
Sheldon — "

"*I'm* taking it easy, Sergeant. It's at home — " 150

Grossbart had finished on the line, and was dusting his fatigues with one
hand. I called to him. "Grossbart, the Captain wants to see you."

He came toward us. His eyes blazed and twinkled. "Hi!"

"Don't point that rifle!" I said.

"I wouldn't shoot you, Sarge." He gave me a smile as wide as a pumpkin,
and turned the barrel aside.

"Damn you, Grossbart, this is no joke! Follow me." 155

I walked ahead of him, and had the awful suspicion that, behind me,
Grossbart was *marching*, his rifle on his shoulder as though he were a one-
man detachment. At the jeep, he gave the Captain a rifle salute. "Private
Sheldon Grossbart, sir."

"At ease, Grossman." The Captain sat down, slid over into the empty
seat, and, crooking a finger, invited Grossbart closer.

"Bart, sir. Sheldon Gross*bart*. It's a common error." Grossbart nodded at
me; *I* understood, he indicated. I looked away just as the mess truck pulled
up to the range, disgorging a half-dozen K.P.s with rolled-up sleeves. The
mess sergeant screamed at them while they set up the chow line equipment.

"Grossbart, your mama wrote some congressman that we don't feed you
right. Do you know that?" the Captain said.

"It was my father, sir. He wrote to Representative Franconi that my 160
religion forbids me to eat certain foods."

"What religion is that, Grossbart?"

"Jewish."

"'Jewish, *sir*,'" I said to Grossbart.

"Excuse me, sir, Jewish, sir."

165 "What have you been living on?" the Captain asked. "You've been in the Army a month already. You don't look to me like you're falling to pieces."

"I eat because I have to, sir. But Sergeant Marx will testify to the fact that I don't eat one mouthful more than I need to in order to survive."

"Is that so, Marx?" Barrett asked.

"I've never seen Grossbart eat, sir," I said.

"But you heard the rabbi," Grossbart said. "He told us what to do, and I listened."

170 The Captain looked at me. "Well, Marx?"

"I still don't know what he eats and doesn't eat, sir."

Grossbart raised his arms to plead with me, and it looked for a moment as though he were going to hand me his weapon to hold. "But, Sergeant —"

"Look, Grossbart, just answer the Captain's questions," I said sharply.

Barrett smiled at me, and I resented it. "All right, Grossbart," he said. "What is it you want? The little piece of paper? You want out?"

175 "No, sir. Only to be allowed to live as a Jew. And for the others, too."

"What others?"

"Fishbein, sir, and Halpern."

"They don't like the way we serve, either?"

"Halpern throws up, sir. I've seen it."

180 "I thought *you* throw up."

"Just once, sir. I didn't know the sausage was sausage."

"We'll give menus, Grossbart. We'll show training films about the food, so you can identify when we're trying to poison you."

Grossbart did not answer. The men had been organized into two long chow lines. At the tail end of one, I spotted Fishbein — or, rather, his glasses spotted me. They winked sunlight back at me. Halpern stood next to him, patting the inside of his collar with a khaki handkerchief. They moved with the line as it began to edge up toward the food. The mess sergeant was still screaming at the K.P.s. For a moment, I was actually terrified by the thought that somehow the mess sergeant was going to become involved in Grossbart's problem.

"Marx," the Captain said, "you're a Jewish fella — am I right?"

185 I played straight man. "Yes, sir."

"How long you been in the Army? Tell this boy."

"Three years and two months."

"A year in combat, Grossbart. Twelve goddam months in combat all through Europe. I admire this man." The Captain snapped a wrist against my chest. "Do you hear him peeping about the food? Do you? I want an answer, Grossbart. Yes or no."

"No, sir."

"And why not? He's a Jewish fella." 190

"Some things are more important to some Jews than other things to other Jews."

Barrett blew up. "Look, Grossbart. Marx, here, is a good man—a goddam hero. When you were in high school, Sergeant Marx was killing Germans. Who does more for the Jews—you, by throwing up over a lousy piece of sausage, a piece of first-cut meat, or Marx, by killing those Nazi bastards? If I was a Jew, Grossbart, I'd kiss this man's feet. He's a goddam hero, and *he* eats what we give him. Why do you have to cause trouble is what I want to know! What is it you're buckin' for—a discharge?"

"No, sir."

"I'm talking to a wall! Sergeant, get him out of my way." Barrett swung himself back into the driver's seat. "I'm going to see the chaplain." The engine roared, the jeep spun around in a whirl of dust, and the Captain was headed back to camp.

For a moment, Grossbart and I stood side by side, watching the jeep. 195 Then he looked at me and said, "I don't want to start trouble. That's the first thing they toss up to us."

When he spoke, I saw that his teeth were white and straight, and the sight of them suddenly made me understand that Grossbart actually did have parents—that once upon a time someone had taken little Sheldon to the dentist. He was their son. Despite all the talk about his parents, it was hard to believe in Grossbart as a child, an heir—as related by blood to anyone, mother, father, or, above all, to me. This realization led me to another.

"What does your father do, Grossbart?" I asked as we started to walk back toward the chow line.

"He's a tailor."

"An American?"

"Now, yes. A son in the Army," he said, jokingly. 200

"And your mother?" I asked.

He winked. "A *ballabusta*.° She practically sleeps with a dustcloth in her hand."

"She's also an immigrant?"

"All she talks is Yiddish, still."

"And your father, too?" 205

"A little English. 'Clean,' 'Press,' 'Take the pants in.' That's the extent of it. But they're good to me."

"Then, Grossbart—" I reached out and stopped him. He turned toward me, and when our eyes met, his seemed to jump back, to shiver in their sockets. "Grossbart—you were the one who wrote that letter, weren't you?"

It took only a second or two for his eyes to flash happy again. "Yes." He walked on, and I kept pace. "It's what my father *would* have written if he had

ballabusta: housewife

known how. It was his name, though. *He* signed it. He even mailed it. I sent it home. For the New York postmark."

I was astonished, and he saw it. With complete seriousness, he thrust his right arm in front of me. "Blood is blood, Sergeant," he said, pinching the blue vein in his wrist.

210 "What the hell *are* you trying to do, Grossbart?" I asked. "I've seen you eat. Do you know that? I told the Captain I don't know what you eat, but I've seen you eat like a hound at chow."

"We work hard, Sergeant. We're in training. For a furnace to work, you've got to feed it coal."

"Why did you say in the letter that you threw up all the time?"

"I was really talking about Mickey there. I was talking *for* him. He would never write, Sergeant, though I pleaded with him. He'll waste away to nothing if I don't help. Sergeant, I used my name — my father's name — but it's Mickey, and Fishbein, too, I'm watching out for."

"You're a regular Messiah, aren't you?"

215 We were at the chow line now.

"That's a good one, Sergeant," he said, smiling. "But who knows? Who can tell? Maybe you're the Messiah — a little bit. What Mickey says is the Messiah is a collective idea. He went to Yeshiva,° Mickey, for a while. He says *together* we're the Messiah. Me a little bit, you a little bit. You should hear that kid talk, Sergeant, when he gets going."

"Me a little bit, you a little bit," I said. "You'd like to believe that, wouldn't you, Grossbart? That would make everything so clean for you."

"It doesn't seem too bad a thing to believe, Sergeant. It only means we should all *give* a little, is all."

I walked off to eat my rations with the other noncoms.

220 Two days later, a letter addressed to Captain Barrett passed over my desk. It had come through the chain of command — from the office of Congressman Franconi, where it had been received, to General Lyman, to Colonel Sousa, to Major Lamont, now to Captain Barrett. I read it over twice. It was dated May 14, the day Barrett had spoken with Grossbart on the rifle range.

Dear Congressman:

First let me thank you for your interest in behalf of my son, Private Sheldon Grossbart. Fortunately, I was able to speak with Sheldon on the phone the other night, and I think I've been able to solve our problem. He is, as I mentioned in my last letter, a very religious boy, and it was only with the greatest difficulty that I could persuade him that the religious thing to do — what God Himself would want

Yeshiva: seminary

Sheldon to do — would be to suffer the pangs of religious remorse for the good of his country and all mankind. It took some doing, Congressman, but finally he saw the light. In fact, what he said (and I wrote down the words on a scratch pad so as never to forget), what he said was "I guess you're right, Dad. So many millions of my fellow-Jews gave up their lives to the enemy, the least I can do is live for a while minus a bit of my heritage so as to help end this struggle and regain for all the children of God dignity and humanity." That, Congressman, would make any father proud.

By the way, Sheldon wanted me to know — and to pass on to you — the name of a soldier who helped him reach this decision: SERGEANT NATHAN MARX. Sergeant Marx is a combat veteran who is Sheldon's first sergeant. This man has helped Sheldon over some of the first hurdles he's had to face in the Army, and is in part responsible for Sheldon's changing his mind about the dietary laws. I know Sheldon would appreciate any recognition Marx could receive.

Thank you and good luck. I look forward to seeing your name on the next election ballot.

Respectfully,
Samuel E. Grossbart

Attached to the Grossbart communiqué was another, addressed to General Marshall Lyman, the post commander, and signed by Representative Charles E. Franconi, of the House of Representatives. The communiqué informed General Lyman that Sergeant Nathan Marx was a credit to the U.S. Army and the Jewish people.

What was Grossbart's motive in recanting? Did he feel he'd gone too far? Was the letter a strategic retreat — a crafty attempt to strengthen what he considered our alliance? Or had he actually changed his mind, via an imaginary dialogue between Grossbart *père* and Grossbart *fils?* I was puzzled, but only for a few days — that is, only until I realized that, whatever his reasons, he had actually decided to disappear from my life; he was going to allow himself to become just another trainee. I saw him at inspection, but he never winked; at chow formations, but he never flashed me a sign. On Sunday, with the other trainees, he would sit around watching the noncoms' softball team, for which I pitched, but not once did he speak an unnecessary word to me. Fishbein and Halpern retreated, too — at Grossbart's command, I was sure. Apparently he had seen that wisdom lay in turning back before he plunged over into the ugliness of privilege undeserved. Our separation allowed me to forgive him our past encounters, and finally, to admire him for his good sense.

Meanwhile, free of Grossbart, I grew used to my job and my administrative tasks. I stepped on a scale one day, and discovered I had truly become a noncombatant; I had gained seven pounds. I found patience to get past the first three pages of a book. I thought about the future more and more, and wrote letters to girls I'd known before the war. I even got a few answers. I sent away to Columbia for a Law School catalogue. I continued to follow the war in the Pacific, but it was not my war. I thought I could see the end, and sometimes, at night, I dreamed that I was walking on the streets of Manhattan — Broadway, Third Avenue, 116th Street, where I had lived the three years I attended Columbia. I curled myself around these dreams and I began to be happy.

And then, one Sunday, when everybody was away and I was alone in the orderly room reading a month-old copy of the *Sporting News*, Grossbart reappeared.

"You a baseball fan, Sergeant?"

230 I looked up. "How are you?"

"Fine," Grossbart said. "They're making a soldier out of me."

"How are Fishbein and Halpern?"

"Coming along," he said. "We've got no training this afternoon. They're at the movies."

"How come you're not with them?"

235 "I wanted to come over and say hello."

He smiled — a shy, regular-guy smile, as though he and I well knew that our friendship drew its sustenance from unexpected visits, remembered birthdays, and borrowed lawnmowers. At first it offended me, and then the feeling was swallowed by the general uneasiness I felt at the thought that everyone on the post was locked away in a dark movie theater and I was here alone with Grossbart. I folded up my paper.

"Sergeant," he said, "I'd like to ask a favor. It is a favor, and I'm making no bones about it."

He stopped, allowing me to refuse him a hearing — which, of course, forced me into a courtesy I did not intend. "Go ahead."

"Well, actually, it's two favors."

240 I said nothing.

"The first one's about these rumors. Everybody says we're going to the Pacific."

"As I told your friend Fishbein, I don't know," I said. "You'll just have to wait to find out. Like everybody else."

"You think there's a chance of any of us going East?"

"Germany?" I said. "Maybe."

245 "I meant New York."

"I don't think so, Grossbart. Offhand."

"Thanks for the information, Sergeant," he said.

"It's not information, Grossbart. Just what I surmise."

"It certainly would be good to be near home. My parents — you know."

He took a step toward the door and then turned back. "Oh, the other thing. May I ask the other?"

250 "What is it?"

"The other thing is — I've got relatives in St. Louis, and they say they'll give me a whole Passover dinner if I can get down there. God, Sergeant, that'd mean an awful lot to me."

I stood up. "No passes during basic, Grossbart."

"But we're off from now till Monday morning, Sergeant. I could leave the post and no one would even know."

"I'd know. You'd know."

"But that's all. Just the two of us. Last night, I called my aunt, and you should have heard her. 'Come — come,' she said. 'I got gefilte fish, *chrain*° — the works!' Just a day, Sergeant. I'd take the blame if anything happened."

"The Captain isn't here to sign a pass."

"You could sign."

"Look, Grossbart — "

"Sergeant, for two months, practically, I've been eating *trafe* till I want to die."

"I thought you'd made up your mind to live with it. To be minus a little bit of heritage."

He pointed a finger at me. "You!" he said. "That wasn't for you to read."

"I read it. So what?"

"The letter was addressed to a congressman."

"Grossbart, don't feed me any baloney. You *wanted* me to read it."

"Why are you persecuting me, Sergeant?"

"Are you kidding!"

"I've run into this before," he said, "but never from my own!"

"Get out of here, Grossbart! Get the hell out of my sight!"

He did not move. "Ashamed, that's what you are," he said. "So you take it out on the rest of us. They say Hitler himself was half a Jew. Hearing you, I wouldn't doubt it."

"What are you trying to do with me, Grossbart?" I asked him. "What are you after? You want me to give you special privileges, to change the food, to find out about your orders, to give you weekend passes."

"You even talk like a goy!"° Grossbart shook his fist. "Is this just a weekend pass I'm asking for? Is a Seder° sacred, or not?"

Seder! It suddenly occurred to me that Passover had been celebrated weeks before. I said so.

"That's right," he replied. "Who says no? A month ago — and I was in the field eating hash! And now all I ask is a simple favor. A Jewish boy I thought would understand. My aunt's willing to go out of her way — to make a Seder a month later . . ." He turned to go, mumbling.

"Come back here!" I called. He stopped and looked at me. "Grossbart, why can't you be like the rest? Why do you have to stick out like a sore thumb?"

---

chrain: horseradish   **goy:** gentile   **Seder:** ceremonial dinner on first day of Passover

"Because I'm a Jew, Sergeant. I *am* different. Better, maybe not. But different."

"This is a war, Grossbart. For the time being *be* the same."

"I refuse."

"What?"

"I refuse. I can't stop being me, that's all there is to it." Tears came to his eyes. "It's a hard thing to be a Jew. But now I understand what Mickey says — it's a harder thing to stay one." He raised a hand sadly toward me. "Look at *you*."

"Stop crying!"

"Stop this, stop that, stop the other thing! *You* stop, Sergeant. Stop closing your heart to your own!" And, wiping his face with his sleeve, he ran out the door. "The least we can do for one another — the least . . ."

An hour later, looking out of the window, I saw Grossbart headed across the field. He wore a pair of starched khakis and carried a little leather ditty bag. I went out into the heat of the day. It was quiet; not a soul was in sight except, over by the mess hall, four K.P.s sitting around a pan, sloped forward from their waists, gabbing and peeling potatoes in the sun.

"Grossbart!" I called.

He looked toward me and continued walking.

"Grossbart, get over here!"

He turned and came across the field. Finally, he stood before me.

"Where are you going?" I asked.

"St. Louis. I don't care."

"You'll get caught without a pass."

"So I'll get caught without a pass."

"You'll go to the stockade."

"I'm *in* the stockade." He made an about-face and headed off.

I let him go only a step or two. "Come back here," I said, and he followed me into the office, where I typed out a pass and signed the Captain's name, and my own initials after it.

He took the pass and then, a moment later, reached out and grabbed my hand. "Sergeant, you don't know how much this means to me."

"O.K.," I said. "Don't get in any trouble."

"I wish I could show you how much this means to me."

"Don't do me any favors. Don't write any more congressmen for citations."

He smiled. "You're right. I won't. But let me do something."

"Bring me a piece of that gefilte fish. Just get out of here."

"I will!" he said. "With a slice of carrot and a little horseradish. I won't forget."

"All right. Just show your pass at the gate. And don't tell *anybody*."

"I won't. It's a month late, but a good Yom Tov° to you."

"Good Yom Tov, Grossbart," I said.

Yom Tov: holiday (literally, good day)

"You're a good Jew, Sergeant. You like to think you have a hard heart, but underneath you're a fine, decent man. I mean that."

Those last three words touched me more than any words from Grossbart's mouth had the right to. "All right, Grossbart," I said. "Now call me 'sir,' and get the hell out of here."

He ran out the door and was gone. I felt very pleased with myself; it was a great relief to stop fighting Grossbart, and it had cost me nothing. Barrett would never find out, and if he did, I could manage to invent some excuse. For a while, I sat at my desk, comfortable in my decision. Then the screen door flew back and Grossbart burst in again. "Sergeant!" he said. Behind him I saw Fishbein and Halpern, both in starched khakis, both carrying ditty bags like Grossbart's.

"Sergeant, I caught Mickey and Larry coming out of the movies. I almost missed them."

"Grossbart—did I say to tell no one?" I said.

"But my aunt said I could bring friends. That I should, in fact."

"*I'm* the Sergeant, Grossbart—not your aunt!"

Grossbart looked at me in disbelief. He pulled Halpern up by his sleeve. "Mickey, tell the Sergeant what this would mean to you."

Halpern looked at me and, shrugging, said, "A lot."

Fishbein stepped forward without prompting. "This would mean a great deal to me and my parents, Sergeant Marx."

"No!" I shouted.

Grossbart was shaking his head. "Sergeant, I could see you denying me, but how can you deny Mickey, a Yeshiva boy—that's beyond me."

"I'm not denying Mickey anything," I said. "You just pushed a little too hard, Grossbart. *You* denied him."

"I'll give him my pass, then," Grossbart said. "I'll give him my aunt's address and a little note. At least let him go."

In a second, he had crammed the pass into Halpern's pants pocket. Halpern looked at me, and so did Fishbein. Grossbart was at the door, pushing it open. "Mickey, bring me a piece of gefilte fish, at least," he said, and then he was outside again.

The three of us looked at one another, and then I said, "Halpern, hand that pass over."

He took it from his pocket and gave it to me. Fishbein had now moved to the doorway, where he lingered. He stood there for a moment with his mouth slightly open, and then he pointed to himself. "And me?" he asked.

His utter ridiculousness exhausted me. I slumped down in my seat and felt pulses knocking at the back of my eyes. "Fishbein," I said, "you understand I'm not trying to deny you anything, don't you? If it was my Army, I'd serve gefilte fish in the mess hall. I'd sell *kugel*° in the PX, honest to God."

Halpern smiled.

"You understand, don't you, Halpern?"

kugel: noodle pudding

"Yes, Sergeant."

325 "And you, Fishbein? I don't want enemies. I'm just like you—I want to serve my time and go home. I miss the same things you miss."

"Then, Sergeant," Fishbein said, "why don't you come, too?"

"Where?"

"To St. Louis. To Shelly's aunt. We'll have a regular Seder. Play hide-the-matzoh."° He gave me a broad, black-toothed smile.

I saw Grossbart again, on the other side of the screen.

330 "Psst!" He waved a piece of paper. "Mickey, here's the address. Tell her I couldn't get away."

Halpern did not move. He looked at me, and I saw the shrug moving up his arms into his shoulders again. I took the cover off my typewriter and made out passes for him and Fishbein. "Go," I said. "The three of you."

I thought Halpern was going to kiss my hand.

That afternoon, in a bar in Joplin, I drank beer and listened with half an ear to the Cardinal game. I tried to look squarely at what I'd become involved in, and began to wonder if perhaps the struggle with Grossbart wasn't as much my fault as his. What was I that I had to *muster* generous feelings? Who was I to have been feeling so grudging, so tight-hearted? After all, I wasn't being asked to move the world. Had I a right, then, or a reason, to clamp down on Grossbart, when that meant clamping down on Halpern, too? And Fishbein—that ugly, agreeable soul? Out of the many recollections of my childhood that had tumbled over me these past few days I heard my grandmother's voice: "What are you making a *tsimmes?*"° It was what she would ask my mother when, say, I had cut myself while doing something I shouldn't have done, and her daughter was busy bawling me out. I needed a hug and a kiss, and my mother would moralize. But my grandmother knew—mercy overrides justice. I should have known it, too. Who was Nathan Marx to be such a penny pincher with kindness? Surely, I thought, the Messiah himself—if He should ever come—won't niggle over nickels and dimes. God willing, he'll hug and kiss.

The next day, while I was playing softball over on the parade ground, I decided to ask Bob Wright, who was noncom in charge of Classification and Assignment, where he thought our trainees would be sent when their cycle ended, in two weeks. I asked casually, between innings, and he said, "They're pushing them all into the Pacific. Shulman cut the orders on your boys the other day."

335 The news shocked me, as though I were the father of Halpern, Fishbein, and Grossbart.

That night, I was just sliding into sleep when someone tapped on my door. "Who is it?" I asked.

"Sheldon."

matzoh: unleavened bread eaten at Passover   *tsimmes:* a to-do

He opened the door and came in. For a moment, I felt his presence without being able to see him. "How was it?" I asked.

He popped into sight in the near-darkness before me. "Great, Sergeant." Then he was sitting on the edge of the bed. I sat up.

"How about you?" he asked. "Have a nice weekend?" 340

"Yes."

"The others went to sleep." He took a deep, paternal breath. We sat silent for a while, and a homey feeling invaded my ugly little cubicle; the door was locked, the cat was out, the children were safely in bed.

"Sergeant, can I tell you something? Personal?"

I did not answer, and he seemed to know why. "Not about me. About Mickey. Sergeant, I never felt for anybody like I feel for him. Last night I heard Mickey in the bed next to me. He was crying so, it could have broken your heart. Real sobs."

"I'm sorry to hear that." 345

"I had to talk to him to stop him. He held my hand, Sergeant — he wouldn't let it go. He was almost hysterical. He kept saying if he only knew where we were going. Even if he knew it *was* the Pacific, that would be better than nothing. Just to know."

Long ago, someone had taught Grossbart the sad rule that only lies can get the truth. Not that I couldn't believe in the fact of Halpern's crying; his eyes *always* seemed red-rimmed. But, fact or not, it became a lie when Grossbart uttered it. He was entirely strategic. But then — it came with the force of indictment — so was I! There are strategies of aggression, but there are strategies of retreat as well. And so, recognizing that I myself had not been without craft and guile, I told him what I knew. "It is the Pacific."

He let out a small gasp, which was not a lie. "I'll tell him. I wish it was otherwise."

"So do I."

He jumped on my words. "You mean you think you could do something? 350 A change, maybe?"

"No, I couldn't do a thing."

"Don't you know anybody over at C. and A.?"

"Grossbart, there's nothing I can do," I said. "If your orders are for the Pacific, then it's the Pacific."

"But Mickey —"

"Mickey, you, me — everybody, Grossbart. There's nothing to be done. 355 Maybe the war'll end before you go. Pray for a miracle."

"But —"

"Good night, Grossbart." I settled back, and was relieved to feel the springs unbend as Grossbart rose to leave. I could see him clearly now; his jaw had dropped, and he looked like a dazed prizefighter. I noticed for the first time a little paper bag in his hand.

"Grossbart." I smiled. "My gift?"

"Oh, yes, Sergeant. Here — from all of us." He handed me the bag. "It's egg roll."

"Egg roll?" I accepted the bag and felt a damp grease spot on the bottom. I opened it, sure that Grossbart was joking.

"We thought you'd probably like it. You know — Chinese egg roll. We thought you'd probably have a taste for — "

"Your aunt served egg roll?"

"She wasn't home."

"Grossbart, she invited you. You told me she invited you and your friends."

365 "I know," he said. "I just reread the letter. *Next* week."

I got out of bed and walked to the window. "Grossbart," I said. But I was not calling to him.

"What?"

"What are you, Grossbart? Honest to God, what are you?"

I think it was the first time I'd asked him a question for which he didn't have an immediate answer.

370 "How can you do this to people?" I went on.

"Sergeant, the day away did us all a world of good. Fishbein, you should see him, he *loves* Chinese food."

"But the Seder," I said.

"We took second best, Sergeant."

Rage came charging at me. I didn't sidestep. "Grossbart, you're a liar!" I said. "You're a schemer and a crook. You've got no respect for anything. Nothing at all. Not for me, the truth — not even for poor Halpern! You use us all — "

375 "Sergeant, Sergeant, I feel for Mickey. Honest to God, I do. I *love* Mickey. I try — "

"You try! You feel!" I lurched toward him and grabbed his shirt front. I shook him furiously. "Grossbart, get out! Get out and stay the hell away from me. Because if I see you, I'll make your life miserable. *You understand that?*"

"Yes."

I let him free, and when he walked from the room, I wanted to spit on the floor where he had stood. I couldn't stop the fury. It engulfed me, owned me, till it seemed I could only rid myself of it with tears or an act of violence. I snatched from the bed the bag Grossbart had given me and, with all my strength, threw it out the window. And the next morning, as the men policed the area around the barracks, I heard a great cry go up from one of the trainees, who had been anticipating only his morning handful of cigarette butts and candy wrappers. "Egg roll!" he shouted. "Holy Christ, Chinese goddam egg roll!"

A week later, when I read the orders that had come down from C. and A., I couldn't believe my eyes. Every single trainee was to be shipped to Camp Stoneman, California, and from there to the Pacific — every trainee but one. Private Sheldon Grossbart. He was to be sent to Fort Monmouth, New Jersey. I read the mimeographed sheet several times. Dee, Farrell, Fishbein,

Fuselli, Fylypowycz, Glinicki, Gromke, Gucwa, Halpern, Hardy, Hele-brandt, right down to Anton Zygadlo — all were to be headed West before the month was out. All except Grossbart. He had pulled a string, and I wasn't it.

I lifted the phone and called C. and A.

The voice on the other end said smartly, "Corporal Shulman, sir."

"Let me speak to Sergeant Wright."

"Who is this calling, sir?"

"Sergeant Marx."

And, to my surprise, the voice said, "*Oh!*" Then, "Just a minute, Sergeant."

Shulman's "*Oh!*" stayed with me while I waited for Wright to come to the phone. Why "*Oh!*"? Who was Shulman? And then, so simply, I knew I'd discovered the string that Grossbart had pulled. In fact, I could hear Grossbart the day he'd discovered Shulman in the PX, or in the bowling alley, or maybe even at services. "Glad to meet you. Where you from? Bronx? Me, too. Do you know So-and-So? And So-and-So? Me, too! You work at C. and A.? Really? Hey, how's chances of getting East? Could you do something? Change something? Swindle, cheat, lie? We gotta help each other, you know. If the Jews in Germany . . ."

Bob Wright answered the phone. "How are you, Nate? How's the pitching arm?"

"Good. Bob, I wonder if you could do me a favor." I heard clearly my own words, and they so reminded me of Grossbart that I dropped more easily than I could have imagined into what I had planned. "This may sound crazy, Bob, but I got a kid here on orders to Monmouth who wants them changed. He had a brother killed in Europe, and he's hot to go to the Pacific. Says he'd feel like a coward if he wound up Stateside. I don't know, Bob — can anything be done? Put somebody else in the Monmouth slot?"

"Who?" he asked cagily.

"Anybody. First guy in the alphabet. I don't care. The kid just asked if something could be done."

"What's his name?"

"Grossbart, Sheldon."

Wright didn't answer.

"Yeah," I said. "He's a Jewish kid, so he thought I could help him out. You know."

"I guess I can do something," he finally said. "The Major hasn't been around for weeks. Temporary duty to the golf course. I'll try, Nate, that's all I can say."

"I'd appreciate it, Bob. See you Sunday." And I hung up, perspiring.

The following day, the corrected orders appeared: Fishbein, Fuselli, Fylypowycz, Glinicki, Gromke, Grossbart, Gucwa, Halpern, Hardy . . . Lucky Private Harley Alton was to go to Fort Monmouth, New Jersey, where, for some reason or other, they wanted an enlisted man with infantry training.

After chow that night, I stopped back at the orderly room to straighten out the guard-duty roster. Grossbart was waiting for me. He spoke first.

"You son of a bitch!"

I sat down at my desk, and while he glared at me, I began to make the necessary alterations in the duty roster.

"What do you have against me?" he cried. "Against my family? Would it kill you for me to be near my father, God knows how many months he has left to him?"

"Why so?"

"His heart," Grossbart said. "He hasn't had enough troubles in a lifetime, you've got to add to them. I curse the day I ever met you, Marx! Shulman told me what happened over there. There's no limit to your anti-Semitism, is there? The damage you've done here isn't enough. You have to make a special phone call! You really want me dead!"

I made the last notations in the duty roster and got up to leave. "Good night, Grossbart."

"You owe me an explanation!" He stood in my path.

"Sheldon, you're the one who owes explanations."

He scowled. "To *you?*"

"To me, I think so — yes. Mostly to Fishbein and Halpern."

"That's right, twist things around. I owe nobody nothing. I've done all I could for them. Now I think I've got the right to watch out for myself."

"For each other we have to learn to watch out, Sheldon. You told me yourself."

"You call this watching out for me — what you did?"

"No. For all of us."

I pushed him aside and started for the door. I heard his furious breathing behind me, and it sounded like steam rushing from an engine of terrible strength.

"*You'll* be all right," I said from the door. And, I thought, so would Fishbein and Halpern be all right, even in the Pacific, if only Grossbart continued to see — in the obsequiousness of the one, the soft spirituality of the other — some profit for himself.

I stood outside the orderly room, and I heard Grossbart weeping behind me. Over in the barracks, in the lighted windows, I could see the boys in their T shirts sitting on their bunks talking about their orders, as they'd been doing for the past two days. With a kind of quiet nervousness, they polished shoes, shined belt buckles, squared away underwear, trying as best they could to accept their fate. Behind me, Grossbart swallowed hard, accepting his. And then, resisting with all my will an impulse to turn and seek pardon for my vindictiveness, I accepted my own.

QUESTIONS

1. More use of dilemma is made in this story than in any other in this text. Identify some of the dilemmas the protagonist finds himself in. Are they

used primarily to create suspense, to reveal character, or to illuminate theme? Might all of these dilemmas be classified as specific applications of one general dilemma? If so, how might this general dilemma be described? (One suggestion for an answer is contained in the wisdom shown by Nathan Marx's grandmother in paragraph 333.)

2. Sergeant Marx finds himself in so many dilemmas because he is trying to reconcile three roles — top sergeant, Jew, and human being. To what extent do these roles conflict? Point out places where Marx is thinking or acting primarily as a sergeant, as a Jew, as a human being.

3. The plot has four major episodes, centering in conflicts over (a) attendance at Friday night services, (b) company food, (c) pass to St. Louis, (d) shipping orders. Insofar as these involve conflict between Sergeant Marx and Grossbart, which is the victor in each?

4. "What are you, Grossbart? Honest to God, what are you?" asks Sergeant Marx. Answer this question as precisely as possible. What is Grossbart's philosophy? Catalogue the various methods he uses to achieve his goals.

5. Even more important to Sergeant Marx is the question, Who is Sergeant Marx? What does the fact that he asks this question (paragraph 333) tell us about him? By what principles does he try to govern his conduct? In paragraph 347, Marx speaks of "strategies of aggression" and "strategies of retreat"; on what occasions does *he* use strategies similar to Grossbart's?

6. What are Sergeant Marx's motivations in his final decision? In which of his roles — sergeant, Jew, human being — is he acting at this point? Is his decision right?

7. What is meant by Sergeant Marx's final statement that he accepted his fate? What *is* his fate?

8. Describe as precisely as possible Captain Barrett's attitude toward Jews.

9. Differentiate Grossbart, Fishbein, and Halpern. How would you rank these three, Captain Barrett, and Sergeant Marx on a scale of human worth?

10. To what character (or characters) does the title refer? Is it used straightforwardly or ironically?

11. This story — by a Jewish author about Jewish characters — has a complex theme. Does the theme at its most general level necessarily involve the idea of Jewishness? Is it more crucial to the story that Nathan Marx is a Jew or a top sergeant? Try stating the theme without mentioning the idea of Jewishness. Now expand it to include the idea of Jewishness. Can it be stated without mentioning the idea of responsibility for command and judgment?

CHAPTER FIVE

Point of View

The primitive storyteller, unbothered by considerations of form, simply spun a tale. "Once upon a time," he began, and proceeded to narrate the story to his listeners, describing the characters when necessary, telling what they thought and felt as well as what they did, and interjecting comments and ideas of his own. Modern fiction writers are artistically more self-conscious. They realize that there are many ways of telling a story; they decide upon a method before they begin, or discover one while in the act of writing, and may even set up rules for themselves. Instead of telling the story themselves, they may let one of the characters tell it; they may tell it by means of letters or diaries; they may confine themselves to recording the thoughts of one of the characters. With the growth of artistic consciousness, the question of **point of view**, of who tells the story, and, therefore, of how it gets told, has assumed especial importance.

To determine the point of view of a story we ask, "Who tells the story?" and "How much is this person allowed to know?" and, especially, "To what extent does the narrator look inside the characters and report their thoughts and feelings?"

Though many variations and combinations are possible, the basic points of view are four, as follows:

1. Omniscient	
2. Limited omniscient	{ (a) Major character { (b) Minor character
3. First person	{ (a) Major character { (b) Minor character
4. Objective	

1. In the **omniscient point of view**, the story is told in the third person by a narrator whose knowledge and prerogatives are unlimited. Such narrators are free to go wherever they wish, to peer inside the minds and hearts of characters at will and tell us what they are thinking or feeling. They can interpret behavior and can comment, if they wish, on the significance of their stories. They know all. They can tell us as much or as little as they please.

The following version of Aesop's fable "The Ant and the Grasshopper" is told from the omniscient point of view. Notice that in it we are told not only what both characters do and say, but also what they think and feel; also, that the narrator comments at the end on the significance of the story. (The phrases in which the narrator enters into the thoughts or feelings of the ant and the grasshopper have been italicized; the comment by the author is printed in small capitals.)

> *Weary in every limb*, the ant tugged over the snow a piece of corn he had stored up last summer. *It would taste mighty good at dinner tonight.*
>
> A grasshopper, *cold and hungry*, looked on. *Finally he could bear it no longer.* "Please, friend ant, may I have a bite of corn?"
>
> "What were you doing all last summer?" asked the ant. He looked the grasshopper up and down. *He knew its kind.*
>
> "I sang from dawn till dark," replied the grasshopper, *happily unaware of what was coming next.*
>
> "Well," said the ant, *hardly bothering to conceal his contempt*, "since you sang all summer, you can dance all winter."
>
> HE WHO IDLES WHEN HE'S YOUNG
> WILL HAVE NOTHING WHEN HE'S OLD

Stories told from the omniscient point of view may differ widely in the amount of omniscience the narrator is allowed. In "The Son from America," we enter the consciousnesses, not only of Berl, Berlcha, and Samuel, but, briefly, even that of the goat, who "gazed with surprise at this strange man [Samuel] — his height and his bizarre clothes." In "The Destructors," though we are taken into the minds of Blackie, Mike, the gang as a group, Old Misery, and the lorry driver, we are not taken into the mind of Trevor — the most important character. In "The Most Dangerous Game," we are confined to the thoughts and feelings of Rainsford, except for the brief passage between Rainsford's leap into the sea and his waking in Zaroff's bed, during which the point of view shifts to General Zaroff.

The omniscient is the most flexible point of view and permits the widest scope. It is also the most subject to abuse. It offers constant danger that the narrator may come between the readers and the story, or that the continual shifting of viewpoint from character to character may cause a breakdown in coherence or unity. Used skillfully it enables the author to achieve simultaneous breadth and depth. Unskillfully used, it can destroy the illusion of reality that the story attempts to create.

2. In the **limited omniscient point of view**, the story is told in the third person, but from the viewpoint of one character in the story. Such point-of-view characters are filters through whose eyes and minds writers look at the events. Authors employing this perspective may move both inside and outside these characters but never leave their sides. They tell us what these characters see and hear and what they think and feel; they possibly interpret the characters' thoughts and behavior. They know everything about their point-of-view characters — often more than the characters know about themselves. But they limit themselves to these characters' perceptions, and show no direct knowledge of what *other* characters are thinking or feeling or doing, except for what the point-of-view character knows or can infer about them. The chosen character may be either a major or a minor character, a participant or an observer, and this choice also will be a very important one for the story. "Prue" and "Miss Brill" are told from the limited omniscient point of view, from the perspective of the main character. The use of this viewpoint with a minor character is rare in the short story, and is not illustrated in this book.

Here is "The Ant and the Grasshopper" told, in the third person, from the point of view of the ant. Notice that this time we are told nothing of what the grasshopper thinks or feels. We see and hear and know of him only what the ant sees and hears and knows.

> *Weary in every limb*, the ant tugged over the snow a piece of corn he had stored up last summer. *It would taste mighty good at dinner tonight. It was then that he noticed the grasshopper, looking cold and pinched.*
>
> "Please, friend ant, may I have a bite of your corn?" asked the grasshopper.
>
> He looked the grasshopper up and down. "What were you doing all last summer?" he asked. *He knew its kind.*
>
> "I sang from dawn till dark," replied the grasshopper.
>
> "Well," said the ant, *hardly bothering to conceal his contempt*, "since you sang all summer, you can dance all winter."

The limited omniscient point of view, since it acquaints us with the world through the mind and senses of only one person, approximates more closely than the omniscient the conditions of real life; it also offers a ready-made unifying element, since all details of the story are the experience of one person. And it affords an additional device of characterization, since what a point-of-view character does or does not find noteworthy, and the inferences that such a character draws about other characters' actions and motives, may reveal biases or limitations in the observer. At the same time it offers a limited field of observation, for the readers can go nowhere except where the chosen character goes, and there may be difficulty in having the character naturally cognizant of all important events. Clumsy writers will constantly have the focal character listening at keyholes, accidentally overhearing important conversations, or coincidentally being present when important events occur.

3. In the **first-person point of view**, the author disappears into one of the characters, who tells the story in the first person. This character, again, may be either a major or minor character, protagonist or observer, and it will make considerable difference whether the protagonist tells the story or someone else tells it. In "I'm a Fool" and "Defender of the Faith," the protagonist tells the story in the first person. In "The Child by Tiger" and "Spotted Horses" (page 349), the story is told by an observer.

Our fable is retold below in the first person from the point of view of the grasshopper. (The whole story is italicized because it all comes out of the grasshopper's mind.)

> *Cold and hungry, I watched the ant tugging over the snow a piece of corn he had stored up last summer. My feelers twitched, and I was conscious of a tic in my left hind leg. Finally I could bear it no longer. "Please, friend ant," I asked, "may I have a bite of your corn?"*
>
> *He looked me up and down. "What were you doing all last summer?" he asked, rather too smugly it seemed to me.*
>
> *"I sang from dawn till dark," I said innocently, remembering the happy times.*
>
> *"Well," he said, with a priggish sneer, "since you sang all summer, you can dance all winter."*

The first-person point of view shares the virtues and limitations of the limited omniscient. It offers, sometimes, a gain in immediacy and reality, since we get the story directly from a participant, the author as intermediary being eliminated. It offers no opportunity, however, for *direct* interpretation by the author, and there is constant danger that narrators may be made to transcend their own sensitivity, their knowledge, or their powers of language in telling a story. Good authors, however, can make tremendous literary capital out of the very limitations of their narrators. The first-person point of view offers excellent opportunities for dramatic irony and for studies in limited or blunted human perceptivity. Often, as in "I'm a Fool," the very heart of the story may lie in the difference between what the narrator perceives and what the reader perceives. In such stories authors offer interpretations of the material *indirectly*, through the use of irony. They may also indicate their own judgment, more straightforwardly though still indirectly, by expressing it through the lips of a discerning and sympathetic narrator. In "Defender of the Faith" the reader is disposed to accept Sergeant Marx's interpretation of characters and events as being largely the author's own. Such identifications of a narrator's attitude with the author's, however, must always be undertaken with extreme caution; they are justified only if the total material of the story supports them. In "Defender of the Faith" the moral sensitivity and intelligence of the narrator reflects the author's own; nevertheless, much of the interest of the story arises from Marx's own uncertainty about his judgments — the nagging apprehension that he may be mistaken.

4. In the **objective point of view**, the narrator disappears into a kind of roving sound camera. This camera can go anywhere but can record only what is seen and heard. It cannot comment, interpret, or enter a character's mind. With this point of view (sometimes called also the **dramatic point of view**) readers are placed in the position of spectators at a movie or play. They see what the characters do and hear what they say but must infer what they think or feel and what they are like. Authors are not there to explain. The purest example of a story told from the objective point of view would be one written entirely in dialogue, for as soon as authors add words of their own, they begin to interpret through their very choice of words. Actually, few stories using this point of view are antiseptically pure, for the limitations it imposes on the author are severe. "Hills Like White Elephants" (page 171) is an excellent example, however, and "The Lottery" (page 436) is essentially objective in its narration.

The following version of "The Ant and the Grasshopper" is also told from the objective point of view. (Since we are nowhere taken into the thoughts or feelings of the characters, none of this version is printed in italics.)

The ant tugged over the snow a piece of corn he had stored up last summer, perspiring in spite of the cold.

A grasshopper, its feelers twitching and with a tic in his left hind leg, looked on for some time. Finally he asked, "Please, friend ant, may I have a bite of your corn?"

The ant looked the grasshopper up and down. "What were you doing all last summer?" he snapped.

"I sang from dawn till dark," replied the grasshopper, not changing his tone.

"Well," said the ant, and a faint smile crept into his face, "since you sang all summer, you can dance all winter."

The objective point of view has the most speed and the most action; also, it requires readers to draw their own inferences. But it must rely heavily on external action and dialogue, and it offers no opportunities for direct interpretation by the author.

Each of the points of view has its advantages, its limitations, and its peculiar uses. Ideally the choice of the author will depend upon the materials and the purpose of a story. Authors choose the point of view that enables them to present their particular materials most effectively in terms of their purposes. Writers of murder mysteries with suspense and thrills as the purpose will ordinarily avoid using the point of view of the murderer or the brilliant detective: otherwise they would have to reveal at the beginning the secrets they wish to conceal till the end. On the other hand, if they are interested in exploring criminal psychology, the murderer's point of view might be by far the most effective. In the Sherlock Holmes stories, A. Conan Doyle effectively uses the somewhat imperceptive Dr. Watson as his narrator, so that the reader may be kept in the dark as long as possible and then be as amazed as Watson is by Holmes's deductive powers. In Dostoevsky's *Crime and Punishment*, however, the author is interested not in mystifying and surprising but in illuminating the moral and psychological operations of the human soul in the act of taking life; he therefore tells the story from the viewpoint of a sensitive and intelligent murderer.

For readers, the examination of point of view may be important both for understanding and for evaluating the story. First, they should know whether the events of the story are being interpreted by the narrator or by one of the characters. If the latter, they must ask how this character's mind and personality affect the interpretation, whether the character is perceptive or imperceptive, and whether the interpretation can be accepted at face value or must be discounted because of ignorance, stupidity, or self-deception. Often, as in "I'm a Fool," an author achieves striking and significant effects by using a narrator not aware of the full import of the events he is reporting.

Next, readers should ask whether the writer has chosen the point of view for maximum revelation of the material or for another reason. The author may choose the point of view mainly to conceal certain information till the end of the story and thus maintain suspense and create surprise. The author may even deliberately mislead readers by presenting the events through a character who puts a false interpretation on them. Such a false interpretation may be justified if it leads eventually to more effective revelation of character and theme. If it is there merely to trick readers, it is obviously less justifiable.

Finally, readers should ask whether the author has used the selected point of view fairly and consistently. Even in escape literature, we have a right to demand fair treatment. If the person to whose thoughts and feelings we are admitted has pertinent information that is not revealed, we legitimately feel cheated. To have a chance to solve a murder mystery, we must know what the detective learns. A writer also should be consistent in the point of view; if it shifts, it should do so for a just artistic reason. Serious interpretive writers choose and use point of view so as to yield ultimately the greatest possible insight, either in fullness or in intensity.

Willa Cather
Paul's Case

It was Paul's afternoon to appear before the faculty of the Pittsburgh High School to account for his various misdemeanors. He had been suspended a week ago, and his father had called at the Principal's office and confessed his perplexity about his son. Paul entered the faculty room suave and smiling. His clothes were a trifle outgrown, and the tan velvet on the collar of his open overcoat was frayed and worn; but for all that there was something of a dandy about him, and he wore an opal pin in his neatly knotted black four-in-hand, and a red carnation in his buttonhole. This latter adornment the faculty somehow felt was not properly significant of the contrite spirit befitting a boy under the ban of suspension.

Paul was tall for his age and very thin, with high, cramped shoulders and a narrow chest. His eyes were remarkable for a certain hysterical brilliancy, and he continually used them in a conscious, theatrical sort of way, peculiarly offensive in a boy. The pupils were abnormally large, as though he were addicted to belladonna, but there was a glassy glitter about them which that drug does not produce.

PAUL'S CASE   Written in 1904, first published in 1905. Willa Cather (1873–1947), born in Virginia, grew up and was educated in Nebraska. From 1895 to 1905 she lived and worked in Pittsburgh, first as a journalist, writing drama and music criticism, later as a teacher of English and Latin in two Pittsburgh high schools. In 1902 she traveled in Europe.

When questioned by the Principal as to why he was there, Paul stated, politely enough, that he wanted to come back to school. This was a lie, but Paul was quite accustomed to lying; found it, indeed, indispensable for overcoming friction. His teachers were asked to state their respective charges against him, which they did with such a rancor and aggrievedness as evinced that this was not a usual case. Disorder and impertinence were among the offences named, yet each of his instructors felt that it was scarcely possible to put into words the real cause of the trouble, which lay in a sort of hysterically defiant manner of the boy's; in the contempt which they all knew he felt for them, and which he seemingly made not the least effort to conceal. Once, when he had been making a synopsis of a paragraph at the blackboard, his English teacher had stepped to his side and attempted to guide his hand. Paul had started back with a shudder and thrust his hands violently behind him. The astonished woman could scarcely have been more hurt and embarrassed had he struck at her. The insult was so involuntary and definitely personal as to be unforgettable. In one way and another, he had made all his teachers, men and women alike, conscious of the same feeling of physical aversion. In one class he habitually sat with his hand shading his eyes; in another he always looked out of the window during the recitation; in another he made a running commentary on the lecture, with humorous intent.

His teachers felt this afternoon that his whole attitude was symbolized by his shrug and his flippantly red carnation flower, and they fell upon him without mercy, his English teacher leading the pack. He stood through it smiling, his pale lips parted over his white teeth. (His lips were continually twitching, and he had a habit of raising his eyebrows that was contemptuous and irritating to the last degree.) Older boys than Paul had broken down and shed tears under that ordeal, but his set smile did not once desert him, and his only sign of discomfort was the nervous trembling of the fingers that toyed with the buttons of his overcoat, and an occasional jerking of the other hand which held his hat. Paul was always smiling, always glancing about him, seeming to feel that people might be watching him and trying to detect something. This conscious expression, since it was as far as possible from boyish mirthfulness, was usually attributed to insolence or "smartness."

As the inquisition proceeded, one of his instructors repeated an impertinent remark of the boy's, and the Principal asked him whether he thought that a courteous speech to make to a woman. Paul shrugged his shoulders slightly and his eyebrows twitched. 5

"I don't know," he replied. "I didn't mean to be polite or impolite, either. I guess it's a sort of way I have, of saying things regardless."

The Principal asked him whether he didn't think that a way it would be well to get rid of. Paul grinned and said he guessed so. When he was told that he could go, he bowed gracefully and went out. His bow was like a repetition of the scandalous red carnation.

His teachers were in despair, and his drawing-master voiced the feeling of them all when he declared there was something about the boy which none of them understood. He added: "I don't really believe that smile of his comes altogether from insolence; there's something sort of haunted about it. The boy is not strong for one thing. There is something wrong about the fellow."

The drawing-master had come to realize that, in looking at Paul, one saw only his white teeth and the forced animation of his eyes. One warm afternoon the boy had gone to sleep at his drawing-board, and his master had noted with amazement what a white, blue-veined face it was; drawn and wrinkled like an old man's about the eyes, the lips twitching even in his sleep.

His teachers left the building dissatisfied and unhappy; humiliated to have felt so vindictive toward a mere boy, to have uttered this feeling in cutting terms, and to have set each other on, as it were, in the gruesome game of intemperate reproach. One of them remembered having seen a miserable street cat set at bay by a ring of tormentors.

As for Paul, he ran down the hill whistling the Soldiers' Chorus from *Faust*, looking behind him now and then to see whether some of his teachers were not there to witness his light-heartedness. As it was now late in the afternoon and Paul was on duty that evening as usher at Carnegie Hall, he decided that he would not go home to supper.

When he reached the concert hall, the doors were not yet open. It was chilly outside, and he decided to go up into the picture gallery — always deserted at this hour — where there were some of Raffelli's gay studies of Paris streets and an airy blue Venetian scene or two that always exhilarated him. He was delighted to find no one in the gallery but the old guard, who sat in the corner, a newspaper on his knee, a black patch over one eye and the other closed. Paul possessed himself of the place and walked confidently up and down, whistling under his breath. After a while he sat down before a blue Rico and lost himself. When he bethought him to look at his watch, it was after seven o'clock and he rose with a start and ran downstairs, making a face at Augustus Caesar, peering out from the cast-room, and an evil gesture at the Venus of Milo as he passed her on the stairway.

When Paul reached the ushers' dressing-room, half a dozen boys were there already, and he began excitedly to tumble into his uniform. It was one of the few that at all approached fitting, and Paul thought it very becoming — though he knew the tight, straight coat accentuated his narrow chest, about which he was exceedingly sensitive. He was always excited while he dressed, twanging all over to the tuning of the strings and the preliminary flourishes of the horns in the music-room; but tonight he seemed quite beside himself, and he teased and plagued the boys until, telling him that he was crazy, they put him down on the floor and sat on him.

Somewhat calmed by his suppression, Paul dashed out to the front of the house to seat the early comers. He was a model usher. Gracious and smiling he ran up and down the aisles. Nothing was too much trouble for him; he carried messages and brought programs as though it were his greatest pleasure in life, and all the people in his section thought him a charming boy, feeling that he remembered and admired them. As the house filled, he grew more and more vivacious and animated, and the color came to his cheeks and lips. It was very much as though this were a great reception and Paul were the host. Just as the musicians came out to take their places, his English teacher arrived with checks for the seats which a prominent manufacturer had taken for the season. She betrayed some embarrassment when she handed Paul the tickets, and a *hauteur* which subsequently made her feel very foolish. Paul was startled for a moment, and had the feeling of wanting to put her out; what business had she here among all these fine people and gay colors? He looked her over and decided that she was not appropriately dressed and must be a fool to sit downstairs in such togs. The tickets had probably been sent her out of kindness, he reflected, as he put down a seat for her, and she had about as much right to sit there as he had.

When the symphony began, Paul sank into one of the rear seats with a   15
long sigh of relief, and lost himself as he had done before the Rico. It was not that symphonies, as such, meant anything in particular to Paul, but the first sight of the instruments seemed to free some hilarious spirit within him; something that struggled there like the Genius in the bottle found by the Arab fisherman. He felt a sudden zest of life; the lights danced before his eyes and the concert hall blazed into unimaginable splendor. When the soprano soloist came on, Paul forgot even the nastiness of his teacher's being there, and gave himself up to the peculiar intoxication such personages always had for him. The soloist chanced to be a German woman, by no means in her first youth, and the mother of many children; but she wore a satin gown and a tiara, and she had that indefinable air of achievement, that world-shine upon her, which always blinded Paul to any possible defects.

After a concert was over, Paul was often irritable and wretched until he got to sleep — and tonight he was even more than usually restless. He had the feeling of not being able to let down; of its being impossible to give up his delicious excitement which was the only thing that could be called living at all. During the last number he withdrew and, after hastily changing his clothes in the dressing-room, slipped out to the side door where the singer's carriage stood. Here he began pacing rapidly up and down the walk, waiting to see her come out.

Over yonder the Schenley, in its vacant stretch, loomed big and square through the fine rain, the windows of its twelve stories glowing like those of a lighted cardboard house under a Christmas tree. All the actors and singers of any importance stayed there when they were in Pittsburgh, and a number of the big manufacturers of the place lived there in the winter. Paul had often hung about the hotel, watching the people go in and out, longing to enter and leave schoolmasters and dull care behind him forever.

At last the singer came out, accompanied by the conductor, who helped her into her carriage and closed the door with a cordial *auf wiedersehen* — which set Paul to wondering whether she were not an old sweetheart of his. Paul followed the carriage over to the hotel, walking so rapidly as not to be far from the entrance when the singer alighted and disappeared behind the swinging glass doors which were opened by a Negro in a tall hat and a long coat. In the moment that the door was ajar, it seemed to Paul that he, too, entered. He seemed to feel himself go after her up the steps, into the warm, lighted building, into an exotic, a tropical world of shiny, glistening surfaces and basking ease. He reflected upon the mysterious dishes that were brought into the dining-room, the green bottles in buckets of ice, as he had seen them in the supper-party pictures of the Sunday supplement. A quick gust of wind brought the rain down with sudden vehemence, and Paul was startled to find that he was still outside in the slush of the gravel driveway; that his boots were letting in the water and his scanty overcoat was clinging wet about him; that the lights in front of the concert hall were out, and that the rain was driving in sheets between him and the orange glow of the windows above him. There it was, what he wanted — tangibly before him, like the fairy world of a Christmas pantomime; as the rain beat in his face, Paul wondered whether he were destined always to shiver in the black night outside, looking up at it.

He turned and walked reluctantly toward the car tracks. The end had to come sometime; his father in his night-clothes at the top of the stairs, explanations that did not explain, hastily improvised fictions that were forever tripping him up, his upstairs room and its horrible yellow wallpaper, the creaking bureau with the greasy plush collar-box, and over his painted wooden bed the pictures of George Washington and John Calvin, and the framed motto, 'Feed my Lambs,' which had been worked in red worsted by his mother, whom Paul could not remember.

20   Half an hour later, Paul alighted from the Negley Avenue car and went slowly down one of the side streets off the main thoroughfare. It was a highly respectable street, where all the houses were exactly alike, and where business men of moderate means begot and reared large families of children, all of whom went to Sabbath School and learned the shorter catechism, and were interested in arithmetic; all of whom were as exactly alike as their homes, and of a piece with the monotony in which they lived. Paul never went up Cordelia Street without a shudder of loathing. His home was next the house of the Cumberland minister. He approached it tonight with the nerveless sense of defeat, the hopeless feeling of sinking back forever into ugliness and commonness that he had always had when he came home. The moment he turned into Cordelia Street he felt the waters close above his head. After each of these orgies of living, he experienced all the physical depression which follows a debauch; the loathing of respectable beds, of common food, of a house permeated by kitchen odors; a shuddering repulsion for the flavorless, colorless mass of everyday existence; a morbid desire for cool things and soft lights and fresh flowers.

The nearer he approached the house, the more absolutely unequal Paul felt to the sight of it all: his ugly sleeping chamber; the old bathroom with the grimy zinc tub, the cracked mirror, the dripping spigots; his father, at the top of the stairs, his hairy legs sticking out from his nightshirt, his feet thrust into carpet slippers. He was so much later than usual that there would certainly be enquiries and reproaches. Paul stopped short before the door. He felt that he could not be accosted by his father tonight; that he could not toss again on that miserable bed. He would not go in. He would tell his father that he had no carfare, and it was raining so hard he had gone home with one of the boys and stayed all night.

Meanwhile, he was wet and cold. He went around to the back of the house and tried one of the basement windows, found it open, and raised it cautiously, and scrambled down the cellar wall to the floor. There he stood, holding his breath, terrified by the noise he had made; but the floor above him was silent, and there was no creak on the stairs. He found a soap-box, and carried it over to the soft ring of light that streamed from the furnace door, and sat down. He was horribly afraid of rats, so he did not try to sleep, but sat looking distrustfully at the dark, still terrified lest he might have awakened his father.

In such reactions, after one of the experiences which made days and nights out of the dreary blanks of the calendar, when his senses were deadened, Paul's head was always singularly clear. Suppose his father had heard him getting in at the window and had come down and shot him for a burglar? Then, again, suppose his father had come down, pistol in hand, and he had cried out in time to save himself, and his father had been horrified to think how nearly he had killed him? Then again, suppose a day should come when his father would remember that night, and wish there had been no warning cry to stay his hand? With this last supposition Paul entertained himself until daybreak.

The following Sunday was fine; the sodden November chill was broken by the last flash of autumnal summer. In the morning Paul had to go to church and Sabbath School, as always. On seasonable Sunday afternoons the burghers of Cordelia Street usually sat out on their front "stoops," and talked to their neighbors on the next stoop, or called to those across the street in neighborly fashion. The men sat placidly on gay cushions placed upon the steps that led down to the sidewalk, while the women, in their Sunday "waists," sat in rockers on the cramped porches, pretending to be greatly at their ease. The children played in the streets; there were so many of them that the place resembled the recreation grounds of a kindergarten. The men on the steps, all in their shirt-sleeves, their vests unbuttoned, sat with their legs well apart, their stomachs comfortably protruding, and talked of the prices of things, or told anecdotes of the sagacity of their various chiefs and overlords. They occasionally looked over the multitude of squabbling children, listened affectionately to their high-pitched, nasal voices, smiling to see their own proclivities reproduced in their offspring, and interspersed their legends of the iron kings with remarks about their sons' progress at school, their grades in arithmetic, and the amounts they had saved in their toy banks.

On this last Sunday of November, Paul sat all afternoon on the lowest step of his "stoop," staring into the street, while his sisters, in their rockers, were talking to the minister's daughters next door about how many shirt-waists they had made in the last week, and how many waffles someone had eaten at the last church supper. When the weather was warm, and his father was in a particularly jovial frame of mind, the girls made lemonade, which was always brought out in a red-glass pitcher, ornamented with forget-me-nots in blue enamel. This the girls thought very fine, and the neighbors joked about the suspicious color of the pitcher.

Today Paul's father, on the top step, was talking to a young man who shifted a restless baby from knee to knee. He happened to be the young man who was daily held up to Paul as a model, and after whom it was his father's dearest hope that he would pattern. This young man was of a ruddy complexion, with a compressed, red mouth, and faded, nearsighted eyes, over which he wore thick spectacles, with gold bows that curved about his ears. He was clerk to one of the magnates of a great steel corporation, and was looked upon in Cordelia Street as a young man with a future. There was a story that, some five years ago — he was now barely twenty-six — he had been a trifle "dissipated," but in order to curb his appetites and save the loss of time and strength that a sowing of wild oats might have entailed, he had taken his chief's advice, oft reiterated to his employees, and at twenty-one had married the first woman whom he could persuade to share his fortunes. She happened to be an angular schoolmistress, much older than he, who also wore thick glasses, and who had now borne him four children, all near-sighted like herself.

The young man was relating how his chief, now cruising in the Mediter-ranean, kept in touch with all the details of the business, arranging his office hours on his yacht just as though he were at home, and "knocking off work enough to keep two stenographers busy." His father told, in turn, the plan his corporation was considering, of putting in an electric railway plant at Cairo. Paul snapped his teeth; he had an awful apprehension that they might spoil it all before he got there. Yet he rather liked to hear these legends of the iron kings, that were told and retold on Sundays and holidays; these stories of palaces in Venice, yachts on the Mediterranean, and high play at Monte Carlo appealed to his fancy, and he was interested in the triumphs of cash-boys who had become famous, though he had no mind for the cash-boy stage.

After supper was over, and he had helped to dry the dishes, Paul ner-vously asked his father whether he could go to George's to get some help in his geometry, and still more nervously asked for carfare. This latter request he had to repeat, as his father, on principle, did not like to hear requests for money, whether much or little. He asked Paul whether he could not go to some boy who lived nearer, and told him that he ought not to leave his school work until Sunday; but he gave him the dime. He was not a poor man, but he had a worthy ambition to come up in the world. His only reason for allowing Paul to usher was that he thought a boy ought to be earning a little.

Paul bounded upstairs, scrubbed the greasy odor of the dishwater from his hands with the ill-smelling soap he hated, and then shook over his fingers a few drops of violet water from the bottle he kept hidden in his drawer. He left the house with his geometry conspicuously under his arm, and the moment he got out of Cordelia Street and boarded a downtown car, he shook off the lethargy of two deadening days, and began to live again.

The leading juvenile of the permanent stock company which played at one of the downtown theaters was an acquaintance of Paul's, and the boy had been invited to drop in at the Sunday-night rehearsals whenever he could. For more than a year Paul had spent every available moment loitering about Charley Edwards's dressing-room. He had won a place among Edwards's following not only because the young actor, who could not afford to employ a dresser, often found him useful, but because he recognized in Paul something akin to what churchmen term "vocation."

It was at the theater and at Carnegie Hall that Paul really lived; the rest was but a sleep and a forgetting. This was Paul's fairy tale, and it had for him all the allurement of a secret love. The moment he inhaled the gassy, painty, dusty odor behind the scenes, he breathed like a prisoner set free, and felt within him the possibility of doing or saying splendid, brilliant things. The moment the cracked orchestra beat out the overture from *Martha*, or jerked at the serenade from *Rigoletto*, all stupid and ugly things slid from him, and his senses were deliciously, yet delicately fired.

Perhaps it was because, in Paul's world, the natural nearly always wore the guise of ugliness, that a certain element of artificiality seemed to him necessary in beauty. Perhaps it was because his experience of life elsewhere was so full of Sabbath-School picnics, petty economies, wholesome advice as to how to succeed in life, and the unescapable odors of cooking, that he found this existence so alluring, these smartly clad men and women so attractive, that he was so moved by these starry apple orchards that bloomed perennially under the limelight. It would be difficult to put it strongly enough how convincingly the stage entrance of the theater was for Paul the actual portal of Romance. Certainly none of the company ever suspected it, least of all Charley Edwards. It was very like the old stories that used to float about London of fabulously rich Jews, who had subterranean halls, with palms, and fountains, and soft lamps and richly appareled women who never saw the disenchanting light of London day. So, in the midst of that smoke-palled city, enamored of figures and grimy toil, Paul had his secret temple, his wishing-carpet, his bit of blue-and-white Mediterranean shore bathed in perpetual sunshine.

Several of Paul's teachers had a theory that his imagination had been perverted by garish fiction; but the truth was he scarcely ever read at all. The books at home were not such as would either tempt or corrupt a youthful mind, and as for reading the novels that some of his friends urged upon him — well, he got what he wanted much more quickly from music; any sort of music, from an orchestra to a barrel-organ. He needed only the spark, the indescribable thrill that made his imagination master of his senses, and he could make plots and pictures enough of his own. It was equally true that he was not stage-struck — not, at any rate, in the usual acceptation of the expression. He had no desire to become an actor, any more than he had to become a musician. He felt no necessity to do any of these things; what he wanted was to see, to be in the atmosphere, float on the wave of it, to be carried out, blue league after league, away from everything.

After a night behind the scenes, Paul found the schoolroom more than ever repulsive; the bare floors and naked walls; the prosy men who never wore frock coats, or violets in their buttonholes; the women with their dull gowns, shrill voices, and pitiful seriousness about prepositions that govern the dative. He could not bear to have the other pupils think, for a moment, that he took these people seriously; he must convey to them that he considered it all trivial, and was there only by the way of a joke, anyway. He had autographed pictures of all the members of the stock company which he showed his classmates, telling them the most incredible stories of his familiarity with these people, of his acquaintance with the soloists who came to Carnegie Hall, his suppers with them and the flowers he sent them. When these stories lost their effect, and his audience grew listless, he would bid all the boys goodbye, announcing that he was going to travel for a while; going to Naples, to California, to Egypt. Then, next Monday, he would slip back, conscious and nervously smiling; his sister was ill, and he would have to defer his voyage until spring.

Matters went steadily worse with Paul at school. In the itch to let his instructors know how heartily he despised them, and how thoroughly he was appreciated elsewhere, he mentioned once or twice that he had no time to fool with theorems; adding — with a twitch of the eyebrows and a touch of that nervous bravado which so perplexed them — that he was helping the people down at the stock company; they were old friends of his.

The upshot of the matter was that the Principal went to Paul's father, and Paul was taken out of school and put to work. The manager at Carnegie Hall was told to get another usher in his stead; the doorkeeper at the theater was warned not to admit him to the house; and Charley Edwards remorsefully promised the boy's father not to see him again.

The members of the stock company were vastly amused when some of Paul's stories reached them — especially the women. They were hard-working women, most of them supporting indolent husbands or brothers, and they laughed rather bitterly at having stirred the boy to such fervid and florid inventions. They agreed with the faculty and with his father, that Paul's was a bad case.

The east-bound train was plowing through a January snowstorm; the dull dawn was beginning to show grey when the engine whistled a mile out of Newark. Paul started up from the seat where he had lain curled in uneasy slumber, rubbed the breath-misted window-glass with his hand, and peered out. The snow was whirling in curling eddies above the white bottom lands, and the drifts lay already deep in the fields and along the fences, while here and there the tall dead grass and dried weed stalks protruded black above it. Lights shone from the scattered houses, and a gang of laborers who stood beside the track waved their lanterns.

Paul had slept very little, and he felt grimy and uncomfortable. He had made the all-night journey in a day coach because he was afraid if he took a Pullman he might be seen by some Pittsburgh business man who had noticed him in Denny and Carson's office. When the whistle woke him, he clutched quickly at his breast pocket, glancing about him with an uncertain smile. But the little, clay-bespattered Italians were still sleeping, the slatternly women across the aisle were in open-mouthed oblivion, and even the crumby, crying babies were for the time stilled. Paul settled back to struggle with his impatience as best he could.

When he arrived at the Jersey City station, he hurried through his break- $\qquad$ 40 fast, manifestly ill at ease and keeping a sharp eye about him. After he reached the Twenty-Third Street station, he consulted a cabman, and had himself driven to a men's furnishing establishment which was just opening for the day. He spent upward of two hours there, buying with endless reconsidering and great care. His new street suit he put on in the fitting-room; the frock coat and dress clothes he had bundled into the cab with his new shirts. Then he drove to a hatter's and a shoe house. His next errand was at Tiffany's, where he selected silver-mounted brushes and a scarf-pin. He would not wait to have his silver marked, he said. Lastly, he stopped at a trunk shop on Broadway, and had his purchases packed into various traveling-bags.

It was a little after one o'clock when he drove up to the Waldorf, and, after settling with the cabman, went into the office. He registered from Washington; said his mother and father had been abroad, and that he had come down to await the arrival of their steamer. He told his story plausibly and had no trouble, since he offered to pay for them in advance, in engaging his rooms; a sleeping-room, sitting-room, and bath.

Not once, but a hundred times Paul had planned this entry into New York. He had gone over every detail of it with Charley Edwards, and in his scrapbook at home there were pages of description about New York hotels, cut from the Sunday papers.

When he was shown to his sitting-room on the eighth floor, he saw at a glance that everything was as it should be; there was but one detail in his mental picture that the place did not realize, so he rang for the bell-boy and sent him down for flowers. He moved about nervously until the boy returned, putting away his new linen and fingering it delightedly as he did so. When the flowers came, he put them hastily into water, and then tumbled into a hot bath. Presently he came out of his white bathroom, resplendent in his new silk underwear, and playing with the tassels of his red robe. The snow was whirling so fiercely outside his windows that he could scarcely see across the street; but within, the air was deliciously soft and fragrant. He put the violets and jonquils on the taboret beside the couch, and threw himself down with a long sigh, covering himself with a Roman blanket. He was thoroughly tired; he had been in such haste, he had stood up to such a strain, covered so much ground in the last twenty-four hours, that he wanted to think how it had all come about. Lulled by the sound of the wind, the warm air, and the cool fragrance of the flowers, he sank into deep, drowsy retrospection.

It had been wonderfully simple; when they had shut him out of the theater and concert hall, when they had taken away his bone, the whole thing was virtually determined. The rest was a mere matter of opportunity. The only thing that at all surprised him was his own courage — for he realized well enough that he had always been tormented by fear, a sort of apprehensive dread which, of late years, as the meshes of the lies he had told closed about him, had been pulling the muscles of his body tighter and tighter. Until now, he could not remember a time when he had not been dreading something. Even when he was a little boy, it was always there — behind him, or before, or on either side. There had always been the shadowed corner, the dark place into which he dared not look, but from which something seemed always to be watching him — and Paul had done things that were not pretty to watch, he knew.

45   But now he had a curious sense of relief, as though he had at last thrown down the gauntlet to the thing in the corner.

Yet it was but a day since he had been sulking in the traces; but yesterday afternoon that he had been sent to the bank with Denny and Carson's deposit, as usual — but this time he was instructed to leave the book to be balanced. There was above two thousand dollars in checks, and nearly a thousand in the banknotes which he had taken from the book and quietly transferred to his pocket. At the bank he had made out a new deposit slip. His nerves had been steady enough to permit of his returning to the office, where he had finished his work and asked for a full day's holiday tomorrow, Saturday, giving a perfectly reasonable pretext. The bank book, he knew, would not be returned before Monday or Tuesday, and his father would be out of town for the next week. From the time he slipped the banknotes into his pocket until he boarded the night train for New York, he had not known a moment's hesitation.

How astonishingly easy it had all been; here he was, the thing done; and this time there would be no awakening, no figure at the top of the stairs. He watched the snowflakes whirling by his window until he fell asleep.

When he awoke, it was four o'clock in the afternoon. He bounded up with a start; one of his precious days gone already! He spent nearly an hour in dressing, watching every stage of his toilet carefully in the mirror. Everything was quite perfect; he was exactly the kind of boy he had always wanted to be.

When he went downstairs, Paul took a carriage and drove up Fifth Avenue toward the Park. The snow had somewhat abated; carriages and tradesmen's wagons were hurrying soundlessly to and fro in the winter twilight; boys in woolen mufflers were shoveling off the doorsteps; the Avenue stages made fine spots of color against the white street. Here and there on the corners whole flower gardens blooming behind glass windows, against which the snowflakes stuck and melted; violets, roses, carnations, lilies-of-the-valley — somehow vastly more lovely and alluring that they blossomed thus unnaturally in the snow. The Park itself was a wonderful stage winter-piece.

When he returned, the pause of the twilight had ceased, and the tune of the streets had changed. The snow was falling faster, lights streamed from the hotels that reared their many stories fearlessly up into the storm, defying the raging Atlantic winds. A long, black stream of carriages poured down the Avenue, intersected here and there by other streams, tending horizontally. There were a score of cabs about the entrance of his hotel, and his driver had to wait. Boys in livery were running in and out of the awning stretched across the sidewalk, up and down the red velvet carpet laid from the door to the street. Above, about, within it all, was the rumble and roar, the hurry and toss of thousands of human beings as hot for pleasure as himself, and on every side of him towered the glaring affirmation of the omnipotence of wealth.

The boy set his teeth and drew his shoulders together in a spasm of realization; the plot of all dramas, the text of all romances, the nerve-stuff of all sensations was whirling about him like the snowflakes. He burnt like a fagot in a tempest.

When Paul came down to dinner, the music of the orchestra floated up the elevator shaft to greet him. As he stepped into the thronged corridor, he sank back into one of the chairs against the wall to get his breath. The lights, the chatter, the perfumes, the bewildering medley of color — he had, for a moment, the feeling of not being able to stand it. But only for a moment; these were his own people, he told himself. He went slowly about the corridors, through the writing-rooms, smoking-rooms, reception-rooms, as though he were exploring the chambers of an enchanted palace, built and peopled for him alone.

When he reached the dining-room he sat down at a table near a window. The flowers, the white linen, the many-colored wine-glasses, the gay toilettes of the women, the low popping of corks, the undulating repetitions of the "Blue Danube" from the orchestra, all flooded Paul's dream with bewildering radiance. When the roseate tinge of his champagne was added — that cold, precious, bubbling stuff that creamed and foamed in his glass — Paul wondered that there were honest men in the world at all. This was what all the world was fighting for, he reflected; this was what all the struggle was about. He doubted the reality of his past. Had he ever known a place called Cordelia Street, a place where fagged-looking business men boarded the early car? Mere rivets in a machine they seemed to Paul — sickening men, with combings of children's hair always hanging to their coats, and the smell of cooking in their clothes. Cordelia Street — Ah, that belonged to another time and country! Had he not always been thus, had he not sat here night after night, from as far back as he could remember, looking pensively over just such shimmering textures, and slowly twirling the stem of a glass like this one between his thumb and middle finger? He rather thought he had.

He was not in the least abashed or lonely. He had no especial desire to meet or to know any of these people; all he demanded was the right to look on and conjecture, to watch the pageant. The mere stage properties were all he contended for. Nor was he lonely later in the evening, in his loge at the Opera. He was entirely rid of his nervous misgivings, of his forced aggressiveness, of the imperative desire to show himself different from his surroundings. He felt now that his surroundings explained him. Nobody questioned the purple; he had only to wear it passively. He had only to glance down at his dress coat to reassure himself that here it would be impossible for anyone to humiliate him.

55 He found it hard to leave his beautiful sitting-room to go to bed that night, and sat long watching the raging storm from his turret window. When he went to sleep, it was with the lights turned on in his bedroom; partly because of his old timidity, and partly so that, if he should wake in the night, there would be no wretched moment of doubt, no horrible suspicion of yellow wallpaper, or of Washington and Calvin above his bed.

On Sunday morning the city was practically snowbound. Paul breakfasted late, and in the afternoon he fell in with a wild San Francisco boy, a freshman at Yale, who said he had run down for a "little flyer" over Sunday. The young man offered to show Paul the night side of the town, and the two boys went off together after dinner, not returning to the hotel until seven o'clock the next morning. They had started out in the confiding warmth of a champagne friendship, but their parting in the elevator was singularly cool. The freshman pulled himself together to make his train, and Paul went to bed. He awoke at two o'clock in the afternoon, very thirsty and dizzy, and rang for ice-water, coffee, and the Pittsburgh papers.

On the part of the hotel management, Paul excited no suspicion. There was this to be said for him, that he wore his spoils with dignity and in no way made himself conspicuous. His chief greediness lay in his ears and eyes, and his excesses were not offensive ones. His dearest pleasures were the grey winter twilights in his sitting-room; his quiet enjoyment of his flowers, his clothes, his wide divan, his cigarette, and his sense of power. He could not remember a time when he had felt so at peace with himself. The mere release from the necessity of petty lying, lying every day and every day, restored his self-respect. He had never lied for pleasure, even at school; but to make himself noticed and admired, to assert his difference from other Cordelia Street boys; and he felt a good deal more manly, more honest, even, now that he had no need for boastful pretensions, now that he could, as his actor friends used to say, "dress the part." It was characteristic that remorse did not occur to him. His golden days went by without a shadow, and he made each as perfect as he could.

On the eighth day after his arrival in New York, he found the whole affair exploited in the Pittsburgh papers, exploited with a wealth of detail which indicated that local news of a sensational nature was at a low ebb. The firm of Denny and Carson announced that the boy's father had refunded the full amount of his theft, and that they had no intention of prosecuting. The

Cumberland minister had been interviewed, and expressed his hope of yet reclaiming the motherless lad, and Paul's Sabbath-School teacher declared that she would spare no effort to that end. The rumor had reached Pittsburgh that the boy had been seen in a New York hotel, and his father had gone East to find him and bring him home.

Paul had just come in to dress for dinner; he sank into the chair, weak in the knees, and clasped his head in his hands. It was to be worse than jail, even; the tepid waters of Cordelia Street were to close over him finally and forever. The grey monotony stretched before him in hopeless, unrelieved years; — Sabbath School, Young People's Meeting, the yellow-papered room, the damp dish-towels; it all rushed back upon him with sickening vividness. He had the old feeling that the orchestra had suddenly stopped, the sinking sensation that the play was over. The sweat broke out on his face, and he sprang to his feet, looked about him with his white, conscious smile, and winked at himself in the mirror. With something of the childish belief in miracles with which he had so often gone to class, all his lessons unlearned, Paul dressed and dashed whistling down the corridor to the elevator.

He had no sooner entered the dining-room and caught the measure of the music than his remembrance was lightened by his old elastic power of claiming the moment, mounting with it, and finding it all-sufficient. The glare and glitter about him, the mere scenic accessories had again, and for the last time, their old potency. He would show himself that he was game, he would finish the thing splendidly. He doubted, more than ever, the existence of Cordelia Street, and for the first time he drank his wine recklessly. Was he not, after all, one of these fortunate beings? Was he not still himself, and in his own place? He drummed a nervous accompaniment to the music and looked about him, telling himself over and over that it had paid. 60

He reflected drowsily, to the swell of the violin and the chill sweetness of his wine, that he might have done it more wisely. He might have caught an outbound steamer and been well out of their clutches before now. But the other side of the world had seemed too far away and too uncertain then; he could not have waited for it; his need had been too sharp. If he had to choose over again, he would do the same thing tomorrow. He looked affectionately about the dining-room, now gilded with a soft mist. Ah, it had paid indeed!

Paul was awakened next morning by a painful throbbing in his head and feet. He had thrown himself across the bed without undressing, and had slept with his shoes on. His limbs and hands were lead-heavy, and his tongue and throat were parched. There came upon him one of those fateful attacks of clear-headedness that never occurred except when he was physically exhausted and his nerves hung loose. He lay still and closed his eyes and let the tide of realities wash over him.

His father was in New York; "stopping at some joint or other," he told himself. The memory of successive summers on the front stoop fell upon him like a weight of black water. He had not a hundred dollars left; and he knew now, more than ever, that money was everything, the wall that stood between all he loathed and all he wanted. The thing was winding itself up; he had thought of that on his first glorious day in New York, and had even provided a way to snap the thread. It lay on his dressing-table now; he had got it out last night when he came blindly up from dinner — but the shiny metal hurt his eyes, and he disliked the look of it, anyway.

He rose and moved about with a painful effort, succumbing now and again to attacks of nausea. It was the old depression exaggerated; all the world had become Cordelia Street. Yet somehow he was not afraid of anything, was absolutely calm; perhaps because he had looked into the dark corner at last, and knew. It was bad enough, what he saw there; but somehow not so bad as his long fear of it had been. He saw everything clearly now. He had a feeling that he had made the best of it, that he had lived the sort of life he was meant to live, and for half an hour he sat staring at the revolver. But he told himself that was not the way, so he went downstairs and took a cab to the ferry.

65   When Paul arrived at Newark, he got off the train and took another cab, directing the driver to follow the Pennsylvania tracks out of town. The snow lay heavy on the roadways and had drifted deep in the open fields. Only here and there the dead grass or dried weed stalks projected, singularly black, above it.

Once well into the country, Paul dismissed the carriage and walked, floundering along the tracks, his mind a medley of irrelevant things. He seemed to hold in his brain an actual picture of everything he had seen that morning. He remembered every feature of both his drivers, the toothless old woman from whom he had bought the red flowers in his coat, the agent from whom he had got his ticket, and all of his fellow-passengers on the ferry. His mind, unable to cope with vital matters near at hand, worked feverishly and deftly at sorting and grouping these images. They made for him a part of the ugliness of the world, of the ache in his head, and the bitter burning on his tongue. He stooped and put a handful of snow into his mouth as he walked, but that, too, seemed hot. When he reached a little hillside, where the tracks ran through a cut some twenty feet below him, he stopped and sat down.

The carnations in his coat were drooping with cold, he noticed; all their red glory over. It occurred to him that all the flowers he had seen in the show windows that first night must have gone the same way, long before this. It was only one splendid breath they had, in spite of their brave mockery at the winter outside the glass. It was a losing game in the end, it seemed, this revolt against the homilies by which the world is run. Paul took one of the blossoms carefully from his coat and scooped a little hole in the snow, where he covered it up. Then he dozed awhile, from his weak condition, seeming insensible to the cold.

The sound of an approaching train woke him and he started to his feet, remembering only his resolution, and afraid lest he should be too late. He stood watching the approaching locomotive, his teeth chattering, his lips drawn away from them in a frightened smile; once or twice he glanced nervously sidewise, as though he were being watched. When the right moment came, he jumped. As he fell, the folly of his haste occurred to him with merciless clearness, the vastness of what he had left undone. There flashed through his brain, clearer than ever before, the blue of Adriatic water, the yellow of Algerian sands.

He felt something strike his chest — his body being thrown swiftly through the air, on and on, immeasurably far and fast, while his limbs gently relaxed. Then, because the picture-making mechanism was crushed, the disturbing visions flashed into black, and Paul dropped back into the immense design of things.

QUESTIONS

1. Technically we should classify the author's point of view as omniscient, for she enters into the minds of characters at will. Nevertheless early in the story the focus changes rather abruptly. Locate the point where the change occurs. Through whose eyes do we see Paul prior to this point? Through whose eyes do we see him afterward? What is the purpose of this shift? Does it offer any clue to the purpose of the story?
2. What details of Paul's appearance and behavior, as his teachers see him, indicate that he is abnormal?
3. Explain Paul's behavior. Why does he lie? What does he hate? What does he want? Contrast the world of Cordelia Street with the worlds that Paul finds at Carnegie Hall, at the Schenley, at the stock theater, and in New York.
4. Is Paul artistic? Describe his reactions to music, to painting, to literature, and to the theater. What value does he find in the arts?
5. Is Paul a static or a developing character? If the latter, at what points does he change? Why?
6. What do Paul's clandestine trips to the stock theater, his trip to New York, and his suicide have in common?
7. Compare Paul and the college boy he meets in New York (paragraph 56). Are they two of a kind? If not, how do they differ?
8. What are the implications of the title? What does the last sentence of the story do to the reader's focus of vision?
9. Are there any clues to the causes of Paul's abnormality? How many? In what is the author chiefly interested?
10. In what two cities is the story set? Does this choice of setting have any symbolic value? Could the story have been set as validly in Cleveland and Detroit? In San Francisco and Los Angeles? In New Orleans and Birmingham?

Margaret Atwood
Rape Fantasies

The way they're going on about it in the magazines you'd think it was just invented, and not only that but it's something terrific, like a vaccine for cancer. They put it in capital letters on the front cover, and inside they have

RAPE FANTASIES   First published in 1977. Margaret Atwood was born in 1939 in Ottawa, and grew up there, in Sault Ste. Marie, and in Toronto, all in Ontario. She was educated at the University of Toronto, Radcliffe, and Harvard. She has published several novels, collections of short stories, and volumes of poetry.

these questionnaires like the ones they used to have about whether you were a good enough wife or an endomorph or an ectomorph, remember that? with the scoring upside down on page 73, and then these numbered do-it-yourself dealies, you know? RAPE, TEN THINGS TO DO ABOUT IT, like it was ten new hairdos or something. I mean, what's so new about it?

So at work they all have to talk about it because no matter what magazine you open, there it is, staring you right between the eyes, and they're beginning to have it on the television, too. Personally I'd prefer a June Allyson movie anytime but they don't make them any more and they don't even have them that much on the Late Show. For instance, day before yesterday, that would be Wednesday, thank god it's Friday as they say, we were sitting around in the women's lunch room — the *lunch* room, I mean you'd think you could get some peace and quiet in there — and Chrissy closes up the magazine she's been reading and says, "How about it, girls, do you have rape fantasies?"

The four of us were having our game of bridge the way we always do, and I had a bare twelve points counting the singleton with not that much of a bid in anything. So I said one club, hoping Sondra would remember about the one club convention, because the time before when I used that she thought I really meant clubs and she bid us up to three, and all I had was four little ones with nothing higher than a six, and we went down two and on top of that we were vulnerable. She is not the world's best bridge player. I mean, neither am I but there's a limit.

Darlene passed but the damage was done, Sondra's head went round like it was on ball bearings and she said, "*What* fantasies?"

"Rape fantasies," Chrissy said. She's a receptionist and she looks like one; she's pretty but cool as a cucumber, like she's been painted all over with nail polish, if you know what I mean. Varnished. "It says here all women have rape fantasies."

"For Chrissake, I'm eating an egg sandwich," I said, "and I bid one club and Darlene passed."

"You mean, like some guy jumping you in an alley or something," Sondra said. She was eating her lunch, we all eat our lunches during the game, and she bit into a piece of that celery she always brings and started to chew away on it with this thoughtful expression in her eyes and I knew we might as well pack it in as far as the game was concerned.

"Yeah, sort of like that," Chrissy said. She was blushing a little, you could see it even under her makeup.

"I don't think you should go out alone at night," Darlene said, "you put yourself in a position," and I may have been mistaken but she was looking at me. She's the oldest, she's forty-one though you wouldn't know it and neither does she, but I looked it up in the employees' file. I like to guess a person's age and then look it up to see if I'm right. I let myself have an extra pack of cigarettes if I am, though I'm trying to cut down. I figure it's harmless as long as you don't tell. I mean, not everyone has access to that file, it's more or less confidential. But it's all right if I tell you, I don't expect you'll ever meet her, though you never know, it's a small world. Anyway.

"For *heaven's* sake, it's only *Toronto*," Greta said. She worked in Detroit for three years and she never lets you forget it, it's like she thinks she's a war hero or something, we should all admire her just for the fact that she's still walking this earth, though she was really living in Windsor the whole time, she just worked in Detroit. Which for me doesn't really count. It's where you sleep, right?

"Well, do you?" Chrissy said. She was obviously trying to tell us about hers but she wasn't about to go first, she's cautious, that one.

"I certainly don't," Darlene said, and she wrinkled up her nose, like this, and I had to laugh. "I think it's disgusting." She's divorced, I read that in the file too, she never talks about it. It must've been years ago anyway. She got up and went over to the coffee machine and turned her back on us as though she wasn't going to have anything more to do with it.

"Well," Greta said. I could see it was going to be between her and Chrissy. They're both blondes, I don't mean that in a bitchy way but they do try to outdress each other. Greta would like to get out of Filing, she'd like to be a receptionist too so she could meet more people. You don't meet much of anyone in Filing except other people in Filing. Me, I don't mind it so much, I have outside interests.

"Well," Greta said, "I sometimes think about, you know my apartment? It's got this little balcony, I like to sit out there in the summer and I have a few plants out there. I never bother that much about locking the door to the balcony, it's one of those sliding glass ones, I'm on the eighteenth floor for heaven's sake, I've got a good view of the lake and the CN Tower and all. But I'm sitting around one night in my housecoat, watching TV with my shoes off, you know how you do, and I see this guy's feet, coming down past the window, and the next thing you know he's standing on the balcony, he's let himself down by a rope with a hook on the end of it from the floor above, that's the nineteenth, and before I can even get up off the chesterfield he's inside the apartment. He's all dressed in black with black gloves on" — I knew right away what show she got the black gloves off because I saw the same one — "and then he, well, you know."

"You know what?" Chrissy said, but Greta said, "And afterwards he tells me that he goes all over the outside of the apartment building like that, from one floor to another, with his rope and his hook . . . and then he goes out to the balcony and tosses his rope, and he climbs up it and disappears."

"Just like Tarzan," I said, but nobody laughed.

"Is that all?" Chrissy said. "Don't you ever think about, well, I think about being in the bathtub, with no clothes on . . ."

"So who takes a bath in their clothes?" I said, you have to admit it's stupid when you come to think of it, but she just went on, ". . . with lots of bubbles, what I use is Vitabath, it's more expensive but it's so relaxing, and my hair pinned up, and the door opens and this fellow's standing there. . . ."

"How'd he get in?" Greta said.

"Oh, I don't know, through a window or something. Well, I can't very well get out of the bathtub, the bathroom's too small and besides he's blocking the doorway, so I just *lie* there, and he starts to very slowly take his own clothes off, and then he gets into the bathtub with me."

"Don't you scream or anything?" said Darlene. She'd come back with her cup of coffee, she was getting really interested. "I'd scream like bloody murder."

"Who'd hear me?" Chrissy said. "Besides, all the articles say it's better not to resist, that way you don't get hurt."

"Anyway you might get bubbles up your nose," I said, "from the deep breathing," and I swear all four of them looked at me like I was in bad taste, like I'd insulted the Virgin Mary or something. I mean, I don't see what's wrong with a little joke now and then. Life's too short, right?

"Listen," I said, "those aren't *rape* fantasies. I mean, you aren't getting *raped*, it's just some guy you haven't met formally who happens to be more attractive than Derek Cummins" — he's the Assistant Manager, he wears elevator shoes or at any rate they have these thick soles and he has this funny way of talking, we call him Derek Duck — "and you have a good time. Rape is when they've got a knife or something and you don't want to."

"So what about you, Estelle," Chrissy said, she was miffed because I laughed at her fantasy, she thought I was putting her down. Sondra was miffed too, by this time she'd finished her celery and she wanted to tell about hers, but she hadn't got in fast enough.

"All right, let me tell you one," I said. "I'm walking down this dark street at night and this fellow comes up and grabs my arm. Now it so happens that I have a plastic lemon in my purse, you know how it always says you should carry a plastic lemon in your purse? I don't really do it, I tried it once but the darn thing leaked all over my checkbook, but in this fantasy I have one, and I say to him, 'You're intending to rape me, right?' and he nods, so I open my purse to get the plastic lemon, and I can't find it! My purse is full of all this junk, Kleenex and cigarettes and my change purse and my lipstick and my driver's license, you know the kind of stuff; so I ask him to hold out his hands, like this, and I pile all this junk into them and down at the bottom there's the plastic lemon, and I can't get the top off. So I hand it to him and he's very obliging, he twists the top off and hands it back to me, and I squirt him in the eye."

I hope you don't think that's too vicious. Come to think of it, it is a bit mean, especially when he was so polite and all.

"*That's* your rape fantasy?" Chrissy says. "I don't believe it."

"She's a card," Darlene says, she and I are the ones that've been here the longest and she never will forget the time I got drunk at the office party and insisted I was going to dance under the table instead of on top of it, I did a sort of Cossack number but then I hit my head on the bottom of the table — actually it was a desk — when I went to get up, and I knocked myself out cold. She's decided that's the mark of an original mind and she tells everyone new about it and I'm not sure that's fair. Though I did do it.

"I'm being totally honest," I say. I always am and they know it. There's ₃₀ no point in being anything else, is the way I look at it, and sooner or later the truth will get out so you might as well not waste the time, right? "You should hear the one about the Easy-Off Oven Cleaner."

But that was the end of the lunch hour, with one bridge game shot to hell, and the next day we spent most of the time arguing over whether to start a new game or play out the hands we had left over from the day before, so Sondra never did get a chance to tell about her rape fantasy.

It started me thinking though, about my own rape fantasies. Maybe I'm abnormal or something, I mean I have fantasies about handsome strangers coming in through the window too, like Mr. Clean, I wish one would, please god somebody without flat feet and big sweat marks on his shirt, and over five feet five, believe me being tall is a handicap though it's getting better, tall guys are starting to like someone whose nose reaches higher than their belly button. But if you're being totally honest you can't count those as rape fantasies. In a real rape fantasy, what you should feel is this anxiety, like when you think about your apartment building catching on fire and whether you should use the elevator or the stairs or maybe just stick your head under a wet towel, and you try to remember everything you've read about what to do but you can't decide.

For instance, I'm walking along this dark street at night and this short, ugly fellow comes up and grabs my arm, and not only is he ugly, you know, with a sort of puffy nothing face, like those fellows you have to talk to in the bank when your account's overdrawn — of course I don't mean they're all like that — but he's absolutely covered in pimples. So he gets me pinned against the wall, he's short but he's heavy, and he starts to undo himself and the zipper gets stuck. I mean, one of the most significant moments in a girl's life, it's almost like getting married or having a baby or something, and he sticks the zipper.

So I say, kind of disgusted, "Oh for Chrissake," and he starts to cry. He tells me he's never been able to get anything right in his entire life, and this is the last straw, he's going to go jump off a bridge.

"Look," I say, I feel so sorry for him, in my rape fantasies I always end up ₃₅ feeling sorry for the guy, I mean there has to be something *wrong* with them, if it was Clint Eastwood it'd be different but worse luck it never is. I was the kind of little girl who buried dead robins, know what I mean? It used to drive my mother nuts, she didn't like me touching them, because of the germs I guess. So I say, "Listen, I know how you feel. You really should do something about those pimples, if you got rid of them you'd be quite good looking, honest; then you wouldn't have to go around doing stuff like this. I had them myself once," I say, to comfort him, but in fact I did, and it ends up I give him the name of my old dermatologist, the one I had in high school, that was back in Leamington, except I used to go to St. Catharines for the dermatologist. I'm telling you, I was really lonely when I first came here; I thought it was going to be such a big adventure and all, but it's a lot harder to meet people in a city. But I guess it's different for a guy.

Or I'm lying in bed with this terrible cold, my face is all swollen up, my eyes are red and my nose is dripping like a leaky tap, and this fellow comes in through the window and *he* has a terrible cold too, it's a new kind of flu that's been going around. So he says, "I'b goig do rabe you" — I hope you don't mind me holding my nose like this but that's the way I imagine it — and he lets out this terrific sneeze, which slows him down a bit, also I'm no object of beauty myself, you'd have to be some kind of pervert to want to rape someone with a cold like mine, it'd be like raping a bottle of LePage's mucilage the way my nose is running. He's looking wildly around the room, and I realize it's because he doesn't have a piece of Kleenex! "Id's ride here," I say, and I pass him the Kleenex, god knows why he even bothered to get out of bed, you'd think if you were going to go around climbing in windows you'd wait till you were healthier, right? I mean, that takes a certain amount of energy. So I ask him why doesn't he let me fix him a Neo-Citran and scotch, that's what I always take, you still have the cold but you don't feel it, so I do and we end up watching the Late Show together. I mean, they aren't all sex maniacs, the rest of the time they must lead a normal life. I figure they enjoy watching the Late Show just like anybody else.

I do have a scarier one though . . . where the fellow says he's hearing angel voices that're telling him he's got to kill me, you know, you read about things like that all the time in the papers. In this one I'm not in the apartment where I live now, I'm back in my mother's house in Leamington and the fellow's been hiding in the cellar, he grabs my arm when I go downstairs to get a jar of jam and he's got hold of the axe too, out of the garage, that one is really scary. I mean, what do you say to a nut like that?

So I start to shake but after a minute I get control of myself and I say, is he sure the angel voices have got the right person, because I hear the same angel voices and they've been telling me for some time that I'm going to give birth to the reincarnation of St. Anne who in turn has the Virgin Mary and right after that comes Jesus Christ and the end of the world, and he wouldn't want to interfere with that, would he? So he gets confused and listens some more, and then he asks for a sign and I show him my vaccination mark, you can see it's sort of an odd-shaped one, it got infected because I scratched the top off, and that does it, he apologizes and climbs out the coal chute again, which is how he got in in the first place, and I say to myself there's some advantage in having been brought up a Catholic even though I haven't been to church since they changed the service into English, it just isn't the same, you might as well be a Protestant. I must write to Mother and tell her to nail up that coal chute, it always has bothered me. Funny, I couldn't tell you at all what this man looks like but I know exactly what kind of shoes he's wearing, because that's the last I see of him, his shoes going up the coal chute, and they're the old-fashioned kind that lace up the ankles, even though he's a young fellow. That's strange, isn't it?

Let me tell you though I really sweat until I see him safely out of there and I go upstairs right away and make myself a cup of tea. I don't think about that one much. My mother always said you shouldn't dwell on unpleasant things and I generally agree with that, I mean, dwelling on them doesn't make them go away. Though not dwelling on them doesn't make them go away either, when you come to think of it.

Sometimes I have these short ones where the fellow grabs my arm but 40
I'm really a Kung-Fu expert, can you believe it, in real life I'm sure it would just be a conk on the head and that's that, like getting your tonsils out, you'd wake up and it would be all over except for the sore places, and you'd be lucky if your neck wasn't broken or something, I could never even hit the volleyball in gym and a volleyball is fairly large, you know? — and I just go *zap* with my fingers into his eyes and that's it, he falls over, or I flip him against a wall or something. But I could never really stick my fingers in anyone's eyes, could you? It would feel like hot jello and I don't even like cold jello, just thinking about it gives me the creeps. I feel a bit guilty about that one, I mean how would you like walking around knowing someone's been blinded for life because of you?

But maybe it's different for a guy.

The most touching one I have is when the fellow grabs my arm and I say, sad and kind of dignified, "You'd be raping a corpse." That pulls him up short and I explain that I've just found out I have leukemia and the doctors have only given me a few months to live. That's why I'm out pacing the streets alone at night, I need to think, you know, come to terms with myself. I don't really have leukemia but in the fantasy I do, I guess I chose that particular disease because a girl in my grade four class died of it, the whole class sent her flowers when she was in the hospital. I didn't understand then that she was going to die and I wanted to have leukemia too so I could get flowers. Kids are funny, aren't they? Well, it turns out that he has leukemia himself, and *he* only has a few months to live, that's why he's going around raping people, he's very bitter because he's so young and his life is being taken from him before he's really lived it. So we walk along gently under the street lights, it's spring and sort of misty, and we end up going for coffee, we're happy we've found the only other person in the world who can understand what we're going through, it's almost like fate, and after a while we just sort of look at each other and our hands touch, and he comes back with me and moves into my apartment and we spend our last months together before we die, we just sort of don't wake up in the morning, though I've never decided which one of us gets to die first. If it's him I have to go on and fantasize about the funeral, if it's me I don't have to worry about that, so it just about depends on how tired I am at the time. You may not believe this but sometimes I even start crying. I cry at the ends of movies, even the ones that aren't all that sad, so I guess it's the same thing. My mother's like that too.

The funny thing about these fantasies is that the man is always someone I don't know, and the statistics in the magazines, well, most of them anyway, they say it's often someone you do know, at least a little bit, like your boss or something — I mean, it wouldn't be *my* boss, he's over sixty and I'm sure he couldn't rape his way out of a paper bag, poor old thing, but it might be someone like Derek Duck, in his elevator shoes, perish the thought — or someone you just met, who invites you up for a drink, it's getting so you can hardly be sociable any more, and how are you supposed to meet people if you can't trust them even that basic amount? You can't spend your whole life in the Filing Department or cooped up in your own apartment with all the doors and windows locked and the shades down. I'm not what you would call a drinker but I like to go out now and then for a drink or two in a nice place, even if I am by myself, I'm with Women's Lib on that even though I can't agree with a lot of other things they say. Like here for instance, the waiters all know me and if anyone, you know, bothers me. . . . I don't know why I'm telling you all this, except I think it helps you get to know a person, especially at first, hearing some of the things they think about. At work they call me the office worry wart, but it isn't so much like worrying, it's more like figuring out what you should do in an emergency, like I said before.

Anyway, another thing about it is that there's a lot of conversation, in fact I spend most of my time, in the fantasy that is, wondering what I'm going to say and what he's going to say, I think it would be better if you could get a conversation going. Like, how could a fellow do that to a person he's just had a long conversation with, once you let them know you're human, you have a life too, I don't see how they could go ahead with it, right? I mean, I know it happens but I just don't understand it, that's the part I really don't understand.

QUESTIONS

1. Characterize Estelle, the narrator. Include as much information as you can about her age, education, background, physical characteristics, attitudes, social and professional life. How does the point of view of this story both hinder and aid you in drawing up your characterization?
2. Characterize the other women who work with Estelle. What qualities in her own personality does Estelle reveal in her way of describing them?
3. To whom is Estelle speaking? Where, and on what occasion? How long has Estelle been acquainted with the person she is addressing? What can you infer about Estelle's reasons for talking about this subject?
4. What do the "rape fantasies" of Greta and Chrissy have in common? Why does Estelle object to her co-workers' fantasies?
5. What are the common characteristics of Estelle's own "rape fantasies"? How, taken together, do they reveal her personality?
6. What is "rape"? What are "fantasies"? Is this story concerned with rape?

Ernest Hemingway
Hills Like White Elephants

The hills across the valley of the Ebro were long and white. On this side there was no shade and no trees and the station was between two lines of rails in the sun. Close against the side of the station there was the warm shadow of the building and a curtain, made of strings of bamboo beads, hung across the open door into the bar, to keep out flies. The American and the girl with him sat at a table in the shade, outside the building. It was very hot and the express from Barcelona would come in forty minutes. It stopped at this junction for two minutes and went on to Madrid.

"What should we drink?" the girl asked. She had taken off her hat and put it on the table.

"It's pretty hot," the man said.

"Let's drink beer."

"Dos cervezas," the man said into the curtain. 5

"Big ones?" a woman asked from the doorway.

"Yes. Two big ones."

The woman brought two glasses of beer and two felt pads. She put the felt pads and the beer glasses on the table and looked at the man and the girl. The girl was looking off at the line of hills. They were white in the sun and the country was brown and dry.

"They look like white elephants," she said.

"I've never seen one," the man drank his beer. 10

"No, you wouldn't have."

"I might have," the man said. "Just because you say I wouldn't have doesn't prove anything."

The girl looked at the bead curtain. "They've painted something on it," she said. "What does it say?"

"Anis del Toro. It's a drink."

"Could we try it?" 15

The man called "Listen" through the curtain. The woman came out from the bar.

"Four reales."

"We want two Anis del Toro."

"With water?"

"Do you want it with water?" 20

"I don't know," the girl said. "Is it good with water?"

"It's all right."

HILLS LIKE WHITE ELEPHANTS   First published in 1927. Ernest Hemingway (1899–1961) was born and grew up in Oak Park, Illinois, with summer vacations in northern Michigan. By the time he wrote this story he had been wounded in Italy during World War I; had traveled extensively in Europe as a newspaper correspondent and writer; had married, fathered a son, been divorced, and remarried.

"You want them with water?" asked the woman.

"Yes, with water."

25 "It tastes like licorice," the girl said and put the glass down.

"That's the way with everything."

"Yes," said the girl. "Everything tastes of licorice. Especially all the things you've waited so long for, like absinthe."

"Oh, cut it out."

"You started it," the girl said. "I was being amused. I was having a fine time."

30 "Well, let's try to have a fine time."

"All right. I was trying. I said the mountains looked like white elephants. Wasn't that bright?"

"That was bright."

"I wanted to try this new drink. That's all we do, isn't it — look at things and try new drinks."

"I guess so."

35 The girl looked across at the hills.

"They're lovely hills," she said. "They don't really look like white elephants. I just meant the coloring of their skin through the trees."

"Should we have another drink?"

"All right."

The warm wind blew the bead curtain against the table.

40 "The beer's nice and cool," the man said.

"It's lovely," the girl said.

"It's really an awfully simple operation, Jig," the man said. "It's not really an operation at all."

The girl looked at the ground the table legs rested on.

"I know you wouldn't mind it, Jig. It's really not anything. It's just to let the air in."

45 The girl did not say anything.

"I'll go with you and I'll stay with you all the time. They just let the air in and then it's all perfectly natural."

"Then what will we do afterward?"

"We'll be fine afterward. Just like we were before."

"What makes you think so?"

50 "That's the only thing that bothers us. It's the only thing that's made us unhappy."

The girl looked at the bead curtain, put her hand out and took hold of two of the strings of beads.

"And you think then we'll be all right and be happy."

"I know we will. You don't have to be afraid. I've known lots of people that have done it."

"So have I," said the girl. "And afterward they were all so happy."

55 "Well," the man said, "if you don't want to you don't have to. I wouldn't have you do it if you didn't want to. But I know it's perfectly simple."

"And you really want to?"

"I think it's the best thing to do. But I don't want you to do it if you don't really want to."

"And if I do it you'll be happy and things will be like they were and you'll love me?"

"I love you now. You know I love you."

"I know. But if I do it, then it will be nice again if I say things are like white elephants, and you'll like it?"

"I'll love it. I love it now but I just can't think about it. You know how I get when I worry."

"If I do it you won't ever worry."

"I won't worry about that because it's perfectly simple."

"Then I'll do it. Because I don't care about me."

"What do you mean?"

"I don't care about me."

"Well, I care about you."

"Oh, yes. But I don't care about me. And I'll do it and then everything will be fine."

"I don't want you to do it if you feel that way."

The girl stood up and walked to the end of the station. Across, on the other side, were fields of grain and trees along the banks of the Ebro. Far away, beyond the river, were mountains. The shadow of a cloud moved across the field of grain and she saw the river through the trees.

"And we could have all this," she said. "And we could have everything and every day we make it more impossible."

"What did you say?"

"I said we could have everything."

"We can have everything."

"No, we can't."

"We can have the whole world."

"No, we can't."

"We can go everywhere."

"No, we can't. It isn't ours any more."

"It's ours."

"No, it isn't. And once they take it away, you never get it back."

"But they haven't taken it away."

"We'll wait and see."

"Come on back in the shade," he said. "You mustn't feel that way."

"I don't feel any way," the girl said. "I just know things."

"I don't want you to do anything that you don't want to do — "

"Nor that isn't good for me," she said. "I know. Could we have another beer."

"All right. But you've got to realize — "

"I realize," the girl said. "Can't we stop talking?"

They sat down at the table and the girl looked across at the hills on the dry side of the valley and the man looked at her and at the table.

"You've got to realize," he said, "that I don't want you to do it if you don't want to. I'm perfectly willing to go through with it if it means anything to you."

"Doesn't it mean anything to you? We could get along."

"Of course it does. But I don't want anybody but you. I don't want any one else. And I know it's perfectly simple."

"Yes, you know it's perfectly simple."

"It's all right for you to say that, but I do know it."

"Would you do something for me now?"

"I'd do anything for you."

"Would you please please please please please please please stop talking?"

He did not say anything but looked at the bags against the wall of the station. There were labels on them from all the hotels where they had spent nights.

"But I don't want you to," he said. "I don't care anything about it."

"I'll scream," said the girl.

The woman came out through the curtains with two glasses of beer and put them down on the damp felt pads. "The train comes in five minutes," she said.

"What did she say?" asked the girl.

"That the train is coming in five minutes."

The girl smiled brightly at the woman, to thank her.

"I'd better take the bags over to the other side of the station," the man said. She smiled at him.

"All right. Then come back and we'll finish the beer."

He picked up the two heavy bags and carried them around the station to the other tracks. He looked up the tracks but could not see the train. Coming back, he walked through the barroom, where people waiting for the train were drinking. He drank an Anis at the bar and looked at the people. They were all waiting reasonably for the train. He went out through the bead curtain. She was sitting at the table and smiled at him.

"Do you feel better?" he asked.

"I feel fine," she said. "There's nothing wrong with me. I feel fine."

QUESTIONS

1. The main topic of discussion between the man and the girl is never named. What is the "awfully simple operation"? Why is it not named? What different attitudes are taken toward it by the man and the girl? Why?

2. What is indicated about the past life of the man and the girl? How? What has happened to the quality of their relationship? Why? How do we know? How accurate is the man's judgment about their future?

3. Though the story consists mostly of dialogue, and though it contains strong emotional conflict, it is entirely without adverbs indicating the tone of the remarks. How does Hemingway indicate tone? At what points are the characters insincere? Self-deceived? Ironic or sarcastic? To what extent do they give

open expression to their feelings? Does either want an open conflict? Why or why not? Trace the various phases of emotion in the girl.

4. How sincere is the man in his insistence that he would not have the girl undergo the operation if she does not want to and that he is "perfectly willing to go through with it" (what is "it"?) if it means anything to the girl? How many times does he repeat these ideas? What significance has the man's drinking an Anis by himself before rejoining the girl at the end of the story?

5. Much of the conversation seems to be about trivial things (ordering drinks, the weather, and so on). What purposes does this conversation serve? What relevance has the girl's remark about absinthe?

6. What is the point of the girl's comparison of the hills to white elephants? Does the remark assume any significance for the reader beyond its significance for the characters? Why does the author use it for his title?

7. What purpose does the setting serve — the hills across the valley, the treeless railroad tracks and station? What is contributed by the precise information about time at the end of the first paragraph?

8. Which of the two characters is more "reasonable"? Which "wins" the conflict between them? The point of view is objective. Does this mean that we cannot tell whether the sympathy of the author lies more with one character than with the other? Explain your answer.

Ernest J. Gaines
Just Like a Tree

> I shall not;
> I shall not be moved.
> I shall not;
> I shall not be moved.
> Just like a tree that's
> planted 'side the water.
> Oh, I shall not be moved.
>
> I made my home in glory;
> I shall not be moved.
> Made my home in glory;
> I shall not be moved.
> Just like a tree that's
> planted 'side the water.
> Oh, I shall not be moved.
> *(from an old Negro spiritual)*

JUST LIKE A TREE   First published in 1968. The quoted spiritual became an anthem of the civil rights movement. Ernest J. Gaines was born in 1933 in rural southern Louisiana, an area that remains central to his fiction, although he was educated at San Francisco State College and Stanford University.

Chuckkie

Pa hit him on the back and he jeck in them chains like he pulling, but ever'body in the wagon knew he ain't, and Pa hit him on the back again. He jeck again like he pulling, but even Big Red know he ain't doing a thing.

"That's why I'm go'n get a horse," Pa say. "He'll kill that other mule. Get up there, Mr. Bascom."

"Oh, let him alone," Gran'mon say. "How would you like it if you was pulling a wagon in all that mud?"

Pa don't answer Gran'mon; he just hit Mr. Bascom on the back again.

"That's right, kill him," Gran'mon say. "See where you get mo' money to buy another one."

"Get up there, Mr. Bascom," Pa say.

"You hear me talking to you, Emile?" Gran'mon say. "You want me hit you with something?"

"Ma, he ain't pulling," Pa say.

"Leave him alone," Gran'mon say.

Pa shake the lines little bit, but Mr. Bascom don't even feel it, and you can see he letting Big Red do all the pulling again. Pa say something kind o' low to hisself, and I can't make out what it is.

I low' my head little bit, 'cause that wind and fine rain was hitting me in the face, and I can feel Mama pressing close to me to keep me warm. She sitting on one side o' me and Pa sitting on the other side o' me, and Gran'mon in the back o' me in her setting chair. Pa didn't want bring the setting chair, telling Gran'mon there was two boards in that wagon already and she could sit on one of 'em all by herself if she wanted to, but Gran'mon say she was taking her setting chair with her if Pa liked it or not. She say she didn't ride in no wagon on nobody board, and if Pa liked it or not, that setting chair was going.

"Let her take her setting chair," Mama say. "What's wrong with taking her setting chair?"

"Ehhh, Lord," Pa say, and picked up the setting chair and took it out to the wagon. "I guess I'll have to bring it back in the house, too, when we come back from there."

Gran'mon went and clambed in the wagon and moved her setting chair back little bit and sat down and folded her arms, waiting for us to get in, too. I got in and knelt down 'side her and Pa so I could stay warm. Soon 's I sat down, Pa hit Mr. Bascom on the back, saying what a trifling thing Mr. Bascom was, and soon 's he got some mo' money he was getting rid o' Mr. Bascom and getting him a horse.

I raise my head to look see how far we is.

"That's it, yonder," I say.

"Stop pointing," Mama say, "and keep your hand in your pocket."

"Where?" Gran'mon say, back there in her setting chair.

"'Cross the ditch, yonder," I say.

"Can't see a thing for this rain," Gran'mon say.

"Can't hardly see it," I say. "But you can see the light little bit. That chinaball tree standing in the way."

"Poor soul," Gran'mon say. "Poor soul."

I know Gran'mon was go'n say "poor soul, poor soul," 'cause she had been saying "poor soul, poor soul," ever since she heard Aunt Fe was go'n leave from back there.

Emile

Darn cane crop to finish getting in and only a mule and a half to do it. If I had my way I'd take that shotgun and a load o' buckshots and — but what's the use.

"Get up, Mr. Bascom — please," I say to that little dried-up, long-eared, tobacco-color thing. "Please, come up. Do your share for God sake — if you don't mind. I know it's hard pulling in all that mud, but if you don't do your share, then Big Red'll have to do his and yours, too. So, please, if it ain't asking you too much to — "

"Oh, Emile, shut up," Leola say.

"I can't hit him," I say, "or Mama back there'll hit me. So I have to talk to him. Please, Mr. Bascom, if you don't mind it. For my sake. No, not for mine; for God sake. No, not even for His'n; for Big Red sake. A fellow mule just like yourself is. Please, come up."

"Now, you hear that boy blaspheming God right in front o' me there," Mama say. "Ehhh, Lord — just keep it up. All this bad weather there like this whole world coming apart — a clap o' thunder come there and knock the fool out you. Just keep it up."

Maybe she right, and I stop. I look at Mr. Bascom there doing nothing, and I just give up. That mule know long 's Mama's alive he go'n do just what he want to do. He know when Papa was dying he told Mama to look after him, and he know no matter what he do, no matter what he don't do, Mama ain't go'n never let me do him anything. Sometimes I even feel Mama care mo' for Mr. Bascom 'an she care for me her own son.

We come up to the gate and I pull back on the lines.

"Whoa up, Big Red," I say. "You don't have to stop, Mr. Bascom. You never started."

I can feel Mama looking at me back there in that setting chair, but she don't say nothing.

"Here," I say to Chuckkie.

He take the lines and I jump down on the ground to open the old beat-up gate. I see Etienne's horse in the yard, and I see Chris new red tractor 'side the house, shining in the rain. When Mama die, I say to myself, Mr. Bascom, you going. Ever'body getting tractors and horses and I'm still stuck with you. You going, brother.

"Can you make it through?" I ask Chuckkie. "That gate ain't too wide."
"I can do it," he say.
"Be sure to make Mr. Bascom pull," I say.
"Emile, you better get back up here and drive 'em through," Leola say. "Chuckkie might break up that wagon."
"No, let him stay down there and give orders," Mama say, back there in that setting chair.
"He can do it," I say. "Come on, Chuckkie boy."
"Come up here, mule," Chuckkie say.
And soon 's he say that, Big Red make a lunge for the yard, and Mr. Bascom don't even move, and 'fore I can bat my eyes I hear *pow-wow; sagg-sagg; pow-wow*. But above all that noise, Leola up there screaming her head off. And Mama — not a word; just sitting in that chair, looking at me with her arms still folded.
"Pull Big Red," I say. "Pull Big Red, Chuckkie."
Poor little Chuckkie up there pulling so hard till one of his little arms straight out in back; and Big Red throwing his shoulders and ever'thing else in it, and Mr. Bascom just walking there just 's loose and free, like he's suppose to be there just for his good looks. I move out the way just in time to let the wagon go by me, pulling half o' the fence in the yard behind it. I glance up again, and there's Leola still hollering and trying to jump out, but Mama not saying a word — just sitting there in that setting chair with her arms still folded.
"Whoa," I hear little Chuckkie saying. "Whoa up, now."
Somebody open the door and a bunch o' people come out on the gallery.
"What the world — ?" Etienne say. "Thought the whole place was coming to pieces there."
"Chuckkie had a little trouble coming in the yard," I say.
"Goodness," Etienne say. "Anybody hurt?"
Mama just sit there about ten seconds, then she say something to herself and start clambing out the wagon.
"Let me help you there, Aunt Lou," Etienne say, coming down the steps.
"I can make it," Mama say. When she get on the ground she look up at Chuckkie. "Hand me my chair there, boy."
Poor little Chuckkie, up there with the lines in one hand, get the chair and hold it to the side, and Etienne catch it just 'fore it hit the ground. Mama start looking at me again, and it look like for at least a' hour she stand there looking at nobody but me. Then she say, "Ehhh, Lord," like that again, and go inside with Leola and the rest o' the people.
I look back at half o' the fence laying there in the yard, and I jump back on the wagon and guide the mules to the side o' the house. After unhitching 'em and tying 'em to the wheels, I look at Chris pretty red tractor again, and me and Chuckkie go inside: I make sure he kick all that mud off his shoes 'fore he go in the house.

Leola

Sitting over there by that fireplace, trying to look joyful when ever'body there know she ain't. But she trying, you know; smiling and bowing when people say something to her. How can she be joyful, I ask you; how can she be? Poor thing, she been here all her life — or the most of it, let's say. 'Fore they moved in this house, they lived in one back in the woods 'bout a mile from here. But for the past twenty-five or thirty years, she been right in this one house. I know ever since I been big enough to know people I been seeing her right here.

Aunt Fe, Aunt Fe, Aunt Fe, Aunt Fe; the name's been 'mongst us just like us own family name. Just like the name o' God. Like the name of town — the city. Aunt Fe, Aunt Fe, Aunt Fe, Aunt Fe.

Poor old thing; how many times I done come here and washed clothes for her when she couldn't do it herself. How many times I done hoed in that garden, ironed her clothes, wrung a chicken neck for her. You count the days in the year and you'll be pretty close. And I didn't mind it a bit. No, I didn't mind it a bit. She there trying to pay me. Proud — Lord, talking 'bout pride. "Here." "No, Aunt Fe; no." "Here, here; you got a child there, you can use it." "No, Aunt Fe. No. No. What would Mama think if she knowed I took money from you? Aunt Fe, Mama would never forgive me. No. I love doing these thing for you. I just wish I could do more."

And there, now, trying to make 'tend she don't mind leaving. Ehhh, Lord.

I hear a bunch o' rattling round in the kitchen and I go back there. I see Louise stirring this big pot o' eggnog.

"Louise," I say.

"Leola," she say.

We look at each other and she stir the eggnog again. She know what I'm go'n say next, and she can't even look in my face.

"Louise, I wish there was some other way."

"There's no other way," she say.

"Louise, moving her from here's like moving a tree you been used to in your front yard all your life."

"What else can I do?"

"Oh, Louise, Louise."

"Nothing else but that."

"Louise, what people go'n do without her here?"

She stir the eggnog and don't answer.

"Louise, us'll take her in with us."

"You all no kin to Auntie. She go with me."

"And us'll never see her again."

She stir the eggnog. Her husband come back in the kitchen and kiss her on the back o' the neck and then look at me and grin. Right from the start I can see I ain't go'n like that nigger.

"Almost ready, honey?" he say.

"Almost."

He go to the safe and get one o' them bottles of whiskey he got in there and come back to the stove.

"No," Louise say. "Everybody don't like whiskey in it. Add the whiskey after you've poured it up."

"Okay, hon."

He kiss her on the back o' the neck again. Still don't like that nigger. Something 'bout him ain't right.

"You one o' the family?" he say.

"Same as one," I say. "And you?"

He don't like the way I say it, and I don't care if he like it or not. He look at me there a second, and then he kiss her on the ear.

"Un-unnn," she say, stirring the pot.

"I love your ear, baby," he say.

"Go in the front room and talk with the people," she say.

He kiss her on the other ear. A nigger do all that front o' public got something to hide. He leave the kitchen. I look at Louise.

"Ain't nothing else I can do," she say.

"You sure, Louise? You positive?"

"I'm positive," she say.

The front door open and Emile and Chuckkie come in. A minute later Washington and Adrieu come in, too. Adrieu come back in the kitchen, and I can see she been crying. Aunt Fe is her godmother, you know.

"How you feel, Adrieu?"

"That weather out there," she say.

"Y'all walked?"

"Yes."

"Us here in the wagon. Y'all can go back with us."

"Y'all the one tore the fence down?" she ask.

"Yes, I guess so. That brother-in-law o' yours in there letting Chuckkie drive that wagon."

"Well, I don't guess it'll matter too much. Nobody go'n be here, anyhow."

And she start crying again. I take her in my arms and pat her on the shoulder, and I look at Louise stirring the eggnog.

"What I'm go'n do and my nan-nane gone? I love her so much."

"Ever'body love her."

"Since my mama died, she been like my mama."

"Shhh," I say. "Don't let her hear you. Make her grieve. You don't want her grieving, now, do you?"

She sniffs there 'gainst my dress few times.

"Oh, Lord," she say. "Lord, have mercy."

"Shhh," I say. "Shhh. That's what life's 'bout."

"That ain't what life's 'bout," she say. "It ain't fair. This been her home all her life. These the people she know. She don't know them people she going to. It ain't fair."

"Shhh, Adrieu," I say. "Now, you saying things that ain't your business."

She cry there some mo'. 110

"Oh, Lord, Lord," she say.

Louise turn from the stove.

"About ready now," she say, going to the middle door. "James, tell everybody to come back and get some."

James

Let me go on back here and show these country niggers how to have a good time. All they know is talk, talk, talk. Talk so much they make me buggy round here. Damn this weather — wind, rain. Must be a million cracks in this old house.

I go to that old beat-up safe in that corner and get that fifth of Mr. Harper 115 (in the South now; got to say Mister), give the seal one swipe, the stopper one jerk, and head back to that old wood stove. (Man, like, these cats are primitive — goodness. You know what I mean? I mean like wood stoves. Don't mention TV, man, these cats here never heard of that.) I start to dump Mr. Harper in the pot and Baby catches my hand again and say not all of them like it. You ever heard of anything like that? I mean a stud's going to drink eggnog, and he's not going to put whiskey in it. I mean he's going to drink it straight. I mean, you ever heard anything like that? Well, I wasn't pressing none of them on Mr. Harper. I mean, me and Mr. Harper get along too well together for me to go around there pressing.

I hold my cup there and let Baby put a few drops of this egg stuff in it; then I jerk my cup back and let Mr. Harper run a while. Couple of these cats come over (some of them aren't so lame) and set their cups, and I let Mr. Harper run for them. Then this cat says he's got 'nough. I let Mr. Harper run for this other stud, and pretty soon he says, "Hold it. Good." Country cat, you know. "Hold it. Good." Real country cat. So I raise the cup to see what Mr. Harper's doing. He's just right. I raise the cup again. Just right, Mr. Harper; just right.

I go to the door with Mr. Harper under my arm and the cup in my hand and I look into the front room where they all are. I mean, there's about ninety-nine of them in there. Old ones, young ones, little ones, big ones, yellow ones, black ones, brown ones — you name them, brother, and they were there. And what for? Brother, I'll tell you what for. Just because me and Baby are taking this old chick out of these sticks. Well, I'll tell you where I'd be at this moment if I was one of them. With that weather out there like it is, I'd be under about five blankets with some little warm belly pressing against mine. Brother, you can bet your hat I wouldn't be here. Man, listen to that thing out there. You can hear that rain beating on that old house like grains of rice; and that wind coming through them cracks like it does in those old Charlie Chaplin movies. Man, like you know — like *whooo-ee; whooo-ee.* Man, you talking about some weird cats.

I can feel Mr. Harper starting to massage my wig and I bat my eyes twice and look at the old girl over there. She's still sitting in that funny-looking little old rocking chair, and not saying a word to anybody. Just sitting there looking into the fireplace at them two pieces of wood that aren't giving out enough heat to warm a baby, let alone ninety-nine grown people. I mean, you know, like that sleet's falling out there like all get-up-and-go, and them two pieces of wood are lying there just as dead as the rest of these way-out cats.

One of the old cats — I don't know which one he is — Mose, Sam, or something like that — leans over and pokes in the fire a minute; then a little blaze shoots up, and he raises up, too, looking as satisfied as if he'd just sent a rocket into orbit. I mean, these cats are like that. They do these little bitty things, and they feel like they've really done something. Well, back in these sticks, I guess there just isn't nothing big to do.

I feel Mr. Harper touching my skull now — and I notice this little chick passing by me with these two cups of eggnog. She goes over to the fireplace and gives one to each of these old chicks. The one sitting in that setting chair she brought with her from God knows where, and the other cup to the old chick that Baby and I are going to haul from here sometime tomorrow morning. Wait, man, I mean like, you ever heard of anybody going to somebody else's house with a chair? I mean, wouldn't you call that an insult at the basest point? I mean, now, like tell me what you think of that? I mean — dig — here I am at my pad, and in you come with your own stool. I mean, now, like man, you know. I mean that's an insult at the basest point. I mean, you know . . . you know, like way out. . . .

Mr. Harper, what you trying to do, boy? — I mean, *sir.* (Got to watch myself, I'm in the South. Got to keep watching myself.)

This stud touches me on the shoulder and raise his cup and say, "How 'bout a taste?" I know what the stud's talking about, so I let Mr. Harper run for him. But soon 's I let a drop get in, the stud say, "'Nough." I mean I let about two drops get in, and already the stud's got enough. Man, I mean, like you know. I mean these studs are 'way out. I mean like 'way back there.

This stud takes a swig of his eggnog and say, "Ahhh." I mean this real down-home way of saying "Ahhhh." I mean, man, like these studs — I notice this little chick passing by me again, and this time she's crying. I mean weeping, you know. And just because this old ninety-nine-year-old chick's packing up and leaving. I mean, you ever heard of anything like that? I mean, here she is pretty as the day is long and crying because Baby and I are hauling this old chick away. Well, I'd like to make her cry. And I can assure you, brother, it wouldn't be from leaving her.

I turn and look at Baby over there by the stove, pouring eggnog in all these cups. I mean, there're about twenty of these cats lined up there. And I bet you not half of them will take Mr. Harper along. Some way-out cats, man. Some way-out cats.

I go up to Baby and kiss her on the back of the neck and give her a little pat where she likes for me to pat her when we're in the bed. She say, "Uh-uh," but I know she likes it anyhow.

Ben O

I back under the bed and touch the slop jar, and I pull back my leg and back somewhere else, and then I get me a good sight on it. I spin my aggie couple times and sight again and then I shoot. I hit it right square in the middle and it go flying over the fireplace. I crawl over there to get it and I see 'em all over there drinking they eggnog and they didn't even offer me and Chuckkie none. I find my marble on the bricks, and I go back and tell Chuckkie they over there drinking eggnog.

"You want some?" I say.

"I want shoot marble," Chuckkie say. "Yo' shot. Shoot up."

"I want some eggnog," I say.

"Shoot up, Ben O," he say. "I'm getting cold staying in one place so long. You feel that draft?"

"Coming from that crack under that bed," I say.

"Where?" Chuckkie say, looking for the crack.

"Over by that bedpost over there," I say.

"This sure's a beat-up old house," Chuckkie say.

"I want me some eggnog," I say.

"Well, you ain't getting none," Gran'mon say, from the fireplace. "It ain't good for you."

"I can drink eggnog," I say. "How come it ain't good for me? It ain't nothing but eggs and milk. I eat chicken, don't I? I eat beef, don't I?"

Gran'mon don't say nothing.

"I want me some eggnog," I say.

Gran'mon still don't say no more. Nobody else don't say nothing, neither.

"I want me some eggnog," I say.

"You go'n get a eggnog," Gran'mon say. "Just keep that noise up."

"I want me some eggnog," I say; "and I 'tend to get me some eggnog tonight."

Next thing I know, Gran'mon done picked up a chip out o' that corner and done sailed it back there where me and Chuckkie is. I duck just in time, and the chip catch old Chuckkie side the head.

"Hey, who that hitting me?" Chuckkie say.

"Move, and you won't get hit," Gran'mon say.

I laugh at old Chuckkie over there holding his head, and next thing I know here's Chuckkie done haul back there and hit me in my side. I jump up from there and give him two just to show him how it feel, and he jump up and hit me again. Then we grab each other and start tussling on the floor.

"You, Ben O," I hear Gran'mon saying. "You, Ben O, cut that out. Y'all cut that out."

But we don't stop, 'cause neither one o' us want be first. Then I feel somebody pulling us apart.

150 "What I ought to do is whip both o' you," Mrs. Leola say. "Is that what y'all want?"

"No'm," I say.

"Then shake hand."

Me and Chuckkie shake hand.

"Kiss," Mrs. Leola say.

155 "No, ma'am," I say. "I ain't kissing no boy. I ain't that crazy."

"Kiss him, Chuckkie," she say.

Old Chuckkie kiss me on the jaw.

"Now, kiss him, Ben O."

"I ain't kissing no Chuckkie," I say. "No'm. Uh-uh. You kiss girls."

160 And the next thing I know, Mama done tipped up back o' me and done whop me on the leg with Daddy belt.

"Kiss Chuckkie," she say.

Chuckkie turn his jaw to me and I kiss him. I almost wipe my mouth. I even feel like spitting.

"Now, come back here and get you some eggnog," Mama say.

"That's right, spoil 'em," Gran'mon say. "Next thing you know, they be drinking from bottles."

165 "Little eggnog won't hurt 'em, Mama," Mama say.

"That's right, never listen," Gran'mon say. "It's you go'n suffer for it. I be dead and gone, me."

Aunt Clo

Be just like wrapping a chain round a tree and jecking and jecking, and then shifting the chain little bit and jecking and jecking some in that direction, and then shifting it some mo' and jecking and jecking in that direction. Jecking and jecking till you get it loose, and then pulling with all your might. Still it might not be loose enough and you have to back the tractor up some and fix the chain round the tree again and start jecking all over. Jeck, jeck, jeck. Then you hear the roots crying, and then you keep on jecking, and then it give, and you jeck some mo', and then it falls. And not till then that you see what you done done. Not till then you see the big hole in the ground and piece of the taproot still way down in it—a piece you won't never get out no matter if you dig till doomsday. Yes, you got the tree — least got it down on the ground, but did you get the taproot? No. No, sir, you didn't get the taproot. You stand there and look down in this hole at it and you grab yo' axe and jump down in it and start chopping at the taproot, but do you get the taproot? No. You don't get the taproot, sir. You never get the taproot. But, sir, I tell you what you do get. You get a big hole in the ground, sir; and you get another big hole in the air where the lovely branches been all these years. Yes, sir, that's what you get. The holes, sir, the holes. Two holes, sir, you can't never fill no matter how hard you try.

So you wrap yo' chain round yo' tree again, sir, and you start dragging it. But the dragging ain't so easy, sir, 'cause she's a heavy old tree — been there a long time, you know — heavy. And you make yo' tractor strain, sir, and the elements work 'gainst you, too, sir, 'cause the elements, they on her side, too, 'cause she part o' the elements, and the elements, they part o' her. So the elements, they do they little share to discourage you — yes, sir, they does. But you will not let the elements stop you. No, sir, you show the elements that they just elements, and man is stronger than elements, and you jeck and jeck on the chain, and soon she start to moving with you, sir, but if you look over yo' shoulder one second you see her leaving a trail — a trail, sir, that can be seen from miles and miles away. You see her trying to hook her little fine branches in different little cracks, in between pickets, round hills o' grass, round anything they might brush 'gainst. But you is a determined man, sir, and you jeck and you jeck, and she keep on grabbing and trying to hold, but you stronger, sir — course you the strongest — and you finally get her out on the pave road. But what you don't notice, sir, is just 'fore she get on the pave road she leave couple her little branches to remind the people that it ain't her that want leave, but you, sir, that think she ought to. So you just drag her and drag her, sir, and the folks that live in the houses 'side the pave road, they come out on they gallery and look at her go by, and then they go back in they house and sit by the fire and forget her. So you just go on, sir, and you just go and you go — and for how many days? I don't know. I don't have the least idea. The North to me, sir, is like the elements. It mystify me. But never mind, you finally get there, and then you try to find a place to set her. You look in this corner and you look in that corner, but no corner is good. She kind o' stand in the way no matter where you set her. So finally, sir, you say, "I just stand her up here a little while and see, and if it don't work out, if she keep getting in the way, I guess we'll just have to take her to the dump."

Chris

Just like him, though, standing up there telling them lies when every-body else feeling sad. I don't know what you do without people like him. And, yet, you see him there, he sad just like the rest. But he just got to be funny. Crying on the inside, but still got to be funny.

He didn't steal it, though; didn't steal it a bit. His grandpa was just like him. Mat? Mat Jefferson? Just like that. Mat could make you die laughing. 'Member once at a wake. Who was dead? Yes — Robert Lewis. Robert Lewis laying up in his coffin dead as a door nail. Everybody sad and droopy. Mat look at that and start his lying. Soon, half o' the place laughing. Funniest wake I ever went to, and yet —

Just like now. Look at 'em. Look at 'em laughing. Ten minutes ago you would 'a' thought you was at a funeral. But look at 'em now. Look at her there in that little old chair. How long she had it? Fifty years — a hundred? It ain't a chair no mo', it's little bit o' her. Just like her arm, just like her leg.

You know, I couldn't believe it. I couldn't. Emile passed the house there the other day, right after the bombing, and I was in my yard digging a water drain to let the water run out in the ditch. Emile, he stopped the wagon there 'fore the door. Little Chuckkie, he in there with him with that little rain cap buckled up over his head. I go out to the gate and I say, "Emile, it's the truth?"

"The truth," he say. And just like that he say it. "The truth."

I look at him there, and he looking up the road to keep from looking back at me. You know, they been pretty close to Aunt Fe ever since they was children coming up. His own mon, Aunt Lou, and Aunt Fe, they been like sisters, there, together.

Me and him, we talk there little while 'bout the cane cutting, then he say he got to get on to the back. He shake the lines and drive on.

Inside me, my heart feel like it done swole up ten times the size it ought to be. Water come in my eyes, and I got to 'mit I cried right there. Yes sir, I cried right there by that front gate.

Louise come in the room and whisper something to Leola, and they go back in the kitchen. I can hear 'em moving things round back there, still getting things together they go'n be taking along. If they offer me anything, I'd like that big iron pot out there in the back yard. Good for boiling water when you killing hog, you know.

You can feel the sadness in the room again. Louise brought it in when she come in and whispered to Leola. Only, she didn't take it out when her and Leola left. Every pan they move, every pot they unhook keep telling you she leaving, she leaving.

Etienne turn over one o' them logs to make the fire pick up some, and I see that boy, Lionel, spreading out his hands over the fire. Watch out, I think to myself, here come another lie. People, he just getting started.

Anne-Marie Duvall

"You're not going?"

"I'm not going," he says, turning over the log with the poker. "And if you were in your right mind, you wouldn't go, either."

"You just don't understand, do you?"

"Oh, I understand. She cooked for your daddy. She nursed you when your mama died."

"And I'm trying to pay her back with a seventy-nine-cents scarf. Is that too much?"

He is silent, leaning against the mantel, looking down at the fire. The fire throws strange shadows across the big, old room. Father looks down at me from against the wall. His eyes do not say go nor stay. But I know what he would do.

"Please go with me, Edward."

"You're wasting your breath."

I look at him a long time, then I get the small package from the coffee table.

"You're still going?"

"I am going."

"Don't call for me if you get bogged down anywhere back there."

I look at him and go out to the garage. The sky is black. The clouds are moving fast and low. A fine drizzle is falling, and the wind coming from the swamps blows in my face. I cannot recall a worse night in all my life.

I hurry into the car and drive out of the yard. The house stands big and black in back of me. Am I angry with Edward? No, I'm not angry with Edward. He's right. I should not go out into this kind of weather. But what he does not understand is I must. Father definitely would have gone if he were alive. Grandfather definitely would have gone, also. And, therefore, I must. Why? I cannot answer why. Only, I must go.

As soon as I turn down that old muddy road, I begin to pray. Don't let me go into that ditch, I pray. Don't let me go into that ditch. Please, don't let me go into that ditch.

The lights play on the big old trees along the road. Here and there the lights hit a sagging picket fence. But I know I haven't even started yet. She lives far back into the fields. Why? God, why does she have to live so far back? Why couldn't she have lived closer to the front? But the answer to that is as hard for me as is the answer to everything else. It was ordained before I—before father—was born—that she should live back there. So why should I try to understand it now?

The car slides towards the ditch, and I stop it dead and turn the wheel, and then come back into the road again. Thanks, father. I know you're with me. Because it was you who said that I must look after her, didn't you? No, you did not say it directly, father. You said it only with a glance. As grandfather must have said it to you, and as his father must have said it to him.

But now that she's gone, father, now what? I know. I know. Aunt Lou, Aunt Clo, and the rest.

The lights shine on the dead, wet grass along the road. There's an old pecan tree, looking dead and all alone. I wish I was a little nigger gal so I could pick pecans and eat them under the big old dead tree.

The car hits a rut, but bounces right out of it. I am frightened for a moment, but then I feel better. The windshield wipers are working well, slapping the water away as fast as it hits the glass. If I make the next half mile all right, the rest of the way will be good. It's not much over a mile now.

200   That was too bad about that bombing — killing that woman and her two children. That poor woman; poor children. What is the answer? What will happen? What do they want? Do they know what they want? Do they really know what they want? Are they positively sure? Have they any idea? Money to buy a car, is that it? If that is all, I pity them. Oh, how I pity them.

Not much farther. Just around that bend and — there's a water hole. Now what?

I stop the car and just stare out at the water a minute; then I get out to see how deep it is. The cold wind shoots through my body like needles. Lightning comes from towards the swamps and lights up the place. For a split second the night is as bright as day. The next second it is blacker than it has ever been.

I look at the water, and I can see that it's too deep for the car to pass through. I must turn back or I must walk the rest of the way. I stand there a while wondering what to do. Is it worth it all? Can't I simply send the gift by someone tomorrow morning? But will there be someone tomorrow morning? Suppose she leaves without getting it, then what? What then? Father would never forgive me. Neither would grandfather or great-grandfather, either. No, they wouldn't.

The lightning flashes again and I look across the field, and I can see the tree in the yard a quarter of a mile away. I have but one choice: I must walk. I get the package out of the car and stuff it in my coat and start out.

205   I don't make any progress at first, but then I become a little warmer and I find I like walking. The lightning flashes just in time to show up a puddle of water, and I go around it. But there's no light to show up the second puddle, and I fall flat on my face. For a moment I'm completely blind, then I get slowly to my feet and check the package. It's dry, not harmed. I wash the mud off my raincoat, wash my hands, and I start out again.

The house appears in front of me, and as I come into the yard, I can hear the people laughing and talking. Sometimes I think niggers can laugh and joke even if they see somebody beaten to death. I go up on the porch and knock and an old one opens the door for me. I swear, when he sees me he looks as if he's seen a ghost. His mouth drops open, his eyes bulge — I swear.

I go into the old crowded and smelly room, and every one of them looks at me the same way the first one did. All the joking and laughing has ceased. You would think I was the devil in person.

"Done, Lord," I hear her saying over by the fireplace. They move to the side and I can see her sitting in that little rocking chair I bet you she's had since the beginning of time. "Done, Master," she says. "Child, what you doing in weather like this? Y'all move; let her get to that fire. Y'all move. Move, now. Let her warm herself."

They start scattering everywhere.

210   "I'm not cold, Aunt Fe," I say. "I just brought you something — something small — because you're leaving us. I'm going right back."

"Done, Master," she says. Fussing over me just like she's done all her life. "Done, Master. Child, you ain't got no business in a place like this. Get close to this fire. Get here. Done, Master."

I move closer, and the fire does feel warm and good.

"Done, Lord," she says.

I take out the package and pass it to her. The other niggers gather around with all kinds of smiles on their faces. Just think of it — a white lady coming through all of this for one old darky. It is all right for them to come from all over the plantation, from all over the area, in all kinds of weather: this is to be expected of them. But a white lady, a white lady. They must think we white people don't have their kind of feelings.

She unwraps the package, her bony little fingers working slowly and deliberately. When she sees the scarf — the seventy-nine-cents scarf — she brings it to her mouth and kisses it.

"Y'all look," she says. "Y'all look. Ain't it the prettiest little scarf y'all ever did see? Y'all look."

They move around her and look at the scarf. Some of them touch it.

"I go'n put it on right now," she says. "I go'n put it on right now, my lady."

She unfolds it and ties it round her head and looks up at everybody and smiles.

"Thank you, my lady," she says. "Thank you, ma'am, from the bottom of my heart."

"Oh, Aunt Fe," I say, kneeling down beside her. "Oh, Aunt Fe."

But I think about the other niggers there looking down at me, and I get up. But I look into that wrinkled old face again, and I must go back down again. And I lay my head in that bony old lap, and I cry and I cry — I don't know how long. And I feel those old fingers, like death itself, passing over my hair and my neck. I don't know how long I kneel there crying, and when I stop, I get out of there as fast as I can.

Etienne

The boy come in, and soon, right off, they get quiet, blaming the boy. If people could look little farther than the tip of they nose — No, they blame the boy. Not that they ain't behind the boy, what he doing, but they blame him for what she must do. What they don't know is that the boy didn't start it, and the people that bombed the house didn't start it, neither. It started a million years ago. It started when one man envied another man for having a penny mo' 'an he had, and then the man married a woman to help him work the field so he could get much 's the other man, but when the other man saw the man had married a woman to get much 's him, he, himself, he married a woman, too, so he could still have mo'. Then they start having children — not from love; but so the children could help 'em work so they could have mo'. But even with the children one man still had a penny mo' 'an the other, so the other man went and bought him a ox, and the other man did the same — to keep ahead of the other man. And soon the other man had bought him a slave to work the ox so he could get ahead of the other man. But the other man went out and bought him two slaves so he could stay ahead of the other man, and the other man went out and bought him three slaves. And soon they had a thousand slaves apiece, but they still wasn't satisfied. And one day the slaves all rose and kill the masters, but the masters (knowing slaves was men just like they was, and kind o' expected they might do this) organized theyself a good police force, and the police force, they come out and killed the two thousand slaves.

So it's not this boy you see standing here 'fore you, 'cause it happened a million years ago. And this boy here's just doing something the slaves done a million years ago. Just that this boy here ain't doing it they way. 'Stead of raising arms 'gainst the masters, he bow his head.

225   No, I say; don't blame the boy 'cause she must go. 'Cause when she's dead, and that won't be long after they get her up there, this boy's work will still be going on. She's not the only one that's go'n die from this boy's work. Many mo' of 'em go'n die 'fore it's over with. The whole place — everything. A big wind is rising, and when a big wind rise, the sea stirs, and the drop o' water you see laying on top the sea this day won't be there tomorrow. 'Cause that's what wind do, and that's what life is. She ain't nothing but one little drop o' water laying on top the sea, and what this boy's doing is called the wind . . . and she must be moved. No, don't blame the boy. Go out and blame the wind. No, don't blame him, 'cause tomorrow, what he's doing today, somebody go'n say he ain't done a thing. 'Cause tomorrow will be his time to be turned over just like it's hers today. And after that, be somebody else time to turn over. And it keep going like that till it ain't nothing left to turn — and nobody left to turn it.

"Sure, they bombed the house," he say; "because they want us to stop. But if we stopped today, then what good would we have done? What good? Those who have already died for the cause would have just died in vain."

"Maybe if they had bombed your house you wouldn't be so set on keeping this up."

"If they had killed my mother and my brothers and sisters, I'd press just that much harder. I can see you all point. I can see it very well. But I can't agree with you. You blame me for their being bombed. You blame me for Aunt Fe's leaving. They died for you and for your children. And I love Aunt Fe as much as anybody in here does. Nobody in here loves her more than I do. Not one of you." He looks at her. "Don't you believe me, Aunt Fe?"

She nods — that little white scarf still tied round her head.

230   "How many times have I eaten in your kitchen, Aunt Fe? A thousand times? How many times have I eaten tea cakes and drank milk on the back steps, Aunt Fe? A thousand times? How many times have I sat at this same fireplace with you, just the two of us, Aunt Fe? Another thousand times — two thousand times? How many times have I chopped wood for you, chopped grass for you, ran to the store for you? Five thousand times? How

many times have we walked to church together, Aunt Fe? Gone fishing at the river together — how many times? I've spent as much time in this house as I've spent in my own. I know every crack in the wall. I know every corner. With my eyes shut, I can go anywhere in here without bumping into anything. How many of you can do that? Not many of you." He looks at her. "Aunt Fe?"

She looks at him.

"Do you think I love you, Aunt Fe?"

She nods.

"I love you, Aunt Fe, much as I do my own parents. I'm going to miss you much as I'd miss my own mother if she were to leave me now. I'm going to miss you, Aunt Fe, but I'm not going to stop what I've started. You told me a story once, Aunt Fe, about my great-grandpa. Remember? Remember how he died?

She looks in the fire and nods.

"Remember how they lynched him — chopped him into pieces?"

She nods.

"Just the two of us were sitting here beside the fire when you told me that. I was so angry I felt like killing. But it was you who told me get killing out of my mind. It was you who told me I would only bring harm to myself and sadness to the others if I killed. Do you remember that, Aunt Fe?"

She nods, still looking in the fire.

"You were right. We cannot raise our arms. Because it would mean death for ourselves, as well as for the others. But we will do something else — and that's what we will do." He looks at the people standing round him. "And if they were to bomb my own mother's house tomorrow, I would still go on."

"I'm not saying for you not to go on," Louise says. "That's up to you. I'm just taking Auntie from here before hers is the next house they bomb."

The boy look at Louise, and then at Aunt Fe. He go up to the chair where she sitting.

"Good-bye, Aunt Fe," he say, picking up her hand. The hand done shriveled up to almost nothing. Look like nothing but loose skin's covering the bones. "I'll miss you," he say.

"Good-bye, Emmanuel," she say. She look at him a long time. "God be with you."

He stand there holding the hand a while longer, then he nods his head, and leaves the house. The people stir round little bit, but nobody say anything.

Aunt Lou

They tell her good-bye, and half of 'em leave the house crying, or want cry, but she just sit there 'side the fireplace like she don't mind going at all. When Leola ask me if I'm ready to go, I tell her I'm staying right there till Fe leave that house. I tell her I ain't moving one step till she go out that door. I been knowing her for the past fifty some years now, and I ain't 'bout to leave her on her last night here.

That boy, Chuckkie, want stay with me, but I make him go. He follow his mon and paw out the house and soon I hear that wagon turning round. I hear Emile saying something to Mr. Bascom even 'fore that wagon get out the yard. I tell myself, well, Mr. Bascom, you sure go'n catch it, and me not there to take up for you—and I get up from my chair and go to the door.

"Emile?" I call.

"Whoa," he say.

250 "You leave that mule 'lone, you hear me?"

"I ain't done Mr. Bascom a thing, Mama," he say.

"Well, you just mind you don't," I say. "I'll sure find out."

"Yes'm," he say. "Come up here, Mr. Bascom."

"Now, you hear that boy. Emile?" I say.

255 "I'm sorry, Mama," he say. "I didn't mean no harm."

They go out in the road, and I go back to the fireplace and sit down again. Louise stir round in the kitchen a few minutes, then she come in the front where we at. Everybody else gone. That husband o' hers, there, got drunk long 'fore midnight, and Emile and them had to put him to bed in the other room.

She come there and stand by the fire.

"I'm dead on my feet," she say.

"Why don't you go to bed," I say. "I'm go'n be here."

260 "You all won't need anything?"

"They got wood in that corner?"

"Plenty."

"Then we won't need a thing."

She stand there and warm, and then she say good night and go round the other side.

265 "Well, Fe?" I say.

"I ain't leaving here tomorrow, Lou," she say.

"'Course you is," I say. "Up there ain't that bad."

She shake her head. "No, I ain't going nowhere."

I look at her over in her chair, but I don't say nothing. The fire pops in the fireplace, and I look at the fire again. It's a good little fire—not too big, not too little. Just 'nough there to keep the place warm.

270 "You want sing, Lou?" she say, after a while. "I feel like singing my 'termination song."

"Sure," I say.

She start singing in that little light voice she got there, and I join with her. We sing two choruses, and then she stop.

"My 'termination for Heaven," she say. "Now—now—"

"What's the matter, Fe?" I say.

275 "Nothing," she say. "I want get in my bed. My gown hanging over there."

I get the gown for her and bring it back to the firehalf. She get out of her dress slowly, like she don't even have 'nough strength to do it. I help her on with her gown, and she kneel down there 'side the bed and say her prayers. I sit in my chair and look at the fire again.

She pray there a long time — half out loud, half to herself. I look at her kneeling down there, little like a little old girl. I see her making some kind o' jecking motion there, but I feel she crying 'cause this her last night here, and 'cause she got to go and leave ever'thing behind. I look at the fire.

She pray there ever so long, and then she start to get up. But she can't make it by herself. I go to help her, and when I put my hand on her shoulder, she say, "Lou? Lou?"

I say, "What's the matter, Fe?"

"Lou?" she say. "Lou?"   280

I feel her shaking in my hand with all her might. Shaking, shaking, shaking — like a person with the chill. Then I hear her take a long breath, longest I ever heard anybody take before. Then she ease back on the bed — calm, calm, calm.

"Sleep on, Fe," I tell her. "When you get up there, tell 'em all I ain't far behind."

QUESTIONS

1. Define the types of conflict in this story and locate their causes.
2. The narrative method here is called **stream of consciousness**, which presents the private thoughts of a character (usually in a first-person or limited-omniscient narration) without direct commentary or interpretation by the author. This story complicates that method by presenting the thoughts of several characters. It should be possible to infer motives and past histories for most of the narrators in this story. Can you also supply them for characters who do not narrate — in particular, for Aunt Fe, Louise, and Emmanuel? Why doesn't the author give monologues to these characters?
3. All of the narrators but two are blacks from the local area. Which two are not? What do the perspectives of these "outsiders" contribute to the story?
4. What is the import of the story's haziness about blood- and marriage-links between the characters? Does your inability to chart all the relationships have a positive value for the story's theme?
5. Given the emotional effects of the story, is it possible to say whether Emmanuel's actions are right? Whether Louise's are right?
6. What happens to Aunt Fe? What does she mean by repeating "Done, Lord" and "Done, Master" when Anne-Marie arrives? Supposing that the song quoted at the beginning of the story is Aunt Fe's "'termination song" (paragraph 270), what meanings does the author imply for the word *'termination*?
7. Compare this story to other first-person narrations (including those by Anderson, Walker, Roth, and Atwood). To what extent do these authors allow their narrators to analyze events? What are the advantages and disadvantages of Gaines's method?

CHAPTER SIX

Symbol and Irony

Most successful stories are characterized by compression. The writer's aim is to say as much as possible as briefly as possible. This does not mean that most good stories are brief. It means only that nothing is wasted and that each word and detail is chosen for maximum effectiveness. The force of an explosion is proportionate to the strength and amount of powder used and the smallness of the space it is confined in.

Good writers achieve compression by exercising a rigid selectivity. They choose the details and incidents that contribute most to the meaning they are after; they omit those whose usefulness is minimal. As far as possible they choose details that are multi-valued — that serve a variety of purposes at once. A detail that expresses character at the same time that it advances plot is more useful than a detail that does only one or the other.

This chapter will discuss two contributory resources of the writer for gaining compression: symbol and irony. Both of them may increase the explosive force of a story, but both demand awareness and maturity on the part of the reader.

A literary **symbol*** is something that means *more* than what it is. It is an object, a person, a situation, an action, or some other item that has a literal meaning in the story but suggests or represents other meanings as well. A very simple illustration is to be found in name symbolism. Most names are simply labels. Seldom does a name tell anything about the person to whom it is attached, except possibly the individual's nationality. In a story, however, authors may choose names for their characters that serve not only to label them but also to suggest something about

---

*Literary symbols are to be distinguished from *arbitrary* symbols, like letters of the alphabet, numbers, and algebraic signs, which have no meaning in and of themselves but which mean only something *else*, not something *more* than what they are.

them. The name of the young civil rights activist in "Just Like a Tree," Emmanuel, is derived from the Hebrew for "God with us," and is identified with the Messiah in Isaiah 7:14. When in parting from him, Aunt Fe blesses him, "God be with you," the symbolism is made overt. In "Everyday Use," Dee's rejection of her name and her adoption of the alternative "Wangero" symbolizes for her a changed perspective on her heritage. The name of General Zaroff in "The Most Dangerous Game" is fitting for a former "officer of the Czar" who now behaves like a czar himself. Trevor's name in Greene's "The Destructors" suggests his upper-class origins. Equally meaningful in that story is the name of the Wormsley Common Gang. First, the word "Common," here designating a small public park or green, also suggests the "common people" or the lower middle and laboring classes as opposed to the upper class. More significant, when Trevor advocates his plan for gutting the old house — "We'd do it from inside. . . . We'd be like worms, don't you see, in an apple" (paragraph 52), we see that Greene's choice of the name Wormsley was quite deliberate, and that it is appropriate also (as well as perfectly natural) that Wormsley Common should have an Underground Station. (The word "apple," in Trevor's speech, also has symbolic resonances. Though it is often a mistake to push symbolism too hard, the reader may well ask whether anything would be lost if Trevor had compared the gang's activities to those of worms in a peach or a pear.)

More important than name symbolism is the symbolic use of objects and actions. In some stories these symbols will fit so naturally into the literal context that their symbolic value will not at first be apparent except to the most perceptive reader. In other stories — usually stories with a less realistic surface — they will be so central and so obvious that they will demand symbolical interpretation if the story is to yield significant meaning. In the first kind of story the symbols *reinforce* and *add* to the meaning. In the second kind of story they *carry* the meaning.

In "Hills Like White Elephants" a man and a girl sit waiting for the train to Madrid, where the girl is to have an abortion. But the girl is not fully persuaded that she wants an abortion (at the deepest levels of her being, she does not). The man is aware of this, and seeks to reassure her: "It's really an awfully simple operation. . . . It's not really an operation at all. . . . But I don't want you to do it if you don't really want to." The man *does* want her to do it even if she doesn't really want to; nevertheless, the decision is not irrevocable. They are at a railroad junction, a place where one can change directions. Symbolically it represents a juncture where they can change the direction of their lives. Their bags, with "labels on them from all the hotels where they had spent nights," indicate the kind of rootless, pleasure-seeking existence without responsibility they have hitherto lived. The man wants the girl to have the abortion so that they can go on living as they have before.

The railway station is situated in a river valley between two mountain ranges. On one side of the valley there is no shade and no trees and the country is "brown and dry." It is on this side, "the dry side," that the station sits in the heat, "between two lines of rails." It is also this side which the couple see from their table and which prompts the girl's remark that the hills look "like white elephants." On the other side of the valley, which the girl can see when she walks to the end of the station, lies the river, with "fields of grain and trees" along its banks, the "shadow of a cloud" moving across a field of grain, and another range of mountains in the distance. Looking in this direction, the girl remarks, "And we could have all this." The two landscapes, on opposite sides of the valley, have symbolic meaning in relation to the decision that the girl is being asked to reconfirm. The hot arid side of the valley represents sterility; the other side, with water in the river and the cloud, a hint of coolness in the cloud's moving shadow, and growing things along the river banks, represents fertility. The girl's remark about this other side shows a conscious recognition of its symbolism.

But what does the girl mean by her remark that the mountains on the dry side of the valley look "like white elephants"? Perhaps nothing at all. It is intended as a "bright" remark, a clever if far-fetched comparison made to amuse the man, as it would have in their earlier days together. But whether or not the girl means anything by it, almost certainly Hemingway means something. Or perhaps several things. Clearly the child begun in the girl's womb is a "white elephant" for the man, who says, "I don't want anybody but you. I don't want any one else." For the girl, on the other hand, the abortion itself, the decision to continue living as they have been living, without responsibility, may be considered a "white elephant." We already know that this life has lost its savor for her. When she remarks that the Anis del Toro "tastes like licorice," the man's response — "That's the way with everything" — is probably meant to apply only to the drinks and food in this section of the country, but the girl's confirmation of his observation seems to enlarge its meaning to the whole life they have been living together, which consists, she says, only of looking at things and trying new drinks. Thus the licorice flavor, suggesting tedium and disillusion, joins the "hills like white elephants," the opposed sides of the river valley, and the railroad junction in a network of symbols that intensify the meaning and impact of the story.*

The ability to recognize and identify symbols requires perception and tact. The great danger facing readers when they first become aware of symbolic values is a tendency to run wild — to find symbols everywhere and to read into the details of a story all sorts of fanciful meanings not legitimately supported by it. Less-experienced readers need to remember that most stories operate almost wholly at the literal level and that, even in highly symbolic stories, the majority of the details are purely literal. A story is not an excuse for an exercise in ingenuity. It is better, indeed, to miss the symbolic meanings of a story than to pervert its meaning by discovering symbols that are nonexistent. Better to miss the boat than to jump wildly for it and drown.

The ability to intepret symbols is nevertheless essential for a full understanding of literature. Less-experienced readers should be alert for symbolic meanings but should observe the following cautions:

1. The story itself must furnish a clue that a detail is to be taken symbolically. In Mansfield's story, Miss Brill's fur is given prominence at the beginning of the story, when it is taken out of its box; at the climax of the story, when the girl on the bench compares it to "a fried whiting"; and at the end of the story, when Miss Brill puts it back in the box and thinks she hears it crying. The fur is clearly a symbol for Miss Brill herself. It comes out of a box like a dark little room or a cupboard, it is old and in need of repair, it is ridiculed by the boy and the girl on the park bench, and it is returned to its box at the end of the story. Symbolically, it is herself whom Miss Brill hears crying. In Hemingway's story, the comparison of the hills to white elephants is used for the title of the story and is mentioned four times within the story, while the opposed sides of the river valley are rather pointedly described in a story that otherwise has very little description in it. Both items are given emphasis, yet neither has any part in the action. Even greater emphasis is given to the quilts in the story by Walker. Symbols nearly always signal their existence by *emphasis, repetition*, or *position*. In the absence of such signals, we should be reluctant to identify an idea as symbolic.

2. The meaning of a literary symbol must be established and supported by the entire context of the story. The symbol has its meaning *in* the story, not *outside* it. Our meaning, for instance, in "Hills Like White

---

*Some critics have found symbolism also in the bead curtain that separates the bar from the table where the man and girl are sitting. But there is not space here, nor need, to discuss all symbolic implications of the story.

Elephants" for the "shadow of a cloud" moving over the field of grain, is supported by and dependent on its relation to other elements in the story, the river, the field of grain, the stifling heat at the station, the brown, dry country on the near side of the valley, and so on. In another work of literature, in another context, a shadow or a cloud might have an almost opposite meaning, or no symbolic meaning at all. The cloud in the ancient saying "Every cloud has a silver lining," and the shadow in the Twenty-third Psalm — "though I walk through the valley of the shadow of death" — have entirely different meanings than they have here. Here, by suggesting the possibility of rain, a spot of shade from the sun, and the existence of a breeze, the moving cloud shadow extends the meaning of the fertility symbol of which it is a part.

3. To be called a symbol, an item must suggest a meaning different in *kind* from its literal meaning; a symbol is something more than the representative of a class or type. Miss Brill, for instance, is an old, odd, silent, friendless person, set in her ways, who does not realize (until the climax of the story) that she herself is old, odd, and set in her ways — like other elderly people she observes in the park each Sunday. But to say this is to say no more than that the story has a theme. Every interpretive story suggests a generalization about life, is more than an accounting of the specific fortunes of specific individuals. There is no point, therefore, in calling Miss Brill a *symbol* of odd, self-deluded, elderly people; she *is* an odd, self-deluded elderly person: a member of the class of odd, self-deluded elderly persons. Her fur is a symbol, but she is not. We ought not to use the phrase *is a symbol of* when we can easily use *is*, or *is an example of*, or *is an evidence of*. Dick Prosser, in "The Child by Tiger," through his association with the tiger in Blake's poem, and by the way he is spoken of in the story's concluding paragraphs, is clearly meant to be something more than an *example* of any class of men, or of mankind in general; he is a symbol of something *in* man, of hidden possibilities that are latent in us all.

In "Hills Like White Elephants" the railroad junction is neither an example nor an evidence of a point in time in the characters' lives when a crucial decision must be made, nor are the opposed sides of the valley examples or evidences of the two kinds of future that might result from their choice. The meanings these things suggest are different from what they are. The label-covered suitcases of the traveling couple, on the other hand, are an *evidence* or sign of their past and should not properly be called a symbol of their past.

4. A symbol may have more than one meaning. It may suggest a cluster of meanings. At its most effective a symbol is like a many-faceted

jewel: it flashes different colors when turned in the light. This is not to say that it can mean anything we want it to: the area of possible meanings is always controlled by the context. Nevertheless, this possibility of complex meaning, plus concreteness and emotional power, gives the symbol its peculiar compressive value. We have identified the far side of the valley in "Hills Like White Elephants" with fertility, but it suggests also pleasantness, growth, beauty, fulfillment — everything that the girl vaguely includes in her statement, "And we could have all this." The quilts in Walker's story have an equally wide range of meaning — inherited values, family attachments, independence and self-reliance, the beauty of useful objects, the virtue of craftsmanship — all in contrast to the shallow, monetary meaning expressed in Dee's acquisitive demand for them. When she says "But they're *priceless!*" she means that they are worth a great deal of money, but in the truer sense their symbolic values cannot be reckoned at any price. The meaning is not confined to any one of these qualities: it is all of them, and therein lies the symbol's value.

Irony is a term with a range of meanings, all of them involving some sort of discrepancy or incongruity. It is a contrast in which one term of the contrast in some ways mocks the other term. It is not to be confused with sarcasm, however, which is simply language designed to cause pain. The story writer uses irony to suggest the complexity of experience, to furnish indirectly an evaluation of the material, and at the same time to achieve compression.

Three kinds of irony may be distinguished here. **Verbal irony,** the simplest and, for the story writer, the least important kind, is a figure of speech in which the opposite is said from what is intended. The discrepancy is between what is said and what is meant. In "The Child by Tiger," when the narrator tells us that the man who fired the first shot into Dick Prosser was "telling the story of his own heroic accomplishments" and refers to him as "the hero," he is using the words "heroic" and "hero" ironically, for it is clear that he feels only contempt for both the man and his actions. In "Defender of the Faith," when Sergeant Marx says to Grossbart, "You're a regular Messiah, aren't you?" he is speaking ironically — and sarcastically — for he thinks Grossbart's motives are self-interested rather than Messianic. Another use of irony for sarcastic purposes is made by the girl in "Hills Like White Elephants." The man has been assuring her that, after the operation, they will be "just like" they were before, for her pregnancy has been the only thing making them unhappy:

"And you think then we'll be all right and be happy."

"I know we will. You don't have to be afraid. I've known lots of people that have done it."

"So have I," said the girl. "And afterward they were all so happy." Abortions, the girl means, make couples anything but "all so happy" afterward. She also speaks ironically at the very end of the story, when she says: "I feel fine . . . There's nothing wrong with me. I feel fine."

In **dramatic irony** the contrast is between what a character says and what the reader knows to be true. The value of this kind of irony lies in the comment it implies on the speaker or the speaker's expectations. Miss Brill, sitting in the park, thinks about others doing the same as she: "Other people sat on the benches and green chairs, but they were nearly always the same, Sunday after Sunday, and — Miss Brill had often noticed — there was something funny about nearly all of them. . . . from the way they stared they looked as though they'd just come from dark little rooms or even — even cupboards!" It is ironic that the judgment she makes of them is what the story makes of her — even including the word "funny," which the young girl later uses about her. She is unaware that her phrase "nearly always the same, Sunday after Sunday," describes her own behavior, which she unwittingly reveals when she thinks that she "had *often* noticed" them. And of course the irony of the statement about the "cupboards" they must have come from is made overt when she returns at the end of the story to "her room like a cupboard." Perhaps the most poignant of the dramatic ironies surrounding Miss Brill is contained in her boastful thought, " 'Yes, I have been an actress for a long time,' " for she has indeed created a fictitious role that she lives in — not that of a glamorous stage actress in a romantic musical play, but that of a perceptive, happy, and self-sufficient woman. Another effective example occurs in "I'm a Fool" when the swipe blames his lie at the race track on the whiskey he had drunk and the man in the Windsor tie. The readers sees, as the swipe does not, that *these are simply additional symptoms of his plight, not its cause.*

In **irony of situation**, usually the most important kind for the story writer, the discrepancy is between appearance and reality, or between expectation and fulfillment, or between what is and what would seem appropriate. In "The Most Dangerous Game," it is ironic that Rainsford, "the celebrated hunter," should become the hunted, for this is a reversal of his expected and appropriate role. In "The Destructors," it is ironic that Old Misery's horoscope should read, "Abstain from any dealings in first half of week. Danger of serious crash," for the horoscope is valid in a sense that is quite different from that which the words seem to indicate. In "Rape Fantasies," all of Estelle's fantasies result in ironic reversals, as she admits: "in my rape fantasies I always end up feeling sorry for the guy," so her stories conclude not in cruelty and violence but in sad forgiveness of the imaginary attackers who have been abashed by the way she talks to them. In "There Are a Lot of Ways to Die," Joseph comes to realize the irony of his hopes and ambitions as he discovers that his native island does not match his recollection or expectation.

As a final example, the title of "Defender of the Faith" points to a complex irony, partly verbal, partly situational. The phrase "defender of the faith" ordinarily suggests a staunch religious champion and partisan, but, insofar as Sergeant Marx fills this role, he does so against his will, even against his intention, for his motivation is to give fair and equal treatment to all his men — he does not want to be partial to Jews. Unwillingly, he is trapped into being a "defender of the faith" by Private Grossbart.

> The next morning, while chatting with Captain Barrett, I recounted the incident of the previous evening. Somehow, in the telling, it must have seemed to the Captain that I was not so much explaining Grossbart's position as defending it.

At the end of the story, however, when Marx has Grossbart's orders changed to the Pacific, the irony is that he becomes most truly a defender of his faith when he seems to be turning against it. "You call this watching out for me — what you did?" asks Grossbart. "No," answers Marx. "For all of us." The cause of the whole Jewish faith is set back when Jews like Grossbart get special favors for themselves, for other people will mistakenly attribute Grossbart's objectionable qualities to the Jewish people as a whole. Thus Marx is unwillingly a "defender of the faith" when he helps his coreligionist, and becomes truly a defender of the faith when he turns against him. These ironies underscore the difficulties involved in being at the same time a good Jew and a good person in a world where Jews are so often the objects of prejudice and persecution.

In all these examples, irony enables the author to gain power with economy. Like symbolism, irony makes it possible to suggest meanings without stating them. Simply by juxtaposing two discordant facts in the right contextual mix, the writer can start a current of meaning flowing between them, as between the two poles of an electric battery. We do not *need* to be told how difficult it is for an aging, solitary woman to cope with being alone; we see it. We do not need to be told that the race-track swipe is lacking in self-knowledge; we see it. We do not need to be told how difficult it is for a Jewish sergeant to balance justice and mercy in a position of command; we feel it. The ironic contrast generates meaning.

Albert Camus
The Guest

The schoolmaster was watching the two men climb toward him. One was on horseback, the other on foot. They had not yet tackled the abrupt rise leading to the schoolhouse built on the hillside. They were toiling onward, making slow progress in the snow, among the stones, on the vast expanse of the high, deserted plateau. From time to time the horse stumbled. He could not be heard yet but the breath issuing from his nostrils could be seen. The schoolmaster calculated that it would take them a half hour to get onto the hill. It was cold; he went back into the school to get a sweater.

He crossed the empty, frigid classroom. On the blackboard the four rivers of France, drawn with four different colored chalks, had been flowing toward their estuaries for the past three days. Snow had suddenly fallen in mid-October after eight months of drought without the transition of rain, and the twenty pupils, more or less, who lived in the villages scattered over the plateau had stopped coming. With fair weather they would return. Daru now heated only the single room that was his lodging, adjoining the classroom. One of the windows faced, like the classroom windows, the south. On that side the school was a few kilometers from the point where the plateau began to slope toward the south. In clear weather the purple mass of the mountain range where the gap opened onto the desert could be seen.

Somewhat warmed, Daru returned to the window from which he had first noticed the two men. They were no longer visible. Hence they must have tackled the rise. The sky was not so dark, for the snow had stopped falling during the night. The morning had dawned with a dirty light which had scarcely become brighter as the ceiling of clouds lifted. At two in the afternoon it seemed as if the day were merely beginning. But still this was better than those three days when the thick snow was falling amidst unbroken darkness with little gusts of wind that rattled the double door of the classroom. Then Daru had spent long hours in his room, leaving it only to go to the shed and feed the chickens or get some coal. Fortunately the delivery truck from Tadjid, the nearest village to the north, had brought his supplies two days before the blizzard. It would return in forty-eight hours.

Besides, he had enough to resist a siege, for the little room was cluttered with bags of wheat that the administration had left as a supply to distribute to

THE GUEST   First published in 1957. Translated into English by Justin O'Brien. Algeria, now a republic, was until mid-century a French territory with a population about 88 percent Moslem (either Arab or Berger). Daru and Balducci, in the story, are French civil servants. Algeria gained its independence as a result of the Algerian War, 1954–1962, a Moslem revolt against French rule. Albert Camus (1913–1960), though a Frenchman, was born in northeastern Algeria, was educated in Algiers, and did not see France until 1939. In 1940, with the fall of France to Germany, he returned to Algiers and taught for two years in a private school in Oran, on the seacoast. In 1942 he returned to Paris and engaged actively in the resistance movement by writing for the underground press. He continued his residence in Paris after World War II.

those of his pupils whose families had suffered from the drought. Actually they had all been victims because they were all poor. Every day Daru would distribute a ration to the children. They had missed it, he knew, during these bad days. Possibly one of the fathers or big brothers would come this afternoon and he could supply them with grain. It was just a matter of carrying them over to the next harvest. Now shiploads of wheat were arriving from France and the worst was over. But it would be hard to forget that poverty, that army of ragged ghosts wandering in the sunlight, the plateaus burned to a cinder month after month, the earth shriveled up little by little, literally scorched, every stone bursting into dust under one's foot. The sheep had died then by thousands, and even a few men, here and there, sometimes without anyone's knowing.

In contrast with such poverty, he who lived almost like a monk, in his remote schoolhouse, had felt like a lord with his whitewashed walls, his narrow couch, his unpainted shelves, his well, and his weekly provisioning with water and food. And suddenly this snow, without warning, without the foretaste of rain. This is the way the region was, cruel to live in, even without men, who didn't help matters either. But Daru had been born here. Everywhere else, he felt exiled.

He went out and stepped forward on the terrace in front of the schoolhouse. The two men were now halfway up the slope. He recognized the horseman to be Balducci, the old gendarme he had known for a long time. Balducci was holding at the end of a rope an Arab walking behind him with hands bound and head lowered. The gendarme waved a greeting to which Daru did not reply, lost as he was in contemplation of the Arab dressed in a faded blue *jellaba*, his feet in sandals but covered with socks of heavy raw wool, his head crowned with a narrow, short *chèche*. Balducci was holding back his horse in order not to hurt the Arab, and the group was advancing slowly.

Within earshot, Balducci shouted, "One hour to do the three kilometers from El Ameur!" Daru did not answer. Short and square in his thick sweater, he watched them climb. Not once had the Arab raised his head. "Hello," said Daru when they got up onto the terrace. "Come in and warm up." Balducci painfully got down from his horse without letting go of the rope. He smiled at the schoolmaster from under his bristling mustache. His little dark eyes, deepset under a tanned forehead, and his mouth surrounded with wrinkles made him look attentive and studious. Daru took the bridle, led the horse to the shed, and came back to the two men who were now waiting for him in the school. He led them into his room. "I am going to heat up the classroom," he said. "We'll be more comfortable there."

When he entered the room again, Balducci was on the couch. He had undone the rope tying him to the Arab, who had squatted near the stove. His hands still bound, the *chèche* pushed back on his head, the Arab was looking toward the window. At first Daru noticed only his huge lips, fat, smooth, almost Negroid; yet his nose was straight, his eyes dark and full of fever. The *chèche* uncovered an obstinate forehead and, under the weathered skin now rather discolored by the cold, the whole face had a restless and rebellious look. "Go into the outer room," said the schoolmaster, "and I'll make you some mint tea." "Thanks," Balducci said. "What a chore! How I long for retirement." And addressing his prisoner in Arabic, he said, "Come on, you." The Arab got up and, slowly, holding his bound wrists in front of him, went into the classroom.

With the tea, Daru brought a chair. But Balducci was already sitting in state at the nearest pupil's desk, and the Arab had squatted against the teacher's platform facing the stove, which stood between the desk and the window. When he held out the glass of tea to the prisoner, Daru hesitated at the sight of his bound hands. "He might perhaps be untied." "Sure," said Balducci. "That was for the trip." He started to get to his feet. But Daru, setting the glass on the floor, had knelt beside the Arab. Without saying anything, the Arab watched him with his feverish eyes. Once his hands were free, he rubbed his swollen wrists against each other, took the glass of tea and sucked up the burning liquid in swift little sips.

10 "Good," said Daru. "And where are you headed?"

Balducci withdrew his mustache from the tea. "Here, son."

"Odd pupils! And you're spending the night?"

"No. I'm going back to El Ameur. And you will deliver this fellow to Tinguit. He is expected at police headquarters."

Balducci was looking at Daru with a friendly little smile.

15 "What's this story?" asked the schoolmaster. "Are you pulling my leg?"

"No, son. Those are the orders."

"The orders? I'm not . . ." Daru hesitated, not wanting to hurt the old Corsican. "I mean, that's not my job."

"What! What's the meaning of that? In wartime people do all kinds of jobs."

"Then I'll wait for the declaration of war!"

20 Balducci nodded. "O.K. But the orders exist and they concern you too. Things are bubbling, it appears. There is talk of a forthcoming revolt. We are mobilized in a way."

Daru still had his obstinate look.

"Listen, son," Balducci said. "I like you and you've got to understand. There's only a dozen of us at El Ameur to patrol the whole territory of a small department and I must be back in a hurry. He couldn't be kept there. His village was beginning to stir; they wanted to take him back. You must take him to Tinguit tomorrow before the day is over. Twenty kilometers shouldn't faze a husky fellow like you. After that, all will be over. You'll come back to your pupils and your comfortable life."

Behind the wall the horse could be heard snorting and pawing the earth. Daru was looking out the window. Decidedly the weather was clearing and the light was increasing over the snowy plateau. When all the snow was melted, the sun would take over again and once more would burn the fields of stone. For days still, the unchanging sky would shed its dry light on the solitary expanse where nothing had any connection with man.

"After all," he said, turning around toward Balducci, "what did he do?" And, before the gendarme had opened his mouth, he asked, "Does he speak French?"

"No, not a word. We had been looking for him for a month, but they were hiding him. He killed his cousin."

"Is he against us?"

"I don't think so. But you can never be sure."

"Why did he kill?"

"A family squabble, I think. One owed grain to the other, it seems. It's not at all clear. In short, he killed his cousin with a billhook. You know, like a sheep, *kreezk!*"

Balducci made the gesture of drawing a blade across his throat, and the Arab, his attention attracted, watched him with a sort of anxiety. Daru felt a sudden wrath against the man, against all men with their rotten spite, their tireless hates, their blood lust.

But the kettle was singing on the stove. He served Balducci more tea, hesitated, then served the Arab again, who drank avidly a second time. His raised arms made the *jellaba* fall open, and the schoolmaster saw his thin, muscular chest.

"Thanks, son," Balducci said. "And now I'm off."

He got up and went toward the Arab, taking a small rope from his pocket.

"What are you doing?" Daru asked dryly.

Balducci, disconcerted, showed him the rope.

"Don't bother."

The old gendarme hesitated. "It's up to you. Of course, you are armed?"

"I have my shotgun."

"Where?"

"In the trunk."

"You ought to have it near your bed."

"Why? I have nothing to fear."

"You're crazy, son. If there's an uprising, no one is safe; we're all in the same boat."

"I'll defend myself. I'll have time to see them coming."

Balducci began to laugh, then suddenly the mustache covered the white teeth. "You'll have time? O.K. That's just what I was saying. You always have been a little cracked. That's why I like you; my son was like that."

At the same time he took out his revolver and put it on the desk. "Keep it; I don't need two weapons from here to El Ameur."

The revolver shone against the black paint of the table. When the gendarme turned toward him, the schoolmaster caught his smell of leather and horseflesh.

"Listen, Balducci," Daru said suddenly, "all this disgusts me, beginning with your fellow here. But I won't hand him over. Fight, yes, if I have to. But not that."

The old gendarme stood in front of him and looked at him severely.

50   "You're being a fool," he said slowly. "I don't like it either. You don't get used to putting a rope on a man even after years of it, and you're even ashamed — yes, ashamed. But you can't let them have their way."

    "I won't hand him over," Daru said again.

    "It's an order, son, and I repeat it."

    "That's right. Repeat to them what I've said to you: I won't hand him over."

    Balducci made a visible effort to reflect. He looked at the Arab and at Daru. At last he decided.

55   "No, I won't tell them anything. If you want to drop us, go ahead; I'll not denounce you. I have an order to deliver the prisoner and I'm doing so. And now you'll just sign this paper for me."

    "There's no need. I'll not deny that you left him with me."

    "Don't be mean with me. I know you'll tell the truth. You're from around these parts and you are a man. But you must sign; that's the rule."

    Daru opened his drawer, took out a little square bottle of purple ink, the red wooden penholder with the "sergeant-major" pen he used for models of handwriting, and signed. The gendarme carefully folded the paper and put it into his wallet. Then he moved toward the door.

    "I'll see you off," Daru said.

60   "No," said Balducci. "There's no use being polite. You insulted me."

    He looked at the Arab, motionless in the same spot, sniffed peevishly, and turned away toward the door. "Good-bye, son," he said. The door slammed behind him. His footsteps were muffled by the snow. The horse stirred on the other side of the wall and several chickens fluttered in fright. A moment later Balducci reappeared outside the window leading the horse by the bridle. He walked toward the little rise without turning around and disappeared from sight with the horse following him.

    Daru walked back toward the prisoner, who, without stirring, never took his eyes off him. "Wait," the schoolmaster said in Arabic and went toward the bedroom. As he was going through the door, he had a second thought, went to the desk, took the revolver, and stuck it in his pocket. Then, without looking back, he went into his room.

    For some time he lay on his couch watching the sky gradually close over, listening to the silence. It was this silence that had seemed painful to him during the first days here, after the war. He had requested a post in the little town at the base of the foothills separating the upper plateaus from the desert. There rocky walls, green and black to the north, pink and lavender to the south, marked the frontier of eternal summer. He had been named to a post farther north, on the plateau itself. In the beginning, the solitude and the silence had been hard for him on these wastelands peopled only by stones. Occasionally, furrows suggested cultivation, but they had been dug to uncover a certain kind of stone good for building. The only plowing here was to harvest rocks. Elsewhere a thin layer of soil accumulated in the hollows would be scraped out to enrich paltry village gardens. This is the way it was: bare rock covered three quarters of the region. Towns sprang up, flourished, then disappeared; men came by, loved one another or fought bitterly, then died. No one in this desert, neither he nor his guest, mattered. And yet, outside this desert neither of them, Daru knew, could have really lived.

When he got up, no noise came from the classroom. He was amazed at the unmixed joy he derived from the mere thought that the Arab might have fled and that he would be alone with no decision to make. But the prisoner was there. He had merely stretched out between the stove and the desk and he was staring at the ceiling. In that position, his thick lips were particularly noticeable, giving him a pouting look. "Come," said Daru. The Arab got up and followed him. In the bedroom the schoolmaster pointed to a chair near the table under the window. The Arab sat down without ceasing to watch Daru.

"Are you hungry?"

"Yes," the prisoner said.

Daru set the table for two. He took flour and oil, shaped a cake in a frying pan, and lighted the little stove that functioned on bottled gas. While the cake was cooking, he went out to the shed to get cheese, eggs, dates, and condensed milk. When the cake was done he set it on the window sill to cool, heated some condensed milk diluted with water, and beat up the eggs into an omelette. In one of his motions he bumped into the revolver stuck in his right pocket. He set the bowl down, went into the classroom, and put the revolver in his desk drawer. When he came back to the room, night was falling. He put on the light and served the Arab. "Eat," he said. The Arab took a piece of the cake, lifted it eagerly to his mouth, and stopped short.

"And you?" he asked.

"After you. I'll eat too."

The thick lips opened slightly. The Arab hesitated, then bit into the cake determinedly.

The meal over, the Arab looked at the schoolmaster. "Are you the judge?"

"No, I'm simply keeping you until tomorrow."

"Why do you eat with me?"

"I'm hungry."

The Arab fell silent. Daru got up and went out. He brought back a camp cot from the shed and set it up between the table and the stove, at right angles to his own bed. From a large suitcase which, upright in a corner, served as a shelf for papers, he took two blankets and arranged them on the cot. Then he stopped, felt useless, and sat down on his bed. There was nothing more to do or to get ready. He had to look at this man. He looked at him therefore, trying to imagine his face bursting with rage. He couldn't do so. He could see nothing but the dark yet shining eyes and the animal mouth.

"Why did you kill him?" he asked in a voice whose hostile tone surprised him.

The Arab looked away. "He ran away. I ran after him."

He raised his eyes to Daru again and they were full of a sort of woeful interrogation. "Now what will they do to me?"

"Are you afraid?"

The Arab stiffened, turning his eyes away.

"Are you sorry?"

The Arab stared at him openmouthed. Obviously he did not understand. Daru's annoyance was growing. At the same time he felt awkward and self-conscious with his big body wedged between the two beds.

"Lie down there," he said impatiently. "That's your bed."

The Arab didn't move. He cried out, "Tell me!"

The schoolmaster looked at him.

"Is the gendarme coming back tomorrow?"

"I don't know."

"Are you coming with us?"

"I don't know. Why?"

The prisoner got up and stretched out on top of the blankets, his feet toward the window. The light from the electric bulb shone straight into his eyes and he closed them at once.

"Why?" Daru repeated, standing beside the bed.

The Arab opened his eyes under the blinding light and looked at him, trying not to blink. "Come with us," he said.

In the middle of the night, Daru was still not asleep. He had gone to bed after undressing completely; he generally slept naked. But when he suddenly realized that he had nothing on, he wondered. He felt vulnerable and the temptation came to him to put his clothes back on. Then he shrugged his shoulders; after all, he wasn't a child and, if it came to that, he could break his adversary in two. From his bed, he could observe him lying on his back, still motionless, his eyes closed under the harsh light. When Daru turned out the light, the darkness seemed to congeal all of a sudden. Little by little, the night came back to life in the window where the starless sky was stirring gently. The schoolmaster soon made out the body lying at his feet. The Arab was still motionless but his eyes seemed open. A faint wind was prowling about the schoolhouse. Perhaps it would drive away the clouds and the sun would reappear.

During the night the wind increased. The hens fluttered a little and then were silent. The Arab turned over on his side with his back to Daru, who thought he heard him moan. Then he listened for his guest's breathing, which had become heavier and more regular. He listened to that breathing so close to him and mused without being able to go to sleep. In the room where he had been sleeping alone for a year, this presence bothered him. But it bothered him also because it imposed on him a sort of brotherhood he refused to accept in the present circumstances; yet he was familiar with it. Men who share the same rooms, soldiers or prisoners, develop a strange alliance as if, having cast off their armor with their clothing, they fraternized every evening, over and above their differences, in the ancient community of dream and fatigue. But Daru shook himself; he didn't like such musings, and it was essential for him to sleep.

A little later, however, when the Arab stirred slightly, the schoolmaster was still not asleep. When the prisoner made a second move, he stiffened, on the alert. The Arab was lifting himself slowly on his arms with almost the motion of a sleepwalker. Seated upright in bed, he waited motionless without turning his head toward Daru, as if he were listening attentively. Daru did not stir; it had just occurred to him that the revolver was still in the drawer of his desk. It was better to act at once. Yet he continued to observe the prisoner, who, with the same slithery motion, put his feet on the ground, waited again, then stood up slowly. Daru was about to call out to him when the Arab began to walk, in a quite natural but extraordinarily silent way. He was heading toward the door at the end of the room that opened into the shed. He lifted the latch with precaution and went out, pushing the door behind him but without shutting it.

Daru had not stirred. "He is running away," he merely thought. "Good riddance!" Yet he listened attentively. The hens were not fluttering; the guest must be on the plateau. A faint sound of water reached him, and he didn't know what it was until the Arab again stood framed in the doorway, closed the door carefully, and came back to bed without a sound. Then Daru turned his back on him and fell asleep. Still later he seemed from the depths of his sleep, to hear furtive steps around the schoolhouse. "I'm dreaming! I'm dreaming!" he repeated to himself. And he went on sleeping.

When he awoke, the sky was clear; the loose window let in a cold, pure air. The Arab was asleep, hunched up under the blankets now, his mouth open, utterly relaxed. But when Daru shook him he started dreadfully, staring at Daru with wild eyes as if he had never seen him and with such a frightened expression that the schoolmaster stepped back. "Don't be afraid. It is I. You must eat." The Arab nodded his head and said yes. Calm had returned to his face, but his expression was vacant and listless.

The coffee was ready. They drank it seated together on the cot as they munched their pieces of the cake. Then Daru led the Arab under the shed and showed him the faucet where he washed. He went back into the room, folded the blankets on the cot, made his own bed, and put the room in order. Then he went through the classroom and out onto the terrace. The sun was already riding in the blue sky; a soft, bright light enveloped the deserted plateau. On the ridge the snow was melting in spots. The stones were about to reappear. Crouched on the edge of the plateau, the schoolmaster looked at the deserted expanse. He thought of Balducci. He had hurt him, for he had sent him off as though he didn't want to be associated with him. He could still hear the gendarme's farewell and, without knowing why, he felt strangely empty and vulnerable.

At that moment, from the other side of the schoolhouse, the prisoner coughed. Daru listened to him almost despite himself and then, furious, threw a pebble that whistled through the air before sinking into the snow. That man's stupid crime revolted him, but to hand him over was contrary to honor; just thinking of it made him boil with humiliation. He simultaneously cursed his own people who had sent him this Arab and the Arab who had dared to kill and not managed to get away. Daru got up, walked in a circle on the terrace, waited motionless, and then went back into the schoolhouse.

The Arab, leaning over the cement floor of the shed, was washing his teeth with two fingers. Daru looked at him and said, "Come." He went back into the room ahead of the prisoner. He slipped a hunting jacket on over his sweater and put on walking shoes. Standing, he waited until the Arab had put on his *chèche* and sandals. They went into the classroom, and the schoolmaster pointed to the exit saying, "Go ahead." The fellow didn't budge. "I'm coming," said Daru. The Arab went out. Daru went back into the room and made a package with pieces of rusk, dates, and sugar in it. In the classroom, before going out, he hesitated a second in front of his desk, then crossed the threshold and locked the door. "That's the way," he said. He started toward the east, followed by the prisoner. But a short distance from the schoolhouse he thought he heard a slight sound behind him. He retraced his steps and examined the surroundings of the house; there was no one there. The Arab watched him without seeming to understand. "Come on," said Daru.

They walked for an hour and rested beside a sharp needle of limestone. The snow was melting faster and faster and the sun was drinking up the puddles just as quickly, rapidly cleaning the plateau, which gradually dried and vibrated like the air itself. When they resumed walking, the ground rang under their feet. From time to time a bird rent the space in front of them with a joyful cry. Daru felt a sort of rapture before the vast familiar expanse, now almost entirely yellow under its dome of blue sky. They walked an hour more, descending toward the south. They reached a sort of flattened elevation made up of crumbly rocks. From there on, the plateau sloped down — eastward toward a low plain on which could be made out a few spindly trees, and to the south toward outcroppings of rock that gave the landscape a chaotic look.

Daru surveyed the two directions. Not a man could be seen. He turned toward the Arab, who was looking at him blankly. Daru offered the package to him. "Take it," he said. "There are dates, bread, sugar. You can hold out for two days. Here are a thousand francs too."

The Arab took the package and the money but kept his full hands at chest level as if he didn't know what to do with what was being given him.

"Now look," the schoolmaster said as he pointed in the direction of the east, "there's the way to Tinguit. You have a two-hour walk. At Tinguit are the administration and the police. They are expecting you."

The Arab looked toward the east, still holding the package and the money against his chest. Daru took his elbow and turned him rather roughly toward the south. At the foot of the elevation on which they stood could be seen a faint path. "That's the trail across the plateau. In a day's walk from here you'll find pasturelands and the first nomads. They'll take you in and shelter you according to their law."

The Arab had now turned toward Daru, and a sort of panic was visible in his expression. "Listen," he said.

Daru shook his head. "No, be quiet. Now I'm leaving you." He turned his back on him, took two long steps in the direction of the school, looked hesitantly at the motionless Arab, and started off again. For a few minutes he heard nothing but his own step resounding on the cold ground, and he did not turn his head. A moment later, however, he turned around. The Arab was still there on the edge of the hill, his arms hanging now, and he was looking at the schoolmaster. Daru felt something rise in his throat. But he swore with impatience, waved vaguely, and started off again. He had already gone a distance when he again stopped and looked. There was no longer anyone on the hill.

Daru hesitated. The sun was now rather high in the sky and beginning to beat down on his head. The schoolmaster retraced his steps, at first somewhat uncertainly, then with decision. When he reached the little hill, he was bathed in sweat. He climbed it as fast as he could and stopped, out of breath, on the top. The rock fields to the south stood out sharply against the blue sky, but on the plain to the east a steamy heat was rising. And in that slight haze, Daru, with heavy heart, made out the Arab walking slowly on the road to prison.

A little later, standing before the window of the classroom, the schoolmaster was watching the clear light bathing the whole surface of the plateau. Behind him on the blackboard, among the winding French rivers, sprawled the clumsily chalked up words he had just read: "You handed over our brother. You will pay for this." Daru looked at the sky, the plateau, and beyond, the invisible lands stretching all the way to the sea. In this vast landscape he had loved so much, he was alone.

QUESTIONS

1. What is the central conflict of the story? Is it external or internal? Can it be defined in terms of dilemma?
2. Compare and contrast the attitudes of Daru and Balducci toward the prisoner and the situation. What is their attitude toward each other? Is either a bad or a cruel man? How does the conflict between Daru and Balducci intensify the central conflict?
3. Why does Daru give the prisoner his freedom? What reasons are there for not giving him his freedom?
4. In what respect is the title ironic? Why does "The Guest" make a better title than "The Prisoner"? And why does the French title, "L'Hôte" (which can mean either "The Guest" or "The Host") make an even better title than its English translation?
5. This story contains the materials of explosive action — a revolver, a murderer, a state of undeclared war, an incipient uprising, a revenge note — but no violence occurs in the story. In what aspect of the situation is Camus principally interested?
6. This story has as its background a specific political situation — the French Algerian crisis in the years following World War II. How does Daru reflect France's plight? Is the story's meaning limited to this situation? What does the story tell us about good and evil and the nature of moral choice? How does

the story differ in its treatment of these things from the typical Western story or the patriotic editorial?

7. In what respect is the ending of the story ironic? What kind of irony is this? What does it contribute to the meaning of the story?

8. Besides the ironies of the title and the ending, there are other ironies in the story. Find and explain them. Daru uses verbal irony in paragraph 12 when he exclaims, "Odd pupils!" Is verbal irony the same thing as sarcasm?

9. Comment on the following: (a) Daru's behavior toward firearms and how it helps reveal him; (b) Camus's reason for making the Arab a murderer; (c) the Arab's reason for taking the road to prison.

Flannery O'Connor
Greenleaf

Mrs. May's bedroom window was low and faced on the east and the bull, silvered in the moonlight, stood under it, his head raised as if he listened — like some patient god come down to woo her — for a stir inside the room. The window was dark and the sound of her breathing too light to be carried outside. Clouds crossing the moon blackened him and in the dark he began to tear at the hedge. Presently they passed and he appeared again in the same spot, chewing steadily, with a hedge-wreath that he had ripped loose for himself caught in the tips of his horns. When the moon drifted into retirement again, there was nothing to mark his place but the sound of steady chewing. Then abruptly a pink glow filled the window. Bars of light slid across him as the venetian blind was slit. He took a step backward and lowered his head as if to show the wreath across his horns.

For almost a minute there was no sound from inside, then as he raised his crowned head again, a woman's voice, guttural as if addressed to a dog, said, "Get away from here, Sir!" and in a second muttered, "Some nigger's scrub bull."

The animal pawed the ground and Mrs. May, standing bent forward behind the blind, closed it quickly lest the light make him charge into the shrubbery. For a second she waited, still bent forward, her nightgown hanging loosely from her narrow shoulders. Green rubber curlers sprouted neatly over her forehead and her face beneath them was smooth as concrete with an egg-white paste that drew the wrinkles out while she slept.

She had been conscious in her sleep of a steady rhythmic chewing as if something were eating one wall of the house. She had been aware that whatever it was had been eating as long as she had the place and had eaten every-

GREENLEAF   First published in 1956. Flannery O'Connor (1925–1964), Roman Catholic by birth and belief, was born in Savannah and lived, from 1938 until 1945, in Milledgeville, Georgia. After five years spent writing in Iowa, New York, and Connecticut, she was stricken with an incurable disease (which had already killed her father) and spent several months in an Atlanta hospital. In the summer of 1951, with the disease only partially checked, she and her mother moved to a dairy farm a few miles outside of Milledgeville, which her mother managed, while she continued to write.

thing from the beginning of her fence line up to the house and now was eating the house and calmly with the same steady rhythm would continue through the house, eating her and the boys, and then on, eating everything but the Greenleafs, on and on, eating everything until nothing was left but the Greenleafs on a little island all their own in the middle of what had been her place. When the munching reached her elbow, she jumped up and found herself, fully awake, standing in the middle of her room. She identified the sound at once: a cow was tearing at the shrubbery under the window. Mr. Greenleaf had left the lane gate open and she didn't doubt that the entire herd was on her lawn. She turned on the dim pink table lamp and then went to the window and slit the blind. The bull, gaunt and long-legged, was standing about four feet from her, chewing calmly like an uncouth country suitor.

For fifteen years, she thought as she squinted at him fiercely, she had been having shiftless people's hogs root up her oats, their mules wallow on her lawn, their scrub bulls breed her cows. If this one was not put up now, he would be over the fence, ruining her herd before morning — and Mr. Greenleaf was soundly sleeping a half mile down the road in the tenant house. There was no way to get him unless she dressed and got in her car and rode down there and woke him up. He would come but his expression, his whole figure, his every pause, would say: "Hit looks to me like one or both of them boys would not make their maw ride out in the middle of the night thisaway. If hit was my boys, they would have got the bull up theirself."

The bull lowered his head and shook it and the wreath slipped down to the base of his horns where it looked like a menacing prickly crown. She had closed the blind then; in a few seconds she heard him move off heavily.

Mr. Greenleaf would say, "If hit was my boys they would never have allowed their maw to go after the hired help in the middle of the night. They would have did it theirself."

Weighing it, she decided not to bother Mr. Greenleaf. She returned to bed thinking that if the Greenleaf boys had risen in the world it was because she had given their father employment when no one else would have him. She had had Mr. Greenleaf fifteen years but no one else would have had him five minutes. Just the way he approached an object was enough to tell anybody with eyes what kind of a worker he was. He walked with a high-shouldered creep and he never appeared to come directly forward. He walked on the perimeter of some invisible circle and if you wanted to look him in the face, you had to move and get in front of him. She had not fired him because she had always doubted she could do better. He was too shiftless to go out and look for another job; he didn't have the initiative to steal, and after she had told him three or four times to do a thing, he did it; but he never told her about a sick cow until it was too late to call the veterinarian and if her barn had caught fire, he would have called his wife to see the flames before he began to put them out. And of the wife, she didn't even like to think. Beside the wife, Mr. Greenleaf was an aristocrat.

"If hit had been my boys," he would have said, "they would have cut off their right arm before they would have allowed their maw to . . ."

"If your boys had any pride, Mr. Greenleaf," she would like to say to him some day, "there are many things that they would not *allow* their mother to do."

The next morning as soon as Mr. Greenleaf came to the back door, she told him there was a stray bull on the place and that she wanted him penned up at once.

"Done already been here three days," he said, addressing his right foot which he held forward, turned slightly as if he were trying to look at the sole. He was standing at the bottom of the three back steps while she leaned out the kitchen door, a small woman with pale near-sighted eyes and grey hair that rose on top like the crest of some disturbed bird.

"Three days!" she said in the restrained screech that had become habitual with her.

Mr. Greenleaf, looking into the distance over the near pasture, removed a package of cigarets from his shirt pocket and let one fall into his hand. He put the package back and stood for a while looking at the cigaret. "I put him in the bull pen but he torn out of there," he said presently. "I didn't see him none after that." He bent over the cigaret and lit it and then turned his head briefly in her direction. The upper part of his face sloped gradually into the lower which was long and narrow, shaped like a rough chalice. He had deep-set fox-colored eyes shadowed under a grey felt hat that he wore slanted forward following the line of his nose. His build was insignificant.

"Mr. Greenleaf," she said, "get the bull up this morning before you do anything else. You know he'll ruin the breeding schedule. Get him up and keep him up and the next time there's a stray bull on this place, tell me at once. Do you understand?"

"Where do you want him put at?" Mr. Greenleaf asked.

"I don't care where you put him," she said. "You are supposed to have some sense. Put him where he can't get out. Whose bull is he?"

For a moment Mr. Greenleaf seemed to hesitate between silence and speech. He studied the air to the left of him. "He must be somebody's bull," he said after a while.

"Yes, he must!" she said and shut the door with a precise little slam.

She went into the dining room where the two boys were eating breakfast and sat down on the edge of her chair at the head of the table. She never ate breakfast but she sat with them to see that they had what they wanted. "Honestly!" she said, and began to tell about the bull, aping Mr. Greenleaf saying, "It must be *somebody's* bull."

Wesley continued to read the newspaper folded beside his plate but Scofield interrupted his eating from time to time to look at her and laugh. The two boys never had the same reaction to anything. They were as different, she said, as night and day. The only thing they did have in common was neither of them cared what happened on the place. Scofield was a business type and Wesley was an intellectual.

Wesley, the younger child, had had rheumatic fever when he was seven and Mrs. May thought that this was what had caused him to be an intellectual. Scofield, who had never had a day's sickness in his life, was an insurance salesman. She would not have minded his selling insurance if he had sold a nicer kind but he sold the kind that only Negroes buy. He was what Negroes call a "policy man." He said there was more money in nigger-insurance than any other kind, and before company, he was very loud about it. He would shout, "Mama don't like to hear me say it but I'm the best nigger-insurance salesman in this county!"

Scofield was thirty-six and he had a broad pleasant face but he was not married. "Yes," Mrs. May would say, "and if you sold decent insurance, some *nice* girl would be willing to marry you. What nice girl wants to marry a nigger-insurance man? You'll wake up some day and it'll be too late."

And at this Scofield would yodel and say, "Why Mamma, I'm not going to marry until you're dead and gone and then I'm going to marry me some nice fat girl that can take over this place!" And once he had added, " — some nice lady like Mrs. Greenleaf." When he had said this Mrs. May had risen from her chair, her back stiff as a rake handle, and had gone to her room. There she had sat down on the edge of her bed for some time with her small face drawn. Finally she had whispered, "I work and slave, I struggle and sweat to keep this place for them and as soon as I'm dead, they'll marry trash and bring it in here and ruin everything. They'll marry trash and ruin everything I've done," and she had made up her mind at that moment to change her will. The next day she had gone to her lawyer and had had the property entailed so that if they married, they could not leave it to their wives.

The idea that one of them might marry a woman even remotely like Mrs. Greenleaf was enough to make her ill. She had put up with Mr. Greenleaf for fifteen years, but the only way she had endured his wife had been by keeping entirely out of her sight. Mrs. Greenleaf was large and loose. The yard around her house looked like a dump and her five girls were always filthy; even the youngest one dipped snuff. Instead of making a garden or washing their clothes, her preoccupation was what she called "prayer healing."

Every day she cut all the morbid stories out of the newspaper — the accounts of women who had been raped and criminals who had escaped and children who had been burned and of train wrecks and plane crashes and the divorces of movie stars. She took these to the woods and dug a hole and buried them and then she fell on the ground over them and mumbled and groaned for an hour or so, moving her huge arms back and forth under her and out again and finally just lying down flat and, Mrs. May suspected, going to sleep in the dirt.

She had not found out about this until the Greenleafs had been with her a few months. One morning she had been out to inspect a field that she wanted planted in rye but that had come up in clover because Mr. Greenleaf had used the wrong seeds in the grain drill. She was returning through a wooded path that separated two pastures, muttering to herself and hitting the ground

25

methodically with a long stick she carried in case she saw a snake. "Mr. Greenleaf," she was saying in a low voice, "I cannot afford to pay for your mistakes. I am a poor woman and this place is all I have. I have two boys to educate. I cannot . . ."

Out of nowhere a guttural agonized voice groaned, "Jesus! Jesus!" In a second it came again with a terrible urgency. "Jesus! Jesus!"

Mrs. May stopped still, one hand lifted to her throat. The sound was so piercing that she felt as if some violent unleashed force had broken out of the ground and was charging toward her. Her second thought was more reasonable: somebody had been hurt on the place and would sue her for everything she had. She had no insurance. She rushed forward and turning a bend in the path, she saw Mrs. Greenleaf sprawled on her hands and knees off the side of the road, her head down.

30   "Mrs. Greenleaf!" she shrilled, "what's happened?"

Mrs. Greenleaf raised her head. Her face was a patchwork of dirt and tears and her small eyes, the color of two field peas, were red-rimmed and swollen, but her expression was as composed as a bulldog's. She swayed back and forth on her hands and knees and groaned, "Jesus, Jesus."

Mrs. May winced. She thought the word, Jesus, should be kept inside the church building like other words inside the bedroom. She was a good Christian woman with a large respect for religion, though she did not, of course, believe any of it was true. "What is the matter with you?" she asked sharply.

"You broke my healing," Mrs. Greenleaf said, waving her aside. "I can't talk to you until I finish."

Mrs. May stood, bent forward, her mouth open and her stick raised off the ground as if she were not sure what she wanted to strike with it.

35   "Oh, Jesus, stab me in the heart!" Mrs. Greenleaf shrieked. "Jesus, stab me in the heart!" and she fell back flat in the dirt, a huge human mound, her legs and arms spread out as if she were trying to wrap them around the earth.

Mrs. May felt as furious and helpless as if she had been insulted by a child. "Jesus," she said, drawing herself back, "would be *ashamed* of you. He would tell you to get up from there this instant and go wash your children's clothes!" and she had turned and walked off as fast as she could.

Whenever she thought of how the Greenleaf boys had advanced in the world, she had only to think of Mrs. Greenleaf sprawled obscenely on the ground, and say to herself, "Well, no matter how far they go, they *came* from that."

She would like to have been able to put in her will that when she died, Wesley and Scofield were not to continue to employ Mr. Greenleaf. She was capable of handling Mr. Greenleaf; they were not. Mr. Greenleaf had pointed out to her once that her boys didn't know hay from silage. She had pointed out to him that they had other talents, that Scofield was a successful businessman and Wesley a successful intellectual. Mr. Greenleaf did not comment, but he never lost an opportunity of letting her see, by his expression or some simple gesture, that he held the two of them in infinite contempt. As scrub-human as the Greenleafs were, he never hesitated to let her know that in any like circumstance in which his own boys might have been involved, they — O. T. and E. T. Greenleaf — would have acted to better advantage.

The Greenleaf boys were two or three years younger than the May boys. They were twins and you never knew when you spoke to one of them whether you were speaking to O. T. or E. T., and they never had the politeness to enlighten you. They were long-legged and raw-boned and red-skinned, with bright grasping fox-colored eyes like their father's. Mr. Greenleaf's pride in them began with the fact that they were twins. He acted, Mrs. May said, as if this were something smart they had thought of themselves. They were energetic and hard-working and she would admit to anyone that they had come a long way — and that the Second World War was responsible for it.

They had both joined the service and, disguised in their uniforms,   40
they could not be told from other people's children. You could tell, of course, when they opened their mouths but they did that seldom. The smartest thing they had done was to get sent overseas and there to marry French wives. They hadn't married French trash either. They had married nice girls who naturally couldn't tell that they murdered the king's English or that the Greenleafs were who they were.

Wesley's heart condition had not permitted him to serve his country but Scofield had been in the army for two years. He had not cared for it and at the end of his military service, he was only a Private First Class. The Greenleaf boys were both some kind of sergeants, and Mr. Greenleaf, in those days, had never lost an opportunity of referring to them by their rank. They had both managed to get wounded and now they both had pensions. Further, as soon as they were released from the army, they took advantage of all the benefits and went to the school of agriculture at the university — the tax-payers meanwhile supporting their French wives. The two of them were living now about two miles down the highway on a piece of land that the government had helped them to buy and in a brick duplex bungalow that the government had helped to build and pay for. If the war had made anyone, Mrs. May said, it had made the Greenleaf boys. They each had three little children apiece, who spoke Greenleaf English and French, and who, on account of their mothers' background, would be sent to the convent school and brought up with manners. "And in twenty years," Mrs. May asked Scofield and Wesley, "do you know what those people will be?

"*Society*," she said blackly.

She had spent fifteen years coping with Mr. Greenleaf and, by now, handling him had become second nature with her. His disposition on any particular day was as much a factor in what she could and couldn't do as the weather was, and she had learned to read his face the way real country people read the sunrise and sunset.

She was a country woman only by persuasion. The late Mr. May, a businessman, had bought the place when land was down, and when he died it was all he had to leave her. The boys had not been happy to move to the country to a broken-down farm, but there was nothing else for her to do. She had the timber on the place cut and with the proceeds had set herself up in the dairy business after Mr. Greenleaf had answered her ad. "i seen yor add and i will come have 2 boys," was all his letter said, but he arrived the next day in a pieced-together truck, his wife and five daughters sitting on the floor in the back, himself and the two boys in the cab.

45   Over the years they had been on her place, Mr. and Mrs. Greenleaf had aged hardly at all. They had no worries, no responsibilities. They lived like the lilies of the field, off the fat that she struggled to put into the land. When she was dead and gone from overwork and worry, the Greenleafs, healthy and thriving, would be just ready to begin draining Scofield and Wesley.

Wesley said the reason Mrs. Greenleaf had not aged was because she released all her emotions in prayer healing. "You ought to start praying, Sweetheart," he had said in the voice that, poor boy, he could not help making deliberately nasty.

Scofield only exasperated her beyond endurance but Wesley caused her real anxiety. He was thin and nervous and bald and being an intellectual was a terrible strain on his disposition. She doubted if he would marry until she died but she was certain that then the wrong woman would get him. Nice girls didn't like Scofield but Wesley didn't like nice girls. He didn't like anything. He drove twenty miles every day to the university where he taught and twenty miles back every night, but he said he hated the twenty-mile drive and he hated the second-rate university and he hated the morons who attended it. He hated the country and he hated the life he lived; he hated living with his mother and his idiot brother and he hated hearing about the damn dairy and the damn help and the damn broken machinery. But in spite of all he said, he never made any move to leave. He talked about Paris and Rome but he never went even to Atlanta.

"You'd go to those places and you'd get sick," Mrs. May would say. "Who in Paris is going to see that you get a salt-free diet? And do you think if you married one of those odd numbers you take out that *she* would cook a salt-free diet for you? No indeed, she would not!" When she took this line, Wesley would turn himself roughly around in his chair and ignore her. Once when she had kept it up too long, he had snarled, "Well, why don't you do something practical, Woman? Why don't you pray for me like Mrs. Greenleaf would?"

"I don't like to hear you boys make jokes about religion," she had said. "If you would go to church, you would meet some nice girls."

50   But it was impossible to tell them anything. When she looked at the two of them now, sitting on either side of the table, neither one caring the least if a stray bull ruined her herd — which was their herd, their future — when she looked at the two of them, one hunched over a paper and the other teetering back in his chair, grinning at her like an idiot, she wanted to jump up and beat her fist on the table and shout, "You'll find out one of these days, you'll find out what *Reality* is when it's too late!"

"Mamma," Scofield said, "don't you get excited now but I'll tell you whose bull that is." He was looking at her wickedly. He let his chair drop forward and he got up. Then with his shoulders bent and his hands held up to cover his head, he tiptoed to the door. He backed into the hall and pulled the door almost to so that it hid all of him but his face. "You want to know, Sugar-pie?" he asked.

Mrs. May sat looking at him coldly.

"That's O. T. and E. T.'s bull," he said. "I collected from their nigger yesterday and he told me they were missing it," and he showed her an exaggerated expanse of teeth and disappeared silently.

Wesley looked up and laughed.

Mrs. May turned her head forward again, her expression unaltered. "I am the only *adult* on this place," she said. She leaned across the table and pulled the paper from the side of his plate. "Do you see how it's going to be when I die and you boys have to handle him?" she began. "Do you see why he didn't know whose bull that was? Because it was theirs. Do you see what I have to put up with? Do you see that if I hadn't kept my foot on his neck all these years, you boys might be milking cows every morning at four o'clock?"

Wesley pulled the paper back toward his plate and staring at her full in the face, he murmured, "I wouldn't milk a cow to save your soul from hell."

"I know you wouldn't," she said in a brittle voice. She sat back and began rapidly turning her knife over at the side of her plate. "O. T. and E. T. are fine boys," she said. "They ought to have been my sons." The thought of this was so horrible that her vision of Wesley was blurred at once by a wall of tears. All she saw was his dark shape, rising quickly from the table. "And you two," she cried, "you two should have belonged to that woman!"

He was heading for the door.

"When I die," she said in a thin voice, "I don't know what's going to become of you."

"You're always yapping about when-you-die," he growled as he rushed out, "but you look pretty healthy to me."

For some time she sat where she was, looking straight ahead through the window across the room into a scene of indistinct grays and greens. She stretched her face and her neck muscles and drew in a long breath but the scene in front of her flowed together anyway into a watery gray mass. "They needn't think I'm going to die any time soon," she muttered, and some more defiant voice in her added: I'll die when I get good and ready.

She wiped her eyes with the table napkin and got up and went to the window and gazed at the scene in front of her. The cows were grazing on two pale green pastures across the road and behind them, fencing them in, was a black wall of trees with a sharp sawtooth edge that held off the indifferent sky. The pastures were enough to calm her. When she looked out any window in her house, she saw the reflection of her own character. Her city friends said she was the most remarkable woman they knew, to go, practically penniless and with no experience, out to a rundown farm and make a success of it. "Everything is against you," she would say, "the weather is against you and the dirt is against you and the help is against you. They're all in league against you. There's nothing for it but an iron hand!"

"Look at Mamma's iron hand!" Scofield would yell and grab her arm and hold it up so that her delicate blue-veined little hand would dangle from her wrist like the head of a broken lily. The company always laughed.

The sun, moving over the black and white grazing cows, was just a little brighter than the rest of the sky. Looking down, she saw a darker shape that might have been its shadow cast at an angle, moving among them. She uttered a sharp cry and turned and marched out of the house.

Mr. Greenleaf was in the trench silo, filling a wheelbarrow. She stood on the edge and looked down at him. "I told you to get up that bull. Now he's in with the milk herd."

"You can't do two thangs at oncet," Mr. Greenleaf remarked.

"I told you to do that first."

He wheeled the barrow out of the open end of the trench toward the barn and she followed close behind him. "And you needn't think, Mr. Greenleaf," she said, "that I don't know exactly whose bull that is or why you haven't been in any hurry to notify me he was here. I might as well feed O. T. and E. T.'s bull as long as I'm going to have him here ruining my herd."

Mr. Greenleaf paused with the wheelbarrow and looked behind him "Is that them boys' bull?" he asked in an incredulous tone.

She did not say a word. She merely looked away with her mouth taut.

"They told me their bull was out but I never known that was him," he said.

"I want that bull put up now," she said, "and I'm going to drive over to O. T. and E. T.'s and tell them they'll have to come get him today. I ought to charge for the time he's been here — then it wouldn't happen again."

"They didn't pay but seventy-five dollars for him," Mr. Greenleaf offered.

"I wouldn't have had him as a gift," she said.

"They was just going to beef him," Mr. Greenleaf went on, "but he got loose and run his head into their pickup truck. He don't like cars and trucks. They had a time getting his horn out the fender and when they finally got him loose, he took off and they was too tired to run after him — but I never known that was him there."

"It wouldn't have paid you to know, Mr. Greenleaf," she said. "But you know now. Get a horse and get him."

In a half hour, from her front window she saw the bull, squirrel-colored, with jutting hips and long light horns, ambling down the dirt road that ran in front of the house. Mr. Greenleaf was behind him on the horse. "That's a Greenleaf bull if I ever saw one," she muttered. She went out on the porch and called, "Put him where he can't get out."

"He likes to bust loose," Mr. Greenleaf said, looking with approval at the bull's rump. "This gentleman is a sport."

"If those boys don't come for him, he's going to be a dead sport," she said. "I'm just warning you."

He heard her but he didn't answer.

"That's the awfullest looking bull I ever saw," she called but he was too far down the road to hear.

It was mid-morning when she turned into O. T. and E. T.'s driveway. The house, a new red-brick, low-to-the-ground building that looked like a warehouse with windows, was on top of a treeless hill. The sun was beating down directly on the white roof of it. It was the kind of house that everybody built now and nothing marked it as belonging to Greenleafs except three dogs, part hound and part spitz, that rushed out from behind it as soon as she stopped her car. She reminded herself that you could always tell the class of people by the class of dog, and honked her horn. While she sat waiting for someone to come, she continued to study the house. All the windows were down and she wondered if the government could have air-conditioned the thing. No one came and she honked again. Presently a door opened and several children appeared in it and stood looking at her, making no move to come forward. She recognized this as a true Greenleaf trait — they could hang in the door, looking at you for hours.

"Can't one of you children come here?" she called.

After a minute they all began to move forward, slowly. They had on overalls and were barefooted but they were not as dirty as she might have expected. There were two or three that looked distinctly like Greenleafs; the others not so much so. The smallest child was a girl with untidy black hair. They stopped about six feet from the automobile and stood looking at her.

"You're mighty pretty," Mrs. May said, addressing herself to the small- est girl.

There was no answer. They appeared to share one dispassionate expression between them.

"Where's your Mamma?" she asked.

There was no answer to this for some time. Then one of them said something in French. Mrs. May did not speak French.

"Where's your daddy?" she asked.

After a while, one of the boys said, "He ain't hyar neither."

"Ahhhh," Mrs. May said as if something had been proven. "Where's the colored man?"

She waited and decided no one was going to answer. "The cat has six little tongues," she said. "How would you like to come home with me and let me teach you how to talk?" She laughed and her laugh died on the silent air. She felt as if she were on trial for her life, facing a jury of Greenleafs. "I'll go down and see if I can find the colored man," she said.

"You can go if you want to," one of the boys said.

"Well, thank you," she murmured and drove off.

The barn was down the lane from the house. She had not seen it before but Mr. Greenleaf had described it in detail for it had been built according to the latest specifications. It was a milking parlor arrangement where the cows are milked from below. The milk ran in pipes from the machines to the milk house and was never carried in no bucket, Mr. Greenleaf said, by no human hand. "When you gonter get you one?" he had asked.

"Mr. Greenleaf," she had said, "I have to do for myself. I am not assisted hand and foot by the government. It would cost me $20,000 to install a milking parlor. I barely make ends meet as it is."

"My boys done it," Mr. Greenleaf had murmured and then — "but all boys ain't alike."

"No indeed!" she had said. "I thank God for that!"

"I thank Gawd for ever-thang," Mr. Greenleaf had drawled.

100   You might as well, she had thought in the fierce silence that followed; you've never done anything for yourself.

She stopped by the side of the barn and honked but no one appeared. For several minutes she sat in the car, observing the various machines parked around, wondering how many of them were paid for. They had a forage harvester and a rotary hay baler. She had those too. She decided that since no one was here, she would get out and have a look at the milking parlor and see if they kept it clean.

She opened the milking room door and stuck her head in and for the first second she felt as if she were going to lose her breath. The spotless white concrete room was filled with sunlight that came from a row of windows head-high along both walls. The metal stanchions gleamed ferociously and she had to squint to be able to look at all. She drew her head out the room quickly and closed the door and leaned against it, frowning. The light outside was not so bright but she was conscious that the sun was directly on top of her head, like a silver bullet ready to drop into her brain.

A Negro carrying a yellow calf-feed bucket appeared from around the corner of the machine shed and came toward her. He was a light yellow boy dressed in the cast-off army clothes of the Greenleaf twins. He stopped at a respectable distance and set the bucket on the ground.

"Where's Mr. O. T. and Mr. E. T.?" she asked.

105   "Mist O. T. he in town, Mist E. T. he off yonder in the field," the Negro said, pointing first to the left and then to the right as if he were naming the position of two planets.

"Can you remember a message?" she asked, looking as if she thought this doubtful.

"I'll remember it if I don't forget it," he said with a touch of sullenness.

"Well, I'll write it down then," she said. She got in her car and took a stub of pencil from her pocket book and began to write on the back of an empty envelope. The Negro came and stood at the window. "I'm Mrs. May," she said as she wrote. "Their bull is on my place and I want him off *today*. You can tell them I'm furious about it."

"That bull lef here Sareday," the Negro said, "and none of us ain't seen him since. We ain't knowed where he was."

110   "Well, you know now," she said, "and you can tell Mr. O. T. and Mr. E. T. that if they don't come get him today, I'm going to have their daddy

shoot him the first thing in the morning. I can't have that bull ruining my herd." She handed him the note.

"If I knows Mist O. T. and Mist E. T.," he said, taking it, "they goin to say go ahead on and shoot him. He done busted up one of our trucks already and we be glad to see the last of him."

She pulled her head back and gave him a look from slightly bleared eyes. "Do they expect me to take my time and my worker to shoot their bull?" she asked. "They don't want him so they just let him loose and expect somebody else to kill him? He's eating my oats and ruining my herd and I'm expected to shoot him too?"

"I speck you is," he said softly. "He done busted up . . ."

She gave him a very sharp look and said, "Well, I'm not surprised. That's just the way some people are," and after a second she asked, "Which is boss, Mr. O. T. or Mr. E. T.?" She had always suspected that they fought between themselves secretly.

"They never quarls," the boy said. "They like one man in two skins." 115

"Hmp. I expect you just never heard them quarrel."

"Nor nobody else heard them neither," he said, looking away as if this insolence were addressed to someone else.

"Well," she said, "I haven't put up with their father for fifteen years not to know a few things about Greenleafs."

The Negro looked at her suddenly with a gleam of recognition. "Is you my policy man's mother?" he asked.

"I don't know who your policy man is," she said sharply. "You give them 120 that note and tell them if they don't come for that bull today, they'll be making their father shoot it tomorrow," and she drove off.

She stayed at home all afternoon waiting for the Greenleaf twins to come for the bull. They did not come. I might as well be working for them, she thought furiously. They are simply going to use me to the limit. At the supper table, she went over it again for the boys' benefit because she wanted them to see exactly what O. T. and E. T. would do. "They don't want that bull," she said, " — pass the butter — so they simply turn him loose and let somebody else worry about getting rid of him for them. How do you like that? I'm the victim. I've always been the victim."

"Pass the butter to the victim," Wesley said. He was in a worse humor than usual because he had had a flat tire on the way home from the university.

Scofield handed her the butter and said, "Why, Mamma, ain't you ashamed to shoot an old bull that ain't done nothing but give you a little scrub strain in your herd? I declare," he said, "with the Mamma I got it's a wonder I turned out to be such a nice boy!"

"You ain't her boy, Son," Wesley said.

She eased back in her chair, her fingertips on the edge of the table. 125

"All I know is," Scofield said, "I done mighty well to be as nice as I am seeing what I come from."

When they teased her they spoke Greenleaf English but Wesley made his own particular tone come through it like a knife edge. "Well lemme tell you one thang, Brother," he said, leaning over the table, "that if you had half a mind you would already know."

"What's that, Brother?" Scofield asked, his broad face grinning into the thin constricted one across from him.

"That is," Wesley said, "that neither you nor me is her boy . . .," but he stopped abruptly as she gave a kind of hoarse wheeze like an old horse lashed unexpectedly. She reared up and ran from the room.

"Oh, for God's sake," Wesley growled, "what did you start her off for?"

"I never started her off," Scofield said. "You started her off."

"Hah."

"She's not as young as she used to be and she can't take it."

"She can only give it out," Wesley said. "I'm the one that takes it."

His brother's pleasant face had changed so that an ugly family resemblance showed between them. "Nobody feels sorry for a lousy bastard like you," he said and grabbed across the table for the other's shirtfront.

From her room she heard a crash of dishes and she rushed back through the kitchen into the dining room. The hall door was open and Scofield was going out of it. Wesley was lying like a large bug on his back with the edge of the over-turned table cutting him across the middle and broken dishes scattered on top of him. She pulled the table off him and caught his arm to help him rise but he scrambled up and pushed her off with a furious charge of energy and flung himself out the door after his brother.

She would have collapsed but a knock on the door stiffened her and she swung around. Across the kitchen and back porch, she could see Mr. Greenleaf peering eagerly through the screenwire. All her resources returned in full strength as if she had only needed to be challenged by the devil himself to regain them. "I heard a thump," he called, "and I thought the plastering might have fell on you."

If he had been wanted someone would have had to go on a horse to find him. She crossed the kitchen and the porch and stood inside the screen and said, "No, nothing happened but the table turned over. One of the legs was weak," and without pausing, "the boys didn't come for the bull so tomorrow you'll have to shoot him."

The sky was crossed with thin red and purple bars and behind them the sun was moving down slowly as if it were descending a ladder. Mr. Greenleaf squatted down on the step, his back to her, the top of his hat on a level with her feet. "Tomorrow I'll drive him home for you," he said.

"Oh no, Mr. Greenleaf," she said in a mocking voice, "you drive him home tomorrow and next week he'll be back here. I know better than that." Then in a mournful tone, she said, "I'm surprised at O. T. and E. T. to treat me this way. I thought they'd have more gratitude. Those boys spent some mighty happy days on this place, didn't they, Mr. Greenleaf?"

Mr. Greenleaf didn't say anything.

"I think they did," she said. "I think they did. But they've forgotten all the nice little things I did for them now. If I recall, they wore my boys' old clothes and played with my boys' old toys and hunted with my boys' old guns. They swam in my pond and shot my birds and fished in my stream and I never forgot their birthday and Christmas seemed to roll around very often if I remember it right. And do they think of any of those things now?" she asked. "NOOOOO," she said.

For a few seconds she looked at the disappearing sun and Mr. Greenleaf examined the palms of his hands. Presently as if it had just occurred to her, she asked, "Do you know the real reason they didn't come for that bull?"

"Naw I don't," Mr. Greenleaf said in a surly voice.

"They didn't come because I'm a woman," she said. "You can get away   145
with anything when you're dealing with a woman. If there were a man running this place . . ."

Quick as a snake striking Mr. Greenleaf said, "You got two boys. They know you got two men on the place."

The sun had disappeared behind the tree line. She looked down at the dark crafty face, upturned now, and at the wary eyes, bright under the shadow of the hatbrim. She waited long enough for him to see that she was hurt and then she said, "Some people learn gratitude too late, Mr. Greenleaf, and some never learn it at all," and she turned and left him sitting on the steps.

Half the night in her sleep she heard a sound as if some large stone were grinding a hole on the outside wall of her brain. She was walking on the inside, over a succession of beautiful rolling hills, planting her stick in front of each step. She became aware after a time that the noise was the sun trying to burn through the tree line and she stopped to watch, safe in the knowledge that it couldn't, that it had to sink the way it always did outside of her property. When she first stopped it was a swollen red ball, but as she stood watching it began to narrow and pale until it looked like a bullet. Then suddenly it burst through the tree line and raced down the hill toward her. She woke up with her hand over her mouth and the same noise, diminished but distinct, in her ear. It was the bull munching under her window. Mr. Greenleaf had let him out.

She got up and made her way to the window in the dark and looked out through the slit blind, but the bull had moved away from the hedge and at first she didn't see him. Then she saw a heavy form some distance away, paused as if observing her. This is the last night I am going to put up with this, she said, and watched until the iron shadow moved away in the darkness.

The next morning she waited until exactly eleven o'clock. Then she got   150
in her car and drove to the barn. Mr. Greenleaf was cleaning milk cans. He had seven of them standing up outside the milk room to get the sun. She had been telling him to do this for two weeks. "All right, Mr. Greenleaf," she said, "go get your gun. We're going to shoot that bull."

"I thought you wanted theseyer cans . . ."

"Go get your gun, Mr. Greenleaf," she said. Her voice and face were expressionless.

"That gentleman torn out of there last night," he murmured in a tone of regret and bent again to the can he had his arm in.

"Go get your gun, Mr. Greenleaf," she said in the same triumphant toneless voice. "The bull is in the pasture with the dry cows. I saw him from my upstairs window. I'm going to drive you up to the field and you can run him into the empty pasture and shoot him there."

155   He detached himself from the can slowly. "Ain't nobody ever ast me to shoot my boys' own bull!" he said in a high rasping voice. He removed a rag from his back pocket and began to wipe his hands violently, then his nose.

She turned as if she had not heard this and said, "I'll wait for you in the car. Go get your gun."

She sat in the car and watched him stalk off toward the harness room where he kept a gun. After he had entered the room, there was a crash as if he had kicked something out of his way. Presently he emerged again with the gun, circled behind the car, opened the door violently and threw himself onto the seat beside her. He held the gun between his knees and looked straight ahead. He'd like to shoot me instead of the bull, she thought, and turned her face away so that he could not see her smile.

The morning was dry and clear. She drove through the woods for a quarter of a mile and then out into the open where there were fields on either side of the narrow road. The exhilaration of carrying her point had sharpened her senses. Birds were screaming everywhere, the grass was almost too bright to look at, the sky was an even piercing blue. "Spring is here!" she said gaily. Mr. Greenleaf lifted one muscle somewhere near his mouth as if he found this the most asinine remark ever made. When she stopped at the second pasture gate, he flung himself out of the car door and slammed it behind him. Then he opened the gate and she drove through. He closed it and flung himself back in, silently, and she drove around the rim of the pasture until she spotted the bull, almost in the center of it, grazing peacefully among the cows.

"The gentleman is waiting on you," she said and gave Mr. Greenleaf's furious profile a sly look. "Run him into that next pasture and when you get him in, I'll drive in behind you and shut the gate myself."

160   He flung himself out again, this time deliberately leaving the car door open so that she had to lean across the seat and close it. She sat smiling as she watched him make his way across the pasture toward the opposite gate. He seemed to throw himself forward at each step and then pull back as if he were calling on some power to witness that he was being forced. "Well," she said aloud as if he were still in the car, "it's your own boys who are making you do this, Mr. Greenleaf." O. T. and E. T. were probably splitting their sides laughing at him now. She could hear their identical nasal voices saying, "Made Daddy shoot our bull for us. Daddy don't know no better than to think that's a fine bull he's shooting. Gonna kill Daddy to shoot that bull!"

"If those boys cared a thing about you, Mr. Greenleaf," she said. "they would have come for that bull. I'm surprised at them."

He was circling around to open the gate first. The bull, dark among the spotted cows, had not moved. He kept his head down, eating constantly. Mr. Greenleaf opened the gate and then began circling back to approach him from the rear. When he was about ten feet behind him, he flapped his arms at his sides. The bull lifted his head indolently and then lowered it again and continued to eat. Mr. Greenleaf stooped again and picked up something and threw it at him with a vicious swing. She decided it was a sharp rock for the bull leapt and then began to gallop until he disappeared over the rim of the hill. Mr. Greenleaf followed at his leisure.

"You needn't think you're going to lose him!" she cried and started the car straight across the pasture. She had to drive slowly over the terraces and when she reached the gate, Mr. Greenleaf and the bull were nowhere in sight. This pasture was smaller than the last, a green arena, encircled almost entirely by woods. She got out and closed the gate and stood looking for some sign of Mr. Greenleaf but he had disappeared completely. She knew at once that his plan was to lose the bull in the woods. Eventually, she would see him emerge somewhere from the circle of trees and come limping toward her and when he finally reached her, he would say, "If you can find that gentleman in them woods, you're better than me."

She was going to say, "Mr. Greenleaf, if I have to walk into those woods with you and stay all afternoon, we are going to find that bull and shoot him. You are going to shoot him if I have to pull the trigger for you." When he saw she meant business, he would return and shoot the bull quickly himself.

She got back into the car and drove to the center of the pasture where he would not have so far to walk to reach her when he came out of the woods. At this moment she could picture him sitting on a stump, making lines in the ground with a stick. She decided she would wait exactly ten minutes by her watch. Then she would begin to honk. She got out of the car and walked around a little and then sat down on the front bumper to wait and rest. She was very tired and she lay her head back against the hood and closed her eyes. She did not understand why she should be so tired when it was only mid-morning. Through her closed eyes, she could feel the sun, red-hot overhead. She opened her eyes slightly but the white light forced her to close them again.

For some time she lay back against the hood, wondering drowsily why she was so tired. With her eyes closed, she didn't think of time as divided into days and nights but into past and future. She decided she was tired because she had been working continuously for fifteen years. She decided she had every right to be tired, and to rest for a few minutes before she began working again. Before any kind of judgment seat, she would be able to say: I've worked, I have not wallowed. At this very instant while she was recalling a lifetime of work, Mr. Greenleaf was loitering in the woods and Mrs.Greenleaf was probably flat on the ground, asleep over her holeful of clippings. The woman had got worse over the years and Mrs. May believed that now she was actually demented. "I'm afraid your wife has let religion warp her," she said once tactfully to Mr. Greenleaf. "Everything in moderation, you know."

"She cured a man oncet that half his gut was eat out with worms," Mr. Greenleaf said, and she had turned away, half-sickened. Poor souls, she thought now, so simple. For a few seconds she dozed.

When she sat up and looked at her watch, more than ten minutes had passed. She had not heard any shot. A new thought occurred to her; suppose Mr. Greenleaf had aroused the bull chunking stones at him and the animal had turned on him and run him up against a tree and gored him? The irony of it deepened: O. T. and E. T. would then get a shyster lawyer and sue her. It would be the fitting end to her fifteen years with the Greenleafs. She thought of it almost with pleasure as if she had hit on the perfect ending for a story she was telling her friends. Then she dropped it, for Mr. Greenleaf had a gun with him and she had insurance.

She decided to honk. She got up and reached inside the car window and gave three sustained honks and two or three shorter ones to let him know she was getting impatient. Then she went back and sat down on the bumper again.

In a few minutes something emerged from the tree line, a black heavy shadow that tossed its head several times and then bounded forward. After a second she saw it was the bull. He was crossing the pasture toward her at a slow gallop, a gay almost rocking gait as if he were overjoyed to find her again. She looked beyond him to see if Mr. Greenleaf was coming out of the woods too but he was not. "Here he is, Mr. Greenleaf!" she called and looked on the other side of the pasture to see if he could be coming out there but he was not in sight. She looked back and saw that the bull, his head lowered, was racing toward her. She remained perfectly still, not in fright, but in a freezing disbelief. She stared at the violent black streak bounding toward her as if she had no sense of distance, as if she could not decide at once what his intention was, and the bull had buried his head in her lap, like a wild tormented lover, before her expression changed. One of his horns sank until it pierced her heart and the other curved around her side and held her in an unbreakable grip. She continued to stare straight ahead but the entire scene in front of her had changed — the tree line was a dark wound in a world that was nothing but sky — and she had the look of a person whose sight has been suddenly restored but who finds the light unbearable.

Mr. Greenleaf was running toward her from the side with his gun raised and she saw him coming though she was not looking in his direction. She saw him approaching on the outside of some invisible circle, the tree line gaping behind him and nothing under his feet. He shot the bull four times through the eye. She did not hear the shots but she felt the quake in the huge body as it sank, pulling her forward on its head, so that she seemed, when Mr. Greenleaf reached her, to be bent over whispering some last discovery into the animal's ear.

QUESTIONS

1. The characters and events of the story are all seen as reflected through Mrs. May's mind. How objective are her evaluations? How far are they reliable testimony and how far only an index of her own mind?
2. What is Mrs. May's mental image of herself? How does it compare with the image her sons have of her? How does it compare with the reader's image?
3. What is Mrs. May's dominant emotion? What is the consuming preoccupation of her mind? Are there any occasions on which she feels joy? What are they?
4. Describe the behavior of Mrs. May and Greenleaf toward each other. Why does Mrs. May keep Greenleaf on when she despises him so?
5. The two families — the Mays and the Greenleafs — are obviously contrasted. Describe this contrast as fully as possible, considering especially the following: (a) their social and economic status — past, present, and future, (b) their religious attitudes, (c) the attitudes of Mrs. May and Greenleaf respectively toward their children, (d) Wesley and Scofield versus O. T. and E. T. What are the reasons for Mrs. May's feelings toward the Greenleafs?
6. The turning point of the story comes when Mrs. May commands Greenleaf to get his gun. What emotional reversal takes place at this point? What are Mrs. May's motivations in having the bull shot?
7. "Suppose [thinks Mrs. May in paragraph 168] Mr. Greenleaf had aroused the bull chunking stones at him and the animal had turned on him and run him up against a tree and gored him? . . . She thought of it almost with pleasure as if she had hit on the perfect ending for a story she was telling her friends." From what perspective is the actual ending of the story a perfect ending? Is the ending of the story purely chance, or is there a sense in which Mrs. May has brought this on herself?
8. What symbolic implications, if any, have the following: (a) the name Greenleaf, (b) the bull, (c) the sun, (d) Mrs. May's two dreams (paragraphs 4/148), (e) the name May? How important is symbolism to the final effect of the story?
9. What kinds of irony predominate in the story? Identify examples of each of the three kinds of irony. How important is irony to the final effect of the story?

Anton Chekhov
Gooseberries

The sky had been overcast since early morning; it was a still day, not hot, but tedious, as it usually is when the weather is gray and dull, when clouds have been hanging over the fields for a long time, and you wait for the rain

GOOSEBERRIES   First published in 1898. Translated from the Russian by Avrahm Yarmolinsky. Anton Chekhov (1860–1904) was raised in semi-poverty in the town of Taganrog on the Black Sea. A scholarship enabled him to take a medical degree from Moscow University, but writing plays, stories, and sketches was his main source of income. Partly because of ill health, in 1892 he purchased a small country estate for his family near Moscow, where he enjoyed the gregariousness of country life. The onset of tuberculosis sent him to the warmer climate of Yalta on the sea, where "Gooseberries" was written.

that does not come. Ivan Ivanych*, a veterinary, and Burkin, a high school teacher, were already tired with walking, and the plain seemed endless to them. Far ahead were the scarcely visible windmills of the village of Mironositzkoe; to the right lay a range of hills that disappeared in the distance beyond the village, and both of them knew that over there were the river, and fields, green willows, homesteads, and if you stood on one of the hills, you could see from there another vast plain, telegraph poles, and a train that from afar looked like a caterpillar crawling, and in clear weather you could even see the town. Now, when it was still and when nature seemed mild and pensive, Ivan Ivanych and Burkin were filled with love for this plain, and both of them thought what a beautiful land it was.

"Last time when we were in Elder Prokofy's barn," said Burkin, "you were going to tell me a story."

"Yes; I wanted to tell you about my brother."

Ivan Ivanych heaved a slow sigh and lit his pipe before beginning his story, but just then it began to rain. And five mintues later there was a downpour, and it was hard to tell when it would be over. The two men halted, at a loss; the dogs, already wet, stood with their tails between their legs and looked at them feelingly.

5   "We must find shelter somewhere," said Burkin. "Let's go to Alyohin's; it's quite near."

"Let's."

They turned aside and walked across a mown meadow, now going straight ahead, now bearing to the right, until they reached the road. Soon poplars came into view, a garden, then the red roofs of barns; the river gleamed, and the view opened on a broad expanse of water with a mill and a white bathing-cabin. That was Sofyino, Alyohin's place.

The mill was going, drowning out the sound of the rain; the dam was shaking. Wet horses stood near the carts, their heads drooping, and men were walking about, their heads covered with sacks. It was damp, muddy, dreary; and the water looked cold and unkind. Ivan Ivanych and Burkin felt cold and messy and uncomfortable through and through; their feet were heavy with mud and when, having crossed the dam, they climbed up to the barns, they were silent as though they were cross with each other.

The noise of a winnowing-machine came from one of the barns, the door was open, and clouds of dust were pouring from within. On the threshold stood Alyohin himself, a man of forty, tall and rotund, with long hair, looking more like a professor or an artist than a gentleman farmer. He was wearing a white blouse, badly in need of washing, that was belted with a rope, and

---

A note on Russian names: In Russia a person was identified by three names — a given name (such as Ivan), a patronymic middle name (Ivanych), and a family or surname (Chimsha-Himalaisky). The patronymic indicated one's father's given name, and for men was formed by adding the suffix -ch, ych (or -ich), or -ovich; for women, the suffixes were -evna or -ovna. "Ivan Ivanych" is thus Ivan, son of Ivan Chimsha-Himalaisky. As in English, nicknames abound.

drawers, and his high boots were plastered with mud and straw. His eyes and nose were black with dust. He recognized Ivan Ivanych and Burkin and was apparently very glad to see them.

"Please go up to the house, gentlemen," he said, smiling; "I'll be there directly, in a moment." 10

It was a large structure of two stories. Alyohin lived downstairs in what was formerly the stewards' quarters: two rooms that had arched ceilings and small windows; the furniture was plain, and the place smelled of rye bread, cheap vodka, and harness. He went into the showy rooms upstairs only rarely, when he had guests. Once in the house, the two visitors were met by a chambermaid, a young woman so beautiful that both of them stood still at the same moment and glanced at each other.

"You can't imagine how glad I am to see you, gentlemen," said Alyohin, joining them in the hall. "What a surprise! Pelageya," he said, turning to the chambermaid, "give the guests a change of clothes. And, come to think of it, I will change, too. But I must go and bathe first, I don't think I've had a wash since spring. Don't you want to go into the bathing-cabin? In the meanwhile things will be got ready here."

The beautiful Pelageya, with her soft, delicate air, brought them bath towels and soap, and Alyohin went to the bathing-cabin with his guests.

"Yes, it's a long time since I've bathed," he said, as he undressed. "I've an excellent bathing-cabin, as you see — it was put up by my father — but somehow I never find time to use it." He sat down on the steps and lathered his long hair and neck, and the water aound him turned brown.

"I say — " observed Ivan Ivanych significantly, looking at his head. 15

"I haven't had a good wash for a long time," repeated Alyohin, embarrassed, and soaped himself once more; the water about him turned dark-blue, the color of ink.

Ivan Ivanych came out of the cabin, plunged into the water with a splash and swam in the rain, thrusting his arms out wide; he raised waves on which white lilies swayed. He swam out to the middle of the river and dived and a minute later came up in another spot and swam on and kept diving, trying to touch bottom. "By God!" he kept repeating delightedly, "by God!" He swam to the mill, spoke to the peasants there, and turned back and in the middle of the river lay floating, exposing his face to the rain. Burkin and Alyohin were already dressed and ready to leave, but he kept on swimming and diving. "By God!" he kept exclaiming. "Lord, have mercy on me."

"You've had enough!" Burkin shouted to him.

They returned to the house. And only when the lamp was lit in the big drawing room upstairs, and the two guests, in silk dressing-gowns and warm slippers, were lounging in armchairs, and Alyohin himself, washed and combed, wearing a new jacket, was walking about the room, evidently savoring the warmth, the cleanliness, the dry clothes and light footwear, and when pretty Pelageya, stepping noiselessly across the carpet and smiling softly, brought in a tray with tea and jam, only then did Ivan Ivanych begin his story, and it was as though not only Burkin and Alyohin were listening, but also the ladies, old and young, and the military men who looked down upon them, calmly and severely, from their gold frames.

20 "We are two brothers," he began, "I, Ivan Ivanych, and my brother, Nikolay Ivanych, who is two years my junior. I went in for a learned profession and became a veterinary; Nikolay at nineteen began to clerk in a provincial branch of the Treasury. Our father was a *kantonist*,° but he rose to be an officer and so a nobleman, a rank that he bequeathed to us together with a small estate. After his death there was a lawsuit and we lost the estate to creditors, but be that as it may, we spent our childhood in the country. Just like peasant children we passed days and nights in the fields and the woods, herded horses, stripped bast from the trees, fished, and so on. And, you know, whoever even once in his life has caught a perch or seen thrushes migrate in the autumn, when on clear, cool days they sweep in flocks over the village, will never really be a townsman and to the day of his death will have a longing for the open. My brother was unhappy in the government office. Years passed, but he went on warming the same seat, scratching away at the same papers, and thinking of one and the same thing: how to get away to the country. And little by little this vague longing turned into a definite desire, into a dream of buying a little property somewhere on the banks of a river or a lake.

"He was a kind and gentle soul and I loved him, but I never sympathized with his desire to shut himself up for the rest of his life on a little property of his own. It is a common saying that a man needs only six feet of earth. But six feet is what a corpse needs, not a man. It is also asserted that if our educated class is drawn to the land and seeks to settle on farms, that's a good thing. But these farms amount to the same six feet of earth. To retire from the city, from the struggle, from the hubbub, to go off and hide on one's own farm — that's not life, it is selfishness, sloth, it is a kind of monasticism, but monasticism without works. Man needs not six feet of earth, but the whole globe, all of Nature, where unhindered he can display all the capacities and peculiarities of his free spirit.

"My brother Nikolay, sitting in his office, dreamed of eating his own *shchi*,° which would fill the whole farmyard with a delicious aroma, of picnicking on the green grass, of sleeping in the sun, of sitting for hours on the seat by the gate gazing at field and forest. Books on agriculture and the farming items in almanacs were his joy, the delight of his soul. He liked newspapers too, but the only things he read in them were advertisements of land for sale, so many acres of tillable land and pasture, with house, garden, river, mill, and millpond. And he pictured to himself garden paths, flowers, fruit, bird-houses with starlings in them, crucians° in the pond, and all that

kantonist: the son of a private, registered at birth in the army and trained in a military school.   *shchi:* a peasant soup   **crucians:** Central European goldfish

sort of thing, you know. These imaginary pictures varied with the advertisements he came upon, but somehow gooseberry bushes figured in every one of them. He could not picture to himself a single country-house, a single rustic nook, without gooseberries.

" 'Country life has its advantages,' he used to say. 'You sit on the veranda having tea, and your ducks swim in the pond, and everything smells delicious and — the gooseberries are ripening.'

"He would draw a plan of his estate and invariably it would contain the following features: a) the master's house; b) servants' quarters; c) kitchen-garden; d) a gooseberry patch. He lived meagerly: he deprived himself of food and drink; he dressed God knows how, like a beggar, but he kept on saving and salting money away in the bank. He was terribly stingy. It was painful for me to see it, and I used to give him small sums and send him something on holidays, but he would put that away too. Once a man is possessed by an idea, there is no doing anything with him.

"Years passed. He was transferred to another province, he was already past forty, yet he was still reading newspaper advertisements and saving up money. Then I heard that he was married. Still for the sake of buying a property with a gooseberry patch he married an elderly, homely widow, without a trace of affection for her, but simply because she had money. After marrying her, he went on living parsimoniously, keeping her half-starved, and he put her money in the bank in his own name. She had previously been the wife of a postmaster, who had got her used to pies and cordials. This second husband did not even give her enough black bread. She began to sicken, and some three years later gave up the ghost. And, of course, it never for a moment occurred to my brother that he was to blame for her death. Money, like vodka, can do queer things to a man. Once in our town a merchant lay on his deathbed; before he died, he ordered a plateful of honey and he ate up all his money and lottery tickets with the honey, so that no one should get it. One day when I was inspecting a drove of cattle at a railway station, a cattle dealer fell under a locomotive and it sliced off his leg. We carried him in to the infirmary, the blood was gushing from the wound — a terrible business, but he kept begging us to find his leg and was very anxious about it: he had twenty rubles in the boot that was on that leg, and he was afraid they would be lost."

"That's a tune from another opera," said Burkin.

Ivan Ivanych paused a moment and then continued:

"After his wife's death, my brother began to look around for a property. Of course, you may scout about for five years and in the end make a mistake, and buy something quite different from what you have been dreaming of. Through an agent my brother bought a mortgaged estate of three hundred acres with a house, servants' quarters, a park, but with no orchard, no gooseberry patch, no duck-pond. There was a stream, but the water in it was the color of coffee, for on one of its banks there was a brickyard and on the other a glue factory. But my brother was not at all disconcerted: he ordered a score of gooseberry bushes, planted them, and settled down to the life of a country gentleman.

"Last year I paid him a visit. I thought I would go and see how things were with him. In his letter to me my brother called his estate 'Chumbaroklov Waste, or Himalaiskoe' (our surname was Chimsha-Himalaisky). I reached the place in the afternoon. It was hot. Everywhere there were ditches, fences, hedges, rows of fir trees, and I was at a loss as to how to get to the yard and where to leave my horse. I made my way to the house and was met by a fat dog with reddish hair that looked like a pig. It wanted to bark, but was too lazy. The cook, a fat, barelegged woman, who also looked like a pig, came out of the kitchen and said that the master was resting after dinner. I went in to see my brother, and found him sitting up in bed, with a quilt over his knees. He had grown older, stouter, flabby; his cheeks, his nose, his lips jutted out: it looked as though he might grunt into the quilt at any moment.

30 "We embraced and dropped tears of joy and also of sadness at the thought that the two of us had once been young, but were now gray and nearing death. He got dressed and took me out to show me his estate.

"'Well, how are you getting on here?' I asked.

"'Oh, all right, thank God. I am doing very well.'

"He was no longer the poor, timid clerk he used to be but a real landowner, a gentleman. He had already grown used to his new manner of living and developed a taste for it. He ate a great deal, steamed himself in the bathhouse, was growing stout, was already having a lawsuit with the village commune and the two factories and was very much offended when the peasants failed to address him as 'Your Honor.' And he concerned himself with his soul's welfare too in a substantial, upper-class manner, and performed good deeds not simply, but pompously. And what good works! He dosed the peasants with bicarbonate and castor oil for all their ailments and on his name day he had a thanksgiving service celebrated in the center of the village, and then treated the villagers to a gallon of vodka, which he thought was the thing to do. Oh, those horrible gallons of vodka! One day a fat landowner hauls the peasants up before the rural police officer for trespasssing, and the next, to mark a feast day, treats them to a gallon of vodka, and they drink and shout 'Hurrah' and when they are drunk bow down at his feet. A higher standard of living, overeating and idleness develop the most insolent self-conceit in a Russian. Nikolay Ivanych, who when he was a petty official was afraid to have opinions of his own even if he kept them to himself, now uttered nothing but incontrovertible truths and did so in the tone of a minister of state: 'Education is necessary, but the masses are not ready for it; corporal punishment is generally harmful, but in some cases it is useful and nothing else will serve.'

"'I know the common people, and I know how to deal with them,' he would say. 'They love me. I only have to raise my little finger, and they will do anything I want.'

"And all this, mark you, would be said with a smile that bespoke kindness and intelligence. Twenty times over he repeated: 'We, of the gentry,' 'I,
as a member of the gentry.' Apparently he no longer remembered that our
grandfather had been a peasant and our father just a private. Even our surname, 'Chimsha-Himalaisky,' which in reality is grotesque, seemed to him
sonorous, distinguished, and delightful.

"But I am concerned now not with him, but with me. I want to tell you
about a change that took place in me during the few hours that I spent on his
estate. In the evening when we were having tea, the cook served a plateful of
gooseberries. They were not bought, they were his own gooseberries, the
first ones picked since the bushes were planted. My brother gave a laugh and
for a minute looked at the gooseberries in silence, with tears in his eyes — he
could not speak for excitement. Then he put one berry in his mouth, glanced
at me with the triumph of a child who has at last been given a toy he was
longing for and said: 'How tasty!' And he ate the gooseberries greedily, and
kept repeating: 'Ah, how delicious! Do taste them!'

"They were hard and sour, but as Pushkin has it,

> The falsehood that exalts we cherish more
> Than meaner truths that are a thousand strong.

I saw a happy man, one whose cherished dream had so obviously come true,
who had attained his goal in life, who had got what he wanted, who was
satisfied with his lot and with himself. For some reason an element of sadness
had always mingled with my thoughts of human happiness, and now at the
sight of a happy man I was assailed by an oppressive feeling bordering on
despair. It weighed on me particularly at night. A bed was made up for me in
a room next to my brother's bedroom, and I could hear that he was wakeful,
and that he would get up again and again, go to the plate of gooseberries and
eat one after another. I said to myself: how many contented, happy people
there really are! What an overwhelming force they are! Look at life: the
insolence and idleness of the strong, the ignorance and brutishness of the
weak, horrible poverty everywhere, overcrowding, degeneration, drunkenness, hypocrisy, lying . . . Yet in all the houses and on all the streets there is
peace and quiet; of the fifty thousand people who live in our town there is not
one who would cry out, who would vent his indignation aloud. We see the
people who go to market, eat by day, sleep by night, who babble nonsense,
marry, grow old, good-naturedly drag their dead to the cemetery, but we do
not see or hear those who suffer, and what is terrible in life goes on somewhere behind the scenes. Everything is peaceful and quiet and only mute
statistics protest: so many people gone out of their minds, so many gallons of
vodka drunk, so many children dead from malnutrition . . . And such a state
of things is evidently necessary; obviously the happy man is at ease only
because the unhappy ones bear their burdens in silence, and if there were not

this silence, happiness would be impossible. It is a general hypnosis. Behind the door of every contented, happy man there ought to be someone standing with a little hammer and continually reminding him with a knock that there are unhappy people, that however happy he may be, life will sooner or later show him its claws, and trouble will come to him — illness, poverty, losses, and then no one will see or hear him, just as now he neither sees nor hears others. But there is no man with a hammer. The happy man lives at his ease, faintly fluttered by small daily cares, like an aspen in the wind — and all is well.

"That night I came to understand that I too had been contented and happy," Ivan Ivanych continued, getting up. "I too over the dinner table or out hunting would hold forth on how to live, what to believe, the right way to govern the people. I too would say that learning was the enemy of darkness, that education was necessary but that for the common people the three R's were sufficient for the time being. Freedom is a boon, I used to say, it is as essential as air, but we must wait awhile. Yes, that's what I used to say, and now I ask: Why must we wait?" said Ivan Ivanych, looking wrathfully at Burkin. "Why must we wait, I ask you? For what reason? I am told that nothing can be done all at once, that every idea is realized gradually, in its own time. But who is it that says so? Where is the proof that it is just? You cite the natural order of things, the law governing all phenomena, but is there law, is there order in the fact that I, a living, thinking man, stand beside a ditch and wait for it to close up of itself or fill up with silt, when I could jump over it or throw a bridge across it? And again, why must we wait? Wait, until we have no strength to live, and yet we have to live and are eager to live!

"I left my brother's place early in the morning, and ever since then it has become intolerable for me to stay in town. I am oppressed by the peace and the quiet, I am afraid to look at the windows, for there is nothing that pains me more than the spectacle of a happy family sitting at table having tea. I am an old man now and unfit for combat, I am not even capable of hating. I can only grieve inwardly, get irritated, worked up, and at night my head is ablaze with the rush of ideas and I cannot sleep. Oh, if I were young!"

Ivan Ivanych paced up and down the room excitedly and repeated, "If I were young!"

He suddenly walked up to Alyohin and began to press now one of his hands, now the other.

"Paval Konstantinych," he said imploringly, "don't quiet down, don't let yourself be lulled to sleep! As long as you are young, strong, alert, do not cease to do good! There is no happiness and there should be none, and if life has a meaning and a purpose, that meaning and purpose is not our happiness but something greater and more rational. Do good!"

All this Ivan Ivanych said with a pitiful, imploring smile, as though he were asking a personal favor.

Afterwards all three of them sat in armchairs in different corners of the drawing room and were silent. Ivan Ivanych's story satisfied neither Burkin nor Alyohin. With the ladies and generals looking down from the golden frames, seeming alive in the dim light, it was tedious to listen to the story of the poor devil of a clerk who ate gooseberries. One felt like talking about elegant people, about women. And the fact that they were sitting in a drawing room where everything — the chandelier under its cover, the armchairs, the carpets underfoot — testified that the very people who were now looking down from the frames had once moved about here, sat and had tea, and the fact that the lovely Pelageya was noiselessly moving about — that was better than any story.

Alyohin was very sleepy; he had gotten up early, before three o'clock in the morning, to get some work done, and now he could hardly keep his eyes open, but he was afraid his visitors might tell an interesting story in his absence, and he would not leave. He did not trouble to ask himself if what Ivan Ivanych had just said was intelligent or right. The guests were not talking about groats, or hay, or tar, but about something that had no direct bearing on his life, and he was glad of it and wanted them to go on. 45

"However, it's bedtime," said Burkin, rising. "Allow me to wish you good night."

Alyohin took leave of his guests and went downstairs to his own quarters, while they remained upstairs. They were installed for the night in a big room in which stood two old wooden beds decorated with carvings and in the corner was an ivory crucifix. The wide cool beds which had been made by the lovely Pelageya gave off a pleasant smell of clean linen.

Ivan Ivanych undressed silently and got into bed.

"Lord forgive us sinners!" he murmured, and drew the bedclothes over his head.

His pipe, which lay on the table, smelled strongly of burnt tobacco, and Burkin, who could not sleep for a long time, kept wondering where the unpleasant odor came from. 50

The rain beat against the window panes all night.

QUESTIONS

1. Distinguish between the "frame story" (what happens to Ivan Ivanych, Burkin, and Alyohin at Alyohin's estate) and the story that Ivan tells about his brother. What are the major events and actions in each? What are the characteristics of the characters in each? What are the plot conflicts in each? What themes does each story have?
2. What correspondences exist between the frame story and Ivan's narration? What parallels are there between Nikolay's estate and Alyohin's?
3. In the opening paragraph, the same landscape is interpreted thus: "tedious . . . gray and dull . . . you wait for rain that does not come . . . mild and pensive . . . love for this plain . . . beautiful land." Account for these

contradictory descriptions, and find other passages in the story that are equally self-contradictory. Are such contradictions characteristic of both the frame story and the narrative?

4. What does Ivan Ivanych see as the lesson to be learned from his brother's history? Why does he urge that lesson on Alyohin? What does Alyohin think of Ivan's story and its lesson? Is either Ivan or Alyohin entirely right or wrong?

5. Explore the symbolism of (a) Ivan's swim, (b) Ivan's pipe, and (c) the gooseberries.

6. Having answered the five preceding questions, re-read question 1 again, and use your answers to it to form a statement that combines the themes of the frame and those of the narrative into a coherent theme for Chekhov's story.

CHAPTER SEVEN

Emotion and Humor

Interpretive fiction presents the reader with significant and therefore durable insights into life. But these insights represent something more than mere intellectual comprehension; otherwise, the story does nothing that cannot be done as well or better by psychology, history, or philosophy. Fiction derives its unique value from its power to give *felt* insights. Its truths take a deeper hold on our minds because they are conveyed through our feelings. Its effectiveness in awakening a sensuous and emotional apprehension of experience that enriches understanding is what distinguishes imaginative literature from other forms of discourse.

All successful stories arouse emotions in the reader. The adventure thriller causes fear, excitement, suspense, anxiety, exultation, surprise. Some stories make us laugh; some cause us to thrill with horror; some make us cry. We value all the arts precisely because they enrich and diversify our emotional life.

A truly significant story pursues emotion indirectly, not directly. Emotion accompanying and producing insight, not emotion for itself, is the aim of the interpretive story. It presents a sample of experience truthfully; the emotions it arouses flow naturally from the experience presented.

Over a century ago, in a review of Hawthorne's *Tales*, Edgar Allan Poe made a famous but misleading pronouncement about the short story:

A skilful literary artist has constructed a tale. If wise, he has not fashioned his thoughts to accommodate his incidents; but having conceived with deliberate care, a certain unique or single *effect* to be brought out, he then invents such incidents — he then combines such events as may best aid him in establishing this preconceived effect. If his very initial sentence tend not to the outbringing of this effect, then he has failed in his first step. In the whole composition there should be no word written, of which the tendency, direct or indirect, is not to the one preestablished design.

Poe's formulation has been enormously influential, for both good and bad. Historically it is important as one of the first discussions of the short story as a unique form. Critically it is important because Poe so clearly enunciates here the basic critical principle of all art—the principle of artistic unity, requiring all details and elements of a piece to contribute harmoniously to the total design. Its influence has been deleterious because of the emphasis Poe put on a "unique" and "preconceived" *effect*.

The serious writer is an interpreter, not an inventor. Like a good actor, the writer is an intermediary between a segment of experience and an audience. The actor must pay some consideration to the audience—being careful, for instance, to face *toward* it, not away from it. But the great actor is the one who is wrapped up in the thoughts and feelings of a role, not the one who is continually stealing glances at the audience to determine the effect of a gesture or bit of business. The actor who begins taking cues from the audience rather than from the script soon becomes a "ham," exaggerating and falsifying for the sake of effects. The writer, too, though paying some consideration to the reader, focuses primarily on the subject. The writer who begins to think primarily of the effect of the tale on the reader begins to manipulate the material, to heighten reality, to contrive and falsify for the sake of effects. The serious writer selects and arranges material in order to convey most effectively the feeling or truth of a human situation. The commercial writer selects and arranges the material so as to stimulate a response in the reader.

Discriminating readers, then, will distinguish between contrived emotion and that which springs naturally from a human story truly told. They will mark a difference between the story that attempts to "play upon" the feelings directly, as if readers were pianos, and one that draws emotion forth as naturally as a plucked string draws forth sympathetic vibrations from another instrument in a room. The difference between the two types of story is the difference between escape and interpretation. In interpretive fiction, emotion is the by-product, not the goal.

No doubt there is pleasure in having our emotions directly stimulated, and in some forms such pleasure is both delightful and innocent. We all enjoy the laugh that follows a good joke, and the story that attempts no more than to provoke laughter may be both pleasant and harmless. There is a difference, nevertheless, between the story written for humor's sake and that in which humor springs from a way of viewing experience. Humor may be as idle as the wisecrack or as vicious as the practical joke; it becomes of significant value when it flows from a comic perception of life.

Most of us enjoy the gooseflesh and the tingle along the spine produced by the successful ghost story. There is something agreeable in letting our blood be chilled by bats in the moonlight, guttering candles, creaking doors, eerie shadows, piercing screams, inexplicable bloodstains, and weird noises. But the terror aroused by tricks and external "machinery" is a far cry from the terror evoked by some terrifying treatment of the human situation. The horror we experience in watching the Werewolf or Dracula or the Frankenstein monster is far less significant than that we get from watching the bloody ambition of Macbeth or the jealousy of Othello. In the first, terror is the end-product; in the second, it is the natural accompaniment of a powerful revelation of life. In the first, we are always aware of a basic unreality; in the second, reality is terrifying.

The story designed merely to provoke laughter or to arouse terror may be an enjoyable and innocent pleasure. The story directed at stimulating tears belongs to a less innocent category. The difference is that the humor story and the terror story seldom ask to be taken for more than what they are: pleasant diversions to help us pass the time agreeably. We enjoy the custard pie in the face and the ghost in the moonlight without taking them seriously. The fiction that depends on such ingredients is pure escape. The tear-jerker, however, asks to be taken seriously. Like the fraudulent street beggar who artfully disposes his rags, puts on dark glasses over perfectly good eyes, holds out a tin cup and wails about his seven starving children (there are really only two, and he doesn't know what has become of them), the tear-jerker cheats us. It is escape literature posing as its opposite; it is counterfeit interpretation. It cheats us by exaggerating and falsifying reality by asking for compassion that is not deserved.

The quality in a story that aims at drawing forth unmerited tender feeling is known as **sentimentality**. Sentimentality is not the same as genuine emotion. Sentimentality is contrived or excessive or faked emotion. A story contains genuine emotion when it treats life faithfully and perceptively. The sentimentalized story oversimplifies and sweetens life to get its feeling. It exaggerates, manipulates, and prettifies. It mixes tears with sugar.

Genuine emotion, like character, is presented *indirectly* — it is *dramatized*. It cannot be produced by words that *identify* emotions, like *angry, sad, pathetic, heart-breaking,* or *passionate*. A writer draws forth genuine emotion by producing a character in a situation that deserves our sympathy, and showing us enough about the character and the situation to make them real and convincing.

Sentimental writers are recognizable by a number of characteristics. First, they often try to make words do what the situation faithfully presented by itself will not do. They *editorialize* — that is, comment on the story and, in a manner, instruct us how to feel. Or they overwrite and *poeticize* — use an immoderately heightened and distended language to accomplish their effects. Second, they make an excessively selective use of detail. All artists, of course, must be selective in their use of detail, but good writers use representative details while sentimentalists use details that all point one way — toward producing emotion rather than conveying truth. The little child that dies will be shown as always uncomplaining and cheerful under adversity, never as naughty, querulous, or ungrateful. It will possibly be an orphan or the only child of a mother who loves it dearly; in addition, it may be lame, hungry, ragged, and possessed of one toy, from which it cannot be parted. The villain will be all-villain, with a cruel laugh and a sharp whip, though he may reform at the end, for sentimentalists are firm believers in the heart of gold beneath the rough exterior. In short, reality will be unduly heightened and drastically over-simplified. Third, sentimentalists rely heavily on the stock response — an emotion that has its source outside the facts established by the story. In some readers certain situations and objects — babies, mothers, grandmothers, young love, patriotism, worship — produce an almost automatic response, whether the immediate situation warrants it or not. Sentimental writers, to affect such readers, have only to draw out certain stops, as on an organ, to produce an easily anticipated effect. They depend on stock materials to produce a stock response. They thus need not go to the trouble of picturing the situation in realistic and convincing detail. Finally, sentimental writers present, nearly always, a fundamentally "sweet" picture of life. They rely not only on stock characters and situations but also on stock themes. For them every cloud has its silver lining, every bad event its good side, every storm its rainbow. If the little child dies, it goes to heaven or makes some life better by its death. Virtue is characteristically triumphant: the villain is defeated, the ne'er-do-well redeemed. True love is rewarded in some fashion; it is love — never hate — that makes the world go round. In short, sentimental writers specialize in the sad but sweet. The tears called for are warm tears, never bitter. There is always sugar at the bottom of the cup.

For experienced readers, emotion is a highly valued but not easily achieved component of a story. It is a by-product, not the end-product. It is gained by honestly portrayed characters in honestly drawn situations that reflect the complexity, the ambiguity, and the endless variety of life. It is produced by a carefully exercised restraint on the part of the writer rather than by "pulling out all the stops." It is one of the chief rewards of art.

EXERCISES

The six stories that follow are paired. In the first pair each story depicts terror; in the second pair each story is humorous; in the third pair each story contains sentiment. In each of the first two pairs, one story is more purely interpretive than the other; in the third pair, one story is guilty of sentimentality. For each pair decide which story is more authentic or significant, and give reasons for your choice.

McKnight Malmar
The Storm

She inserted her key in the lock and turned the knob. The March wind snatched the door out of her hand and slammed it against the wall. It took strength to close it against the pressure of the gale, and she had no sooner closed it than the rain came in a pounding downpour, beating noisily against the windows as if trying to follow her in. She could not hear the taxi as it started up and went back down the road.

She breathed a sigh of thankfulness at being home again and in time. In rain like this, the crossroads always were flooded. Half an hour later her cab could not have got through the rising water, and there was no alternative route.

There was no light anywhere in the house. Ben was not home, then. As she turned on the lamp by the sofa she had a sense of anticlimax. All the way home — she had been visiting her sister — she had seen herself going into a lighted house, to Ben, who would be sitting by the fire with his paper. She had taken delight in picturing his happy surprise at seeing her, home a week earlier than he had expected her. She had known just how his round face would light up, how his eyes would twinkle behind his glasses, how he would catch her by the shoulders and look down into her face to see the changes a month had made in her, and then kiss her resoundingly on both cheeks, like a French general bestowing a decoration. Then she would make coffee and find a piece of cake, and they would sit together by the fire and talk.

But Ben wasn't here. She looked at the clock on the mantel and saw it was nearly ten. Perhaps he had not planned to come home tonight, as he was not expecting her; even before she had left he frequently was in the city all

THE STORM   First published in 1944. McKnight Malmar was born in 1903 in Albany, New York, and grew up in suburban New York, later residing in Virginia.

night because business kept him too late to catch the last train. If he did not come soon, he would not be able to make it at all.

5   She did not like the thought. The storm was growing worse. She could hear the wild lash of the trees, the whistle of the wind around the corners of the little house. For the first time she regretted this move to the far suburbs. There had been neighbors at first, a quarter-mile down the road; but they moved away several months ago, and now their house stood empty.

She had thought nothing of the lonesomeness. It was perfect here — for two. She had taken such pleasure in fixing up her house — her very own house — and caring for it that she had not missed company other than Ben. But now, alone and with the storm trying to batter its way in, she found it frightening to be so far away from other people. There was no one this side of the crossroads; the road that passed the house wandered past farmland into nothingness in the thick woods a mile farther on.

She hung her hat and her coat in the closet and went to stand before the hall mirror to pin up the soft strands of hair that the wind had loosened. She did not really see the pale face with its blunt nose, the slender, almost childish figure in its grown-up black dress, or the big brown eyes that looked back at her.

She fastened the last strands into the pompadour and turned away from the mirror. Her shoulders drooped a little. There was something childlike about her, like a small girl craving protection, something immature and yet appealing, in spite of her plainness. She was thirty-one and had been married for fifteen months. The fact that she had married at all still seemed a miracle to her.

Now she began to walk through the house, turning on lights as she went. Ben had left it in fairly good order. There was very little trace of an untidy masculine presence; but then, he was a tidy man. She began to realize that the house was cold. Of course, Ben would have lowered the thermostat. He was very careful about things like that. He would not tolerate waste.

10   No wonder it was cold; the thermostat was set at fifty-eight. She pushed the little needle up to seventy, and the motor in the cellar started so suddenly and noisily that it frightened her for a moment.

She went into the kitchen and made some coffee. While she waited for it to drip she began to prowl around the lower floor. She was curiously restless and could not relax. Yet it was good to be back again among her own things, in her own home. She studied the living-room with fresh eyes. Yes, it was a pleasant room even though it was small. The bright, flowered chintzes on the furniture and at the windows were cheerful and pretty, and the lowboy she had bought three months ago was just right for the middle of the long wall. But her plants, set so bravely along the window sill, had died. Ben had forgotten to water them, in spite of all her admonitions, and now they drooped, shrunken and pale, in whitened, powdery soil. The sight of them added to the depression that was beginning to blot out all the pleasure of homecoming.

She returned to the kitchen and poured herself a cup of coffee, wishing that Ben would come home to share it with her. She carried her cup into the living-room and set it on the small, round table beside Ben's special big chair. The furnace was still mumbling busily, sending up heat, but she was colder than ever. She shivered and got an old jacket of Ben's from the closet and wrapped it around her before she sat down.

The wind hammered at the door and the windows, and the air was full of the sound of water, racing in the gutters, pouring from the leaders, thudding on the roof. Listening, she wished for Ben almost feverishly. She never had felt so alone. And he was such a comfort. He had been so good about her going for this long visit, made because her sister was ill. He had seen to everything and had put her on the train with her arms loaded with books and candy and fruit. She knew those farewell gifts had meant a lot to him — he didn't spend money easily. To be quite honest, he was a little close.

But he was a good husband. She sighed unconsciously, not knowing it was because of youth and romance missed. She repeated it to herself, firmly, as she sipped her coffee. He was a good husband. Suppose he was ten years older than she, and a little set in his ways; a little — perhaps — dictatorial at times, and moody. He had given her what she thought she wanted, security and a home of her own; if security were not enough, she could not blame him for it.

Her eye caught a shred of white protruding under a magazine on the table beside her. She put out a hand toward it, yet her fingers were almost reluctant to grasp it. She pulled it out nevertheless and saw that it was, as she had known instinctively, another of the white envelopes. It was empty, and it bore, as usual, the neat, typewritten address: *Benj. T. Willsom, Esq., Wildwood Road, Fairport, Conn.* The postmark was *New York City.* It never varied.

She felt the familiar constriction about the heart as she held it in her hands. What these envelopes contained she never had known. What she did know was their effect on Ben. After receiving one — one came every month or two — he was irritable, at times almost ugly. Their peaceful life together fell apart. At first she had questioned him, had striven to soothe and comfort him; but she soon had learned that this only made him angry, and of late she had avoided any mention of them. For a week after one came they shared the same room and the same table like two strangers, in a silence that was morose on his part and a little frightened on hers.

This one was postmarked three days before. If Ben got home tonight he would probably be cross, and the storm would not help his mood. Just the same she wished he would come.

She tore the envelope into tiny pieces and tossed them into the fireplace. The wind shook the house in its giant grip, and a branch crashed on the roof. As she straightened, a movement at the window caught her eye.

She froze there, not breathing, still half-bent toward the cold fireplace, her hand still extended. The glimmer of white at the window behind the sheeting blur of rain had been — she was sure of it — a human face. There had been eyes. She was certain there had been eyes staring in at her.

20 The wind's shout took on a personal, threatening note. She was rigid for a long time, never taking her eyes from the window. But nothing moved there now except the water on the windowpane; beyond it there was blackness, and that was all. The only sounds were the thrashing of the trees, the roar of water, and the ominous howl of the wind.

She began to breathe again, at last found courage to turn out the light and go to the window. The darkness was a wall, impenetrable and secret, and the blackness within the house made the storm close in, as if it were a pack of wolves besieging the house. She hastened to put on the light again.

She must have imagined those staring eyes. Nobody could be out on a night like this. Nobody. Yet she found herself terribly shaken.

If only Ben would come home. If only she were not so alone.

She shivered and pulled Ben's coat tighter about her and told herself she was becoming a morbid fool. Nevertheless, she found the aloneness intolerable. Her ears strained to hear prowling footsteps outside the windows. She became convinced that she did hear them, slow and heavy.

25 Perhaps Ben could be reached at the hotel where he sometimes stayed. She no longer cared whether her homecoming was a surprise to him. She wanted to hear his voice. She went to the telephone and lifted the receiver.

The line was quite dead.

The wires were down, of course.

She fought panic. The face at the window had been an illusion, a trick of the light reflected on the sluicing pane; and the sound of footsteps was an illusion, too. Actual ones would be inaudible in the noise made by the wild storm. Nobody would be out tonight. Nothing threatened her, really. The storm was held at bay beyond these walls, and in the morning the sun would shine again.

The thing to do was to make herself as comfortable as possible and settle down with a book. There was no use going to bed — she couldn't possibly sleep. She would only lie there wide awake and think of that face at the window, hear the footsteps.

30 She would get some wood for a fire in the fireplace. She hesitated at the top of the cellar stairs. The light, as she switched it on, seemed insufficient; the concrete wall at the foot of the stairs was dank with moisture and somehow gruesome. And wind was chilling her ankles. Rain was beating in through the outside door to the cellar, because that door was standing open.

The inner bolt sometimes did not hold, she knew very well. If it had not been carefully closed, the wind could have loosened it. Yet the open door increased her panic. It seemed to argue the presence of something less impersonal than the gale. It took her a long minute to nerve herself to go down the steps and reach out into the darkness for the doorknob.

In just that instant she was soaked; but her darting eyes could find nothing outdoors but the black, wavering shapes of the maples at the side of the house. The wind helped her and slammed the door resoundingly. She jammed the bolt home with all her strength and then tested it to make sure it would hold. She almost sobbed with the relief of knowing it to be firm against any intruder.

She stood with her wet clothes clinging to her while the thought came that turned her bones to water. Suppose — suppose the face at the window had been real, after all. Suppose its owner had found shelter in the only shelter to be had within a quarter-mile — this cellar.

She almost flew up the stairs again, but then she took herself firmly in hand. She must not let herself go. There had been many storms before; just because she was alone in this one, she must not let morbid fancy run away with her. But she could not throw off the reasonless fear that oppressed her, although she forced it back a little. She began to hear again the tread of the prowler outside the house. Although she knew it to be imagination, it was fearfully real — the crunch of feet on gravel, slow, persistent, heavy, like the patrol of a sentinel.

She had only to get an armful of wood. Then she could have a fire, she would have light and warmth and comfort. She would forget these terrors. 35

The cellar smelled of dust and old moisture. The beams were fuzzed with cobwebs. There was only one light, a dim one in the corner. A little rivulet was running darkly down the wall and already had formed a foot-square pool on the floor.

The woodpile was in the far corner away from the light. She stopped and peered around. Nobody could hide here. The cellar was too open, the supporting stanchions too slender to hide a man.

The oil burner went off with a sharp click. Its mutter, she suddenly realized, had had something human and companionable about it. Nothing was down here with her now but the snarl of the storm.

She almost ran to the woodpile. Then something made her pause and turn before she bent to gather the logs.

What was it? Not a noise. Something she had seen as she hurried across 40 that dusty floor. Something odd.

She searched with her eyes. It was a spark of light she had seen, where no spark should be.

An inexplicable dread clutched at her heart. Her eyes widened, round and dark as a frightened deer's. Her old trunk that stood against the wall was open just a crack; from the crack came this tiny pinpoint of reflected light to prick the cellar's gloom.

She went toward it like a woman hypnotized. It was only one more insignificant thing, like the envelope on the table, the vision of the face at the window, the open door. There was no reason for her to feel smothered in terror.

Yet she was sure she had not only closed, but clamped the lid on the trunk; she was sure because she kept two or three old coats in it, wrapped in newspapers and tightly shut away from moths.

45 Now the lid was raised perhaps an inch. And the twinkle of light was still there.

She threw back the lid.

For a long moment she stood looking down into the trunk, while each detail of its contents imprinted itself on her brain like an image on a film. Each tiny detail was indelibly clear and never to be forgotten.

She could not have stirred a muscle in that moment. Horror was a black cloak thrown around her, stopping her breath, hobbling her limbs.

Then her face dissolved into formlessness. She slammed down the lid and ran up the stairs like a mad thing. She was breathing again, in deep, sobbing breaths that tore at her lungs. She shut the door at the top of the stairs with a crash that shook the house; then she turned the key. Gasping she clutched one of the sturdy maple chairs by the kitchen table and wedged it under the knob with hands she could barely control.

50 The wind took the house in its teeth and shook it as a dog shakes a rat.

Her first impulse was to get out of the house. But in the time it took to get to the front door she remembered the face at the window.

Perhaps she had not imagined it. Perhaps it was the face of a murderer — a murderer waiting for her out there in the storm; ready to spring on her out of the dark.

She fell into the big chair, her huddled body shaken by great tremors. She could not stay here — not with that thing in her trunk. Yet she dared not leave. Her whole being cried out for Ben. He would know what to do. She closed her eyes, opened them again, rubbed them hard. The picture still burned into her brain as if it had been etched with acid. Her hair, loosened, fell in soft straight wisps about her forehead, and her mouth was slack with terror.

Her old trunk had held the curled-up body of a woman.

55 She had not seen the face; the head had been tucked down into the hollow of the shoulder, and a shower of fair hair had fallen over it. The woman had worn a red dress. One hand had rested near the edge of the trunk, and on its third finger there had been a man's ring, a signet bearing the raised figure of a rampant lion with a small diamond between its paws. It had been the diamond that caught the light. The little bulb in the corner of the cellar had picked out this ring from the semidarkness and made it stand out like a beacon.

She never would be able to forget it. Never forget how the woman looked: the pale, luminous flesh of her arms; her doubled-up knees against the side of the trunk, with their silken covering shining softly in the gloom; the strands of hair that covered her face . . .

Shudders continued to shake her. She bit her tongue and pressed her hand against her jaw to stop the chattering of her teeth. The salty taste of blood in her mouth steadied her. She tried to force herself to be rational, to plan; yet all the time the knowledge that she was imprisoned with the body of a murdered woman kept beating at her nerves like a flail.

She drew the coat closer about her, trying to dispel the mortal cold that held her. Slowly something beyond the mere fact of murder, of death, began to penetrate her mind. Slowly she realized that beyond this fact there would be consequences. That body in the cellar was not an isolated phenomenon; some train of events had led to its being there and would follow its discovery there.

There would be policemen.

At first the thought of policemen was a comforting one; big, brawny men in blue, who would take the thing out of her cellar, take it away so she never need think of it again.

Then she realized it was *her* cellar — hers and Ben's; and policemen are suspicious and prying. Would they think *she* killed the woman? Could they be made to believe she never had seen her before?

Or would they think Ben had done it? Would they take the letters in the white envelopes, and Ben's absences on business, and her own visit to her sister, about which Ben was so helpful, and out of them build a double life for him? Would they insist that the woman had been a discarded mistress, who had hounded him with letters until out of desperation he had killed her? That was a fantastic theory, really; but the police might do that.

They might.

Now a sudden new panic invaded her. The dead woman must be taken out of the cellar, must be hidden. The police must never connect her with this house.

Yet the dead woman was bigger than she herself was; she could never move her.

Her craving for Ben became a frantic need. If only he would come home! Come home and take that body away, hide it somewhere so the police could not connect it with this house. He was strong enough to do it.

Even with the strength to move the body by herself she would not dare do it, because there was the prowler — real or imaginary — outside the house. Perhaps the cellar door had not been open by chance. Or perhaps it had been, and the murderer, seeing it so welcoming, had seized the opportunity to plant the evidence of his crime upon the Willsoms' innocent shoulders.

She crouched there, shaking. It was as if the jaws of a great trap had closed on her: on one side the storm and the silence of the telephone, on the other the presence of the prowler and of that still, cramped figure in her trunk. She was caught between them, helpless.

As if to accent her helplessness, the wind stepped up its shriek and a tree crashed thunderously out in the road. She heard glass shatter.

Her quivering body stiffened like a drawn bow. Was it the prowler attempting to get in? She forced herself to her feet and made a round of the windows on the first floor and the one above. All the glass was intact, staunchly resisting the pounding of the rain.

Nothing could have made her go into the cellar to see if anything had happened there.

The voice of the storm drowned out all other sounds, yet she could not rid herself of the fancy that she heard footsteps going round and round the house, that eyes sought an opening and spied upon her.

She pulled the shades down over the shiny black windows. It helped a little to make her feel more secure, more sheltered; but only a very little. She told herself sternly that the crash of glass had been nothing more than a branch blown through a cellar window.

The thought brought her no comfort — just the knowledge that it would not disturb that other woman. Nothing could comfort her now but Ben's plump shoulder and his arms around her and his neat, capable mind planning to remove the dead woman from this house.

75 A kind of numbness began to come over her, as if her capacity for fear were exhausted. She went back to the chair and curled up in it. She prayed mutely for Ben and for daylight.

The clock said half-past twelve.

She huddled there, not moving and not thinking, not even afraid, only numb for another hour. Then the storm held its breath for a moment, and in the brief space of silence she heard footsteps on the walk — actual footsteps, firm and quick and loud. A key turned in the lock. The door opened and Ben came in.

He was dripping, dirty, and white with exhaustion. But it was Ben. Once she was sure of it she flung herself on him, babbling incoherently of what she had found.

He kissed her lightly on the cheek and took her arms down from around his neck. "Here, here, my dear. You'll get soaked. I'm drenched to the skin." He removed his glasses and handed them to her, and she began to dry them for him. His eyes squinted at the light. "I had to walk in from the crossroads. What a night!" He began to strip off rubbers and coat and shoes. "You'll never know what a difference it made, finding the place lighted. Lord, but it's good to be home."

80 She tried again to tell him of the past hours, but again he cut her short. "Now, wait a minute, my dear. I can see you're bothered about something. Just wait until I get into some dry things; then I'll come down and we'll straighten it out. Suppose you rustle up some coffee and toast. I'm done up — the whole trip out was a nightmare, and I didn't know if I'd ever make it from the crossing. I've been hours."

He did look tired, she thought with concern. Now that he was back, she could wait. The past hours had taken on the quality of a nightmare, horrifying but curiously unreal. With Ben here, so solid and commonplace and cheerful, she began to wonder if the hours *were* nightmare. She even began to doubt the reality of the woman in the trunk, although she could see her as vividly as ever. Perhaps only the storm was real.

She went to the kitchen and began to make fresh coffee. The chair, still wedged against the kitchen door, was a reminder of her terror. Now that Ben was home it seemed silly, and she put it back in its place by the table.

He came down very soon, before the coffee was ready. How good it was to see him in that old gray bathrobe of his, his hands thrust into its pockets. How normal and wholesome he looked with his round face rubbed pink by a rough towel and his hair standing up in damp little spikes around his bald spot. She was almost shamefaced when she told him of the face at the window, the open door, and finally of the body in the trunk. None of it, she saw quite clearly now, could possibly have happened.

Ben said so, without hesitation. But he came to put an arm around her. "You poor child. The storm scared you to death, and I don't wonder. It's given you the horrors."

She smiled dubiously. "Yes. I'm almost beginning to think so. Now that you're back, it seems so safe. But — but you will *look* in the trunk, Ben? I've got to *know*. I can see her so plainly. How could I imagine a thing like that?"

He said indulgently, "Of course I'll look, if it will make you feel better. I'll do it now. Then I can have my coffee in peace."

He went to the cellar door and opened it and snapped on the light. Her heart began to pound once more, a deafening roar in her ears. The opening of the cellar door opened, again, the whole vista of fear: the body, the police, the suspicions that would cluster about her and Ben. The need to hide this evidence of somebody's crime.

She could not have imagined it; it was incredible that she could have believed, for a minute, that her mind had played such tricks on her. In another moment Ben would know it, too.

She heard the thud as he threw back the lid of the trunk. She clutched at the back of a chair, waiting for his voice. It came in an instant.

She could not believe it. It was as cheerful and reassuring as before. He said, "There's nothing here but a couple of bundles. Come take a look."

Nothing!

Her knees were weak as she went down the stairs, down into the cellar again.

It was still musty and damp and draped with cobwebs. The rivulet was still running down the wall, but the pool was larger now. The light was still dim.

It was just as she remembered it except that the wind was whistling through a broken window and rain was splattering in on the bits of shattered glass on the floor. The branch lying across the sill had removed every scrap of glass from the frame and left not a single jagged edge.

Ben was standing by the open trunk, waiting for her. His stocky body was a bulwark. "See," he said, "there's nothing. Just some old clothes of yours, I guess."

She went to stand beside him. Was she losing her mind? Would she, now, see that crushed figure in there, see the red dress and the smooth shining knees, when Ben could not? And the ring with the diamond between the lion's paws?

Her eyes looked, almost reluctantly, into the trunk. "It *is* empty!"

There were the neat, newspaper-wrapped packages she had put away so carefully, just as she had left them deep in the bottom of the trunk. And nothing else.

She must have imagined the body. She was light with the relief the knowledge brought her, and yet confused and frightened, too. If her mind could play such tricks, if she could imagine anything so gruesome in the complete detail with which she had seen the dead woman in the trunk, the thought of the future was terrifying. When might she not have another such hallucination?

The actual, physical danger did not exist, however, and never existed. The threat of the law hanging over Ben had been based on a dream.

"I — dreamed it all, I must have," she admitted. "Yet it was so horribly clear and I wasn't asleep." Her voice broke. "I thought — oh, Ben, I thought — "

"What did you think, my dear?" His voice was odd, not like Ben's at all. It had a cold cutting edge to it.

He stood looking down at her with an immobility that chilled her more than the cold wind that swept in through the broken window. She tried to read his face, but the light from the little bulb was too weak. It left his features shadowed in broad, dark planes that made him look like a stranger, and somehow sinister.

She said, "I — " and faltered.

He still did not move, but his voice hardened. "What was it you thought?"

She backed away from him.

He moved, then. It was only to take his hands from his pockets to stretch his arms toward her; but she stood for an instant staring at the thing that left her stricken, with a voiceless scream forming in her throat.

She was never to know whether his arms had been outstretched to take her within their shelter or to clutch at her white neck. For she turned and fled, stumbling up the stairs in a mad panic of escape.

He shouted, "Janet! Janet!" His steps were heavy behind her. He tripped on the bottom step and fell on one knee and cursed.

Terror lent her strength and speed. She could not be mistaken. Although she had seen it only once, she knew that on the little finger of his left hand there had been the same, the unmistakable ring the dead woman had worn.

The blessed wind snatched the front door from her and flung it wide, and she was out in the safe, dark shelter of the storm.

QUESTIONS

1. By what means does this story create and build suspense? What uses does it make of mystery? At what points does it employ surprise?
2. Is the ending of the story determinate or indeterminate?

3. From what point of view is the story told? What advantages has this point of view for this story? Are there any places where the contents of Janet's consciousness are suppressed, at least temporarily? For what purpose?
4. Put together an account of Ben's activities that will explain as many as possible of the phenomena that Janet observes — or thinks she observes — during the course of the evening. Are any left unexplained? Is any motivation provided for the murder of the woman in the trunk? How?
5. What are the chief features of Ben's characterization? Why is he characterized as he is? Has the characterization been fashioned to serve the story or the story to serve the characterization?
6. To what extent does the story depend on coincidence?
7. What is the main purpose of the story? Does it have a theme? If so, what?
8. What do you find most effective in the story?

Nadine Gordimer
Once Upon a Time

Someone has written to ask me to contribute to an anthology of stories for children. I reply that I don't write children's stories; and he writes back that at a recent congress/book fair/seminar a certain novelist said every writer ought to write a least one story for children. I think of sending a postcard saying I don't accept that I "ought" to write anything.

And then last night I woke up — or rather was awakened without knowing what had roused me.

A voice in the echo-chamber of the subconscious?

A sound.

A creaking of the kind made by the weight carried by one foot after another along a wooden floor. I listened. I felt the apertures of my ears distend with concentration. Again: the creaking. I was waiting for it; waiting to hear if it indicated that feet were moving from room to room, coming up the passage — to my door. I have no burglar bars, no gun under the pillow, but I have the same fears as people who do take these precautions, and my windowpanes are thin as rime, could shatter like a wineglass. A woman was murdered (how do they put it) in broad daylight in a house two blocks away, last year, and the fierce dogs who guarded an old widower and his collection of antique clocks were strangled before he was knifed by a casual laborer he had dismissed without pay.

ONCE UPON A TIME   First published in 1989. Nadine Gordimer was born in 1923 in a small town near Johannesburg, South Africa, and graduated from the University of Witwatersrand. She has taught at several American universities, but continues to reside in her native country. A prolific writer, Gordimer has published ten novels and ten short story collections. In addition to England's prestigious Booker Prize for Fiction (1974), she received the Nobel Prize for Literature in 1991.

I was staring at the door, making it out in my mind rather than seeing it, in the dark. I lay quite still — a victim already — the arrhythmia of my heart was fleeing, knocking this way and that against its body-cage. How finely tuned the senses are, just out of rest, sleep! I could never listen intently as that in the distractions of the day; I was reading every faintest sound, identifying and classifying its possible threat.

But I learned that I was to be neither threatened nor spared. There was no human weight pressing on the boards, the creaking was a buckling, an epicenter of stress. I was in it. The house that surrounds me while I sleep is built on undermined ground; far beneath my bed, the floor, the house's foundations, the stopes and passages of gold mines have hollowed the rock, and when some face trembles, detaches and falls, three thousand feet below, the whole house shifts slightly, bringing uneasy strain to the balance and counterbalance of brick, cement, wood and glass that hold it as a structure around me. The misbeats of my heart tailed off like the last muffled flourishes on one of the wooden xylophones made by the Chopi and Tsonga° migrant miners who might have been down there, under me in the earth at that moment. The stope where the fall was could have been disused, dripping water from its ruptured veins; or men might now be interred there in the most profound of tombs.

I couldn't find a position in which my mind would let go of my body — release me to sleep again. So I began to tell myself a story; a bedtime story.

In a house, in a suburb, in a city, there were a man and his wife who loved each other very much and were living happily ever after. They had a little boy, and they loved him very much. They had a cat and a dog that the little boy loved very much. They had a car and a caravan trailer for holidays, and a swimming-pool which was fenced so that the little boy and his playmates would not fall in and drown. They had a housemaid who was absolutely trustworthy and an itinerant gardener who was highly recommended by the neighbors. For when they began to live happily ever after they were warned, by that wise old witch, the husband's mother, not to take on anyone off the street. They were inscribed in a medical benefit society, their pet dog was licensed, they were insured against fire, flood damage and theft, and subscribed to the local Neighborhood Watch, which supplied them with a plaque for their gates lettered YOU HAVE BEEN WARNED over the silhouette of a would-be intruder. He was masked; it could not be said if he was black or white, and therefore proved the property owner was no racist.

It was not possible to insure the house, the swimming pool or the car against riot damage. There were riots, but these were outside the city, where people of another color were quartered. These people were not allowed into the suburb except as reliable housemaids and gardeners, so there was nothing to fear, the husband told the wife. Yet she was afraid that some day such

Chopi and Tsonga: two peoples from Mozambique, northeast of South Africa

people might come up the street and tear off the plaque YOU HAVE BEEN WARNED and open the gates and stream in . . . Nonsense, my dear, said the husband, there are police and soldiers and tear-gas and guns to keep them away. But to please her — for he loved her very much and buses were being burned, cars stoned, and schoolchildren shot by the police in those quarters out of sight and hearing of the suburb — he had electronically controlled gates fitted. Anyone who pulled off the sign YOU HAVE BEEN WARNED and tried to open the gates would have to announce his intentions by pressing a button and speaking into a receiver relayed to the house. The little boy was fascinated by the device and used it as a walkie-talkie in cops and robbers play with his small friends.

The riots were suppressed, but there were many burglaries in the suburb and somebody's trusted housemaid was tied up and shut in a cupboard by thieves while she was in charge of her employers' house. The trusted housemaid of the man and wife and little boy was so upset by this misfortune befalling a friend left, as she herself often was, with responsibility for the possessions of the man and his wife and the little boy that she implored her employers to have burglar bars attached to the doors and windows of the house, and an alarm system installed. The wife said, She is right, let us take heed of her advice. So from every window and door in the house where they were living happily ever after they now saw the trees and sky through bars, and when the little boy's pet cat tried to climb in by the fanlight to keep him company in his little bed at night, as it customarily had done, it set off the alarm keening through the house.

The alarm was often answered — it seemed — by other burglar alarms, in other houses, that had been triggered by pet cats or nibbling mice. The alarms called to one another across the gardens in shrills and bleats and wails that everyone soon became accustomed to, so that the din roused the inhabitants of the suburb no more than the croak of frogs and musical grating of cicadas' legs. Under cover of the electronic harpies' discourse intruders sawed the iron bars and broke into homes, taking away hi-fi equipment, television sets, cassette players, cameras and radios, jewelry and clothing, and sometimes were hungry enough to devour everything in the refrigerator or paused audaciously to drink the whiskey in the cabinets or patio bars. Insurance companies paid no compensation for single malt,° a loss made keener by the property owner's knowledge that the thieves wouldn't even have been able to appreciate what it was they were drinking.

Then the time came when many of the people who were not trusted housemaids and gardeners hung about the suburb because they were unemployed. Some importuned for a job: weeding or painting a roof; anything, *baas*,° madam. But the man and his wife remembered the warning about taking on anyone off the street. Some drank liquor and fouled the street with discarded bottles. Some begged, waiting for the man or his wife to drive the

single malt: an expensive Scotch whiskey   *baas:* boss

car out of the electronically operated gates. They sat about with their feet in the gutters, under the jacaranda trees that made a green tunnel of the street — for it was a beautiful suburb, spoilt only by their presence — and sometimes they fell asleep lying right before the gates in the midday sun. The wife could never see anyone go hungry. She sent the trusted housemaid out with bread and tea, but the trusted housemaid said these were loafers and *tsotsis*,° who would come and tie her and shut her in a cupboard. The husband said, She's right. Take heed of her advice. You only encourage them with your bread and tea. They are looking for their chance . . . And he brought the little boy's tricycle from the garden into the house every night, because if the house was surely secure, once locked and with the alarm set, someone might still be able to climb over the wall or the electronically closed gates into the garden.

You are right, said the wife, then the wall should be higher. And the wise old witch, the husband's mother, paid for the extra bricks as her Christmas present to her son and his wife — the little boy got a Space Man outfit and a book of fairy tales.

15   But every week there were more reports of intrusion: in broad daylight and the dead of night, in the early hours of the morning, and even in the lovely summer twilight — a certain family was at dinner while the bedrooms were being ransacked upstairs. The man and his wife, talking of the latest armed robbery in the suburb, were distracted by the sight of the little boy's pet cat effortlessly arriving over the seven-foot wall, descending first with a rapid bracing of extended forepaws down on the sheer vertical surface, and then a graceful launch, landing with swishing tail within the property. The whitewashed wall was marked with the cat's comings and goings; and on the street side of the wall there were larger red-earth smudges that could have been made by the kind of broken running shoes, seen on the feet of unemployed loiterers, that had no innocent destination.

When the man and wife and little boy took the pet dog for its walk round the neighborhood streets they no longer paused to admire this show of roses or that perfect lawn; these were hidden behind an array of different varieties of security fences, walls and devices. The man, wife, little boy and dog passed a remarkable choice: there was the low-cost option of pieces of broken glass embedded in cement along the top of walls, there were iron grilles ending in lance-points, there were attempts at reconciling the aesthetics of prison architecture with the Spanish Villa style (spikes painted pink) and with the plaster urns of neoclassical façades (twelve-inch pikes finned like zigzags of lightning and painted pure white). Some walls had a small board affixed, giving the name and telephone number of the firm responsible for the installation of the devices. While the little boy and the pet dog raced ahead, the husband and wife found themselves comparing the possible effectiveness of each style against its appearance; and after several weeks when they paused before this barricade or that without needing to speak, both

tsotsis: hooligans

came out with the conclusion that only one was worth considering. It was the ugliest but the most honest in its suggestion of the pure concentration-camp style, no frills, all evident efficacy. Placed the length of walls, it consisted of a continuous coil of stiff and shining metal serrated into jagged blades, so that there would be no way of climbing over it and no way through its tunnel without getting entangled in its fangs. There would be no way out, only a struggle getting bloodier and bloodier, a deeper and sharper hooking and tearing of flesh. The wife shuddered to look at it. You're right, said the husband, anyone would think twice . . . And they took heed of the advice on a small board fixed to the wall: Consult DRAGON'S TEETH The People For Total Security.

Next day a gang of workmen came and stretched the razor-bladed coils all round the walls of the house where the husband and wife and little boy and pet dog and cat were living happily ever after. The sunlight flashed and slashed, off the serrations, the cornice of razor thorns encircled the home, shining. The husband said, Never mind. It will weather. The wife said, You're wrong. They guarantee it's rust-proof. And she waited until the little boy had run off to play before she said, I hope the cat will take heed . . . The husband said, Don't worry, my dear, cats always look before they leap. And it was true that from that day on the cat slept in the little boy's bed and kept to the garden, never risking a try at breaching security.

One evening, the mother read the little boy to sleep with a fairy story from the book the wise old witch had given him at Christmas. Next day he pretended to be the Prince who braves the terrible thicket of thorns to enter the palace and kiss the Sleeping Beauty back to life: he dragged a ladder to the wall, the shining coiled tunnel was just wide enough for his little body to creep in, and with the first fixing of its razor-teeth in his knees and hands and head he screamed and struggled deeper into its tangle. The trusted house-maid and the itinerant gardener, whose "day" it was, came running, the first to see and to scream with him, and the itinerant gardener tore his hands trying to get at the little boy. Then the man and his wife burst wildly into the garden and for some reason (the cat, probably) the alarm set up wailing against the screams while the bleeding mass of the little boy was hacked out of the security coil with saws, wire-cutters, choppers, and they carried it — the man, the wife, the hysterical trusted housemaid and the weeping gardener — into the house.

QUESTIONS

1. The opening section of the story is told by a writer who is awakened by a frightening sound in the night. What two causes for the sound does she consider? Ultimately, which is the more significant cause for fear? How do these together create an emotional background for the "children's story" that she tells?
2. What stylistic devices does the writer use to create the atmosphere of children's stories?

3. To what extent does the story explore the motives for the behavior of the wife and husband, the husband's mother, the servants, and the people who surround the suburb and the house? What motives can you infer for these people? What ironies do they display in their actions?
4. Why do the wife and husband keep increasing the security devices of their home? What is ironic about the conclusion of the story?
5. Can you fix the blame for the calamity that befalls the child? What are the possible meanings for the repeated phrase "YOU HAVE BEEN WARNED"?
6. What details in the introductory section and in the children's story imply the nature of the social order in which both occur?
7. Compare this story with "The Storm" as a study in fear. What are the most significant differences? What are the themes of the two stories?

James Thurber
The Catbird Seat

Mr. Martin bought the pack of Camels on Monday night in the most crowded cigar store on Broadway. It was theater time and seven or eight men were buying cigarettes. The clerk didn't even glance at Mr. Martin, who put the pack in his overcoat pocket and went out. If any of the staff at F & S had seen him buy the cigarettes, they would have been astonished, for it was generally known that Mr. Martin did not smoke, and never had. No one saw him.

It was just a week to the day since Mr. Martin had decided to rub out Mrs. Ulgine Barrows. The term "rub out" pleased him because it suggested nothing more than the correction of an error — in this case an error of Mr. Fitweiler. Mr. Martin had spent each night of the past week working out his plan and examining it. As he walked home now he went over it again. For the hundredth time he resented the element of imprecision, the margin of guesswork that entered into the business. The project as he had worked it out was casual and bold, the risks were considerable. Something might go wrong anywhere along the line. And therein lay the cunning of his scheme. No one would ever see in it the cautious, painstaking hand of Erwin Martin, head of the filing department at F & S of whom Mr. Fitweiler had once said, "Man is fallible but Martin isn't." No one would see his hand, that is, unless it were caught in the act.

Sitting in his apartment, drinking a glass of milk, Mr. Martin reviewed his case against Mrs. Ulgine Barrows, as he had every night for seven nights. He began at the beginning. Her quacking voice and braying laugh had first

THE CATBIRD SEAT   First published in 1942 in *The New Yorker*. At that time the "Dodgers" were located in Brooklyn, and Red Barber, originally from Mississippi, was the beloved radio announcer for all the Dodgers' games. James Thurber (1894–1961), cartoonist and writer, was born and grew up in Columbus, Ohio. In 1925, after a year's sojourn in France, he joined the staff of *The New Yorker*, with which he was associated until his death.

profaned the halls of F & S on March 7, 1941 (Mr. Martin had a head for dates). Old Roberts, the personnel chief, had introduced her as the newly appointed special adviser to the president of the firm, Mr. Fitweiler. The woman had appalled Mr. Martin instantly, but he hadn't shown it. He had given her his dry hand, a look of studious concentration, and a faint smile. "Well," she had said, looking at the papers on his desk, "are you lifting the oxcart out of the ditch?" As Mr. Martin recalled the moment, over his milk, he squirmed slightly. He must keep his mind on her crimes as a special adviser, not on her peccadillos as a personality. This he found difficult to do, in spite of entering an objection and sustaining it. The faults of the woman as a woman kept chattering on in his mind like an unruly witness. She had, for almost two years now, baited him. In the halls, in the elevator, even in his own office, into which she romped now and then like a circus horse, she was constantly shouting these silly questions at him. "Are you lifting the oxcart out of the ditch? Are you tearing up the pea patch? Are you hollering down the rain barrel? Are you scraping around the bottom of the pickle barrel? Are you sitting in the catbird seat?"

It was Joey Hart, one of Mr. Martin's two assistants, who had explained what the gibberish meant. "She must be a Dodger fan," he had said. "Red Barber announces the Dodger games over the radio and he uses those expressions — picked 'em up down South." Joey had gone on to explain one or two. "Tearing up the pea patch" meant going on a rampage; "sitting in the catbird seat" meant sitting pretty, like a batter with three balls and no strikes on him. Mr. Martin dismissed all this with an effort. It had been annoying, it had driven him near to distraction, but he was too solid a man to be moved to murder by anything so childish. It was fortunate, he reflected as he passed on to the important charges against Mrs. Barrows, that he had stood up under it so well. He had maintained always an outward appearance of polite tolerance. "Why, I even believe you like the woman," Miss Paird, his other assistant, had once said to him. He had simply smiled.

A gavel rapped in Mr. Martin's mind and the case was resumed. Mrs. Ulgine Barrows stood charged with willful, blatant, and persistent attempts to destroy the efficiency and system of F & S. It was competent, material, and relevant to review her advent and rise to power. Mr. Martin had got the story from Miss Paird, who seemed always able to find things out. According to her, Mrs. Barrows had met Mr. Fitweiler at a party, where she had rescued him from the embraces of a powerfully built drunken man who had mistaken the president of F & S for a famous retired Middle Western football coach. She had led him to a sofa and somehow worked upon him a monstrous magic. The aging gentleman had jumped to the conclusion there and then that this was a woman of singular attainments, equipped to bring out the best in him and the firm. A week later he had introduced her into F & S as his special adviser. On that day confusion got its foot in the door. After Miss Tyson, Mr. Brundage and Mr. Bartlett had been fired and Mr. Munson had taken his hat and stalked out, mailing in his resignation later, old Roberts had been emboldened to speak to Mr. Fitweiler. He mentioned that Mr. Munson's department had been "a little disrupted" and hadn't they perhaps better resume the old system there? Mr. Fitweiler had said certainly not. He had the greatest faith in Mrs. Barrows's ideas. "They require a little seasoning, a little seasoning, is all," he had added. Mr. Roberts had given it up. Mr. Martin reviewed in detail all the changes wrought by Mrs. Barrows. She had begun chipping at the cornices of the firm's edifice and now she was swinging at the foundation with a pickaxe.

Mr. Martin came now, in his summing up, to the afternoon of Monday, November 2, 1942 — just one week ago. On that day, at 3 P.M., Mrs. Barrows had bounced into his office. "Boo!" she had yelled. "Are you scraping around the bottom of the pickle barrel?" Mr. Martin had looked at her from under his green eyeshade, saying nothing. She had begun to wander about the office, taking it in with her great, popping eyes. "Do you really need *all* these filing cabinets?" she had demanded suddenly. Mr. Martin's heart had jumped. "Each of these files," he had said, keeping his voice even, "plays an indispensable part in the system of F & S." She had brayed at him, "Well, don't tear up the pea patch!" and gone to the door. From there she had bawled, "But you sure have got a lot of fine scrap in here!" Mr. Martin could no longer doubt that the finger was on his beloved department. Her pickaxe was on the upswing, poised for the first blow. It had not come yet; he had received no blue memo from the enchanted Mr. Fitweiler bearing nonsensical instructions deriving from the obscene woman. But there was no doubt in Mr. Martin's mind that one would be forthcoming. He must act quickly. Already a precious week had gone by. Mr. Martin stood up in his living room, still holding his milk glass. "Gentlemen of the jury," he said to himself, "I demand the death penalty for this horrible person."

The next day Mr. Martin followed his routine, as usual. He polished his glasses more often and once sharpened an already sharp pencil, but not even Miss Paird noticed. Only once did he catch sight of his victim; she swept past him in the hall with a patronizing "Hi!" At five-thirty he walked home, as usual, and had a glass of milk, as usual. He had never drunk anything stronger in his life — unless you could count ginger ale. The late Sam Schlosser, the S of F & S, had praised Mr. Martin at a staff meeting several years before for his temperate habits. "Our most efficient worker neither drinks nor smokes," he had said. "The results speak for themselves." Mr. Fitweiler had sat by, nodding approval.

Mr. Martin was still thinking about that red-letter day as he walked over to the Schrafft's on Fifth Avenue near Forty-sixth Street. He got there, as he always did, at eight o'clock. He finished his dinner and the financial page of the *Sun* at a quarter to nine, as he always did. It was his custom after dinner to take a walk. This time he walked down Fifth Avenue at a casual pace. His gloved hands felt moist and warm, his forehead cold. He transferred the Camels from his overcoat to a jacket pocket. He wondered, as he did so, if they did not represent an unnecessary note of strain. Mrs. Barrows smoked only Luckies. It was his idea to puff a few puffs on a Camel (after the rubbing-out), stub it out in the ashtray holding her lipstick-stained Luckies, and thus drag a small red herring across the trail. Perhaps it was not a good idea. It would take time. He might even choke, too loudly.

Mr. Martin had never seen the house on West Twelfth Street where Mrs. Barrows lived, but he had a clear enough picture of it. Fortunately, she had bragged to everybody about her ducky first-floor apartment in the perfectly darling three-story red-brick. There would be no doorman or other attendants; just the tenants of the second and third floors. As he walked along, Mr. Martin realized that he would get there before nine-thirty. He had considered walking north on Fifth Avenue from Schrafft's to a point from which it would take him until ten o'clock to reach the house. At that hour people were less likely to be coming in or going out. But the procedure would have made an awkward loop in the straight thread of his casualness, and he had abandoned it. It was impossible to figure when people would be entering or leaving the house, anyway. There was a great risk at any hour. If he ran into anybody, he would simply have to place the rubbing-out of Ulgine Barrows in the inactive file forever. The same thing would hold true if there were someone in her apartment. In that case he would just say that he had been passing by, recognized her charming house, and thought to drop in.

It was eighteen minutes after nine when Mr. Martin turned into Twelfth Street. A man passed him, and a man and a woman, talking. There was no one within fifty paces when he came to the house, halfway down the block. He was up the steps and in the small vestibule in no time, pressing the bell under the card that said "Mrs. Ulgine Barrows." When the clicking in the lock started he jumped forward against the door. He got inside fast, closing the door behind him. A bulb in a lantern hung from the hall ceiling on a chain seemed to give a monstrously bright light. There was nobody on the stair, which went up ahead of him along the left wall. A door opened down the hall in the wall on the right. He went toward it swiftly, on tiptoe.

"Well, for God's sake, look who's here!" bawled Mrs. Barrows, and her braying laugh rang out like the report of a shotgun. He rushed past her like a football tackle, bumping her. "Hey, quit shoving!" she said, closing the door behind them. They were in her living room, which seemed to Mr. Martin to be lighted by a hundred lamps. "What's after you?" she said. "You're as jumpy as a goat." He found he was unable to speak. His heart was wheezing in his throat. "I — yes," he finally brought out. She was jabbering and laughing as she started to help him off with his coat. "No, no," he said. "I'll put it here." He took it off and put it on a chair near the door. "Your hat and gloves, too," she said. "You're in a lady's house." He put his hat on top of the coat. Mrs. Barrows seemed larger than he had thought. He kept his gloves on. "I was passing by," he said. "I recognized — is there anyone here?" She laughed louder than ever. "No," she said, "we're all alone. You're as white as a sheet, you funny man. Whatever *has* come over you? I'll mix you a toddy." She started toward a door across the room. "Scotch-and-soda be all right? But say, you don't drink, do you?" She turned and gave him her amused look. Mr. Martin pulled himself together. "Scotch-and-soda will be all right," he heard himself say. He could hear her laughing in the kitchen.

Mr. Martin looked quickly around the living room for the weapon. He had counted on finding one there. There were andirons and a poker and something in a corner that looked like an Indian club. None of them would do. It couldn't be that way. He began to pace around. He came to a desk. On it lay a metal paper knife with an ornate handle. Would it be sharp enough? He reached for it and knocked over a small brass jar. Stamps spilled out of it and it fell to the floor with a clatter. "Hey," Mrs. Barrows yelled from the kitchen, "are you tearing up the pea patch?" Mr. Martin gave a strange laugh. Picking up the knife, he tried its point against his left wrist. It was blunt. It wouldn't do.

When Mrs. Barrows reappeared, carrying two highballs, Mr. Martin, standing there with his gloves on, became acutely conscious of the fantasy he had wrought. Cigarettes in his pocket, a drink prepared for him — it was all too grossly improbable. It was more than that; it was impossible. Somewhere in the back of his mind a vague idea stirred, sprouted. "For heaven's sake, take off those gloves," said Mrs. Barrows. "I always wear them in the house," said Mr. Martin. The idea began to bloom, strange and wonderful. She put the glasses on a coffee table in front of a sofa and sat on the sofa. "Come over here, you odd little man," she said. Mr. Martin went over and sat beside her. It was difficult getting a cigarette out of the pack of Camels, but he managed it. She held a match for him, laughing. "Well," she said, handing him his drink, "this is perfectly marvelous. You with a drink and a cigarette."

Mr. Martin puffed, not too awkwardly, and took a gulp of the highball. "I drink and smoke all the time," he said. He clinked his glass against hers. "Here's nuts to that old windbag, Fitweiler," he said, and gulped again. The stuff tasted awful, but he made no grimace. "Really, Mr. Martin," she said, her voice and posture changing, "you are insulting our employer." Mrs. Barrows was now all special adviser to the president. "I am preparing a bomb," said Mr. Martin, "which will blow the old goat higher than hell." He had only had a little of the drink, which was not strong. It couldn't be that. "Do you take dope or something?" Mrs. Barrows asked coldly. "Heroin," said Mr. Martin. "I'll be coked to the gills when I bump the old buzzard off." "Mr. Martin!" she shouted, getting to her feet. "That will be all of that. You must go at once." Mr. Martin took another swallow of his drink. He tapped his cigarette out in the ashtray and put the pack of Camels on the coffee table. Then he got up. She stood glaring at him. He walked over and put on his hat and coat. "Not a word about this," he said, and laid an index finger against his lips. All Mrs. Barrows could bring out was "Really!" Mr. Martin put his hand on the doorknob. "I'm sitting in the catbird seat," he said. He stuck his tongue out at her and left. Nobody saw him go.

15 Mr. Martin got to his apartment, walking, well before eleven. No one saw him go in. He had two glasses of milk after brushing his teeth, and he felt

elated. It wasn't tipsiness, because he hadn't been tipsy. Anyway, the walk had worn off all effects of the whiskey. He got in bed and read a magazine for a while. He was asleep before midnight.

Mr. Martin got to the office at eight-thirty the next morning, as usual. At a quarter to nine, Ulgine Barrows, who had never before arrived at work before ten, swept into his office. "I'm reporting to Mr. Fitweiler now!" she shouted. "If he turns you over to the police, it's no more than you deserve!" Mr. Martin gave her a look of shocked surprise. "I beg your pardon?" he said. Mrs. Barrows snorted and bounced out of the room, leaving Miss Paird and Joey Hart staring after her. "What's the matter with that old devil now?" asked Miss Paird. "I have no idea," said Mr. Martin, resuming his work. The other two looked at him and then at each other. Miss Paird got up and went out. She walked slowly past the closed door of Mr. Fitweiler's office. Mrs. Barrows was yelling inside, but she was not braying. Miss Paird could not hear what the woman was saying. She went back to her desk.

Forty-five minutes later, Mrs. Barrows left the president's office and went into her own, shutting the door. It wasn't until half an hour later that Mr. Fitweiler sent for Mr. Martin. The head of the filing department, neat, quiet, attentive, stood in front of the old man's desk. Mr. Fitweiler was pale and nervous. He took his glasses off and twiddled them. He made a small, bruffing sound in his throat. "Martin," he said, "you have been with us more than twenty years." "Twenty-two, sir," said Mr. Martin. "In that time," pursued the president, "your work and your — uh — manner have been exemplary." "I trust so, sir," said Mr. Martin. "I have understood, Martin," said Mr. Fitweiler, "that you have never taken a drink or smoked." "That is correct, sir," said Mr. Martin. "Ah, yes," Mr. Fitweiler polished his glasses. "You may describe what you did after leaving the office yesterday, Martin," he said. Mr. Martin allowed less than a second for his bewildered pause. "Certainly, sir," he said. "I walked home. Then went to Schrafft's for dinner. Afterward I walked home again. I went to bed early, sir, and read a magazine for a while. I was asleep before eleven." "Ah, yes," said Mr. Fitweiler again. He was silent for a moment, searching for the proper words to say to the head of the filing department. "Mrs. Barrows," he said finally, "Mrs. Barrows has worked hard, Martin, very hard. It grieves me to report that she has suffered a severe breakdown. It has taken the form of a persecution complex accompanied by distressing hallucinations." "I am very sorry, sir," said Mr. Martin. "Mrs. Barrows is under the delusion," continued Mr. Fitweiler, "that you visited her last evening and behaved yourself in an — uh — unseemly manner." He raised his hand to silence Mr. Martin's little pained outcry. "It is the nature of these psychological diseases," Mr. Fitweiler said, "to fix upon the least likely and most innocent party as the — uh — source of persecution. These matters are not for the lay mind to grasp, Martin. I've just had my psychiatrist, Dr. Fitch, on the phone. He would not, of course, commit himself, but he made enough generalizations to substantiate my suspicions. I suggested to Mrs. Barrows, when she had completed her — uh — story to me this morning, that she visit Dr. Fitch, for I suspected a condition at once. She flew, I regret to say, into a rage, and demanded — uh — requested that I call you on the carpet. You may not know, Martin, but Mrs. Barrows had planned a reorganization of your department — subject to my approval, of course, subject to my approval. This brought you, rather than anyone else, to her mind — but again that is a phenomenon for Dr. Fitch and not for us. So, Martin, I am afraid Mrs. Barrows's usefulness here is at an end." "I am dreadfully sorry, sir," said Mr. Martin.

It was at this point that the door to the office blew open with the suddenness of a gas-main explosion and Mrs. Barrows catapulted through it. "Is the little rat denying it?" she screamed. "He can't get away with that!" Mr. Martin got up and moved discreetly to a point beside Mr. Fitweiler's chair. "You drank and smoked at my apartment," she bawled at Mr. Martin, "and you know it! You called Mr. Fitweiler an old windbag and said you were going to blow him up when you got coked to the gills on your heroin!" She stopped yelling to catch her breath and a new glint came into her popping eyes. "If you weren't such a drab, ordinary little man," she said, "I'd think you'd planned it all. Sticking your tongue out, saying you were sitting in the catbird seat, because you thought no one would believe me when I told it! My God, it's really too perfect!" She brayed loudly and hysterically, and the fury was on her again. She glared at Mr. Fitweiler. "Can't you see how he has tricked us, you old fool? Can't you see his little game?" But Mr. Fitweiler had been surreptitiously pressing all the buttons under the top of his desk and employees of F & S began pouring into the room. "Stockton," said Mr. Fitweiler, "you and Fishbein will take Mrs. Barrows to her home. Mrs. Powell, you will go with them." Stockton, who had played a little football in high school, blocked Mrs. Barrows as she made for Mr. Martin. It took him and Fishbein together to force her out of the door into the hall, crowded with stenographers and office boys. She was still screaming imprecations at Mr. Martin, tangled and contradictory imprecations. The hubbub finally died out down the corridor.

"I regret that this has happened," said Mr. Fitweiler. "I shall ask you to dismiss it from your mind, Martin." "Yes sir," said Mr. Martin, anticipating his chief's "That will be all" by moving to the door. "I will dismiss it." He went out and shut the door, and his step was light and quick in the hall. When he entered his department he had slowed down to his customary gait, and he walked quietly across the room to the W20 file, wearing a look of studious concentration.

QUESTIONS

1. How is suspense aroused and maintained in the story? What is the story's principal surprise?
2. Through whose consciousness are the events of the story chiefly seen? Are there any departures from this strictly limited point of view? Where in the story are we taken most fully into Mr. Martin's mind? For what purpose?

3. At what point in the story do Mr. Martin's plans change? What happens to the point of view at this point? What does Thurber's handling of the point of view here tell us about the seriousness of the story's purpose?
4. Characterize Mr. Martin and Mrs. Barrows respectively. In what ways are they character foils?
5. Analyze the story in terms of its conflicts. What kinds of conflict are involved? Is there any internal conflict? What kind of conflict that *might* be expected in a murder story is missing?
6. Evaluate the surprise ending of the story by the criteria suggested on page 45.
7. What insights into the life of a business office does the story provide? What kind of insight does the story not provide? What is the story's greatest improbability?
8. What are the main sources of the story's humor?
9. Why does Thurber choose this particular expression of Mrs. Barrows's for his title rather than one of her others?

Frank O'Connor
The Drunkard

It was a terrible blow to Father when Mr. Dooley on the terrace died. Mr. Dooley was a commercial traveler with two sons in the Dominicans and a car of his own, so socially he was miles ahead of us, but he had no false pride. Mr. Dooley was an intellectual, and, like all intellectuals, the thing he loved best was conversation, and in his own limited way Father was a well-read man and could appreciate an intelligent talker. Mr. Dooley was remarkably intelligent. Between business acquaintances and clerical contacts, there was very little he didn't know about what went on in town, and evening after evening he crossed the road to our gate to explain to Father the news behind the news. He had a low, palavering voice and a knowing smile, and Father would listen in astonishment, giving him a conversational lead now and again, and then stump triumphantly in to Mother with his face aglow and ask: "Do you know what Mr. Dooley is after telling me?" Ever since, when somebody has given me some bit of information off the record I have found myself on the point of asking: "Was it Mr. Dooley told you that?"

Till I actually saw him laid out in his brown shroud with the rosary beads entwined between his waxy fingers I did not take the report of his death seriously. Even then I felt there must be a catch and that some summer evening Mr. Dooley must reappear at our gate to give us the lowdown on the next world. But Father was very upset, partly because Mr. Dooley was about

THE DRUNKARD   First published in 1948. Frank O'Connor (1903–1966) was born Michael O'Donovan, the only child of very poor, Roman Catholic parents in Cork, Ireland. He used his mother's maiden name as a pseudonym when he began to publish. "The Drunkard" is based on an incident from his boyhood in Cork, as revealed in the first two chapters of his autobiographical volume, *An Only Son* (1961).

one age with himself, a thing that always gives a distinctly personal turn to another man's demise; partly because now he would have no one to tell him what dirty work was behind the latest scene at the Corporation.° You could count on your fingers the number of men in Blarney Lane who read the papers as Mr. Dooley did, and none of these would have overlooked the fact that Father was only a laboring man. Even Sullivan, the carpenter, a mere nobody, thought he was a cut above Father. It was certainly a solemn event.

"Half past two to the Curragh," Father said meditatively, putting down the paper.

"But you're not thinking of going to the funeral?" Mother asked in alarm.

5   "'Twould be expected," Father said, scenting opposition. "I wouldn't give it to say to them."

"I think," said Mother with suppressed emotion, "it will be as much as anyone will expect if you go to the chapel with him."

("Going to the chapel," of course, was one thing, because the body was removed after work, but going to a funeral meant the loss of a half-day's pay.)

"The people hardly know us," she added.

"God between us and all harm," Father replied with dignity, "we'd be glad if it was our own turn."

10   To give Father his due, he was always ready to lose a half day for the sake of an old neighbor. It wasn't so much that he liked funerals as that he was a conscientious man who did as he would be done by, and nothing could have consoled him so much for the prospect of his own death as the assurance of a worthy funeral. And, to give Mother her due, it wasn't the half-day's pay she begrudged, badly as we could afford it.

Drink, you see, was Father's great weakness. He could keep steady for months, even for years, at a stretch, and while he did he was as good as gold. He was first up in the morning and brought the mother a cup of tea in bed, stayed home in the evenings and read the paper; saved money and bought himself a new blue serge suit and bowler hat. He laughed at the folly of men who, week in, week out, left their hard-earned money with the publicans; and sometimes, to pass an idle hour, he took pencil and paper and calculated precisely how much he saved each week through being a teetotaller. Being a natural optimist he sometimes continued this calculation through the whole span of his prospective existence and the total was breathtaking. He would die worth hundreds.

If I had only known it, this was a bad sign; a sign he was becoming stuffed up with spiritual pride and imagining himself better than his neighbors. Sooner or later, the spiritual pride grew till it called for some form of celebration. Then he took a drink — not whiskey, of course; nothing like that — just a glass of some harmless drink like lager beer. That was the end of

---

Corporation: the officials of the city (mayor, aldermen, councillors)

Father. By the time he had taken the first he already realized that he had made a fool of himself, took a second to forget it and a third to forget that he couldn't forget, and at last came home reeling drunk. From this on it was "The Drunkard's Progress," as in the moral prints. Next day he stayed in from work with a sick head while Mother went off to make his excuses at the works, and inside a fortnight he was poor and savage and despondent again. Once he began he drank steadily through everything down to the kitchen clock. Mother and I knew all the phases and dreaded all the dangers. Funerals were one.

"I have to go to Dunphy's to do a half-day's work," said Mother in distress. "Who's to look after Larry?"

"I'll look after Larry," Father said graciously. "The little walk will do him good."

There was no more to be said, though we all knew I didn't need anyone to look after me, and that I could quite well have stayed home and looked after Sonny, but I was being attached to the party to act as a brake on Father. As a brake I had never achieved anything, but Mother still had great faith in me.

Next day, when I got home from school, Father was there before me and made a cup of tea for both of us. He was very good at tea, but too heavy in the hand for anything else; the way he cut bread was shocking. Afterwards, we went down the hill to the church, Father wearing his best blue serge and a bowler cocked to one side of his head with the least suggestion of the masher. To his great joy he discovered Peter Crowley among the mourners. Peter was another danger signal, as I knew well from certain experiences after Mass on Sunday morning: a mean man, as Mother said, who only went to funerals for the free drinks he could get at them. It turned out that he hadn't even known Mr. Dooley! But Father had a sort of contemptuous regard for him as one of the foolish people who wasted their good money in public-houses when they could be saving it. Very little of his own money Peter Crowley wasted!

It was an excellent funeral from Father's point of view. He had it all well studied before we set off after the hearse in the afternoon sunlight.

"Five carriages!" he exclaimed. "Five carriages and sixteen covered cars! There's one alderman, two councillors and 'tis unknown how many priests. I didn't see a funeral like this from the road since Willie Mack, the publican, died."

"Ah, he was well liked," said Crowley in his husky voice.

"My goodness, don't I know that?" snapped Father. "Wasn't the man my best friend? Two nights before he died — only two nights — he was over telling me the goings-on about the housing contract. Them fellows in the Corporation are night and day robbers. But even I never imagined he was as well connected as that."

Father was stepping out like a boy, pleased with everything: the other mourners, and the fine houses along Sunday's Well. I knew danger signals were there in full force: a sunny day, a fine funeral and a distinguished company of clerics and public men were bringing out all the natural vanity and flightiness of Father's character. It was with something like genuine pleasure that he saw his old friend lowered into the grave; with the sense of having performed a duty and the pleasant awareness that however much he would miss poor Mr. Dooley in the long summer evenings, it was he and not poor Mr. Dooley who would do the missing.

"We'll be making tracks before they break up," he whispered to Crowley as the gravediggers tossed in the first shovelfuls of clay, and away he went, hopping like a goat from grassy hump to hump. The drivers, who were probably in the same state as himself, though without months of abstinence to put an edge on it, looked up hopefully.

"Are they nearly finished, Mick?" bawled one.

"All over now bar the last prayers," trumpeted Father in the tone of one who brings news of great rejoicing.

25 The carriages passed us in a lather of dust several hundred yards from the public-house, and Father, whose feet gave him trouble in hot weather, quickened his pace, looking nervously over his shoulder for any sign of the main body of mourners crossing the hill. In a crowd like that a man might be kept waiting.

When we did reach the pub the carriages were drawn up outside, and solemn men in black ties were cautiously bringing out consolation to mysterious females whose hands reached out modestly from behind the drawn blinds of the coaches. Inside the pub there were only the drivers and a couple of shawly women. I felt if I was to act as a brake at all, this was the time, so I pulled Father by the coattails.

"Dadda, can't we go home now?" I asked.

"Two minutes now," he said, beaming affectionately. "Just a bottle of lemonade and we'll go home."

This was a bribe, and I knew it, but I was always a child of weak character. Father ordered lemonade and two pints. I was thirsty and swallowed my drink at once. But that wasn't Father's way. He had long months of abstinence behind him and an eternity of pleasure before. He took out his pipe, blew through it, filled it, and then lit it with loud pops, his eyes bulging above it. After that he deliberately turned his back on the pint, leaned one elbow on the counter in the attitude of a man who did not know there was a pint behind him, and deliberately brushed the tobacco from his palms. He had settled down for the evening. He was steadily working through all the important funerals he had ever attended. The carriages departed and the minor mourners drifted in till the pub was half full.

30 "Dadda," I said, pulling his coat again, "can't we go home now?"

"Ah, your mother won't be in for a long time yet," he said benevolently enough. "Run out in the road and play, can't you."

It struck me very cool, the way grown-ups assumed that you could play all by yourself on a strange road. I began to get bored as I had so often been bored before. I knew Father was quite capable of lingering there till nightfall. I knew I might have to bring him home, blind drunk, down Blarney Lane, with all the old women at their doors, saying: "Mick Delaney is on it again." I knew that my mother would be half crazy with anxiety; that next day Father wouldn't go out to work; and before the end of the week she would be running down to the pawn with the clock under her shawl. I could never get over the lonesomeness of the kitchen without a clock.

I was still thirsty. I found if I stood on tiptoe I could just reach Father's glass, and the idea occurred to me that it would be interesting to know what the contents were like. He had his back to it and wouldn't notice. I took down the glass and sipped cautiously. It was a terrible disappointment. I was astonished that he could even drink such stuff. It looked as if he had never tried lemonade.

I should have advised him about lemonade but he was holding forth himself in great style. I heard him say that bands were a great addition to a funeral. He put his arms in the position of someone holding a rifle in reverse and hummed a few bars of Chopin's Funeral March. Crowley nodded reverently. I took a longer drink and began to see that porter might have its advantages. I felt pleasantly elevated and philosophic. Father hummed a few bars of the Dead March in *Saul*. It was a nice pub and a very fine funeral, and I felt sure that poor Mr. Dooley in Heaven must be highly gratified. At the same time I thought they might have given him a band. As Father said, bands were a great addition.

But the wonderful thing about porter was the way it made you stand aside, or rather float aloft like a cherub rolling on a cloud, and watch yourself with your legs crossed, leaning against a bar counter, not worrying about trifles but thinking deep, serious, grown-up thoughts about life and death. Looking at yourself like that, you couldn't help thinking after a while how funny you looked, and suddenly you got embarrassed and wanted to giggle. But by the time I had finished the pint, that phase too had passed; I found it hard to put back the glass, the counter seemed to have grown so high. Melancholia was supervening again. 35

"Well," Father said reverently, reaching behind him for his drink, "God rest the poor man's soul, wherever he is!" He stopped, looked first at the glass, and then at the people around him. "Hello," he said in a fairly good-humored tone, as if he were just prepared to consider it a joke, even if it was in bad taste, "who was at this?"

There was silence for a moment while the publican and the old women looked first at Father and then at his glass.

"There was no one at it, my good man," one of the women said with an offended air. "Is it robbers you think we are?"

"Ah, there's no one here would do a thing like that, Mick," said the publican in a shocked tone.

"Well, someone did it," said Father, his smile beginning to wear off. 40

"If they did, they were them that were nearer it," said the woman darkly, giving me a dirty look; and at the same moment the truth began to dawn on Father. I suppose I must have looked a bit starry-eyed. He bent and shook me.

"Are you all right, Larry?" he asked in alarm.

Peter Crowley looked down at me and grinned.

"Could you beat that?" he exclaimed in a husky voice.

I could and without difficulty. I started to get sick. Father jumped back in holy terror that I might spoil his good suit, and hastily opened the back door.

"Run! run! run!" he shouted.

I saw the sunlit wall outside with the ivy overhanging it, and ran. The intention was good but the performance was exaggerated, because I lurched right into the wall, hurting it badly, as it seemed to me. Being always very polite, I said "Pardon" before the second bout came on me. Father, still concerned for his suit, came up behind and cautiously held me while I got sick.

"That's a good boy!" he said encouragingly. "You'll be grand when you get that up."

Begor, I was not grand! Grand was the last thing I was. I gave one unmerciful wail out of me as he steered me back to the pub and put me sitting on the bench near the shawlies. They drew themselves up with an offended air, still sore at the suggestion that they had drunk his pint.

"God help us!" moaned one, looking pityingly at me. "Isn't it the likes of them would be fathers?"

"Mick," said the publican in alarm, spraying sawdust on my tracks, "that child isn't supposed to be in here at all. You'd better take him home quick in case a bobby would see him."

"Merciful God!" whimpered Father, raising his eyes to heaven and clapping his hands silently as he only did when distraught. "What misfortune was on me? Or what will his mother say? . . . If women might stop at home and look after their children themselves!" he added in a snarl for the benefit of the shawlies. "Are them carriages all gone, Bill?"

"The carriages are finished long ago, Mick," replied the publican.

"I'll take him home," Father said despairingly. . . . "I'll never bring you out again," he threatened me. "Here," he added, giving me the clean handkerchief from his breast pocket, "put that over your eye."

The blood on the handkerchief was the first indication I got that I was cut, and instantly my temple began to throb and I set up another howl. "Whisht, whisht, whisht!" Father said testily, steering me out the door.

"One'd think you were killed. That's nothing. We'll wash it when we get home."

"Steady now, old scout!" Crowley said, taking the other side of me. "You'll be all right in a minute."

I never met two men who knew less about the effects of drink. The first breath of fresh air and the warmth of the sun made me groggier than ever and I pitched and rolled between wind and tide till Father started to whimper again.

"God Almighty, and the whole road out! What misfortune was on me didn't stop at my work! Can't you walk straight?"

I couldn't. I saw plain enough that, coaxed by the sunlight, every woman old and young in Blarney Lane was leaning over her half-door or sitting on her doorstep. They all stopped gabbling to gape at the strange spectacle of two sober, middle-aged men bringing home a drunken small boy with a cut over his eye. Father, torn between the shamefast desire to get me home as quick as he could, and the neighborly need to explain that it wasn't his fault, finally halted outside Mrs. Roche's. There was a gang of old women outside a door at the opposite side of the road. I didn't like the look of them from the first. They seemed altogether too interested in me. I leaned against the wall of Mrs. Roche's cottage with my hands in my trousers pockets, thinking mournfully of poor Mr. Dooley in his cold grave on the Curragh, who would never walk down the road again, and, with great feeling, I began to sing a favorite song of Father's.

> Though lost to Mononia and cold in the grave
> He returns to Kincora no more.

"Wisha, the poor child!" Mrs. Roche said, "Haven't he a lovely voice,   60
God bless him!"

That was what I thought myself, so I was the more surprised when Father said "Whisht!" and raised a threatening finger at me. He didn't seem to realize the appropriateness of the song, so I sang louder than ever.

"Whisht, I tell you!" he snapped, and then tried to work up a smile for Mrs. Roche's benefit. "We're nearly home now. I'll carry you the rest of the way."

But, drunk and all as I was, I knew better than to be carried home ignominiously like that.

"Now," I said severely, "can't you leave me alone? I can walk all right. 'Tis only my head. All I want is a rest."

"But you can rest at home in bed," he said viciously, trying to pick me   65
up, and I knew by the flush on his face that he was very vexed.

"Ah, Jasus," I said crossly, "what do I want to go home for? Why the hell can't you leave me alone?"

For some reason the gang of old women at the other side of the road thought this was very funny. They nearly split their sides over it. A gassy fury began to expand in me at the thought that a fellow couldn't have a drop taken without the whole neighborhood coming out to make game of him.

"Who are ye laughing at?" I shouted, clenching my fists at them. "I'll make ye laugh at the other side of yeer faces if ye don't let me pass."

They seemed to think this funnier still; I had never seen such ill-mannered people.

"Go away, ye bloody bitches!" I said.   70

"Whisht, whisht, whisht, I tell you!" snarled Father, abandoning all pretence of amusement and dragging me along behind him by the hand. I was maddened by the women's shrieks of laughter. I was maddened by

Father's bullying. I tried to dig in my heels but he was too powerful for me, and I could only see the women by looking back over my shoulder.

"Take care or I'll come back and show ye!" I shouted. "I'll teach ye to let decent people pass. Fitter for ye to stop at home an wash yeer dirty faces."

"'Twill be all over the road," whimpered Father. "Never again, never again, not if I live to be a thousand!"

To this day I don't know whether he was forswearing me or the drink. By way of a song suitable to my heroic mood I bawled "The Boys of Wexford," as he dragged me in home. Crowley, knowing he was not safe, made off and Father undressed me and put me to bed. I couldn't sleep because of the whirling in my head. It was very unpleasant, and I got sick again. Father came in with a wet cloth and mopped up after me. I lay in a fever, listening to him chopping sticks to start a fire. After that I heard him lay the table.

Suddenly the front door banged open and Mother stormed in with Sonny in her arms, not her usual gentle, timid self, but a wild, raging woman. It was clear that she had heard it all from the neighbors.

"Mick Delaney," she cried hysterically, "what did you do to my son?"

"Whisht, woman, whisht, whisht!" he hissed, dancing from one foot to the other. "Do you want the whole road to hear?"

"Ah," she said with a horrifying laugh, "the road knows all about it by this time. The road knows the way you filled your unfortunate innocent child with drink to make sport for you and that other rotten, filthy brute."

"But I gave him no drink," he shouted, aghast at the horrifying interpretation the neighbors had chosen to give his misfortune. "He took it while my back was turned. What the hell do you think I am?"

"Ah," she replied bitterly, "everyone knows what you are now. God forgive you, wasting our hard-earned few ha'pence on drink, and bringing up your child to be a drunken corner-boy like yourself."

Then she swept into the bedroom and threw herself on her knees by the bed. She moaned when she saw the gash over my eye. In the kitchen Sonny set up a loud bawl on his own, and a moment later Father appeared in the bedroom door with his cap over his eyes, wearing an expression of the most intense self-pity.

"That's a nice way to talk to me after all I went through," he whined. "That's a nice accusation, that I was drinking. Not one drop of drink crossed my lips the whole day. How could it when he drank it all? I'm the one that ought to be pitied, with my day ruined on me, and I after being made a show for the whole road."

But the next morning, when he got up and went out quietly to work with his dinner-basket, Mother threw herself on me in the bed and kissed me. It seemed it was all my doing, and I was being given a holiday till my eye got better.

"My brave little man!" she said with her eyes shining. "It was God did it you were there. You were his guardian angel."

QUESTION

1. What are the sources of humor in this story? Does the humor arise from observation of life or from distortion of life? What elements of the story seem to you funniest?
2. Is this a purely humorous story, or are there undertones of pathos in it? If the latter, from what does the pathos arise?
3. List what seem to you the chief insights into life and character presented by the story.
4. Is the title seriously meant? To whom does it refer?
5. The boy's drunkenness is seen from four perspectives. What are they, and how do they differ?
6. What is the principal irony in the story?
7. The story is told in retrospect by a man recalling an incident from his boyhood. What does this removal in time do to the treatment of the material?
8. Which story — this one or "The Catbird Seat" — is more purely an interpretive story? Discuss.
9. *Did* Larry's father forswear liquor? Support your answer with evidence from the story.

Truman Capote
A Christmas Memory

Imagine a morning in late November. A coming of winter morning more than twenty years ago. Consider the kitchen of a spreading old house in a country town. A great black stove is its main feature; but there is also a big round table and a fireplace with two rocking chairs placed in front of it. Just today the fireplace commenced its seasonal roar.

A woman with shorn white hair is standing at the kitchen window. She is wearing tennis shoes and a shapeless gray sweater over a summery calico dress. She is small and sprightly, like a bantam hen; but, due to a long youthful illness, her shoulders are pitifully hunched. Her face is remarkable — not unlike Lincoln's, craggy like that, and tinted by sun and wind; but it is delicate too, finely boned, and her eyes are sherry-colored and timid. "Oh my," she exclaims, her breath smoking the windowpane, "it's fruitcake weather!"

The person to whom she is speaking is myself. I am seven; she is sixty-something. We are cousins, very distant ones, and we have lived together — well, as long as I can remember. Other people inhabit the house, relatives; and though they have power over us, and frequently make us cry, we are not,

A CHRISTMAS MEMORY   First published in 1956. Truman Capote (1924–1984) was born in New Orleans. His parents divorced when he was four, and Capote lived until he was nine or ten with a family of distant and elderly cousins in the small town of Monroeville, Alabama. Miss Sook Faulk, the real-life distant cousin on whom this story is based, died in 1938 while Capote was a student in a military academy in New York State.

on the whole, too much aware of them. We are each other's best friend. She calls me Buddy, in memory of a boy who was formerly her best friend. The other Buddy died in the 1880's, when she was still a child. She is still a child.

"I knew it before I got out of bed," she says, turning away from the window with a purposeful excitement in her eyes. "The courthouse bell sounded so cold and clear. And there were no birds singing; they've gone to warmer country, yes indeed. Oh, Buddy, stop stuffing biscuit and fetch our buggy. Help me find my hat. We've thirty cakes to bake."

5   It's always the same: a morning arrives in November, and my friend, as though officially inaugurating the Christmas time of year that exhilarates her imagination and fuels the blaze of her heart, announces: "It's fruitcake weather! Fetch our buggy. Help me find my hat."

The hat is found, a straw cartwheel corsaged with velvet roses out-of-doors has faded: it once belonged to a more fashionable relative. Together, we guide our buggy, a dilapidated baby carriage, out to the garden and into a grove of pecan trees. The buggy is mine; that is, it was bought for me when I was born. It is made of wicker, rather unraveled, and the wheels wobble like a drunkard's legs. But it is a faithful object; springtimes, we take it to the woods and fill it with flowers, herbs, wild fern for our porch pots; in the summer, we pile it with picnic paraphernalia and sugar-cane fishing poles and roll it down to the edge of a creek; it has its winter uses, too: as a truck for hauling firewood from the yard to the kitchen, as a warm bed for Queenie, our tough little orange and white rat terrier who has survived distemper and two rattlesnake bites. Queenie is trotting beside it now.

Three hours later we are back in the kitchen hulling a heaping buggyload of windfall pecans. Our backs hurt from gathering them: how hard they were to find (the main crop having been shaken off the trees and sold by the orchard's owners, who are not us) among the concealing leaves, the frosted, deceiving grass. Caarackle! A cheery crunch, scraps of miniature thunder sound as the shells collapse and the golden mound of sweet oily ivory meat mounts in the milk-glass bowl. Queenie begs to taste, and now and again my friend sneaks her a mite, though insisting we deprive ourselves. "We mustn't, Buddy. If we start, we won't stop. And there's scarcely enough as there is. For thirty cakes." The kitchen is growing dark. Dusk turns the window into a mirror: our reflections mingle with the rising moon as we work by the fireside in the firelight. At last, when the moon is quite high, we toss the final hull into the fire and, with joined sighs, watch it catch flame. The buggy is empty, the bowl is brimful.

We eat our supper (cold biscuits, bacon, blackberry jam) and discuss tomorrow. Tomorrow the kind of work I like best begins: buying. Cherries and citron, ginger and vanilla and canned Hawaiian pineapple, rinds and raisins and walnuts and whiskey and oh, so much flour, butter, so many eggs, spices, flavoring: why we'll need a pony to pull the buggy home.

But before these purchases can be made, there is the question of money. Neither of us has any. Except for skinflint sums persons in the house occasionally provide (a dime is considered very big money); or what we earn ourselves from various activities: holding rummage sales, selling buckets of hand-picked blackberries, jars of homemade jam and apple jelly and peach preserves, rounding up flowers for funerals and weddings. Once we won seventy-ninth prize, five dollars, in a national football contest. Not that we know a fool thing about football. It's just that we enter any contest we hear about: at the moment our hopes are centered on the fifty-thousand-dollar Grand Prize being offered to name a new brand of coffee (we suggest "A.M."; and, after some hesitation, for my friend thought it perhaps sacrilegious, the slogan "A.M.! Amen!"). To tell the truth, our only *really* profitable enterprise was the Fun and Freak Museum we conducted in a backyard woodshed two summers ago. The Fun was a stereopticon with slide views of Washington and New York lent us by a relative who had been to those places (she was furious when she discovered why we'd borrowed it); the Freak was a three-legged biddy chicken hatched by one of our hens. Everyone hereabouts wanted to see that biddy: we charged grownups a nickel, kids two cents. And took in a good twenty dollars before the museum shut down due to the decease of the main attraction.

But one way and another we do each year accumulate Christmas savings, a Fruitcake Fund. These moneys we keep hidden in an ancient bead purse under a loose board under the floor under a chamber pot under my friend's bed. The purse is seldom removed from this safe location except to make a deposit, or, as happens every Saturday, a withdrawal; for on Saturdays I am allowed ten cents to go to the picture show. My friend has never been to a picture show, nor does she intend to: "I'd rather hear you tell the story, Buddy. That way I can imagine it more. Besides, a person my age shouldn't squander their eyes. When the Lord comes, let me see him clear." In addition to never having seen a movie, she has never: eaten in a restaurant, traveled more than five miles from home, received or sent a telegram, read anything except funny papers and the Bible, worn cosmetics, cursed, wished someone harm, told a lie on purpose, let a hungry dog go hungry. Here are a few things she has done, does do: killed with a hoe the biggest rattlesnake ever seen in this county (sixteen rattles), dip snuff (secretly), tame hummingbirds (just try it) till they balance on her finger, tell ghost stories (we both believe in ghosts) so tingling they chill you in July, talk to herself, take walks in the rain, grow the prettiest japonicas in town, know the recipe for every sort of old-time Indian cure, including a magical wart remover.

Now, with supper finished, we retire to the room in a faraway part of the house where my friend sleeps in a scrap-quilt-covered iron bed painted rose pink, her favorite color. Silently, wallowing in the pleasures of conspiracy, we take the bead purse from its secret place and spill its contents on the scrap quilt. Dollar bills, tightly rolled and green as May buds. Somber fifty-cent pieces, heavy enough to weight a dead man's eyes. Lovely dimes, the liveliest coin, the one that really jingles. Nickels and quarters, worn smooth as creek pebbles. But mostly a hateful heap of bitter-odored pennies. Last summer

10

others in the house contracted to pay us a penny for every twenty-five flies we killed. Oh, the carnage of August: the flies that flew to heaven! Yet it was not work in which we took pride. And, as we sit counting pennies, it is as though we were back tabulating dead flies. Neither of us has a head for figures; we count slowly, lose track, start again. According to her calculation, we have $12.73. According to mine, exactly $13. "I do hope you're wrong, Buddy. We can't mess around with thirteen. The cakes will fall. Or put somebody in the cemetery. Why, I wouldn't dream of getting out of bed on the thirteenth." This is true: she always spends thirteenths in bed. So, to be on the safe side, we subtract a penny and toss it out the window.

Of the ingredients that go into our fruitcakes, whiskey is the most expensive, as well as the hardest to obtain: State laws forbid its sale. But everybody knows you can buy a bottle from Mr. Haha Jones. And the next day, having completed our more prosaic shopping, we set out for Mr. Haha's business address, a "sinful" (to quote public opinion) fish-fry and dancing café down by the river. We've been there before, and on the same errand; but in previous years our dealings have been with Haha's wife, an iodine-dark Indian woman with brazzy peroxided hair and a dead-tired disposition. Actually, we've never laid eyes on her husband, though we've heard that he's an Indian too. A giant with razor scars across his cheeks. They call him Haha because he's so gloomy, a man who never laughs. As we approach his café (a large log cabin festooned inside and out with chains of garish-gay naked lightbulbs and standing by the river's muddy edge under the shade of river trees where moss drifts through the branches like gray mist) our steps slow down. Even Queenie stops prancing and sticks close by. People have been murdered in Haha's café. Cut to pieces. Hit on the head. There's a case coming up in court next month. Naturally these goings-on happen at night when the colored lights cast crazy patterns and the victrola wails. In the daytime Haha's is shabby and deserted. I knock at the door, Queenie barks, my friend calls: "Mrs. Haha, ma'am? Anyone to home?"

Footsteps. The door opens. Our hearts overturn. It's Mr. Haha Jones himself! And he *is* a giant; he *does* have scars; he *doesn't* smile. No, he glowers at us through Satan-tilted eyes and demands to know: "What you want with Haha?"

For a moment we are too paralyzed to tell. Presently my friend half-finds her voice, a whispery voice at best: "If you please, Mr. Haha, we'd like a quart of your finest whiskey."

His eyes tilt more. Would you believe it? Haha is smiling! Laughing, too. "Which one of you is a drinkin' man?"

"It's for making fruitcakes, Mr. Haha. Cooking."

This sobers him. He frowns. "That's no way to waste good whiskey." Nevertheless, he retreats into the shadowed café and seconds later appears carrying a bottle of daisy yellow unlabeled liquor. He demonstrates its sparkle in the sunlight and says: "Two dollars."

We pay him with nickels and dimes and pennies. Suddenly, jangling the coins in his hands like a fistful of dice, his face softens. "Tell you what," he proposes, pouring the money back into our bead purse, "just send me one of them fruitcakes instead."

"Well," my friend remarks on our way home, "there's a lovely man. We'll put an extra cup of raisins in *his* cake."

The black stove, stoked with coal and firewood, glows like a lighted [20] pumpkin. Eggbeaters whirl, spoons spin round in bowls of butter and sugar, vanilla sweetens the air, ginger spices it; melting, nose-tingling odors saturate the kitchen, suffuse the house, drift out to the world on puffs of chimney smoke. In four days our work is done. Thirty-one cakes, dampened with whiskey, bask on window sills and shelves.

Who are they for?

Friends. Not necessarily neighbor friends: indeed, the larger share are intended for persons we've met maybe once, perhaps not at all. People who've struck our fancy. Like President Roosevelt. Like the Reverend and Mrs. J. C. Lucey, Baptist missionaries to Borneo who lectured here last winter. Or the little knife grinder who comes through town twice a year. Or Abner Packer, the driver of the six o'clock bus from Mobile, who exchanges waves with us every day as he passes in a dust-cloud whoosh. Or the young Wistons, a California couple whose car one afternoon broke down outside the house and who spent a pleasant hour chatting with us on the porch (young Mr. Wiston snapped our picture, the only one we've ever had taken). Is it because my friend is shy with everyone *except* strangers that these strangers, and merest acquaintances, seem to us our truest friends? I think yes. Also, the scrapbooks we keep of thank-you's on White House stationery, time-to-time communications from California and Borneo, the knife grinder's penny post cards, make us feel connected to eventful worlds beyond the kitchen with its view of a sky that stops.

Now a nude December fig branch grates against the window. The kitchen is empty, the cakes are gone; yesterday we carted the last of them to the post office, where the cost of stamps turned our purse inside out. We're broke. That rather depresses me, but my friend insists on celebrating — with two inches of whiskey left in Haha's bottle. Queenie has a spoonful in a bowl of coffee (she likes her coffee chicory-flavored and strong). The rest we divide between a pair of jelly glasses. We're both quite awed at the prospect of drinking straight whiskey; the taste of it brings screwed-up expressions and sour shudders. But by and by we begin to sing, the two of us singing different songs simultaneously. I don't know the words to mine, just: *Come on along, come on along, to the dark-town strutters' ball.* But I can dance: that's what I mean to be, a tap dancer in the movies. My dancing shadow rollicks on the walls; our voices rock the chinaware; we giggle: as if unseen hands were tickling us. Queenie rolls on her back, her paws plow the air, something like a grin stretches her black lips. Inside myself, I feel warm and sparky as those crumbling logs, carefree as the wind in the chimney. My friend waltzes round the stove, the hem of her poor calico skirt pinched between her fingers as though it were a party dress: *Show me the way to go home*, she sings, her tennis shoes squeaking on the floor. *Show me the way to go home.*

Enter: two relatives. Very angry. Potent with eyes that scold, tongues that scald. Listen to what they have to say, the words tumbling together into a wrathful tune: "A child of seven! whiskey on his breath! are you out of your mind? feeding a child of seven! must be loony! road to ruination! remember Cousin Kate? Uncle Charlie? Uncle Charlie's brother-in-law? shame! scandal! humiliation! kneel, pray, beg the Lord!"

25   Queenie sneaks under the stove. My friend gazes at her shoes, her chin quivers, she lifts her skirt and blows her nose and runs to her room. Long after the town has gone to sleep and the house is silent except for the chimings of clocks and the sputter of fading fires, she is weeping into a pillow already as wet as a widow's handkerchief.

"Don't cry," I say, sitting at the bottom of her bed and shivering despite my flannel nightgown that smells of last winter's cough syrup, "Don't cry," I beg, teasing her toes, tickling her feet, "you're too old for that."

"It's because," she hiccups, "I *am* too old. Old and funny."

"Not funny. Fun. More fun than anybody. Listen. If you don't stop crying you'll be so tired tomorrow we can't go cut a tree."

She straightens up. Queenie jumps on the bed (where Queenie is not allowed) to lick her cheeks. "I know where we'll find pretty trees, Buddy. And holly, too. With berries big as your eyes. It's way off in the woods. Farther than we've ever been. Papa used to bring us Christmas trees from there: carry them on his shoulder. That's fifty years ago. Well now: I can't wait for morning."

30   Morning. Frozen rime lusters the grass; the sun, round as an orange and orange as hot-weather moons, balances on the horizon, burnishes the silvered winter woods. A wild turkey calls. A renegade hog grunts in the undergrowth. Soon, by the edge of knee-deep, rapid-running water, we have to abandon the buggy. Queenie wades the stream first, paddles across barking complaints at the swiftness of the current, the pneumonia-making coldness of it. We follow, holding our shoes and equipment (a hatchet, a burlap sack) above our heads. A mile more: of chastising thorns, burs and briers that catch at our clothes; of rusty pine needles brilliant with gaudy fungus and molted feathers. Here, there, a flash, a flutter, an ecstasy of shrillings remind us that not all the birds have flown south. Always, the path unwinds through lemony sun pools and pitch vine tunnels. Another creek to cross: a disturbed armada of speckled trout froths the water round us, and frogs the size of plates practice belly flops; beaver workmen are building a dam. On the farther shore, Queenie shakes herself and trembles. My friend shivers, too: not with cold but enthusiasm. One of her hat's ragged roses sheds a petal as she lifts her head and inhales the pine-heavy air. "We're almost there; can you smell it, Buddy?" she says, as though we were approaching an ocean.

And, indeed, it is a kind of ocean. Scented acres of holiday trees, prickly-leafed holly. Red berries shiny as Chinese bells: black crows swoop upon them screaming. Having stuffed our burlap sacks with enough greenery and crimson to garland a dozen windows, we set about choosing a tree. "It should be," muses my friend, "twice as tall as a boy. So a boy can't steal the star." The one we pick is twice as tall as me. A brave handsome brute that survives thirty hatchet strokes before it keels with a creaking rending cry. Lugging it like a kill, we commence the long trek out. Every few yards we abandon the struggle, sit down and pant. But we have the strength of triumphant huntsmen; that and the tree's virile, icy perfume revive us, goad us on. Many compliments accompany our sunset return along the red clay road to town; but my friend is sly and noncommital when passers-by praise the treasure perched on our buggy: what a fine tree and where did it come from? "Yonderways," she murmurs vaguely. Once a car stops and the rich mill owner's lazy wife leans out and whines: "Giveya two-bits cash for that ol tree." Ordinarily my friend is afraid of saying no; but on this occasion she promptly shakes her head: "We wouldn't take a dollar." The mill owner's wife persists. "A dollar, my foot! Fifty cents. That's my last offer. Goodness, woman, you can get another one." In answer, my friend gently reflects: "I doubt it. There's never two of anything."

Home: Queenie slumps by the fire and sleeps till tomorrow, snoring loud as a human.

A trunk in the attic contains: a shoebox of ermine tails (off the opera cape of a curious lady who once rented a room in the house), coils of frazzled tinsel gone gold with age, one silver star, a brief rope of dilapidated, undoubtedly dangerous candy-like bulbs. Excellent decorations, as far as they go, which isn't far enough: my friend wants our tree to blaze "like a Baptist window," droop with weighty snows of ornament. But we can't afford the made-in-Japan splendors at the five-and-dime. So we do what we've always done: sit for days at the kitchen table with scissors and crayons and stacks of colored paper. I make sketches and my friend cuts them out: lots of cats, fish too (because they're easy to draw), some apples, some watermelons, a few winged angels devised from saved-up sheets of Hershey-bar tin foil. We use safety pins to attach these creations to the tree; as a final touch, we sprinkle the branches with shredded cotton (picked in August for this purpose). My friend, surveying the effects, clasps her hands together. "Now honest, Buddy. Doesn't it look good enough to eat?" Queenie tries to eat an angel.

After weaving and ribboning holly wreaths for all the front windows, our next project is the fashioning of family gifts. Tie-dye scarves for the ladies, for the men a home-brewed lemon and licorice and aspirin syrup to be taken "at the first Symptoms of a Cold and after Hunting." But when it comes time for making each other's gift, my friend and I separate to work secretly. I would like to buy her a pearl-handled knife, a radio, a whole pound of chocolate-covered cherries (we tasted some once, and she always swears: "I could live on them, Buddy, Lord yes I could — and that's not taking His name in vain"). Instead, I am building her a kite. She would like to give me a bicycle (she's said so on several million occasions: "If only I could, Buddy. It's bad enough in life to do without something *you* want; but confound it, what gets my goat is not being able to give somebody something you want *them* to have. Only one of these days I will, Buddy. Locate you a bike. Don't ask how. Steal it, maybe"). Instead, I'm fairly certain that she is building me a kite — the same as last year, and the year before: the year before that we exchanged slingshots. All of which is fine by me. For we are champion kite-fliers who study the wind like sailors; my friend, more accomplished than I, can get a kite aloft when there isn't enough breeze to carry clouds.

40   Christmas Eve afternoon we scrape together a nickel and go to the butcher's to buy Queenie's traditional gift, a good gnawable beef bone. The bone, wrapped in funny paper, is placed high in the tree near the silver star. Queenie knows it's there. She squats at the foot of the tree staring up in a trance of greed: when bedtime arrives she refuses to budge. Her excitement is equaled by my own. I kick the covers and turn my pillow as though it were a scorching summer's night. Somewhere a rooster crows: falsely, for the sun is still on the other side of the world.

"Buddy, are you awake?" It is my friend, calling from her room, which is next to mine; and an instant later she is sitting on my bed holding a candle. "Well, I can't sleep a hoot," she declares. "My mind's jumping like a jack rabbit. Buddy, do you think Mrs. Roosevelt will serve our cake at dinner?" We huddle in the bed, and she squeezes my hand I-love-you. "Seems like your hand used to be so much smaller. I guess I hate to see you grow up. When you're grown up, will we still be friends?" I say always. "But I feel so bad, Buddy. I wanted so bad to give you a bike. I tried to sell my cameo Papa gave me. Buddy" — she hesitates, as though embarrassed — "I made you another kite." Then I confess that I made her one, too; and we laugh. The candle burns too short to hold. Out it goes, exposing the starlight, the stars spinning at the window like a visible caroling that slowly, slowly daybreak silences. Possibly we doze; but the beginnings of dawn splash us like cold water: we're up, wide-eyed and wandering while we wait for others to waken. Quite deliberately my friend drops a kettle on the kitchen floor. I tap-dance in front of closed doors. One by one the household emerges, looking as though they'd like to kill us both; but it's Christmas, so they can't. First, a gorgeous breakfast: just everything you can imagine — from flapjacks and fried squirrel to hominy grits and honey-in-the-comb. Which puts everyone in a good humor except my friend and I. Frankly, we're so impatient to get at the presents we can't eat a mouthful.

Well, I'm disappointed. Who wouldn't be? With socks, a Sunday school shirt, some handkerchiefs, a hand-me-down sweater and a year's subscription to a religious magazine for children. *The Little Shepherd*. It makes me boil. It really does.

My friend has a better haul. A sack of Satsumas, that's her best present. She is proudest, however, of a white wool shawl knitted by her married sister. But she *says* her favorite gift is the kite I built her. And it *is* very beautiful; though not as beautiful as the one she made me, which is blue and scattered with gold and green Good Conduct stars; moreover, my name is painted on it, "Buddy."

"Buddy, the wind is blowing."

The wind is blowing, and nothing will do till we've run to a pasture below the house where Queenie has scooted to bury her bone (and where, a winter hence, Queenie will be buried, too). There, plunging through the healthy waist-high grass, we unreel our kites, feel them twitching at the string like sky fish as they swim into the wind. Satisfied, sun-warmed, we sprawl in the grass and peel Satsumas and watch our kites cavort. Soon I forget the socks and hand-me-down sweater. I'm as happy as if we'd already won the fifty-thousand-dollar Grand Prize in that coffee-naming contest.

"My, how foolish I am!" my friend cries, suddenly alert, like a woman remembering too late she has biscuits in the oven. "You know what I've always thought?" she asks in a tone of discovery, and not smiling at me but a point beyond. "I've always thought a body would have to be sick and dying before they saw the Lord. And I imagined that when He came it would be like looking at the Baptist window: pretty as colored glass with the sun pouring through, such a shine you don't know it's getting dark. And it's been a comfort: to think of that shine taking away all the spooky feeling. But I'll wager it never happens. I'll wager at the very end a body realizes the Lord has already shown Himself. That things as they are" — her hand circles in a gesture that gathers clouds and kites and grass and Queenie pawing earth over her bone — "just what they've always seen, was seeing Him. As for me, I could leave the world with today in my eyes."

This is our last Christmas together.

Life separates us. Those who Know Best decide that I belong in a military school. And so follows a miserable succession of bugle-blowing prisons, grim reveille-ridden summer camps. I have a new home too. But it doesn't count. Home is where my friend is, and there I never go.

And there she remains, puttering around the kitchen. Alone with Queenie. Then alone. ("Buddy dear," she writes in her wild hard-to-read script, "yesterday Jim Macy's horse kicked Queenie bad. Be thankful she didn't feel much. I wrapped her in a Fine Linen sheet and rode her in the buggy down to Simpson's pasture where she can be with all her Bones . . ."). For a few Novembers she continues to bake her fruitcakes single-handed; not as many, but some: and, of course, she always sends me "the best of the batch." Also, in every letter she encloses a dime wadded in toilet paper: "See a picture show and write me the story." But gradually in her letters she tends to confuse me with her other friend, the Buddy who died in the 1880's; more and more thirteenths are not the only days she stays in bed: a morning arrives in November, a leafless birdless coming of winter morning, when she cannot rouse herself to exclaim: "Oh my, it's fruitcake weather!"

45 And when that happens, I know it. A message saying so merely confirms a piece of news some secret vein had already received, severing from me an irreplaceable part of myself, letting it loose like a kite on a broken string. That is why, walking across a school campus on this particular December morning, I keep searching the sky. As if I expected to see, rather like hearts, a lost pair of kites hurrying toward heaven.

QUESTIONS

1. Although the Christmas memory of the title is more than twenty years old, it is recollected in the present tense. How is this managed? What advantages has it for the story?
2. What does the narrator mean by saying that his more than sixty-year-old friend "is still a child"? Is she like a child in more than one sense? Cite instances of behavior to support different meanings. What does she herself mean when she says that she is "old and funny" (paragraph 27)? What are her chief sources of pleasure? Why does she make a perfect companion for the narrator? Are there places where she exhibits a superior wisdom to that of the adults in the story? Is she in any sense a developing character?
3. If the narrator and his friend — and Queenie — be taken as the protagonists of the story, who are the antagonists? At what points do they enter the story, and with what results? What are the sources of conflict? Who ultimately have the upper hand?
4. Where does the primary interest of the story lie? What are the principal sources of its appeal? Does it illuminate human character?
5. Can you formulate a theme for the story?

Benjamin Capps
The Night Old Santa Claus Came

Imagine a white schoolhouse sitting on a hill. It had two large rooms. The one on the north was full of desks, blackboards, a bookshelf, a teacher's desk, a pedal organ, and everything needed for the seventeen pupils who attended Mama's school. It smelled like chalk dust and ink and glue.

The other room in the schoolhouse was ours. It was the only place at Anarene for us to live, but it was a good home. It had a kitchen and closet

THE NIGHT OLD SANTA CLAUS CAME   First published in 1981. Benjamin Capps was born in 1922 in Dundee near Wichita Falls, Texas, and from the age of eight was raised on a ranch nearby. He attended Texas Tech, and in 1944 was commissioned a second lieutenant in the Air Corps and flew forty bombing missions in the Pacific. After the war he completed his education at the University of Texas. He is the author of eight novels and has been honored by the Western Writers of America and by the Cowboy Hall of Fame and Western Heritage Center. He lives in Grand Prairie, Texas.

curtained off at one end, with a kerosene cook stove and linoleum on the floor; the rest of our room had a lumber floor and two beds, one for me and Bill, one for Mama and Roy, and in between our wood-burning heater stove.

Roy was five years old. I was going on eight. Bill was nine. Mama was ancient, at least thirty, maybe even thirty-one. The pupils who came were different ages, two in highschool, two in the first grade, the rest scattered in between. They walked in across the prairie and through the mesquite brush from every direction each school morning. From schoolhouse hill you could only see where four other families lived; the other kids had long walks, and one rode horseback.

At one end of the white painted schoolhouse rose a flagpole, where we flew the U.S. flag on good days; at the other end stood the cistern with its squeaky pully and fuzzy rope to draw drinking water. Out on the flat ground we had three swings and a see-saw, a baseball field to play scrub, a garage for Mama's Model-T, and the woodpile and toilets. From schoolhouse hill you could see a long way, and it looked lonely out there — not much happening, except a few white-face cattle grazing.

That winter Mama said she hoped it would snow at the right time so we would have a white Christmas, but we would take whatever God sent. He did not often send the best snow to West Texas, but usually north wind and blowing sleet.

Mama was rich. Since she was the principal as well as the teacher and also mopped the schoolhouse floor, she got paid a hundred dollars a month. They had said when we first came there that you could not be a teacher at Anarene unless you could whip the biggest boy in school. They did not know her; she had fierce eyes. She was beautiful, but she could look at a big boy and say, "I thought you were older and more responsible than that," and he would start blushing and stammering.

But usually she gave rewards. If a big girl made ninety on spelling, Mama would let her sit in one of the long desks and teach a smaller kid his reading lesson. Or if a big boy did good in Geography, Mama would let him bring in wood or stoke the fire or draw water for the water keg.

We had been thinking about Christmas and one Saturday Mama gave me and Bill and Roy each fifty cents for gift money. We could spend it any way we wanted to, but Mama said, "Remember, it's better to give than to receive." Even more exciting, we were going shopping that day to the great city of Wichita Falls. She needed to buy some bright crepe paper and things for decorations. She did not ask the school trustees about such things, but used her own money because she made such a big salary.

Mama knew how to get to Wichita Falls and all the streets and stores, for she went up there sometimes to junior college. She had got her certificate that showed she was smart enough to teach school a long time ago by taking a test at the capitol of Archer County. But she said that in her spare time she might as well further her education. So she got assignments from Wichita Falls and did them at night after us kids went to bed and sent them in through the mail. Anyway, me and Bill and Roy found ourselves in the biggest nickel and dime store in the world with fifty cents in our pockets.

Everything looked bright and colorful and shiny, hundreds of things in trays and hanging up wherever you looked. And the store smelled good. I could have walked around in there for weeks just looking.

Roy was dumb. He could not see past his own nose. We were not supposed to spy on what each other bought, but I could not take care of him and not let him get lost without seeing what he did. And here's exactly what he did. He bought himself a thirty-five-cent wind-up caterpillar tractor made out of tin with rubber tracks. Then he lost a dime and never could find it. The last nickel he spent for a sack of yellow candy corn, which he stuffed down before he even got back to the car. Me and Bill told him how dumb he was and said, "Boy, you're going to be sorry when it comes time to put gifts on the Christmas tree." It didn't seem to bother him, but we said, "You wait and see!"

I got Mama a new spatula to turn pancakes and Bill got her a handkerchief with flowers embroidered in the corner. I got the other two kids a pewter whistle with a bird on top; you could put a little water in it and it would make a tweeting sound. But I didn't know whether I wanted to give Roy a present or not; a kid of five ought to be more responsible than that.

The school days got long during the week before Christmas, but we all had to work decorating the room for the tree and program the night all the parents would come. Mama said that our studies must not stop, so each pupil must show each day that he learned some lessons before he could help decorate. By the time for the last recess each day we had all earned the right to work on green and red pasted chains or twisted crepe-paper chains or Christmas posters for the walls or little cut-out figures for the tree. A big girl named Myrtle Farmer made a star and put silver tinfoil on it. A boy named Tots, who could draw real good, made beautiful scenes on the blackboards with colored chalk. Some girls got to string popcorn which Mama popped, and we all teased them and accused them of eating some.

During those days Mama changed our breakfast Bible reading too. Each morning in our room when we washed our hands and sat down to eat, she would read a few verses, then say a short prayer. Usually she read straight through the Bible, including somebody begat somebody and they begat somebody else. Then we would eat our oatmeal with canned milk and maybe have hot chocolate. Now she skipped over to Isaiah and explained that it meant that Jesus was coming. Three days before Christmas she started reading about the Christ in the New Testament.

The last school day before the holiday was the day to get the tree. Two big boys, Auzy Brown and Garland Andrews, went to hunt it on a creek a long way off. They had got their Algebra and other lessons caught up, so they left early. The only trees with leaves were chaparral bushes, but Mama said leaves didn't matter, except we had to have a tree that could come in the door and would not be too high for the ceiling. The smaller boys could not go, because the big boys were taking an axe. We watched from the schoolhouse hill and when we saw them dragging the tree over the prairie, we ran to help bring it. We struggled and pushed from every side to get it in the door and stood up. Later in the day some boys went to get mistletoe.

Mama had a habit of going with a coal oil lamp into the schoolroom to work on her college after us kids went to bed. Bill said part of the time she prayed in there and asked God to make her know how to be a good father as well as a mother and to be a good teacher of young minds. Bill could have been wrong; a boy of nine is not so smart, but it could be true. Anyway, before the holidays Mama practiced on the organ at night in her spare time. She could play good enough for us to sing in school, but she was afraid Mrs. Meaders, the lady who usually played for community programs, would not get over her flu before Christmas, so she had to be ready. We would lay in bed nearly asleep and listen to her away over there in the other half of the schoolhouse, softly playing, "Oh, Little Town of Bethlehem" and "Silent Night."

On Christmas Eve morning before breakfast Mama said we would read a little more than usual. She read: "And there were in the same country shepherds abiding in the field, keeping watch over their flock by night. And, lo, the angel of the Lord came upon them, and the glory of the Lord shone round about them; and they were sore afraid. And the angel said unto them, Fear not: for, behold, I bring you good tidings of great joy, which shall be to all people." And she read all of it about the shepherds coming to visit the new baby Jesus.

After breakfast we started wrapping presents, each one working in a different place, me on one bed, Mama on one, and Bill behind the kitchen curtain, to keep the presents a surprise. Roy tried to play with his caterpillar tractor, which now had the spring broken and one track lost. Then he played with the stove wood some. Finally he stood out in the middle of the room and started bawling.

After a minute Mama went over to him and asked, "What's the matter, honey? Don't cry."

He didn't want to say. She knelt down and petted him and kept saying, "Don't cry. What's the matter?" 20

Finally he said, "I love you, Mama."

"I know you do, honey. Don't cry."

"I would give you my tractor, but you already seen it and it wouldn't be a surprise."

She got the whole story out of him and said, "I ought to spank you good." But she smiled a little and went to her purse hanging on the nail. She got out a nickel for him to buy her a present and asked me if I would go down to the store with him.

We put on our coats. Roy no sooner got out the door than he started 25 running. It was about a minute run to the store. Before we got there he was laughing and talking just like he'd never done anything wrong in his life. He bought Mama a Peanut Pattie candy bar about the size of a pancake, only thicker, with peanuts sticking out of the top and wrapped in clear paper.

On the way back up the hill he began to open the sack and I said, "What are you doing?"

"Nothing, I'm just going to look at it."

I said, "Leave it in the sack. What are you doing?" I had thought at first that it was useless for me to go with him, since there are no rattlesnakes in winter and you won't get on a cactus if you stay in the road; but it was a good thing I went — to protect Mama's present.

He said, "I just want to smell of it."

30   "Roy," I told him, "don't you unwrap that! What do you think you're doing?"

"I'm just going to take a little bite. Mama won't care."

"Don't you dare! Haven't you got a lick of sense?" I got tough with him. "You put that back in that sack and don't you touch it! I'll knock you right on the seat of your pants!"

He knew I meant it. I watched him all the way home and until he got it wrapped in red paper and tied with a string and had put Mama's name on it.

God did not send us a white Christmas that day, but the air was still and cold and clear, like you could see a hundred miles. Later, when dark came, the sky was like purple velvet and the stars were like diamonds, and you could imagine looking up there that you could hear the tune of "Silent Night."

35   Mama had pumped up and lighted the two gasoline lanterns in the schoolroom, and the schoolhouse hill seemed the most wonderful place a person could possibly be when the people started coming in across the prairie from every direction, driving and walking, most of them laughing. There must have been a hundred, or at least forty. They brought presents to put on the tree for each other. Everyone said how great the schoolroom looked with all our decoration.

It looked as good as a five and ten cent store, not so shiny, but happier. Our chains and ribbons, mostly red and green, looped around on the walls, and the popcorn looked like snow. It was a whole roomful of people, all smiling, and everyone talking at once, until the program started. The lady with the flu was well, so she played the pedal organ and Mama announced. We all sang "Jingle Bells" and other songs. Then the kids who had practiced up gave readings. Two girls and a boy, who could sing good together, sang "Hark, the Herald Angels Sing." Bill, who was good at memory, said, "'Twas the Night Before Christmas."

When Santa Claus came in, dressed in red and white, saying "Ho! Ho! Ho! Have all you boys and girls been good this year?" it was thrilling, but us big kids knew it was Mr. Charlie Graham dressed up that way. The dumb little kids like Roy thought he had just got in on his sled from the North Pole.

I had learned about Santa Claus a long time ago, before our daddy died. I even knew where Mama kept the red suit and beard, in a box on top of the green metal bookcase.

The program lasted real late, at least till ten o'clock. All the grown people told Mama thank you before they left. You could hear their voices and laughter going away into the clear, cold night. When we got in our room, after we had looked at our gifts a minute, Roy began talking about hanging up stockings; he'd been talking to the other kids about it.

Mama said, "Boys, we've had a big Christmas. I don't think we need to hang up our stockings this year. We will have some goodies to eat in the next few days."

Roy said, "Well, I want to hang mine up."   40

"We've had a big Christmas," she said. "Don't you think we should just go to bed and have a good, lazy night's sleep?"

He didn't know what she meant about getting a night's sleep; she meant she didn't have to practice the organ or do any college lessons tonight and she didn't want any other duties in her spare time. See, she had several things to do all the time, being principal, like getting the trustees to haul firewood and getting all the right textbooks and getting chalk and stuff, then keeping up with all the lessons with two in highschool, and making state reports, and getting the broken window fixed, and entertaining the community, and practicing the organ, and furthering her education, and doing all the things mamas like to do such as wash clothes and cook oatmeal and make stew and put patches on your overalls. So she said to us, like it was the last word, "Well, I'm going to bed. Tomorrow I'm going to bake chicken and make dressing." Me and Bill sniggered.

Roy, that dumb kid, took his socks up to the curtain which marked off the kitchen, got two clothes pins, stood on a chair, and hung his socks to the top of the curtain. I could read his dumb mind; this was between him and Santa Claus. After Mama blew out the lamp, me and Bill lay there laughing. Boy, was that kid going to learn something! If your mama says Old Santa Claus ain't coming, then he sure ain't coming anymore tonight! I would have laughed forever if I hadn't been so sleepy.

We nearly always waked up when Mama was building the fire in the morning, because the stove clanked. When she saw us sitting up in bed, she said, "Christmas gift!" It was a joke meaning you had to give them a gift if they said it first, but nobody really did it. Suddenly Roy hopped out of bed and ran toward his socks. I and Bill got to sniggering again.

About that time Roy squealed. His socks were so full he had to take them   45 down one at a time. He ran and started spilling goodies out onto the bed.

Me and Bill looked at Mama. Why in the world had she done that? How could she be such a traitor? It wasn't fair. We liked candy and things as much as him, and he was the one who hadn't acted grown up, but he got a reward for being dumb.

"Jump up, lazy bones," Mama said to me and Bill. How could she be so cheerful when she had acted like a traitor to us? "It's a nice day," she said. "Get your clothes on."

I didn't even want to speak to her as I walked over the cold floor to the chair where I left my clothes. A crazy thought was going through my mind: Could it be possible that there really is a Santa Claus who fills up the stockings of dumb little kids? I got my shoes and socks out from under the chair. I couldn't get my socks on. Something was the matter with them. Lumpy. I nearly cried as old as I was because my mind was still going over the idea if there is really a Santa Claus for dumb little kids.

In my socks was one orange, one apple, fourteen pecans, nine little pieces of hard candy, one big piece of wavy ribbon candy, eleven English walnuts, four Brazil nuts, twelve almonds, and a third of a Peanut Pattie.

We all offered Mama a piece of our candy, and she said she would take a small piece of peppermint, because she didn't care for anything that was too sweet. When she got a chance, she winked at me and Bill. I believe it was a year before Roy ever figured out how come Old Santa Claus put a third of a Peanut Pattie in his sock that night.

QUESTIONS

1. Who is the protagonist of this story — the narrator, the mother, or little Roy? Characterize each of them. How does the story judge any failings or weaknesses that they display?
2. What period in time is the narrator remembering? (What date is implied by "Mama's Model-T" in paragraph 4?) What details of the story give a sense of the quality of life that the narrator is recalling? How are we expected to feel about the family's deprivations?
3. Explore the ironic contrasts between the narrator's present evaluation of himself as a child and the child's self-evaluations. Is there any blame attached to the child's?
4. What was the narrator's evaluation of Roy's behavior? What does he feel about it now?
5. What are the similarities between this story and Truman Capote's "A Christmas Memory"? Consider character (including stock characters), plot, point of view, and theme.
6. Which of these two stories is designed to leave us with a happy glow? Which takes us into a deeper understanding of life?

CHAPTER EIGHT

Fantasy

Truth in fiction is not the same as fidelity to fact. Fiction, after all, is the opposite of fact. It is a game of make-believe — though, at its best, a serious game — in which the author imaginatively conceives characters and situations and sets them down on paper. And yet these characters and situations, if deeply imagined, may embody truths of human life and behavior more fully and significantly than any number of the miscellaneous facts reported on the front pages of our morning papers. The purpose of the interpretive artist is to communicate truths by means of imagined facts.

The story writer begins, then, by saying "Let's suppose. . . ." "Let's suppose," for instance, "that a fair-minded, conscientious, but not cold-hearted Jewish top sergeant, during World War II, is placed in charge of a training company in which a Jewish recruit tries to play on their common Jewishness to obtain special favors for himself and his friends." From this initial assumption the author goes on to develop a story ("Defender of the Faith") which, though entirely imaginary in the sense that it never happened, nevertheless reveals convincingly to us some truths of human behavior.

But now, what if the author goes a step further and supposes not just something that might very well have happened though it didn't but something highly improbable — something that could happen, say, only as the result of a very surprising coincidence? What if he begins, "Let's suppose that a misogynist and a charming woman find themselves alone on a desert island"? This initial supposition causes us to stretch our imaginations a bit further, but is not this situation just as capable of revealing human truths as the former? The psychologist puts a rat in a maze (certainly an improbable situation for a rat), observes its reactions to the maze, and discovers some truth of rat nature. The author may put imaginary characters on an imagined desert island, imaginatively study their reactions, and reveal some truth of human nature. The improbable initial situation may yield as much truth as the probable one.

From the improbable it is but one step further to the impossible (as we know it in this life). Why should not our author begin "Let's suppose that a miser and his termagant wife find themselves in hell" or "Let's suppose that a timid but ambitious man discovers how to make himself invisible" or "Let's suppose that in the course of an afternoon a man experiences the next year of his life" or "Let's suppose that a primitive scapegoat ritual still survives in contemporary America." Could not these situations also be used to exhibit human truth?

The nonrealistic story, or **fantasy**, is one that transcends the bounds of known reality. Commonly, it conjures up a strange and marvelous world, which one enters by falling down a rabbit hole or climbing up a beanstalk or getting shipwrecked in an unfamiliar ocean or dreaming a dream; or else it introduces strange powers and occult forces into the world of ordinary reality, allowing one to foretell the future or communicate with the dead or separate the mind from the body or turn into a monster. It introduces human beings into a world where the ordinary laws of nature are suspended or superseded and where the landscape and its creatures are unfamiliar, or it introduces ghosts or fairies or dragons or werewolves or talking animals or invaders from Mars or miraculous occurrences into the normal world of human beings. Fables, ghost stories, science fiction — all are types of fantasy.

Fantasy may be escapist or interpretive, true or false. The space ship on its way to a distant planet may be filled with stock characters or with human beings. The story may be designed chiefly to exhibit mechanical marvels or to provide thrills or adventures, or it may be a means of creating exacting circumstances in which human behavior may be sharply observed and studied. Fantasy, like other elements of fiction, may be employed sheerly for its own sake or as a means of communicating an important insight. The appeal may be to our taste for the strange or to our need for the true. The important point to remember is that truth in fiction is not to be identified with realism in method. Stories that never depart from the three dimensions of actuality — like "The Catbird Seat" or "The Storm" — may distort and falsify life. Stories that fly on the wings of fantasy may be vehicles for truth. Fantasy may convey truth through symbolism or allegory or simply by providing an unusual setting for the observation of human beings. Some of the world's greatest works of literature have been partly or wholly fantasy: *The Odyssey, The Book of Job, The Divine Comedy, The Tempest, Pilgrim's Progress, Gul-*

liver's Travels, Faust, Alice in Wonderland. All these have had important things to say about the human condition.

We must not judge a story, then, by whether or not it stays within the limits of the possible. Rather, we begin by granting every story a "Let's suppose" — an initial assumption. The initial assumption may be plausible or implausible. The writer may begin with an ordinary, everyday situation or with a far-fetched, improbable coincidence. Or the writer may be allowed to suspend a law of nature or to create a marvelous being or machine or place. But once we have granted the impossibility, we have a right to demand probability in the treatment of it. The realm of fantasy is not a realm in which *all* laws of logic are suspended. We need to ask, too, for what reason the story employs the element of fantasy. Is it used simply for its own strangeness or for thrills or surprises or laughs? Or is it used to illumine the more normal world of our experience? What is the purpose of the author's invention? Is it, like a roller coaster, simply a machine for producing thrills? Or does it, like an observation balloon, provide a vantage point from which we may view the world?

D. H. Lawrence
The Rocking-Horse Winner

There was a woman who was beautiful, who started with all the advantages, yet she had no luck. She married for love, and the love turned to dust. She had bonny children, yet she felt they had been thrust upon her, and she could not love them. They looked at her coldly, as if they were finding fault with her. And hurriedly she felt she must cover up some fault in herself. Yet what it was that she must cover up she never knew. Nevertheless, when her children were present, she always felt the center of her heart go hard. This troubled her, and in her manner she was all the more gentle and anxious for her children, as if she loved them very much. Only she herself knew that at the center of her heart was a hard little place that could not feel love, no, not for anybody. Everybody else said of her: "She is such a good mother. She adores her children." Only she herself, and her children themselves, knew it was not so. They read it in each other's eyes.

There were a boy and two little girls. They lived in a pleasant house, with a garden, and they had discreet servants, and felt themselves superior to anyone in the neighborhood.

THE ROCKING-HORSE WINNER   First published in 1933. D. H. Lawrence (1855–1930), son of a coal miner and a school teacher, was born and grew up in Nottinghamshire, England, was rejected for military service in World War I because of lung trouble, and lived most of his adult life abroad, including part of three years in New Mexico.

Although they lived in style, they felt always an anxiety in the house. There was never enough money. The mother had a small income, and the father had a small income, but not nearly enough for the social position which they had to keep up. The father went into town to some office. But though he had good prospects, these prospects never materialized. There was always the grinding sense of the shortage of money, though the style was always kept up.

At last the mother said: "I will see if I can't make something." But she did not know where to begin. She racked her brains, and tried this thing and the other, but could not find anything successful. The failure made deep lines come into her face. Her children were growing up, they would have to go to school. There must be more money, there must be more money. The father, who was always very handsome and expensive in his tastes, seemed as if he never would be able to do anything worth doing. And the mother, who had a great belief in herself, did not succeed any better, and her tastes were just as expensive.

5 And so the house came to be haunted by the unspoken phrase: There must be more money! There must be more money! The children could hear it all the time, though nobody said it aloud. They heard it at Christmas, when the expensive and splendid toys filled the nursery. Behind the shining modern rocking horse, behind the smart doll's-house, a voice would start whispering: "There must be more money! There must be more money!" And the children would stop playing, to listen for a moment. They would look into each other's eyes, to see if they had all heard. And each one saw in the eyes of the other two that they too had heard. "There must be more money! There must be more money!"

It came whispering from the springs of the still-swaying rocking horse, and even the horse, bending his wooden, champing head, heard it. The big doll, sitting so pink and smirking in her new pram, could hear it quite plainly, and seemed to be smirking all the more self-consciously because of it. The foolish puppy, too, that took the place of the Teddy bear, he was looking so extraordinarily foolish for no other reason but that he heard the secret whisper all over the house: "There must be more money!"

Yet nobody ever said it aloud. The whisper was everywhere, and therefore no one spoke it. Just as no one ever says: "We are breathing!" in spite of the fact that breath is coming and going all the time.

"Mother," said the boy Paul one day, "why don't we keep a car of our own? Why do we always use uncle's, or else a taxi?"

"Because we're the poor members of the family," said the mother.

10 "But why are we, mother?"

"Well—I suppose," she said slowly and bitterly, "it's because your father has no luck."

The boy was silent for some time.

"Is luck money, mother?" he asked, rather timidly.

"No, Paul. Not quite. It's what causes you to have money."

"Oh!" said Paul vaguely. "I thought when Uncle Oscar said filthy lucker, it meant money." 15

"Filthy lucre° does mean money," said the mother. "But it's lucre, not luck."

"Oh!" said the boy. "Then what is luck, mother?"

"It's what causes you to have money. If you're lucky you have money. That's why it's better to be born lucky than rich. If you're rich, you may lose your money. But if you're lucky, you will always get more money."

"Oh! Will you? And is father not lucky?"

"Very unlucky, I should say," she said bitterly. 20

The boy watched her with unsure eyes.

"Why?" he asked.

"I don't know. Nobody ever knows why one person is lucky and another unlucky."

"Don't they? Nobody at all? Does nobody know?"

"Perhaps God. But He never tells." 25

"He ought to, then. And aren't you lucky either, mother?"

"I can't be, if I married an unlucky husband."

"But by yourself, aren't you?"

"I used to think I was, before I married. Now I think I am very unlucky indeed."

"Why?" 30

"Well—never mind! Perhaps I'm not really," she said.

The child looked at her, to see if she meant it. But he saw, by the lines of her mouth, that she was only trying to hide something from him.

"Well, anyhow," he said stoutly, "I'm a lucky person."

"Why?" said his mother, with a sudden laugh.

He stared at her. He didn't even know why he had said it. 35

"God told me," he asserted, brazening it out.

"I hope He did, dear!" she said, again with a laugh, but rather bitter.

"He did, mother!"

"Excellent!" said the mother, using one of her husband's exclamations.

The boy saw she did not believe him; or, rather, that she paid no atten- 40 tion to his assertion. This angered him somewhat, and made him want to compel her attention.

He went off by himself, vaguely, in a childish way, seeking for the clue to "luck." Absorbed, taking no heed of other people, he went about with a sort of stealth, seeking inwardly for luck. He wanted luck, he wanted it, he wanted it. When the two girls were playing dolls in the nursery, he would sit on his big rocking horse, charging madly into space, with a frenzy that made the little girls peer at him uneasily. Wildly the horse careered, the waving dark hair of the boy tossed, his eyes had a strange glare in them. The little girls dared not speak to him.

filthy lucre: see New Testament, I Timothy 3:3

When he had ridden to the end of his mad little journey, he climbed down and stood in front of his rocking horse, staring fixedly into its lowered face. Its red mouth was slightly open, its big eye was wide and glassy-bright.

"Now!" he would silently command the snorting steed. "Now, take me to where there is luck! Now take me!"

And he would slash the horse on the neck with the little whip he had asked Uncle Oscar for. He knew the horse could take him to where there was luck, if only he forced it. So he would mount again, and start on his furious ride, hoping at last to get there. He knew he could get there.

45 "You'll break your horse, Paul!" said the nurse.

"He's always riding like that! I wish he'd leave off!" said his elder sister Joan.

But he only glared down on them in silence. Nurse gave him up. She could make nothing of him. Anyhow he was growing beyond her.

One day his mother and his Uncle Oscar came in when he was on one of his furious rides. He did not speak to them.

"Hallo, you young jockey! Riding a winner?" said his uncle.

50 "Aren't you growing too big for a rocking horse? You're not a very little boy any longer, you know," said his mother.

But Paul only gave a blue glare from his big, rather close-set eyes. He would speak to nobody when he was in full tilt. His mother watched him with an anxious expression on her face.

At last he suddenly stopped forcing his horse into the mechanical gallop, and slid down.

"Well, I got there!" he announced fiercely, his blue eyes still flaring, and his sturdy long legs straddling apart.

"Where did you get to?" asked his mother.

55 "Where I wanted to go," he flared back at her.

"That's right, son!" said Uncle Oscar. "Don't you stop till you get there. What's the horse's name?"

"He doesn't have a name," said the boy.

"Gets on without all right?" asked the uncle.

"Well, he has different names. He was called Sansovino last week."

60 "Sansovino, eh? Won the Ascot. How did you know his name?"

"He always talks about horse races with Bassett," said Joan.

The uncle was delighted to find that his small nephew was posted with all the racing news. Bassett, the young gardener, who had been wounded in the left foot in the war and got his present job through Oscar Cresswell, whose batman he had been, was a perfect blade of the "turf." He lived in the racing events, and the small boy lived with him.

Oscar Cresswell got it all from Bassett.

"Master Paul comes and asks me, so I can't do more than tell him, sir," said Bassett, his face terribly serious, as if he were speaking of religious matters.

65 "And does he ever put anything on a horse he fancies?"

"Well—I don't want to give him away—he's a young sport, a fine sport, sir. Would you mind asking him yourself? He sort of takes a pleasure in it, and perhaps he'd feel I was giving him away, sir, if you don't mind."

Bassett was serious as a church.

The uncle went back to his nephew, and took him off for a ride in the car.

"Say, Paul, old man, do you ever put anything on a horse?" the uncle asked.

The boy watched the handsome man closely. 70

"Why, do you think I oughtn't to?" he parried.

"Not a bit of it! I thought perhaps you might give me a tip for the Lincoln."

The car sped on into the country, going down to Uncle Oscar's place in Hampshire.

"Honor bright?" said the nephew.

"Honor bright, son!" said the uncle. 75

"Well, then, Daffodil."

"Daffodil! I doubt it, sonny. What about Mirza?"

"I only know the winner," said the boy. "That's Daffodil."

"Daffodil, eh?"

There was a pause. Daffodil was an obscure horse comparatively. 80

"Uncle!"

"Yes, son?"

"You won't let it go any further, will you? I promised Bassett."

"Bassett be damned, old man! What's he got to do with it?"

"We're partners. We've been partners from the first. Uncle, he lent me 85 my first five shillings, which I lost. I promised him, honor bright, it was only between me and him; only you gave me that ten-shilling note I started winning with, so I thought you were lucky. You won't let it go any further, will you?"

The boy gazed at his uncle from those big, hot, blue eyes, set rather close together. The uncle stirred and laughed uneasily.

"Right you are, son! I'll keep your tip private. Daffodil, eh? How much are you putting on him?"

"All except twenty pounds," said the boy. "I keep that in reserve."

The uncle thought it a good joke.

"You keep twenty pounds in reserve, do you, you young romancer? 90 What are you betting, then?"

"I'm betting three hundred," said the boy gravely. "But it's between you and me, Uncle Oscar! Honor bright?"

The uncle burst into a roar of laughter.

"It's between you and me all right, you young Nat Gould,"° he said, laughing. "But where's your three hundred?"

"Bassett keeps it for me. We're partners."

Nat Gould: a journalist and novelist (1857–1919) who wrote about horse racing

"You are, are you! And what is Bassett putting on Daffodil?"

"He won't go quite as high as I do, I expect. Perhaps he'll go a hundred and fifty."

"What, pennies?" laughed the uncle.

"Pounds," said the child, with a surprised look at his uncle. "Bassett keeps a bigger reserve than I do."

Between wonder and amusement Uncle Oscar was silent. He pursued the matter no further, but he determined to take his nephew with him to the Lincoln races.

"Now, son," he said, "I'm putting twenty on Mirza, and I'll put five for you on any horse you fancy. What's your pick?"

"Daffodil, uncle."

"No, not the fiver on Daffodil!"

"I should if it was my own fiver," said the child.

"Good! Good! Right you are! A fiver for me and a fiver for you on Daffodil."

The child had never been to a race meeting before, and his eyes were blue fire. He pursed his mouth tight, and watched. A Frenchman just in front had put his money on Lancelot. Wild with excitement, he flayed his arms up and down, yelling "Lancelot! Lancelot!" in his French accent.

Daffodil came in first, Lancelot second, Mirza third. The child, flushed and with eyes blazing, was curiously serene. His uncle brought him four five-pound notes, four to one.

"What am I to do with these?" he cried, waving them before the boy's eyes.

"I suppose we'll talk to Bassett," said the boy. "I expect I have fifteen hundred now; and twenty in reserve; and this twenty."

His uncle studied him for some moments.

"Look here, son!" he said. "You're not serious about Bassett and that fifteen hundred, are you?"

"Yes, I am. But it's between you and me, uncle. Honor bright!"

"Honor bright all right, son! But I must talk to Bassett."

"If you'd like to be a partner, uncle, with Bassett and me, we could all be partners. Only, you'd have to promise, honor bright, uncle, not to let it go beyond us three. Bassett and I are lucky, and you must be lucky, because it was your ten shillings I started winning with . . ."

Uncle Oscar took both Bassett and Paul into Richmond Park for an afternoon, and there they talked.

"It's like this, you see, sir," Bassett said. "Master Paul would get me talking about racing events, spinning yarns, you know, sir. And he was always keen on knowing if I'd made or if I'd lost. It's about a year since, now, that I put five shillings on Blush of Dawn for him — and we lost. Then the luck turned, with that ten shillings he had from you, that we put on Singhalese. And since that time, it's been pretty steady, all things considering. What do you say, Master Paul?"

"We're all right when we're sure," said Paul. "It's when we're not quite sure that we go down."

"Oh, but we're careful then," said Bassett.

"But when are you sure?" smiled Uncle Oscar.

"It's Master Paul, sir," said Bassett, in a secret, religious voice. "It's as if he had it from heaven. Like Daffodil, now, for the Lincoln. That was as sure as eggs."

"Did you put anything on Daffodil?" asked Oscar Cresswell.

"Yes, sir, I made my bit."

"And my nephew?"

Bassett was obstinately silent, looking at Paul.

"I made twelve hundred, didn't I, Bassett? I told uncle I was putting three hundred on Daffodil."

"That's right," said Bassett, nodding.

"But where's the money?" asked the uncle.

"I keep it safe locked up, sir. Master Paul he can have it any minute he likes to ask for it."

"What, fifteen hundred pounds?"

"And twenty! and forty, that is, with the twenty he made on the course."

"It's amazing!" said the uncle.

"If Master Paul offers you to be partners, sir, I would, if I were you; if you'll excuse me," said Bassett.

Oscar Cresswell thought about it.

"I'll see the money," he said.

They drove home again, and sure enough, Bassett came round to the garden-house with fifteen hundred pounds in notes. The twenty pounds reserve was left with Joe Glee, in the Turf Commission deposit.

"You see, it's all right, uncle, when I'm sure! Then we go strong, for all we're worth. Don't we Bassett?"

"We do that, Master Paul."

"And when are you sure?" said the uncle, laughing.

"Oh, well, sometimes I'm absolutely sure, like about Daffodil," said the boy; "and sometimes I have an idea; and sometimes I haven't even an idea, have I, Bassett? Then we're careful, because we mostly go down."

"You do, do you! And when you're sure, like about Daffodil, what makes you sure, sonny?"

"Oh, well, I don't know," said the boy uneasily. "I'm sure, you know, uncle; that's all."

"It's as if he had it from heaven, sir," Bassett reiterated.

"I should say so!" said the uncle.

But he became a partner. And when the Leger was coming on, Paul was "sure" about Lively Spark, which was a quite inconsiderable horse. The boy insisted on putting a thousand on the horse, Bassett went for five hundred, and Oscar Cresswell two hundred. Lively Spark came in first, and the betting had been ten to one against him. Paul had made ten thousand.

"You see," he said, "I was absolutely sure of him."

Even Oscar Cresswell had cleared two thousand.

"Look here son," he said, "this sort of thing makes me nervous."

"It needn't, uncle! Perhaps I shan't be sure again for a long time."

"But what are you going to do with your money?" asked the uncle.

"Of course," said the boy, "I started it for mother. She said she had no luck, because father is unlucky, so I thought if I was lucky, it might stop whispering."

"What might stop whispering?"

"Our house. I hate our house for whispering."

"What does it whisper?"

"Why — why" — the boy fidgeted — "why, I don't know. But it's always short of money, you know, uncle."

"I know it, son, I know it."

"You know people send mother writs, don't you, uncle?"

"I'm afraid I do," said the uncle.

"And then the house whispers, like people laughing at you behind your back. It's awful, that is! I thought if I was lucky . . ."

"You might stop it," added the uncle.

The boy watched him with big blue eyes that had an uncanny cold fire in them, and he said never a word.

"Well, then!" said the uncle. "What are we doing?"

"I shouldn't like mother to know I was lucky," said the boy.

"Why not, son?"

"She'd stop me."

"I don't think she would."

"Oh!" — and the boy writhed in an odd way — "I don't want her to know, uncle."

"All right, son! We'll manage it without her knowing."

They managed it very easily. Paul, at the other's suggestion, handed over five thousand pounds to his uncle, who deposited it with the family lawyer, who was then to inform Paul's mother that a relative had put five thousand pounds into his hands, which sum was to be paid out a thousand pounds at a time, on the mother's birthday, for the next five years.

"So she'll have a birthday present of a thousand pounds for five successive years," said Uncle Oscar. "I hope it won't make it all the harder for her later."

Paul's mother had her birthday in November. The house had been "whispering" worse than ever lately, and, even in spite of his luck, Paul could not bear up against it. He was very anxious to see the effect of the birthday letter, telling his mother about the thousand pounds.

When there were no visitors, Paul now took his meals with his parents, as he was beyond the nursery control. His mother went into town nearly every day. She had discovered that she had an odd knack of sketching furs and dress materials, so she worked secretly in the studio of a friend who was the chief "artist" for the leading drapers. She drew the figures of ladies in furs and ladies in silk and sequins for the newspaper advertisements. This young woman artist earned several thousand pounds a year, but Paul's mother only made several hundreds, and she was again dissatisfied. She so wanted to be first in something, and she did not succeed, even in making sketches for drapery advertisements.

She was down to breakfast on the morning of her birthday. Paul watched her face as she read her letters. He knew the lawyer's letter. As his mother read it, her face hardened and became more expressionless. Then a cold, determined look came on her mouth. She hid the letter under the pile of others, and said not a word about it.

"Didn't you have anything nice in the post for your birthday, mother?" said Paul.

"Quite moderately nice," she said, her voice cold and absent.

She went away to town without saying more.

But in the afternoon Uncle Oscar appeared. He said Paul's mother had had a long interview with the lawyer, asking if the whole five thousand could be advanced at once, as she was in debt.

"What do you think, uncle?" said the boy.

"I leave it to you, son."

"Oh, let her have it, then! We can get some more with the other," said the boy.

"A bird in the hand is worth two in the bush, laddie!" said Uncle Oscar.

"But I'm sure to know for the Grand National; or the Lincolnshire; or else the Derby. I'm sure to know for one of them," said Paul.

So Uncle Oscar signed the agreement, and Paul's mother touched the whole five thousand. Then something very curious happened. The voices in the house suddenly went mad, like a chorus of frogs on a spring evening. There were certain new furnishings, and Paul had a tutor. He was really going to Eton,° his father's school, in the following autumn. There were flowers in the winter, and a blossoming of the luxury Paul's mother had been used to. And yet the voices in the house, behind the sprays of mimosa and almond blossom, and from under the piles of iridescent cushions, simply trilled and screamed in a sort of ecstasy: "There must be more money! Oh-h-h, there must be more money. Oh, now, now-w! Now-w-w — there must be more money — more than ever! More than ever!"

It frightened Paul terribly. He studied away at his Latin and Greek with his tutor. But his intense hours were spent with Bassett. The Grand National had gone by: he had not "known," and had lost a hundred pounds. Summer was at hand. He was in agony for the Lincoln. But even for the Lincoln he didn't "know" and he lost fifty pounds. He became wild-eyed and strange, as if something were going to explode in him.

"Let it alone, son! Don't you bother about it!" urged Uncle Oscar. But it was as if the boy couldn't really hear what his uncle was saying.

Eton: England's most prestigious privately supported secondary school

"I've got to know for the Derby! I've got to know for the Derby!" the child reiterated, his big blue eyes blazing with a sort of madness.

185 His mother noticed how overwrought he was.

"You'd better go to the seaside. Wouldn't you like to go now to the seaside, instead of waiting? I think you'd better," she said, looking down at him anxiously, her heart curiously heavy because of him.

But the child lifted his uncanny blue eyes.

"I couldn't possibly go before the Derby, mother!" he said. "I couldn't possibly!"

"Why not?" she said, her voice becoming heavy when she was opposed. "Why not? You can still go from the seaside to see the Derby with your Uncle Oscar, if that's what you wish. No need for you to wait here. Besides, I think you care too much about these races. It's a bad sign. My family has been a gambling family, and you won't know till you grow up how much damage it has done. But it has done damage. I shall have to send Bassett away, and ask Uncle Oscar not to talk racing to you, unless you promise to be reasonable about it; go away to the seaside and forget it. You're all nerves!"

190 "I'll do what you like, mother, so long as you don't send me away till after the Derby," the boy said.

"Send you away from where? Just from this house?"

"Yes," he said, gazing at her.

"Why, you curious child, what makes you care about this house so much, suddenly? I never knew you loved it."

He gazed at her without speaking. He had a secret within a secret, something he had not divulged, even to Bassett or to his Uncle Oscar.

195 But his mother, after standing undecided and a little bit sullen for some moments, said:

"Very well, then! Don't go to the seaside till after the Derby, if you don't wish it. But promise me you won't let your nerves go to pieces. Promise you won't think so much about horse racing and events, as you call them!"

"Oh, no," said the boy casually. "I won't think much about them, mother. You needn't worry. I wouldn't worry, mother, if I were you."

"If you were me and I were you," said his mother, "I wonder what we should do!"

"But you know you needn't worry, mother, don't you?" the boy repeated.

200 "I should be awfully glad to know it," she said wearily.

"Oh, well, you can, you know. I mean, you ought to know you needn't worry," he insisted.

"Ought I? Then I'll see about it," she said.

Paul's secret of secrets was his wooden horse, that which had no name. Since he was emancipated from a nurse and a nursery-governess, he had had his rocking horse removed to his own bedroom at the top of the house.

"Surely, you're too big for a rocking horse!" his mother had remonstrated.

205 "Well, you see mother, till I can have a real horse, I like to have some sort of animal about," had been his quaint answer.

"Do you feel he keeps you company?" she laughed.

"Oh, yes! He's very good, he always keeps me company, when I'm there," said Paul.

So the horse, rather shabby, stood in an arrested prance in the boy's bedroom.

The Derby was drawing near, and the boy grew more and more tense. He hardly heard what was spoken to him, he was very frail, and his eyes were really uncanny. His mother had sudden seizures of uneasiness about him. Sometimes, for half-an-hour, she would feel a sudden anxiety about him that was almost anguish. She wanted to rush to him at once, and know he was safe.

Two nights before the Derby, she was at a big party in town, when one of her rushes of anxiety about her boy, her first-born, gripped her heart till she could hardly speak. She fought with the feeling, might and main, for she believed in common sense. But it was too strong. The children's nursery-governess was terribly surprised and startled at being rung up in the night.

"Are the children all right, Miss Wilmot?"

"Oh, yes, they are quite all right."

"Master Paul? Is he all right?"

"He went to bed as right as a trivet. Shall I run up and look at him?"

"No," said Paul's mother reluctantly. "No! Don't trouble. It's all right. Don't sit up. We shall be home fairly soon." She did not want her son's privacy intruded upon.

"Very good," said the governess.

It was about one o'clock when Paul's mother and father drove up to their house. All was still. Paul's mother went to her room and slipped off her white fur coat. She had told her maid not to wait up for her. She heard her husband downstairs, mixing a whiskey-and-soda.

And then, because of the strange anxiety at her heart, she stole upstairs to her son's room. Noiselessly she went along the upper corridor. Was there a faint noise? What was it?

She stood, with arrested muscles, outside his door listening. There was a strange, heavy, and yet not loud noise. Her heart stood still. It was a sound-less noise, yet rushing and powerful. Something huge, in violent, hushed motion. What was it? What in God's name was it? She ought to know. She felt that she knew the noise. She knew what it was.

Yet she could not place it. She couldn't say what it was. And on and on it went, like madness.

Softly, frozen with anxiety and fear, she turned the door handle.

The room was dark. Yet in the space near the window, she heard and saw something plunging to and fro. She gazed in fear and amazement.

Then suddenly she switched on the light, and saw her son, in his green pajamas, madly surging on the rocking horse. The blaze of light suddenly lit him up, as he urged the wooden horse, and lit her up, as she stood, blonde, in her dress of pale green and crystal, in the doorway.

"Paul!" she cried. "Whatever are you doing?"

225 "It's Malabar!" he screamed, in a powerful, strange voice. "It's Malabar."

His eyes blazed at her for one strange and senseless second, as he ceased urging his wooden horse. Then he fell with a crash to the ground, and she, all her tormented motherhood flooding upon her, rushed to gather him up.

But he was unconscious, and unconscious he remained, with some brain-fever. He talked and tossed, and his mother sat stonily by his side.

"Malabar! It's Malabar! Bassett, Bassett, I know it! It's Malabar!"

So the child cried, trying to get up and urge the rocking horse that gave him his inspiration.

230 "What does he mean by Malabar?" asked the heart-frozen mother.

"I don't know," said his father stonily.

"What does he mean by Malabar?" she asked her brother Oscar.

"It's one of the horses running for the Derby," was the answer.

And, in spite of himself, Oscar Cresswell spoke to Bassett, and himself put a thousand on Malabar: at fourteen to one.

235 The third day of the illness was critical: they were waiting for a change. The boy, with his rather long, curly hair, was tossing ceaselessly on the pillow. He neither slept nor regained consciousness, and his eyes were like blue stones. His mother sat, feeling her heart had gone, turned actually into a stone.

In the evening, Oscar Cresswell did not come, but Bassett sent a message, saying could he come up for one moment, just one moment? Paul's mother was very angry at the intrusion, but on second thought she agreed. The boy was the same. Perhaps Bassett might bring him to consciousness.

The gardener, a shortish fellow with a brown mustache, and sharp little brown eyes, tiptoed into the room, touched his imaginary cap to Paul's mother, and stole to the bedside, staring with glittering, smallish eyes, at the tossing, dying child.

"Master Paul!" he whispered. "Master Paul! Malabar came in first all right, a clean win. I did as you told me. You've made over seventy thousand pounds, you have; you've got over eighty thousand. Malabar came in all right, Master Paul."

"Malabar! Malabar! Did I say Malabar, mother? Did I say Malabar? Do you think I'm lucky, mother? I knew Malabar, didn't I? Over eighty thousand pounds! I call that lucky, don't you, mother? Over eighty thousand pounds! I knew, didn't I know I knew? Malabar came in all right. If I ride my horse till I'm sure, then I tell you, Bassett, you can go as high as you like. Did you go for all you were worth, Bassett?"

240 "I went a thousand on it, Master Paul."

"I never told you, mother, that if I can ride my horse, and get there, then I'm absolutely sure — oh, absolutely! Mother, did I ever tell you? I'm lucky."

"No, you never did," said the mother.

But the boy died in the night.

And even as he lay dead, his mother heard her brother's voice saying to her: "My God, Hester, you're eighty-odd thousand to the good and a poor devil of a son to the bad. But, poor devil, poor devil, he's best gone out of a life where he rides his rocking horse to find a winner."

QUESTIONS

1. In the phraseology of its beginning ("There was a woman . . ."), its simple style, its direct characterization, and its use of the wish motif — especially that of the wish that is granted only on conditions that nullify its desirability (compare the story of King Midas) — this story has the qualities of a fairy tale. Its differences, however — in characterization, setting, and ending — are especially significant. What do they tell us about the purpose of the story?
2. Characterize the mother fully. How does she differ from the stepmothers in fairy tales like "Cinderella" and "Hansel and Gretel"? How does the boy's mistake about *filthy lucker* clarify her thinking and her motivations? Why had her love for her husband turned to dust? Why is she "unlucky"?
3. What kind of a child is Paul? What are his motivations?
4. The initial assumptions of the story are that (a) a boy might get divinatory powers by riding a rocking horse, (b) a house can whisper. Could the second of these be accepted as little more than a metaphor? Once we have granted these initial assumptions, does the story develop plausibly?
5. It is ironic that the boy's attempt to stop the whispers should only increase them. Is this a plausible irony? Why? What does it tell us about the theme of the story? Why is it ironic that the whispers should be especially audible at Christmas time? What irony is contained in the boy's last speech?
6. In what way is the boy's furious riding on the rocking horse an appropriate symbol for materialistic pursuits?
7. How might a sentimental writer have ended the story?
8. How many persons in the story are affected (or infected) by materialism?
9. What is the theme of the story?

Nathaniel Hawthorne
Young Goodman Brown

Young Goodman Brown came forth at sunset into the street of Salem village, but put his head back, after crossing the threshold, to exchange a parting kiss with his young wife. And Faith, as the wife was aptly named,

YOUNG GOODMAN BROWN   First published in 1835. "Goodman" was a title of respect, but at a social rank lower than "gentleman." "Goody" (or "Goodwife") was the feminine equivalent. Deacon Gookin in the story is a historical personage (1612–1687), as are also Goody Cloyse, Goody Cory, and Martha Carrier, all three executed at the Salem witchcraft trials in 1692. Nathaniel Hawthorne (1804–1864) was born and grew up in Salem, Massachusetts, where Hawthornes had lived since the seventeenth century. One ancestor had been a judge at the Salem witch trials; another had been a leader in the persecution of Quakers. "Young Goodman Brown" is one of several stories in which Hawthorne explored the Puritan past of New England.

thrust her own pretty head into the street, letting the wind play with the pink ribbons of her cap while she called to Goodman Brown.

"Dearest heart," whispered she softly and rather sadly when her lips were close to his ear, "prithee, put off your journey until sunrise, and sleep in your own bed tonight. A lone woman is troubled with such dreams and such thoughts that she's afeard of herself, sometimes. Pray, tarry with me this night, dear husband, of all nights in the year!"

"My love and my Faith," replied young Goodman Brown, "of all nights in the year this one must I tarry away from thee. My journey, as thou callest it, forth and back again must needs be done 'twixt now and sunrise. What, my sweet, pretty wife, dost thou doubt me already, and we but three months married!"

"Then God bless you!" said Faith with the pink ribbons, "and may you find all well when you come back."

5   "Amen!" cried Goodman Brown. "Say thy prayers, dear Faith, and go to bed at dusk, and no harm will come to thee."

So they parted; and the young man pursued his way until, being about to turn the corner by the meeting-house, he looked back and saw the head of Faith still peeping after him with a melancholy air in spite of her pink ribbons.

"Poor little Faith!" thought he, for his heart smote him. "What a wretch am I, to leave her on such an errand! She talks of dreams, too. Methought, as she spoke, there was trouble in her face, as if a dream had warned her what work is to be done tonight. But no, no! 'twould kill her to think it. Well; she's a blessed angel on earth and after this one night I'll cling to her skirts and follow her to Heaven."

With this excellent resolve for the future, Goodman Brown felt himself justified in making more haste on his present evil purpose. He had taken a dreary road, darkened by all the gloomiest trees of the forest, which barely stood aside to let the narrow path creep through, and closed immediately behind. It was all as lonely as could be; and there is this peculiarity in such a solitude, that the traveler knows not who may be concealed by the innumerable trunks and the thick boughs overhead, so that with lonely footsteps he may be passing through an unseen multitude.

"There may be a devilish Indian behind every tree," said Goodman Brown to himself; and he glanced fearfully behind him as he added, "What if the devil himself should be at my very elbow!"

10   His head being turned back, he passed a crook of the road, and looking forward again beheld the figure of a man in grave and decent attire, seated at the foot of an old tree. He rose at Goodman Brown's approach and walked onward side by side with him.

"You are late, Goodman Brown," said he. "The clock of the Old South was striking as I came through Boston, and that is full fifteen minutes agone."°

full fifteen minutes agone: The distance from the center of Boston to the forest was over 20 miles.

"Faith kept me back awhile," replied the young man with a tremor in his voice caused by the sudden appearance of his companion, though not wholly unexpected.

It was now deep dusk in the forest, and deepest in that part of it where these two were journeying. As nearly as could be discerned, the second traveler was about fifty years old, apparently in the same rank of life as Goodman Brown, and bearing a considerable resemblance to him, though perhaps more in expression than features. Still, they might have been taken for father and son. And yet, though the elder person was as simply clad as the younger, and as simple in manner too, he had an indescribable air of one who knew the world and would not have felt abashed at the governor's dinner table or in King William's court,° were it possible that his affairs should call him thither. But the only thing about him that could be fixed upon as remarkable was his staff, which bore the likeness of a great black snake, so curiously wrought that it might almost be seen to twist and wriggle itself like a living serpent. This, of course, must have been an ocular deception, assisted by the uncertain light.

"Come, Goodman Brown!" cried his fellow-traveler, "this is a dull pace for the beginning of a journey. Take my staff if you are so soon weary."

"Friend," said the other, exchanging his slow pace for a full stop, "having kept covenant by meeting thee here, it is my purpose now to return whence I came. I have scruples touching the matter thou wot'st of." 15

"Sayest thou so?" replied he of the serpent, smiling apart. "Let us walk on nevertheless, reasoning as we go, and if I convince thee not, thou shalt turn back. We are but a little way in the forest yet."

"Too far, too far!" exclaimed the goodman, unconsciously resuming his walk. "My father never went into the woods on such an errand, nor his father before him. We have been a race of honest men and good Christians since the days of the martyrs. And shall I be the first of the name of Brown that ever took this path and kept—"

"Such company, thou wouldst say," observed the elder person interrupting his pause. "Well said, Goodman Brown! I have been as well acquainted with your family as with ever a one among the Puritans, and that's no trifle to say. I helped your grandfather the constable when he lashed the Quaker woman so smartly through the streets of Salem. And it was I that brought your father a pitch-pine knot kindled at my own hearth, to set fire to an Indian village, in King Philip's war.° They were my good friends, both; and many a pleasant walk have we had along this path and returned merrily after midnight. I would fain be friends with you, for their sake."

"If it be as thou sayest," replied Goodman Brown, "I marvel they never spoke of these matters. Or, verily, I marvel not, seeing that the least rumor of the sort would have driven them from New England. We are a people of prayer, and good works to boot, and abide no such wickedness."

King Williams's court: William III, King of England, 1689–1702 **King Philip's War:** a war between the colonists and Indians, 1675–1676

"Wickedness or not," said the traveler with twisted staff, "I have a general acquaintance here in New England. The deacons of many a church have drunk the communion wine with me, the selectmen of divers towns make me their chairman, and a majority of the Great and General Court° are firm supporters of my interest. The governor and I, too — but these are state secrets."

"Can this be so!" cried Goodman Brown with a stare of amazement at his undisturbed companion. "Howbeit, I have nothing to do with the governor and council; they have their own ways and are no rule for a simple husbandman like me. But were I to go on with thee, how should I meet the eye of that good old man, our minister, at Salem village? Oh, his voice would make me tremble, both Sabbath-day and lecture-day!"

Thus far, the elder traveler had listened with due gravity but now burst into a fit of irrepressible mirth, shaking himself so violently that his snake-like staff actually seemed to wriggle in sympathy.

"Ha! ha! ha!" shouted he, again and again; then composing himself, "Well, go on, Goodman Brown, go on; but prithee, don't kill me with laughing!"

"Well, then, to end the matter at once," said Goodman Brown, considerably nettled, "there is my wife, Faith. It would break her dear little heart, and I'd rather break my own!"

"Nay, if that be the case," answered the other, "e'en go thy ways, Goodman Brown. I would not for twenty old women like the one hobbling before us that Faith should come to any harm."

As he spoke he pointed his staff at a female figure on the path in whom Goodman Brown recognized a very pious and exemplary dame who had taught him his catechism in youth and was still his moral and spiritual adviser, jointly with the minister and Deacon Gookin.

"A marvel, truly, that Goody Cloyse should be so far in the wilderness at nightfall!" said he. "But with your leave, friend, I shall take a cut through the woods until we have left this Christian woman behind. Being a stranger to you, she might ask whom I was consorting with and whither I was going."

"Be it so," said his fellow-traveler. "Betake you to the woods and let me keep the path."

Accordingly, the young man turned aside, but took care to watch his companion who advanced softly along the road until he had come within a staff's length of the old dame. She, meanwhile, was making the best of her way, with singular speed for so aged a woman, and mumbling some indistinct words, a prayer, doubtless, as she went. The traveler put forth his staff and touched her withered neck with what seemed the serpent's tail.

"The devil!" screamed the pious old lady.

"Then Goody Cloyse knows her old friend?" observed the traveler confronting her and leaning on his writhing stick.

Great and General Court: the legislature of the Massachusetts Bay Colony

"Ah, forsooth, and is it your worship indeed?" cried the good dame. "Yea, truly is it, and in the very image of my old gossip, Goodman Brown, the grandfather of the silly fellow that now is. But would your worship believe it? my broomstick hath strangely disappeared, stolen as I suspect by that un-hanged witch, Goody Cory, and that, too, when I was all anointed with the juice of smallage and cinque-foil and wolf's-bane—"

"Mingled with fine wheat and the fat of a new-born babe," said the shape of old Goodman Brown.

"Ah, your worship knows the recipe," cried the old lady, cackling aloud. "So, as I was saying, being all ready for the meeting, and no horse to ride on, I made up my mind to foot it; for they tell me there is a nice young man to be taken into communion tonight. But now your good worship will lend me your arm and we shall be there in a twinkling."

"That can hardly be," answered her friend. "I may not spare you my arm, Goody Cloyse, but here is my staff, if you will."

So saying, he threw it down at her feet where, perhaps, it assumed life, being one of the rods which its owner had formerly lent to the Egyptian Magi. Of this fact, however, Goodman Brown could not take cognizance. He had cast up his eyes in astonishment, and looking down again beheld neither Goody Cloyse nor the serpentine staff, but his fellow-traveler alone, who waited for him as calmly as if nothing had happened.

"That old woman taught me my catechism!" said the young man, and there was a world of meaning in this simple comment.

They continued to walk onward while the elder traveler exhorted his companion to make good speed and persevere in the path, discoursing so aptly that his arguments seemed rather to spring up in the bosom of his auditor than to be suggested by himself. As they went he plucked a branch of maple to serve for a walking-stick, and began to strip it of the twigs and little boughs which were wet with evening dew. The moment his fingers touched them they became strangely withered and dried up, as with a week's sun-shine. Thus the pair proceeded at a good free pace, until suddenly, in a gloomy hollow of the road, Goodman Brown sat himself down on the stump of a tree and refused to go any farther.

"Friend," said he stubbornly, "my mind is made up. Not another step will I budge on this errand. What if a wretched old woman do choose to go to the devil when I thought she was going to Heaven! Is that any reason why I should quit my dear Faith and go after her?"

"You will think better of this by and by," said his acquaintance compos-edly. "Sit here and rest yourself awhile, and when you feel like moving again, there is my staff to help you along."

Without more words, he threw his companion the maple stick and was as speedily out of sight as if he had vanished into the deepening gloom. The young man sat a few moments by the roadside, applauding himself greatly and thinking with how clear a conscience he should meet the minister in his morning walk, nor shrink from the eye of good old Deacon Gookin. And what calm sleep would be his that very night, which was to have been spent so wickedly, but purely and sweetly now, in the arms of Faith! Amidst these pleasant and praiseworthy meditations, Goodman Brown heard the tramp of horses along the road and deemed it advisable to conceal himself within the verge of the forest, conscious of the guilty purpose that had brought him thither, though now so happily turned from it.

On came the hoof-tramps and the voices of the riders, two grave old voices conversing soberly as they drew near. These mingled sounds appeared to pass along the road within a few yards of the young man's hiding place; but owing, doubtless, to the depth of the gloom at that particular spot, neither the travelers nor their steeds were visible. Though their figures brushed the small boughs by the wayside, it could not be seen that they intercepted even for a moment the faint gleam from the strip of bright sky athwart which they must have passed. Goodman Brown alternately crouched and stood on tip-toe, pulling aside the branches and thrusting forth his head as far as he durst, without discerning so much as a shadow. It vexed him the more because he could have sworn, were such a thing possible, that he recognized the voices of the minister and Deacon Gookin, jogging along quietly as they were wont to do when bound to some ordination or ecclesiastical council. While yet within hearing, one of the riders stopped to pluck a switch.

"Of the two, reverend Sir," said the voice like the deacon's, "I had rather miss an ordination dinner than tonight's meeting. They tell me that some of our community are to be here from Falmouth and beyond, and others from Connecticut and Rhode Island, besides several of the Indian powwows who, after their fashion, know almost as much deviltry as the best of us. Moreover, there is a goodly young woman to be taken into communion."

"Mighty well, Deacon Gookin!" replied the solemn old tones of the minister. "Spur up, or we shall be late. Nothing can be done, you know, until I get on the ground."

45   The hoofs clattered again, and the voices talking so strangely in the empty air passed on through the forest where no church had ever been gathered nor solitary Christian prayed. Whither, then, could these holy men be journeying, so deep into the heathen wilderness? Young Goodman Brown caught hold of a tree for support, being ready to sink down on the ground, faint and over-burthened with the heavy sickness of his heart. He looked up to the sky, doubting whether there really was a Heaven above him. Yet there was the blue arch, and the stars brightening in it.

"With Heaven above, and Faith below, I will yet stand firm against the devil!" cried Goodman Brown.

While he still gazed upward into the deep arch of the firmament and had lifted his hands to pray, a cloud, though no wind was stirring, hurried across the zenith and hid the brightening stars. The blue sky was still visible except directly overhead, where this black mass of cloud was sweeping swiftly northward. Aloft in the air, as if from the depths of the cloud, came a confused and doubtful sound of voices. Once the listener fancied that he could distinguish the accents of townspeople of his own, men and women, both pious and ungodly, many of whom he had met at the communion-table, and had seen others rioting at the tavern. The next moment, so indistinct were the sounds, he doubted whether he had heard aught but the murmur of the old forest whispering without a wind. Then came a stronger swell of those familiar tones heard daily in the sunshine at Salem village, but never, until now, from a cloud at night. There was one voice, of a young woman uttering lamentations yet with an uncertain sorrow, and entreating for some favor, which, perhaps, it would grieve her to obtain. And all the unseen multitude, both saints and sinners, seemed to encourage her onward.

"Faith!" shouted Goodman Brown in a voice of agony and desperation; and the echoes of the forest mocked him, crying — "Faith! Faith!" as if bewildered wretches were seeking her all through the wilderness.

The cry of grief, rage, and terror was yet piercing the night when the unhappy husband held his breath for a response. There was a scream, drowned immediately in a louder murmur of voices fading into far-off laughter as the dark cloud swept away leaving the clear and silent sky above Goodman Brown. But something fluttered lightly down through the air and caught on the branch of a tree. The young man seized it and beheld a pink ribbon.

"My Faith is gone!" cried he, after one stupefied moment. "There is no good on earth, and sin is but a name. Come, devil! for to thee is this world given." 50

And maddened with despair, so that he laughed loud and long, did Goodman Brown grasp his staff and set forth again at such a rate that he seemed to fly along the forest path rather than to walk or run. The road grew wilder and drearier and more faintly traced, and vanished at length, leaving him in the heart of the dark wilderness, still rushing onward with the instinct that guides mortal man to evil. The whole forest was peopled with frightful sounds — the creaking of the trees, the howling of wild beasts, and the yell of Indians; while sometimes the wind tolled like a distant church bell, and sometimes gave a broad roar around the traveler, as if all Nature were laughing him to scorn. But he was himself the chief horror of the scene, and shrank not from its other horrors.

"Ha! ha! ha!" roared Goodman Brown when the wind laughed at him. "Let us hear which will laugh loudest! Think not to frighten me with your deviltry! come witch, come wizard, come Indian powwow, come devil himself! and here comes Goodman Brown. You may as well fear him as he fear you!"

In truth, all through the haunted forest there could be nothing more frightful than the figure of Goodman Brown. On he flew among the black pines, brandishing his staff with frenzied gestures, now giving vent to an inspiration of horrid blasphemy, and now shouting forth such laughter as set all the echoes of the forest laughing like demons around him. The fiend in his own shape is less hideous than when he rages in the breast of man. Thus sped the demoniac on his course until, quivering among the trees, he saw a red light before him, as when the felled trunks and branches of a clearing have been set on fire and throw up their lurid blaze against the sky at the hour of midnight. He paused in a lull of the tempest that had driven him onward, and heard the swell of what seemed a hymn rolling solemnly from a distance with the weight of many voices. He knew the tune. It was a familiar one in the choir of the village meeting-house. The verse died heavily away, and was lengthened by a chorus not of human voices but of all the sounds of the benighted wilderness pealing in awful harmony together. Goodman Brown cried out, and his cry was lost to his own ear by its unison with the cry of the desert.

In the interval of silence he stole forward until the light glared full upon his eyes. At one extremity of an open space, hemmed in by the dark wall of the forest, arose a rock bearing some rude, natural resemblance either to an altar or a pulpit, and surrounded by four blazing pines, their tops aflame, their stems untouched, like candles at an evening meeting. The mass of foliage that had overgrown the summit of the rock was all on fire, blazing high into the night and fitfully illuminating the whole field. Each pendent twig and leafy festoon was in a blaze. As the red light arose and fell, a numerous congregation alternately shone forth, then disappeared in shadow, and again grew, as it were, out of the darkness, peopling the heart of the solitary woods at once.

55   "A grave and dark-clad company!" quoth Goodman Brown.

In truth they were such. Among them, quivering to and fro between gloom and splendor, appeared faces that would be seen next day at the council-board of the province, and others which Sabbath after Sabbath looked devoutly heavenward and benignantly over the crowded pews from the holiest pulpits in the land. Some affirm that the lady of the governor was there. At least, there were high dames well known to her, and wives of honored husbands, and widows a great multitude, and ancient maidens, all of excellent repute, and fair young girls who trembled lest their mothers should espy them. Either the sudden gleams of light flashing over the obscure field bedazzled Goodman Brown, or he recognized a score of the church members of Salem village famous for their especial sanctity. Good old Deacon Gookin had arrived and waited at the skirts of that venerable saint, his reverend pastor. But irreverently consorting with these grave, reputable, and pious people, these elders of the church, these chaste dames and dewy virgins, there were men of dissolute lives and women of spotted fame, wretches given over to all mean and filthy vice and suspected even of horrid crimes. It was strange to see that the good shrank not from the wicked, nor were the sinners abashed by the saints. Scattered also among their pale-faced enemies were the Indian priests or powwows who had often scared their native forest with more hideous incantations than any known to English witchcraft.

"But where is Faith?" thought Goodman Brown; and as hope came into his heart he trembled.

Another verse of the hymn arose, a slow and mournful strain such as the pious love, but joined to words which expressed all that our nature can conceive of sin, and darkly hinted at far more. Unfathomable to mere mortals is the lore of fiends. Verse after verse was sung, and still the chorus of the desert swelled between, like the deepest tone of a mighty organ. And with the final peal of that dreadful anthem, there came a sound as if the roaring wind, the rushing streams, the howling beasts, and every other voice of the unconverted wilderness were mingling and according with the voice of guilty man in homage to the prince of all. The four blazing pines threw up a loftier flame and obscurely discovered shapes and visages of horror on the smoke-wreaths above the impious assembly. At the same moment the fire on the rock shot redly forth and formed a glowing arch above its base, where now appeared a figure. With reverence be it spoken, the apparition bore no slight similitude both in garb and manner to some grave divine of the New England churches.

"Bring forth the converts!" cried a voice that echoed through the field and rolled into the forest.

At the word, Goodman Brown stepped forth from the shadow of the trees and approached the congregation, with whom he felt a loathful brotherhood by the sympathy of all that was wicked in his heart. He could have well-nigh sworn that the shape of his own dead father beckoned him to advance, looking downward from a smoke-wreath, while a woman with dim features of despair threw out her hand to warn him back. Was it his mother? But he had no power to retreat one step nor to resist, even in thought, when the minister and good old Deacon Gookin seized his arms and led him to the blazing rock. Thither came also the slender form of a veiled female led between Goody Cloyse, that pious teacher of the catechism, and Martha Carrier, who had received the devil's promise to be queen of hell. A rampant hag was she! And there stood the proselytes beneath the canopy of fire.

"Welcome, my children," said the dark figure, "to the communion of your race! Ye have found, thus young, your nature and your destiny. My children, look behind you!"

They turned, and flashing forth as it were in a sheet of flame, the fiend-worshippers were seen; the smile of welcome gleamed darkly on every visage.

"There," resumed the sable form, "are all whom ye have reverenced from youth. Ye deemed them holier than yourselves and shrank from your own sin, contrasting it with their lives of righteousness and prayerful aspirations heavenward. Yet here are they all in my worshipping assembly! This night it shall be granted you to know their secret deeds: how hoary-bearded elders of the church have whispered wanton words to the young maids of their households; how many a woman eager for widow's weeds has given her husband a drink at bedtime, and let him sleep his last sleep in her bosom; how beardless youths have made haste to inherit their father's wealth; and how fair damsels — blush not, sweet ones! — have dug little graves in the garden and bidden me, the sole guest, to an infant's funeral. By the sympathy of your human hearts for sin, ye shall scent out all the places — whether in church, bedchamber, street, field, or forest — where crime has been committed, and shall exult to behold the whole earth one stain of guilt, one mighty blood-spot. Far more than this! It shall be yours to penetrate in every bosom the deep mystery of sin, the fountain of all wicked arts, and which inexhaustibly supplies more evil impulses than human power — than my power, at its utmost! — can make manifest in deeds. And now, my children, look upon each other."

They did so, and by the blaze of the hell-kindled torches the wretched man beheld his Faith, and the wife her husband trembling before that unhallowed altar.

65 "Lo! there ye stand, my children," said the figure in a deep solemn tone, almost sad with its despairing awfulness, as if his once angelic nature could yet mourn for our miserable race. "Depending upon one another's hearts, ye had still hoped that virtue were not all a dream! Now are ye undeceived — Evil is the nature of mankind. Evil must be your only happiness. Welcome, again, my children, to the communion of your race!"

"Welcome!" repeated the fiend-worshippers in one cry of despair and triumph.

And there they stood, the only pair as it seemed who were yet hesitating on the verge of wickedness in this dark world. A basin was hollowed naturally in the rock. Did it contain water, reddened by the lurid light? or was it blood? or, perchance, a liquid flame? Herein did the Shape of Evil dip his hand and prepare to lay the mark of baptism upon their foreheads, that they might be partakers of the mystery of sin, more conscious of the secret guilt of others both in deed and thought than they could now be of their own. The husband cast one look at his pale wife, and Faith at him. What polluted wretches would the next glance show them to each other, shuddering alike at what they disclosed and what they saw!

"Faith! Faith!" cried the husband. "Look up to Heaven, and resist the Wicked One!"

Whether Faith obeyed he knew not. Hardly had he spoken when he found himself amid calm night and solitude, listening to a roar of the wind which died heavily away through the forest. He staggered against the rock and felt it chill and damp, while a hanging twig that had been all on fire besprinkled his cheek with the coldest dew.

70 The next morning, young Goodman Brown came slowly into the street of Salem village staring around him like a bewildered man. The good old minister was taking a walk along the graveyard to get an appetite for breakfast and meditate his sermon, and bestowed a blessing as he passed on Goodman Brown. He shrank from the venerable saint as if to avoid an anathema. Old Deacon Gookin was at domestic worship, and the holy words of his prayer were heard through the open window. "What God doth the wizard pray to?" quoth Goodman Brown. Goody Cloyse, that excellent old Christian, stood in

the early sunshine at her own lattice catechizing a little girl who had brought her a pint of morning's milk. Goodman Brown snatched away the child as from the grasp of the fiend himself. Turning the corner by the meeting-house, he spied the head of Faith with the pink ribbons gazing anxiously forth, and bursting into such joy at sight of him that she skipped along the street and almost kissed her husband before the whole village. But Goodman Brown looked sternly and sadly into her face and passed on without a greeting.

Had Goodman Brown fallen asleep in the forest and only dreamed a wild dream of a witch-meeting?

Be it so, if you will. But, alas! it was a dream of evil omen for young Goodman Brown. A stern, a sad, a darkly meditative, a distrustful, if not a desperate man did he become from the night of that fearful dream. On the Sabbath-day when the congregation were singing a holy psalm, he could not listen because an anthem of sin rushed loudly upon his ear and drowned all the blessed strain. When the minister spoke from the pulpit with power and fervid eloquence and with his hand on the open Bible, of the sacred truths of our religion, and of saint-like lives and triumphant deaths, and of future bliss or misery unutterable, then did Goodman Brown turn pale, dreading lest the roof should thunder down upon the gray blasphemer and his hearers. Often awaking suddenly at midnight, he shrank from the bosom of Faith, and at morning or eventide when the family knelt down at prayer, he scowled and muttered to himself and gazed sternly at his wife and turned away. And when he had lived long and was borne to his grave a hoary corpse, followed by Faith, an aged woman, and children and grandchildren, a goodly procession, besides neighbors not a few, they carved no hopeful verse upon his tombstone, for his dying hour was gloom.

QUESTIONS

1. During what period in history does the story take place? What does Hawthorne gain by including the names of actual persons (Goody Cloyse, Goody Cory, Deacon Gookin, Martha Carrier) and places (Salem village, Boston, Old South Church)? What religion is practiced by the townspeople?
2. What is the point of view? Where does it change, and what is the result of the change?
3. What allegorical meanings may be given to Goodman Brown? His wife? The forest? Night (as opposed to day)? Brown's journey?
4. What is Brown's motive for going into the forest? What results does he expect from his journey? What does he expect the rest of his life to be like?
5. After he keeps his appointment with the traveler in the forest, Brown announces that he plans to return home. Why does he not do so immediately, and why at each stage when he renews his intention to do so does he proceed deeper into the forest? Is there any reason to suppose he does not actually see and hear what he thinks he perceives?

6. What details of the "witch-meeting" parallel those of a church communion service? Why does the congregation include "grave, reputable, and pious people" as well as known sinners?

7. What prevents Goodman Brown from receiving baptism? What does the devil promise as the result of baptism? Is that what you usually suppose is the reward for selling your soul to the devil? Why is it an appropriate reward for Goodman Brown? Since he does not receive baptism, how do you account for his behavior when he returns to the village?

8. "Had Goodman Brown . . . only dreamed a wild dream of a witch-meeting?" How are we to answer this question? Point out other places where Hawthorne leaves the interpretation of the story ambiguous. How is such ambiguity related to the story's theme?

9. Characterize the behavior of Faith and the other townspeople after Brown's return to the village. Is Brown's attitude and behavior thereafter the result of conviction or doubt? Is he completely misanthropic?

10. Does the story demonstrate the devil's claim that "Evil is the nature of mankind"?

CHAPTER NINE

The Scale of Value

Our purpose in the preceding chapters has been to develop not literary critics but proficient readers — readers who choose wisely and read well. Yet good reading involves criticism, for choice necessitates judgment. Though we need not, to read well, be able to settle the relative claims of Chekhov and Mansfield or of Welty and Faulkner, we do need to discriminate between the genuine and the spurious, the consequential and the trivial, the significant and the merely entertaining. Our first object, naturally, is enjoyment; but full development as human beings requires that we enjoy most what is most worth enjoying.

There are no easy rules for literary judgment. Such judgment depends ultimately on our perceptivity, intelligence, and experience; it is a product of how much and how alertly we have lived and how much and how well we have read. Yet at least two basic principles may be set up. First, *every story is to be initially judged by how fully it achieves its central purpose.* Each element in the story is to be judged by the effectiveness of its contribution to the central purpose. In a good story every element works with every other element for the accomplishment of this central purpose. It follows that no element in the story may be judged in isolation.

Perhaps the most frequent mistake made by inexperienced readers when called upon for a judgment is to judge the elements of the story in isolation, independently of each other. For example, a student once wrote of "I'm a Fool" that it is not a very good story "because it is not written in good English." And certainly the style of the story, if judged by itself, is very poor indeed: the language is slangy and ungrammatical; the sentences are often disjointed and broken-backed; the narrator constantly digresses and is at times so incapable of expressing himself that he can only say "etc., etc., you know." But no high level of discrimination is needed to see that just such a style is essential to the purpose of the story. The uneducated race-track swipe, whose failure in school life has made him feel both scornful and envious of boys who "go to high schools and college," can hardly speak otherwise than as he does here; the digressions, moreover, are not truly digressions, for each of them supplies additional insight into the character of the swipe, which is the true subject of the story. Similarly, the varieties of "substandard" English displayed by the various characters in "Just Like a Tree" enrich rather than diminish the characterizations.

The principle of judgment just applied to style may be applied to every other element in a story. We cannot say that "Miss Brill" is a poor story because it does not have an exciting plot full of action and conflict: plot can only be judged in relation to the other elements in a story and to the story's central purpose, and in this relationship the plot of "Miss Brill" is a good one. We cannot say that "Just Like a Tree" is a poor story because it contains no such complex characterization as is to be found in "Gooseberries." The purpose of "Just Like a Tree" is to demonstrate the variety of human responses to a single event, each springing from an essentially flat characterization.

Every first-rate story is an organic whole. All its parts are related, and all are necessary to the central purpose. Near the beginning of "The Most Dangerous Game" there is a suggestion of theme. When Whitney declares that hunting is a great sport — for hunter, not for the jaguar — Rainsford replies, "Who cares how a jaguar feels? . . . They've no understanding." To this, Whitney counters: "I rather think they understand one thing — fear. The fear of pain and the fear of death." Evidently Rainsford has something to learn about how it feels to be hunted, and presumably during the hunt Rainsford learns it, for when General Zaroff turns back the first time — playing cat and mouse — we are told, "Then it was that Rainsford knew the full meaning of terror." Later, on the morning of the third day, Rainsford is awakened by the baying of hounds — "a sound that made him know that he had new things to learn about fear." But, really, little is made of Rainsford's terror during the hunt. The main interest focuses on Malay mancatchers, Burmese tiger pits, Uganda knife-throwers — in short, on what Zaroff refers to as "Your brain against mine. Your woodcraft against mine. Your strength and stamina against mine. Outdoor chess!" The story ends with the physical triumph of Rainsford over Zaroff. Has Rainsford been altered by the experience? Has he learned anything significant? Has he changed his attitudes toward hunting? We cannot answer, for the author's interest has been elsewhere. What connection has the final sentence — "He had never slept in a better bed, Rainsford decided" — to the question "Who cares how a jaguar feels?"

In "The Storm" we are presented with an experience of mounting terror in a woman who (1) returns to an empty, lonely house during the outbreak of a storm and (2) discovers that her husband is a murderer. There is, of course, no logical connection between the storm and the fact that her husband is a murderer or her discovery of that fact: the coincidence of the storm and the discovery is simply that — a coincidence. This coincidence and the author's manipulation of point of view (her temporary suppression of Janet Willsom's consciousness, in order to prolong suspense, when she sees the body in the trunk and when she recognizes the ring on her husband's finger) are partial clues that the author's purpose is not really to provide insight into human terror so much as to produce terror in the reader. In the light of this purpose, the storm and the discovery of the murder are both justified in the story, for both help to produce terror in the reader. At the same time, their co-presence largely prevents the story from being more meaningful, for what might have been either (1) a study of irrational terror in a woman left alone in an isolated house during a storm or (2) a study of rational terror in a woman who discovers that her husband is a murderer is prevented from being either. Thus "The Storm" is a skillfully written suspense story rather than a story of human insight.

Once a story has been judged successful in achieving its central purpose, we may apply a second principle of judgment. *A story, if successful, may be judged by the significance of its purpose.* If every story is to be judged by how successfully it integrates its materials into an organic unity, it is also to be judged by the extent, the range, and the value of the materials integrated. This principle returns us to our distinction between escape and interpretation. If a story's only aim is to entertain, whether by mystifying, surprising, thrilling, provoking to laughter or tears, or furnishing a substitute dream life, we may judge it of less value than a story whose aim is to *reveal*. "Once Upon a Time," "The Storm," "The Drunkard," and "The Catbird Seat" are all successful stories if we judge them by the degree to which they fulfill their central purpose. But "Once Upon a Time" has a more significant purpose than "The Storm" and "The Drunkard," a more significant purpose than "The Catbird Seat." When a story does provide some revelation — does make some serious statement about life — we may measure it by the breadth and depth of that revelation. "The Drunkard" and "Once Upon a Time" are both fine stories, but "Once Upon a Time" attempts a deeper probing than does "The Drunkard." The situation with which it is concerned is more crucial, cuts deeper. The story reveals a more significant range and depth of life.

Some stories, then, like "The Storm" and "The Catbird Seat" provide good fun and innocent merriment, and even may convey some measure of interpretation along the way. Others, like "The Drunkard" and

"Once Upon a Time" afford the reader a deeper enjoyment through the profounder and more consistent insights they give into life. A third type, like many of the soap operas of television, offers a cheaper and less innocent pleasure by providing escape under the guise of interpretation. Such stories, while professing to present real-life situations and everyday people and happenings, actually, by their shallowness of characterization, their falsifications of plot, their use of stock themes and stock emotions, present us with dangerous oversimplifications and distortions. They seriously misrepresent life and are harmful to the extent that they keep us from a more sensitive, more discriminating response to experience.

The above types of stories do not fall into sharp, distinct categories. There are no fortified barriers running between them to inform us when we are passing from one realm into another. There are no appointed officials to whom we can apply for certain information. Our only passports are our own good judgments, based on our accumulated experience with both literature and life. Nevertheless, certain questions, if asked wisely and with consideration for the two principles developed in this chapter, may help us both to understand the stories we read and to place them with rough accuracy on a scale of value that rises through many gradations from "poor" to "good" to "great." These questions, most of them explored in the previous chapters of this book, are, for convenience, summarized here.

GENERAL QUESTIONS FOR ANALYSIS AND EVALUATION

Plot
1. Who is the protagonist of the story? What are the conflicts? Are they physical, intellectual, moral, or emotional? Is the main conflict between sharply differentiated good and evil, or is it more subtle and complex?
2. Does the plot have unity? Are all the episodes relevant to the total meaning or effect of the story? Does each incident grow logically out of the preceding incident and lead naturally to the next? Is the ending happy, unhappy, or indeterminate? Is it fairly achieved?
3. What use does the story make of chance and coincidence? Are these occurrences used to initiate, to complicate, or to resolve the story? How improbable are they?
4. How is suspense created in the story? Is the interest confined to "What happens next?" or are larger concerns involved? Can you find examples of mystery? Of dilemma?
5. What use does the story make of surprise? Are the surprises achieved fairly? Do they serve a significant purpose? Do they divert the reader's attention from weaknesses in the story?
6. To what extent is this a "formula" story?

Characters

7. What means does the author use to reveal character? Are the characters sufficiently dramatized? What use is made of character contrasts?
8. Are the characters consistent in their actions? Adequately motivated? Plausible? Does the author successfully avoid stock characters?
9. Is each character fully enough developed to justify its role in the story? Are the main characters round or flat?
10. Is any of the characters a developing character? If so, is the change a large or a small one? Is it a plausible change for such a person? Is it sufficiently motivated? Is it given sufficient time?

Theme

11. Does the story have a theme? What is it? Is it implicit or explicit?
12. Does the theme reinforce or oppose popular notions of life? Does it furnish a new insight or refresh or deepen an old one?

Point of View

13. What point of view does the story use? Is it consistent in its use of this point of view? If shifts are made, are they justified?
14. What advantages has the chosen point of view? Does it furnish any clues as to the purpose of the story?
15. If the point of view is that of one of the characters, does this character have any limitations that affect his interpretation of events or persons?
16. Does the author use point of view primarily to reveal or conceal? Is important information known to the focal character ever unfairly withheld?

Symbol and Irony

17. Does the story make use of symbols? If so, do the symbols carry or merely reinforce the meaning of the story?
18. Does the story anywhere utilize irony of situation? Dramatic irony? Verbal irony? What functions do the ironies serve?

Emotion and Humor

19. Does the story aim directly at an emotional *effect*, or is emotion merely its natural by-product?
20. Is the emotion sufficiently dramatized? Is the author anywhere guilty of sentimentality?

Fantasy

21. Does the story employ fantasy? If so, what is the initial assumption? Does the story operate logically from this assumption?
22. Is the fantasy employed for its own sake or to express some human truth? If the latter, what truth?

General

23. Is the primary interest of the story in plot, character, theme, or some other element?
24. What contribution to the story is made by its setting? Is the particular setting essential, or could the story have happened anywhere?
25. What are the characteristics of the author's style? Are they appropriate to the nature of the story?

26. What light is thrown on the story by its title?
27. Do all the elements of the story work together to support a central purpose? Is any part irrelevant or inappropriate?
28. What do you conceive to be the story's central purpose? How fully has it achieved that purpose?
29. Does the story offer chiefly escape or interpretation? How significant is the story's purpose?
30. Does the story gain or lose on a second reading?

EXERCISE

The two stories that follow have a number of plot features in common; in purpose, however, they are quite different. One attempts to reveal certain truths about aspects of human life and succeeds in doing so. The other attempts to do little more than entertain the reader, and, in achieving this end, it falsifies human life. Which story is which? Support your decision by making a thorough analysis of both.

O. Henry
A Municipal Report

> The cities are full of pride,
> Challenging each to each —
> This from her mountainside,
> That from her burthened beach.
> — R. KIPLING

Fancy a novel about Chicago or Buffalo, let us say, or Nashville, Tennessee! There are just three big cities in the United States that are "story cities" — New York, of course, New Orleans, and, best of the lot, San Francisco. — FRANK NORRIS.

East is east°, and west is San Francisco, according to Californians. Californians are a race of people; they are not merely inhabitants of a State. They are the Southerners of the West. Now, Chicagoans are no less loyal to their city; but when you ask them why, they stammer and speak of lake fish and the new Odd Fellows Building. But Californians go into detail.

A MUNICIPAL REPORT   First published in 1909. Rand McNally and Co. (see end of second paragraph), founded in 1856, is a well-known publisher of atlases and gazeteers. The statistical and historical notes about Nashville in the story are such as might be excerpted from one of their books. Generals Hood, Thomas, Sherman, and Longstreet, Fort Sumter and Appomattox, are all names connected with the Civil War, during which, in 1863, the slaves were emancipated. William Sydney Porter (1862–1919), who wrote under the pseudonym O. Henry, was born in North Carolina, but his immensely varied life took him to Texas, Central and South America, Mexico, Ohio, and Pittsburgh, before he arrived in New York City in 1901 to become a writer very much in demand for his short stories.

East is east . . . : cf. Rudyard Kipling's poem "The Ballad of East and West"

Of course they have, in the climate, an argument that is good for half an hour while you are thinking of your coal bills and heavy underwear. But as soon as they come to mistake your silence for conviction, madness comes upon them, and they picture the city of the Golden Gate as the Bagdad of the New World. So far, as a matter of opinion, no refutation is necessary. But dear cousins all (from Adam and Eve descended), it is a rash one who will lay his finger on the map and say "In this town there can be no romance — what could happen here?" Yes, it is a bold and a rash deed to challenge in one sentence history, romance, and Rand and McNally.

Nashville. — A city, port of delivery, and the capital of the State of Tennessee, is on the Cumberland River and on the N.C. & St.L. and the L. & N. railroads. This city is regarded as the most important educational center in the South.

I stepped off the train at 8 P.M. Having searched the thesaurus in vain for adjectives, I must, as a substitution, hie me to comparison in the form of a recipe.

Take of London fog 30 parts; malaria 10 parts; gas leaks 20 parts; dewdrops gathered in a brick yard at sunrise, 25 parts; odor of honeysuckle 15 parts. Mix.

The mixture will give you an approximate conception of a Nashville drizzle. It is not so fragrant as a moth-ball nor as thick as peasoup; but 'tis enough — 'twill serve.°

I went to a hotel in a tumbril. It required strong self-suppression for me to keep from climbing to the top of it and giving an imitation of Sidney Carton.° The vehicle was drawn by beasts of a bygone era and driven by something dark and emancipated.

I was sleepy and tired, so when I got to the hotel I hurriedly paid it the fifty cents it demanded (with approximate lagniappe, I assure you). I knew its habits; and I did not want to hear it prate about its old "marster" or anything that happened "befo' de wah."

The hotel was one of the kind described as "renovated." That means $20,000 worth of new marble pillars, tiling, electric lights and brass cuspidors in the lobby, and a new L. & N. time table and a lithograph of Lookout Mountain in each one of the great rooms above. The management was without reproach, the attention full of exquisite Southern courtesy, the service as slow as the progress of a snail and as good-humored as Rip Van Winkle. The food was worth traveling a thousand miles for. There is no other hotel in the world where you can get such chicken livers *en brochette*.

At dinner I asked a Negro waiter if there was anything doing in town. He pondered gravely for a minute, and then replied: "Well, boss, I don't really reckon there's anything at all doin' after sundown."

not so fragrant . . . 'twill serve: cf. Mercutio's dying speech, *Romeo and Juliet*, 3.1. 99–100 **Sidney Carton:** a dissipated character who dies nobly on the guillotine in Dickens's novel *A Tale of Two Cities*

Sundown had been accomplished: it had been drowned in drizzle long before. So that spectacle was denied me. But I went forth upon the streets in the drizzle to see what might be there.

It is built on undulating grounds; and the streets are lighted by electricity at a cost of $32,470 per annum.

As I left the hotel there was a race riot. Down upon me charged a company of freedmen, or Arabs, or Zulus, armed with — no, I saw with relief that they were not rifles, but whips. And I saw dimly a caravan of black, clumsy vehicles; and at the reassuring shouts, "Kyar you anywhere in the town, boss, fuh fifty cents," I reasoned that I was merely a "fare" instead of a victim.

I walked through long streets, all leading uphill. I wondered how those streets ever came down again. Perhaps they didn't until they were "graded." On a few of the "main streets" I saw lights in stores here and there; saw street cars go by conveying worthy burghers hither and yon; saw people pass engaged in the art of conversation, and heard a burst of semi-lively laughter issuing from a soda-water and ice-cream parlor. The streets other than "main" seemed to have enticed upon their borders houses consecrated to peace and domesticity. In many of them lights shone behind discreetly drawn window shades, in a few pianos tinkled orderly and irreproachable music. There was indeed, little "doing." I wished I had come before sundown. So I returned to my hotel.

15 *In November, 1864, the Confederate General Hood advanced against* 15
Nashville, where he shut up a National force under General Thomas. The latter then sallied forth and defeated the Confederates in a terrible conflict.

All my life I have heard of, admired, and witnessed the fine marksmanship of the South in its peaceful conflicts in the tobacco-chewing regions. But in my hotel a surprise awaited me. There were twelve bright, new, imposing, capacious brass cuspidors in the great lobby, tall enough to be called urns and so wide-mouthed that the crack pitcher of a lady baseball team should have been able to throw a ball into one of them at five paces distant. But, although a terrible battle had raged and was still raging, the enemy had not suffered. Bright, new, imposing, capacious, untouched, they stood. But, shades of Jefferson Brick!° the tile floor — the beautiful tile floor! I could not avoid thinking of the battle of Nashville, and trying to draw, as is my foolish habit, some deductions about hereditary marksmanship.

Here I first saw Major (by misplaced courtesy) Wentworth Caswell. I knew him for a type the moment my eyes suffered from the sight of him. A

Jefferson Brick: an American journalist, "unwholesomely pale" from "excessive use of [chewing] tobacco" in Dickens's novel *Martin Chuzzlewit*

rat has no geographical habitat. My old friend, A. Tennyson,° said, as he so well said almost everything:

> *Prophet, curse me the blabbing lip,*
> *And curse me the British vermin, the rat.*

Let us regard the word "British" as interchangeable *ad lib*. A rat is a rat. This man was hunting about the hotel lobby like a starved dog that had forgotten where he had buried a bone. He had a face of great acreage, red, pulpy, and with a kind of sleepy massiveness like that of Buddha. He possessed one single virtue—he was very smoothly shaven. The mark of the beast is not indelible upon a man until he goes about with a stubble. I think that if he had not used his razor that day I would have repulsed his advances, and the criminal calendar of the world would have been spared the addition of one murder.

I happened to be standing within five feet of a cuspidor when Major Caswell opened fire upon it. I had been observant enough to perceive that the attacking force was using Gatlings instead of squirrel rifles, so I sidestepped so promptly that the major seized the opportunity to apologize to a noncombatant. He had the blabbing lip. In four minutes he had become my friend and had dragged me to the bar.

I desire to interpolate here that I am a Southerner. But I am not one by profession or trade. I eschew the string tie, the slouch hat, the Prince Albert, the number of bales of cotton destroyed by Sherman, and plug chewing. When the orchestra plays "Dixie" I do not cheer. I slide a little lower on the leather-cornered seat and, well, order another Würzburger and wish that Longstreet had—but what's the use?

Major Caswell banged the bar with his fist, and the first gun at Fort Sumter re-echoed. When he fired the last one at Appomattox I began to hope. But then he began on family trees, and demonstrated that Adam was only a third cousin of a collateral branch of the Caswell family. Genealogy disposed of, he took up, to my distaste, his private family matters. He spoke of his wife, traced her descent back to Eve, and profanely denied any possible rumor that she may have had relations in the land of Nod.°

By this time I began to suspect that he was trying to obscure by noise the fact that he had ordered the drinks, on the chance that I would be bewildered into paying for them. But when they were down he crashed a silver dollar loudly upon the bar. Then, of course, another serving was obligatory. And when I had paid for that I took leave of him brusquely; for I wanted no more of him. But before I had obtained my release he had prated loudly of an income that his wife received, and showed a handful of silver money.

When I got my key at the desk the clerk said to me courteously: "If that man Caswell has annoyed you, and if you would like to make a complaint, we

---

A. Tennyson: The quoted lines are from Tennyson's *Maud*, Part 2. 5. 6   **land of Nod:** where Cain, the exiled son of Adam and Eve, found a wife (Genesis 4. 16ff.)

will have him ejected. He is a nuisance, a loafer, and without any known means of support, although he seems to have some money most of the time. But we don't seem to be able to hit upon any means of throwing him out legally."

25   "Why, no," said I, after some reflection; "I don't see my way clear to making a complaint. But I would like to place myself on record as asserting that I do not care for his company. Your town," I continued, "seems to be a quiet one. What manner of entertainment, adventure, or excitement, have you to offer to the stranger within your gates?"°

"Well, sir," said the clerk, "there will be a show here next Thursday. It is — I'll look it up and have the announcement sent up to your room with the ice water. Good-night."

After I went up to my room I looked out the window. It was only about ten o'clock, but I looked upon a silent town. The drizzle continued, spangled with dim lights, as far apart as currants in a cake sold at the Ladies' Exchange.

"A quiet place," I said to myself, as my first shoe struck the ceiling of the occupant of the room beneath mine. "Nothing of the life here that gives color and good variety to the cities in the East and West. Just a good, ordinary, humdrum, business town."

Nashville occupies a foremost place among the manufacturing centers of the country. It is the fifth boot and shoe market in the United States, the largest candy and cracker manufacturing city in the South, and does an enormous wholesale drygoods, grocery, and drug business.

30   I must tell you how I came to be in Nashville, and I assure you the digression brings as much tedium to me as it does to you. I was traveling elsewhere on my own business, but I had a commission from a Northern literary magazine to stop over there and establish a personal connection between the publication and one of its contributors, Azalea Adair.

Adair (there was no clue to the personality except the handwriting) had sent in some essays (lost art!) and poems that had made the editors swear approvingly over their one o'clock luncheon. So they had commissioned me to round up said Adair and corner by contract his or her output at two cents a word before some other publisher offered her ten or twenty.

At nine o'clock the next morning, after my chicken livers *en brochette* (try them if you can find that hotel), I strayed out into the drizzle, which was still on for an unlimited run. At the first corner I came upon Uncle Caesar. He was a stalwart Negro, older than the pyramids, with gray wool and a face that reminded me of Brutus,° and a second afterwards of the late King Cettiwayo.° He wore the most remarkable coat that I ever had seen or expect to

stranger within your gates: cf. Exodus 20.10   **Brutus:** tragic hero of Shakespeare's *Julius Caesar*   **King Cettiwayo:** king of the Zulus (1872–1884)

see. It reached to his ankles and had once been a confederate gray in color. But rain and sun and age had so variegated it that Joseph's coat,° beside it, would have faded to a pale monochrome. I must linger with that coat, for it has to do with the story — the story that is so long in coming, because you can hardly expect anything to happen in Nashville.

Once it must have been the military coat of an officer. The cape of it had vanished, but all adown its front it had been frogged and tasseled magnificently. But now the frogs and tassels were gone. In their stead had been patiently stitched (I surmised by some surviving "black mammy") new frogs made of cunningly twisted common hempen twine. This twine was frayed and disheveled. It must have been added to the coat as a substitute for vanished splendors, with tasteless but painstaking devotion, for it followed faithfully the curves of the long-missing frogs. And, to complete the comedy and pathos of the garment, all its buttons were gone save one. The second button from the top alone remained. The coat was fastened by other twine strings tied through the buttonholes and other holes rudely pierced in the opposite side. There was never such a weird garment so fantastically bedecked and of so many mottled hues. The lone button was the size of a half-dollar, made of yellow horn and sewed on with coarse twine.

This Negro stood by a carriage so old that Ham° himself might have started a hack line with it after he left the ark with the two animals hitched to it. As I approached he threw open the door, drew out a feather duster, waved it without using it, and said in deep, rumbling tones:

"Step right in, suh; ain't a speck of dust in it — jus' got back from a funeral, suh." 35

I inferred that on such gala occasions carriages were given an extra cleaning. I looked up and down the street and perceived that there was little choice among the vehicles for hire that lined the curb. I looked in my memorandum book for the address of Azalea Adair.

"I want to go to 861 Jessamine Street," I said, and was about to step into the hack. But for an instant the thick, long, gorilla-like arm of the Negro barred me. On his massive and saturnine face a look of sudden suspicion and enmity flashed for a moment. Then, with quickly returning conviction, he asked, blandishingly: "What are you gwine there for, boss?"

"What is that to you?" I asked, a little sharply.

"Nothin', suh, jus' nothin'. Only it's a lonesome kind of part of town and few folks ever has business out there. Step right in. The seats is clean — jus' got back from a funeral, suh."

A mile and a half it must have been to our journey's end. I could hear 40 nothing but the fearful rattle of the ancient hack over the uneven brick paving; I could smell nothing but the drizzle, now further flavored with coal smoke and something like a mixture of tar and oleander blossoms.

Joseph's coat: cf. Genesis 37   **Ham:** son of Noah who, according to tradition, settled in Africa and was the ancestor of the black races

All I could see through the streaming windows were two rows of dim houses.

The city has an area of 10 square miles; 181 miles of streets, of which 137 miles are paved; a system of waterworks that cost $2,000,000, with 77 miles of mains.

Eight-six-one Jessamine Street was a decayed mansion. Thirty yards back from the street it stood, outmerged in a splendid grove of trees and untrimmed shrubbery. A row of box bushes overflowed and almost hid the paling fence from sight; the gate was kept closed by a rope noose that encircled the gate post and the first paling of the gate. But when you got inside you saw that 861 was a shell, a shadow, a ghost of former grandeur and excellence. But in the story, I have not yet got inside.

When the hack had ceased from rattling and the weary quadrupeds came to a rest I handed my jehu° his fifty cents with an additional quarter, feeling a glow of conscious generosity as I did so. He refused it.

"It's two dollars, suh," he said.

45   "How's that?" I asked, "I plainly heard you call at the hotel. 'Fifty cents to any part of town.'"

"It's two dollars, suh," he repeated obstinately. "It's a long ways from the hotel."

"It is within the city limits and well within them," I argued. "Don't think that you have picked up a greenhorn Yankee. Do you see those hills over there?" I went on, pointing toward the east (I could not see them, myself, for the drizzle); "well, I was born and raised on their other side. You old fool nigger, can't you tell people from other people when you see 'em?"

The grim face of King Cettiwayo softened. "Is you from the South, suh? I reckon it was them shoes of yourn' fooled me. They is somethin' sharp in the toes for a Southern gen'l'man to wear."

"Then the charge is fifty cents, I suppose?" said I, inexorably.

50   His former expression, a mingling of cupidity and hostility, returned, remained ten seconds, and vanished.

"Boss," he said, "fifty cents is right; but I *needs* two dollars, suh; I'm *obleeged* to have two dollars. I ain't *demandin'* it now, suh; after I knows whar you's from; I'm jus' sayin' that I *has* to have two dollars to-night and business is mighty po'."

Peace and confidence settled upon his heavy features. He had been luckier than he had hoped. Instead of having picked up a greenhorn, ignorant of rates, he had come upon an inheritance.

"You confounded old rascal," I said, reaching down to my pocket, "you ought to be turned over to the police."

For the first time I saw him smile. He knew; *he knew;* HE KNEW.

jehu: a fast driver (cf. 2 Kings 9.20)

I gave him two one-dollar bills. As I handed them over I noticed that one ⁵⁵ of them had seen parlous times. Its upper right-hand corner was missing and it had been torn through in the middle, but joined again. A strip of blue tissue paper, pasted over the split, preserved its negotiability.

Enough of the African bandit for the present: I left him happy, lifted the rope, and opened the creaky gate.

The house, as I said, was a shell. A paint brush had not touched it in twenty years. I could not see why a strong wind should not have bowled it over like a house of cards until I looked again at the trees that hugged it close — the trees that saw the battle of Nashville and still drew their protecting branches around it against storm and enemy and cold.

Azalea Adair, fifty years old, white-haired, a descendant of the cavaliers, as thin and frail as the house she lived in, robed in the cheapest and cleanest dress I ever saw, with an air as simple as a queen's, received me.

The reception room seemed a mile square, because there was nothing in it except some rows of books on unpainted white-pine bookshelves, a cracked marble-topped table, a rag rug, a hairless horsehair sofa, and two or three chairs. Yes, there was a picture on the wall, a colored crayon drawing of a cluster of pansies. I looked around for the portrait of Andrew Jackson and the pine-cone hanging basket but they were not there.

Azalea Adair and I had conversation, a little of which will be repeated to ⁶⁰ you. She was a product of the old South, gently nurtured in the sheltered life. Her learning was not broad, but was deep and of splendid originality in its somewhat narrow scope. She had been educated at home, and her knowledge of the world was derived from inference and by inspiration. Of such is the precious, small group of essayists made. While she talked to me I kept brushing my fingers, trying, unconsciously, to rid them guiltily of the absent dust from the half-calf backs of Lamb, Chaucer, Hazlitt, Marcus Aurelius, Montaigne, and Hood. She was exquisite, she was a valuable discovery. Nearly everybody nowadays knows too much — oh, so much too much — of real life.

I could perceive clearly that Azalea Adair was very poor. A house and a dress she had, not much else, I fancied. So, divided between my duty to the magazine and my loyalty to the poets and essayists who fought Thomas in the valley of the Cumberland, I listened to her voice which was like a harpsichord's and found that I could not speak of contracts. In the presence of the nine Muses and the three Graces one hesitated to lower the topic to two cents. There would have to be another colloquy after I had regained my commercialism. But I spoke of my mission, and three o'clock of the next afternoon was set for the discussion of the business proposition.

"Your town," I said, as I began to make ready to depart (which is the time for smooth generalities), "seems to be a quiet, sedate place. A home town, I should say, where few things out of the ordinary ever happen."

It carries on an extensive trade in stoves and hollow ware with the West and South, and its flouring mills have a daily capacity of more than 2,000 barrels.

Azaela Adair seemed to reflect.

"I have never thought of it that way," she said, with a kind of sincere intensity that seemed to belong to her. "Isn't it in the still, quiet places that things do happen? I fancy that when God began to create the earth on the first Monday morning one could have leaned out one's window and heard the drops of mud splashing from His trowel as He built up the everlasting hills. What did the noisiest project in the world — I mean the building of the tower of Babel — result in finally? A page and a half of Esperanto in the *North American Review*."

"Of course," said I, platitudinously, "human nature is the same everywhere; but there is more color — er — more drama and movement and — er — romance in some cities than in others."

"On the surface," said Azalea Adair. "I have traveled many times around the world in a golden airship wafted on two wings — print and dreams. I have seen (on one of my imaginary tours) the Sultan of Turkey bowstring° with his own hands one of his wives who had uncovered her face in public. I have seen a man in Nashville tear up his theater tickets because his wife was going out with her face covered — with rice powder. In San Francisco's Chinatown I saw the slave girl Sing Yee dipped slowly, inch by inch, in boiling almond oil to make her swear she would never see her American lover again. She gave in when the boiling oil had reached three inches above her knees. At a euchre party in East Nashville the other night I saw Kitty Morgan cut dead by seven of her schoolmates and lifelong friends because she had married a house painter. The boiling oil was sizzling as high as her heart; but I wish you could have seen the fine little smile that she carried from table to table. Oh, yes, it is a humdrum town. Just a few miles of red brick houses and mud and stores and lumber yards."

Someone had knocked hollowly at the back of the house. Azalea Adair breathed a soft apology and went to investigate the sound. She came back in three minutes with brightened eyes, a faint flush on her cheeks, and ten years lifted from her shoulders.

"You must have a cup of tea before you go," she said, "and a sugar cake."

She reached and shook a little iron bell. In shuffled a small Negro girl about twelve, barefoot, not very tidy, glowering at me with thumb in mouth and bulging eyes.

Azalea Adair opened a tiny, worn purse and drew out a dollar bill, a dollar bill with the upper right-hand corner missing, torn in two pieces and pasted together again with a strip of blue tissue paper. It was one of those bills I had given the piratical Negro — there was no doubt of it.

"Go up to Mr. Baker's store on the corner, Impy," she said, handing the girl the dollar bill, "and get a quarter pound of tea — the kind he always sends me — and ten cents' worth of sugar cakes. Now, hurry. The supply of tea in the house happens to be exhausted," she explained to me.

bowstring: strangle with a bowstring

Impy left by the back way. Before the scrape of her hard, bare feet had died away on the back porch, a wild shriek — I was sure it was hers — filled the hollow house. Then the deep, gruff tones of an angry man's voice mingled with the girl's further squeals and unintelligible words.

Azalea Adair rose without surprise or emotion and disappeared. For two minutes I heard the hoarse rumble of the man's voice; then something like an oath and a slight scuffle, and she returned calmly to her chair.

"This is a roomy house," she said, "and I have a tenant for part of it. I am sorry to have to rescind my invitation to tea. It is impossible to get the kind I always use at the store. Perhaps tomorrow Mr. Baker will be able to supply me." 75

I was sure that Impy had not had time to leave the house. I inquired concerning street-car lines and took my leave. After I was well on my way I remembered that I had not learned Azalea Adair's name. But tomorrow would do.

The same day I started in on the course of iniquity that this uneventful city forced upon me. I was in the town only two days, but in that time I managed to lie shamelessly by telegraph, and to be an accomplice — after the fact, if that is the correct legal term — to a murder.

As I rounded the corner nearest my hotel the Afrite coachman of the polychromatic, nonpareil coat seized me, swung open the dungeony door of his peripatetic sarcophagus, flirted his feather duster and began his ritual: "Step right in, boss. Carriage is clean — jus' got back from a funeral. Fifty cents to any — "

And then he knew me and grinned broadly. "'Scuse me, boss; you is de gen'l'man what rid out with me dis mawnin'.' Thank you kindly, suh."

"I am going out to 861 again to-morrow afternoon at three," said I, "and if you will be here, I'll let you drive me. So you know Miss Adair?" I concluded, thinking of my dollar bill. 80

"I belonged to her father, Judge Adair, suh," he replied.

"I judge that she is pretty poor," I said. "She hasn't much money to speak of, has she?"

For an instant I looked again at the fierce countenance of King Cettiwayo, and then he changed back to an extortionate old Negro hack driver.

"She ain't gwine to starve, suh," he said. "She has reso'ces, suh; she has reso'ces."

"I shall pay you fifty cents for the trip," said I. 85

"Dat is puffeckly correct, suh," he answered, humbly. "I just *had* to have dat two dollars dis mawnin', boss."

I went to the hotel and lied by electricity. I wired the magazine: "A. Adair holds out for eight cents a word."

The answer that came back was: "Give it to her quick, you duffer."

Just before dinner "Major" Wentworth Caswell bore down upon me with greetings of a long-lost friend. I have seen few men whom I have so instantaneously hated, and of whom it was so difficult to be rid. I was standing at the bar when he invaded me; therefore I could not wave the white ribbon in his face. I would have paid gladly for the drinks, hoping thereby to escape another; but he was one of those despicable, roaring, advertising bibbers who must have brass bands and fireworks attend upon every cent that they waste in their follies.

With an air of producing millions he drew two one-dollar bills from a pocket and dashed one of them upon the bar. I looked once more at the dollar bill with the upper right-hand corner missing, torn through the middle, and patched with a strip of blue tissue paper. It was my dollar again. It could have been no other.

I went up to my room. The drizzle and the monotony of a dreary, eventless Southern town had made me tired and listless. I remember that just before I went to bed I mentally disposed of the mysterious dollar bill (which might have formed the clue to a tremendously fine detective story of San Francisco) by saying to myself sleepily: "Seems as if a lot of people here own stock in the Hack-Drivers' Trust. Pays dividends promptly, too. Wonder if—" Then I fell asleep.

King Cettiwayo was at his post the next day, and rattled my bones over the stones out to 861. He was to wait and rattle me back again when I was ready.

Azalea Adair looked paler and cleaner and frailer than she had looked on the day before. After she had signed the contract at eight cents per word she grew still paler and began to slip out of her chair. Without much trouble I managed to get her up on the antediluvian horsehair sofa and then I ran out to the sidewalk and yelled to the coffee-colored Pirate to bring a doctor. With a wisdom that I had not suspected in him, he abandoned his team and struck off up the street afoot, realizing the value of speed. In ten minutes he returned with a grave, gray-haired, and capable man of medicine. In a few words (worth much less than eight cents each) I explained to him my presence in the hollow house of mystery. He bowed with stately understanding, and turned to the old Negro.

"Uncle Caesar," he said, calmly, "run up to my house and ask Miss Lucy to give you a cream pitcher full of fresh milk and half a tumbler of port wine. And hurry back. Don't drive—run. I want you to get back sometime this week."

It occurred to me that Dr. Merriman also felt a distrust as to the speeding powers of the land-pirate's steeds. After Uncle Caesar was gone, lumberingly, but swiftly, up the street, the doctor looked me over with great politeness and as much careful calculation until he had decided that I might do.

"It is only a case of insufficient nutrition," he said. "In other words, the result of poverty, pride, and starvation. Mrs. Caswell has many devoted friends who would be glad to aid her, but she will accept nothing except from that old Negro, Uncle Caesar, who was once owned by her family."

"Mrs. Caswell!" said I, in surprise. And then I looked at the contract and saw that she had signed it "Azalea Adair Caswell."

"I thought she was Miss Adair," I said.

"Married to a drunken, worthless loafer, sir," said the doctor. "It is said that he robs her even of the small sums that her old servant contributes toward her support."

When the milk and wine had been brought the doctor soon revived Azalea Adair. She sat up and talked of the beauty of the autumn leaves that were then in season and their height of color. She referred lightly to her fainting seizure as the outcome of an old palpitation of her heart. Impy fanned her as she lay on the sofa. The doctor was due elsewhere, and I followed him to the door. I told him that it was within my power and intentions to make a reasonable advance of money to Azalea Adair on future contributions to the magazine, and he seemed pleased.

"By the way," he said, "perhaps you would like to know that you have had royalty for a coachman. Old Caesar's grandfather was a king in Congo. Caesar himself has royal ways, as you may have observed."

As the doctor was moving off I heard Uncle Caesar's voice inside: "Did he get bofe of dem two dollars from you, Mis' Zalea?"

"Yes, Caesar," I heard Azalea Adair answer, weakly. And then I went in and concluded business negotiations with our contributor. I assumed the responsibility of advancing fifty dollars, putting it as a necessary formality in binding our bargin. And then Uncle Caesar drove me back to the hotel.

Here ends all of the story as far as I can witness. The rest must be only bare statements of facts.

At about six o'clock I went out for a stroll. Uncle Caesar was at his corner. He threw open the door of his carriage, flourished his duster, and began his depressing formula: "Step right in, suh. Fifty cents to anywhere in the city — hack's puffickly clean, suh — jus' got back from a funeral — "

And then he recognized me. I think his eyesight was getting bad. His coat had taken on a few more faded shades of color, the twine strings were more frayed and ragged, the last remaining button — the button of yellow horn — was gone. A motley descendant of kings was Uncle Caesar!

About two hours later I saw an excited crowd besieging the front of the drug store. In a desert where nothing happens this was manna; so I wedged my way inside. On an extemporized couch of empty boxes and chairs was stretched the mortal corporeality of Major Wentworth Caswell. A doctor was testing him for the mortal ingredient. His decision was that it was conspicuous by its absence.

The erstwhile Major had been found dead on a dark street and brought by curious and ennuied citizens to the drug store. The late human being had been engaged in terrific battle — the details showed that. Loafer and reprobate though he had been, he had been also a warrior. But he had lost. His hands were yet clinched so tightly that his fingers could not be opened. The gentle citizens who had known him stood about and searched their vocabularies to find some good words, if it were possible, to speak of him. One kindlooking man said, after much thought: "When 'Cas' was about fo'teen he was one of the best spellers in the school."

While I stood there the fingers of the right hand of "the man that was," which hung down the side of a white pine box, relaxed, and dropped something at my feet. I covered it with one foot quietly, and a little later on I picked it up and pocketed it. I reasoned that in his last struggle his hand must have seized that object unwittingly and held it in a death grip.

110   At the hotel that night the main topic of conversation, with the possible exceptions of politics and prohibition, was the demise of Major Caswell. I heard one man say to a group of listeners:

"In my opinion, gentlemen, Caswell was murdered by some of these no-account niggers for his money. He had fifty dollars this afternoon which he showed to several gentlemen in the hotel. When he was found the money was not on his person."

I left the city the next morning at nine, and as the train was crossing the bridge over the Cumberland River I took out of my pocket a yellow horn overcoat button the size of a fifty-cent piece, with frayed ends of coarse twine hanging from it, and cast it out of the window into the slow, muddy waters below.

I wonder what's doing in Buffalo!

Susan Glaspell
A Jury of Her Peers

When Martha Hale opened the storm-door and got a cut of the north wind, she ran back for her big woolen scarf. As she hurriedly wound that round her head her eye made a scandalized sweep of her kitchen. It was no ordinary thing that called her away—it was probably farther from ordinary than anything that had ever happened in Dickson County. But what her eye took in was that her kitchen was in no shape for leaving: her bread all ready for mixing, half the flour sifted and half unsifted.

She hated to see things half done; but she had been at that when the team from town stopped to get Mr. Hale, and then the sheriff came running in to say his wife wished Mrs. Hale would come too—adding, with a grin, that he guessed she was getting scarey and wanted another woman along. So she had dropped everything right where it was.

"Martha!" now came her husband's impatient voice. "Don't keep folks waiting out here in the cold."

She again opened the storm-door, and this time joined the three men and the one woman waiting for her in the big two-seated buggy.

A JURY OF HER PEERS First published in 1917, the story is based on the author's one-act play *Trifles*, written in 1916 for the Provincetown Players. Susan Glaspell (1882–1948) lived for the first thirty-two years of her life in Iowa. She has said that *Trifles* (and hence this short story) was suggested to her by an experience she had while working for a Des Moines newspaper.

After she had the robes tucked around her she took another look at the woman who sat beside her on the back seat. She had met Mrs. Peters the year before at the county fair, and the thing she remembered about her was that she didn't seem like a sheriff's wife. She was small and thin and didn't have a strong voice. Mrs. Gorman, sheriff's wife before Gorman went out and Peters came in, had a voice that somehow seemed to be backing up the law with every word. But if Mrs. Peters didn't look like a sheriff's wife, Peters made it up in looking like a sheriff. He was to a dot the kind of man who could get himself elected sheriff—a heavy man with a big voice, who was particularly genial with the law-abiding, as if to make it plain that he knew the difference between criminals and non-criminals. And right there it came into Mrs. Hale's mind, with a stab, that this man who was so pleasant and lively with all of them was going to the Wrights' now as a sheriff.

"The country's not very pleasant this time of year," Mrs. Peters at last ventured, as if she felt they ought to be talking as well as the men.

Mrs. Hale scarcely finished her reply, for they had gone up a little hill and could see the Wright place now, and seeing it did not make her feel like talking. It looked very lonesome this cold March morning. It had always been a lonesome-looking place. It was down in a hollow, and the poplar trees around it were lonesome-looking trees. The men were looking at it and talking about what had happened. The county attorney was bending to one side of the buggy, and kept looking steadily at the place as they drew up to it.

"I'm glad you came with me," Mrs. Peters said nervously, as the two women were about to follow the men in through the kitchen door.

Even after she had her foot on the door-step, her hand on the knob, Martha Hale had a moment of feeling she could not cross the threshold. And the reason it seemed she couldn't cross it now was simply because she hadn't crossed it before. Time and time again it had been in her mind, "I ought to go over and see Minnie Foster"—she still thought of her as Minnie Foster, though for twenty years she had been Mrs. Wright. And then there was always something to do and Minnie Foster would go from her mind. But *now* she could come.

The men went over to the stove. The women stood close together by the door. Young Henderson, the county attorney, turned around and said, "Come up to the fire, ladies."

Mrs. Peters took a step forward, then stopped. "I'm not—cold," she said.

And so the two women stood by the door, at first not even so much as looking around the kitchen.

The men talked for a minute about what a good thing it was the sheriff had sent his deputy out that morning to make a fire for them, and then Sheriff Peters stepped back from the stove, unbuttoned his outer coat, and leaned his hands on the kitchen table in a way that seemed to mark the beginning of official business. "Now, Mr. Hale," he said in a sort of semiofficial voice, "before we move things about, you tell Mr. Henderson just what it was you saw when you came here yesterday morning."

The county attorney was looking around the kitchen.

15 "By the way," he said, "has anything been moved?" He turned to the sheriff. "Are things just as you left them yesterday?"

Peters looked from cupboard to sink; from that to a small worn rocker a little to one side of the kitchen table.

"It's just the same."

"Somebody should have been left here yesterday," said the county attorney.

"Oh — yesterday," returned the sheriff, with a little gesture as of yesterday having been more than he could bear to think of. "When I had to send Frank to Morris Center for that man who went crazy — let me tell you, I had my hands full *yesterday*. I knew you could get back from Omaha by today, George, and as long as I went over everything here myself — "

20 "Well, Mr. Hale," said the county attorney, in a way of letting what was past and gone go, "tell just what happened when you came here yesterday morning."

Mrs. Hale, still leaning against the door, had that sinking feeling of the mother whose child is about to speak a piece. Lewis often wandered along and got things mixed up in a story. She hoped he would tell this straight and plain, and not say unnecessary things that would just make things harder for Minnie Foster. He didn't begin at once, and she noticed that he looked queer — as if standing in that kitchen and having to tell what he had seen there yesterday morning made him almost sick.

"Yes, Mr. Hale?" the county attorney reminded.

"Harry and I had started to town with a load of potatoes," Mrs. Hale's husband began.

Harry was Mrs. Hale's oldest boy. He wasn't with them now, for the very good reason that those potatoes never got to town yesterday and he was taking them this morning, so he hadn't been home when the sheriff stopped to say he wanted Mr. Hale to come over to the Wright place and tell the county attorney his story there, where he could point it all out. With all Mrs. Hale's other emotions came the fear that maybe Harry wasn't dressed warm enough — they hadn't any of them realized how that north wind did bite.

25 "We come along this road," Hale was going on, with a motion of his hand to the road over which they had just come, "and as we got in sight of the house I says to Harry, 'I'm goin' to see if I can't get John Wright to take a telephone.' You see," he explained to Henderson, "unless I can get somebody to go in with me they won't come out this branch road except for a price *I* can't pay. I'd spoke to Wright about it once before; but he put me off, saying folks talked too much anyway, and all he asked was peace and quiet — guess you know about how much he talked himself. But I thought maybe if I went to the house and talked about it before his wife, and said all the women-folks liked the telephones, and that in this lonesome stretch of road it would

be a good thing — well, I said to Harry that that was what I was going to say — though I said at the same time that I didn't know as what his wife wanted made much difference to John — "

Now, there he was! — saying things he didn't need to say. Mrs. Hale tried to catch her husband's eye, but fortunately the county attorney interrupted with:

"Let's talk about that a little later, Mr. Hale. I do want to talk about that, but I'm anxious now to get along to just what happened when you got here."

When he began this time, it was very deliberately and carefully:

"I didn't see or hear anything. I knocked at the door. And still it was all quiet inside. I knew they must be up — it was past eight o'clock. So I knocked again, louder, and I thought I heard somebody say 'Come in.' I wasn't sure — I'm not sure yet. But I opened the door — this door," jerking a hand toward the door by which the two women stood, "and there, in that rocker" — pointing to it — "sat Mrs. Wright."

Every one in the kitchen looked at the rocker. It came into Mrs. Hale's mind that that rocker didn't look in the least like Minnie Foster — the Minnie Foster of twenty years before. It was a dingy red, with wooden rungs up the back, and the middle rung was gone, and the chair sagged to one side.

"How did she — look?" the county attorney was inquiring.

"Well," said Hale, "she looked — queer."

"How do you mean — queer?"

As he asked it he took out a note-book and pencil. Mrs. Hale did not like the sight of that pencil. She kept her eye fixed on her husband, as if to keep him from saying unnecessary things that would go into that note-book and make trouble.

Hale did speak guardedly, as if the pencil had affected him too.

"Well, as if she didn't know what she was going to do next. And kind of — done up."

"How did she seem to feel about your coming?"

"Why, I don't think she minded — one way or other. She didn't pay much attention. I said, 'Ho' do, Mrs. Wright? It's cold, ain't it?' And she said, 'Is it?' — and went on pleatin' at her apron.

"Well, I was surprised. She didn't ask me to come up to the stove, or to sit down, but just set there, not even lookin' at me. And so I said: 'I want to see John.'

"And then she — laughed. I guess you would call it a laugh.

"I thought of Harry and the team outside, so I said, a little sharp, 'Can I see John?' 'No,' says she — kind of dull like. 'Ain't he home?' says I. Then she looked at me. 'Yes,' says she, 'he's home.' 'Then why can't I see him?' I asked her, out of patience with her now. ''Cause he's dead,' says she, just as quiet and dull — and fell to pleatin' her apron. 'Dead?' says I, like you do when you can't take in what you've heard.

"She just nodded her head, not getting a bit excited, but rockin' back and forth.

"'Why — where is he?' says I, not knowing *what* to say.

"She just pointed upstairs — like this" — pointing to the room above.

"I got up, with the idea of going up there myself. By this time I — didn't know what to do. I walked from there to here; then I says: 'Why, what did he die of?'

"'He died of a rope around his neck,' says she; and just went on pleatin' at her apron."

Hale stopped speaking, and stood staring at the rocker, as if he were still seeing the woman who had sat there the morning before. Nobody spoke; it was as if every one were seeing the woman who had sat there the morning before.

"And what did you do then?" the county attorney at last broke the silence.

"I went out and called Harry. I thought I might — need help. I got Harry in, and we went upstairs." His voice fell almost to a whisper. "There he was — lying over the — "

"I think I'd rather have you go into that upstairs," the county attorney interrupted, "where you can point it all out. Just go on now with the rest of the story."

"Well, my first thought was to get that rope off. It looked — "

He stopped, his face twitching.

"But Harry, he went up to him, and he said, 'No, he's dead all right, and we'd better not touch anything.' So we went downstairs.

"She was still sitting that same way. 'Has anybody been notified?' I asked. 'No,' says she, unconcerned."

"'Who did this, Mrs. Wright?' said Harry. He said it business-like, and she stopped pleatin' at her apron. 'I don't know,' she says. 'You don't *know?*' says Harry. 'Weren't you sleepin' in the bed with him?' 'Yes,' says she, 'but I was on the inside.' 'Somebody slipped a rope round his neck and strangled him, and you didn't wake up?' says Harry. 'I didn't wake up,' she said after him.

"We may have looked as if we didn't see how that could be, for after a minute she said, 'I sleep sound.'

"Harry was going to ask her more questions, but I said maybe that weren't our business; maybe we ought to let her tell her story first to the coroner or the sheriff. So Harry went fast as he could over to High Road — the Rivers's place, where there's a telephone."

"And what did she do when she knew you had gone for the coroner?" The attorney got his pencil in his hand all ready for writing.

"She moved from that chair to this one over here" — Hale pointed to a small chair in the corner — "and just sat there with her hands held together and looking down. I got a feeling that I ought to make some conversation, so I said I had come in to see if John wanted to put in a telephone; and at that she started to laugh, and then she stopped and looked at me — scared."

At the sound of a moving pencil the man who was telling the story looked up.

"I dunno — maybe it wasn't scared," he hastened; "I wouldn't like to say it was. Soon Harry got back, and then Dr. Lloyd came, and you, Mr. Peters, and so I guess that's all I know that you don't."

He said that last with relief, and moved a little, as if relaxing. Every one moved a little. The county attorney walked toward the stair door.

"I guess we'll go upstairs first — then out to the barn and around there." He paused and looked around the kitchen.

"You're convinced there was nothing important here?" he asked the sheriff. "Nothing that would — point to any motive?"

The sheriff too looked all around, as if to re-convince himself.

"Nothing here but kitchen things," he said, with a little laugh for the insignificance of kitchen things.

The county attorney was looking at the cupboard — a peculiar, ungainly structure, half closet and half cupboard, the upper part of it being built in the wall, and the lower part just the old-fashioned kitchen cupboard. As if its queerness attracted him, he got a chair and opened the upper part and looked in. After a moment he drew his hand away sticky.

"Here's a nice mess," he said resentfully.

The two women had drawn nearer, and now the sheriff's wife spoke.

"Oh — her fruit," she said, looking to Mrs. Hale for sympathetic understanding. She turned back to the county attorney and explained: "She worried about that when it turned so cold last night. She said the fire would go out and her jars might burst."

Mrs. Peters's husband broke into a laugh.

"Well, can you beat the women! Held for murder, and worrying about her preserves!"

The young attorney set his lips.

"I guess before we're through with her she may have something more serious than preserves to worry about."

"Oh, well," said Mrs. Hale's husband, with good-natured superiority, "women are used to worrying over trifles."

The two women moved a little closer together. Neither of them spoke. The county attorney seemed suddenly to remember his manners — and think of his future.

"And yet," said he, with the gallantry of a young politician, "for all their worries, what would we do without the ladies?"

The women did not speak, did not unbend. He went to the sink and began washing his hands. He turned to wipe them on the roller wheel — whirled it for a cleaner place.

"Dirty towels! Not much of a housekeeper, would you say, ladies?"

He kicked his foot against some dirty pans under the sink.

"There's a great deal of work to be done on a farm," said Mrs. Hale stiffly.

"To be sure. And yet" — with a little bow to her — "I know there are some Dickson County farm-houses that do not have such roller towels." He gave it a pull to expose its full length again.

"Those towels get dirty awful quick. Men's hands aren't always as clean as they might be."

"Ah, loyal to your sex, I see," he laughed. He stopped and gave her a keen look. "But you and Mrs. Wright were neighbors. I suppose you were friends, too."

Martha Hale shook her head.

"I've seen little enough of her of late years. I've not been in this house — it's more than a year."

"And why was that? You didn't like her?"

"I liked her well enough," she replied with spirit. "Farmers' wives have their hands full, Mr. Henderson. And then" — She looked around the kitchen.

"Yes?" he encouraged.

"It never seemed a very cheerful place," said she, more to herself than to him.

"No," he agreed; "I don't think any one would call it cheerful. I shouldn't say she had the home-making instinct."

"Well, I don't know as Wright had, either," she muttered.

"You mean they didn't get on very well?" he was quick to ask.

"No; I don't mean anything," she answered, with decision. As she turned a little away from him, she added: "But I don't think a place would be any the cheerfuler for John Wright's bein' in it."

"I'd like to talk to you about that a little later, Mrs. Hale," he said. "I'm anxious to get the lay of things upstairs now."

He moved toward the stair door, followed by the two men.

"I suppose anything Mrs. Peters does'll be all right?" the sheriff inquired. "She was to take in some clothes for her, you know — and a few little things. We left in such a hurry yesterday."

The county attorney looked at the two women whom they were leaving alone there among the kitchen things.

"Yes — Mrs. Peters," he said, his glance resting on the woman who was not Mrs. Peters, the big farmer woman who stood behind the sheriff's wife. "Of course Mrs. Peters is one of us," he said, in a manner of entrusting responsibility. "And keep your eye out, Mrs. Peters, for anything that might be of use. No telling; you women might come upon a clue to the motive — and that's the thing we need."

Mr. Hale rubbed his face after the fashion of a show man getting ready for a pleasantry.

"But would the women know a clue if they did come upon it?" he said; and, having delivered himself of this, he followed the others through the stair door.

The women stood motionless and silent, listening to the footsteps, first upon the stairs, then in the room above them.

Then, as if releasing herself from something strange, Mrs. Hale began to arrange the dirty pans under the sink, which the county attorney's disdainful push of the foot had deranged.

"I'd hate to have men comin' into my kitchen," she said testily — "snoopin' round and criticizin'." 105

"Of course it's no more than their duty," said the sheriff's wife, in her manner of timid acquiescence.

"Duty's all right," replied Mrs. Hale bluffly; "but I guess that deputy sheriff that come out to make the fire might have got a little of this on." She gave the roller towel a pull. "Wish I'd thought of that sooner! Seems mean to talk about her for not having things slicked up, when she had to come away in such a hurry."

She looked around the kitchen. Certainly it was not "slicked up." Her eye was held by a bucket of sugar on a low shelf. The cover was off the wooden bucket, and beside it was a paper bag — half full.

Mrs. Hale moved toward it.

"She was putting this in here," she said to herself — slowly. 110

She thought of the flour in her kitchen at home — half sifted, half not sifted. She had been interrupted, and had left things half done. What had interrupted Minnie Foster? Why had that work been left half done? She made a move as if to finish it, — unfinished things always bothered her, — and then she glanced around and saw that Mrs. Peters was watching her — and she didn't want Mrs. Peters to get that feeling she had got of work begun and then — for some reason — not finished.

"It's a shame about her fruit," she said, and walked toward the cupboard that the county attorney had opened, and got on the chair, murmuring: "I wonder if it's all gone."

It was a sorry enough looking sight, but "Here's one that's all right," she said at last. She held it toward the light. "This is cherries, too." She looked again. "I declare I believe that's the only one."

With a sigh, she got down from the chair, went to the sink, and wiped off the bottle.

"She'll feel awful bad, after all her hard work in the hot weather. I re- 115 member the afternoon I put up my cherries last summer."

She set the bottle on the table, and, with another sigh, started to sit down in the rocker. But she did not sit down. Something kept her from sitting down in that chair. She straightened — stepped back, and, half turned away, stood looking at it, seeing the woman who sat there "pleatin' at her apron."

The thin voice of the sheriff's wife broke in upon her: "I must be getting those things from the front room closet." She opened the door into the other room, started in, stepped back. "You coming with me, Mrs. Hale?" she asked nervously. "You — you could help me get them."

They were soon back — the stark coldness of that shut-up room was not a thing to linger in.

"My!" said Mrs. Peters, dropping the things on the table and hurrying to the stove.

120   Mrs. Hale stood examining the clothes the woman who was being detained in town had said she wanted.

"Wright was close!" she exclaimed, holding up a shabby black skirt that bore the marks of much making over. "I think maybe that's why she kept so much to herself. I s'pose she felt she couldn't do her part; and then, you don't enjoy things when you feel shabby. She used to wear pretty clothes and be lively — when she was Minnie Foster, one of the town girls, singing in the choir. But that — oh, that was twenty years ago."

With a carefulness in which there was something tender, she folded the shabby clothes and piled them at one corner of the table. She looked at Mrs. Peters, and there was something in the other woman's look that irritated her.

"She don't care," she said to herself. "Much difference it makes to her whether Minnie Foster had pretty clothes when she was a girl."

Then she looked again, and she wasn't so sure; in fact, she hadn't at any time been perfectly sure about Mrs. Peters. She had that shrinking manner, and yet her eyes looked as if they could see a long way into things.

125   "This all you was to take in?" asked Mrs. Hale.

"No," said the sheriff's wife; "she said she wanted an apron. Funny thing to want," she ventured in her nervous little way, "for there's not much to get you dirty in jail, goodness knows. But I suppose just to make her feel more natural. If you're used to wearing an apron — . She said they were in the bottom drawer of this cupboard. Yes — here they are. And then her little shawl that always hung on the stair door."

She took the small gray shawl from behind the door leading upstairs, and stood a minute looking at it.

Suddenly Mrs. Hale took a quick step toward the other woman.

"Mrs. Peters!"

130   "Yes, Mrs. Hale?"

"Do you think she — did it?"

A frightened look blurred the other things in Mrs. Peters's eyes.

"Oh, I don't know," she said, in a voice that seemed to shrink away from the subject.

"Well, I don't think she did," affirmed Mrs. Hale stoutly. "Asking for an apron, and her little shawl. Worryin' about her fruit."

135   "Mr. Peters says — ." Footsteps were heard in the room above; she stopped, looked up, then went on in a lowered voice: "Mr. Peters says — it looks bad for her. Mr. Henderson is awful sarcastic in a speech, and he's going to make fun of her saying she didn't — wake up."

For a moment Mrs. Hale had no answer. Then, "Well, I guess John Wright didn't wake up — when they was slippin' that rope under his neck," she muttered.

"No, it's *strange*," breathed Mrs. Peters. "They think it was such a — funny way to kill a man."

She began to laugh; at the sound of the laugh, abruptly stopped.

"That's just what Mr. Hale said," said Mrs. Hale, in a resolutely natural voice. "There was a gun in the house. He says that's what he can't understand."

"Mr. Henderson said, coming out, that what was needed for the case was a motive. Something to show anger — or sudden feeling." 140

"Well, I don't see any signs of anger around here," said Mrs. Hale. "I don't — "

She stopped. It was as if her mind tripped on something. Her eye was caught by a dish-towel in the middle of the kitchen table. Slowly she moved toward the table. One half of it was wiped clean, the other half messy. Her eyes made a slow, almost unwilling turn to the bucket of sugar and the half empty bag beside it. Things begun — and not finished.

After a moment she stepped back, and said, in that manner of releasing herself:

"Wonder how they're finding things upstairs? I hope she had it a little more red up° up there. You know," — she paused, and feeling gathered, — "it seems kind of *sneaking;* locking her up in town and coming out here to get her own house to turn against her!"

"But, Mrs. Hale," said the sheriff's wife, "the law is the law." 145

"I s'pose 'tis," answered Mrs. Hale shortly.

She turned to the stove, saying something about that fire not being much to brag of. She worked with it a minute, and when she straightened up she said aggressively:

"The law is the law — and a bad stove is a bad stove. How'd you like to cook on this?" — pointing with the poker to the broken lining. She opened the oven door and started to express her opinion of the oven; but she was swept into her own thoughts, thinking of what it would mean, year after year, to have that stove to wrestle with. The thought of Minnie Foster trying to bake in that oven — and the thought of her never going over to see Minnie Foster — .

She was startled by hearing Mrs. Peters say: "A person gets discouraged — and loses heart."

The sheriff's wife had looked from the stove to the sink — to the pail of water which had been carried in from outside. The two women stood there silent, above them the footsteps of the men who were looking for evidence against the woman who had worked in that kitchen. That look of seeing into things, of seeing through a thing to something else, was in the eyes of the sheriff's wife now. When Mrs. Hale next spoke to her, it was gently: 150

"Better loosen up your things, Mrs. Peters. We'll not feel them when we go out."

red up: neatened, readied (dialectical)

Mrs. Peters went to the back of the room to hang up the fur tippet she was wearing. A moment later she exclaimed, "Why, she was piecing a quilt," and held up a large sewing basket piled high with quilt pieces.

Mrs. Hale spread some of the blocks on the table.

"It's log-cabin pattern," she said, putting several of them together. "Pretty, isn't it?"

155 They were so engaged with the quilt that they did not hear the footsteps on the stairs. Just as the stair door opened Mrs. Hale was saying:

"Do you suppose she was going to quilt it or just knot it?"

The sheriff threw up his hands.

"They wonder whether she was going to quilt it or just knot it!"

There was a laugh for the ways of women, a warming of hands over the stove, and then the county attorney said briskly:

160 "Well, let's go right out to the barn and get that cleared up."

"I don't see as there's anything so strange," Mrs. Hale said resentfully, after the outside door had closed on the three men — "our taking up our time with little things while we're waiting for them to get the evidence. I don't see as it's anything to laugh about."

"Of course they've got awful important things on their minds," said the sheriff's wife apologetically.

They returned to an inspection of the blocks for the quilt. Mrs. Hale was looking at the fine, even sewing, and preoccupied with thoughts of the woman who had done that sewing, when she heard the sheriff's wife say, in a queer tone:

"Why, look at this one."

165 She turned to take the block held out to her.

"The sewing," said Mrs. Peters, in a troubled way. "All the rest of them have been so nice and even — but — this one. Why, it looks as if she didn't know what she was about!"

Their eyes met — something flashed to life, passed between them; then, as if with an effort, they seemed to pull away from each other. A moment Mrs. Hale sat there, her hands folded over that sewing which was so unlike all the rest of the sewing. Then she had pulled a knot and drawn the threads.

"Oh, what are you doing, Mrs. Hale?" asked the sheriff's wife, startled.

"Just pulling out a stitch or two that's not sewed very good," said Mrs. Hale mildly.

170 "I don't think we ought to touch things," Mrs. Peters said, a little helplessly.

"I'll just finish up this end," answered Mrs. Hale, still in that mild, matter-of-fact fashion.

She threaded a needle and started to replace bad sewing with good. For a little while she sewed in silence. Then, in that thin, timid voice, she heard:

"Mrs. Hale!"

"Yes, Mrs. Peters?"

175 "What do you suppose she was so — nervous about?"

"Oh, *I* don't know," said Mrs. Hale, as if dismissing a thing not important enough to spend much time on. "I don't know as she was — nervous. I sew awful queer sometimes when I'm just tired."

She cut a thread, and out of the corner of her eye looked up at Mrs. Peters. The small, lean face of the sheriff's wife seemed to have tightened up. Her eyes had that look of peering into something. But the next moment she moved, and said in her thin, indecisive way:

"Well, I must get those clothes wrapped. They may be through sooner than we think. I wonder where I could find a piece of paper — and string."

"In that cupboard, maybe," suggested Mrs. Hale, after a glance around.

One piece of the crazy sewing remained unripped. Mrs. Peters's back turned, Martha Hale now scrutinized that piece, compared it with the dainty, accurate sewing of the other blocks. The difference was startling. Holding this block made her feel queer, as if the distracted thoughts of the woman who had perhaps turned to it to try and quiet herself were communicating themselves to her.   180

Mrs. Peters's voice roused her.

"Here's a bird-cage," she said. "Did she have a bird, Mrs. Hale?"

"Why, I don't know whether she did or not." She turned to look at the cage Mrs. Peters was holding up. "I've not been here in so long." She sighed. "There was a man round last year selling canaries cheap — but I don't know as she took one. Maybe she did. She used to sing real pretty herself."

Mrs. Peters looked around the kitchen.

"Seems kind of funny to think of a bird here." She half laughed — an attempt to put up a barrier. "But she must have had one — or why would she have a cage? I wonder what happened to it."   185

"I suppose maybe the cat got it," suggested Mrs. Hale, resuming her sewing.

"No, she didn't have a cat. She's got that feeling some people have about cats — being afraid of them. When they brought her to our house yesterday, my cat got in the room, and she was real upset and asked me to take it out."

"My sister Bessie was like that," laughed Mrs. Hale.

The sheriff's wife did not reply. The silence made Mrs. Hale turn around. Mrs. Peters was examining the bird-cage.

"Look at this door," she said slowly. "It's broke. One hinge has been pulled apart."   190

Mrs. Hale came nearer.

"Looks as if some one must have been — rough with it."

Again their eyes met — startled, questioning, apprehensive. For a moment neither spoke nor stirred. Then Mrs. Hale, turning away, said brusquely:

"If they're going to find any evidence, I wish they'd be about it. I don't like this place."

195   "But I'm awful glad you came with me, Mrs. Hale." Mrs. Peters put the bird-cage on the table and sat down. "It would be lonesome for me — sitting here alone."

"Yes, it would, wouldn't it?" agreed Mrs. Hale, a certain determined naturalness in her voice. She picked up the sewing, but now it dropped in her lap, and she murmured in a different voice: "But I tell you what I *do* wish, Mrs. Peters. I wish I had come over sometimes when she was here. I wish — I had."

"But of course you were awful busy, Mrs. Hale. Your house — and your children."

"I could've come," retorted Mrs. Hale shortly. "I stayed away because it weren't cheerful — and that's why I ought to have come. I" — she looked around — "I've never liked this place. Maybe because it's down in a hollow and you don't see the road. I don't know what it is, but it's a lonesome place, and always was. I wish I had come over to see Minnie Foster sometimes. I can see now — " She did not put it into words.

"Well, you mustn't reproach yourself," counseled Mrs. Peters. "Somehow, we just don't see how it is with other folks till — something comes up."

200   "Not having children makes less work," mused Mrs. Hale, after a silence, "but it makes a quiet house — and Wright out to work all day — and no company when he did come in. Did you know John Wright, Mrs. Peters?"

"Not to know him. I've seen him in town. They say he was a good man."

"Yes — good," conceded John Wright's neighbor grimly. "He didn't drink, and kept his word as well as most, I guess, and paid his debts. But he was a hard man, Mrs. Peters. Just to pass the time of day with him — ." She stopped, shivered a little. "Like a raw wind that gets to the bone." Her eye fell upon the cage on the table before her, and she added, almost bitterly: "I should think she would've wanted a bird!"

Suddenly she leaned forward, looking intently at the cage. "But what do you s'pose went wrong with it?"

"I don't know," returned Mrs. Peters; "unless it got sick and died."

205   But after she said it she reached over and swung the broken door. Both women watched it as if somehow held by it.

"You didn't know — her?" Mrs. Hale asked, a gentler note in her voice.

"Not till they brought her yesterday," said the sheriff's wife.

"She — come to think of it, she was kind of like a bird herself. Real sweet and pretty, but kind of timid and — fluttery. How — she — did — change."

That held her for a long time. Finally, as if struck with a happy thought and relieved to get back to everyday things, she exclaimed:

210   "Tell you what, Mrs. Peters, why don't you take the quilt in with you? It might take up her mind."

"Why, I think that's a real nice idea, Mrs. Hale," agreed the sheriff's wife, as if she too were glad to come into the atmosphere of a simple kindness. "There couldn't possibly be any objection to that, could there? Now, just what will I take? I wonder if her patches are in here — and her things."

They turned to the sewing basket.

"Here's some red," said Mrs. Hale, bringing out a roll of cloth. Underneath that was a box. "Here, maybe her scissors are in here — and her things." She held it up. "What a pretty box! I'll warrant that was something she had a long time ago — when she was a girl."

She held it in her hand a moment; then, with a little sigh, opened it. Instantly her hand went to her nose.

"Why — !"

Mrs. Peters drew nearer — then turned away.

"There's something wrapped up in this piece of silk," faltered Mrs. Hale.

"This isn't her scissors," said Mrs. Peters in a shrinking voice.

Her hand not steady, Mrs. Hale raised the piece of silk. "Oh, Mrs. Peters!" she cried. "It's — "

Mrs. Peters bent closer.

"It's the bird," she whispered.

"But, Mrs. Peters!" cried Mrs. Hale. "*Look* at it! Its neck — look at its neck! It's all — other side *to*."

She held the box away from her.

The sheriff's wife again bent closer.

"Somebody wrung its neck," said she, in a voice that was slow and deep.

And then again the eyes of the two women met — this time clung together in a look of dawning comprehension, of growing horror. Mrs. Peters looked from the dead bird to the broken door of the cage. Again their eyes met. And just then there was a sound at the outside door.

Mrs. Hale slipped the box under the quilt pieces in the basket, and sank into the chair before it. Mrs. Peters stood holding to the table. The county attorney and the sheriff came in from outside.

"Well, ladies," said the county attorney, as one turning from serious things to little pleasantries, "have you decided whether she was going to quilt it or knot it?"

"We think," began the sheriff's wife in a flurried voice, "that she was going to — knot it."

He was too preoccupied to notice the change that came in her voice on that last.

"Well, that's very interesting, I'm sure," he said tolerantly. He caught sight of the bird-cage. "Has the bird flown?"

"We think the cat got it," said Mrs. Hale in a voice curiously even.

He was walking up and down, as if thinking something out.

"Is there a cat?" he asked absently.

Mrs. Hale shot a look up at the sheriff's wife.

"Well, not *now*," said Mrs. Peters. "They're superstitious, you know; they leave."

She sank into the chair.

The county attorney did not heed her. "No sign at all of any one having come in from the outside," he said to Peters, in the manner of continuing an interrupted conversation. "Their own rope. Now let's go upstairs again and go over it, piece by piece. It would have to have been some one who knew just the —"

The stair door closed behind them and their voices were lost.

The two women sat motionless, not looking at each other, but as if peering into something and at the same time holding back. When they spoke now it was as if they were afraid of what they were saying, but as if they could not help saying it.

"She liked the bird," said Martha Hale, low and slowly. "She was going to bury it in that pretty box."

"When I was a girl," said Mrs. Peters, under her breath, "my kitten — there was a boy took a hatchet, and before my eyes — before I could get there —" She covered her face an instant. "If they hadn't held me back I would have" — she caught herself, looked upstairs where footsteps were heard, and finished weakly — "hurt him."

Then they sat without speaking or moving.

"I wonder how it would seem," Mrs. Hale at last began, as if feeling her way over strange ground — "never to have had any children around?" Her eyes made a slow sweep of the kitchen, as if seeing what that kitchen had meant through all the years. "No, Wright wouldn't like the bird," she said after that — "a thing that sang. She used to sing. He killed that too." Her voice tightened.

Mrs. Peters moved uneasily.

"Of course we don't know who killed the bird."

"I knew John Wright," was Mrs. Hale's answer.

"It was an awful thing was done in this house that night, Mrs. Hale," said the sheriff's wife. "Killing a man while he slept — slipping a thing round his neck that choked the life out of him."

Mrs. Hale's hand went out to the bird-cage.

"His neck. Choked the life out of him."

"We don't *know* who killed him," whispered Mrs. Peters wildly. "We don't *know*."

Mrs. Hale had not moved. "If there had been years and years of — nothing, then a bird to sing to you, it would be awful — still — after the bird was still."

It was as if something within her not herself had spoken, and it found in Mrs. Peters something she did not know as herself.

"I know what stillness is," she said, in a queer, monotonous voice. "When we homesteaded in Dakota, and my first baby died — after he was two years old — and me with no other then —"

Mrs. Hale stirred.

"How soon do you suppose they'll be through looking for evidence?"

"I know what stillness is," repeated Mrs. Peters, in just that same way. Then she too pulled back. "The law has got to punish crime, Mrs. Hale," she said in her tight little way.

"I wish you'd seen Minnie Foster," was the answer, "when she wore a white dress with blue ribbons, and stood up there in the choir and sang."

The picture of that girl, the fact that she had lived neighbor to that girl 260
for twenty years, and had let her die for lack of life, was suddenly more than
she could bear.

"Oh, I *wish* I'd come over here once in a while!" she cried. "That was a
crime! That was a crime! Who's going to punish that?"

"We mustn't take on," said Mrs. Peters, with a frightened look toward
the stairs.

"I might 'a' *known* she needed help! I tell you, it's *queer*, Mrs. Peters. We
live close together, and we live far apart. We all go through the same things —
it's all just a different kind of the same thing! If it weren't — why do you and I
understand? Why do we *know* — what we know this minute?"

She dashed her hand across her eyes. Then, seeing the jar of fruit on the
table, she reached for it and choked out:

"If I was you I wouldn't *tell* her her fruit was gone! Tell her it *ain't.* Tell 265
her it's all right — all of it. Here — take this in to prove it to her! She — she
may never know whether it was broke or not."

She turned away.

Mrs. Peters reached out for the bottle of fruit as if she were glad to take
it — as if touching a familiar thing, having something to do, could keep her
from something else. She got up, looked about for something to wrap the
fruit in, took a petticoat from the pile of clothes she had brought from the
front room, and nervously started winding that round the bottle.

"My!" she began, in a high, false voice, "it's a good thing the men
couldn't hear us! Getting all stirred up over a little thing like a — dead
canary." She hurried over that. "As if that could have anything to do with —
with — My, wouldn't they *laugh?*"

Footsteps were heard on the stairs.

"Maybe they would," muttered Mrs. Hale — "maybe they wouldn't." 270

"No, Peters," said the county attorney incisively; "it's all perfectly clear,
except the reason for doing it. But you know juries when it comes to women.
If there was some definite thing — something to show. Something to make a
story about. A thing that would connect up with this clumsy way of doing it."

In a covert way Mrs. Hale looked at Mrs. Peters. Mrs. Peters was looking
at her. Quickly they looked away from each other. The outer door opened
and Mr. Hale came in.

"I've got the team round now," he said. "Pretty cold out there."

"I'm going to stay here awhile by myself," the county attorney suddenly
announced. "You can send Frank out for me, can't you?" he asked the sheriff. "I want to go over everything. I'm not satisfied we can't do better."

Again, for one brief moment, the two women's eyes found one another. 275
The sheriff came up to the table.

"Did you want to see what Mrs. Peters was going to take in?"

The county attorney picked up the apron. He laughed.

"Oh, I guess they're not very dangerous things the ladies have picked out."

Mrs. Hale's hand was on the sewing basket in which the box was con- 280
cealed. She felt that she ought to take her hand off the basket. She did not

seem able to. He picked up one of the quilt blocks which she had piled on to cover the box. Her eyes felt like fire. She had a feeling that if he took up the basket she would snatch it from him.

But he did not take it up. With another little laugh, he turned away, saying:

"No; Mrs. Peters doesn't need supervising. For that matter, a sheriff's wife is married to the law. Ever think of it that way, Mrs. Peters?"

Mrs. Peters was standing beside the table. Mrs. Hale shot a look up at her; but she could not see her face. Mrs. Peters had turned away. When she spoke, her voice was muffled.

"Not — just that way," she said.

285 "Married to the law!" chuckled Mrs. Peters's husband. He moved toward the door into the front room, and said to the county attorney:

"I just want you to come in here a minute, George. We ought to take a look at these windows."

"Oh — windows," said the county attorney scoffingly.

"We'll be right out, Mr. Hale," said the sheriff to the farmer, who was still waiting by the door.

Hale went to look after the horses. The sheriff followed the county attorney into the other room. Again — for one moment — the two women were alone in that kitchen.

290 Martha Hale sprang up, her hands tight together, looking at that other woman, with whom it rested. At first she could not see her eyes, for the sheriff's wife had not turned back since she turned away at that suggestion of being married to the law. But now Mrs. Hale made her turn back. Her eyes made her turn back. Slowly, unwillingly, Mrs. Peters turned her head until her eyes met the eyes of the other woman. There was a moment when they held each other in a steady, burning look in which there was no evasion nor flinching. Then Martha Hale's eyes pointed the way to the basket in which was hidden the thing that would make certain the conviction of the other woman — that woman who was not there and yet who had been there with them all through the hour.

For a moment Mrs. Peters did not move. And then she did it. With a rush forward, she threw back the quilt pieces, got the box, tried to put it in her handbag. It was too big. Desperately she opened it, started to take the bird out. But there she broke — she could not touch the bird. She stood helpless, foolish.

There was the sound of a knob turning in the inner door. Martha Hale snatched the box from the sheriff's wife, and got it in the pocket of her big coat just as the sheriff and the county attorney came back into the kitchen.

"Well, Henry," said the county attorney facetiously, "at least we found out that she was not going to quilt it. She was going to — what is it you call it, ladies?"

Mrs. Hale's hand was against the pocket of her coat.

295 "We call it — knot it, Mr. Henderson."

The two stories by William Faulkner that follow, both revolving around an animal chase and financial transactions related thereto, are both comic interpretive stories of indisputable merit. The majority of qualified judges, however, would rank one story higher on the scale of literary value than the other. Which story, in your estimation, deserves the higher ranking? Support your decision with a reasoned and thorough analysis, using the study questions for what help they may provide.

William Faulkner
Spotted Horses

1

Yes, sir. Flem Snopes has filled that whole country full of spotted horses. You can hear folks running them all day and all night, whooping and hollering, and the horses running back and forth across them little wooden bridges ever now and then kind of like thunder. Here I was this morning pretty near half way to town, with the team ambling along and me setting in the buckboard about half asleep, when all of a sudden something come swurging up outen the bushes and jumped the road clean, without touching hoof to it. It flew right over my team, big as a billboard and flying through the air like a hawk. It taken me thirty minutes to stop my team and untangle the harness and the buckboard and hitch them up again.

That Flem Snopes. I be dog if he ain't a case, now. One morning about ten years ago, the boys was just getting settled down on Varner's porch for a little talk and tobacco, when here come Flem from behind the counter, with his coat off and his hair all parted, like he might have been clerking for Varner for ten years already. Folks all knowed him; it was a big family of them about five miles down the bottom. That year, at least. Sharecropping. They never stayed on any place over a year. Then they would move on to another place, with the chap or maybe the twins of that year's litter. It was a regular nest of them. But Flem. The rest of them stayed tenant farmers, moving every year, but here come Flem one day, walking out from behind Jody Varner's counter like he owned it. And he wasn't there but a year or two before folks knowed

SPOTTED HORSES   First published in 1931. An expanded, considerably altered version of the story constitutes book 4, chapter 1, of *The Hamlet* (1940), part of a trilogy with *The Town* and *The Mansion*. These three books chart the spread of the Snopes tribe and the rise of Flem Snopes, son of a tenant farmer, to the foremost position of power and wealth in the county. For the setting of many of his novels and stories Faulkner created the mythical Yoknapatawpha County, Mississippi, where this story takes place. Its county seat, "Jefferson," is roughly based on Oxford, Mississippi, of which Faulkner (1897–1962) was a lifelong resident.

that, if him and Jody was both still in that store in ten years more, it would be Jody clerking for Flem Snopes. Why, that fellow could make a nickel where it wasn't but four cents to begin with. He skun me in two trades, myself, and the fellow that can do that, I just hope he'll get rich before I do; that's all.

All right. So here Flem was, clerking at Varner's, making a nickel here and there and not telling nobody about it. No, sir. Folks never knowed when Flem got the better of somebody lessen the fellow he beat told it. He'd just set there in the store-chair, chewing his tobacco and keeping his own business to hisself, until about a week later we'd find out it was somebody else's business he was keeping to hisself — provided the fellow he trimmed was mad enough to tell it. That's Flem.

We give him ten years to own ever thing Jody Varner had. But he never waited no ten years. I reckon you-all know that gal of Uncle Billy Varner's, the youngest one; Eula. Jody's sister. Ever Sunday ever yellow-wheeled buggy and curried riding horse in that country would be hitched to Bill Varner's fence, and the young bucks setting on the porch, swarming around Eula like bees around a honey pot. One of these here kind of big, soft-looking gals that could giggle richer than plowed new-ground. Wouldn't none of them leave before the others, and so they would set there on the porch until time to go home, with some of them with nine or ten miles to ride and then get up tomorrow and go back to the field. So they would all leave together and they would ride in a clump down to the creek ford and hitch them curried horses and yellow-wheeled buggies and get out and fight one another. Then they would get in the buggies again and go on home.

5   Well, one day about a year ago, one of them yellow-wheeled buggies and one of them curried saddle-horses quit this country. We heard they was heading for Texas. The next day Uncle Billy and Eula and Flem come in to town in Uncle Bill's surrey, and when they come back, Flem and Eula was married. And on the next day we heard that two more of them yellow-wheeled buggies had left the country. They mought have gone to Texas, too. It's a big place.

Anyway, about a month after the wedding, Flem and Eula went to Texas, too. They was gone pretty near a year. Then one day last month, Eula come back, with a baby. We figgured up, and we decided that it was as well-growed a three-months-old baby as we ever see. It can already pull up on a chair. I reckon Texas makes big men quick, being a big place. Anyway, if it keeps on like it started, it'll be chewing tobacco and voting time it's eight years old.

And so last Friday here come Flem himself. He was on a wagon with another fellow. The other fellow had one of these two-gallon hats and a ivory-handled pistol and a box of gingersnaps sticking out of his hind pocket, and tied to the tail-gate of the wagon was about two dozen of them Texas ponies, hitched to one another with barbed wire. They was colored like parrots and they was quiet as doves, and ere a one of them would kill you quick as a rattlesnake. Nere a one of them had two eyes the same color, and nere a one of them had ever see a bridle, I reckon; and when that Texas man got down offen the wagon and walked up to them to show how gentle they was, one of them cut his vest clean offen him, same as with a razor.

Flem had done already disappeared; he had went on to see his wife, I reckon, and to see if that ere baby had done gone on to the field to help Uncle Billy plow maybe. It was the Texas man that taken the horses on to Mrs. Littlejohn's lot. He had a little trouble at first, when they come to the gate, because they hadn't never see a fence before, and when he finally got them in and taken a pair of wire cutters and unhitched them and got them into the barn and poured some shell corn into the trough, they durn nigh tore down the barn. I reckon they thought that shell corn was bugs, maybe. So he left them in the lot and he announced that the auction would begin at sunup to-morrow.

That night we was setting on Mrs. Littlejohn's porch. You-all mind the moon was nigh full that night, and we could watch them spotted varmints swirling along the fence and back and forth across the lot same as minnows in a pond. And then now and then they would all kind of huddle up against the barn and rest themselves by biting and kicking one another. We would hear a squeal, and then a set of hoofs would go Bam! against the barn, like a pistol. It sounded just like a fellow with a pistol, in a nest of cattymounts, taking his time.

2

It wasn't ere a man knowed yet if Flem owned them things or not. They just knowed one thing: that they wasn't never going to know for sho if Flem did or not, or if maybe he didn't just get on that wagon at the edge of town, for the ride or not. Even Eck Snopes didn't know, Flem's own cousin. But wasn't nobody surprised at that. We knowed that Flem would skin Eck quick as he would ere a one of us.

They was there by sunup next morning, some of them come twelve and sixteen miles, with seed-money tied up in tobacco sacks in their overalls, standing along the fence, when the Texas man come out of Mrs. Littlejohn's after breakfast and clumb onto the gate post with that ere white pistol butt sticking outen his hind pocket. He taken a new box of gingersnaps outen his pocket and bit the end offen it like a cigar and spit out the paper, and said the auction was open. And still they was coming up in wagons and a horse- and mule-back and hitching the teams across the road and coming to the fence. Flem wasn't nowhere in sight.

But he couldn't get them started. He began to work on Eck, because Eck holp him last night to get them into the barn and feed them that shell corn. Eck got out just in time. He come outen that barn like a chip on the crest of a busted dam of water, and clumb into the wagon just in time.

He was working on Eck when Henry Armstid come up in his wagon. Eck was saying he was skeered to bid on one of them, because he might get it, and the Texas man says, "Them ponies? Them little horses?" He clumb down offen the gate post and went toward the horses. They broke and run, and him following them, kind of chirping to them, with his hand out like he was fixing to catch a fly, until he got three or four of them cornered. Then he jumped into them, and then we couldn't see nothing for a while because of the dust. It was a big cloud of it, and them blare-eyed, spotted things swoaring outen it twenty foot to a jump, in forty directions without counting up. Then the dust settled and there they was, the Texas man and the horse. He had its head twisted clean around like a owl's head. Its legs was braced and it was trembling like a bride and groaning like a saw mill, and him holding its head wrung clean around on its neck so it was snuffing sky. "Look it over," he says, with his heels dug too and that white pistol sticking outen his pocket and his neck swole up like a spreading adder's until you could just tell what he was saying, cussing the horse and talking to us all at once: "Look him over, the fiddle-headed son of fourteen fathers. Try him, buy him; you will get the best — " Then it was all dust again, and we couldn't see nothing but spotted hide and mane, and that ere Texas man's boot-heels like a couple of walnuts on two strings, and after a while that two-gallon hat come sailing out like a fat old hen crossing a fence.

When the dust settled again, he was just getting outen the far fence corner, brushing himself off. He come and got his hat and brushed it off and come and clumb onto the gate post again. He was breathing hard. He taken the gingersnap box outen his pocket and et one, breathing hard. The hammer-head horse was still running round and round the lot like a merry-go-round at a fair. That was when Henry Armstid come shoving up to the gate in them patched overalls and one of them dangle-armed shirts of hisn. Hadn't nobody noticed him until then. We was all watching the Texas man and the horses. Even Mrs. Littlejohn; she had done come out and built a fire under the wash-pot in her back yard, and she would stand at the fence a while and then go back into the house and come out again with a arm full of wash and stand at the fence again. Well, here come Henry shoving up, and then we see Mrs. Armstid right behind him, in that ere faded wrapper and sunbonnet and them tennis shoes. "Git on back to that wagon," Henry says.

"Henry," she says.

"Here, boys," the Texas man says; "make room for missus to git up and see. Come on, Henry," he says; "here's your chance to buy that saddle-horse missus has been wanting. What about ten dollars, Henry?"

"Henry," Mrs. Armstid says. She put her hand on Henry's arm. Henry knocked her hand down.

"Git on back to that wagon, like I told you," he says.

Mrs. Armstid never moved. She stood behind Henry, with her hands rolled into her dress, not looking at nothing. "He hain't no more despair than to buy one of them things," she says. "And us not five dollars ahead of the pore house, he hain't no more despair." It was the truth, too. They ain't never made more than a bare living offen that place of theirs, and them with four chaps and the very clothes they wears she earns by weaving by the firelight at night while Henry's asleep.

"Shut your mouth and git on back to that wagon," Henry says. "Do you 20 want I taken a wagon stake to you here in the big road?"

Well, that Texas man taken one look at her. Then he begun on Eck again, like Henry wasn't even there. But Eck was skeered. "I can git me a snapping turtle or a water moccasin for nothing. I ain't going to buy none."

So the Texas man said he would give Eck a horse. "To start the auction, and because you holp me last night. If you'll start the bidding on the next horse," he says, "I'll give you that fiddle-head horse."

I wish you could have seen them, standing there with their seed-money in their pockets, watching that Texas man give Eck Snopes a live horse, all fixed to call him a fool if he taken it or not. Finally Eck says he'll take it. "Only I just starts the bidding," he says. "I don't have to buy the next one lessen I ain't overtopped." The Texas man said all right, and Eck bid a dollar on the next one, with Henry Armstid standing there with his mouth already open, watching Eck and the Texas man like a mad-dog or something. "A dollar," Eck says.

The Texas man looked at Eck. His mouth was already open too, like he had started to say something and what he was going to say had up and died on him. "A dollar?" he says. "One dollar? You mean, *one* dollar, Eck?"

"Durn it," Eck says; "two dollars, then." 25

Well, sir, I wish you could a seen that Texas man. He taken out that gingersnap box and held it up and looked into it, careful, like it might have been a diamond ring in it, or a spider. Then he throwed it away and wiped his face with a bandanna. "Well," he says. "Well. Two dollars. Two dollars. Is your pulse all right, Eck?" he says. "Do you have ager-sweats at night, maybe?" he says. "Well," he says, "I got to take it. But are you boys going to stand there and see Eck get two horses at a dollar a head?"

That done it. I be dog if he wasn't nigh as smart as Flem Snopes. He hadn't no more than got the words outen his mouth before here was Henry Armstid, waving his hand. "Three dollars," Henry says. Mrs. Armstid tried to hold him again. He knocked her hand off, shoving up to the gate post.

"Mister," Mrs. Armstid says, "we got chaps in the house and not corn to feed the stock. We got five dollars I earned my chaps a-weaving after dark, and him snoring in the bed. And he hain't no more despair."

"Henry bids three dollars," the Texas man says. "Raise him a dollar, Eck, and the horse is yours."

"Henry," Mrs. Armstid says. 30

"Raise him, Eck," the Texas man says.

"Four dollars," Eck says.

"Five dollars," Henry says, shaking his fist. He shoved up right under the gate post. Mrs. Armstid was looking at the Texas man too.

"Mister," she says, "if you take that five dollars I earned my chaps a-weaving for one of them things, it'll be a curse onto you and yourn during all the time of man."

But it wasn't no stopping Henry. He had shoved up, waving his fist at the 35 Texas man. He opened it; the money was in nickels and quarters, and one dollar bill that looked like a cow's cud. "Five dollars," he says. "And the man that raises it'll have to beat my head off, or I'll beat hisn."

"All right," the Texas man says. "Five dollars is bid. But don't you shake your hand at me."

3

It taken till nigh sundown before the last one was sold. He got them hotted up once and the bidding got up to seven dollars and a quarter, but most of them went around three or four dollars, him setting on the gate post and picking the horses out one at a time by mouth-word, and Mrs. Littlejohn pumping up and down at the tub and stopping and coming to the fence for a while and going back to the tub again. She had done got done too, and the wash was hung on the line in the back yard, and we could smell supper cooking. Finally they was all sold; he swapped the last two and the wagon for a buckboard.

We was all kind of tired, but Henry Armstid looked more like a mad-dog then ever. When he bought, Mrs. Armstid had went back to the wagon, setting in it behind them two rabbit-sized bone-pore mules, and the wagon itself looking like it would fall all to pieces soon as the mules moved. Henry hadn't even waited to pull it outen the road; it was still in the middle of the road and her setting in it, not looking at nothing, ever since this morning.

Henry was right up against the gate. He went up to the Texas man. "I bought a horse and I paid cash," Henry says. "And yet you expect me to stand around here until they are all sold before I can get my horse. I'm going to take my horse outen that lot."

40 The Texas man looked at Henry. He talked like he might have been asking for a cup of coffee at the table. "Take your horse," he says.

Then Henry quit looking at the Texas man. He begun to swallow, holding onto the gate. "Ain't you going to help me?" he says.

"It ain't my horse," the Texas man says.

Henry never looked at the Texas man again, he never looked at nobody. "Who'll help me catch my horse?" he says. Never nobody said nothing. "Bring the plowline," Henry says. Mrs. Armstid got outen the wagon and brought the plowline. The Texas man got down off the post. The woman made to pass him, carrying the rope.

"Don't you go in there, missus," the Texas man says.

45 Henry opened the gate. He didn't look back. "Come on here," he says.

"Don't you go in there, missus," the Texas man says.

Mrs. Armstid wasn't looking at nobody, neither, with her hands across her middle, holding the rope. "I reckon I better," she says. Her and Henry went into the lot. The horses broke and run. Henry and Mrs. Armstid followed.

"Get him into the corner," Henry says. They got Henry's horse cornered finally, and Henry taken the rope, but Mrs. Armstid let the horse get out. They hemmed it up again, but Mrs. Armstid let it get out again, and Henry turned and hit her with the rope. "Why didn't you head him back?" Henry says. He hit her again. "Why didn't you?" It was about that time I looked around and see Flem Snopes standing there.

It was the Texas man that done something. He moved fast for a big man. He caught the rope before Henry could hit the third time, and Henry whirled and made like he would jump at the Texas man. But he never jumped. The Texas man went and taken Henry's arm and led him outen the lot. Mrs. Armstid come behind them and the Texas man taken some money outen his pocket and he give it into Mrs. Armstid's hand. "Get him into the wagon and take him on home," the Texas man says, like he might have been telling them he enjoyed his supper.

Then here come Flem. "What's that for, Buck?" Flem says.

"Thinks he bought one of them ponies," the Texas man says. "Get him on away, missus."

But Henry wouldn't go. "Give him back that money," he says. "I bought that horse and I aim to have him if I have to shoot him."

And there was Flem, standing there with his hands in his pockets, chewing, like he had just happened to be passing.

"You take your money and I take my horse," Henry says. "Give it back to him," he says to Mrs. Armstid.

"You don't own no horse of mine," the Texas man says. "Get him on home, missus."

Then Henry seen Flem. "You got something to do with these horses," he says. "I bought one. Here's the money for it." He taken the bill outen Mrs. Armstid's hand. He offered it to Flem. "I bought one. Ask him. Here. Here's the money," he says, giving the bill to Flem.

When Flem taken the money, the Texas man dropped the rope he had snatched outen Henry's hand. He had done sent Eck Snopes's boy up to the store for another box of gingersnaps, and he taken the box outen his pocket and looked into it. It was empty and he dropped it on the ground. "Mr. Snopes will have your money for you to-morrow," he says to Mrs. Armstid. "You can get it from him to-morrow. He don't own no horse. You get him into the wagon and get him on home." Mrs. Armstid went back to the wagon and got in. "Where's that ere buckboard I bought?" the Texas man says. It was after sundown then. And then Mrs. Littlejohn come out on the porch and rung the supper bell.

50

55

4

I come on in and et supper. Mrs. Littlejohn would bring in a pan of bread or something, then she would go out to the porch a minute and come back and tell us. The Texas man had hitched his team to the buckboard he had swapped them last two horses for, and him and Flem had gone, and then she told that the rest of them that never had ropes had went back to the store with I. O. Snopes to get some ropes, and wasn't nobody at the gate but Henry Armstid, and Mrs. Armstid setting in the wagon in the road, and Eck Snopes and that boy of hisn. "I don't care how many of them fool men gets killed by them things," Mrs. Littlejohn says, "but I ain't going to let Eck Snopes take that boy into that lot again." So she went down to the gate, but she come back without the boy or Eck neither.

"It ain't no need to worry about that boy," I says. "He's charmed." He was right behind Eck last night when Eck went to help feed them. The whole drove of them jumped clean over that boy's head and never touched him. It was Eck that touched him. Eck snatched him into the wagon and taken a rope and frailed the tar out of him.

So I had done et and went to my room and was undressing, long as I had a long trip to make the next day; I was trying to sell a machine to Mrs. Bundren up past Whiteleaf; when Henry Armstid opened that gate and went in by hisself. They couldn't make him wait for the balance of them to get back with their ropes. Eck Snopes said he tried to make Henry wait, but Henry wouldn't do it. Eck said Henry walked right up to them and that when they broke, they run clean over Henry like a hay-mow breaking down. Eck said he snatched that boy of hisn out of the way just in time and that them things went through the gate like a creek flood and into the wagons and teams hitched side the road, busting wagon tongues and snapping harness like it was fishing-line, with Mrs. Armstid still setting in their wagon in the middle of it like something carved outen wood. Then they scattered, wild horses and tame mules with pieces of harness and single-trees dangling offen them, both ways up and down the road.

"There goes ourn, paw!" Eck says his boy said. "There it goes, into Mrs. Littlejohn's house." Eck says it run right up the steps and into the house like a boarder late for supper. I reckon so. Anyway, I was in my room, in my underclothes, with one sock on and one sock in my hand, leaning out the window when the commotion busted out, when I heard something run into the melodeon in the hall; it sounded like a railroad engine. Then the door to my room come sailing in like when you throw a tin bucket top into the wind and I looked over my shoulder and see something that looked like a fourteen-foot pinwheel a-blaring its eyes at me. It had to blare them fast, because I was already done jumped out the window.

I reckon it was anxious, too. I reckon it hadn't never seen barbed wire or shell corn before, but I know it hadn't never seen underclothes before, or maybe it was a sewing-machine agent it hadn't never seen. Anyway, it swirled and turned to run back up the hall and outen the house, when it met Eck Snopes and that boy just coming in, carrying a rope. It swirled again and run down the hall and out the back door just in time to meet Mrs. Littlejohn. She had just gathered up the clothes she had washed, and she was coming onto the back porch with a armful of washing in one hand and a scrubbing-board in the other, when the horse skidded up to her, trying to stop and swirl again. It never taken Mrs. Littlejohn no time a-tall.

"Git outen here, you son," she says. She hit it across the face with the scrubbing board; that ere scrubbing-board split as neat as ere a axe could have done it, and when the horse swirled to run back up the hall, she hit it again with what was left of the scrubbing-board, not on the head this time. "And stay out," she says.

Eck and that boy was half-way down the hall by this time. I reckon that horse looked like a pinwheel to Eck too. "Git to hell outen here, Ad!" Eck says. Only there wasn't time. Eck dropped flat on his face, but the boy never moved. The boy was about a yard tall maybe, in overhalls just like Eck's; that horse swoared over his head without touching a hair. I saw that, because I was just coming back up the front steps, still carrying that ere sock and still in my underclothes, when the horse come onto the porch again. It taken one look at me and swirled again and run to the end of the porch and jumped the banisters and the lot fence like a hen-hawk and lit in the lot running and went out the gate again and jumped eight or ten upside-down wagons and went on down the road. It was a full moon then. Mrs. Armstid was still setting in the wagon like she had done been carved outen wood and left there and forgot.

That horse. It ain't never missed a lick. It was going about forty miles a hour when it come to the bridge over the creek. It would have had a clear road, but it so happened that Vernon Tull was already using the bridge when it got there. He was coming back from town; he hadn't heard about the auction; him and his wife and three daughters and Mrs. Tull's aunt, all setting in chairs in the wagon bed, and all asleep, including the mules. They waked up when the horse hit the bridge one time, but Tull said the first he knew was when the mules tried to turn the wagon around in the middle of the bridge and he seen that spotted varmint run right twixt the mules and run up the wagon tongue like a squirrel. He said he just had time to hit it across the face with his whip-stock, because about that time the mules turned the wagon around on that ere one-way bridge and that horse clumb across one of the mules and jumped down onto the bridge again and went on, with Vernon standing up in the wagon and kicking at it.

Tull said the mules turned in the harness and clumb back into the wagon too, with Tull trying to beat them out again, with the reins wrapped around his wrist. After that he says all he seen was overturned chairs and women-folks' legs and white drawers shining in the moonlight, and his mules and that spotted horse going on up the road like a ghost.

The mules jerked Tull outen the wagon and drug him a spell on the bridge before the reins broke. They thought at first that he was dead, and while they was kneeling around him, picking the bridge splinters outen him, here come Eck and that boy, still carrying the rope. They was running and breathing a little hard. "Where'd he go?" Eck says.

5

I went back and got my pants and shirt and shoes on just in time to go and help get Henry Armstid outen the trash in the lot. I be dog if he didn't look like he was dead, with his head hanging back and his teeth showing in the moonlight, and a little rim of white under his eyelids. We could still hear them horses, here and there; hadn't none of them got more than four-five miles away yet, not knowing the country, I reckon. So we could hear them and folks yelling now and then: "Whooey. Head him!"

We toted Henry into Mrs. Littlejohn's. She was in the hall; she hadn't put down the armful of clothes. She taken one look at us, and she laid down the busted scrubbing-board and taken up the lamp and opened a empty door. "Bring him in here," she says.

70 We toted him in and laid him on the bed. Mrs. Littlejohn set the lamp on the dresser, still carrying the clothes. "I'll declare, you men," she says. Our shadows was way up the wall, tiptoeing too; we could hear ourselves breathing. "Better get his wife," Mrs. Littlejohn says. She went out, carrying the clothes.

"I reckon we had," Quick says. "Go get her, somebody."

"Whyn't you go?" Winterbottom says.

"Let Ernest git her," Durley says. "He lives neighbors with them."

Ernest went to fetch her. I be dog if Henry didn't look like he was dead. Mrs. Littlejohn come back, with a kettle and some towels. She went to work on Henry, and then Mrs. Armstid and Ernest come in. Mrs. Armstid come to the foot of the bed and stood there, with her hands rolled into her apron, watching what Mrs. Littlejohn was doing, I reckon.

75 "You men git outen the way," Mrs. Littlejohn says. "Git outside," she says. "See if you can't find something else to play with that will kill some more of you."

"Is he dead?" Winterbottom says.

"It ain't your fault if he ain't," Mrs. Littlejohn says. "Go tell Will Varner to come up here. I reckon a man ain't so different from a mule, come long come short. Except maybe a mule's got more sense."

We went to get Uncle Billy. It was a full moon. We could hear them, now and then, four mile away: "Whooey. Head him." The country was full of them, one on ever wooden bridge in the land, running across it like thunder: "Whooey. There he goes. Head him."

We hadn't got far before Henry begun to scream. I reckon Mrs. Littlejohn's water had brung him to; anyway, he wasn't dead. We went on to Uncle Billy's. The house was dark. We called to him, and after a while the window opened and Uncle Billy put his head out, peart as a peckerwood, listening. "Are they still trying to catch them durn rabbits?" he says.

80 He come down, with his britches on over his night-shirt and his suspenders dangling, carrying his horse-doctoring grip. "Yes, sir," he says, cocking his head like a woodpecker; "they're still a-trying."

We could hear Henry before we reached Mrs. Littlejohn's. He was going Ah-Ah-Ah. We stopped in the yard. Uncle Billy went on in. We could hear Henry. We stood in the yard, hearing them on the bridges, this-a-way and that: "Whooey. Whooey."

"Eck Snopes ought to caught hisn," Ernest says.

"Looks like he ought," Winterbottom said.

Henry was going Ah-Ah-Ah steady in the house; then he begun to scream. "Uncle Billy's started," Quick says. We looked into the hall. We could see the light where the door was. Then Mrs. Littlejohn come out.

"Will needs some help," she says. "You, Ernest. You'll do." Ernest went ⁸⁵ into the house.

"Hear them?" Quick said. "That one was on Four Mile bridge." We could hear them; it sounded like thunder a long way off; it didn't last long. "Whooey."

We could hear Henry: "Ah-Ah-Ah-Ah-Ah."

"They are both started now," Winterbottom says. "Ernest too."

That was early in the night. Which was a good thing, because it taken a ⁹⁰ long night for folks to chase them things right and for Henry to lay there and holler, being as Uncle Billy never had none of this here chloryfoam to set Henry's leg with. So it was considerate in Flem to get them started early. And what do you reckon Flem's com-ment was?

That's right. Nothing. Because he wasn't there. Hadn't nobody see him since that Texas man left.

6

That was Saturday night. I reckon Mrs. Armstid got home about daylight, to see about the chaps. I don't know where they thought her and Henry was. But lucky the oldest one was a gal, about twelve, big enough to take care of the little ones. Which she did for the next two days. Mrs. Armstid would nurse Henry all night and work in the kitchen for hern and Henry's keep, and in the afternoon she would drive home (it was about four miles) to see to the chaps. She would cook up a pot of victuals and leave it on the stove, and the gal would bar the house and keep the little ones quiet. I would hear Mrs. Littlejohn and Mrs. Armstid talking in the kitchen. "How are the chaps making out?" Mrs. Littlejohn says.

"All right," Mrs. Armstid says.

"Don't they git skeered at night?" Mrs. Littlejohn says.

"Ina May bars the door when I leave," Mrs. Armstid says. "She's got the ⁹⁵ axe in bed with her. I reckon she can make out."

I reckon they did. And I reckon Mrs. Armstid was waiting for Flem to come back to town; hadn't nobody seen him until this morning; to get her money the Texas man said Flem was keeping for her. Sho. I reckon she was.

Anyway, I heard Mrs. Armstid and Mrs. Littlejohn talking in the kitchen this morning while I was eating breakfast. Mrs. Littlejohn had just told Mrs. Armstid that Flem was in town. "You can ask him for that five dollars," Mrs. Littlejohn says.

"You reckon he'll give it to me?" Mrs. Armstid says.

Mrs. Littlejohn was washing dishes, washing them like a man, like they was made out of iron. "No," she says. "But asking him won't do no hurt. It might shame him. I don't reckon it will, but it might."

"If he wouldn't give it back, it ain't no use to ask," Mrs. Armstid says. ¹⁰⁰

"Suit yourself," Mrs. Littlejohn says. "It's your money."

I could hear the dishes.

"Do you reckon he might give it back to me?" Mrs. Armstid says. "That Texas man said he would. He said I could get it from Mr. Snopes later."

"Then go and ask him for it," Mrs. Littlejohn says.

105 I could hear the dishes.

"He won't give it back to me," Mrs. Armstid says.

"All right," Mrs. Littlejohn says. "Don't ask him for it, then."

I could hear the dishes; Mrs. Armstid was helping. "You don't reckon he would, do you?" she says. Mrs. Littlejohn never said nothing. It sounded like she was throwing the dishes at one another. "Maybe I better go and talk to Henry about it," Mrs. Armstid says.

"I would," Mrs. Littlejohn says. I be dog if it didn't sound like she had two plates in her hands, beating them together. "Then Henry can buy another five-dollar horse with it. Maybe he'll buy one next time that will out and out kill him. If I thought that, I'd give you back the money, myself."

110 "I reckon I better talk to him first," Mrs. Armstid said. Then it sounded like Mrs. Littlejohn taken up all the dishes and throwed them at the cookstove and I come away.

That was this morning. I had been up to Bundren's and back, and I thought that things would have kind of settled down. So after breakfast, I went up to the store. And there was Flem, setting in the store-chair and whittling, like he might not have ever moved since he come to clerk for Jody Varner. I. O. was leaning in the door, in his shirt sleeves and with his hair parted too, same as Flem was before he turned the clerking job over to I. O. It's a funny thing about them Snopes: they all looks alike, yet there ain't ere a two of them that claims brothers. They're always just cousins, like Flem and Eck and Flem and I. O. Eck was there too, squatting against the wall, him and that boy, eating cheese and crackers outen a sack; they told me that Eck hadn't been home a-tall. And that Lon Quick hadn't got back to town, even. He followed his horse clean down to Samson's Bridge, with a wagon and a camp outfit. Eck finally caught one of hisn. It run into a blind lane at Freeman's and Eck and the boy taken and tied their rope across the end of the lane, about three foot high. The horse come to the end of the lane and whirled and run back without ever stopping. Eck says it never seen the rope a-tall. He says it looked just like one of these here Christmas pinwheels. "Didn't it try to run again?" I says.

"No," Eck says, eating a bite of cheese offen his knife blade. "Just kicked some."

"Kicked some?" I says.

"It broke its neck," Eck says.

115 Well, they was squatting there, about six of them, talking, talking at Flem; never nobody knowed yet if Flem had ere a interest in them horses or not. So finally I come right out and asked him. "Flem's done skun all of us so much," I says, "that we're proud of him. Come on, Flem," I says, "how much did you and that Texas man make offen them horses? You can tell us. Ain't nobody here but Eck that bought one of them; the others ain't got back

to town yet, and Eck's your own cousin; he'll be proud to hear, too. How much did you-all make?"

They was all whittling, not looking at Flem, making like they was studying. But you could a heard a pin drop. And I. O. He had been rubbing his back up and down on the door, but he stopped now, watching Flem like a pointing dog. Flem finished cutting the sliver offen his stick. He spit across the porch, into the road. "'Twarn't none of my horses," he says.

I. O. cackled, like a hen, slapping his legs with both hands. "You boys might just as well quit trying to get ahead of Flem," he said.

Well, about that time I see Mrs. Armstid come outen Mrs. Littlejohn's gate, coming up the road. I never said nothing. I says, "Well, if a man can't take care of himself in a trade, he can't blame the man that trims him."

Flem never said nothing, trimming at the stick. He hadn't seen Mrs. Armstid. "Yes, sir," I says. "A fellow like Henry Armstid ain't got nobody but hisself to blame."

"Course he ain't," I. O. says. He ain't seen her, neither. "Henry Armstid's a born fool. Always is been. If Flem hadn't a got his money, somebody else would." 120

We looked at Flem. He never moved. Mrs. Armstid come on up the road.

"That's right," I says. "But, come to think of it, Henry never bought no horse." We looked at Flem; you could a heard a match drop. "That Texas man told her to get that five dollars back from Flem next day. I reckon Flem's done already taken that money to Mrs. Littlejohn's and give it to Mrs. Armstid."

We watched Flem. I. O. quit rubbing his back against the door again. After a while Flem raised his head and spit across the porch, into the dust. I. O. cackled, just like a hen. "Ain't he a beating fellow, now?" I. O. says.

Mrs. Armstid was getting closer, so I kept on talking, watching to see if Flem would look up and see her. But he never looked up. I went on talking about Tull, about how he was going to sue Flem, and Flem setting there, whittling his stick, not saying nothing else after he said they wasn't none of his horses.

Then I. O. happened to look around. He seen Mrs. Armstid. "Pssssst!" 125 he says. Flem looked up. "Here she comes!" I. O. says. "Go out the back. I'll tell her you done went in to town to-day."

But Flem never moved. He just set there, whittling, and we watched Mrs. Armstid come up onto the porch, in that ere faded sunbonnet and wrapper and them tennis shoes that made a kind of hissing noise on the porch. She come onto the porch and stopped, her hands rolled into her dress in front, not looking at nothing.

"He said Saturday," she says, "that he wouldn't sell Henry no horse. He said I could get the money from you."

Flem looked up. The knife never stopped. It went on trimming off a sliver same as if he was watching it. "He taken that money off with him when he left," Flem says.

Mrs. Armstid never looked at nothing. We never looked at her, neither, except that boy of Eck's. He had a half-et cracker in his hand, watching her, chewing.

130 "He said Henry hadn't bought no horse," Mrs. Armstid says. "He said for me to get the money from you to-day."

"I reckon he forgot about it," Flem said. "He taken that money off with him Saturday." He whittled again. I. O. kept on rubbing his back, slow. He licked his lips. After a while the woman looked up the road, where it went on up the hill, toward the graveyard. She looked up that way for a while, with that boy of Eck's watching her and I. O. rubbing his back slow against the door. Then she turned back toward the steps.

"I reckon it's time to get dinner started," she says.

"How's Henry this morning, Mrs. Armstid?" Winterbottom says.

She looked at Winterbottom; she almost stopped. "He's resting, I thank you kindly," she says.

135 Flem got up, outen the chair, putting the knife away. He spit across the porch. "Wait a minute, Mrs. Armstid," he says. She stopped again. She didn't look at him. Flem went on into the store, with I. O. done quit rubbing his back now, with his head craned after Flem, and Mrs. Armstid standing there with her hands rolled into her dress, not looking at nothing. A wagon come up the road and passed; it was Freeman, on the way to town. Then Flem come out again, with I. O. still watching him. Flem had one of these little striped sacks of Jody Varner's candy; I bet he still owes Jody that nickel, too. He put the sack into Mrs. Armstid's hand, like he would have put it into a hollow stump. He spit again across the porch. "A little sweetening for the chaps," he says.

"You're right kind," Mrs. Armstid says. She held the sack of candy in her hand, not looking at nothing. Eck's boy was watching the sack, the half-et cracker in his hand; he wasn't chewing now. He watched Mrs. Armstid roll the sack into her apron. "I reckon I better get on back and help with dinner," she says. She turned and went back across the porch. Flem set down in the chair again and opened his knife. He spit across the porch again, past Mrs. Armstid where she hadn't went down the steps yet. Then she went on, in that ere sunbonnet and wrapper all the same color, back down the road toward Mrs. Littlejohn's. You couldn't see her dress move, like a natural woman walking. She looked like a old snag still standing up and moving along on a high water. We watched her turn in at Mrs. Littlejohn's and go outen sight. Flem was whittling. I. O. begun to rub his back on the door. Then he begun to cackle, just like a durn hen.

"You boys might just as well quit trying," I. O. says. "You can't git ahead of Flem. You can't touch him. Ain't he a sight, now?"

I be dog if he ain't. If I had brung a herd of wild cattymounts into town and sold them to my neighbors and kinfolks, they would have lynched me. Yes, sir.

QUESTIONS

1. Characterize Flem Snopes and trace his history in the story. What is his principal motivation? What inferences may be drawn about his marriage? About his involvement in the auction? Is there any point in the story where Flem can be proved to be lying? Are any of his actions motivated by generosity? How is he regarded by his cousins? Why?
2. Who is the narrator of the story? Characterize him as a person, and comment on his abilities as a story-teller, illustrating particularly by an analysis of some single paragraph (e.g., the opening one). What kind of story, as he tells it, is this — comic? tragic? pathetic? horrifying? What kind would it be if told by Mrs. Armstid? By Mr. Armstid? How does the narrator regard his characters? What is his attitude toward Flem? What are the chief sources of his humor?
3. Characterize the Texan. How is he different from Flem? What details of his characterization make him memorable?
4. Characterize Mrs. Armstid. What characteristics individuate her and make her more than just a "victim" of social and marital injustice? Is she a sympathetic character? What are her values and loyalties? How is she regarded by (a) her husband, (b) the Texan, (c) Flem, (d) Mrs. Littlejohn, (e) the narrator?
5. For a story of its length, this story has an unusual number of characters. How many are more than mere names? Identify each of the following, characterize each briefly, and comment on characteristics that make them memorable in any way: (a) Henry Armstid, (b) Mrs. Littlejohn, (c) Eck Snopes, (d) Eck's son, Ad, (e) I. O. Snopes, (f) Eula Varner, (g) "Uncle" Billy Varner, (h) the spotted horses. What is the irony of Vernon Tull's role in the story?
6. Who is the protagonist? Who are the antagonists? Who is victorious in their conflict? Does the story have a happy ending?

William Faulkner
Mule in the Yard

It was a gray day in late January, though not cold because of the fog. Old Het, just walked in from the poorhouse, ran down the hall toward the kitchen, shouting in a strong, bright, happy voice. She was about seventy probably, though by her own counting, calculated from the ages of various housewives in the town from brides to grandmothers whom she claimed to have nursed in infancy, she would have to be around a hundred and at least triplets. Tall, lean, fog-beaded, in tennis shoes and a long rat-colored cloak trimmed with what forty or fifty years ago had been fur, a modish though not

MULE IN THE YARD   First published in 1934. A considerably altered version of the story is incorporated in Chapter 16 of *The Town* (1957). The action of the story occurs many years after that of "Spotted Horses." The town is Jefferson, the county seat of Yoknapatawpha County.

new purple toque set upon her headrag and carrying (time was when she made her weekly rounds from kitchen to kitchen carrying a brocaded carpet-bag though since the advent of the ten-cent stores the carpetbag became an endless succession of the convenient paper receptacles with which they supply their customers for a few cents) the shopping-bag, she ran into the kitchen and shouted with strong and childlike pleasure: "Miss Mannie! Mule in de yard!"

Mrs. Hait, stooping to the stove, in the act of drawing from it a scuttle of live ashes, jerked upright; clutching the scuttle, she glared at old Het, then she too spoke at once, strong too, immediate. "Them sons of bitches," she said. She left the kitchen, not running exactly, yet with a kind of outraged celerity, carrying the scuttle — a compact woman of forty-odd, with an air of indomitable yet relieved bereavement, as though that which had relicted her had been a woman and a not particularly valuable one at that. She wore a calico wrapper and a sweater coat, and a man's felt hat which they in the town knew had belonged to her ten years' dead husband. But the man's shoes had not belonged to him. They were high shoes which buttoned, with toes like small tulip bulbs, and in the town they knew that she had bought them new for herself. She and old Het ran down the kitchen steps and into the fog. That's why it was not cold: as though there lay supine and prisoned between earth and mist the long winter night's suspiration of the sleeping town in dark, close rooms — the slumber and the rousing; the stale waking thermo-static, by reheating heat-engendered: it lay like a scum of cold grease upon the steps and the wooden entrance to the basement and upon the narrow plank walk which led to a shed building in the corner of the yard: upon these planks, running and still carrying the scuttle of live ashes, Mrs. Hait skated viciously.

"Watch out!" old Het, footed securely by her rubber soles, cried happily. "Dey in de front!" Mrs. Hait did not fall. She did not even pause. She took in the immediate scene with one cold glare and was running again when there appeared at the corner of the house and apparently having been born before their eyes of the fog itself, a mule. It looked taller than a giraffe. Longheaded, with a flying halter about its scissorlike ears, it rushed down upon them with violent and apparitionlike suddenness.

"Dar hit!" old Het cried, waving the shopping-bag. "Hoo!" Mrs. Hait whirled. Again she skidded savagely on the greasy planks as she and the mule rushed parallel with one another toward the shed building, from whose open doorway there now projected the static and astonished face of a cow. To the cow the fog-born mule doubtless looked taller and more incredibly sudden than a giraffe even, and apparently bent upon charging right through the shed as though it were made of straw or were purely and simply mirage. The cow's head likewise had a quality transient and abrupt and unmundane. It vanished, sucked into invisibility like a match flame, though the mind knew and the reason insisted that she had withdrawn into the shed, from which, as proof's burden, there came an indescribable sound of shock and alarm by shed and beast engendered, analogous to a single note from a profoundly struck lyre or harp. Toward this sound Mrs. Hait sprang, immediately, as if by pure reflex, as though in invulnerable compact of female with female against a world of mule and man. She and the mule converged upon the shed at top speed, the heavy scuttle poised lightly in her hand to hurl. Of course it did not take this long, and likewise it was the mule which refused the gambit. Old Het was still shouting "Dar hit! Dar hit!" when it swerved and rushed at her where she stood tall as a stove pipe, holding the shopping-bag which she swung at the beast as it rushed past her and vanished beyond the other corner of the house as though sucked back into the fog which had produced it, profound and instantaneous and without any sound.

With that unhasteful celerity Mrs. Hait turned and set the scuttle down on the brick coping of the cellar entrance and she and old Het turned the corner of the house in time to see the now wraithlike mule at the moment when its course converged with that of a choleric-looking rooster and eight Rhode Island Red hens emerging from beneath the house. Then for an instant its progress assumed the appearance and trappings of an apotheosis: hell-born and hell-returning, in the act of dissolving completely into the fog, it seemed to rise vanishing into a sunless and dimensionless medium borne upon and enclosed by small winged goblins.

"Dey's mo in de front!" old Het cried.

"Them sons of bitches," Mrs. Hait said, again in that grim, prescient voice without rancor or heat. It was not the mules to which she referred; it was not even the owner of them. It was her whole town-dwelling history as dated from that April dawn ten years ago when what was left of Hait had been gathered from the mangled remains of five mules and several feet of new Manila rope on a blind curve of the railroad just out of town; the geographical hap of her very home; the very components of her bereavement — the mules, the defunct husband, and the owner of them. His name was Snopes; in the town they knew about him too — how he bought his stock at the Memphis market and brought it to Jefferson and sold it to farmers and widows and orphans black and white, for whatever he could contrive — down to a certain figure; and about how (usually in the dead season of winter) teams and even small droves of his stock would escape from the fenced pasture where he kept them and, tied one to another with sometimes quite new hemp rope (and which item Snopes included in the subsequent claim), would be annihilated by freight trains on the same blind curve which was to be the scene of Hait's exit from this world; once a town wag sent him through the mail a printed train schedule for the division. A squat, pasty man perennially tieless and with a strained, harried expression, at stated intervals he passed athwart the peaceful and somnolent life of the town in dust and uproar, his advent heralded by shouts and cries, his passing marked by a yellow cloud filled with tossing jug-shaped heads and clattering hooves and the same forlorn and earnest cries of the drovers; and last of all and well back out of the dust, Snopes himself moving at a harried and panting trot, since it was said in the town that he was deathly afraid of the very beasts in which he cleverly dealt.

The path which he must follow from the railroad station to his pasture crossed the edge of town near Hait's home; Hait and Mrs. Hait had not been in the house a week before they waked one morning to find it surrounded by galloping mules and the air filled with the shouts and cries of the drovers. But it was not until that April dawn some years later, when those who reached the scene first found what might be termed foreign matter among the mangled mules and the savage fragments of new rope, that the town suspected that Hait stood in any closer relationship to Snopes and the mules than that of helping at periodical intervals to drive them out of his front yard. After that they believed that they knew; in a three days' recess of interest, surprise, and curiosity they watched to see if Snopes would try to collect on Hait also.

But they learned only that the adjuster appeared and called upon Mrs. Hait and that a few days later she cashed a check for eight thousand five hundred dollars, since this was back in the old halcyon days when even the companies considered their southern branches and divisions the legitimate prey of all who dwelt beside them. She took the cash: she stood in her sweater coat and the hat which Hait had been wearing on the fatal morning a week ago and listened in cold, grim silence while the teller counted the money and the president and the cashier tried to explain to her the virtues of a bond, then of a savings account, then of a checking account, and departed with the money in a salt sack under her apron; after a time she painted her house: that serviceable and time-defying color which the railroad station was painted, as though out of sentiment or (as some said) gratitude.

10   The adjuster also summoned Snopes into conference, from which he emerged not only more harried-looking than ever, but with his face stamped with a bewildered dismay which it was to wear from then on, and that was the last time his pasture fence was ever to give inexplicably away at dead of night upon mules coupled in threes and fours by adequate rope even though not always new. And then it seemed as though the mules themselves knew this, as if, even while haltered at the Memphis block at his bid, they sensed it somehow as they sensed that he was afraid of them. Now, three or four times a year and as though by fiendish concord and as soon as they were freed of the box car, the entire uproar — the dust cloud filled with shouts earnest, harried, and dismayed, with plunging demoniac shapes — would become translated in a single burst of perverse and uncontrollable violence, without any intervening contact with time, space, or earth, across the peaceful and astonished town and into Mrs. Hait's yard, where, in a certain hapless despair which abrogated for the moment even physical fear, Snopes ducked and dodged among the thundering shapes about the house (for whose very impervious paint the town believed that he felt he had paid and whose inmate lived within it a life of idle and queenlike ease on money which he considered at least partly his own) while gradually that section and neighborhood gath-

ered to look on from behind adjacent window curtains and porches screened and not, and from the sidewalks and even from halted wagons and cars in the street — housewives in the wrappers and boudoir caps of morning, children on the way to school, casual Negroes and casual whites in static and entertained repose.

They were all there when, followed by old Het and carrying the stub of a worn-out broom, Mrs. Hait ran around the next corner and onto the handkerchief-sized plot of earth which she called her front yard. It was small; any creature with a running stride of three feet could have spanned it in two paces, yet at the moment, due perhaps to the myopic and distortive quality of the fog, it seemed to be as incredibly full of mad life as a drop of water beneath the microscope. Yet again she did not falter. With the broom clutched in her hand and apparently with a kind of sublime faith in her own invulnerability, she rushed on after the haltered mule which was still in that arrested and wraithlike process of vanishing furiously into the fog, its wake indicated by the tossing and dispersing shapes of the nine chickens like so many jagged scraps of paper in the dying air blast of an automobile, and the madly dodging figure of a man. The man was Snopes; beaded too with moisture, his wild face gaped with hoarse shouting and the two heavy lines of shaven beard descending from the corners of it as though in alluvial retrospect of years of tobacco, he screamed at her: "Fore God, Miz Hait! I done everything I could!" She didn't even look at him.

"Ketch that big un with the bridle on," she said in her cold, panting voice. "Git that big un outen here."

"Sho!" Snopes shrieked. "Jest let um take their time. Jest don't git um excited now."

"Watch out!" old Het shouted. "He headin fer de back again!"

"Git the rope," Mrs. Hait said, running again. Snopes glared back at old Het.

"Fore God, where is ere rope?" he shouted.

"In de cellar fo God!" old Het shouted, also without pausing. "Go roun de udder way en head um." Again she and Mrs. Hait turned the corner in time to see again the still-vanishing mule with the halter once more in the act of floating lightly onward on its cloud of chickens with which, they being able to pass under the house and so on the chord of a circle while it had to go around on the arc, it had once more coincided. When they turned the next corner they were in the back yard again.

"Fo God!" old Het cried. "He fixin' to misuse de cow!" For they had gained on the mule now, since it had stopped. In fact, they came around the corner on a tableau. The cow now stood in the center of the yard. She and the mule faced one another a few feet apart. Motionless, with lowered heads and braced forelegs, they looked like two book ends from two distinct pairs of a general pattern which some one of amateurly bucolic leanings might have purchased, and which some child had salvaged, brought into idle juxtaposition and then forgotten; and, his head and shoulders projecting above the back-flung slant of the cellar entrance where the scuttle still sat, Snopes standing as though buried to the armpits for a Spanish-Indian-American suttee. Only again it did not take this long. It was less than tableau; it was one of those things which later even memory cannot quite affirm. Now and in turn, man and cow and mule vanished beyond the next corner, Snopes now in the lead, carrying the rope, the cow next with her tail rigid and raked slightly like the stern staff of a boat. Mrs. Hait and old Het ran on, passing the open cellar gaping upon its accumulation of human necessities and widowed womanyears — boxes of kindling wood, old papers and magazines, the broken and outworn furniture and utensils which no woman ever throws away; a pile of coal and another of pitch pine for priming fires — and ran on and turned the next corner to see man and cow and mule all vanishing now in the wild cloud of ubiquitous chickens which had once more crossed beneath the house and emerged. They ran on, Mrs. Hait in grim and unflagging silence, old Het with the eager and happy amazement of a child. But when they gained the front again they saw only Snopes. He lay flat on his stomach, his head and shoulders upreared by his outstretched arms, his coat tail swept forward by its own arrested momentum about his head so that from beneath it his slack-jawed face mused in wild repose like that of a burlesqued nun.

"Whar'd dey go?" old Het shouted at him. He didn't answer.

20 "Dey tightenin' on de curves!" she cried. "Dey already in de back again!" That's where they were. The cow made a feint at running into her shed, but deciding perhaps that her speed was too great, she whirled in a final desperation of despair-like valor. But they did not see this, nor see the mule, swerving to pass her, crash and blunder for an instant at the open cellar door before going on. When they arrived, the mule was gone. The scuttle was gone too, but they did not notice it; they saw only the cow standing in the center of the yard as before, panting, rigid, with braced forelegs and lowered head facing nothing, as if the child had returned and removed one of the book ends for some newer purpose or game. They ran on. Mrs. Hait ran heavily now, her mouth too open, her face putty-colored and one hand pressed to her side. So slow was their progress that the mule in its third circuit of the house overtook them from behind and soared past with undiminished speed, with brief demon thunder and a keen ammonia-sweet reek of sweat sudden and sharp as a jeering cry, and was gone. Yet they ran doggedly on around the next corner in time to see it succeed at last in vanishing into the fog; they heard its hoofs, brief, staccato, and derisive, on the paved street, dying away.

"Well," old Het said, stopping. She panted, happily. "Gentlemen, hush! Ain't we had — " Then she became stone still; slowly her head turned, high-nosed, her nostrils pulsing; perhaps for the instant she saw the open cellar door as they had last passed it, with no scuttle beside it. "Fo God I smells smoke!" she said. "Chile, run, git yo money."

That was still early, not yet ten o'clock. By noon the house had burned to the ground. There was a farmers' supply store where Snopes could be usually found; more than one had made a point of finding him there by that time. They told him about how when the fire engine and the crowd reached the scene, Mrs. Hait, followed by old Het carrying her shopping-bag in one hand and a framed portrait of Mr. Hait in the other, emerged with an umbrella and wearing a new, dun-colored, mail-order coat, in one pocket of which lay a fruit jar filled with smoothly rolled banknotes and in the other a heavy, nickel-plated pistol, and crossed the street to the house opposite, where with old Het beside her in another rocker, she had been sitting ever since on the veranda, grim, inscrutable, the two of them rocking steadily, while hoarse and tireless men hurled her dishes and furniture and bedding up and down the street.

"What are you telling me for?" Snopes said. "Hit warn't me that set that ere scuttle of live fire where the first thing that passed would knock hit into the cellar."

"It was you that opened the cellar door, though."

"Sho. And for what? To git that rope, her own rope, where she told me to get it."

"To catch your mule with, that was trespassing on her property. You can't get out of it this time, I. O. There ain't a jury in the county that won't find for her."

"Yes. I reckon not. And just because she is a woman. That's why. Because she is a durn woman. All right. Let her go to her durn jury with hit. I can talk too; I reckon hit's a few things I could tell a jury myself about — " He ceased. They were watching him.

"What? Tell a jury about what?"

"Nothing. Because hit ain't going to no jury. A jury between her and me? Me and Mannie Hait? You boys don't know her if you think she's going to make trouble over a pure acci-dent couldn't nobody help. Why, there ain't a fairer, finer woman in the county than Miz Mannie Hait. I just wisht I had a opportunity to tell her so." The opportunity came at once. Old Het was behind her, carrying the shopping-bag. Mrs. Hait looked once, quietly, about at the faces, making no response to the murmur of curious salutation, then not again. She didn't look at Snopes long either, nor talk to him long.

"I come to buy that mule," she said.

"What mule?" They looked at one another. "You'd like to own that mule?" She looked at him. "Hit'll cost you a hundred and fifty, Miz Mannie."

"You mean dollars?"

"I don't mean dimes nor nickels neither, Miz Mannie."

"Dollars," she said. "That's more than mules was in Hait's time."

"Lots of things is different since Hait's time. Including you and me."

"I reckon so," she said. Then she went away. She turned without a word, old Het following.

"Maybe one of them others you looked at this morning would suit you," Snopes said. She didn't answer. Then they were gone.

"I don't know as I would have said that last to her," one said.

"What for?" Snopes said. "If she was aiming to law something outen me about that fire, you reckon she would have come and offered to pay me money for hit?" That was about one o'clock. About four o'clock he was shouldering his way through a throng of Negroes before a cheap grocery store when one called his name. It was old Het, the now bulging shopping-bag on her arm, eating bananas from a paper sack.

"Fo God I wuz jest dis minute huntin fer you," she said. She handed the banana to a woman beside her and delved and fumbled in the shopping-bag and extended a greenback. "Miz Mannie gimme dis to give you; I wuz just on de way to de sto whar you stay at. Here." He took the bill.

"What's this? From Miz Hait?"

"Fer de mule." The bill was for ten dollars. "You don't need to gimme no receipt. I kin be de witness I give hit to you."

"Ten dollars? For that mule? I told her a hundred and fifty dollars."

"You'll have to fix dat up wid her yo'self. She just gimme dis to give ter you when she sot out to fetch de mule."

"Set out to fetch — She went out there herself and taken my mule outen my pasture?"

"Lawd, chile," old Het said, "Miz Mannie ain't skeered of no mule. Ain't you done foun dat out?"

And then it became late, what with the yet short winter days; when she came in sight of the two gaunt chimneys against the sunset, evening was already finding itself. But she could smell the ham cooking before she came in sight of the cow shed even, though she could not see it until she came around in front where the fire burned beneath an iron skillet set on bricks and where nearby Mrs. Hait was milking the cow. "Well," old Het said, "you is settled down, ain't you?" She looked into the shed, neated and raked and swept even, and floored now with fresh hay. A clean new lantern burned on a box, beside it a pallet bed was spread neatly on the straw and turned neatly back for the night. "Why, you is fixed up," she said with pleased astonishment. Within the door was a kitchen chair. She drew it out and sat down beside the skillet and laid the bulging shopping-bag beside her.

"I'll tend dis meat whilst you milks. I'd offer to strip dat cow fer you ef I wuzn't so wo out wid all dis excitement we been had." She looked around her. "I don't believe I sees yo new mule, dough." Mrs. Hait grunted, her head against the cow's flank. After a moment she said,

"Did you give him that money?"

"I give um ter him. He ack surprise at first, lak maybe he think you didn't aim to trade dat quick. I tole him to settle de details wid you later. He taken de money, dough. So I reckin dat's offen his mine en yo'n bofe." Again Mrs. Hait grunted. Old Het turned the ham in the skillet. Beside it the coffee pot bubbled and steamed. "Cawfee smell good too," she said. "I ain't had no appetite in years now. A bird couldn't live on de vittles I eats. But jest lemme git a whiff er cawfee en seem lak hit always whets me a little. Now, ef you jest had nudder little piece o dis ham, now — Fo God, you got company aready." But Mrs. Hait did not even look up until she had finished. Then she turned without rising from the box on which she sat.

"I reckon you and me better have a little talk," Snopes said. "I reckon I got something that belongs to you and I hear you got something that belongs to me." He looked about, quickly, ceaselessly, while old Het watched him. He turned to her. "You go away, aunty. I don't reckon you want to set here and listen to us."

"Lawd, honey," old Het said. "Don't you mind me. I done already had so much troubles myself dat I kin set en listen to udder folks' widout hit worryin me a-tall. You gawn talk whut you came ter talk; I jest set here en tend de ham." Snopes looked at Mrs. Hait.

"Ain't you going to make her go away?" he said.

"What for?" Mrs. Hait said. "I reckon she ain't the first critter that ever come on this yard when hit wanted and went or stayed when hit liked." Snopes made a gesture, brief, fretted, restrained.

"Well," he said. "All right. So you taken the mule."   55

"I paid you for it. She give you the money."

"Ten dollars. For a hundred-and-fifty-dollar mule. Ten dollars."

"I don't know anything about hundred-and-fifty-dollar mules. All I know is what the railroad paid." Now Snopes looked at her for a full moment.

"What do you mean?"

"Them sixty dollars a head the railroad used to pay for mules back when   60
you and Hait — — "

"Hush," Snopes said; he looked about again, quick, ceaseless. "All right. Even call it sixty dollars. But you just sent me ten."

"Yes. I sent you the difference." He looked at her, perfectly still. "Between that mule and what you owed Hait."

"What I owed — — "

"For getting them five mules onto the tr — — "

"Hush!" he cried. "Hush!" Her voice went on, cold, grim, level.   65

"For helping you. You paid him fifty dollars each time, and the railroad paid you sixty dollars a head for the mules. Ain't that right?" He watched her. "That last time you never paid him. So I taken that mule instead. And I sent you the ten dollars difference."

"Yes," he said in a tone of quiet, swift, profound bemusement; then he cried: "But look! Here's where I got you. Hit was our agreement that I wouldn't never owe him nothing until after the mules was — — "

"I reckon you better hush yourself," Mrs. Hait said.

" — until hit was over. And this time, when over had come, I never owed nobody no money because the man hit would have been owed to wasn't nobody," he cried triumphantly. "You see?" Sitting on the box, motionless, downlooking, Mrs. Hait seemed to muse. "So you just take your ten dollars back and tell me where my mule is and we'll just go back good friends to where we started at. Fore God, I'm as sorry as ere a living man about that fire — — "

"Fo God!" old Het said, "hit was a blaze, wuzn't it?"

" — but likely with all that ere railroad money you still got, you just been wanting a chance to build new, all along. So here. Take hit." He put the money into her hand. "Where's my mule?" But Mrs. Hait didn't move at once.

"You want to give it back to me?" she said.

"Sho. We been friends all the time; now we'll just go back to where we left off being. I don't hold no hard feelings and don't you hold none. Where you got the mule hid?"

"Up at the end of that ravine ditch behind Spilmer's," she said.

"Sho. I know. A good, sheltered place, since you ain't got nere barn. Only if you'd a just left hit in the pasture, hit would a saved us both trouble. But hit ain't no hard feelings though. And so I'll bid you goodnight. You're all fixed up, I see. I reckon you could save some more money by not building no house a-tall."

"I reckon I could," Mrs. Hait said. But he was gone.

"Whut did you leave de mule dar fer?" old Het said.

"I reckon that's far enough," Mrs. Hait said.

"Fer enough?" But Mrs. Hait came and looked into the skillet, and old Het said, "Wuz hit me er you dat mentioned something erbout er nudder piece o dis ham?" So they were both eating when in the not-quite-yet accomplished twilight Snopes returned. He came up quietly and stood, holding his hands to the blaze as if he were quite cold. He did not look at any one now.

"I reckon I'll take that ere ten dollars," he said.

"What ten dollars?" Mrs. Hait said. He seemed to muse upon the fire. Mrs. Hait and old Het chewed quietly, old Het alone watching him.

"You ain't going to give hit back to me?" he said.

"You was the one that said to let's go back to where we started," Mrs. Hait said.

"Fo God you wuz, en dat's de fack," old Het said. Snopes mused upon the fire; he spoke in a tone of musing and amazed despair:

"I go to the worry and the risk and the agoment for years and years and I get sixty dollars. And you, one time, without no trouble and no risk, without even knowing you are going to git it, git eighty-five hundred dollars. I never begrudged hit to you; can't nere a man say I did, even if hit did seem a little strange that you should git it all when he wasn't working for you and you never even knowed where he was at and what doing; that all you done to git it was to be married to him. And now, after all these ten years of not begrudging you hit, you taken the best mule I had and you ain't even going to pay me ten dollars for hit. Hit ain't right. Hit ain't justice."

'You got de mule back, en you ain't satisfried yit," old Het said. "Whut does you want?" Now Snopes looked at Mrs. Hait.

"For the last time I ask hit," he said. "Will you or won't you give hit back?"

"Give what back?" Mrs. Hait said. Snopes turned. He stumbled over something — it was old Het's shopping-bag — and recovered and went on. They could see him in silhouette, as though framed by the two blackened chimneys against the dying west; they saw him fling up both clenched hands in a gesture almost Gallic, of resignation and impotent despair. Then he was gone. Old Het was watching Mrs. Hait.

"Honey," she said. "Whut did you do wid de mule?" Mrs. Hait leaned forward to the fire. On her plate lay a stale biscuit. She lifted the skillet and poured over the biscuit the grease in which the ham had cooked.

"I shot it," she said.   90

"You which?" old Het said. Mrs. Hait began to eat the biscuit. "Well," old Het said, happily, "de mule burnt de house en you shot de mule. Dat's whut I calls justice." It was getting dark fast now, and before her was still the three-mile walk to the poorhouse. But the dark would last a long time in January, and the poorhouse too would not move at once. She sighed with weary and happy relaxation. "Gentlemen, hush! Ain't we had a day!"

QUESTIONS

1. This story has one character in common with "Spotted Horses." Is he a logical projection of the character as seen in that story? How is he like and unlike his cousin Flem? How does he make his living?
2. Characterize Mrs. Hait. Explain in detail her final transactions with I. O.
3. Characterize Old Het. What color is she?
4. From what point of view is this story told? Compare and contrast its narrative style with that of "Spotted Horses." Give specific examples.
5. What are the chief sources of comedy in this story? Is there any difference in the flavor of its humor?
6. Who is the protagonist? Who is the antagonist? Which is successful in their conflict?
7. Like "Spotted Horses," this is a comic story involving an animal chase. Which story is more powerful, broader in scope, deeper in insight and effect? Justify your answer.

PART 2

Stories for Further Reading

Alice Adams

Fog

On an unspeakably cold and foggy night one November in San Francisco, something terrible happens to a woman named Antonia Love. She is a painter, middle-aged, recently successful, who has invited some people to her house for dinner (one of whom she has not even met, as yet). But in the course of tearing greens into the salad bowl and simultaneously shooing off one of her cats — the old favorite, who would like to knead on one of her new brown velvet shoes — Antonia, who is fairly tall, loses her balance and falls, skidding on a fragment of watercress and avoiding the cat but landing, *bang*, on the floor, which is Mexican-tiled, blue and white. Hard. Antonia thinks she heard the crack of a bone.

Just lying there for a moment, shocked, Antonia imagines herself a sprawled, stuffed china-headed doll, her limbs all askew, awry. How incredibly stupid, how dumb, she scolds herself; if I didn't want people to dinner, I could just have not asked them. And then: Well, useless to blame myself, there are accidents. The point is, what to do now?

As she tries to move, it is apparent that her left arm indeed is broken; it won't work, and in the effort of trying to move it Antonia experiences an instant of pain so acute that she reels, almost faints, and only does not by the most excruciating effort of will.

The problem of what to do, then, seems almost out of her hands. Since she can't for the moment get up, she also can't call her doctor, nor 911. Nor, certainly, can she go on with making dinner.

5   Fortunately her coming guests are old close friends (except for the very young man she doesn't know, although he seems to think he has met her somewhere). And, further luck, she is sure that she unlocked the front door, its bell being hard to hear, back here in the kitchen. And so her friends will arrive and they will come on in, calling out to her, and she to them. They will find her ludicrously positioned, they will help — although possibly she is really quite all right, and will manage to get up by herself any minute now.

A new flash of pain as she tries to move convinces Antonia that her arm is really broken, and again she castigates herself for clumsiness, for evident ill will toward her friends, determined self-defeat. For steady progress toward no progress at all — oh, for everything!

In addition to which she has probably scared her cat quite badly. He is nowhere around, although she calls out to him, "Baron! Baron?"

FOG   First published in 1989. Alice Adams was born in 1926 in Fredericksburg, Virginia, and was raised in Chapel Hill, North Carolina. She received her B.A. at Radcliffe in 1945, married and had children, worked at a variety of office jobs, divorced, and eventually was able to support herself by writing. She published the first of her five novels in 1966, and this story is taken from her fourth short story collection. She now lives in San Francisco.

No cat, then, and no live-in lover either, since Reeve is at the moment off on one of his restless trips somewhere; Reeve who in an off-and-on way lives there with Antonia, the arrangement being that both are "free." And just as well he is gone, thinks Antonia; he so hates debility, hates bodily things going wrong. (But in that case why has he chosen to live, more or less, with an "older woman," whose body must inevitably decline?) Antonia wonders if Reeve is alone on this trip (she knows that he sometimes is not), but she finds that she lacks just now the stamina for jealous speculation.

Her arm really hurts badly, though; she wishes someone would come, and she wonders who will be the first—who will come in to find her in this worse than undignified position? Will it be her old friend from school days, Lisa, who is bringing the strange young man? Or will it be Bynum and Phyllis, who are old friends—or Bynum is. He is a sculptor, and Phyllis, his latest wife, a very young lawyer. Antonia believes they are not getting along very well.

Or (at this new notion Antonia grimaces to herself) it could always be   10
tall, thin, sandy Reeve himself, who is given to changing his mind, to turning around and away from trips, and people. Reeve, a painter too, is more apt to come home early from trips on which he is accompanied than from those he takes alone; but even that is not a formulation on which anyone, especially Antonia, should count.

Antonia is aware that her friends wonder why she "puts up" with Reeve, his absences, his occasional flings with young art students. And she considers her private view of him: an exceptional man, of extreme (if occasional) sensitivity, kindness—a painter of the most extraordinary talent. (On the other hand, sometimes she too wonders.)

Antonia knows too that her friends refer to Reeve as "Antonia's cowboy" . . .

Reeve is from Wyoming.

She tries next to lie down, believing that some rest might help, or ease the pain, which now seems to have become a constant. Never mind how appalling the spectacle of herself would be, her oversized body sprawled across the floor. However, she can't get down, can't reach the floor; the broken arm impedes any such changes of position. Antonia finds that the most she can achieve is leaning back against table legs, fortunately a heavy, substantial table.

Perry Loomis, the unmet guest, is a journalist, just getting started, or   15
trying to in New York. He could surely sell an article about such a distinguished, increasingly famous woman, especially since Antonia never gives interviews. Now, having cleverly engineered this meeting, and being driven in from Marin County by Antonia's old friend Lisa, Perry is overexcited, unable not to babble. "It said in *Time* that a lot of speculators are really grabbing up her stuff. Even at thirty or forty thousand per. She must hate all that, but still."

"It's hard to tell how she does feel about it," Lisa responds. "Or anything else, for that matter. I think success has been quite confusing to Antonia."

The bay is heavily fogged, slowing their progress from Mill Valley into town, to Antonia's small house on Telegraph Hill. Not everyone slows, however; an occasional small, smart sports car will zoom from nowhere past Lisa's more practical Ford wagon. Scary, but she does not even think of asking this young man to drive. They met through friends at a recent gallery (not the opening) at which Antonia's work was being shown. Perry described himself as a "tremendous Antonia Love fan" and seemed in his enthusiasm both innocent and appealing. Which led Lisa fatally to say, "Oh, really, I've known her almost all my life." Which was not even quite true, but which, repeated to Antonia, led up to this dinner invitation. "Well, why don't you bring him along when you come next Thursday? I'm almost sure Reeve won't be here, and poor Bynum must be tired of being the token man."

"And she's so beautiful," rattles Perry. "Was she always such a beauty?"

"Well, no," says Lisa, too quickly. "In fact, I don't quite see — but you know how old friends are. As a young woman, she was just so — big. You know, and all that hair."

20   "But I met her," Perry reminds her firmly. "At that thing in New York. She had on the most marvelous dress, she was ravishing, really."

"Oh yes, her green dress. It is good-looking. I think she paid the earth for it. That's one of the points about darling Antonia, really. Her adorable inconsistencies. A dress like that but never a sign of a maid or even a cleaning person in her house." And just why is she sounding so bitchy? Lisa wonders.

"Maybe she thinks they'd get in her way?" Perry's imagination has a practical turn. As a schoolboy, which was not all that long ago, he too meant to be an artist, and was full of vague, romantic plans. However, during college years, in the late seventies, he came to see that journalism might better serve his needs, a judgment seemingly correct. However, his enthusiasm for "artists," in this instance Antonia, is a vestige of that earlier phase.

"Well, she's in any case a marvelous cook," Lisa promises warmly. And then, somewhat less charitably, "Her cooking is surely one of those things that keeps young Reeve around."

"But isn't he a painter too?" Saying this, with an embarrassed twinge Perry realizes that he has imagined Reeve, described in Antonia Love articles as her "young painter companion" as a slightly older version of himself. He had looked forward to seeing just what of himself he would find in Antonia's Reeve.

25   "Of course he's a painter, that's nine-tenths of the problem right there. Reeve's from Wyoming, we call him 'Antonia's cowboy.' But they should never — Oh, look. *Damn.* There must be an accident on the bridge. Damn, we'll never get there."

Before them, on the downward, entirely fog-shrouded approach to the Golden Gate Bridge, what now seems heavy traffic is halted, absolutely. Red brake lights flicker as thick cold moisture condenses and drips in rivulets down windshields, windows, as somewhere out in the depthless, dangerous bay the foghorns croak, and mourn.

"Oh dear," says Perry Loomis. Although this attractive, rather interesting "older woman" was kind enough to bring him to his object, the desired Antonia, he thinks he really doesn't like her very much. (Are she and Antonia Love the same age? he wonders. This one looks younger, he thinks.)

"Indeed," says Lisa. On the whole an honest woman, she now admits to herself that she agreed to bring this Perry along not entirely out of kindness; there was also (she confesses to herself) some element of fantasy involved, specifically a romantic fantasy of herself with a younger lover (Lisa has been twice divorced, most recently two years back, from an especially mean-spirited lawyer). And then: Oh God, she thinks. Do I have to spend my life trying to be Antonia?

Reeve, who did indeed start out for Oregon, and alone, has now made a wide detour via the Richmond-San Rafael Bridge and is headed for Berkeley. Where, as Antonia might have guessed, had she the energy, there is a girl, Sharon, in whom Reeve is "interested." At this moment, heading along the foggy freeway toward the Berkeley exits, he longs to talk to Sharon, talking being so far about all they have done.

It's very difficult living with Antonia, he would like to tell Sharon. Here she is so successful, everything people work for, and she doesn't believe it. In her mind she's still starving and probably lonely. I mean, it's very hard to live with someone whom nothing can convince that she's all right. Nothing can convince her that people love her, including me.

Sharon is one of the most beautiful young women that Reeve has ever seen; he rather suspects that she was hired in the Art Department, where she works, on that basis — she was formerly a model. A darkly creamy blonde, with dreamy, thick-lashed blue-green eyes, Sharon holds her perfect body forward like a prize; she moves like a small queen — and she would not understand a single word of all that Reeve would like to say. To Sharon it would all be the ancient complaints about a wife.

In fact, the only person who could make the slightest sense of his ravings is Antonia herself. Reeve, a somewhat sardonic, self-mocking young man, comes to this conclusion with a twisting, interior smile. And, on an impulse, passing Sharon's exit, which is University, and heading toward the fog-ladened Bay Bridge, he speeds up the car.

"Phyllis and Bynum, Lisa. Perry. I'll be back soon. Sorry. Stew and risotto in the oven. Salad and wine in refrig. Please take and eat. Love, Antonia."

This note, taped to Antonia's door, was found by Phyllis and Bynum, one of whose first remarks to each other then was "Who on earth does she mean by Perry?"

"Oh, some new young man of Lisa's, wouldn't you say?"

"But what could have happened to Antonia?"

"One of her meetings, wouldn't you imagine? One of her good works."
This last from Bynum, Antonia's oldest friend, who has very little patience
with her, generally.

That exchange takes place on the long stairs leading up to the small,
shabby-comfortable living room in which they soon sit, with glasses of wine,
engaged in speculations concerning their hostess.

"Something could be wrong?" Phyllis ventures. A small, blonde, rather
pretty woman, she is much in awe of Antonia, whom she perceives as exceptionally *strong*, in ways that she, Phyllis, believes herself not to be.

"I doubt it." Big, gnarled Bynum frowns.

This room's great feature — to some its only virtue — is the extraordinary
view afforded of the city, even now, despite the thick fog. City lights still are
faintly visible, everywhere, though somewhat muffled, dim, and the loom-
ing shapes of buildings can just be made out against the lighter sky.

Phyllis, who is extremely tired (a grueling day in court; but is she also
tired of Bynum, as she sometimes thinks?), now lounges across a large,
lumpy overstuffed chair, and she sips at the welcome cool wine. (The very
size of Antonia's chair diminishes her to almost nothing, Phyllis feels.) She
says, "Obviously, the view is why Antonia stays here?"

"Contrariness, I'd say," pontificates Bynum, himself most contrary by
nature. "I doubt if she even notices the view anymore."

A familiar annoyance tightens Phyllis's throat as she mildly says, "Oh,
I'll bet she does." She is thinking, if Bynum and I split up, I'll be lucky to get
a place this nice, he doesn't have to keep putting it down. This could cost,
oh, close to a thousand.

"Besides, the rent's still so low," continues Bynum, as though Phyllis
had not spoken, perhaps as though he had read her mind.

A pause ensues.

"God, I'm so hungry," says Phyllis. "Do you think we should really go
ahead with dinner?"

"Baby, I sure do." Bynum too is tired, a long sad day of not being able to
work. And he too is hungry. "Antonia could be forever, and Lisa and her
young man lost somewhere out in the fog."

The immediate prospect of food, however, serves to appease their hunger. They smile pleasantly at each other, like strangers, or those just met.
Phyllis even thinks what a handsome man Bynum is; he looks wonderful for
his age. "Was Antonia good-looking back when you first knew her?" she
asks him.

"Well, she was odd." Bynum seems to ruminate. "She varied so much.
Looking terrific one day, and really bad the next. But she was always, uh,
attractive. Men after her. But the thing is, she doesn't know it."

"Oh, not even now?" Phyllis, disliking her own small scale, her blonde
pallor, admires Antonia's larger, darker style. Antonia is so emphatic, is
what Phyllis thinks.

"Especially not now." Bynum's smile and his tone are indulgent.

"Do you remember that really strange thing she said, when she told a reporter, 'I'm not Antonia Love'?" asks Phyllis. She has wanted to mention this before to Bynum, but they have, seemingly, no time for conversation.

"I think she meant that she could only view herself as created," Bynum explains authoritatively.

Phyllis is not sure whether he is speaking as a fellow artist or simply as an old friend. She asks, "Do you mean by the media?" She is aware of enjoying this conversation, perhaps because it is one, a conversation.

"Oh no, so much more sinister," Bynum assures her. "By herself. She thinks she's someone she's painted." He chuckles a little too loudly.

And loses the momentary sympathy of his young wife. Declining to comment, though, and remembering how hungry she is, Phyllis gets up to her feet. "Well, I don't care how lost Lisa and what's-his-name are. I'm heating up dinner."

She goes out into the kitchen as Bynum calls after her, "I'll be there in a minute."

But several minutes pass, during which Bynum does not follow Phyllis. Instead he stares out the window, out into the dark, the enveloping, thickening fog. Into dimmed yellow lights.

He is fairly sure that Phyllis will leave soon; he knows the signs — the ill-concealed small gestures of impatience, the long speculative looks, the tendencies to argument. How terribly alike they all seem, these girls that he marries. Or is it possible that he sees none of them very sharply, by herself — that he can't differentiate? One of them made this very accusation, referring to what she called his "myopia." In any case, he will probably not miss Phyllis any more than he missed the others, and in a year or so he will find and marry a new young woman who is very much like Phyllis and the rest. He knows that he must be married.

A strong light wind has come up, rattling the windowpanes. Standing there, still looking out, Bynum has a brand-new thought — or, rather, a series of thoughts. He thinks, Why do they always have to be so goddamn young? Just who am I kidding? I'm not a young man. A woman of my own age or nearly might at last be a perfect companion for me. A woman artist, even, and he thinks, Well, why not Antonia? This place is a dump, but she's so successful now we could travel a lot. And I've always liked her really, despite our fights. This Reeve person must surely be on the way out. She won't put up with him much longer — so callow.

"Bynum, come on, it's all ready," Phyllis then calls out as at that same instant the doorbell rings.

It is of course Lisa and the new young man, Perry, who looks, Bynum observes, far too smugly pleased with himself.

Introductions are made, warm greetings exchanged: "But you look marvelous! Have you been here long? Yes, I'm sure we met at the gallery. How very like Antonia not to be here. But whatever could have happened?"

"Actually, it is not at all like Antonia not to be here," Bynum announces. He is experiencing a desire to establish himself as the one of them who knows her best.

Over dinner, which indeed is excellent — a succulent veal stew, with a risotto — Bynum scrutinizes Lisa, and what looks to be her new friend. Lisa is looking considerably less happy than the young man is, this Perry, in Bynum's view. Could they possibly have made it in the car, on the way over here, and now Lisa is feeling regrets? Even to Bynum's somewhat primitive imagination this seems unlikely.

What Lisa regrets is simply having talked as much as she did to Perry as on the way over they remained locked in the fogbound traffic. She not only talked, she exaggerated, overemphasized Antonia's occasional depression, even her worries over Reeve.

And even while going on and on in that way, Lisa was visited by an odd perception, which was that she was really talking about herself. She, Lisa, suffers more than occasional depressions. It is her work, not Antonia's (well, hardly Antonia's), that seems to be going nowhere. And Lisa, with no Reeve or anyone interesting in her life at the moment, is worried that this very attractive young man will not like her (she has always liked small, dark, trimly built men like Perry). Which is really why she said so much about Antonia — gossip as gift, which is something she knows about, having done it far too often.

The truth is — or one truth is — that she is deeply, permanently fond of Antonia. And another truth is that her jealous competitiveness keeps cropping up, like some ugly, uncontrolled weed. She has to face up to it, do something about it, somehow.

"What a superb cook Antonia is," she now says (this is true, but is she atoning?). "Her food is always such a treat."

"The truth is that Antonia does everything quite well," Bynum intones. "Remember that little spate of jewelry design she went into? Therapy, she called it, and she gave it up pretty quickly, but she did some lovely stuff."

"Oh, Bynum," Lisa is unable not to cry out. "How can you even mention that junk? She was so depressed when she did it, and it did not work as therapy. You know perfectly well that she looked dreadful with all those dangles. She's too big."

Perry laughs as she says this, but in a pleasant, rather sympathetic way, so that Lisa thinks that maybe, after all, he understood? understood about love as well as envy?

Below them on the street now are the straining, dissonant, banging sounds of cars: people trying to park, trying to find their houses, to get home to rest. It is hard to separate one sound from another, to distinguish, identify. Thus, steps that must be Antonia's, with whomever she is with, are practically upon them before anyone has time to say, "Oh, that must be Antonia."

It is, though: Antonia, her arm in its bright white muslin sling thrust 75
before her, in a bright new shiny plaster cast. Tall Antonia, looked triumphant, if very pale. And taller Reeve, somewhat disheveled, longish sandy
hair all awry, but also in his own way triumphant, smiling. His arm is around
Antonia's shoulder, in protective possession.

First exclamations are in reaction to the cast. "Antonia, how terrible!
However did you? How lucky that Reeve — How awful, does it still hurt?
Your *left* arm, how lucky!"

Reeve pulls out a chair for Antonia, and in an already practiced gesture
with her good, lucky right arm she places the cast in her lap. In a somewhat
embarrassed way (she has never been fond of center stage), she looks around
at her friends. "I'm glad you went on with dinner" is the first thing she says.
"Now you can feed us. God, I'm really starving."

"I came home and there she was on the floor — " Reeve begins, apparently about to start a speech.

"The damn cat!" Antonia cries out. "I tripped over Baron, I was making
the salad."

Reeve scowls. "It was very scary," he tells everyone present. "Suppose I 80
hadn't come home just then? I could have been traveling somewhere,
although — "

This time he is interrupted by Bynum, who reasonably, if unnecessarily,
states, "In that case, we would have been the ones to find Antonia. Phyllis
and I."

"I do wish someone would just hand me a plate of that stew," Antonia
puts in.

"Oh of course, you must be starved," her friends all chorus. "Poor thing!"

It is Lisa who places the full, steaming plate before Antonia. Lisa asking,
"You can eat okay? You want me to butter some bread?"

"Dear Lisa. Well, actually I do, I guess. God, I hope I don't get to like 85
this helplessness."

"Here," Lisa passes a thick slice of New York rye, all buttered. "Oh, and
this is Perry," she says. "He's been wanting to meet you. You know, we drove
down from Marin together."

Antonia and Perry acknowledge each other with smiles and small murmurs, difficult for Antonia, since she is now eating, ravenously.

"Real bastards in the emergency ward," Reeve is telling everyone; he
obviously relishes his part in this rescue. "They let you wait forever," he
says.

"Among bleeding people on gurneys," Antonia shudders. "You could
die there, and I'm sure some people do, if they're poor enough."

"*Does* it hurt?" asks Lisa. 90

"Not really. Really not at all. I just feel so clumsy. Clumsier than usual,
I mean."

She and Lisa smile at each other: old friends, familiar irony.

ALICE ADAMS   **383**

Now everyone has taken up forks again and begun to eat, along with Antonia. Wine is poured around, glasses refilled with red, or cold white, from pitchers.

Reeve alone seems not to be eating much, or drinking — for whatever reasons of his own: sheer excitement, possibly, anyone who thinks about it could conclude. He seems nervy, geared up by his — their recent experience.

The atmosphere is generally united, convivial, though. People tell their own accident stories, as they will when anyone has had an accident (hospital visitors like to tell the patient about their own operations). Bynum as a boy broke his right arm not once but twice, both times falling out of trees. Lisa broke her leg on some ice. "You remember, Antonia, that awful winter I lived in New York. Everything terrible happened." Perry almost broke his back, "but just a fractured coccyx, as things turned out," falling off a horse, in New Mexico (this story does not go over very well, somehow; a lack of response can be felt around the room). Phyllis broke her arm skiing in Idaho.

Reeve refrains from such reminiscences — although he is such a tall, very vigorous young man; back in Wyoming, he must have broken something, sometime. He has the air of a man who is waiting for the main event, and who in the meantime chooses to distance himself.

In any case, the conversation rambles on in a pleasant way, and no one is quite prepared to hear Antonia's end-of-meal pronouncement. Leaning back and looking around, she says, "It's odd that it's taken me so long to see how much I hate it here."

This is surely something that she has never said before. However, Antonia has a known predilection for the most extreme, the most emotional statement of any given feeling, and so at first no one pays much serious attention.

Lisa only says, "Well, the city's not at its best in all this fog. And then your poor arm."

And Bynum? "You can't mean this apartment. I've always loved it here." (At which Phyllis gives him a speculative, not quite friendly look.)

Looking at them all — at least she has everyone's attention — Antonia says, "Well, I do mean this apartment. It's so small, and so inconvenient having a studio five blocks away. Not to mention paying for both. Oh, I know I can afford it, but I hate to." She looks over at Reeve, and a smile that everyone can read as significant passes between the two of them.

One of Antonia's cats, the guilty old tabby, Baron, has settled on her lap, and she leans to scratch the bridge of his nose, very gently.

And so it is Reeve who announces, "I've talked Antonia into coming back to Wyoming with me. At least to recuperate." He smiles widely (can he be blushing?), in evident pleasure at this continuation of his rescuer role.

"I'm so excited!" Antonia then bursts out. "The Grand Tetons, imagine! I've always wanted to go there, and somehow I never dared. But Reeve has this whole house, and a barn that's already a studio."

"It's actually in Wilson, which is just south of Jackson," Reeve explains. "Much less touristic. It's my folks' old place."

If Antonia expected enthusiasm from her friends about this project, though, she is disappointed.

Of them all Bynum looks most dejected, his big face sags with displeasure, with thwarted hopes. Phyllis also is displeased, visibly so (but quite possibly it is Bynum of whom she disapproves?).

Lisa cries out, "But, Antonia, what'll I do without you? I'll miss you so, I'm not used to your being away. It'll be like New York — "

To which Antonia smilingly, instantly responds, "You must come visit. Do come, we could start some sort of colony. And, Bynum, you can use this place while I'm gone if you want to."

Perry of course is thinking of his article, of which he now can envision 110
the ending: Antonia Love off to the wilds of Wyoming, putting fogbound, dangerous San Francisco behind her. He likes the sound of it, although he is not quite sure that Jackson or even Wilson would qualify as "wilds." But there must be a way to find out.

In any case, he now sees that he has been quite right in his estimate of Antonia: she is beautiful. At this moment, radiantly pale, in the barely candlelit, dim room, her face is stylized, almost abstract, with her broad, heavy forehead and heavy dark brows, her wide-spaced large black eyes and her wide, dark-painted mouth. It will be easy to describe her: stylized, abstract.

She is of course not at all his type (he actually much prefers her friend Lisa whom he has decided that he does like, very much; he plans to see her again) — nor does Perry see himself in Reeve, at all. He senses, however, some exceptional connection between the two of them, some heightened rapport, as though, already in Wyoming, they breathed the same heady, pure, exhilarating air.

Antonia is talking about Wyoming now, her imagined refuge. "Mountains, clouds, water. Wildflowers," she is saying, while near her side Reeve smiles, quite privately.

And Perry believes that he has struck on the first sentence of his article: "Antonia Love these days is a very happy woman."

Raymond Carver
The Bridle

This old station wagon with Minnesota plates pulls into a parking space in front of the window. There's a man and woman in the front seat, two boys in the back. It's July, temperature's one hundred plus. These people look

THE BRIDLE   First published in *The New Yorker* in 1982. Raymond Carver (1939–1988) was born in Clatskanie, Oregon, and married his first wife while attending Humboldt State College in California, from which he graduated in 1963. He spent the next year at the University of Iowa and worked at a number of miscellaneous jobs. The success of his short stories and poems led to many awards and prizes, among them a five-year fellowship from the American Academy of Arts and Letters in 1983 that allowed him to give up his teaching (at Syracuse University) and write full-time.

whipped. There are clothes hanging inside; suitcases, boxes, and such piled in back. From what Harley and I put together later, that's all they had left after the bank in Minnesota took their house, their pickup, their tractor, the farm implements, and a few cows.

The people inside sit for a minute, as if collecting themselves. The air-conditioner in our apartment is going full blast. Harley's around in back cutting grass. There's some discussion in the front seat, and then she and him get out and start for the front door. I pat my hair to make sure that it's in place and wait till they push the doorbell for the second time. Then I go to let them in. "You're looking for an apartment?" I say. "Come on in here where it's cool." I show them into the living room. The living room is where I do business. It's where I collect the rents, write the receipts, and talk to interested parties. I also do hair. I call myself a *stylist*. That's what my cards say. I don't like the word *beautician*. It's an old-time word. I have the chair in a corner of the living room, and a dryer I can pull up to the back of the chair. And there's a sink that Harley put in a few years ago. Alongside the chair, I have a table with some magazines. The magazines are old. The covers are gone from some of them. But people will look at anything while they're under the dryer.

The man says his name.

"My name is Holits."

He tells me she's his wife. But she won't look at me. She looks at her nails instead. She and Holits won't sit down, either. He says they're interested in one of the furnished units.

"How many of you?" But I'm just saying what I always say. I know how many. I saw the two boys in the back seat. Two and two is four.

"Me and her and the boys. The boys are thirteen and fourteen, and they'll share a room, like always."

She has her arms crossed and is holding the sleeves of her blouse. She takes in the chair and the sink as if she's never seen their like before. Maybe she hasn't.

"I do hair," I say.

She nods. Then she gives my prayer plant the once-over. It has exactly five leaves to it.

"That needs watering," I say. I go over and touch one of its leaves. "Everything around here needs water. There's not enough water in the air. It rains three times a year if we're lucky. But you'll get used to it. We had to get used to it. But everything here is air-conditioned."

"How much is the place?" Holits wants to know.

I tell him and he turns to her to see what she thinks. But he may as well have been looking at the wall. She won't give him back his look. "I guess we'll have you show us," he says. So I move to get the key for 17, and we go outside.

I hear Harley before I see him.

Then he comes into sight between the buildings. He's moving along behind the power mower in his Bermudas and T-shirt, wearing the straw hat he bought in Nogales. He spends his time cutting grass and doing the small maintenance work. We work for a corporation, Fulton Terrace, Inc. They own the place. If anything major goes wrong, like air-conditioning trouble or something serious in the plumbing department, we have a list of phone numbers.

I wave. I have to. Harley takes a hand off the mower handle and signals. Then he pulls the hat down over his forehead and gives his attention back to what he's doing. He comes to the end of his cut, makes his turn, and starts back toward the street.

"That's Harley." I have to shout it. We go in at the side of the building and up some stairs. "What kind of work are you in, Mr. Holits?" I ask him.

"He's a farmer," she says.

"No more."

"Not much to farm around here." I say it without thinking. 20

"We had us a farm in Minnesota. Raised wheat. A few cattle. And Holits knows horses. He knows everything there is about horses."

"That's all right, Betty."

I get a piece of the picture then. Holits is unemployed. It's not my affair, and I feel sorry if that's the case — it is, it turns out — but as we stop in front of the unit, I have to say something. "If you decide, it's first month, last month, and one-fifty as security deposit." I look down at the pool as I say it. Some people are sitting in deck chairs, and there's somebody in the water.

Holits wipes his face with the back of his hand. Harley's mower is clacking away. Farther off, cars speed by on Calle Verde. The two boys have got out of the station wagon. One of them is standing at military attention, legs together, arms at his sides. But as I watch, I see him begin to flap his arms up and down and jump, like he intends to take off and fly. The other one is squatting down on the driver's side of the station wagon, doing knee bends.

I turn to Holits. 25

"Let's have a look," he says.

I turn the key and the door opens. It's just a little two-bedroom furnished apartment. Everybody has seen dozens. Holits stops in the bathroom long enough to flush the toilet. He watches till the tank fills. Later, he says, "This could be our room." He's talking about the bedroom that looks out over the pool. In the kitchen, the woman takes hold of the edge of the drainboard and stares out the window.

"That's the swimming pool," I say.

She nods. "We stayed in some motels that had swimming pools. But in one pool they had too much chlorine in the water."

I wait for her to go on. But that's all she says. I can't think of anything 30 else, either.

"I guess we won't waste any more time. I guess we'll take it." Holits looks at her as he says it. This time she meets his eyes. She nods. He lets out breath through his teeth. Then she does something. She begins snapping her fingers. One hand is still holding the edge of the drainboard, but with her other hand she begins snapping her fingers. Snap, snap, snap, like she was calling her dog, or else trying to get somebody's attention. Then she stops and runs her nails across the counter.

I don't know what to make of it. Holits doesn't either. He moves his feet. "We'll walk back to the office and make things official," I say. "I'm glad."

I *was* glad. We had a lot of empty units for this time of year. And these people seemed like dependable people. Down on their luck, that's all. No disgrace can be attached to that.

35   Holits pays in cash — first, last, and the one-fifty deposit. He counts out bills of fifty-dollar denomination while I watch. U. S. Grants, Harley calls them, though he's never seen many. I write out the receipt and give him two keys. "You're all set."

He looks at the keys. He hands her one. "So, we're in Arizona. Never thought you'd see Arizona, did you?"

She shakes her head. She's touching one of the prayer-plant leaves.

"Needs water," I say.

She lets go of the leaf and turns to the window. I go over next to her. Harley is still cutting grass. But he's around in front now. There's been this talk of farming, so for a minute I think of Harley moving along behind a plow instead of behind his Black and Decker power mower.

40   I watch them unload their boxes, suitcases, and clothes. Holits carries in something that has straps hanging from it. It takes a minute, but then I figure out it's a bridle. I don't know what to do next. I don't feel like doing anything. So I take the Grants out of the cashbox. I just put them in there, but I take them out again. The bills have come from Minnesota. Who knows where they'll be this time next week? They could be in Las Vegas. All I know about Las Vegas is what I see on TV — about enough to put into a thimble. I can imagine one of the Grants finding its way out to Waikiki Beach, or else some other place. Miami or New York City. New Orleans. I think about one of those bills changing hands during Mardi Gras. They could go any place, and anything could happen because of them. I write my name in ink across Grant's broad old forehead: MARGE. I print it. I do it on every one. Right over his thick brows. People will stop in the midst of their spending and wonder. Who's this Marge? That's what they'll ask themselves, Who's this Marge?

Harley comes in from outside and washes his hands in my sink. He knows it's something I don't like him to do. But he goes ahead and does it anyway.

"Those people from Minnesota," he says. "The Swedes. They're a long way from home." He dries his hands on a paper towel. He wants me to tell him what I know. But I don't know anything. They don't look like Swedes and they don't talk like Swedes.

"They're not Swedes," I tell him. But he acts like he doesn't hear me.

"So what's he do?"

45   "He's a farmer."

"What do you know about that?"

Harley takes his hat off and puts it on my chair. He runs a hand through his hair. Then he looks at the hat and puts it on again. He may as well be glued to it. "There's not much to farm around here. Did you tell him that?" He gets a can of soda pop from the fridge and goes to sit in his recliner. He picks up the remote-control, pushes something, and the TV sizzles on. He pushes some more buttons until he finds what he's looking for. It's a hospital show. "What else does the Swede do? Besides farm?"

I don't know, so I don't say anything. But Harley's already taken up with his program. He's probably forgotten he asked me the question. A siren goes off. I hear the screech of tires. On the screen, an ambulance has come to a stop in front of an emergency-room entrance, its red lights flashing. A man jumps out and runs around to open up the back.

The next afternoon the boys borrow the hose and wash the station wagon. They clean the outside and the inside. A little later I notice her drive away. She's wearing high heels and a nice dress. Hunting up a job, I'd say. After a while, I see the boys messing around the pool in their bathing suits. One of them springs off the board and swims all the way to the other end underwater. He comes up blowing water and shaking his head. The other boy, the one who'd been doing knee bends the day before, lies on his stomach on a towel at the far side of the pool. But this one boy keeps swimming back and forth from one end of the pool to the other, touching the wall and turning back with a little kick.

There are two other people out there. They're in lounge chairs, one on either side of the pool. One of them is Irving Cobb, a cook at Denny's. He calls himself Spuds. People have taken to calling him that, Spuds, instead of Irv or some other nickname. Spuds is fifty-five and bald. He already looks like beef jerky, but he wants more sun. Right now, his new wife, Linda Cobb, is at work at the K Mart. Spuds works nights. But him and Linda Cobb have it arranged so they take their Saturdays and Sundays off. Connie Nova is in the other chair. She's sitting up and rubbing lotion on her legs. She's nearly naked — just this little two-piece suit covering her. Connie Nova is a cocktail waitress. She moved in here six months ago with her so-called fiancé, an alcoholic lawyer. But she got rid of him. Now she lives with a long-haired student from the college whose name is Rick. I happen to know he's away right now, visiting his folks. Spuds and Connie are wearing dark glasses. Connie's portable radio is going.

Spuds was a recent widower when he moved in, a year or so back. But after a few months of being a bachelor again, he got married to Linda. She's a red-haired woman in her thirties. I don't know how they met. But one night a couple of months ago Spuds and the new Mrs. Cobb had Harley and me over to a nice dinner that Spuds fixed. After dinner, we sat in their living room drinking sweet drinks out of big glasses. Spuds asked if we wanted to see home movies. We said sure. So Spuds set up his screen and his projector.

Linda Cobb poured us more of that sweet drink. Where's the harm? I asked myself. Spuds began to show films of a trip he and his dead wife had made to Alaska. It began with her getting on the plane in Seattle. Spuds talked as he ran the projector. The deceased was in her fifties, good-looking, though maybe a little heavy. Her hair was nice.

"That's Spuds's first wife," Linda Cobb said. "That's the first Mrs. Cobb."

"That's Evelyn," Spuds said.

The first wife stayed on the screen for a long time. It was funny seeing her and hearing them talk about her like that. Harley passed me a look, so I know he was thinking something, too. Linda Cobb asked if we wanted another drink or a macaroon. We didn't. Spuds was saying something about the first Mrs. Cobb again. She was still at the entrance to the plane, smiling and moving her mouth even if all you could hear was the film going through the projector. People had to go around her to get on the plane. She kept waving at the camera, waving at us there in Spuds's living room. She waved and waved. "There's Evelyn again," the new Mrs. Cobb would say each time the first Mrs. Cobb appeared on the screen.

Spuds would have shown films all night, but we said we had to go. Harley made the excuse.

I don't remember what he said.

Connie Nova is lying on her back in the chair, dark glasses covering half of her face. Her legs and stomach shine with oil. One night, not long after she moved in, she had a party. This was before she kicked the lawyer out and took up with the long-hair. She called her party a housewarming. Harley and I were invited, along with a bunch of other people. We went, but we didn't care for the company. We found a place to sit close to the door, and that's where we stayed till we left. It wasn't all that long, either. Connie's boyfriend was giving a door prize. It was the offer of his legal services, without charge, for handling of a divorce. Anybody's divorce. Anybody who wanted to could draw a card out of the bowl he was passing around. When the bowl came our way, everybody began to laugh. Harley and I swapped glances. I didn't draw. Harley didn't draw, either. But I saw him look in the bowl at the pile of cards. Then he shook his head and handed the bowl to the person next to him. Even Spuds and the new Mrs. Cobb drew cards. The winning card had something written across the back. "Entitles bearer to one free uncontested divorce," and the lawyer's signature and the date. The lawyer was a drunk, but I say this is no way to conduct your life. Everybody but us had put his hand into the bowl, like it was a fun thing to do. The woman who drew the winning card clapped. It was like one of those game shows. "Goddamn, this is the first time I ever won anything!" I was told she had a husband in the military. There's no way of knowing if she still has him, or if she got her divorce, because Connie Nova took up with a different set of friends after she and the lawyer went their separate ways.

We left the party right after the drawing. It made such an impression we couldn't say much, except one of us said, "I don't believe I saw what I think I saw."

Maybe I said it.

A week later Harley asks if the Swede — he means Holits — has found work yet. We've just had lunch, and Harley's in his chair with his can of pop. But he hasn't turned his TV on. I say I don't know. And I don't. I wait to see what else he has to say. But he doesn't say anything else. He shakes his head. He seems to think about something. Then he pushes a button and the TV comes to life.

She finds a job. She starts working as a waitress in an Italian restaurant a few blocks from here. She works a split shift, doing lunches and then going home, then back to work again in time for the dinner shift. She's meeting herself coming and going. The boys swim all day, while Holits stays inside the apartment. I don't know what he does in there. Once, I did her hair and she told me a few things. She told me she did waitressing when she was just out of high school and that's where she met Holits. She served him some pancakes in a place back in Minnesota.

She'd walked down that morning and asked me could I do her a favor. She wanted me to fix her hair after her lunch shift and have her out in time for her dinner shift. Could I do it? I told her I'd check the book. I asked her to step inside. It must have been a hundred degrees already.

"I know it's short notice," she said. "But when I came in from work last night, I looked in the mirror and saw my roots showing. I said to myself, 'I need a treatment.' I don't know where else to go."

I find Friday, August 14. There's nothing on the page.

"I could work you in at two-thirty, or else at three o'clock," I say.

"Three would be better," she says. "I have to run for it now before I'm late. I work for a real bastard. See you later."

At two-thirty, I tell Harley I have a customer, so he'll have to take his baseball game into the bedroom. He grumps, but he winds up the cord and wheels the set out back. He closes the door. I make sure everything I need is ready. I fix up the magazines so they're easy to get to. Then I sit next to the dryer and file my nails. I'm wearing the rose-colored uniform that I put on when I do hair. I go on filing my nails and looking up at the window from time to time.

She walks by the window and then pushes the doorbell. "Come on in," I call. "It's unlocked."

She's wearing the black-and-white uniform from her job. I can see how we're both wearing uniforms. "Sit down, honey, and we'll get started." She looks at the nail file. "I give manicures, too," I say.

She settles into the chair and draws a breath.

I say, "Put your head back. That's it. Close your eyes now, why don't you? Just relax. First I'll shampoo you and touch up these roots here. Then we'll go from there. How much time do you have?"

"I have to be back there at five-thirty."

"We'll get you fixed up."

"I can eat at work. But I don't know what Holits and the boys will do for their supper."

75 "They'll get along fine without you."

I start the warm water and then notice Harley's left me some dirt and grass. I wipe up his mess and start over.

I say, "If they want, they can just walk down the street to the hamburger place. It won't hurt them."

"They won't do that. Anyway, I don't want them to have to go there."

It's none of my business, so I don't say any more. I make up a nice lather and go to work. After I've done the shampoo, rinse, and set, I put her under the dryer. Her eyes have closed. I think she could be asleep. So I take one of her hands and begin.

80 "No manicure." She opens her eyes and pulls away her hand.

"It's all right, honey. The first manicure is always no charge."

She gives me back her hand and picks up one of the magazines and rests it in her lap. "They're his boys," she says. "From his first marriage. He was divorced when we met. But I love them like they were my own. I couldn't love them any more if I tried. Not even if I was their natural mother."

I turn the dryer down a notch so that it's making a low, quiet sound. I keep on with her nails. Her hand starts to relax.

"She lit out on them, on Holits and the boys, on New Year's Day ten years ago. They never heard from her again." I can see she wants to tell me about it. And that's fine with me. They like to talk when they're in the chair. I go on using the file. "Holits got the divorce. Then he and I started going out. Then we got married. For a long time, we had us a life. It had its ups and downs. But we thought we were working toward something." She shakes her head. "But something happened. Something happened to Holits, I mean. One thing happened was he got interested in horses. This one particular race horse, he bought it, you know — something down, something each month. He took it around to the tracks. He was still up before daylight, like always, still doing the chores and such. I thought everything was all right. But I don't know anything. If you want the truth, I'm not so good at waiting tables. I think those wops would fire me at the drop of a hat, if I gave them a reason. Or for no reason. What if I got fired? Then what?"

85 I say, "Don't worry, honey. They're not going to fire you."

Pretty soon she picks up another magazine. But she doesn't open it. She just holds it and goes on talking. "Anyway, there's this horse of his. Fast Betty. The Betty part is a joke. But he says it can't help but be a winner if he names it after me. A big winner, all right. The fact is, wherever it ran, it lost. Every race. Betty Longshot — that's what it should have been called. In the beginning, I went to a few races. But the horse always ran ninety-nine to one. Odds like that. But Holits is stubborn if he's anything. He wouldn't give up. He'd bet on the horse and bet on the horse. Twenty dollars to win. Fifty dollars to win. Plus all the other things it costs for keeping a horse. I know it don't sound like a large amount. But it adds up. And when the odds were like that — ninety-nine to one, you know — sometimes he'd buy a combination ticket. He'd ask me if I realized how much money we'd make if the horse came in. But it didn't, and I quit going."

I keep on with what I'm doing. I concentrate on her nails. "You have nice cuticles," I say. "Look here at your cuticles. See these little half-moons? Means your blood's good."

She brings her hand up close and looks. "What do you know about that?" She shrugs. She lets me take her hand again. She's still got things to tell. "Once, when I was in high school, a counselor asked me to come to her office. She did it with all the girls, one of us at a time. 'What dreams do you have?' this woman asked me. 'What do you see yourself doing in ten years? Twenty years?' I was sixteen or seventeen. I was just a kid. I couldn't think what to answer. I just sat there like a lump. This counselor was about the age I am now. I thought she was *old*. She's old, I said to myself. I knew *her* life was half over. And I felt like I knew something she didn't. Something she'd never know. A secret. Something nobody's supposed to know, or ever talk about. So I stayed quiet. I just shook my head. She must've written me off as a dope. But I couldn't say anything. You know what I mean? I thought I knew things she couldn't guess at. Now, if anybody asked me that question again, about my dreams and all, I'd tell them."

"What would you tell them, honey?" I have her other hand now. But I'm not doing her nails. I'm just holding it, waiting to hear.

She moves forward in the chair. She tries to take her hand back.   90
"What would you tell them?"

She sighs and leans back. She lets me keep the hand. "I'd say, 'Dreams, you know, are what you wake up from.' That's what I'd say." She smooths the lap of her skirt. "If anybody asked, that's what I'd say. But they won't ask." She lets out her breath again. "So how much longer?" she says.

"Not long," I say.

"You don't know what it's like."

"Yes, I do," I say. I pull the stool right up next to her legs. I'm starting to   95
tell how it was before we moved here, and how it's still like that. But Harley picks right then to come out of the bedroom. He doesn't look at us. I hear the TV jabbering away in the bedroom. He goes to the sink and draws a glass of water. He tips his head back to drink. His Adam's apple moves up and down in his throat.

I move the dryer away and touch the hair at both sides of her head. I lift one of the curls just a little.

I say, "You look brand-new, honey."

"Don't I wish."

The boys keep on swimming all day, every day, till their school starts. Betty keeps on at her job. But for some reason she doesn't come back to get her hair done. I don't know why this is. Maybe she doesn't think I did a good job. Sometimes I lie awake, Harley sleeping like a grindstone beside me, and try to picture myself in Betty's shoes. I wonder what I'd do then.

100   Holits sends one of his sons with the rent on the first of September, and on the first of October, too. He still pays in cash. I take the money from the boy, count the bills right there in front of him, and then write out the receipt. Holits has found work of some sort. I think so, anyway. He drives off every day with the station wagon. I see him leave early in the morning and drive back late in the afternoon. She goes past the window at ten-thirty and comes back at three. If she sees me, she gives me a little wave. But she's not smiling. Then I see Betty again at five, walking back to the restaurant. Holits drives in a little later. This goes on till the middle of October.

Meanwhile, the Holits couple acquainted themselves with Connie Nova and her long-hair friend, Rick. And they also met up with Spuds and the new Mrs. Cobb. Sometimes, on a Sunday afternoon, I'd see all of them sitting around the pool, drinks in their hands, listening to Connie's portable radio. One time Harley said he saw them all behind the building, in the barbecue area. They were in their bathing suits then, too. Harley said the Swede had a chest like a bull. Harley said they were eating hot dogs and drinking whiskey. He said they were drunk.

It was Saturday, and it was after eleven at night. Harley was asleep in his chair. Pretty soon I'd have to get up and turn off the set. When I did that, I knew he'd wake up. "Why'd you turn it off? I was watching that show." That's what he'd say. That's what he always said. Anyway, the TV was going, I had the curlers in, and there's a magazine on my lap. Now and then I'd look up. But I couldn't get settled on the show. They were all out there in the pool area — Spuds and Linda Cobb, Connie Nova and the long-hair, Holits and Betty. We have a rule against anyone being out there after ten. But this night they didn't care about rules. If Harley woke up, he'd go out and say something. I felt it was all right for them to have their fun, but it was time for it to stop. I kept getting up and going over to the window. All of them except Betty had on bathing suits. She was still in her uniform. But she had her shoes off, a glass in her hand, and she was drinking right along with the rest of them. I kept putting off having to turn off the set. Then one of them shouted something, and another one took it up and began to laugh. I looked and saw Holits finish off his drink. He put the glass down on the deck. Then he walked over to the cabana. He dragged up one of the tables and climbed onto that. Then — he seemed to do it without any effort at all — he lifted up onto the roof of the cabana. It's true, I thought; he's strong. The long-hair claps his hands, like he's all for this. The rest of them are hooting Holits on, too. I know I'm going to have to go out there and put a stop to it.

Harley's slumped in his chair. The TV's still going. I ease the door open, step out, and then push it shut behind me. Holits is up on the roof of the cabana. They're egging him on. They're saying, "Go on, you can do it." "Don't belly-flop, now." "I double-dare you." Things like that.

Then I hear Betty's voice. "Holits, think what you're doing." But Holits just stands there at the edge. He looks down at the water. He seems to be figuring how much of a run he's going to have to make to get out there. He backs up to the far side. He spits in his palm and rubs his hands together. Spuds calls out, "That's it, boy! You'll do it now."

I see him hit the deck. I hear him, too.   105

"Holits!" Betty cries.

They all hurry over to him. By the time I get there, he's sitting up. Rick is holding him by the shoulders and yelling into his face. "Holits! Hey, man!"

Holits has this gash on his forehead, and his eyes are glassy. Spuds and Rick help him into a chair. Somebody gives him a towel. But Holits holds the towel like he doesn't know what he's supposed to do with it. Somebody else hands him a drink. But Holits doesn't know what to do with that, either. People keep saying things to him. Holits brings the towel up to his face. Then he takes it away and looks at the blood. But he just looks at it. He can't seem to understand anything.

"Let me see him." I get around in front of him. It's bad. "Holits, are you all right?" But Holits just looks at me, and then his eyes drift off. "I think he'd best go to the emergency room." Betty looks at me when I say this and begins to shake her head. She looks back at Holits. She gives him another towel. I think she's sober. But the rest of them are drunk. Drunk is the best that can be said for them.

Spuds picks up what I said. "Let's take him to the emergency room." 110

Rick says, "I'll go, too."

"We'll all go," Connie Nova says.

"We better stick together," Linda Cobb says.

"Holits." I say his name again.

"I can't go it," Holits says. 115

"What'd he say?" Connie Nova asks me.

"He said he can't go it," I tell her.

"Go what? What's he talking about?" Rick wants to know.

"Say again?" Spuds says. "I didn't hear."

"He says he can't go it. I don't think he knows what he's talking about. 120 You'd best take him to the hospital," I say. Then I remember Harley and the rules. "You shouldn't have been out here. Any of you. We have rules. Now go on and take him to the hospital."

"Let's take him to the hospital," Spuds says like it's something he's just thought of. He might be farther gone than any of them. For one thing, he can't stand still. He weaves. And he keeps picking up his feet and putting them down again. The hair on his chest is snow white under the overhead pool lights.

"I'll get the car." That's what the long-hair says. "Connie, let me have the keys."

"I can't go it," Holits says. The towel has moved down to his chin. But the cut is on his forehead.

"Get him that terry-cloth robe. He can't go to the hospital that way." Linda Cobb says that. "Holits! Holits, it's us." She waits and then she takes the glass of whiskey from Holits's fingers and drinks from it.

125 I can see people at some of the windows, looking down on the commotion. Lights are going on. "Go to bed!" someone yells.

Finally, the long-hair brings Connie's Datsun from behind the building and drives it up close to the pool. The headlights are on bright. He races the engine.

"For Christ's sake, go to bed!" the same person yells. More people come to their windows. I expect to see Harley come out any minute, wearing his hat, steaming. Then I think, No, he'll sleep through it. Just forget Harley.

Spuds and Connie Nova get on either side of Holits. Holits can't walk straight. He's wobbly. Part of it's because he's drunk. But there's no question he's hurt himself. They get him into the car, and they all crowd inside, too. Betty is the last to get in. She has to sit on somebody's lap. Then they drive off. Whoever it was that has been yelling slams the window shut.

The whole next week Holits doesn't leave the place. And I think Betty must have quit her job, because I don't see her pass the window anymore. When I see the boys go by, I step outside and ask them, point-blank: "How's your dad?"

130 "He hurt his head," one of them says.

I wait in hopes they'll say more. But they don't. They shrug and go on to school with their lunch sacks and binders. Later, I was sorry I hadn't asked after their step-mom.

When I see Holits outside, wearing a bandage and standing on his balcony, he doesn't even nod. He acts like I'm a stranger. It's like he doesn't know me or doesn't want to know me. Harley says he's getting the same treatment. He doesn't like it. "What's with him?" Harley wants to know. "Damn Swede. What happened to his head? Somebody belt him or what?" I don't tell Harley anything when he says that. I don't go into it at all.

Then that Sunday afternoon I see one of the boys carry out a box and put it in the station wagon. He goes back upstairs. But pretty soon he comes back down with another box, and he puts that in, too. It's then I know they're making ready to leave. But I don't say what I know to Harley. He'll know everything soon enough.

Next morning, Betty sends one of the boys down. He's got a note that says she's sorry but they have to move. She gives me her sister's address in Indio where she says we can send the deposit to. She points out they're leaving eight days before their rent is up. She hopes there might be something in the way of a refund there, even though they haven't given the thirty days' notice. She says, "Thanks for everything. Thanks for doing my hair that time." She signs the note, "Sincerely, Betty Holits."

"What's your name?" I ask the boy.   135
"Billy."

"Billy, tell her I said I'm real sorry."

Harley reads what she's written, and says it will be a cold day in hell
before they see any money back from Fulton Terrace. He says he can't understand these people. "People who sail through life like the world owes
them a living." He asks me where they're going. But I don't have any idea
where they're going. Maybe they're going back to Minnesota. How do I
know where they're going? But I don't think they're going back to Minnesota. I think they're going someplace else to try their luck.

Connie Nova and Spuds have their chairs in the usual places, one on
either side of the pool. From time to time, they look over at the Holits boys
carrying things out to the station wagon. Then Holits himself comes out with
some clothes over his arm. Connie Nova and Spuds holler and wave. Holits
looks at them like he doesn't know them. But then he raises up his free hand.
Just raises it, that's all. They wave. Then Holits is waving. He keeps waving
at them, even after they've stopped. Betty comes downstairs and touches his
arm. She doesn't wave. She won't even look at these people. She says something to Holits, and he goes on to the car. Connie Nova lies back in her chair
and reaches over to turn up her portable radio. Spuds holds his sunglasses
and watches Holits and Betty for a while. Then he fixes the glasses over his
ears. He settles himself in the lounge chair and goes back to tanning his
leathery old self.

Finally, they're all loaded and ready to move on. The boys are in the   140
back, Holits behind the wheel, Betty in the seat right up next to him. It's just
like it was when they drove in here.

"What are you looking at?" Harley says.

He's taking a break. He's in his chair, watching the TV. But he gets up
and comes over to the window.

"Well, there they go. They don't know where they're going or what
they're going to do. Crazy Swede."

I watch them drive out of the lot and turn onto the road that's going to
take them to the freeway. Then I look at Harley again. He's settling into his
chair. He has his can of pop, and he's wearing his straw hat. He acts like
nothing has happened or ever will happen.

"Harley?"   145

But, of course, he can't hear me. I go over and stand in front of his chair.
He's surprised. He doesn't know what to make of it. He leans back, just sits
there looking at me.

The phone starts ringing.

"Get that, will you?" he says.

I don't answer him. Why should I?

"Then let it ring," he says.   150

I go find the mop, some rags, S.O.S. pads, and a bucket. The phone
stops ringing. He's still sitting in his chair. But he's turned off the TV. I take

the passkey, go outside and up the stairs to 17. I let myself in and walk through the living room to their kitchen — what used to be their kitchen.

The counters have been wiped down, the sink and cupboards are clean. It's not so bad. I leave the cleaning things on the stove and go take a look at the bathroom. Nothing there a little steel wool can't take care of. Then I open the door to the bedroom that looks out over the pool. The blinds are raised, the bed is stripped. The floor shines. "Thanks," I say out loud. Wherever she's going, I wish her luck. "Good luck, Betty." One of the bureau drawers is open and I go to close it. Back in a corner of the drawer I see the bridle he was carrying in when he first came. It must have been passed over in their hurry. But maybe it wasn't. Maybe the man left it on purpose.

"Bridle," I say. I hold it up to the window and look at it in the light. It's not fancy, it's just an old dark leather bridle. I don't know much about them. But I know that one part of it fits in the mouth. That part's called the bit. It's made of steel. Reins go over the head and up where they're held on the neck between the fingers. The rider pulls the reins this way and that, and the horse turns. It's simple. The bit's heavy and cold. If you had to wear this thing between your teeth, I guess you'd catch on in a hurry. When you felt it pull, you'd know it was time. You'd know you were going somewhere.

John Cheever
The Swimmer

It was one of those midsummer Sundays when everyone sits around saying, " I *drank* too much last night." You might have heard it whispered by the parishioners leaving church, heard it from the lips of the priest himself, struggling with his cassock in the *vestiarium*, heard it from the golf links and the tennis courts, heard it from the wildlife preserve where the leader of the Audubon group was suffering from a terrible hangover. "I *drank* too much," said Donald Westerhazy. "We all *drank* too much," said Lucinda Merrill. "It must have been the wine," said Helen Westerhazy. "I *drank* too much of that claret."

This was at the edge of the Westerhazys' pool. The pool, fed by an artesian well with a high iron content, was a pale shade of green. It was a fine day. In the west there was a massive stand of cumulus clouds so like a city seen from a distance — from the bow of an approaching ship — that it might have had a name. Lisbon. Hackensack. The sun was hot. Neddy Merrill sat by the green water, one hand in it, one around a glass of gin. He was a slender

THE SWIMMER   First published in 1964. John Cheever (1912–1982) was born in Quincy, Massachusetts. After being expelled from a private school at seventeen, he went to New York City and published his first story later that year. He lived in various New England and New York towns, especially in commuter towns near New York City.

man — he seemed to have the especial slenderness of youth — and while he was far from young he had slid down his banister that morning and given the bronze backside of Aphrodite on the hall table a smack, as he jogged toward the smell of coffee in his dining room. He might have been compared to a summer's day, particularly the last hours of one, and while he lacked a tennis racket or a sail bag the impression was definitely one of youth, sport, and clement weather. He had been swimming and now he was breathing deeply, stertorously as if he could gulp into his lungs the components of that moment, the heat of the sun, the intenseness of his pleasure. It all seemed to flow into his chest. His own house stood in Bullet Park, eight miles to the south, where his four beautiful daughters would have had their lunch and might be playing tennis. Then it occurred to him that by taking a dogleg to the southwest he could reach his home by water.

His life was not confining and the delight he took in this observation could not be explained by its suggestion of escape. He seemed to see, with a cartographer's eye, that string of swimming pools, that quasi-subterranean stream that curved across the county. He had made a discovery, a contribution to modern geography; he would name the stream Lucinda after his wife. He was not a practical joker nor was he a fool but he was determinedly original and had a vague and modest idea of himself as a legendary figure. The day was beautiful and it seemed to him that a long swim might enlarge and celebrate its beauty.

He took off a sweater that was hung over his shoulders and dove in. He had an inexplicable contempt for men who did not hurl themselves into pools. He swam a choppy crawl, breathing either with every stroke or every fourth stroke and counting somewhere well in the back of his mind the one-two one-two of a flutter kick. It was not a serviceable stroke for long distances but the domestication of swimming had saddled the sport with some customs and in his part of the world a crawl was customary. To be embraced and sustained by the light green water was less a pleasure, it seemed, than the resumption of a natural condition, and he would have liked to swim without trunks, but this was not possible, considering his project. He hoisted himself up on the far curb — he never used the ladder — and started across the lawn. When Lucinda asked where he was going he said he was going to swim home.

The only maps and charts he had to go by were remembered or imaginary but these were clear enough. First there were the Grahams, the Hammers, the Lears, the Howlands, and the Crosscups. He would cross Ditmar Street to the Bunkers and come, after a short portage, to the Levys, the Welchers, and the public pool in Lancaster. Then there were the Hallorans, the Sachses, the Biswangers, Shirley Adams, the Gilmartins, and the Clydes. The day was lovely, and that he lived in a world so generously supplied with water seemed like a clemency, a beneficence. His heart was high and he ran across the grass. Making his way home by an uncommon route gave him the feeling that he was a pilgrim, an explorer, a man with a destiny, and he knew that he would find friends all along the way; friends would line the banks of the Lucinda River.

He went through a hedge that separated the Westerhazys' land from the Grahams', walked under some flowering apple trees, passed the shed that housed their pump and filter, and came out at the Grahams' pool. "Why, Neddy," Mrs. Graham said, "what a marvelous surprise. I've been trying to get you on the phone all morning. Here, let me get you a drink." He saw then, like any explorer, that the hospitable customs and traditions of the natives would have to be handled with diplomacy if he was ever going to reach his destination. He did not want to mystify or seem rude to the Grahams nor did he have the time to linger there. He swam the length of their pool and joined them in the sun and was rescued, a few minutes later, by the arrival of two carloads of friends from Connecticut. During the uproarious reunions he was able to slip away. He went down by the front of the Grahams' house, stepped over a thorny hedge, and crossed a vacant lot to the Hammers'. Mrs. Hammer, looking up from her roses, saw him swim by although she wasn't quite sure who it was. The Lears heard him splashing past the open windows of their living room. The Howlands and the Crosscups were away. After leaving the Howlands' he crossed Ditmar Street and started for the Bunkers', where he could hear, even at that distance, the noise of a party.

The water refracted the sound of voices and laughter and seemed to suspend it in midair. The Bunkers' pool was on a rise and he climbed some stairs to a terrace where twenty-five or thirty men and women were drinking. The only person in the water was Rusty Towers, who floated there on a rubber raft. Oh, how bonny and lush were the banks of the Lucinda River! Prosperous men and women gathered by the sapphire-colored waters while caterer's men in white coats passed them cold gin. Overhead a red de Haviland trainer was circling around and around and around in the sky with something like the glee of a child in a swing. Ned felt a passing affection for the scene, a tenderness for the gathering, as if it was something he might touch. In the distance he heard thunder. As soon as Enid Bunker saw him she began to scream: "Oh, look who's here! What a marvelous surprise! When Lucinda said that you couldn't come I thought I'd *die*." She made her way to him through the crowd, and when they had finished kissing she led him to the bar, a progress that was slowed by the fact that he stopped to kiss eight or ten other women and shake the hands of as many men. A smiling bartender he had seen at a hundred parties gave him a gin and tonic and he stood by the bar for a moment, anxious not to get stuck in any conversation that would delay his voyage. When he seemed about to be surrounded he dove in and swam close to the side to avoid colliding with Rusty's raft. At the far end of the pool he bypassed the Tomlinsons with a broad smile and jogged up the garden path. The gravel cut his feet but this was the only unpleasantness. The party was confined to the pool, and as he went toward the house he heard the brilliant, watery sound of voices fade, heard the noise of a radio from the Bunkers' kitchen, where someone was listening to a ball game. Sunday afternoon. He made his way through the parked cars and down the grassy border of their driveway to Alewives Lane. He did not want to be seen on the road in his bathing trunks but there was no traffic and he made the short distance to the Levys' driveway, marked with a PRIVATE PROPERTY sign and a green tube for *The New York Times*. All the doors and windows of the big house were open but there were no signs of life; not even a dog barked. He went around the side of the house to the pool and saw that the Levys had only recently left. Glasses and bottles and dishes of nuts were on a table at the deep end, where there was a bathhouse or gazebo, hung with Japanese lanterns. After swimming the pool he got himself a glass and poured a drink. It was his fourth or fifth drink and he had swum nearly half the length of the Lucinda River. He felt tired, clean, and pleased at that moment to be alone; pleased with everything.

It would storm. The stand of cumulus cloud — that city — had risen and darkened, and while he sat there he heard the percussiveness of thunder again. The de Haviland trainer was still circling overhead and it seemed to Ned that he could almost hear the pilot laugh with pleasure in the afternoon; but when there was another peal of thunder he took off for home. A train whistle blew and he wondered what time it had gotten to be. Four? Five? He thought of the provincial station at that hour, where a waiter, his tuxedo concealed by a raincoat, a dwarf with some flowers wrapped in newspaper, and a woman who had been crying would be waiting for the local. It was suddenly growing dark; it was that moment when the pinheaded birds seem to organize their song into some acute and knowledgeable recognition of the storm's approach. Then there was a fine noise of rushing water from the crown of an oak at his back, as if a spigot there had been turned. Then the noise of fountains came from the crowns of all the tall trees. Why did he love storms, what was the meaning of his excitement when the door sprang open and the rain wind fled rudely up the stairs, why had the simple task of shutting the windows of an old house seemed fitting and urgent, why did the first watery notes of a storm wind have for him the unmistakable sound of good news, cheer, glad tidings? Then there was an explosion, a smell of cordite, and rain lashed the Japanese lanterns that Mrs. Levy had bought in Kyoto the year before last, or was it the year before that?

He stayed in the Levys' gazebo until the storm had passed. The rain had cooled the air and he shivered. The force of the wind had stripped a maple of its red and yellow leaves and scattered them over the grass and the water. Since it was midsummer the tree must be blighted, and yet he felt a peculiar sadness at this sign of autumn. He braced his shoulders, emptied his glass, and started for the Welchers' pool. This meant crossing the Lindleys' riding ring and he was surprised to find it overgrown with grass and all the jumps dismantled. He wondered if the Lindleys had sold their horses or gone away for the summer and put them out to board. He seemed to remember having heard something about the Lindleys and their horses but the memory was unclear. On he went, barefoot through the wet grass, to the Welchers', where he found their pool was dry.

This breach in his chain of water disappointed him absurdly, and he felt like some explorer who seeks a torrential headwater and finds a dead stream. He was disappointed and mystified. It was common enough to go away for the summer but no one ever drained his pool. The Welchers had definitely gone away. The pool furniture was folded, stacked, and covered with a tarpaulin. The bathhouse was locked. All the windows of the house were shut, and when he went around to the driveway in front he saw a FOR SALE sign nailed to a tree. When had he last heard from the Welchers — when, that is, had he and Lucinda last regretted an invitation to dine with them? It seemed only a week or so ago. Was his memory failing or had he so disciplined it in the repression of unpleasant facts that he had damaged his sense of the truth? Then in the distance he heard the sound of a tennis game. This cheered him, cleared away all his apprehensions and let him regard the overcast sky and the cold air with indifference. This was the day that Neddy Merrill swam across the county. That was the day! He started off then for his most difficult portage.

Had you gone for a Sunday afternoon ride that day you might have seen him, close to naked, standing on the shoulders of Route 424, waiting for a chance to cross. You might have wondered if he was the victim of foul play, had his car broken down, or was he merely a fool. Standing barefoot in the deposits of the highway — beer cans, rags, and blowout patches — exposed to all kinds of ridicule, he seemed pitiful. He had known when he started that this was a part of his journey — it had been on his maps — but confronted with the lines of traffic, worming through the summery light, he found himself unprepared. He was laughed at, jeered at, a beer can was thrown at him, and he had no dignity or humor to bring to the situation. He could have gone back, back to the Westerhazys', where Lucinda would still be sitting in the sun. He had signed nothing, vowed nothing, pledged nothing, not even to himself. Why, believing as he did, that all human obduracy was susceptible to common sense, was he unable to turn back? Why was he determined to complete his journey even if it meant putting his life in danger? At what point had this prank, this joke, this piece of horseplay become serious? He could not go back, he could not even recall with any clearness the green water at the Westerhazys', the sense of inhaling the day's components, the friendly and relaxed voices saying that they had *drunk* too much. In the space of an hour, more or less, he had covered a distance that made his return impossible.

An old man, tooling down the highway at fifteen miles an hour, let him get to the middle of the road, where there was a grass divider. Here he was exposed to the ridicule of the northbound traffic, but after ten or fifteen minutes he was able to cross. From here he had only a short walk to the Recreation Center at the edge of the village of Lancaster, where there were some handball courts and a public pool.

The effect of the water on voices, the illusion of brilliance and suspense, was the same here as it had been at the Bunkers' but the sounds here were louder, harsher, and more shrill, and as soon as he entered the crowded enclosure he was confronted with regimentation. "ALL SWIMMERS MUST TAKE A SHOWER BEFORE USING THE POOL. ALL SWIMMERS MUST USE THE FOOTBATH. ALL SWIMMERS MUST WEAR THEIR IDENTIFICATION DISKS." He took a shower, washed his feet in a cloudy and bitter solution, and made his way to the edge of the water. It stank of chlorine and looked to him like a sink. A pair of lifeguards in a pair of towers blew police whistles at what seemed to be regular intervals and abused the swimmers through a public address system. Neddy remembered the sapphire water at the Bunkers' with longing and thought that he might contaminate himself — damage his own prosperousness and charm — by swimming in this murk, but he reminded himself that he was an explorer, a pilgrim, and that this was merely a stagnant bend in the Lucinda River. He dove, scowling with distaste, into the chlorine and had to swim with his head above water to avoid collisions, but even so he was bumped into, splashed, and jostled. When he got to the shallow end both lifeguards were shouting at him: "Hey, you, you without the identification disk, get outa the water." He did, but they had no way of pursuing him and he went through the reek of suntan oil and chlorine out through the hurricane fence and passed the handball courts. By crossing the road he entered the wooded part of the Halloran estate. The woods were not cleared and the footing was treacherous and difficult until he reached the lawn and the clipped beech hedge that encircled their pool.

The Hallorans were friends, an elderly couple of enormous wealth who seemed to bask in the suspicion that they might be Communists. They were zealous reformers but they were not Communists, and yet when they were accused, as they sometimes were, of subversion, it seemed to gratify and excite them. Their beech hedge was yellow and he guessed this had been blighted like the Levys' maple. He called hullo, hullo, to warn the Hallorans of his approach, to palliate his invasion of their privacy. The Hallorans, for reasons that had never been explained to him, did not wear bathing suits. No explanations were in order, really. Their nakedness was a detail in their uncompromising zeal for reform and he stepped politely out of his trunks before he went through the opening in the hedge.

Mrs. Halloran, a stout woman with white hair and a serene face, was reading the *Times*. Mr. Halloran was taking beech leaves out of the water with a scoop. They seemed not surprised or displeased to see him. Their pool was perhaps the oldest in the county, a fieldstone rectangle, fed by a brook. It had no filter or pump and its waters were the opaque gold of the stream.

"I'm swimming across the county," Ned said.

"Why, I didn't know one could," exclaimed Mrs. Halloran.

"Well, I've made it from the Westerhazys'," Ned said. "That must be about four miles."

He left his trunks at the deep end, walked to the shallow end, and swam this stretch. As he was pulling himself out of the water he heard Mrs.

Halloran say, "We've been *terribly* sorry to hear about all your misfortunes, Neddy."

20   "My misfortunes?" Ned asked. "I don't know what you mean."

"Why, we heard that you'd sold the house and that your poor children . . ."

"I don't recall having sold the house," Ned said, "and the girls are at home."

"Yes," Mrs. Halloran sighed. "Yes . . ." Her voice filled the air with an unseasonable melancholy and Ned spoke briskly. "Thank you for the swim."

"Well, have a nice trip," said Mrs. Halloran.

25   Beyond the hedge he pulled on his trunks and fastened them. They were loose and he wondered if, during the space of an afternoon, he could have lost some weight. He was cold and he was tired and the naked Hallorans and their dark water had depressed him. The swim was too much for his strength but how could he have guessed this, sliding down the banister that morning and sitting in the Westerhazys' sun? His arms were lame. His legs felt rubbery and ached at the joints. The worst of it was the cold in his bones and the feeling that he might never be warm again. Leaves were falling down around him and he smelled wood smoke on the wind. Who would be burning wood at this time of year?

He needed a drink. Whiskey would warm him, pick him up, carry him through the last of his journey, refresh his feeling that it was original and valorous to swim across the county. Channel swimmers took brandy. He needed a stimulant. He crossed the lawn in front of the Hallorans' house and went down a little path to where they had built a house for their only daughter, Helen, and her husband, Eric Sachs. The Sachses' pool was small and he found Helen and her husband there.

"Oh, *Neddy*," Helen said. "Did you lunch at Mother's?"

"Not *really*," Ned said. "I *did* stop to see your parents." This seemed to be explanation enough. "I'm terribly sorry to break in on you like this but I've taken a chill and I wonder if you'd give me a drink."

"Why, I'd *love* to," Helen said, "but there hasn't been anything in this house to drink since Eric's operation. That was three years ago."

30   Was he losing his memory, had his gift for concealing painful facts let him forget that he had sold his house, that his children were in trouble, and that his friend had been ill? His eyes slipped from Eric's face to his abdomen, where he saw three pale, sutured scars, two of them at least a foot long. Gone was his navel, and what, Neddy thought, would the roving hand, bed-checking one's gifts at 3 A.M., make of a belly with no navel, no link to birth, this breach in the succession?

"I'm sure you can get a drink at the Biswangers'," Helen said. "They're having an enormous do. You can hear it from here. Listen!"

She raised her head and from across the road, the lawns, the gardens, the woods, the fields, he heard again the brilliant noise of voices over water. "Well, I'll get wet," he said, still feeling that he had no freedom of choice about his means of travel. He dove into the Sachses' cold water and, gasping, close to drowning, made his way from one end of the pool to the other. "Lucinda and I want *terribly* to see you," he said over his shoulder, his face set toward the Biswangers'. "We're sorry it's been so long and we'll call you *very* soon."

He crossed some fields to the Biswangers' and the sounds of revelry there. They would be honored to give him a drink, they would be happy to give him a drink. The Biswangers invited him and Lucinda for dinner four times a year, six weeks in advance. They were always rebuffed and yet they continued to send out their invitations, unwilling to comprehend the rigid and undemocratic realities of their society. They were the sort of people who discussed the price of things at cocktails, exchanged market tips during dinner, and after dinner told dirty stories to mixed company. They did not belong to Neddy's set — they were not even on Lucinda's Christmas card list. He went toward their pool with feelings of indifference, charity, and some unease, since it seemed to be getting dark and these were the longest days of the year. The party when he joined it was noisy and large. Grace Biswanger was the kind of hostess who asked the optometrist, the veterinarian, the real-estate dealer, and the dentist. No one was swimming and the twilight, reflected on the water of the pool, had a wintry gleam. There was a bar and he started for this. When Grace Biswanger saw him she came toward him, not affectionately as he had every right to expect, but bellicosely.

"Why, this party has everything," she said loudly, "including a gate crasher."

She could not deal him a social blow — there was no question about this and he did not flinch. "As a gate crasher," he asked politely, "do I rate a drink?"

"Suit yourself," she said. "You don't seem to pay much attention to invitations."

She turned her back on him and joined some guests, and he went to the bar and ordered a whiskey. The bartender served him but he served him rudely. His was a world in which the caterer's men kept the social score, and to be rebuffed by a part-time barkeep meant that he had suffered some loss of social esteem. Or perhaps the man was new and uninformed. Then he heard Grace at his back say: "They went for broke overnight — nothing but income — and he showed up drunk one Sunday and asked us to loan him five thousand dollars. . . ." She was always talking about money. It was worse than eating your peas off a knife. He dove into the pool, swam its length and went away.

The next pool on his list, the last but two, belonged to his old mistress, Shirley Adams. If he had suffered any injuries at the Biswangers' they would be cured here. Love — sexual roughhouse in fact — was the supreme elixir, the pain killer, the brightly colored pill that would put the spring back into his step, the joy of life in his heart. They had had an affair last week, last month, last year. He couldn't remember. It was he who had broken it off, his was the upper hand, and he stepped through the gate of the wall that surrounded her pool with nothing so considered as self-confidence. It seemed in a way to be his pool, as the lover, particularly the illicit lover, enjoys the possessions of his mistress with an authority unknown to holy matrimony. She was there, her hair the color of brass, but her figure, at the edge of the lighted, cerulean water, excited in him no profound memories. It had been, he thought, a lighthearted affair, although she had wept when he broke it off. She seemed confused to see him and he wondered if she was still wounded. Would she, God forbid, weep again?

"What do you want?" she asked.

40 "I'm swimming across the county."

"Good Christ. Will you ever grow up?"

"What's the matter?"

"If you've come here for money," she said, "I won't give you another cent."

"You could give me a drink."

45 "I could but I won't. I'm not alone."

"Well, I'm on my way."

He dove in and swam the pool, but when he tried to haul himself up onto the curb he found that the strength in his arms and shoulders had gone, and he paddled to the ladder and climbed out. Looking over his shoulder he saw, in the lighted bathhouse, a young man. Going out onto the dark lawn he smelled chrysanthemums or marigolds — some stubborn autumnal fragrance — on the night air, strong as gas. Looking overhead he saw that the stars had come out, but why should he seem to see Andromeda, Cepheus, and Cassiopeia? What had become of the constellations of midsummer? He began to cry.

It was probably the first time in his adult life that he had ever cried, certainly the first time in his life that he had ever felt so miserable, cold, tired, and bewildered. He could not understand the rudeness of the caterer's barkeep or the rudeness of a mistress who had come to him on her knees and showered his trousers with tears. He had swum too long, he had been immersed too long, and his nose and his throat were sore from the water. What he needed then was a drink, some company, and some clean, dry clothes, and while he could have cut directly across the road to his home he went on to the Gilmartins' pool. Here, for the first time in his life, he did not dive but went down the steps into the icy water and swam a hobbled sidestroke that he might have learned as a youth. He staggered with fatigue on his way to the Clydes' and paddled the length of their pool, stopping again and again with his hand on the curb to rest. He climbed up the ladder and wondered if he had the strength to get home. He had done what he wanted, he had swum the county, but he was so stupefied with exhaustion that his triumph seemed vague. Stooped, holding on to the gateposts for support, he turned up the driveway of his own house.

The place was dark. Was it so late that they had all gone to bed? Had Lucinda stayed at the Westerhazys' for supper? Had the girls joined her there or gone someplace else? Hadn't they agreed, as they usually did on Sunday, to regret all their invitations and stay at home? He tried the garage doors to see what cars were in but the doors were locked and rust came off the handles onto his hands. Going toward the house, he saw that the force of the thunderstorm had knocked one of the rain gutters loose. It hung down over the front door like an umbrella rib, but it could be fixed in the morning. The house was locked, and he thought that the stupid cook or the stupid maid must have locked the place up until he remembered that it had been some time since they had employed a maid or a cook. He shouted, pounded on the door, tried to force it with his shoulder, and then, looking in at the windows, saw the place was empty.

Stephen Crane
The Bride Comes to Yellow Sky

1

The great Pullman was whirling onward with such dignity of motion that a glance from the window seemed simply to prove that the plains of Texas were pouring eastward. Vast flats of green grass, dull-hued spaces of mesquite and cactus, little groups of frame houses, woods of light and tender trees, all were sweeping into the east, sweeping over the horizon, a precipice.

A newly married pair had boarded this coach at San Antonio. The man's face was reddened from many days in the wind and sun, and a direct result of his new black clothes was that his brick-colored hands were constantly performing in a most conscious fashion. From time to time he looked down respectfully at his attire. He sat with a hand on each knee, like a man waiting in a barber's shop. The glances he devoted to other passengers were furtive and shy.

The bride was not pretty, nor was she very young. She wore a dress of blue cashmere, with small reservations of velvet here and there, and with steel buttons abounding. She continually twisted her head to regard her puff sleeves, very stiff, straight, and high. They embarrassed her. It was quite apparent that she had cooked, and that she expected to cook, dutifully. The blushes caused by the careless scrutiny of some passengers as she had

THE BRIDE COMES TO YELLOW SKY   First published in 1898. Stephen Crane (1871–1900), son of a Methodist minister, grew up in New Jersey and New York State and did his early writing in New York City. A newspaper assignment in the West (including Texas, Arizona, Nevada, and Mexico), in the early months of 1895, provided background for this story.

entered the car were strange to see upon this plain, underclass countenance, which was drawn in placid, almost emotionless lines.

They were evidently very happy. "Ever been in a parlor car before?" he asked, smiling with delight.

5 "No," she answered, "I never was..It's fine, ain't it?"

"Great! And then after a while we'll go forward to the diner, and get a big lay-out. Finest meal in the world. Charge a dollar."

"Oh, do they?" cried the bride. "Charge a dollar? Why, that's too much — for us — ain't it, Jack?"

"Not this trip, anyhow," he answered bravely. "We're going to go the whole thing."

Later he explained to her about the trains. "You see, it's a thousand miles from one end of Texas to the other; and this train runs right across it, and never stops but four times." He had the pride of an owner. He pointed out to her the dazzling fittings of the coach; and in truth her eyes opened wider as she contemplated the sea-green figured velvet, the shining brass, silver, and glass, the wood that gleamed as darkly brilliant as the surface of a pool of oil. At one end a bronze figure sturdily held a support for a separated chamber, and at convenient places on the ceiling were frescos in olive and silver.

10 To the minds of the pair, their surroundings reflected the glory of their marriage that morning in San Antonio; this was the environment of their new estate; and the man's face in particular beamed with an elation that made him appear ridiculous to the Negro porter. This individual at times surveyed them from afar with an amused and superior grin. On other occasions he bullied them with skill in ways that did not make it exactly plain to them that they were being bullied. He subtly used all the manners of the most unconquerable kind of snobbery. He oppressed them; but of this oppression they had small knowledge, and they speedily forgot that infrequently a number of travelers covered them with stares of derisive enjoyment. Historically there was supposed to be something infinitely humorous in their situation.

"We are due in Yellow Sky at 3:42," he said, looking tenderly into her eyes.

"Oh, are we?" she said, as if she had not been aware of it. To evince surprise at her husband's statement was part of her wifely amiability. She took from a pocket a little silver watch; and as she held it before her, and stared at it with a frown of attention, the new husband's face shone.

"I bought it in San Anton' from a friend of mine," he told her gleefully.

"It's seventeen minutes past twelve," she said, looking up at him with a kind of shy and clumsy coquetry. A passenger, noting this play, grew excessively sardonic, and winked at himself in one of the numerous mirrors.

15 At last they went to the dining car. Two rows of Negro waiters, in glowing white suits, surveyed their entrance with the interest, and also the equanimity, of men who had been forewarned. The pair fell to the lot of a waiter

who happened to feel pleasure in steering them through their meal. He viewed them with the manner of a fatherly pilot, his countenance radiant with benevolence. The patronage, entwined with the ordinary deference, was not plain to them. And yet, as they returned to their coach, they showed in their faces a sense of escape.

To the left, miles down a long purple slope, was a little ribbon of mist where moved the keening Rio Grande. The train was approaching it at an angle, and the apex was Yellow Sky. Presently it was apparent that, as the distance from Yellow Sky grew shorter, the husband became commensurately restless. His brick-red hands were more insistent in their prominence. Occasionally he was even rather absent-minded and faraway when the bride leaned forward and addressed him.

As a matter of truth, Jack Potter was beginning to find the shadow of a deed weigh upon him like a leaden slab. He, the town marshal of Yellow Sky, a man known, liked, and feared in his corner, a prominent person, had gone to San Antonio to meet a girl he believed he loved, and there, after the usual prayers, had actually induced her to marry him, without consulting Yellow Sky for any part of the transaction. He was now bringing his bride before an innocent and unsuspecting community.

Of course people in Yellow Sky married as it pleased them, in accordance with a general custom; but such was Potter's thought of his duty to his friends, or of their idea of his duty, or of an unspoken form which does not control men in these matters, that he felt he was heinous. He had committed an extraordinary crime. Face to face with this girl in San Antonio, and spurred by his sharp impulse, he had gone headlong over all the social hedges. At San Antonio he was like a man hidden in the dark. A knife to sever any friendly duty, any form, was easy to his hand in that remote city. But the hour of Yellow Sky — the hour of daylight — was approaching.

He knew full well that his marriage was an important thing to his town. It could only be exceeded by the burning of the new hotel. His friends could not forgive him. Frequently he had reflected on the advisability of telling them by telegraph, but a new cowardice had been upon him. He feared to do it. And now the train was hurrying him toward a scene of amazement, glee, and reproach. He glanced out of the window at the line of haze swinging slowly in toward the train.

Yellow Sky had a kind of brass band, which played painfully, to the delight of the populace. He laughed without heart as he thought of it. If the citizens could dream of his prospective arrival with his bride, they would parade the band at the station and escort them, amid cheers and laughing congratulations, to his adobe home.

He resolved that he would use all the devices of speed and plains-craft in making the journey from the station to his house. Once within that safe citadel, he could issue some sort of vocal bulletin, and then not go among the citizens until they had time to wear off a little of their enthusiasm.

20

The bride looked anxiously at him. "What's worrying you, Jack?"

He laughed again. "I'm not worrying, girl; I'm only thinking of Yellow Sky."

She flushed in comprehension.

A sense of mutual guilt invaded their minds and developed a finer tenderness. They looked at each other with eyes softly aglow. But Potter often laughed the same nervous laugh; the flush upon the bride's face seemed quite permanent.

The traitor to the feelings of Yellow Sky narrowly watched the speeding landscape. "We're nearly there," he said.

Presently the porter came and announced the proximity of Potter's home. He held a brush in his hand, and, with all his airy superiority gone, he brushed Potter's new clothes as the latter slowly turned this way and that way. Potter fumbled out a coin and gave it to the porter, as he had seen others do. It was a heavy and muscle-bound business, as that of a man shoeing his first horse.

The porter took their bag, and as the train began to slow they moved forward to the hooded platform of the car. Presently the two engines and their long string of coaches rushed into the station of Yellow Sky.

"They have to take water here," said Potter, from a constricted throat and in mournful cadence, as one announcing death. Before the train stopped, his eye had swept the length of the platform, and he was glad and astonished to see there was none upon it but the station agent, who, with a slightly hurried and anxious air, was walking toward the water tanks. When the train had halted, the porter alighted first, and placed in position a little temporary step.

"Come on, girl," said Potter, hoarsely. As he helped her down they each laughed on a false note. He took the bag from the Negro, and bade his wife cling to his arm. As they slunk rapidly away, his hangdog glance perceived that they were unloading the two trunks, and also that the station agent, far ahead near the baggage car, had turned and was running toward him, making gestures. He laughed, and groaned as he laughed, when he noted the first effect of his marital bliss upon Yellow Sky. He gripped his wife's arm firmly to his side, and they fled. Behind them the porter stood, chuckling fatuously.

2

The California Express on the Southern Railway was due at Yellow Sky in twenty-one minutes. There were six men at the bar of the Weary Gentleman saloon. One was a drummer° who talked a great deal and rapidly; three were Texans who did not care to talk at that time; and two were Mexican sheepherders, who did not talk as a general practice in the Weary Gentleman

drummer: traveling salesman

saloon. The barkeeper's dog lay on the boardwalk that crossed in front of the door. His head was on his paws, and he glanced drowsily here and there with the constant vigilance of a dog that is kicked on occasion. Across the sandy street were some vivid green grass-plots, so wonderful in appearance, amid the sands that burned near them in a blazing sun, that they caused a doubt in the mind. They exactly resembled the grass mats used to represent lawns on the stage. At the cooler end of the railway station, a man without a coat sat in a tilted chair and smoked his pipe. The fresh-cut bank of the Rio Grande circled near the town, and there could be seen beyond it a great plum-colored plain of mesquite.

Save for the busy drummer and his companions in the saloon, Yellow Sky was dozing. The newcomer leaned gracefully upon the bar, and recited many tales with the confidence of a bard who has come upon a new field.

"— and at the moment that the old man fell downstairs with the bureau in his arms, the old woman was coming up with two scuttles of coal, and of course —"

The drummer's tale was interrupted by a young man who suddenly appeared in the open door. He cried: "Scratchy Wilson's drunk, and has turned loose with both hands." The two Mexicans at once set down their glasses and faded out of the rear entrance of the saloon.

The drummer, innocent and jocular, answered: "All right, old man. S'pose he has? Come in and have a drink, anyhow."

But the information had made such an obvious cleft in every skull in the room that the drummer was obliged to see its importance. All had become instantly solemn. "Say," said he, mystified, "what is this?" His three companions made the introductory gesture of eloquent speech; but the young man at the door forestalled them.

"It means, my friend," he answered, as he came into the saloon, "that for the next two hours this town won't be a health resort."

The barkeeper went to the door, and locked and barred it; reaching out of the window, he pulled in heavy wooden shutters, and barred them. Immediately a solemn, chapel-like gloom was upon the place. The drummer was looking from one to another.

"But say," he cried, "what is this anyhow? You don't mean there is going to be a gun fight?"

"Don't know whether there'll be a fight or not," answered one man, grimly, "but there'll be some shootin' — some good shootin'."

The young man who had warned them waved his hand. "Oh, there'll be a fight fast enough, if anyone wants it. Anybody can get a fight out there in the street. There's a fight just waiting."

The drummer seemed to be swayed between the interest of a foreigner and a perception of personal danger.

"What did you say his name was?" he asked.

"Scratchy Wilson," they answered in chorus.

45   "And will he kill anybody? What are you going to do? Does this happen often? Does he rampage around like this once a week or so? Can he break in that door?"

"No, he can't break down that door," replied the barkeeper. "He's tried it three times. But when he comes you'd better lay down on the floor, stranger. He's dead sure to shoot at it, and a bullet may come through."

Thereafter the drummer kept a strict eye upon the door. The time had not yet been called for him to hug the floor, but, as a minor precaution, he sidled near to the wall. "Will he kill anybody?" he said again.

The men laughed low and scornfully at the question.

"He's out to shoot, and he's out for trouble. Don't see any good in experimentin' with him."

50   "But what do you do in a case like this? What do you do?"

A man responded: "Why, he and Jack Potter — "

"But," in chorus the other men interrupted, "Jack Potter's in San Anton'."

"Well, who is he? What's he got to do with it?"

"Oh, he's the town marshal. He goes out and fights Scratchy when he gets on one of these tears."

55   "Wow!" said the drummer, mopping his brow. "Nice job he's got."

The voices had toned away to mere whisperings. The drummer wished to ask further questions, which were born of an increasing anxiety and bewilderment; but when he attempted them, the men merely looked at him in irritation and motioned him to remain silent. A tense waiting hush was upon them. In the deep shadows of the room their eyes shone as they listened for sounds from the street. One man made three gestures at the barkeeper; and the latter, moving like a ghost, handed him a glass and a bottle. The man poured a full glass of whisky, and set down the bottle noiselessly. He gulped the whisky in a swallow, and turned again toward the door in immovable silence. The drummer saw that the barkeeper, without a sound, had taken a Winchester from beneath the bar. Later he saw this individual beckoning to him, so he tip-toed across the room.

"You better come with me back of the bar."

"No, thanks," said the drummer, perspiring; "I'd rather be where I can make a break for the back door."

Whereupon the man of bottles made a kindly but peremptory gesture. The drummer obeyed it, and, finding himself seated on a box with his head below the level of the bar, balm was laid upon his soul at sight of various zinc and copper fittings that bore a resemblance to armor plate. The barkeeper took a seat comfortably upon an adjacent box.

60   "You see," he whispered, "this here Scratchy Wilson is a wonder with a gun — a perfect wonder; and when he goes on the war-trail, we hunt our holes — naturally. He's about the last one of the old gang that used to hang out along the river here. He's a terror when he's drunk. When he's sober he's

all right — kind of simple — wouldn't hurt a fly — nicest fellow in town. But when he's drunk — whoo!"

There were periods of stillness. "I wish Jack Potter was back from San Anton'," said the barkeeper. "He shot Wilson up once — in the leg — and he would sail in and pull out the kinks in this thing."

Presently they heard from a distance the sound of a shot, followed by three wild yowls. It instantly removed a bond from the men in the darkened saloon. There was a shuffling to feet. They looked at each other. "Here he comes," they said.

3

A man in a maroon-colored flannel shirt, which had been purchased for purposes of decoration, and made principally by some Jewish women on the east side of New York, rounded a corner and walked into the middle of the main street of Yellow Sky. In either hand the man held a long, heavy, blue-black revolver. Often he yelled, and these cries rang through a semblance of a deserted village, shrilly flying over the roofs in a volume that seemed to have no relation to the ordinary vocal strength of a man. It was as if the surrounding stillness formed the arch of a tomb over him. These cries of ferocious challenge rang against walls of silence. And his boots had red tops with gilded imprints, of the kind beloved in winter by little sledding boys on the hillsides of New England.

The man's face flamed in a rage begot of whisky. His eyes, rolling, and yet keen for ambush, hunted the still doorways and windows. He walked with the creeping movement of the midnight cat. As it occurred to him, he roared menacing information. The long revolvers in his hands were as easy as straws; they were moved with an electric swiftness. The little fingers of each hand played sometimes in a musician's way. Plain from the low collar of the shirt, the cords of his neck straightened and sank, straightened and sank, as passion moved him. The only sounds were his terrible invitations. The calm adobes preserved their demeanor at the passing of this small thing in the middle of the street.

There was no offer of fight — no offer of fight. The man called to the sky. 65
There were no attractions. He bellowed and fumed and swayed his revolvers here and everywhere.

The dog of the barkeeper of the Weary Gentleman saloon had not appreciated the advance of events. He yet lay dozing in front of his master's door. At sight of the dog, the man paused and raised his revolver humorously. At sight of the man, the dog sprang up and walked diagonally away, with a sullen head, and growling. The man yelled, and the dog broke into a gallop. As it was about to enter an alley, there was a loud noise, a whistling, and something spat the ground directly before it. The dog screamed, and, wheeling in terror, galloped headlong in a new direction. Again there was a noise, a whistling, and sand was kicked viciously before it. Fear-stricken, the dog turned and flurried like an animal in a pen. The man stood laughing, his weapons at his hips.

Ultimately the man was attracted by the closed door of the Weary Gentleman saloon. He went to it and, hammering with a revolver, demanded drink.

The door remaining imperturbable, he picked a bit of paper from the walk, and nailed it to the framework with a knife. He then turned his back contemptuously upon this popular resort and, walking to the opposite side of the street and spinning there on his heel quickly and lithely, fired at the bit of paper. He missed it by a half-inch. He swore at himself, and went away. Later he comfortably fusilladed the windows of his most intimate friend. The man was playing with this town; it was a toy for him.

But still there was no offer of fight. The name of Jack Potter, his ancient antagonist, entered his mind, and he concluded that it would be a glad thing if he should go to Potter's house, and by bombardment induce him to come out and fight. He moved in the direction of his desire, chanting Apache scalp-music.

70 When he arrived at it, Potter's house presented the same still, calm front as had the other adobes. Taking up a strategic position, the man howled a challenge. But this house regarded him as might a great stone god. It gave no sign. After a decent wait, the man howled further challenges, mingling with them wonderful epithets.

Presently there came the spectacle of a man churning himself into deepest rage over the immobility of a house. He fumed at it as the winter wind attacks a prairie cabin in the North. To the distance there should have gone the sound of a tumult like the fighting of two hundred Mexicans. As necessity bade him, he paused for breath or to reload his revolvers.

4

Potter and his bride walked sheepishly and with speed. Sometimes they laughed together shamefacedly and low.

"Next corner, dear," he said finally.

They put forth the efforts of a pair walking bowed against a strong wind. Potter was about to raise a finger to point the first appearance of the new home when, as they circled the corner, they came face to face with a man in a maroon-colored shirt, who was feverishly pushing cartridges into a large revolver. Upon the instant the man dropped this revolver to the ground and, like lightning, whipped another from its holster. The second weapon was aimed at the bridegroom's chest.

75 There was a silence. Potter's mouth seemed to be merely a grave for his tongue. He exhibited an instinct to at once loosen his arm from the woman's grip, and he dropped the bag to the sand. As for the bride, her face had gone as yellow as old cloth. She was a slave to hideous rites, gazing at the apparitional snake.

The two men faced each other at a distance of three paces. He of the revolver smiled with a new and quiet ferocity.

"Tried to sneak up on me," he said. "Tried to sneak up on me!" His eyes grew more baleful. As Potter made a slight movement, the man thrust his revolver venomously forward. "No, don't you do it, Jack Potter. Don't you move a finger toward a gun just yet. Don't you move an eyelash. The time has come for me to settle with you, and I'm goin' to do it my own way, and loaf along with no interferin'. So if you don't want a gun bent on you, just mind what I tell you."

Potter looked at his enemy. "I ain't got a gun on me, Scratchy," he said. "Honest, I ain't." He was stiffening and steadying, but yet somewhere at the back of his mind a vision of the Pullman floated, the sea-green figured velvet, the shining brass, silver, and glass, the wood that gleamed as darkly brilliant as the surface of a pool of oil — all the glory of the marriage, the environment of the new estate. "You know I fight when it comes to fighting, Scratchy Wilson, but I ain't got a gun on me. You'll have to do all the shootin' yourself."

His enemy's face went livid. He stepped forward and lashed his weapon to and fro before Potter's chest. "Don't you tell me you ain't got no gun on you, you whelp. Don't tell me no lie like that. There ain't a man in Texas ever seen you without no gun. Don't take me for no kid." His eyes blazed with light, and his throat worked like a pump.

"I ain't takin' you for no kid," answered Potter. His heels had not moved an inch backward. "I'm takin' you for a damn fool. I tell you I ain't got a gun, and I ain't. If you're goin' to shoot me up, you better begin now; you'll never get a chance like this again."

So much enforced reasoning had told on Wilson's rage; he was calmer. "If you ain't got a gun, why ain't you got a gun?" he sneered. "Been to Sunday school?"

"I ain't got a gun because I've just come from San Anton' with my wife. I'm married," said Potter. "And if I'd thought there was going to be any galoots like you prowling around when I brought my wife home, I'd had a gun, and don't you forget it."

"Married!" said Scratchy, not at all comprehending.

"Yes, married. I'm married," said Potter, distinctly.

"Married?" said Scratchy. Seemingly for the first time, he saw the drooping, drowning woman at the other man's side. "No!" he said. He was like a creature allowed a glimpse of another world. He moved a pace backward, and his arm with the revolver dropped to his side. "Is this — is this the lady?" he asked.

"Yes, this is the lady," answered Potter.

There was another period of silence.

"Well," said Wilson at last, slowly, "I s'pose it's all off now."

"It's all off if you say so, Scratchy. You know I didn't make the trouble." Potter lifted his valise.

90 "Well, I 'low it's off Jack," said Wilson. He was looking at the ground. "Married!" He was not a student of chivalry; it was merely that in the presence of this foreign condition he was a simple child of the earlier plains. He picked up his starboard revolver, and, placing both weapons in their holsters, he went away. His feet made funnel-shaped tracks in the heavy sand.

Louise Erdrich
A Wedge of Shade

Every place that I could name you, in the whole world around us, has better things about it than Argus, North Dakota. I just happened to grow up there for eighteen years, and the soil got to be part of me, the air has something in it that I breathed. Argus water doesn't taste as good as water in the cities. Still, the first thing I do, walking back into my mother's house, is stand at the kitchen sink and toss down glass after glass.

"Are you filled up?" My mother stands behind me. "Sit down if you are."

She's tall and board-square, French-Chippewa, with long arms and big knuckles. Her face is rawboned, fierce, and almost masculine in its edges and planes. Several months ago, a beauty operator convinced her that she should feminize her look with curls. Now the permanent, grown out in grizzled streaks, bristles like the coat of a terrier. I don't look like her. Not just the hair, since hers is salt-and-pepper and mine is a reddish brown, but my build. I'm short, boxy, more like my Aunt Mary. Like her, I can't seem to shake this town. I keep coming back here.

"There's jobs at the beet plant," my mother says.

5   This rumor, probably false, since the plant is in a slump, drops into the dim, close air of the kitchen. We have the shades drawn because it's a hot June, over a hundred degrees, and we're trying to stay cool. Outside, the water has been sucked from everything. The veins in the leaves are hollow, the ditch grass is crackling. The sky has absorbed every drop. It's a thin whitish-blue veil stretched from end to end over us, a flat gauze tarp. From the depot, I've walked here beneath it, dragging my suitcase.

We're sweating as if we're in an oven, a big messy one. For a week, it's been too hot to clean much or even move, and the crops are stunted, failing. The farmer next to us just sold his field for a subdivision, but the construction workers aren't doing much. They're wearing wet rags on their heads,

A WEDGE OF SHADE   First published in *The New Yorker* in 1989. Louise Erdrich was born in 1954 in Little Falls, Minnesota, a child of German-American Chippewa parents, and was raised in Wahpeton, North Dakota, where her parents worked for the Bureau of Indian Affairs. She graduated from Dartmouth College in 1976, and returned to North Dakota to teach in that state's Poetry in the Schools Program. She earned an M.A. in creative writing at Johns Hopkins in 1979, and has published three novels and a book of poetry as well as short stories. She lives in New Hampshire with her husband and five children.

sitting near the house sites in the brilliance of noon. The studs of wood stand upright over them, but uselessly — nothing casts shadows. The sun has dried them up, too.

"The beet plant," my mother says again.

"Maybe so," I say, and then, because I've got something bigger on my mind, "Maybe I'll go out there and apply."

"Oh?" She is intrigued now.

"God, this is terrible!" I take the glass of water in my hand and tip some onto my head. I don't feel cooler, though; I just feel the steam rising off me.

"The fan broke down," she states. "Both of them are kaput now. The motors or something. If Mary would get the damn tax refund, we'd run out to Pamida, buy a couple more, set up a breeze. Then we'd be cool out here."

"Your garden must be dead," I say, lifting the edge of the pull shade.

"It's sick, but I watered. And I won't mulch; that draws the damn slugs."

"Nothing could live out there, no bug." My eyes smart from even looking at the yard, which is a clear sheet of sun, almost incandescent.

"You'd be surprised."

I wish I could blurt it out, just tell her. Even now, the words swell in my mouth, the one sentence, but I'm scared, and with good reason. There is this about my mother: it is awful to see her angry. Her lips press together and she stiffens herself within, growing wooden, silent. Her features become fixed and remote, she will not speak. It takes a long time, and until she does you are held in suspense. Nothing that she ever says, in the end, is as bad as that feeling of dread. So I wait, half believing that she'll figure out my secret for herself, or drag it out of me, not that she ever tries. If I'm silent, she hardly notices. She's not like Aunt Mary, who forces me to say more than I know is on my mind.

My mother sighs. "It's too hot to bake. It's too hot to cook. But it's too hot to eat anyway."

She's talking to herself, which makes me reckless. Perhaps she is so preoccupied by the heat that I can slip my announcement past her. I should just say it, but I lose nerve, make an introduction that alerts her. "I have something to tell you."

I've cast my lot; there's no going back unless I think quickly. My thoughts hum.

But she waits, forgetting the heat for a moment.

"Ice," I say. "We have to have ice." I speak intensely, leaning toward her, almost glaring, but she is not fooled.

"Don't make me laugh," she says. "There's not a cube in town. The refrigerators can't keep cold enough." She eyes me the way a hunter eyes an animal about to pop from its den and run.

"O.K." I break down. "I really do have something." I stand, turn my back. In this lightless warmth I'm dizzy, almost sick. Now I've gotten to her and she's frightened to hear, breathless.

"Tell me," she urges. "Go on, get it over with."

And so I say it. "I got married." There is a surge of relief, a wind blowing through the room, but then it's gone. The curtain flaps and we're caught again, stunned in an even denser heat. It's now my turn to wait, and I whirl around and sit right across from her. Now is the time to tell her his name, a Chippewa name that she'll know from the papers, since he's notorious. Now is the time to get it over with. But I can't bear the picture she makes, the shock that parts her lips, the stunned shade of hurt in her eyes. I have to convince her, somehow, that it's all right.

"You hate weddings! Just think, just picture it. Me, white net. On a day like this. You, stuffed in your summer wool, and Aunt Mary, God knows . . . and the tux, the rental, the groom . . ."

Her head had lowered as my words fell on her, but now her forehead tips up and her eyes come into view, already hardening. My tongue flies back into my mouth.

She mimics, making it a question, "The groom . . ."

I'm caught, my lips half open, a stuttering noise in my throat. How to begin? I have rehearsed this, but my lines melt away, my opening, my casual introductions. I can think of nothing that would convince her of how much more he is than the captions beneath the photos. There is no picture adequate, no representation that captures him. So I just put my hand across the table and I touch her hand. "Mother," I say, as if we're in a staged drama, "He'll arrive here shortly."

There is something forming in her, some reaction. I am afraid to let it take complete shape. "Let's go out and wait on the steps, Mom. Then you'll see him."

"I do not understand," she says in a frighteningly neutral voice. This is what I mean. Everything is suddenly forced, unnatural — we're reading lines.

"He'll approach from a distance." I can't help speaking like a bad actor. "I told him to give me an hour. He'll wait, then he'll come walking down the road."

We rise and unstick our blouses from our stomachs, our skirts from the backs of our legs. Then we walk out front in single file, me behind, and settle ourselves on the middle step. A scrubby box-elder tree on one side casts a light shade, and the dusty lilacs seem to catch a little breeze on the other. It's not so bad out here, still hot, but not so dim, contained. It is worse past the trees. The heat shimmers in a band, rising off the fields, out of the spars and bones of houses that will wreck our view. The horizon and the edge of town show through the gaps in the framing now, and as we sit we watch the workers move, slowly, almost in a practiced recital, back and forth. Their headcloths hang to their shoulders, their hard hats are dabs of yellow, their white T-shirts blend into the fierce air and sky. They don't seem to be doing anything, although we hear faint thuds from their hammers. Otherwise, except for the whistles of a few birds, there is silence. Certainly we don't speak.

It is a longer wait than I anticipated, maybe because he wants to give me time. At last the shadows creep out, hard, hot, charred, and the heat begins to lengthen and settle. We are going into the worst of the afternoon when a dot at the end of the road begins to form.

Mom and I are both watching. We have not moved our eyes around much, and we blink and squint to try and focus. The dot doesn't change, not for a long while. And then it suddenly springs clear in relief—a silhouette, lost for a moment in the shimmer, reappearing. In that shining expanse he is a little wedge of moving shade. He continues, growing imperceptibly, until there are variations in the outline, and it can be seen that he is large. As he passes the construction workers, they turn and stop, all alike in their hats, stock-still.

Growing larger yet, as if he has absorbed their stares, he nears us. Now we can see the details. He is dark, the first thing. His arms are thick, his chest is huge, and the features of his face are wide and open. He carries nothing in his hands. He wears a black T-shirt, the opposite of the construction workers, and soft jogging shoes. His jeans are held under his stomach by a belt with a star beaded on the buckle. His hair is long, in a tail. I am the wrong woman for him. I am paler, shorter, un-magnificent. But I stand up. Mom joins me, and I answer proudly when she asks, "His name?"

"His name is Gerry—" Even now I can't force his last name through my lips. But Mom is distracted by the sight of him anyway.

We descend one step, and stop again. It is here we will receive him. Our hands are folded at our waists. We're balanced, composed. He continues to stroll toward us, his white smile widening, his eyes filling with the sight of me as mine are filling with him. At the end of the road behind him, another dot has appeared. It is fast-moving and the sun flares off it twice: a vehicle. Now there are two figures—one approaching in a spume of dust from the rear, and Gerry, unmindful, not slackening or quickening his pace, continuing on. It is like a choreography design. They move at parallel speeds in front of our eyes. Then, at the same moment, at the end of our yard, they conclude the performance; both of them halt.

Gerry stands, looking toward us, his thumbs in his belt. He nods respectfully to Mom, looks calmly at me, and half smiles. He raises his brows, and we're suspended. Officer Lovchik emerges from the police car, stooped and tired. He walks up behind Gerry and I hear the snap of handcuffs, then I jump. I'm stopped by Gerry's gaze, though, as he backs away from me, still smiling tenderly. I am paralyzed halfway down the walk. He kisses the air while Lovchik cautiously prods at him, fitting his prize into the car. And then the doors slam, the engine roars, and they back out and turn around. As they move away there is no siren. I think I've heard Lovchik mention questioning. I'm sure it is lots of fuss for nothing, a mistake, but it cannot be denied—this is terrible timing.

I shake my shoulders, smooth my skirt, and turn to my mother with a look of outrage. "How do you like that?" I try.

She's got her purse in one hand, her car keys out.

"Let's go," she says.

"O.K.," I answer. "Fine. Where?"

"Aunt Mary's."

45   "I'd rather go and bail him out, Mom."

"Bail," she says. "*Bail*?"

She gives me such a look of cold and furious surprise that I sink immediately into the front seat, lean back against the vinyl. I almost welcome the sting of the heated plastic on my back, thighs, shoulders.

Aunt Mary lives at the rear of the butcher shop she runs. As we walk toward the "House of Meats," her dogs are rugs in the dirt, flattened by the heat of the day. Not one of them barks at us to warn her. We step over them and get no more reaction than a whine, the slow beat of a tail. Inside, we get no answers either, although we call Aunt Mary up and down the hall. We enter the kitchen and sit at the table, which holds a half-ruined watermelon. By the sink, in a tin box, are cigarettes. My mother takes one and carefully puts a match to it, frowning. "I know what," she says. "Go check the lockers."

There are two — a big freezer full of labelled meats and rental space, and another, smaller one that is just a side cooler. I notice, walking past the meat display counter, that the red beacon beside the outside switch of the cooler is glowing. That tells you when the light is on inside.

50   I pull the long metal handle toward me and the thick door swishes open. I step into the cool, spicy air. Aunt Mary is there, too proud to ever register a hint of surprise. She simply nods and looks away as though I've just been out for a minute, although we've not seen one another in six months or more. She is relaxing on a big can of pepper labelled "Zanzibar," reading a scientific-magazine article. I sit down on a barrel of alum. With no warning, I drop my bomb: "I'm married." It doesn't matter how I tell it to Aunt Mary, because she won't be, refuses to be, surprised.

"What's he do?" she simply asks, putting aside the sheaf of paper. I thought the first thing she'd do was scold me for fooling my mother. But it's odd, for two women who have lived through boring times and disasters, how rarely one comes to the other's defense, and how often they are each willing to take advantage of the other's absence. But I'm benefitting here. It seems that Aunt Mary is truly interested in Gerry. So I'm honest.

"He's something like a political activist. I mean he's been in jail and all. But not for any crime, you see; it's just because of his convictions."

She gives me a long, shrewd stare. Her skin is too tough to wrinkle, but she doesn't look young. All around us hang loops of sausages, every kind you can imagine, every color, from the purple-black of blutwurst to the pale-whitish links that my mother likes best. Blocks of butter and headcheese, a can of raw milk, wrapped parcels, and cured bacons are stuffed onto the shelves around us. My heart has gone still and cool inside me, and I can't stop talking.

"He's the kind of guy it's hard to describe. Very different. People call him a free spirit, but that doesn't say it either, because he's very disciplined in some ways. He learned to be neat in jail." I pause. She says nothing, so I go on. "I know it's sudden, but who likes weddings? I hate them — all that mess with the bridesmaids' gowns, getting material to match. I don't have girl-friends. I mean, how embarrassing, right? Who would sing 'O Perfect Love'? Carry the ring?"

She isn't really listening. 55

"What's he do?" she asks again.

Maybe she won't let go of it until I discover the right answer, like a game with nouns and synonyms.

"He — well, he agitates," I tell her.

"Is that some kind of factory work?"

"Not exactly, no, it's not a nine-to-five job or anything . . ." 60

She lets the magazine fall, now, cocks her head to one side, and stares at me without blinking her cold yellow eyes. She has the look of a hawk, of a person who can see into the future but won't tell you about it. She's lost business for staring at customers, but she doesn't care.

"Are you telling me that he doesn't . . ." Here she shakes her head twice, slowly, from one side to the other, without removing me from her stare. "That he doesn't have regular work?"

"Oh, what's the matter, anyway?" I say roughly. "I'll work. This is the nineteen-seventies."

She jumps to her feet, stands over me — a stocky woman with terse features and short, thin points of gray hair. Her earrings tremble and flash — small fiery opals. Her brown plastic glasses hang crooked on a cord around her neck. I have never seen her become quite so instantly furious, so disturbed. "We're going to fix that," she says.

The cooler immediately feels smaller, the sausages knock at my shoulder, and the harsh light makes me blink. I am as stubborn as Aunt Mary, however, and she knows that I can go head to head with her. "We're married and that's final." I manage to stamp my foot. 65

Aunt Mary throws an arm back, blows air through her cheeks, and waves away my statement vigorously. "You're a little girl. How old is *he*?"

I frown at my lap, trace the threads in my blue cotton skirt, and tell her that age is irrelevant.

"Big word," she says sarcastically. "Let me ask you this. He's old enough to get a job?"

"Of course he is; what do you think? O.K., he's older than me. He's in his thirties."

"Aha, I knew it." 70

"Geez! So what? I mean, haven't you ever been in love, hasn't someone ever gotten you *right here*?" I smash my fist on my chest.

We lock eyes, but she doesn't waste a second in feeling hurt. "Sure, sure I've been in love. You think I haven't? I know what it feels like, you smart-ass. You'd be surprised. But he was no lazy son of a bitch. Now, listen . . ." She stops, draws breath, and I let her. "Here's what I mean by 'fix.' I'll teach the sausage-making trade to him — to you, too — and the grocery business.

I've about had it anyway, and so's your mother. We'll do the same as my aunt and uncle — leave the shop to you and move to Arizona. I like this place." She looks up at the burning safety bulb, down at me again. Her face drags in the light. "But what the hell. I always wanted to travel."

I'm stunned, a little flattened out, maybe ashamed of myself. "You hate going anywhere," I say, which is true.

The door swings open and Mom comes in with us. She finds a milk can and balances herself on it, sighing at the delicious feeling of the air, absorbing from the silence the fact that we have talked. She hasn't anything to add, I guess, and as the coolness hits, her eyes fall shut. Aunt Mary's, too. I can't help it, either, and my eyelids drop, although my brain is conscious and alert. From the darkness, I can see us in the brilliance. The light rains down on us. We sit the way we have been sitting, on our cans of milk and pepper, upright and still. Our hands are curled loosely in our laps. Our faces are blank as the gods'. We could be statues in a tomb sunk into the side of a mountain. We could be dreaming the world up in our brains.

75   It is later, and the weather has no mercy. We are drained of everything but simple thoughts. It's too hot for feelings. Driving home, we see how field after field of beets has gone into shock, and even some of the soybeans. The plants splay, limp, burned into the ground. Only the sunflowers continue to struggle upright, bristling but small.

What drew me in the first place to Gerry was the unexpected. I went to hear him talk just after I enrolled at the university, and then I demonstrated when they came and got him off the stage. He always went so willingly, accommodating everyone. I began to visit him. I sold lunar calendars and posters to raise his bail and eventually free him. One thing led to another, and one night we found ourselves alone in a Howard Johnson's coffee shop downstairs from where they put him up when his speech was finished. There were much more beautiful women after him; he could have had his pick of Swedes or Yankton Sioux girls, who are the best-looking of all. But I was different, he says. He liked my slant on life. And then there was no going back once it started, no turning, as though it was meant. We had no choice.

I have this intuition as we near the house, in the fateful quality of light, as in the turn of the day the heat continues to press and the blackness, into which the warmth usually lifts, lowers steadily: We must come to the end of something; there must be a close to this day.

As we turn into the yard we see that Gerry is sitting on the porch stairs. Now it is our turn to be received. I throw the car door open and stumble out before the motor even cuts. I run to him and hold him, as my mother, pursuing the order of events, parks carefully. Then she walks over, too, holding her purse by the strap. She stands before him and says no word but simply looks into his face, staring as if he's cardboard, a man behind glass who cannot see her. I think she's rude, but then I realize that he is staring back, that they are the same height. Their eyes are level.

He puts his hand out. "My name is Gerry."

"Gerry what?"

"Nanapush."

She nods, shifts her weight. "You're from that line, the old strain, the ones . . ." She does not finish.

"And my father," Gerry says, "was Old Man Pillager."

"Kashpaws," she says, "are my branch, of course. We're probably related through my mother's brother." They do not move. They are like two opponents from the same divided country, staring across the border. They do not shift or blink, and I see that they are more alike than I am like either one of them — so tall, solid, dark-haired. They could be mother and son.

"Well, I guess you should come in," she offers. "You are a distant relative, after all." She looks at me. "Distant enough."

Whole swarms of mosquitoes are whining down, discovering us now, so there is no question of staying where we are. And so we walk into the house, much hotter than outside, with the gathered heat. Instantly the sweat springs from our skin and I can think of nothing else but cooling off. I try to force the windows higher in their sashes, but there's no breeze anyway; nothing stirs, no air.

"Are you sure," I gasp, "about those fans?"

"Oh, they're broke, all right," my mother says, distressed. I rarely hear this in her voice. She switches on the lights, which makes the room seem hotter, and we lower ourselves into the easy chairs. Our words echo, as though the walls have baked and dried hollow.

"Show me those fans," says Gerry.

My mother points toward the kitchen. "They're sitting on the table. I've already tinkered with them. See what you can do."

And so he does. After a while she hoists herself and walks out back to him. Their voices close together now, absorbed, and their tools clank frantically, as if they are fighting a duel. But it is a race with the bell of darkness and their waning energy. I think of ice. I get ice on the brain.

"Be right back," I call out, taking the car keys from my mother's purse. "Do you need anything?"

There is no answer from the kitchen but a furious sputter of metal, the clatter of nuts and bolts spilling to the floor.

I drive out to the Superpumper, a big new gas-station complex on the edge of town, where my mother most likely has never been. She doesn't know about convenience stores, has no credit cards for groceries or gas, pays only with small bills and change. She never has used an ice machine. It would grate on her that a bag of frozen water costs eighty cents, but it doesn't bother me. I take the plastic-foam cooler and I fill it for a couple of dollars. I buy two six-packs of Shasta soda and I plunge them in among the uniform coins of ice. I drink two myself on the way home, and I manage to lift the whole heavy cooler out of the trunk, carry it to the door.

LOUISE ERDRICH **423**

The fans are whirring, beating the air. I hear them going in the living room the minute I come in. The only light shines from the kitchen. Gerry and my mother have thrown the pillows from the couch onto the livingroom floor, and they are sitting in the rippling currents of air. I bring the cooler in and put it near us. I have chosen all dark flavors — black cherry, grape, red berry, cola — so as we drink the darkness swirls inside us with the night air, sweet and sharp, driven by small motors.

I drag more pillows down from the other rooms upstairs. There is no question of attempting the bedrooms, the stifling beds. And so, in the dark, I hold hands with Gerry as he settles down between my mother and me. He is huge as a hill between the two of us, solid in the beating wind.

Richard Ford
Great Falls

This is not a happy story. I warn you.

My father was a man named Jack Russell, and when I was a young boy in my early teens, we lived with my mother in a house to the east of Great Falls, Montana, near the small town of Highwood and the Highwood Mountains and the Missouri River. It is a flat, treeless benchland there, all of it used for wheat farming, though my father was never a farmer, but was brought up near Tacoma, Washington, in a family that worked for Boeing.

He — my father — had been an Air Force sergeant and had taken his discharge in Great Falls. And instead of going home to Tacoma, where my mother wanted to go, he had taken a civilian's job with the Air Force, working on planes, which was what he liked to do. And he had rented the house out of town from a farmer who did not want it left standing empty.

The house itself is gone now — I have been to the spot. But the double row of Russian olive trees and two of the outbuildings are still standing in the milkweeds. It was a plain, two-story house with a porch on the front and no place for the cars. At the time, I rode the school bus to Great Falls every morning, and my father drove in while my mother stayed home.

5   My mother was a tall pretty woman, thin, with black hair and slightly sharp features that made her seem to smile when she wasn't smiling. She had grown up in Wallace, Idaho, and gone to college a year in Spokane, then moved out to the coast, which is where she met Jack Russell. She was two years older than he was, and married him, she said to me, because he was

GREAT FALLS   First published in 1987. Richard Ford was born in Jackson, Mississippi, in 1944, and raised there and in Little Rock. He received a B.A. from Michigan State University and an M.F.A. from the University of California at Irvine in 1970. During the 1970s, he taught writing at Princeton, Williams, and the University of Michigan. In 1981 he gave up teaching to concentrate on writing, and he moved to Missoula, Montana, in 1983 when his wife took a job there. He has published four novels and one collection of stories, and now lives in New Orleans.

young and wonderful looking, and because she thought they could leave the sticks and see the world together—which I suppose they did for a while. That was the life she wanted, even before she knew much about wanting anything else or about the future.

When my father wasn't working on airplanes, he was going hunting or fishing, two things he could do as well as anyone. He had learned to fish, he said, in Iceland, and to hunt ducks up on the DEW line—stations he had visited in the Air Force. And during the time of this—it was 1960—he began to take me with him on what he called his "expeditions." I thought even then, with as little as I knew, that these were opportunities other boys would dream of having but probably never would. And I don't think that I was wrong in that.

It is a true thing that my father did not know limits. In the spring, when we would go east to the Judith River Basin and camp up on the banks, he would catch a hundred fish in a weekend and sometimes more than that. It was all he did from morning until night, and it was never hard for him. He used yellow corn kernels stacked onto a #4 snelled hook, and he would rattle this rig-up along the bottom of a deep pool below a split-shot sinker, and catch fish. And most of the time, because he knew the Judith River and knew how to feel his bait down deep, he could catch fish of good size.

It was the same with ducks, the other thing he liked. When the northern birds were down, usually by mid-October, he would take me and we would build a cattail and wheatstraw blind on one of the tule ponds or sloughs he knew about down the Missouri, where the water was shallow enough to wade. We would set out his decoys to the leeward side of our blind, and he would sprinkle corn on a hunger-line from the decoys to where we were. In the evenings when he came home from the base, we would go and sit out in the blind until the roosting flights came and put down among the decoys— there was never calling involved. And after a while, sometimes it would be an hour and full dark, the ducks would find the corn, and the whole raft of them—sixty, sometimes—would swim in to us. At the moment he judged they were close enough, my father would say to me, "Shine, Jackie," and I would stand and shine a seal-beam car light out onto the pond, and he would stand up beside me and shoot all the ducks that were there, on the water if he could, but flying and getting up as well. He owned a Model 11 Remington with a long-tube magazine that would hold ten shells, and with that many, and shooting straight over the surface rather than down onto it, he could kill or wound thirty ducks in twenty seconds' time. I remember distinctly the report of that gun and the flash of it over the water into the dark air, one shot after another, not even so fast, but measured in a way to hit as many as he could.

What my father did with the ducks he killed, and the fish, too, was sell them. It was against the law then to sell wild game, and it is against the law now. And though he kept some for us, most he would take—his fish laid on ice, or his ducks still wet and bagged in the burlap corn sacks—down to the

Great Northern Hotel, which was still open then on Second Street in Great Falls, and sell them to the Negro caterer who bought them for his wealthy customers and for the dining car passengers who came through. We would drive in my father's Plymouth to the back of the hotel — always this was after dark — to a concrete loading ramp and lighted door that were close enough to the yards that I could sometimes see passenger trains waiting at the station, their car lights yellow and warm inside, the passengers dressed in suits, all bound for someplace far away from Montana — Milwaukee or Chicago or New York City, unimaginable places to me, a boy fourteen years old, with my father in the cold dark selling illegal game.

10   The caterer was a tall, stooped-back man in a white jacket, who my father called "Professor Ducks" or "Professor Fish," and the Professor referred to my father as "Sarge." He paid a quarter per pound for trout, a dime for whitefish, a dollar for a mallard duck, two for a speckle or a blue goose, and four dollars for a Canada. I have been with my father when he took away a hundred dollars for fish he'd caught and, in the fall, more than that for ducks and geese. When he had sold game in that way, we would drive out 10th Avenue and he would drink with some friends he knew there, and they would laugh about hunting and fishing while I played pinball and wasted money in the jukebox.

It was on such a night as this that the unhappy things came about. It was in late October. I remember the time because Halloween had not been yet, and in the windows of the houses that I passed every day on the bus to Great Falls, people had put pumpkin lanterns, and set scarecrows in their yards in chairs.

My father and I had been shooting ducks in a slough on the Smith River, upstream from where it enters on the Missouri. He had killed thirty ducks, and we'd driven them down to the Great Northern and sold them there, though my father had kept two back in his corn sack. And when we had driven away, he suddenly said, "Jackie, let's us go back home tonight. Who cares about those hard-dicks at The Mermaid. I'll cook these ducks on the grill. We'll do something different tonight." He smiled at me in an odd way. This was not a thing he usually said, or the way he usually talked. He liked The Mermaid, and my mother — as far as I knew — didn't mind it if he went there.

"That sounds good," I said.

"We'll surprise your mother," he said. "We'll make her happy."

15   We drove out past the air base on Highway 87, past where there were planes taking off into the night. The darkness was dotted by the green and red beacons, and the tower light swept the sky and trapped planes as they disappeared over the flat landscape toward Canada or Alaska and the Pacific.

"Boy-oh-boy," my father said — just out of the dark. I looked at him and his eyes were narrow, and he seemed to be thinking about something. "You know, Jackie," he said, "your mother said something to me once I've never forgotten. She said, 'Nobody dies of a broken heart.' This was somewhat before you were born. We were living down in Texas and we'd had some big blow-up, and that was the idea she had. I don't know why." He shook his head.

He ran his hand under the seat, found a half-pint bottle of whiskey, and held it up to the lights of the car behind us to see what there was left of it. He unscrewed the cap and took a drink, then held the bottle out to me. "Have a drink, son," he said. "Something oughta be good in life." And I felt that something was wrong. Not because of the whiskey, which I had drunk before and he had reason to know about, but because of some sound in his voice, something I didn't recognize and did not know the importance of, though I was certain it was important.

I took a drink and gave the bottle back to him, holding the whiskey in my mouth until it stopped burning and I could swallow it a little at a time. When we turned out the road to Highwood, the lights of Great Falls sank below the horizon, and I could see the small white lights of farms, burning at wide distances in the dark.

"What do you worry about, Jackie?" my father said. "Do you worry about girls? Do you worry about your future sex life? Is that some of it?" He glanced at me, then back at the road.

"I don't worry about that," I said.

"Well, what then?" my father said. "What else is there?"

"I worry if you're going to die before I do," I said, though I hated saying that, "or if Mother is. That worries me."

"It'd be a miracle if we didn't," my father said, with the half-pint held in the same hand he held the steering wheel. I had seen him drive that way before. "Things pass too fast in your life, Jackie. Don't worry about that. If I were you, I'd worry we might not." He smiled at me, and it was not the worried, nervous smile from before, but a smile that meant he was pleased. And I don't remember him ever smiling at me that way again.

We drove on out behind the town of Highwood and onto the flat field roads toward our house. I could see, out on the prairie, a moving light where the farmer who rented our house to us was disking his field for winter wheat. "He's waited too late with that business," my father said and took a drink, then threw the bottle right out the window. "He'll lose that," he said, "the cold'll kill it." I did not answer him, but what I thought was that my father knew nothing about farming, and if he was right it would be an accident. He knew about planes and hunting game, and that seemed all to me.

"I want to respect your privacy," he said then, for no reason at all that I understood. I am not even certain he said it, only that it is in my memory that way. I don't know what he was thinking of. Just words. But I said to him, I remember well, "It's all right. Thank you."

We did not go straight out the Geraldine Road to our house. Instead my father went down another mile and turned, went a mile and turned back again so that we came home from the other direction. "I want to stop and listen now," he said. "The geese should be in the stubble." We stopped and he cut the lights and engine, and we opened the car windows and listened. It was eight o'clock at night and it was getting colder, though it was dry. But I could hear nothing, just the sound of air moving lightly through the field, and not a goose sound. Though I could smell the whiskey on my father's breath and on mine, could hear the motor ticking, could hear him breathe, hear the sound we made sitting side by side on the car seat, our clothes, our feet, almost our hearts beating. And I could see out in the night the yellow lights of our house, shining through the olive trees south of us like a ship on the sea. "I hear them, by God," my father said, his head stuck out the window. "But they're high up. They won't stop here now, Jackie. They're high flyers, those boys. Long gone geese."

There was a car parked off the road, down the line of wind-break trees, beside a steel thresher the farmer had left there to rust. You could see moonlight off the taillight chrome. It was a Pontiac, a two-door hard-top. My father said nothing about it and I didn't either, though I think now for different reasons.

The floodlight was on over the side door of our house and lights were on inside, upstairs and down. My mother had a pumpkin on the front porch, and the wind chime she had hung by the door was tinkling. My dog, Major, came out of the quonset shed and stood in the car lights when we drove up.

"Let's see what's happening here," my father said, opening the door and stepping out quickly. He looked at me inside the car, and his eyes were wide and his mouth drawn tight.

30   We walked in the side door and up the basement steps into the kitchen, and a man was standing there — a man I had never seen before, a young man with blond hair, who might've been twenty or twenty-five. He was tall and was wearing a short-sleeved shirt and beige slacks with pleats. He was on the other side of the breakfast table, his fingertips just touching the wooden tabletop. His blue eyes were on my father, who was dressed in hunting clothes.

"Hello," my father said.

"Hello," the young man said, and nothing else. And for some reason I looked at his arms, which were long and pale. They looked like a young man's arms, like my arms. His short sleeves had each been neatly rolled up, and I could see the bottom of a small green tattoo edging out from underneath. There was a glass of whiskey on the table, but no bottle.

"What's your name?" my father said, standing in the kitchen under the bright ceiling light. He sounded like he might be going to laugh.

"Woody," the young man said and cleared his throat. He looked at me, then he touched the glass of whiskey, just the rim of the glass. He wasn't nervous, I could tell that. He did not seem to be afraid of anything.

35   "Woody," my father said and looked at the glass of whiskey. He looked at me, then sighed and shook his head. "Where's Mrs. Russell, Woody? I guess you aren't robbing my house, are you?"

Woody smiled. "No," he said. "Upstairs. I think she went upstairs."

"Good," my father said, "that's a good place." And he walked straight out of the room, but came back and stood in the doorway. "Jackie, you and Woody step outside and wait on me. Just stay there and I'll come out." He looked at Woody then in a way I would not have liked him to look at me, a look that meant he was studying Woody. "I guess that's your car," he said.

"That Pontiac," Woody nodded.

"Okay. Right," my father said. Then he went out again and up the stairs. At that moment the phone started to ring in the living room, and I heard my mother say, "Who's that?" And my father say, "It's me. It's Jack." And I decided I wouldn't go answer the phone. Woody looked at me, and I understood he wasn't sure what to do. Run, maybe. But he didn't have run in him. Though I thought he would probably do what I said if I would say it.

"Let's just go outside," I said. 40

And he said, "All right."

Woody and I walked outside and stood in the light of the floodlamp above the side door. I had on my wool jacket, but Woody was cold and stood with his hands in his pockets, and his arms bare, moving from foot to foot. Inside, the phone was ringing again. Once I looked up and saw my mother come to the window and look down at Woody and me. Woody didn't look up or see her, but I did. I waved at her, and she waved back at me and smiled. She was wearing a powder-blue dress. In another minute the phone stopped ringing.

Woody took a cigarette out of his shirt pocket and lit it. Smoke shot through his nose into the cold air, and he sniffed, looked around the ground and threw his match on the gravel. His blond hair was combed backwards and neat on the sides, and I could smell his aftershave on him, a sweet, lemon smell. And for the first time I noticed his shoes. They were two-tones, black with white tops and black laces. They stuck out below his baggy pants and were long and polished and shiny, as if he had been planning on a big occasion. They looked like shoes some country singer would wear, or a salesman. He was handsome, but only like someone you would see beside you in a dime store and not notice again.

"I like it out here," Woody said, his head down, looking at his shoes. "Nothing to bother you. I bet you'd see Chicago if the world was flat. The Great Plains commence here."

"I don't know," I said. 45

Woody looked up at me, cupping his smoke with one hand. "Do you play football?"

"No," I said. I thought about asking him something about my mother. But I had no idea what it would be.

"I *have* been drinking," Woody said, "but I'm not drunk now."

The wind rose then, and from behind the house I could hear Major bark once from far away, and I could smell the irrigation ditch, hear it hiss in the field. It ran down from Highwood Creek to the Missouri, twenty miles away. It was nothing Woody knew about, nothing he could hear or smell. He knew nothing about anything that was here. I heard my father say the words, "That's a real joke," from inside the house, then the sound of a drawer being opened and shut, and a door closing. Then nothing else.

50   Woody turned and looked into the dark toward where the glow of Great Falls rose on the horizon, and we both could see the flashing lights of a plane lowering to land there. "I once passed my brother in the Los Angeles airport and didn't even recognize him," Woody said, staring into the night. "He recognized *me*, though. He said, 'Hey, bro, are you mad at me, or what?' I wasn't mad at him. We both had to laugh."

    Woody turned and looked at the house. His hands were still in his pockets, his cigarette clenched between his teeth, his arms taut. They were, I saw, bigger, stronger arms than I had thought. A vein went down the front of each of them. I wondered what Woody knew that I didn't. Not about my mother—I didn't know anything about that and didn't want to— but about a lot of things, about the life out in the dark, about coming out here, about airports, even about me. He and I were not so far apart in age, I knew that. But Woody was one thing, and I was another. And I wondered how I would ever get to be like him, since it didn't necessarily seem so bad a thing to be.

    "Did you know your mother was married before?" Woody said.

    "Yes," I said. "I knew that."

    "It happens to all of them, now," he said. "They can't wait to get divorced."

55   "I guess so," I said.

    Woody dropped his cigarette into the gravel and toed it out with his black-and-white shoe. He looked up at me and smiled the way he had inside the house, a smile that said he knew something he wouldn't tell, a smile to make you feel bad because you weren't Woody and never could be.

    It was then that my father came out of the house. He still had on his plaid hunting coat and his wool cap, but his face was as white as snow, as white as I have ever seen a human being's face to be. It was odd. I had the feeling that he might've fallen inside, because he looked roughed up, as though he had hurt himself somehow.

    My mother came out the door behind him and stood in the floodlight at the top of the steps. She was wearing the powder-blue dress I'd seen through the window, a dress I had never seen her wear before, though she was also wearing a car coat and carrying a suitcase. She looked at me and shook her head in a way that only I was supposed to notice, as if it was not a good idea to talk now.

    My father had his hands in his pockets, and he walked right up to Woody. He did not even look at me. "What do you do for a living?" he said, and he was very close to Woody. His coat was close enough to touch Woody's shirt.

60   "I'm in the Air Force," Woody said. He looked at me and then at my father. He could tell my father was excited.

"Is this your day off, then?" my father said. He moved even closer to Woody, his hands still in his pockets. He pushed Woody with his chest, and Woody seemed willing to let my father push him.

"No," he said, shaking his head.

I looked at my mother. She was just standing, watching. It was as if someone had given her an order, and she was obeying it. She did not smile at me, though I thought she was thinking about me, which made me feel strange.

"What's the matter with you?" my father said into Woody's face, right into his face — his voice tight, as if it had gotten hard for him to talk. "Whatever in the world is the matter with you? Don't you understand something?" My father took a revolver pistol out of his coat and put it up under Woody's chin, into the soft pocket behind the bone, so that Woody's whole face rose, but his arms stayed at his sides, his hands open. "I don't know what to do with you," my father said. "I don't have any idea what to do with you. I just don't." Though I thought that what he wanted to do was hold Woody there just like that until something important took place, or until he could simply forget about all this.

My father pulled the hammer back on the pistol and raised it tighter under Woody's chin, breathing into Woody's face — my mother in the light with her suitcase, watching them, and me watching them. A half a minute must've gone by.

And then my mother said, "Jack, let's stop now. Let's just stop."

My father stared into Woody's face as if he wanted Woody to consider doing something — moving or turning around or anything on his own to stop this — that my father would then put a stop to. My father's eyes grew narrowed, and his teeth were gritted together, his lips snarling up to resemble a smile. "You're crazy, aren't you?" he said. "You're a goddamned crazy man. Are you in love with her, too? Are you, crazyman? Are you? Do you say you love her? Say you love her! Say you love her so I can blow your fucking brains in the sky."

"All right," Woody said. "No. It's all right."

"He doesn't love me, Jack. For God's sake," my mother said. She seemed so calm. She shook her head at me again. I do not think she thought my father would shoot Woody. And I don't think Woody thought so. Nobody did, I think, except my father himself. But I think he did, and was trying to find out how to.

My father turned suddenly and glared at my mother, his eyes shiny and moving, but with the gun still on Woody's skin. I think he was afraid, afraid he was doing this wrong and could mess all of it up and make matters worse without accomplishing anything.

"You're leaving," he yelled at her. "That's why you're packed. Get out. Go on."

"Jackie has to be at school in the morning," my mother said in just her normal voice. And without another word to any one of us, she walked out of

65

70

the floodlamp light carrying her bag, turned the corner at the front porch steps and disappeared toward the olive trees that ran in rows back into the wheat.

My father looked back at me where I was standing in the gravel, as if he expected to see me go with my mother toward Woody's car. But I hadn't thought about that — though later I would. Later I would think I should have gone with her, and that things between them might've been different. But that isn't how it happened.

"You're sure you're going to get away now, aren't you, mister?" my father said into Woody's face. He was crazy himself, then. Anyone would've been. Everything must have seemed out of hand to him.

75 "I'd like to," Woody said. "I'd like to get away from here."

"And I'd like to think of some way to hurt you," my father said and blinked his eyes. "I feel helpless about it." We all heard the door to Woody's car close in the dark. "Do you think that I'm a fool?" my father said.

"No," Woody said. "I don't think that."

"Do you think you're important?"

"No," Woody said. "I'm not."

80 My father blinked again. He seemed to be becoming someone else at the moment, someone I didn't know. "Where are you from?"

And Woody closed his eyes. He breathed in, then out, a long sigh. It was as if this was somehow the hardest part, something he hadn't expected to be asked to say.

"Chicago," Woody said. "A suburb of there."

"Are your parents alive?" my father said, all the time with his blue magnum pistol pushed under Woody's chin.

"Yes," Woody said. "Yessir."

85 "That's too bad," my father said. "Too bad they have to know what you are. I'm sure you stopped meaning anything to them a long time ago. I'm sure they both wish you were dead. You didn't know that. But I know it. I can't help them out, though. Somebody else'll have to kill you. I don't want to have to think about you anymore. I guess that's it."

My father brought the gun down to his side and stood looking at Woody. He did not back away, just stood, waiting for what I don't know to happen. Woody stood a moment, then he cut his eyes at me uncomfortably. And I know that I looked down. That's all I could do. Though I remember wondering if Woody's heart was broken and what any of this meant to him. Not to me, or my mother, or my father. But to him, since he seemed to be the one left out somehow, the one who would be lonely soon, the one who had done something he would someday wish he hadn't and would have no one to tell him that it was all right, that they forgave him, that these things happen in the world.

Woody took a step back, looked at my father and at me again as if he intended to speak, then stepped aside and walked away toward the front of our house, where the wind chime made a noise in the new cold air.

My father looked at me, his big pistol in his hand. "Does this seem stupid to you?" he said. "All this? Yelling and threatening and going nuts? I wouldn't blame you if it did. You shouldn't even see this. I'm sorry. I don't know what to do now."

"It'll be all right," I said. And I walked out to the road. Woody's car started up behind the olive trees. I stood and watched it back out, its red taillights clouded by exhaust. I could see their two heads inside, with the headlights shining behind them. When they got into the road, Woody touched his brakes, and for a moment I could see that they were talking, their heads turned toward each other, nodding. Woody's head and my mother's. They sat that way for a few seconds, then drove slowly off. And I wondered what they had to say to each other, something important enough that they had to stop right at that moment and say it. Did she say, *I love you?* Did she say, *That is not what I expected to happen?* Did she say, *This is what I've wanted all along?* And did he say, *I'm sorry for all this,* or *I'm glad,* or *None of this matters to me?* These are not the kinds of things you can know if you were not there. And I was not there and did not want to be. It did not seem like I should be there. I heard the door slam when my father went inside, and I turned back from the road where I could still see their taillights disappearing, and went back into the house where I was to be alone with my father.

Things seldom end in one event. In the morning I went to school on the bus as usual, and my father drove in to the air base in his car. We had not said very much about all that had happened. Harsh words, in a sense, are all alike. You can make them up yourself and be right. I think we both believed that we were in a fog we couldn't see through yet, though in a while, maybe not even a long while, we would see lights and know something.

In my third-period class that day a messenger brought a note for me that said I was excused from school at noon, and I should meet my mother at a motel down 10th Avenue South — a place not so far from my school — and we would eat lunch together.

It was a gray day in Great Falls that day. The leaves were off the trees and the mountains to the east of town were obscured by a low sky. The night before had been cold and clear, but today it seemed as if it would rain. It was the beginning of winter in earnest. In a few days there would be snow everywhere.

The motel where my mother was staying was called the Tropicana, and was beside the city golf course. There was a neon parrot on the sign out front, and the cabins made a U shape behind a little white office building. Only a couple of cars were parked in front of cabins, and no car was in front of my mother's cabin. I wondered if Woody would be here, or if he was at the air base. I wondered if my father would see him there, and what they would say.

I walked back to cabin 9. The door was open, though a DO NOT DISTURB sign was hung on the knob outside. I looked through the screen and saw my mother sitting on the bed alone. The television was on, but she was looking at me. She was wearing the powder-blue dress she had had on the night before. She was smiling at me, and I liked the way she looked at the moment, through the screen, in shadows. Her features did not seem as sharp as they had before. She looked comfortable where she was, and I felt like we were going to get along, no matter what had happened, and that I wasn't mad at her—that I had never been mad at her.

95 She sat forward and turned the television off. "Come in, Jackie," she said, and I opened the screen door and came inside. "It's the height of grandeur in here, isn't it?" My mother looked around the room. Her suitcase was open on the floor by the bathroom door, which I could see through and out the window onto the golf course, where three men were playing under the milky sky. "Privacy can be a burden, sometimes," she said, and reached down and put on her high-heeled shoes. "I didn't sleep very well last night, did you?"

"No," I said, though I had slept all right. I wanted to ask her where Woody was, but it occurred to me at that moment that he was gone now and wouldn't be back, that she wasn't thinking in terms of him and didn't care where he was or ever would be.

"I'd like a nice compliment from you," she said. "Do you have one of those to spend?"

"Yes," I said. "I'm glad to see you."

"That's a nice one," she said and nodded. She had both her shoes on now. "Would you like to go have lunch? We can walk across the street to the cafeteria. You can get hot food."

100 "No," I said. "I'm not really hungry now."

"That's okay," she said and smiled at me again. And, as I said before, I liked the way she looked. She looked pretty in a way I didn't remember seeing her, as if something that had had a hold on her had let her go, and she could be different about things. Even about me.

"Sometimes, you know," she said, "I'll think about something I did. Just anything. Years ago in Idaho, or last week, even. And it's as if I'd read it. Like a story. Isn't that strange?"

"Yes," I said. And it did seem strange to me because I was certain then what the difference was between what had happened and what hadn't, and knew I always would be.

"Sometimes," she said, and she folded her hands in her lap and stared out the little side window of her cabin at the parking lot and the curving row of other cabins. "Sometimes I even have a moment when I completely forget what life's like. Just altogether." She smiled. "That's not so bad, finally. Maybe it's a disease I have. Do you think I'm just sick and I'll get well?"

105 "No. I don't know," I said. "Maybe. I hope so." I looked out the bathroom window and saw the three men walking down the golf course fairway carrying golf clubs.

"I'm not very good at sharing things right now," my mother said. "I'm sorry." She cleared her throat, and then she didn't say anything for almost a minute while I stood there. "I *will* answer anything you'd like me to answer, though. Just ask me anything, and I'll answer it with the truth, whether I want to or not. Okay? I will. You don't even have to trust me. That's not a big issue with us. We're both grown-ups now."

And I said, "Were you ever married before?"

My mother looked at me strangely. Her eyes got small, and for a moment she looked the way I was used to seeing her — sharp-faced, her mouth set and taut. "No," she said. "Who told you that? That isn't true. I never was. Did Jack say that to you? Did your father say that? That's an awful thing to say. I haven't been that bad."

"He didn't say that," I said.

"Oh, of course he did," my mother said. "He doesn't know just to let things go when they're bad enough."

"I wanted to know that," I said. "I just thought about it. It doesn't matter."

"No, it doesn't," my mother said. "I could've been married eight times. I'm just sorry he said that to you. He's not generous sometimes."

"He didn't say that," I said. But I'd said it enough, and I didn't care if she believed me or didn't. It was true that trust was not a big issue between us then. And in any event, I know now that the whole truth of anything is an idea that stops existing finally.

"Is that all you want to know, then?" my mother said. She seemed mad, but not at me, I didn't think. Just at things in general. And I sympathized with her. "Your life's your own business, Jackie," she said. "Sometimes it scares you to death it's so much your own business. You just want to run."

"I guess so," I said.

"I'd like a less domestic life, is all." She looked at me, but I didn't say anything. I didn't see what she meant by that, though I knew there was nothing I could say to change the way her life would be from then on. And I kept quiet.

In a while we walked across 10th Avenue and ate lunch in the cafeteria. When she paid for the meal I saw that she had my father's silver-dollar money clip in her purse and that there was money in it. And I understood that he had been to see her already that day, and no one cared if I knew it. We were all of us on our own in this.

When we walked out onto the street, it was colder and the wind was blowing. Car exhausts were visible and some drivers had their lights on, though it was only two o'clock in the afternoon. My mother had called a taxi, and we stood and waited for it. I didn't know where she was going, but I wasn't going with her.

"Your father won't let me come back," she said, standing on the curb. It was just a fact to her, not that she hoped I would talk to him or stand up for her or take her part. But I did wish then that I had never let her go the night before. Things can be fixed by staying; but to go out into the night and not come back hazards life, and everything can get out of hand.

My mother's taxi came. She kissed me and hugged me very hard, then got inside the cab in her powder-blue dress and high heels and her car coat. I smelled her perfume on my cheeks as I stood watching her. "I used to be afraid of more things than I am now," she said, looking at me, and smiled. "I've got a knot in my stomach, of all things." And she closed the cab door, waved at me, and rode away.

I walked back toward my school. I thought I could take the bus home if I got there by three. I walked a long way down 10th Avenue to Second Street, beside the Missouri River, then over to town. I walked by the Great Northern Hotel, where my father had sold ducks and geese and fish of all kinds. There were no passenger trains in the yard and the loading dock looked small. Garbage cans were lined along the edge of it, and the door was closed and locked.

As I walked toward school I thought to myself that my life had turned suddenly, and that I might not know exactly how or which way for possibly a long time. Maybe, in fact, I might never know. It was a thing that happened to you — I knew that — and it had happened to me in this way now. And as I walked on up the cold street that afternoon in Great Falls, the questions I asked myself were these: why wouldn't my father let my mother come back? Why would Woody stand in the cold with me outside my house and risk being killed? Why would he say my mother had been married before, if she hadn't been? And my mother herself — why would she do what she did? In five years my father had gone off to Ely, Nevada, to ride out the oil strike there, and been killed by accident. And in the years since then I have seen my mother from time to time — in one place or another, with one man or other — and I can say, at least, that we know each other. But I have never known the answer to these questions, have never asked anyone their answers. Though possibly it — the answer — is simple: it is just low-life, some coldness in us all, some helplessness that causes us to misunderstand life when it is pure and plain, makes our existence seem like a border between two nothings, and makes us no more or less than animals who meet on the road — watchful, unforgiving, without patience or desire.

Shirley Jackson
The Lottery

The morning of June 27th was clear and sunny, with the fresh warmth of a full-summer day; the flowers were blossoming profusely and the grass was richly green. The people of the village began to gather in the square, between

THE LOTTERY First published in 1948. Shirley Jackson (1919–1965) was born in San Francisco and spent most of her early life in California. After her marriage in 1940 she lived in a quiet rural community in Vermont.

the post office and the bank, around ten o'clock; in some towns there were so many people that the lottery took two days and had to be started on June 26th, but in this village, where there were only about three hundred people, the whole lottery took less than two hours, so it could begin at ten o'clock in the morning and still be through in time to allow the villagers to get home for noon dinner.

The children assembled first, of course. School was recently over for the summer, and the feeling of liberty sat uneasily on most of them; they tended to gather together quietly for a while before they broke into boisterous play, and their talk was still of the classroom and the teacher, of books and reprimands. Bobby Martin had already stuffed his pockets full of stones, and the other boys soon followed his example, selecting the smoothest and roundest stones; Bobby and Harry Jones and Dickie Delacroix — the villagers pronounced this name "Dellacroy" — eventually made a great pile of stones in one corner of the square and guarded it against the raids of the other boys. The girls stood aside, talking among themselves, looking over their shoulders at the boys, and the very small children rolled in the dust or clung to the hands of their older brothers or sisters.

Soon the men began to gather, surveying their own children, speaking of planting and rain, tractors and taxes. They stood together, away from the pile of stones in the corner, and their jokes were quiet and they smiled rather than laughed. The women, wearing faded house dresses and sweaters, came shortly after their menfolk. They greeted one another and exchanged bits of gossip as they went to join their husbands. Soon the women, standing by their husbands, began to call to their children, and the children came reluctantly, having to be called four or five times. Bobby Martin ducked under his mother's grasping hand and ran, laughing, back to the pile of stones. His father spoke up sharply, and Bobby came quickly and took his place between his father and his oldest brother.

The lottery was conducted — as were the square dances, the teen-age club, the Halloween program — by Mr. Summers, who had time and energy to devote to civic activities. He was a round-faced, jovial man and he ran the coal business, and people were sorry for him, because he had no children and his wife was a scold. When he arrived in the square, carrying the black wooden box, there was a murmur of conversation among the villagers, and he waved and called, "Little late today, folks." The postmaster, Mr. Graves, followed him, carrying a three-legged stool, and the stool was put in the center of the square and Mr. Summers set the black box down on it. The villagers kept their distance, leaving a space between themselves and the stool, and when Mr. Summers said, "Some of you fellows want to give me a hand?" there was a hesitation before two men, Mr. Martin and his oldest son, Baxter, came forward to hold the box steady on the stool while Mr. Summers stirred up the papers inside it.

The original paraphernalia for the lottery had been lost long ago, and the black box now resting on the stool had been put into use even before Old Man Warner, the oldest man in town, was born. Mr. Summers spoke frequently to the villagers about making a new box, but no one liked to upset even as much tradition as was represented by the black box. There was a story that the present box had been made with some pieces of the box that had preceded it, the one that had been constructed when the first people settled down to make a village here. Every year, after the lottery, Mr. Summers began talking again about a new box, but every year the subject was allowed to fade off without anything's being done. The black box grew shabbier each year; by now it was no longer completely black but splintered badly along one side to show the original wood color, and in some places faded or stained.

Mr. Martin and his oldest son, Baxter, held the black box securely on the stool until Mr. Summers had stirred the papers thoroughly with his hand. Because so much of the ritual had been forgotten or discarded, Mr. Summers had been successful in having slips of paper substituted for the chips of wood that had been used for generations. Chips of wood, Mr. Summers had argued, had been all very well when the village was tiny, but now that the population was more than three hundred and likely to keep on growing, it was necessary to use something that would fit more easily into the black box. The night before the lottery, Mr. Summers and Mr. Graves made up the slips of paper and put them in the box, and it was then taken to the safe of Mr. Summers's coal company and locked up until Mr. Summers was ready to take it to the square next morning. The rest of the year, the box was put away, sometimes one place, sometimes another; it had spent one year in Mr. Graves's barn and another year underfoot in the post office, and sometimes it was set on a shelf in the Martin grocery and left there.

There was a great deal of fussing to be done before Mr. Summers declared the lottery open. There were the lists to make up — of heads of families, heads of households in each family, members of each household in each family. There was the proper swearing-in of Mr. Summers by the postmaster, as the official of the lottery; at one time, some people remembered, there had been a recital of some sort, performed by the official of the lottery, a perfunctory, tuneless chant that had been rattled off duly each year; some people believed that the official of the lottery used to stand just so when he said or sang it, others believed that he was supposed to walk among the people, but years and years ago this part of the ritual had been allowed to lapse. There had been, also, a ritual salute, which the official of the lottery had had to use in addressing each person who came up to draw from the box, but this also had changed with time, until now it was felt necessary only for the official to speak to each person approaching. Mr. Summers was very good at all this; in his clean white shirt and blue jeans, with one hand resting carelessly on the black box, he seemed very proper and important as he talked interminably to Mr. Graves and the Martins.

Just as Mr. Summers finally left off talking and turned to the assembled villagers, Mrs. Hutchinson came hurriedly along the path to the square, her sweater thrown over her shoulders, and slid into place in the back of the crowd. "Clean forgot what day it was," she said to Mrs. Delacroix, who stood next to her, and they both laughed softly. "Thought my old man was out back stacking wood," Mrs. Hutchinson went on, "and then I looked out the window and the kids were gone, and then I remembered it was the twenty-seventh and came a-running." She dried her hands on her apron, and Mrs. Delacroix said, "You're in time, though. They're still talking away up there."

Mrs. Hutchinson craned her neck to see through the crowd and found her husband and children standing near the front. She tapped Mrs. Delacroix on the arm as a farewell and began to make her way through the crowd. The people separated good-humoredly to let her through; two or three people said, in voices just loud enough to be heard across the crowd, "Here comes your Missus, Hutchinson," and "Bill, she made it after all." Mrs. Hutchinson reached her husband, and Mr. Summers, who had been waiting, said cheerfully, "Thought we were going to have to get on without you, Tessie." Mrs. Hutchinson said, grinning, "Wouldn't have me leave m'dishes in the sink, now, would you, Joe?" and soft laughter ran through the crowd as the people stirred back into position after Mrs. Hutchinson's arrival.

"Well, now," Mr. Summers said soberly, "guess we better get started, ₁₀ get this over with, so's we can go back to work. Anybody ain't here?"

"Dunbar," several people said. "Dunbar, Dunbar."

Mr. Summers consulted his list. "Clyde Dunbar," he said. "That's right. He's broke his leg, hasn't he? Who's drawing for him?"

"Me, I guess," a woman said, and Mrs. Summers turned to look at her. "Wife draws for her husband," Mr. Summers said. "Don't you have a grown boy to do it for you, Janey?" Although Mr. Summers and everyone else in the village knew the answer perfectly well, it was the business of the official of the lottery to ask such questions formally. Mr. Summers waited with an expression of polite interest while Mrs. Dunbar answered.

"Horace's not but sixteen yet," Mrs. Dunbar said regretfully. "Guess I gotta fill in for the old man this year."

"Right," Mr. Summers said. He made a note on the list he was holding. ₁₅ Then he asked, "Watson boy drawing this year?"

A tall boy in the crowd raised his hand. "Here," he said. "I'm drawing for m'mother and me." He blinked his eyes nervously and ducked his head as several voices in the crowd said things like "Good fellow, Jack," and "Glad to see your mother's got a man to do it."

"Well," Mr. Summers said, "guess that's everyone. Old Man Warner make it?"

"Here," a voice said, and Mr. Summers nodded.

A sudden hush fell on the crowd as Mr. Summers cleared his throat and looked at the list. "All ready?" he called. "Now, I'll read the names — heads of families first — and the men come up and take a paper out of the box. Keep the paper folded in your hand without looking at it until everyone has had a turn. Everything clear?"

The people had done it so many times that they only half listened to the directions; most of them were quiet, wetting their lips, not looking around. Then Mr. Summers raised one hand high and said, "Adams." A man disengaged himself from the crowd and came forward. "Hi, Steve," Mr. Summers said, and Mr. Adams said, "Hi, Joe." They grinned at one another humorlessly and nervously. Then Mr. Adams reached into the black box and took out a folded paper. He held it firmly by one corner as he turned and went hastily back to his place in the crowd, where he stood a little apart from his family, not looking down at his hand.

"Allen," Mr. Summers said. "Anderson . . . Bentham."

"Seems like there's no time at all between lotteries any more," Mrs. Delacroix said to Mrs. Graves in the back row. "Seems like we got through with the last one only last week."

"Time sure goes fast," Mrs. Graves said.

"Clark . . . Delacroix."

"There goes my old man," Mrs. Delacroix said. She held her breath while her husband went forward.

"Dunbar," Mrs. Summers said, and Mrs. Dunbar went steadily to the box while one of the women said, "Go on, Janey," and another said, "There she goes."

"We're next," Mrs. Graves said. She watched while Mr. Graves came around from the side of the box, greeted Mr. Summers gravely, and selected a slip of paper from the box. By now, all through the crowd there were men holding the small folded papers in their large hands, turning them over and over nervously. Mrs. Dunbar and her two sons stood together, Mrs. Dunbar holding the slip of paper.

"Harburt . . . Hutchinson."

"Get up there, Bill," Mrs. Hutchinson said, and the people near her laughed.

"Jones."

"They do say," Mr. Adams said to Old Man Warner, who stood next to him, "that over in the north village they're talking of giving up the lottery."

Old Man Warner snorted. "Pack of crazy fools," he said. "Listening to the young folks, nothing's good enough for *them*. Next thing you know, they'll be wanting to go back to living in caves, nobody work any more, live *that* way for a while. Used to be a saying about 'Lottery in June, corn be heavy soon.' First thing you know, we'd all be eating stewed chickweed and acorns. There's *always* been a lottery," he added petulantly. "Bad enough to see young Joe Summers up there joking with everybody."

"Some places have already quit lotteries," Mrs. Adams said.

"Nothing but trouble in *that*," Old Man Warner said stoutly. "Pack of young fools."

"Martin." And Bobby Martin watched his father go forward. "Overdyke ³⁵ . . . Percy."

"I wish they'd hurry," Mrs. Dunbar said to her older son. "I wish they'd hurry."

"They're almost through," her son said.

Mr. Summers called his own name and then stepped forward precisely and selected a slip from the box. Then he called, "Warner."

"Seventy-seventh year I been in the lottery," Old Man Warner said as he ⁴⁰ went through the crowd. "Seventy-seventh time."

"Watson." The tall boy came awkwardly through the crowd. Someone said, "Don't be nervous, Jack," and Mr. Summers said, "Take your time, son."

"Zanini."

After that, there was a long pause, a breathless pause, until Mr. Summers, holding his slip of paper in the air, said, "All right, fellows." For a minute, no one moved, and then all the slips of paper were opened. Suddenly, all the women began to speak at once, saying, "Who is it?" "Who's got it?" "Is it the Dunbars?" "Is it the Watsons?" Then the voices began to say, "It's Hutchinson. It's Bill," "Bill Hutchinson's got it."

"Go tell your father," Mrs. Dunbar said to her older son.

People began to look around to see the Hutchinsons. Bill Hutchinson ⁴⁵ was standing quiet, staring down at the paper in his hand. Suddenly, Tessie Hutchinson shouted to Mr. Summers. "You didn't give him time enough to take any paper he wanted. I saw you. It wasn't fair."

"Be a good sport, Tessie," Mrs. Delacroix called, and Mrs. Graves said, "All of us took the same chance."

"Shut up, Tessie," Bill Hutchinson said.

"Well, everyone," Mr. Summers said, "that was done pretty fast, and now we've got to be hurrying a little more to get done in time." He consulted his next list. "Bill," he said, "you draw for the Hutchinson family. You got any other households in the Hutchinsons?"

"There's Don and Eva," Mrs. Hutchinson yelled. "Make *them* take their chance!"

"Daughters draw with their husband's families, Tessie," Mr. Summers ⁵⁰ said gently. "You know that as well as anyone else."

"It wasn't *fair*," Tessie said.

"I guess not, Joe," Bill Hutchinson said regretfully. "My daughter draws with her husband's family, that's only fair. And I've got no other family except the kids."

"Then, as far as drawing for families is concerned, it's you," Mr. Summers said in explanation, "and as far as drawing for households is concerned, that's you, too. Right?"

"Right," Bill Hutchinson said.

"How many kids, Bill?" Mr. Summers asked formally. ⁵⁵

"Three," Bill Hutchinson said. "There's Bill, Jr., and Nancy, and little Dave. And Tessie and me."

"All right, then," Mr. Summers said. "Harry, you got their tickets back?"

Mr. Graves nodded and held up the slips of paper. "Put them in the box, then," Mr. Summers directed. "Take Bill's and put it in."

"I think we ought to start over," Mrs. Hutchinson said, as quietly as she could. "I tell you it wasn't *fair*. You didn't give him time enough to choose. *Every*body saw that."

Mr. Graves had selected the five slips and put them in the box, and he dropped all the papers but those onto the ground, where the breeze caught them and lifted them off.

"Listen, everybody," Mrs. Hutchinson was saying to the people around her.

"Ready, Bill?" Mr. Summers asked, and Bill Hutchinson, with one quick glance around at his wife and children, nodded.

"Remember," Mr. Summers said, "take the slips and keep them folded until each person has taken one. Harry, you help little Dave." Mr. Graves took the hand of the little boy, who came willingly with him up to the box. "Take a paper out of the box, Davy," Mr. Summers said. Davy put his hand into the box and laughed. "Take just *one* paper," Mr. Summers said. "Harry, you hold it for him." Mr. Graves took the child's hand and removed the folded paper from the tight fist and held it while little Dave stood next to him and looked up at him wonderingly.

"Nancy next," Mr. Summers said. Nancy was twelve, and her school friends breathed heavily as she went forward, switching her skirt, and took a slip daintily from the box. "Bill, Jr.," Mr. Summers said, and Billy, his face red and his feet over-large, nearly knocked the box over as he got a paper out. "Tessie," Mr. Summers said. She hesitated for a minute, looking around defiantly, and then set her lips and went up to the box. She snatched a paper out and held it behind her.

"Bill," Mr. Summers said, and Bill Hutchinson reached into the box and felt around, bringing his hand out at last with the slip of paper in it.

The crowd was quiet. A girl whispered, "I hope it's not Nancy," and the sound of the whisper reached the edges of the crowd.

"It's not the way it used to be," Old Man Warner said clearly. "People ain't the way they used to be."

"All right," Mr. Summers said. "Open the papers. Harry, you open little Dave's."

Mr. Graves opened the slip of paper and there was a general sigh through the crowd as he held it up and everyone could see that it was blank. Nancy and Bill, Jr., opened theirs at the same time, and both beamed and laughed, turning around to the crowd and holding their slips of paper above their heads.

"Tessie," Mr. Summers said. There was a pause, and then Mr. Summers looked at Bill Hutchinson, and Bill unfolded his paper and showed it. It was blank.

"It's Tessie," Mr. Summers said, and his voice was hushed. "Show us her paper, Bill."

Bill Hutchinson went over to his wife and forced the slip of paper out of her hand. It had a black spot on it, the black spot Mr. Summers had made the night before with the heavy pencil in the coal-company office. Bill Hutchinson held it up, and there was a stir in the crowd.

"All right, folks," Mr. Summers said. "Let's finish quickly."

Although the villagers had forgotten the ritual and lost the original black box, they still remembered to use stones. The pile of stones the boys had made earlier was ready; there were stones on the ground with the blowing scraps of paper that had come out of the box. Mrs. Delacroix selected a stone so large she had to pick it up with both hands and turned to Mrs. Dunbar. "Come on," she said. "Hurry up."

Mrs. Dunbar had small stones in both hands, and she said, gasping for breath, "I can't run at all. You'll have to go ahead and I'll catch up with you." 75

The children had stones already, and someone gave little Davy Hutchinson a few pebbles.

Tessie Hutchinson was in the center of a cleared space by now, and she held her hands out desperately as the villagers moved in on her. "It isn't fair," she said. A stone hit her on the side of the head.

Old Man Warner was saying, "Come on, come on, everyone." Steve Adams was in front of the crowd of villagers, with Mrs. Graves beside him.

"It isn't fair, it isn't right," Mrs. Hutchinson screamed, and then they were upon her.

James Joyce
Eveline

She sat at the window watching evening invade the avenue. Her head was leaned against the window curtains and in her nostrils was the odor of dusty cretonne. She was tired.

Few people passed. The man out of the last house passed on his way home; she heard his footsteps clacking along the concrete pavement and afterwards crunching on the cinder path before the new red houses. One time there used to be a field there in which they used to play every evening with other people's children. Then a man from Belfast bought the field and built houses in it — not like their little brown houses but bright brick houses with shining roofs. The children of the avenue used to play together in that field — the Devines, the Waters, the Dunns, little Keogh the cripple, she and

EVELINE First published in 1904. James Joyce (1882–1941) was born and lived in Dublin, Ireland, until 1904 when he went to the continent, and for the rest of his life he lived abroad and wrote about Dublin. Eveline's weekly wages working as a sales clerk in "the Stores" are the equivalent of less than $10. The "night boat" that she and Frank are planning to take departed from a dock called "the North Wall" for Liverpool, England; presumably Frank has planned to take a ship from there to Argentina with her.

her brothers and sisters. Ernest, however, never played: he was too grown up. Her father used often to hunt them in out of the field with his blackthorn stick; but usually little Keogh used to keep *nix* and call out when he saw her father coming. Still they seemed to have been rather happy then. Her father was not so bad then; and besides, her mother was alive. That was a long time ago; she and her brothers and sisters were all grown up; her mother was dead. Tizzie Dunn was dead, too, and the Waters had gone back to England. Everything changes. Now she was going to go away like the others, to leave her home.

Home! She looked round the room, reviewing all its familiar objects which she had dusted once a week for so many years, wondering where on earth all the dust came from. Perhaps she would never see again those familiar objects from which she had never dreamed of being divided. And yet during all those years she had never found out the name of the priest whose yellowing photograph hung on the wall above the broken harmonium beside the colored print of the promises made to Blessed Margaret Mary Alacoque. He had been a school friend of her father. Whenever he showed the photograph to a visitor her father used to pass it with a casual word:

"He is in Melbourne now."

5   She had consented to go away, to leave her home. Was that wise? She tried to weigh each side of the question. In her home anyway she had shelter and food; she had those whom she had known all her life about her. Of course she had to work hard both in the house and at business. What would they say of her in the Stores when they found out that she had run away with a fellow? Say she was a fool, perhaps; and her place would be filled up by advertisement. Miss Gavan would be glad. She had always had an edge on her, especially whenever there were people listening.

"Miss Hill, don't you see these ladies are waiting?"

"Look lively, Miss Hill, please."

She would not cry many tears at leaving the Stores.

But in her new home, in a distant unknown country, it would not be like that. Then she would be married — she, Eveline. People would treat her with respect then. She would not be treated as her mother had been. Even now, though she was over nineteen, she sometimes felt herself in danger of her father's violence. She knew it was that that had given her the palpitations. When they were growing up he had never gone for her, like he used to go for Harry and Ernest, because she was a girl; but latterly he had begun to threaten her and say what he would do to her only for her dead mother's sake. And now she had nobody to protect her. Ernest was dead and Harry, who was in the church decorating business, was nearly always down somewhere in the country. Besides, the invariable squabble for money on Saturday nights had begun to weary her unspeakably. She always gave her entire wages — seven shillings — and Harry always sent up what he could but the trouble was to get any money from her father. He said she used to squander the money, that she had no head, that he wasn't going to give her his hard-earned money to throw about the streets, and much more, for he was usually fairly bad of a Saturday night. In the end he would give her the money and ask her had she any intention of buying Sunday's dinner. Then she had to rush out as quickly as she could and do her marketing, holding her black leather purse tightly in her hand as she elbowed her way through the crowds and returning home late under her load of provisions. She had hard work to keep the house together and to see that the two young children who had been left to her charge went to school regularly and got their meals regularly. It was hard work — a hard life — but now that she was about to leave it she did not find it a wholly undesirable life.

She was about to explore another life with Frank. Frank was very kind, manly, open-hearted. She was to go away with him by the night-boat to be his wife and to live with him in Buenos Aires where he had a home waiting for her. How well she remembered the first time she had seen him; he was lodging in a house on the main road where she used to visit. It seemed a few weeks ago. He was standing at the gate, his peaked cap pushed back on his head and his hair tumbled forward over a face of bronze. Then they had come to know each other. He used to meet her outside the Stores every evening and see her home. He took her to see *The Bohemian Girl* and she felt elated as she sat in an unaccustomed part of the theater with him. He was awfully fond of music and sang a little. People knew that they were courting and, when he sang about the lass that loves a sailor, she always felt pleasantly confused. He used to call her Poppens out of fun. First of all it had been an excitement for her to have a fellow and then she had begun to like him. He had tales of distant countries. He had started as a deck boy at a pound a month on a ship of the Allan Line going out to Canada. He told her the names of the ships he had been on and the names of the different services. He had sailed through the Straits of Magellan and he told her stories of the terrible Patagonians. He had fallen on his feet in Buenos Aires, he said, and had come over to the old country just for a holiday. Of course, her father had found out the affair and had forbidden her to have anything to say to him.

"I know these sailor chaps," he said.

One day he had quarrelled with Frank and after that she had to meet her lover secretly.

The evening deepened in the avenue. The white of two letters in her lap grew indistinct. One was to Harry; the other was to her father. Ernest had been her favorite but she liked Harry too. Her father was becoming old lately, she noticed; he would miss her. Sometimes he could be very nice. Not long before, when she had been laid up for a day, he had read her out a ghost story and made toast for her at the fire. Another day, when their mother was alive, they had all gone for a picnic to the Hill of Howth. She remembered her father putting on her mother's bonnet to make the children laugh.

Her time was running out but she continued to sit by the window, leaning her head against the window curtain, inhaling the odor of dusty cretonne. Down far in the avenue she could hear a street organ playing. She knew the air. Strange that it should come that very night to remind her of the promise to her mother, her promise to keep the home together as long as she could. She remembered the last night of her mother's illness; she was again in the close dark room at the other side of the hall and outside she heard a melancholy air of Italy. The organ-player had been ordered to go away and given sixpence. She remembered her father strutting back into the sickroom saying:

15   "Damned Italians! coming over here!"

As she mused the pitiful vision of her mother's life laid its spell on the very quick of her being — that life of commonplace sacrifices closing in final craziness. She trembled as she heard again her mother's voice saying constantly with foolish insistence:

"Derevaun Seraun! Derevaun Seraun!"°

She stood up in a sudden impulse of terror. Escape! She must escape! Frank would save her. He would give her life, perhaps love, too. But she wanted to live. Why should she be unhappy? She had a right to happiness. Frank would take her in his arms, fold her in his arms. He would save her.

She stood among the swaying crowd in the station at the North Wall. He held her hand and she knew that he was speaking to her, saying something about the passage over and over again. The station was full of soldiers with brown baggages. Through the wide doors of the sheds she caught a glimpse of the black mass of the boat, lying in beside the quay wall, with illumined portholes. She answered nothing. She felt her cheek pale and cold and, out of a maze of distress, she prayed to God to direct her, to show her what was her duty. The boat blew a long mournful whistle into the mist. If she went, tomorrow she would be on the sea with Frank, steaming towards Buenos Aires. Their passage had been booked. Could she still draw back after all he had done for her? Her distress awoke a nausea in her body and she kept moving her lips in silent fervent prayer.

20   A bell clanged upon her heart. She felt him seize her hand:

"Come!"

All the seas of the world tumbled about her heart. He was drawing her into them: he would drown her. She gripped with both hands at the iron railing.

"Come!"

No! No! No! It was impossible. Her hands clutched the iron in frenzy. Amid the seas she sent a cry of anguish!

25   "Eveline! Evvy!"

He rushed beyond the barrier and called to her to follow. He was shouted at to go on but he still called to her. She set her white face to him, passive, like a helpless animal. Her eyes gave him no sign of love or farewell or recognition.

"Derevaun Seraun!": This has been interpreted as a slurred Gaelic phrase meaning either "the end of pleasure is pain," or "the end of song is raving madness."

Walter McDonald
The Track

By noon Bien Dien sweltered, the humid air heavy like deep depression. The clouds had not built far enough to block out the sun, which beat down almost too bright to see. For the first time since the rocket blast last night, the base was quiet, as if totally shut down. I could not hear a jet or bombs or gunfire anywhere. The whole war seemed to have been called off.

I felt my back baking already as Lebowitz guided me, jogging the three blocks to the track, a dirt oval bulldozed around a field laid out for football but covered now in dead yellow grass, a collapsing rusting goalpost at each end. Lebowitz said that in the old days, with a half million Americans in Vietnam, the base was famous as Bien Dien-by-the-Sea, its beaches a favorite R and R° center. But after most of the troops were withdrawn, there weren't enough left for proper patrols, and the VC began mining the beaches. Now the ocean was off limits, and jogging was the best hot way to relax.

A road paralleled the track and cut north to the flight line a few blocks away, hidden by hangars and Quonset huts. Along the other side of the field were wooden bleachers built between the forty-yard lines, a platform at the fifty like a parade reviewing stand. Behind the bleachers a sagging cyclone fence ran the length of the field, and on the other side were rows and rows of tin and wooden shacks where Vietnamese airmen lived with their families. And at the far end of the field, beyond a great wall smothered with vines, there was a huge French mansion with a red roof and trees everywhere around it, like part of the jungle.

There were a dozen or more men in trunks already on the track, some of them jogging fast, some shuffling along with their heads down, their arms hanging. Lebowitz drew the towel from his neck and wiped his face and threw the towel on the field. His thin face was drawn, and his eyes had that haunted, hollow stare from dark sockets, his stiff white hair already glistening.

"Six times around for a mile," he said, not breaking stride.   5

"How many miles do you go?" I asked, my bones heavy in the heat.

"Four, five, I'll let you know."

He ran light on his feet, a thin man with long muscles. He kept his fists straight out in front of him, knuckles up. He was taller than me by several

THE TRACK First published in 1976. Walter McDonald was born in 1934 in Lubbock, Texas, and earned B.A. and M.A. degrees at Texas Tech and a Ph.D. at the University of Iowa. He was a career officer in the U.S. Air Force from 1957–1971, serving as a pilot and also as a member of the faculty at the Air Force Academy, retiring with the rank of major. Since 1971, McDonald has taught at Texas Tech, where he is Director of Creative Writing. He has published eleven books of poetry, as well as a short story collection focusing on the Vietnam War, *A Band of Brothers*, from which this story is taken. The antagonists in that war, after the defeat and withdrawal of the French colonial forces, were American and South Vietnamese military on one side and guerilla Viet Cong ("VC") and regular North Vietnamese military on the other.

R and R: rest and recuperation

inches, his long stride hitting three for my four. His high voice chattered like a separate thing that could not be winded.

"See that guy rounding the end zone? That's Fleming. He runs every day. The only guy here who can outlast me."

"Yeah," I said, still trying to fall in with his pace. "I see him."

Fresh from the States, I was used to handball and an indoor track, and running in this humidity was like treading deep water with boots on.

I watched Fleming round the turn and enter the straightaway, running fast with determined desperate lunges past a group of slower joggers and along the row of Vietnamese shacks. Three children broke from the bushes and ran to the track, whirling and darting away out of sight as Fleming ran past. When the children broke toward the group following him, one of the men lunged at them and the children scattered.

We approached the turn and the old wall of the French estate towered before us, lush with vines and blossoms, shaded by the great limbs of trees beyond the wall.

"The Frenchman's place," Lebowitz said, tossing his thumb at the wall. "It's their private club, now."

I had read about Bien Dien before leaving Saigon. I knew it was one of the American bases built in the sixties, bulldozed not merely out of jungle but out of an old French colonial plantation on the bay. At the peak of U.S. involvement, eighteen thousand Americans crowded the base, along with a handful of French still running their plantation and a few hundred Vietnamese. Now, only four hundred Americans remained and thousands of Vietnamese and still the handful of French, who lived apart and never troubled themselves with Americans except invitations to the base commander and his staff at Christmas and the Fourth of July and Bastille Day.

I heard a board thudding just beyond the wall, and then a splash cut trimly into water.

"Swimming pool," Lebowitz said, not even glancing at the wall, his fists pumping. "Those cats still think they're in the Promised Land."

We turned down the backstretch and came even with the shacks. There was an awful smell, like rotten cabbages and vinegar.

"You numbah ten!" a child's voice screamed, the worst insult possible. "You 'mericans numbah ten!"

Lebowitz never turned his head toward that supreme insult, just kept jogging the same steady pace. And when the child screamed at us again, Lebowitz called back, friendly, "You numbah one! You numbah one, boychild!"

He answered my silence as we jogged on. "Want to trade places with them?"

"No way," I said.

"You're right," he said. "If we can't be friends with the kids, there's no way."

Shackler and Malatesta arrived from the officers' hootches, and we fell in behind them as they entered the track, jogging heavily. Shackler lunged along, leaning forward like a heavyweight, but Malatesta brought his knees high and trotted with his shoulders thrust back as if on parade.

"They hit the village again?" Lebowitz called. ²⁵

"Naw," Shackler replied, not looking back. "Must be getting ready to pound the base."

Rumors. At breakfast someone had said three NVA° divisions had crossed the demilitarized zone and were last seen forty kilometers north of the base. Rumors of casualties from last night's mortar and rocket attacks ran as high as dozens of Americans and hundreds of Vietnamese killed and God knows how many wounded. Someone said the VC had overrun half of Plei Nhon and massacred scores of villagers during the night.

I waited for someone else to talk, but all ran quietly, all alone. Now and then we would fall into step and there would be the thump thump thump of our running. Then the steps would syncopate and break rhythm and in the heavy depressing heat I would find myself having to concentrate to maintain stride.

Fleming caught us in the second lap and passed without looking, his breath puffing, the tendons in his neck stretched tight. He was a good-looking kid with blond hair and flushed cheeks and he looked too young to be out of high school. He raced on, as if trying to outdistance fear.

Each time we passed the wall I listened, and once I thought I heard ³⁰ sensual laughter, and another time I heard music, slow and light and peaceful, like Paris in springtime.

A muscular, middle-aged man ran past us, deeply tanned, an old sergeant or a colonel, his thick white hair glistening with sweat. Around his waist he wore a wide leather back support, gleaming black, a blue .38 holstered on one side and a knife scabbard stitched to the other.

"Watch him," Lebowitz said. "He won't go near the shacks."

Sure enough, the man ran swiftly along the inside of the track, next to the football field.

"Hates kids?" I asked.

"Naw," he said. "Just afraid someone's gonna nail him before it's over. ³⁵ He's not the only one."

After three laps Shackler and Malatesta dropped out, panting heavily, but Lebowitz jogged on, staring ahead. I glanced at them walking slowly back toward the quarters, their arms limp. I felt more like that than running, but something in my legs kept going and after a few paces I caught up with Lebowitz again.

"It all counts toward DEROS," he said grimly. Date of Earliest Return from Overseas: months, impossible months from now.

We must have jogged around that track for an hour. One by one the others dropped out and returned to the barracks for showers and back to duty. After a while there were only Lebowitz and I and, lapping us every two or three rounds, Fleming, haunting the day with his fear.

NVA: North Vietnamese Army

Lebowitz paced me like a record spinning around and around, lap after lap. I caught my mind wandering off the track, dozing, drugged with fatigue and the heat. I no longer heard the children jeering at us, only now and then a woman's high strange scolding from inside the shacks, or a crying baby. I listened for the swimming pool to splash again or for music, but there were not even birds singing in the Frenchman's jungle beyond the wall. After a while even Lebowitz hushed and there was only the thump of our toes jogging on dirt.

40   My lungs numbed in the heat and my legs came to feel like things apart, able to go on and on. My eyes burned with sweat, and I squinted so tight I could hardly see, and because they stung it was impossible to think. I was adjusting, though, lost in rhythm, like a mechanical animal going around and around, getting closer to DEROS. It felt good and I was slipping deep in dreams when I heard a noise with my name on it.

"Moose. It's time, Moose," Lebowitz called.

I jolted to a halt off the track and dropped my arms. My hands were numb. I heard jets roaring from the flight line. Drenched in sweat, tasting salt and iodine, I shuddered. It was overcast, the sky boiling with clouds, and in the distance there was thunder, or bombs, and I knew from the noon sun burning my skull there was still a long, long way to go.

Bobbie Ann Mason
Wish

Sam tried to hold his eyes open. The preacher, a fat-faced boy with a college degree, had a curious way of pronouncing his r's. The sermon was about pollution of the soul and started with a news item about an oil spill. Sam drifted into a dream about a flock of chickens scratching up a bed of petunias. His sister Damson, beside him, knifed him in the ribs with her bony elbow. Snoring, she said with her eyes.

Every Sunday after church, Sam and Damson visited their other sister, Hortense, and her husband, Cecil. Ordinarily, Sam drove his own car, but today Damson gave him a ride because his car was low on gas. Damson lived in town, but Hort and Cecil lived out in the country, not far from the old homeplace, which had been sold twenty years before, when Pap died. As they drove past the old place now, Sam saw Damson shudder. She had stopped saying "Trash" under her breath when they passed by and saw the junk cars that had accumulated around the old house. The yard was bare dirt now, and the large elm in front had split. Many times Sam and his sisters had

WISH   First published in 1985. Bobbie Ann Mason was born in 1940 in Mayfield, Kentucky, the daughter of a dairy farmer. Her university degrees include a B.A. from the University of Kentucky, an M.A. from the State University of New York at Binghamton, and a Ph.D. from the University of Connecticut. Her first two books were critical studies; she began publishing fiction in 1980. She has published a novel, a novella, and three collections of short stories.

wished the new interstate had gone through the homeplace instead. Sam knew he should have bought out his sisters and kept it.

"How are you, Sam?" Hort asked when he and Damson arrived. Damson's husband, Porter, had stayed home today with a bad back.

"About dead." Sam grinned and knuckled his chest, pretending heart trouble and exaggerating the arthritis in his hands.

"Not again!" Hort said, teasing him. "You just like to growl, Sam. You've been that way all your life."

"You ain't even knowed me that long! Why, I remember the night you was born. You come in mad at the world, with your stinger out, and you've been like that ever since."

Hort patted his arm. "Your barn door's open, Sam," she said as they went into the living room.

He zipped up his fly unselfconsciously. At his age, he didn't care.

Hort steered Damson off into the kitchen, murmuring something about a blue dish, and Sam sat down with Cecil to discuss crops and the weather. It was their habit to review the week's weather, then their health, then local news — in that order. Cecil was a small, amiable man who didn't like to argue.

A little later, at the dinner table, Cecil jokingly asked Sam, "Are you sending any money to Jimmy Swaggart?"°

"Hell, no! I ain't sending a penny to that bastard."

"Sam never gave them preachers nothing," Hort said defensively as she sent a bowl of potatoes au gratin Sam's way. "That was Nova."

Nova, Sam's wife, had been dead eight and a half years. Nova was always buying chances on Heaven, Sam thought. There was something squirrelly in her, like the habit she had of saving out extra seed from the garden or putting up more preserves than they could use.

Hort said, "I still think Nova wanted to build on that ground she heired so she could have a house in her own name."

Damson nodded vigorously. "She didn't want you to have your name on the new house, Sam. She wanted it in her name."

"Didn't make no sense, did it?" Sam said, reflecting a moment on Nova. He could see her plainly, holding up a piece of fried chicken like a signal for attention. The impression was so vivid he almost asked her to pass the peas.

Hort said, "You already had a nice house with shade trees and a tobacco patch, and it was close to your kinfolks, but she just *had* to move toward town."

"She told me if she had to get to the hospital the ambulance would get there quicker," said Damson, taking a second biscuit. "Hort, these biscuits ain't as good as you usually make."

"I didn't use self-rising," said Hort.

"It wouldn't make much difference, with that new highway," said Cecil, speaking of the ambulance.

Jimmy Swaggart: television evangelist

On the day they moved to the new house, Sam stayed in bed with the covers pulled up around him and refused to budge. He was still there at four o'clock in the evening, after his cousins had moved out all the furniture. Nova ignored him until they came for the bed. She laid his clothes on the bed and rattled the car keys in his face. She had never learned to drive. That was nearly fifteen years ago. Only a few years after that, Nova died and left him in that brick box she called a dream home. There wasn't a tree in the yard when they built the house. Now there were two flowering crab apples and a flimsy little oak.

After dinner, Hort and Cecil brought out new pictures of their great-grandchildren. The children had changed, and Sam couldn't keep straight which ones belonged to Linda and which ones belonged to Donald. He felt full. He made himself comfortable among the crocheted pillows on Hort's high-backed couch. For ten minutes, Hort talked on the telephone to Linda, in Louisiana, and when she hung up she reported that Linda had a new job at a finance company. Drowsily, Sam listened to the voices rise and fall. Their language was so familiar; his kinfolks never told stories or reminisced when they sat around on a Sunday. Instead, they discussed character. "He's the stingiest man alive." "She was nice to talk to on the street but *H* to work with." "He never would listen when you tried to tell him anything." "She'd do anything for you."

Now, as Sam stared at a picture of a child with a Depression-style bowl haircut, Damson was saying, "Old Will Stone always referred to himself as 'me.' '*Me* did this. *Me* wants that.'"

Hort said, "The Stones were always trying to get you to do something for them. Get around one of them and they'd think of something they wanted you to do." The Stones were their mother's people.

"I never would let 'em tell me what to do," Damson said with a laugh. "I'd say, 'I can't! I've got the nervous trembles.'"

Damson was little then, and her Aunt Rue always complained of nervous trembles. Once, Damson had tried to get out of picking English peas by claiming she had nervous trembles, too. Sam remembered that. He laughed — a hoot so sudden they thought he hadn't been listening and was laughing about something private.

Hort fixed a plate of fried chicken, potatoes, field peas, and stewed apples for Sam to take home. He set it on the back seat of Damson's car, along with fourteen eggs and a sack of biscuits. Damson spurted out of the driveway backwards, scaring the hound dog back to his hole under a lilac bush.

"Hort and Cecil's having a time keeping up this place," Sam said, noticing the weed-clogged pen where they used to keep hogs.

Damson said, "Hort's house always smelled so good, but today it smelled bad. It smelled like fried fish."

"I never noticed it," said Sam, yawning.

"Ain't you sleeping good, Sam?"

"Yeah, but when my stomach sours I get to yawning."

"You ain't getting old on us, are you?"

"No, I ain't old. Old is in your head."

Damson invited herself into Sam's house, saying she wanted to help him put the food away. His sisters wouldn't leave him alone. They checked on his housekeeping, searched for ruined food, made sure his commode was flushed. They had fits when he took in a stray dog one day, and they would have taken her to the pound if she hadn't got hit on the road first.

Damson stored the food in the kitchen and snooped in his refrigerator. Sam was itching to get into his bluejeans and watch something on Ted Turner's channel that he had meant to watch. He couldn't remember now what it was, but he knew it came on at four o'clock. Damson came into the living room and began to peer at all his pictures, exclaiming over each great-grandchild. All Sam's kids and grandkids were scattered around. His son worked in the tire industry in Akron, Ohio, and his oldest granddaughter operated a frozen-yogurt store in Florida. He didn't know why anybody would eat yogurt in any form. His grandson Bobby had arrived from Arizona last year with an Italian woman who spoke in a sharp accent. Sam had to hold himself stiff to keep from laughing. He wouldn't let her see him laugh, but her accent tickled him. Now Bobby had written that she'd gone back to Italy.

Damson paused over an old family portrait — Pap and Mammy and all six children, along with Uncle Clay and Uncle Thomas and their wives, Rosie and Zootie, and Aunt Rue. Sam's three brothers were dead now. Damson, a young girl in the picture, wore a lace collar, and Hort was in blond curls and a pinafore. Pap sat in the center on a chair with his legs set far apart, as if to anchor himself to hold the burden of this wild family. He looked mean and willful, as though he were about to whip somebody.

Suddenly Damson blurted out, "Pap ruined my life."

Sam was surprised. Damson hadn't said exactly that before, but he knew what she was talking about. There had always been a sadness about her, as though she had had the hope knocked out of her years ago.

She said, "He ruined my life — keeping me away from Lyle."

"That was near sixty years ago, Damson. That don't still bother you now, does it?"

She held the picture close to her breast and said, "You know how you hear on the television nowadays about little children getting beat up or treated nasty and it makes such a mark on them? Nowadays they know about that, but they didn't back then. They never knowed how something when you're young can hurt you so long."

"None of that happened to you."

"Not that, but it was just as bad."

"Lyle wouldn't have been good to you," said Sam.

"But I loved him, and Pap wouldn't let me see him."

"Lyle was a drunk and Pap didn't trust him no further than he could throw him."

"And then I married Porter, for pure spite," she went on. "You know good and well I never cared a thing about him."

"How come you've stayed married to him all these years then? Why don't you do like the kids do nowadays — like Bobby out in Arizona? Him and that Italian. They've done quit!"

"But she's a foreigner. I ain't surprised," said Damson, blowing her nose with a handkerchief from her pocketbook. She sat down on Sam's divan. He had towels spread on the upholstery to protect it, a habit of Nova's he couldn't get rid of. That woman was so practical she had even orchestrated her deathbed. She had picked out her burial clothes, arranged for his breakfast. He remembered holding up hangers of dresses from her closet for her to choose from.

"Damson," he said, "if you could do it over, you'd do it different, but it might not be no better. You're making Lyle out to be more than he would have been."

"He wouldn't have shot hisself," she said calmly.

"It was an accident."

She shook her head. "No, I think different."

Damson had always claimed he killed himself over her. That night, Lyle had come over to the homeplace near dark. Sam and his brothers had helped Pap put in a long day suckering tobacco. Sam was already courting Nova, and Damson was just out of high school. The neighborhood boys came over on Sundays after church like a pack of dogs after a bitch. Damson had an eye for Lyle because he was so daresome, more reckless than the rest. That Saturday night when Lyle came by for her, he had been into some moonshine, and he was frisky, like a young bull. Pap wouldn't let her go with him. Sam heard Damson in the attic, crying, and Lyle was outside, singing at the top of his lungs, calling her. "Damson! My fruit pie!" Pap stepped out onto the porch then, and Lyle slipped off into the darkness.

Damson set the family picture back on the shelf and said, "He was different from all the other boys. He knew a lot, and he'd been to Texas once with his daddy — for his daddy's asthma. He had a way about him."

"I remember when Lyle come back late that night," Sam said. "I heard him on the porch. I knowed it must be him. He was loud and acted like he was going to bust in the house after you."

"I heard him," she said. "From my pallet up there at the top. It was so hot I had a bucket of water and a washrag and I'd wet my face and stand in that little window and reach for a breeze. I heard him come, and I heard him thrashing around down there on the porch. There was a loose board you always had to watch out for."

"I remember that!" Sam said. He hadn't thought of that warped plank in years.

"He fell over it," Damson said. "But then he got up and backed down the steps. I could hear him out in the yard. Then — " She clasped her arms around herself and bowed her head. "Then he yelled out, 'Damson!' I can still hear that."

A while later, they had heard the gunshot. Sam always remembered hearing a hollow thump and a sudden sound like cussing, then the explosion. He and his brother Bob rushed out in the dark, and then Pap brought a coal-oil lantern. They found Lyle sprawled behind the barn, with the shotgun kicked several feet away. There was a milk can turned over, and they figured that Lyle had stumbled over it when he went behind the barn. Sam had never forgotten Damson on the living-room floor, bawling. She lay there all the next day, screaming and beating her heavy work shoes against the floor, and people had to step around her. The women fussed over her, but none of the men could say anything.

Sam wanted to say something now. He glared at that big family in the picture. The day the photographer came, Sam's mother made everyone dress up, and they had to stand there as still as stumps for about an hour in that August heat. He remembered the kink in Damson's hair, the way she had fixed it so pretty for Lyle. A blurred chicken was cutting across the corner of the picture, and an old bird dog named Obadiah was stretched out in front, holding a pose better than the fidgety people. In the front row, next to her mother, Damson's bright, upturned face sparkled with a smile. Everyone had admired the way she could hold a smile for the camera.

Pointing to her face in the picture, he said, "Here you are, Damson — a young girl in love."

Frowning, she said, "I just wish life had been different."

He grabbed Damson's shoulders and stared into her eyes. To this day, she didn't even wear glasses and was still pretty, still herself in there, in that puffed-out old face. He said, "You wish! Well, wish in one hand and shit in the other and see which one fills up the quickest!"

He got her. She laughed so hard she had to catch her tears with her handkerchief. "Sam, you old hound. Saying such as that — and on a Sunday."

She rose to go. He thought he'd said the right thing, because she seemed lighter on her feet now. "You've got enough eggs and bacon to last you all week," she said. "And I'm going to bring you some of that popcorn cake my neighbor makes. You'd never guess it had popcorn in it."

She had her keys in her hand, her pocketbook on her arm. She was wearing a pretty color of pink, the shade of baby pigs. She said, "I know why you've lived so long, Sam. You just see what you want to see. You're like Pap, just as hard and plain."

"That ain't the whole truth," he said, feeling a mist of tears come.

That night he couldn't get to sleep. He went to bed at eight-thirty, after a nature special on the television — grizzly bears. He lay in bed and replayed his life with Nova. The times he wanted to leave home. The times he went to a lawyer to inquire about a divorce. (It turned out to cost too much, and anyway he knew his folks would never forgive him.) The time she hauled him out of bed for the move to this house. He had loved their old place, a wood-frame house with a porch and a swing, looking out over tobacco fields and a strip of woods. He always had a dog then, a special dog, sitting on the porch with him. Here he had no porch, just some concrete steps, where he would sit sometimes and watch the traffic. At night, drunk drivers zoomed along, occasionally plowing into somebody's mailbox.

She had died at three-thirty in the morning, and toward the end she didn't want anything — no food, no talk, no news, nothing soft. No kittens to hold, no memories. He stayed up with her in case she needed him, but she went without needing him at all. And now he didn't need her. In the dim light of the street lamp, he surveyed the small room where he had chosen to sleep — the single bed, the bare walls, his jeans hanging up on a nail, his shoes on a shelf, the old washstand that had belonged to his grandmother, the little rag rug beside the bed. He was happy. His birthday was two months from today. He would be eighty-four. He thought of that bird dog, Obadiah, who had been with him on his way through the woods the night he set out to meet someone — the night he first made love to a girl. Her name was Nettie, and at first she had been reluctant to lie down with him, but he had brought a quilt, and he spread it out in the open pasture. The hay had been cut that week, and the grass was damp and sweet-smelling. He could still feel the clean, soft, cool cotton of that quilt, the stubble poking through the patterns of the quilting pressing into his back. Nettie lay there beside him, her breath blowing on his shoulder as they studied the stars far above the field — little pinpoint holes punched through the night sky like the needle holes around the tiny stitches in the quilting. Nettie. Nettie Slade. Her dress had self-covered buttons, hard like seed corn.

Herman Melville

Bartleby the Scrivener

A Story of Wall Street

I am a rather elderly man. The nature of my avocations for the last thirty years has brought me into more than ordinary contact with what would seem an interesting and somewhat singular set of men of whom as yet nothing that I know of has ever been written — I mean the law-copyists or scriveners. I

BARTLEBY THE SCRIVENER First published in 1853. Herman Melville (1819–1891) was born in New York City. After working as a farmhand, clerk, bookkeeper, and teacher, he went to sea in 1837, where his adventures and observations supplied him with the material for several novels of the sea including *Moby Dick* (1851). The lack of financial success of that book and later works of fiction, including *Piazza Tales*, which reprinted "Bartleby the Scrivener," led Melville eventually to write poetry instead. By the time of the story, Wall Street had become the financial and business center of New York City. In the days before the invention of the typewriter, official documents and legal papers had to be copied by hand — the job of a "scrivener." "The Tombs" (paragraph 11 and thereafter) was the vivid nickname of the city prison, properly called the Halls of Justice.

have known very many of them, professionally and privately, and if I pleased could relate diverse histories at which good-natured gentlemen might smile and sentimental souls might weep. But I waive the biographies of all other scriveners for a few passages in the life of Bartleby, who was a scrivener the strangest I ever saw or heard of. While of other law-copyists I might write the complete life, of Bartleby nothing of that sort can be done. I believe that no materials exist for a full and satisfactory biography of this man. It is an irreparable loss to literature. Bartleby was one of those beings of whom nothing is ascertainable except from the original sources, and in his case those are very small. What my own astonished eyes saw of Bartleby, *that* is all I know of him except, indeed, one vague report which will appear in the sequel.

Ere introducing the scrivener as he first appeared to me, it is fit I make some mention of myself, my employees, my business, my chambers, and general surroundings, because some such description is indispensable to an adequate understanding of the chief character about to be presented.

Imprimis: I am a man who from his youth upwards has been filled with a profound conviction that the easiest way of life is the best. Hence, though I belong to a profession proverbially energetic and nervous, even to turbulence at times, yet nothing of that sort have I ever suffered to invade my peace. I am one of those unambitious lawyers who never addresses a jury or in any way draws down public applause, but in the cool tranquility of a snug retreat do a snug business among rich men's bonds and mortgages and title-deeds. All who know me consider me an eminently *safe* man. The late John Jacob Astor, a personage little given to poetic enthusiasm, had no hesitation in pronouncing my first grand point to be prudence; my next, method. I do not speak it in vanity but simply record the fact that I was not unemployed in my profession by the late John Jacob Astor, a name which, I admit, I love to repeat, for it hath a rounded and orbicular sound to it and rings like unto bullion. I will freely add that I was not insensible to the late John Jacob Astor's good opinion.

Sometime prior to the period at which this little history begins, my avocations had been largely increased. The good old office now extinct in the State of New York of a Master in Chancery had been conferred upon me. It was not a very arduous office but very pleasantly remunerative. I seldom lose my temper; much more seldom indulge in dangerous indignation at wrongs and outrages; but I must be permitted to be rash here and declare that I consider the sudden and violent abrogation of the office of Master in Chancery by the new Constitution as a ———— premature act, inasmuch as I had counted upon a life-lease of the profits, whereas I only received those of a few short years. But this is by the way.

My chambers were upstairs at No. — Wall Street. At one end they looked   5 upon the white wall of the interior of a spacious skylight shaft penetrating the building from top to bottom. This view might have been considered rather tame than otherwise, deficient in what landscape painters call "life."

But if so, the view from the other end of my chambers offered at least a contrast, if nothing more. In that direction my windows commanded an unobstructed view of a lofty brick wall, black by age and everlasting shade, which wall required no spy-glass to bring out its lurking beauties, but for the benefit of all near-sighted spectators was pushed up to within ten feet of my window panes. Owing to the great height of the surrounding buildings, and my chambers being on the second floor, the interval between this wall and mine not a little resembled a huge square cistern.

At the period just preceding the advent of Bartleby, I had two persons as copyists in my employment and a promising lad as an office boy. First, Turkey; second, Nippers; third, Ginger Nut. These may seem names the like of which are not usually found in the Directory. In truth they were nicknames mutually conferred upon each other by my three clerks, and were deemed expressive of their respective persons or characters. Turkey was a short, pursy Englishman of about my own age, that is, somewhere not far from sixty. In the morning, one might say, his face was of a fine florid hue, but after twelve o'clock, meridian — his dinner hour — it blazed like a grate full of Christmas coals, and continued blazing — but as it were with a gradual wane — till 6 o'clock P.M. or thereabouts, after which I saw no more of the proprietor of the face, which gaining its meridian with the sun, seemed to set with it, to rise, culminate, and decline the following day, with the like regularity and undiminished glory. There are many singular coincidences I have known in the course of my life, not the least among which was the fact that exactly when Turkey displayed his fullest beams from his red and radiant countenance, just then, too, at the critical moment began the daily period when I considered his business capacities as seriously disturbed for the remainder of the twenty-four hours. Not that he was absolutely idle or averse to business then; far from it. The difficulty was, he was apt to be altogether too energetic. There was a strange, inflamed, flurried, flighty recklessness of activity about him. He would be incautious in dipping his pen into his ink-stand. All his blots upon my documents were dropped there after twelve o'clock, meridian. Indeed not only would he be reckless and sadly given to making blots in the afternoon, but some days he went further and was rather noisy. At such times, too, his face flamed with augmented blazonry, as if cannel coal had been heaped on anthracite. He made an unpleasant racket with his chair; spilled his sand-box°; in mending his pens, impatiently split them all to pieces, and threw them on the floor in a sudden passion; stood up and leaned over his table, boxing his papers about in a most indecorous manner, very sad to behold in an elderly man like him. Nevertheless, as he was in many ways a most valuable person to me, and all the time before twelve o'clock, meridian, was the quickest, steadiest creature too, accomplishing a great deal of work in a style not easy to be matched — for these reasons, I was willing to overlook his eccentricities, though indeed occasionally I remonstrated with him. I did this very gently, however, because

sand-box: sand kept in a shaker and used for blotting wet ink

though the civilest, nay, the blandest and most reverential of men in the morning, yet in the afternoon he was disposed upon provocation to be slightly rash with his tongue, in fact insolent. Now valuing his morning services as I did, and resolved not to lose them; yet at the same time made uncomfortable by his inflamed ways after twelve o'clock; and being a man of peace, unwilling by my admonitions to call forth unseemly retorts from him, I took upon me one Saturday noon (he was always worse on Saturdays) to hint to him very kindly that perhaps now that he was growing old, it might be well to abridge his labors; in short, he need not come to my chambers after twelve o'clock but, dinner over, had best go home to his lodgings and rest himself till tea-time. But no; he insisted upon his afternoon devotions. His countenance became intolerably fervid as he oratorically assured me — gesticulating with a long ruler at the other end of the room — that if his services in the morning were useful, how indispensable, then, in the afternoon?

"With submission, sir," said Turkey on this occasion. "I consider myself your right-hand man. In the morning I but marshal and deploy my columns, but in the afternoon I put myself at their head and gallantly charge the foe, thus!" — and he made a violent thrust with the ruler.

"But the blots, Turkey," intimated I.

"True, — but, with submission, sir, behold these hairs! I am getting old. Surely, sir, a blot or two of a warm afternoon is not to be severely urged against gray hairs. Old age — even if it blot the page — is honorable. With submission, sir, we *both* are getting old."

This appeal to my fellow-feeling was hardly to be resisted. At all events, I saw that go he would not. So I made up my mind to let him stay, resolving nevertheless to see to it that during the afternoon he had to do with my less important papers.

Nippers, the second on my list, was a whiskered, sallow, and upon the whole rather piratical-looking young man of about five and twenty. I always deemed him the victim of two evil powers — ambition and indigestion. The ambition was evinced by a certain impatience of the duties of a mere copyist, an unwarrantable usurpation of strictly professional affairs such as the original drawing up of legal documents. The indigestion seemed betokened in an occasional nervous testiness and grinning irritability causing the teeth to audibly grind together over mistakes committed in copying; unnecessary maledictions hissed rather than spoken in the heat of business; and especially by a continual discontent with the height of the table where he worked. Though of a very ingenious mechanical turn, Nippers could never get this table to suit him. He put chips under it, blocks of various sorts, bits of pasteboard, and at last went so far as to attempt an exquisite adjustment by final pieces of folded blotting-paper. But no invention would answer. If for the sake of easing his back he brought the table lid at a sharp angle well up towards his chin, and wrote there like a man using the steep roof of a Dutch house for his desk, then he declared that it stopped the circulation in his arms. If now he lowered the table to his waistbands and stooped over it in writing, then there was a sore aching in his back. In short, the truth of the matter was Nippers knew not what he wanted. Or if he wanted anything, it was to be rid of a scrivener's table altogether. Among the manifestations of his diseased ambition was a fondness he had for receiving visits from certain ambiguous-looking fellows in seedy coats, whom he called his clients. Indeed I was aware that not only was he at times considerable of a ward-politician, but he occasionally did a little business at the Justices' courts and was not unknown on the steps of the Tombs. I have good reason to believe however that one individual who called upon him at my chambers and who with a grand air he insisted was his client was no other than a dun, and the alleged title-deed, a bill. But with all his failings, and the annoyances he caused me, Nippers, like his compatriot Turkey, was a very useful man to me; wrote a neat, swift hand; and, when he chose, was not deficient in a gentlemanly sort of deportment. Added to this, he always dressed in a gentlemanly sort of way, and so incidentally reflected credit upon my chambers. Whereas with respect to Turkey, I had much ado to keep him from being a reproach to me. His clothes were apt to look oily and smell of eating-houses. He wore his pantaloons very loose and baggy in the summer. His coats were execrable, his hat not to be handled. But while the hat was a thing of indifference to me inasmuch as his natural civility and deference as a dependent Englishman always led him to doff it the moment he entered the room, yet his coat was another matter. Concerning his coats, I reasoned with him, but with no effect. The truth was I suppose that a man with so small an income could not afford to sport such a lustrous face and a lustrous coat at one and the same time. As Nippers once observed, Turkey's money went chiefly for red ink. One winter day I presented Turkey with a highly respectable looking coat of my own, a padded gray coat of a most comfortable warmth and which buttoned straight up from the knee to the neck. I thought Turkey would appreciate the favor and abate his rashness and obstreperousness of afternoons. But no. I verily believe that buttoning himself up in so downy and blanket-like a coat had a pernicious effect upon him, upon the same principle that too much oats are bad for horses. In fact, precisely as a rash, restive horse is said to feel his oats, so Turkey felt his coat. It made him insolent. He was a man whom prosperity harmed.

Though concerning the self-indulgent habits of Turkey I had my own private surmises, yet touching Nippers I was well persuaded that whatever might be his faults in other respects, he was at least a temperate young man. But indeed, nature herself seemed to have been his vintner and at his birth charged him so thoroughly with an irritable, brandy-like disposition that all subsequent potations were needless. When I consider how amid the stillness of my chambers Nippers would sometimes impatiently rise from his seat and stooping over his table spread his arms wide apart, seize the whole desk, and move it, and jerk it, with a grim, grinding motion on the floor, as if the table were a perverse voluntary agent intent on thwarting and vexing him, I plainly perceive that for Nippers, brandy and water were altogether superfluous.

It was fortunate for me that, owing to its peculiar cause — indigestion — the irritability and consequent nervousness of Nippers were mainly observable in the morning, while in the afternoon he was comparatively mild. So that Turkey's paroxysms only coming on about twelve o'clock, I never had to do with their eccentricities at one time. Their fits relieved each other like guards. When Nippers's was on, Turkey's was off, and vice versa. This was a good natural arrangement under the circumstances.

Ginger Nut, the third on my list, was a lad some twelve years old. His father was a carman,° ambitious of seeing his son on the bench instead of a cart before he died. So he sent him to my office as student at law, errand boy, and cleaner and sweeper, at the rate of one dollar a week. He had a little desk to himself but he did not use it much. Upon inspection, the drawer exhibited a great array of the shells of various sorts of nuts. Indeed, to this quick-witted youth the whole noble science of the law was contained in a nutshell. Not the least among the employments of Ginger Nut, as well as one which he discharged with the most alacrity, was his duty as cake and apple purveyor for Turkey and Nippers. Copying law papers being proverbially a dry, husky sort of business, my two scriveners were fain to moisten their mouths very often with Spitzenbergs° to be had at the numerous stalls nigh the Custom House and Post Office. Also, they sent Ginger Nut very frequently for that peculiar cake — small, flat, round, and very spicy — after which he had been named by them. Of a cold morning when business was but dull, Turkey would gobble up scores of these cakes as if they were mere wafers — indeed they sell them at the rate of six or eight for a penny — the scrape of his pen blending with the crunching of the crisp particles in his mouth. Of all the fiery afternoon blunders and flurried rashnesses of Turkey was his once moistening a ginger cake between his lips and clapping it on to a mortgage for a seal. I came within an ace of dismissing him then. But he mollified me by making an oriental bow and saying — "With submission, sir, it was generous of me to find you in stationery on my own account."

Now my original business — that of a conveyancer and title hunter, and drawer-up of recondite documents of all sorts — was considerably increased by receiving the master's office. There was now great work for scriveners. Not only must I push the clerks already with me, but I must have additional help. In answer to my advertisement, a motionless young man one morning stood upon my office threshold, the door being open, for it was summer. I can see that figure now — pallidly neat, pitiably respectable, incurably forlorn! It was Bartleby.

After a few words touching his qualifications I engaged him, glad to have among my corps of copyists a man of so singularly sedate an aspect, which I thought might operate beneficially upon the flighty temper of Turkey and the fiery one of Nippers.

I should have stated before that ground glass folding doors divided my premises into two parts, one of which was occupied by my scriveners, the

15

carman: a cart driver   Spitzenbergs: a variety of apples

other by myself. According to my humor I threw open these doors, or closed them. I resolved to assign Bartleby a corner by the folding doors, but on my side of them so as to have this quiet man within easy call in case any trifling thing was to be done. I placed his desk close up to a small side window in that part of the room, a window which originally had afforded a lateral view of certain grimy backyards and bricks, but which owing to subsequent erections commanded at present no view at all, though it gave some light. Within three feet of the panes was a wall, and the light came down from far above between two lofty buildings as from a very small opening in a dome. Still further to a satisfactory arrangement, I procured a high green folding screen which might entirely isolate Bartleby from my sight though not remove him from my voice. And thus, in a manner privacy and society were conjoined.

At first Bartleby did an extraordinary quantity of writing. As if long famishing for something to copy, he seemed to gorge himself on my documents. There was no pause for digestion. He ran a day and night line, copying by sunlight and by candlelight. I should have been quite delighted with his application had he been cheerfully industrious. But he wrote on silently, palely, mechanically.

It is of course an indispensable part of a scrivener's business to verify the accuracy of his copy, word by word. Where there are two or more scriveners in an office, they assist each other in this examination, one reading from the copy, the other holding the original. It is a very dull, wearisome, and lethargic affair. I can readily imagine that to some sanguine temperaments it would be altogether intolerable. For example, I cannot credit that the mettlesome poet Byron would have contentedly sat down with Bartleby to examine a law document of, say, five hundred pages closely written in a crimpy hand.

20   Now and then in the haste of business, it had been my habit to assist in comparing some brief document myself, calling Turkey or Nippers for this purpose. One object I had in placing Bartleby so handy to me behind the screen was to avail myself of his services on such trivial occasions. It was on the third day, I think, of his being with me, and before any necessity had arisen for having his own writing examined, that being much hurried to complete a small affair I had in hand, I abruptly called to Bartleby. In my haste and natural expectancy of instant compliance, I sat with my head bent over the original on my desk and my right hand sideways and somewhat nervously extended with the copy, so that immediately upon emerging from his retreat Bartleby might snatch it and proceed to business without the least delay.

In this very attitude did I sit when I called to him, rapidly stating what it was I wanted him to do — namely, to examine a small paper with me. Imagine my surprise, nay my consternation, when without moving from his privacy Bartleby in a singularly mild, firm voice replied, "I would prefer not to."

I sat awhile in perfect silence, rallying my stunned faculties. Immediately it occurred to me that my ears had deceived me, or Bartleby had entirely misunderstood my meaning. I repeated my request in the clearest tone I could assume. But in quite as clear a one came the previous reply, "I would prefer not to."

"Prefer not to," echoed I, rising in high excitement and crossing the room with a stride, "What do you mean? Are you moonstruck? I want you to help me compare this sheet here — take it," and I thrust it towards him.

"I would prefer not to," said he.

I looked at him steadfastly. His face was leanly composed, his gray eye dimly calm. Not a wrinkle of agitation rippled him. Had there been the least uneasiness, anger, impatience or impertinence in his manner, in other words had there been anything ordinarily human about him, doubtless I should have violently dismissed him from the premises. But as it was, I should have as soon thought of turning my pale plaster-of-paris bust of Cicero out of doors. I stood gazing at him awhile as he went on with his own writing, and then reseated myself at my desk. This is very strange, thought I. What had one best do? But my business hurried me. I concluded to forget the matter for the present, reserving it for my future leisure. So calling Nippers from the other room, the paper was speedily examined.

A few days after this Bartleby concluded four lengthy documents, being quadruplicates of a week's testimony taken before me in my High Court of Chancery. It became necessary to examine them. It was an important suit and great accuracy was imperative. Having all things arranged I called Turkey, Nippers and Ginger Nut from the next room, meaning to place the four copies in the hands of my four clerks while I should read from the original. Accordingly Turkey, Nippers and Ginger Nut had taken their seats in a row, each with his document in hand, when I called to Bartleby to join this interesting group.

"Bartleby! quick, I am waiting."

I heard a slow scrape of his chair legs on the unscraped floor, and soon he appeared standing at the entrance of his hermitage.

"What is wanted?" said he mildly.

"The copies, the copies," said I hurriedly. "We are going to examine them. There" — and I held towards him the fourth quadruplicate.

"I would prefer not to," he said, and gently disappeared behind the screen.

For a few moments I was turned into a pillar of salt° standing at the head of my seated column of clerks. Recovering myself, I advanced towards the screen and demanded the reason for such extraordinary conduct.

"*Why* do you refuse?"

"I would prefer not to."

With any other man I should have flown outright into a dreadful passion, scorned all further words, and thrust him ignominiously from my presence. But there was something about Bartleby that not only strangely disarmed

pillar of salt: See Genesis 19.26.

me, but in a wonderful manner touched and disconcerted me. I began to reason with him.

"These are your own copies we are about to examine. It is labor saving to you, because one examination will answer for your four papers. It is common usage. Every copyist is bound to help examine his copy. Is it not so? Will you not speak? Answer!"

"I prefer not to," he replied in a flute-like tone. It seemed to me that while I had been addressing him, he carefully revolved every statement that I made, fully comprehended the meaning, could not gainsay the irresistible conclusion, but at the same time some paramount consideration prevailed with him to reply as he did.

"You are decided, then, not to comply with my request — a request made according to common usage and common sense?"

He briefly gave me to understand that on that point my judgment was sound. Yes: his decision was irreversible.

It is not seldom the case that when a man is browbeaten in some unprecedented and violently unreasonable way he begins to stagger in his own plainest faith. He begins, as it were, vaguely to surmise that wonderful as it may be, all the justice and all the reason is on the other side. Accordingly, if any disinterested persons are present he turns to them for some reinforcement for his own faltering mind.

"Turkey," said I, "what do you think of this? Am I not right?"

"With submission, sir," said Turkey with his blandest tone, "I think that you are."

"Nippers," said I, "what do *you* think of it?"

"I think I should kick him out of the office."

(The reader of nice perceptions will here perceive that, it being morning, Turkey's answer is couched in polite and tranquil terms, but Nippers replies in ill-tempered ones. Or, to repeat a previous sentence, Nippers's ugly mood was on duty, and Turkey's off.)

"Ginger Nut," said I, willing to enlist the smallest suffrage in my behalf, "what do *you* think of it?"

"I think, sir, he's a little *loony*," replied Ginger Nut, with a grin.

"You hear what they say," said I, turning towards the screen, "come forth and do your duty."

But he vouchsafed no reply. I pondered a moment in sore perplexity. But once more business hurried me. I determined again to postpone the consideration of this dilemma to my future leisure. With a little trouble we made out to examine the papers without Bartleby, though at every page or two, Turkey deferentially dropped his opinion that this proceeding was quite out of the common, while Nippers, twitching in his chair with a dyspeptic nervousness, ground out between his set teeth occasional hissing maledictions against the stubborn oaf behind the screen. And for his (Nippers's) part, this was the first and the last time he would do another man's business without pay.

Meanwhile Bartleby sat in his hermitage, oblivious to everything but his own peculiar business there.

Some days passed, the scrivener being employed upon another lengthy work. His late remarkable conduct led me to regard his way narrowly. I observed that he never went to dinner, indeed that he never went anywhere. As yet I had never of my personal knowledge known him to be outside of my office. He was a perpetual sentry in the corner. At about eleven o'clock though, in the morning, I noticed that Ginger Nut would advance toward the opening in Bartleby's screen as if silently beckoned thither by a gesture invisible to me where I sat. That boy would then leave the office jingling a few pence and reappear with a handful of ginger nuts which he delivered in the hermitage, receiving two of the cakes for his trouble.

He lives then on ginger nuts, thought I; never eats a dinner, properly speaking; he must be a vegetarian then, but no, he never eats even vegetables, he eats nothing but ginger nuts. My mind then ran on in reveries concerning the probable effects upon the human constitution of living entirely on ginger nuts. Ginger nuts are so called because they contain ginger as one of their peculiar constituents, and the final flavoring one. Now what was ginger? A hot, spicy thing. Was Bartleby hot and spicy? Not at all. Ginger, then, had no effect upon Bartleby. Probably he preferred it should have none.

Nothing so aggravates an earnest person as a passive resistance. If the individual so resisted be of a not inhumane temper, and the resisting one perfectly harmless in his passivity, then in the better moods of the former, he will endeavor charitably to construe to his imagination what proves impossible to be solved by his judgment. Even so for the most part I regarded Bartleby and his ways. Poor fellow! thought I, he means no mischief; it is plain he intends no insolence; his aspect sufficiently evinces that his eccentricities are involuntary. He is useful to me. I can get along with him. If I turn him away, the chances are he will fall in with some less indulgent employer, and then he will be rudely treated and perhaps driven forth miserably to starve. Yes. Here I can cheaply purchase a delicious self-approval. To befriend Bartleby, to humor him in his strange wilfulness, will cost me little or nothing, while I lay up in my soul what will eventually prove a sweet morsel for my conscience. But this mood was not invariable with me. The passiveness of Bartleby sometimes irritated me. I felt strangely goaded on to encounter him in new opposition, to elicit some angry spark from him answerable to my own. But indeed I might as well have essayed to strike fire with my knuckles against a bit of Windsor soap. But one afternoon the evil impulse in me mastered me, and the following little scene ensued:

"Bartleby," said I, "when those papers are all copied I will compare them with you."

"I would prefer not to."

"How? Surely you do not mean to persist in that mulish vagary?"

No answer.

I threw open the folding doors nearby, and turning upon Turkey and Nippers, exclaimed in an excited manner —

"He says, a second time, he won't examine his papers. What do you think of it, Turkey?"

It was afternoon, be it remembered. Turkey sat glowing like a brass boiler, his bald head steaming, his hands reeling among his blotted papers.

"Think of it?" roared Turkey, "I think I'll just step behind his screen and black his eyes for him!"

So saying, Turkey rose to his feet and threw his arms into a pugilistic position. He was hurrying away to make good his promise when I detained him, alarmed at the effect of incautiously rousing Turkey's combativeness after dinner.

"Sit down, Turkey," said I, "and hear what Nippers has to say. What do you think of it, Nippers? Would I not be justified in immediately dismissing Bartleby?"

"Excuse me, that is for you to decide, sir. I think his conduct quite unusual, and indeed unjust as regards Turkey and myself. But it may only be a passing whim."

"Ah," exclaimed I, "you have strangely changed your mind then — you speak very gently of him now."

"All beer," cried Turkey, "gentleness is effects of beer — Nippers and I dined together today. You see how gentle *I* am, sir. Shall I go and black his eyes?"

"You refer to Bartleby, I suppose. No, not today, Turkey," I replied, "pray, put up your fists."

I closed the doors, and again advanced towards Bartleby. I felt additional incentives tempting me to my fate. I burned to be rebelled against again. I remembered that Bartleby never left the office.

"Bartleby," said I, "Ginger Nut is away; just step round to the post office, won't you? (it was but a three minutes walk) and see if there is anything for me."

"I would prefer not to."

"You *will* not?"

"I *prefer* not."

I staggered to my desk and sat there in a deep study. My blind inveteracy returned. Was there any other thing in which I could procure myself to be ignominiously repulsed by this lean, penniless wight? — my hired clerk? What added thing is there, perfectly reasonable, that he will be sure to refuse to do?

"Bartleby!"

No answer.

"Bartleby," in a louder tone.

No answer.

"Bartleby," I roared.

Like a very ghost, agreeably to the laws of magical invocation, at the third summons he appeared at the entrance of his hermitage.

"Go to the next room, and tell Nippers to come to me."

"I prefer not to," he respectfully and slowly said, and mildly disappeared.

"Very good, Bartleby," said I, in a quiet sort of serenely severe self-possessed tone, intimating the unalterable purpose of some terrible retribution very close at hand. At the moment I half intended something of the kind. But upon the whole, as it was drawing towards my dinner hour, I thought it best to put on my hat and walk home for the day, suffering much from perplexity and distress of mind.

Shall I acknowledge it? The conclusion of this whole business was that it soon became a fixed fact of my chambers that a pale young scrivener by the name of Bartleby had a desk there; that he copied for me at the usual rate of four cents a folio (one hundred words); but he was permanently exempt from examining the work done by him, that duty being transferred to Turkey and Nippers, one of compliment doubtless to their superior acuteness; moreover, said Bartleby was never on any account to be dispatched on the most trivial errand of any sort, and that even if entreated to take upon him such a matter, it was generally understood that he would prefer not to — in other words, that he would refuse point-blank.

As days passed on, I became considerably reconciled to Bartleby. His steadiness, his freedom from all dissipation, his incessant industry (except when he chose to throw himself into a standing revery behind his screen), his great stillness, his unalterableness of demeanor under all circumstances, made him a valuable acquisition. One prime thing was this — *he was always there* — first in the morning, continually through the day, and the last at night. I had a singular confidence in his honesty. I felt my most precious papers perfectly safe in his hands. Sometimes to be sure I could not for the very soul of me avoid falling into sudden spasmodic passions with him. For it was exceeding difficult to bear in mind all the time those strange peculiarities, privileges, and unheard of exemptions forming the tacit stipulations on Bartleby's part under which he remained in my office. Now and then in the eagerness of dispatching pressing business, I would inadvertently summon Bartleby, in a short rapid tone, to put his finger, say, on the incipient tie of a bit of red tape with which I was about compressing some papers. Of course, from behind the screen the usual answer, "I prefer not to," was sure to come, and then how could a human creature with the common infirmities of our nature, refrain from bitterly exclaiming upon such perverseness — such unreasonableness? However, every added repulse of this sort which I received only tended to lessen the probability of my repeating the inadvertence.

Here it must be said that according to the custom of most legal gentlemen occupying chambers in densely populated law buildings, there were several keys to my door. One was kept by a woman residing in the attic, which person weekly scrubbed and daily swept and dusted my apartments. Another was kept by Turkey for convenience sake. The third I sometimes carried in my own pocket. The fourth I knew not who had.

Now one Sunday morning I happened to go to Trinity Church° to hear a celebrated preacher, and finding myself rather early on the ground I thought I would walk round to my chambers for a while. Luckily I had my key with me, but upon applying it to the lock, I found it resisted by something inserted from the inside. Quite surprised, I called out, when to my consternation a key was turned from within, and thrusting his lean visage at me and holding the door ajar, the apparition of Bartleby appeared, in his shirt sleeves, and otherwise in a strangely tattered dishabille, saying quietly that he was sorry but he was deeply engaged just then and — preferred not admitting me at present. In a brief word or two, he moreover added that perhaps I had better walk round the block two or three times, and by that time he would probably have concluded his affairs.

Now, the utterly unsurmised appearance of Bartleby tenanting my law-chambers of a Sunday morning with his cadaverously gentlemanly noncha-lance, yet withal firm and self-possessed, had such a strange effect upon me that incontinently I slunk away from my own door and did as desired. But not without sundry twinges of impotent rebellion against the mild effrontery of this unaccountable scrivener. Indeed it was his wonderful mildness chiefly which not only disarmed me but unmanned me, as it were. For I consider that one, for the time, is a sort of unmanned when he tranquilly permits his hired clerk to dictate to him and order him away from his own premises. Furthermore, I was full of uneasiness as to what Bartleby could possibly be doing in my office in his shirt sleeves and in an otherwise dismantled condi-tion of a Sunday morning. Was anything amiss going on? Nay, that was out of the question. It was not to be thought of for a moment that Bartleby was an immoral person. But what could he be doing there? — copying? Nay again, whatever might be his eccentricities, Bartleby was an eminently deco-rous person. He would be the last man to sit down to his desk in any state approaching to nudity. Besides, it was Sunday, and there was something about Bartleby that forbade the supposition that he would by any secular occupation violate the properties of the day.

Nevertheless, my mind was not pacified; and full of a restless curiosity, at last I returned to the door. Without hindrance I inserted my key, opened it, and entered. Bartleby was not to be seen. I looked round anxiously, peeped behind his screen, but it was very plain that he was gone. Upon more closely examining the place, I surmised that for an indefinite period Bartleby must have ate, dressed, and slept in my office, and that too without plate, mirror, or bed. The cushioned seat of a rickety old sofa in one corner bore the faint impress of a lean, reclining form. Rolled away under his desk I found a blanket; under the empty grate, a blacking box and brush; on a chair, a tin basin with soap and a ragged towel; in a newspaper a few crumbs of ginger nuts and a morsel of cheese. Yes, thought I, it is evident enough that Bartleby has been making his home here, keeping bachelor's hall all by

Trinity Church: located at the corner of Broadway and Wall Street

himself. Immediately then the thought came sweeping across me, what miserable friendlessness and loneliness are here revealed! His poverty is great; but his solitude, how horrible! Think of it. Of a Sunday, Wall Street is deserted as Petra, and every night of every day it is an emptiness. This building too which of weekdays hums with industry and life at nightfall echoes with sheer vacancy, and all through Sunday is forlorn. And here Bartleby makes his home, sole spectator of a solitude which he has seen all populous — a sort of innocent and transformed Marius brooding among the ruins of Carthage!

For the first time in my life a feeling of overpowering stinging melancholy seized me. Before I had never experienced aught but a not unpleasing sadness. The bond of a common humanity now drew me irresistibly to gloom. A fraternal melancholy! For both I and Bartleby were sons of Adam. I remembered the bright silks and sparkling faces I had seen that day in gala trim, swan-like sailing down the Mississippi of Broadway; and I contrasted them with the pallid copyist, and thought to myself, Ah, happiness courts the light, so we deem the world is gay; but misery hides aloof, so we deem that misery there is none. These sad fancyings — chimeras doubtless of a sick and silly brain — led on to other and more special thoughts concerning the eccentricities of Bartleby. Presentiments of strange discoveries hovered round me. The scrivener's pale form appeared to me laid out, among uncaring strangers, in its shivering winding sheet.

Suddenly I was attracted by Bartleby's closed desk, the key in open sight left in the lock. 90

I mean no mischief, seek the gratification of no heartless curiosity, thought I; besides, the desk is mine, and its contents too, so I will make bold to look within. Everything was methodically arranged, the papers smoothly placed. The pigeon holes were deep, and removing the files of documents, I groped into their recesses. Presently I felt something there and dragged it out. It was an old bandanna handkerchief, heavy and knotted. I opened it, and saw it was a savings bank.

I now recalled all the quiet mysteries which I had noted in the man. I remembered that he never spoke but to answer; that though at intervals he had considerable time to himself, yet I had never seen him reading — no, not even a newspaper; that for long periods he would stand looking out, at his pale window behind the screen, upon the dead brick wall; I was quite sure he never visited any refectory or eating house, while his pale face clearly indicated that he never drank beer like Turkey, or tea and coffee even, like other men; that he never went anywhere in particular that I could learn, never went out for a walk, unless indeed that was the case at present; that he had declined telling who he was or whence he came or whether he had any relatives in the world; that though so thin and pale, he never complained of ill health. And more than all, I remembered a certain unconscious air of pallid — how shall I call it? — of pallid haughtiness, say, or rather an austere reserve about him, which had positively awed me into my tame compliance with his eccentricities when I had feared to ask him to do the slightest incidental thing for me, even though I might know from his long-continued motionlessness that behind his screen he must be standing in one of those dead-wall reveries of his.

Revolving all these things, and coupling them with the recently discovered fact that he made my office his constant abiding place and home, and not forgetful of his morbid moodiness; revolving all these things, a prudential feeling began to steal over me. My first emotions had been those of pure melancholy and sincerest pity; but just in proportion as the forlornness of Bartleby grew and grew to my imagination, did that same melancholy merge into fear, that pity into repulsion. So true it is, and so terrible too, that up to a certain point the thought or sight of misery enlists our best affections; but in certain special cases, beyond that point it does not. They err who would assert that invariably this is owing to the inherent selfishness of the human heart. It rather proceeds from a certain hopelessness of remedying excessive and organic ill. To a sensitive being, pity is not seldom pain. And when at last it is perceived that such pity cannot lead to effectual succor, common sense bids the soul be rid of it. What I saw that morning persuaded me that the scrivener was the victim of innate and incurable disorder. I might give alms to his body, but his body did not pain him; it was his soul that suffered, and his soul I could not reach.

I did not accomplish the purpose of going to Trinity Church that morning. Somehow, the things I had seen disqualified me for the time from church-going. I walked homeward, thinking what I would do with Bartleby. Finally I resolved upon this: — I would put certain calm questions to him the next morning, touching his history, &c., and if he declined to answer them openly and unreservedly (and I supposed he would prefer not), then to give him a twenty dollar bill over and above whatever I might owe him, and tell him his services were no longer required; but that if in any other way I could assist him, I would be happy to do so, especially if he desired to return to his native place, wherever that might be, I would willingly help to defray the expenses. Moreover, if after reaching home he found himself at any time in want of aid, a letter from him would be sure of a reply.

95   The next morning came.

"Bartleby," said I, in a still gentler tone, "come here; I am not going to ask you to do anything you would prefer not to do — I simply wish to speak to you."

ask you to do anything you would prefer not to do — I simply wish to speak to you.

Upon this he noiselessly slid into view.

100   "Will you tell me, Bartleby, where you were born?"

"I would prefer not to."

"Will you tell me *anything* about yourself?"

"I would prefer not to."

"But what reasonable objection can you have to speak to me? I feel friendly towards you."

He did not look at me while I spoke, but kept his glance fixed upon my bust of Cicero, which as I then sat was directly behind me, some six inches above my head.

"What is your answer, Bartleby?" said I, after waiting a considerable time for a reply, during which his countenance remained immovable, only there was the faintest conceivable tremor of the white attenuated mouth.

"At present I prefer to give no answer," he said, and retired into his hermitage.

It was rather weak in me I confess, but his manner on this occasion nettled me. Not only did there seem to lurk in it a certain disdain, but his perverseness seemed ungrateful, considering the undeniable good usage and indulgence he had received from me.

Again I sat ruminating what I should do. Mortified as I was at his behavior, and resolved as I had been to dismiss him when I entered my office, nevertheless I strangely felt something superstitious knocking at my heart, and forbidding me to carry out my purpose, and denouncing me for a villain if I dared to breathe one bitter word against this forlornest of mankind. At last, familiarly drawing my chair behind his screen, I sat down and said: "Bartleby, never mind then about revealing your history; but let me entreat you, as a friend, to comply as far as may be with the usages of this office. Say now you will help to examine papers tomorrow or next day: in short, say now that in a day or two you will begin to be a little reasonable: — say so, Bartleby."

"At present I would prefer not to be a little reasonable," was his mildly cadaverous reply.

Just then the folding doors opened, and Nippers approached. He seemed suffering from an unusually bad night's rest, induced by severer indigestion than common. He overheard those final words of Bartleby.

"*Prefer not*, eh?" gritted Nippers — "I'd *prefer* him, if I were you, sir," addressing me — "I'd *prefer* him; I'd give him preferences, the stubborn mule! What is it, sir, pray, that he *prefers* not to do now?"

Bartleby moved not a limb.

"Mr. Nippers," said I, "I'd prefer that you would withdraw for the present."

Somehow, of late I had got into the way of involuntarily using this word "prefer" upon all sorts of not exactly suitable occasions. And I trembled to think that my contact with the scrivener had already and seriously affected me in a mental way. And what further and deeper aberration might it not yet produce? This apprehension had not been without efficacy in determining me to summary means.

As Nippers, looking very sour and sulky, was departing, Turkey blandly and deferentially approached.

"With submission, sir," said he, "yesterday I was thinking about Bartleby here, and I think that if he would but prefer to take a quart of good ale every day, it would do much towards mending him and enabling him to assist in examining his papers."

"So you have got the word too," said I, slightly excited.

"With submission, what word, sir?" asked Turkey, respectfully crowding himself into the contracted space behind the screen, and by so doing making me jostle the scrivener. "What word, sir?"

"I would prefer to be left alone here," said Bartleby, as if offended at being mobbed in his privacy.

"*That's* the word, Turkey," said I — "*that's* it."

"Oh, *prefer*? oh yes — queer word. I never use it myself. But, sir, as I was saying, if he would but prefer — "

"Turkey," interrupted I, "you will please withdraw."

"Oh certainly, sir, if you prefer that I should."

As he opened the folding door to retire, Nippers at his desk caught a glimpse of me and asked whether I would prefer to have a certain paper copied on blue paper or white. He did not in the least roguishly accent the word prefer. It was plain that it involuntarily rolled from his tongue. I thought to myself, surely I must get rid of a demented man who already has in some degree turned the tongues if not the heads of myself and clerks. But I thought it prudent not to break the dismission at once.

The next day I noticed that Bartleby did nothing but stand at his window in his dead-wall revery. Upon my asking him why he did not write, he said that he had decided upon doing no more writing.

"Why, how now? what next?" exclaimed I, "do no more writing?"

"No more."

"And what is the reason?"

"Do you not see the reason for yourself?" he indifferently replied.

I looked steadfastly at him, and perceived that his eyes looked dull and glazed. Instantly it occurred to me that his unexampled diligence in copying by his dim window for the first few weeks of his stay with me might have temporarily impaired his vision.

I was touched. I said something in condolence with him. I hinted that of course he did wisely in abstaining from writing for a while, and urged him to embrace that opportunity of taking wholesome exercise in the open air. This, however, he did not do. A few days after this, my other clerks being absent, and being in a great hurry to dispatch certain letters by the mail, I thought that, having nothing else earthly to do, Bartleby would surely be less inflexible than usual and carry these letters to the post office. But he blankly declined. So, much to my inconvenience, I went myself.

Still added days went by. Whether Bartleby's eyes improved or not, I could not say. To all appearance, I thought they did. But when I asked him if they did, he vouchsafed no answer. At all events, he would do no copying. At last, in reply to my urgings, he informed me that he had permanently given up copying.

"What!" exclaimed I; "suppose your eyes should get entirely well — better than ever before — would you not copy then?"

"I have given up copying," he answered, and slid aside.

He remained as ever, a fixture in my chamber. Nay — if that were possible — he became still more of a fixture than before. What was to be done? He would do nothing in the office: why should he stay there? In plain fact, he had now become a millstone to me, not only useless as a necklace but afflictive to bear. Yet I was sorry for him. I speak less than truth when I say that on his own account, he occasioned me uneasiness. If he would but have named a single relative or friend, I would instantly have written and urged their taking the poor fellow away to some convenient retreat. But he seemed alone, absolutely alone in the universe. A bit of wreck in the mid-Atlantic. At length, necessities connected with my business tyrannized over all other considerations. Decently as I could, I told Bartleby that in six days' time he must unconditionally leave the office. I warned him to take measures, in the interval, for procuring some other abode. I offered to assist him in this endeavor, if he himself would but take the first step towards a removal. "And when you finally quit me, Bartleby," added I, "I shall see that you go not away entirely unprovided. Six days from this hour, remember."

At the expiration of that period I peeped behind the screen, and lo! Bartleby was there.

I buttoned up my coat, balanced myself, advanced slowly towards him, touched his shoulder, and said, "The time has come; you must quit this place; I am sorry for you; here is money; but you must go."

"I would prefer not," he replied, with his back still towards me.

"You *must*." 140

He remained silent.

Now I had an unbounded confidence in this man's common honesty. He had frequently restored to me six pences and shillings carelessly dropped upon the floor, for I am apt to be very reckless in such shirt-button affairs. The proceeding then which followed will not be deemed extraordinary.

"Bartleby," said I, "I owe you twelve dollars on account; here are thirty-two; the odd twenty are yours. Will you take it?" and I handed the bills towards him.

But he made no motion.

"I will leave them here then," putting them under a weight on the table. 145 Then taking my hat and cane and going to the door I tranquilly turned and added, "After you have removed your things from these offices, Bartleby, you will of course lock the door — since every one is now gone for the day but you — and if you please, slip your key underneath the mat so that I may have it in the morning. I shall not see you again, so good-bye to you. If hereafter in your new place of abode I can be of any service to you, do not fail to advise me by letter. Good-bye, Bartleby, and fare you well."

But he answered not a word; like the last column of some ruined temple, he remained standing mute and solitary in the middle of the otherwise deserted room.

As I walked home in a pensive mood, my vanity got the better of my pity. I could not but highly plume myself on my masterly management in getting

rid of Bartleby. Masterly I call it, and such it must appear to any dispassionate thinker. The beauty of my procedure seemed to consist in its perfect
quietness. There was no vulgar bullying, no bravado of any sort, no choleric
hectoring and striding to and fro across the apartment, jerking out vehement
commands for Bartleby to bundle himself off with his beggarly traps.° Nothing of the kind. Without loudly bidding Bartleby depart—as an inferior
genius might have done—I *assumed* the ground that depart he must, and
upon the assumption built all I had to say. The more I thought over my
procedure, the more I was charmed with it. Nevertheless, next morning,
upon awakening, I had my doubts—I had somehow slept off the fumes of
vanity. One of the coolest and wisest hours a man has is just after he awakes
in the morning. My procedure seemed as sagacious as ever—but only in
theory. How it would prove in practice—there was the rub. It was truly a
beautiful thought to have assumed Bartleby's departure; but after all, that
assumption was simply my own, and none of Bartleby's. The great point was
not whether I had assumed that he would quit me, but whether he would
prefer so to do. He was more a man of preferences than assumptions.

After breakfast, I walked downtown, arguing the probabilities *pro* and
con. One moment I thought it would prove a miserable failure, and Bartleby
would be found all alive at my office as usual; the next moment it seemed
certain that I should see his chair empty. And so I kept veering about. At the
corner of Broadway and Canal Street, I saw quite an excited group of people
standing in earnest conversation.

"I'll take odds he doesn't," said a voice as I passed.

"Doesn't go?—done!" said I, "put up your money."

I was instinctively putting my hand in my pocket to produce my own,
when I remembered that this was an election day. The words I had overheard
bore no reference to Bartleby, but to the success or non-success of some
candidate for the mayoralty. In my intent frame of mind, I had, as it were,
imagined that all Broadway shared in my excitement and were debating the
same question with me. I passed on, very thankful that the uproar of the
street screened my momentary absent-mindedness.

As I had intended, I was earlier than usual at my office door. I stood
listening for a moment. All was still. He must be gone. I tried the knob. The
door was locked. Yes, my procedure had worked to a charm; he indeed must
be vanished. Yet a certain melancholy mixed with this: I was almost sorry for
my brilliant success. I was fumbling under the door mat for the key which
Bartleby was to have left there for me when accidentally my knee knocked
against a panel, producing a summoning sound, and in response a voice
came to me from within—"Not yet; I am occupied."

It was Bartleby.

I was thunderstruck. For an instant I stood like the man who, pipe in
mouth, was killed one cloudless afternoon long ago in Virginia, by summer
lightning; at his own warm open window he was killed, and remained lean-

traps: belongings

ing out there upon the dreamy afternoon till someone touched him, when he fell.

"Not gone!" I murmured at last. But again obeying that wondrous as- 155 cendancy which the inscrutable scrivener had over me, and from which ascendancy, for all my chafing, I could not completely escape, I slowly went downstairs and out into the street, and while walking round the block, considered what I should next do in this unheard of perplexity. Turn the man out by an actual thrusting I could not; to drive him away by calling him hard names would not do; calling in the police was an unpleasant idea; and yet, permit him to enjoy his cadaverous triumph over me? — this too I could not think of. What was to be done? or if nothing could be done, was there anything further that I could *assume* in the matter? Yes, as before I had prospectively assumed that Bartleby would depart, so now I might retrospectively assume that departed he was. In the legitimate carrying out of this assumption, I might enter my office in a great hurry, and pretending not to see Bartleby at all, walk straight against him as if he were air. Such a proceeding would in a singular degree have the appearance of a home-thrust. It was hardly possible that Bartleby could withstand such an application of the doctrine of assumptions. But upon second thoughts the success of the plan seemed rather dubious. I resolved to argue the matter over with him again.

"Bartleby," said I, entering the office with a quietly severe expression, "I am seriously displeased. I am pained, Bartleby. I had thought better of you. I had imagined you of such a gentlemanly organization that in my delicate dilemma a slight hint would suffice — in short, an assumption. But it appears I am deceived. Why," I added, unaffectedly starting, "you have not even touched that money yet," pointing to it just where I had left it the evening previous.

He answered nothing.

"Will you, or will you not, quit me?" I now demanded in a sudden passion, advancing close to him.

"I would prefer *not* to quit you," he replied, gently emphasizing the *not*.

"What earthly right have you to stay here? Do you pay any rent? Do you 160 pay my taxes? Or is this property yours?"

He answered nothing.

"Are you ready to go on and write now? Are your eyes recovered? Could you copy a small paper for me this morning? or help examine a few lines? or step round to the post office? In a word, will you do anything at all to give a coloring to your refusal to depart the premises?"

He silently retired into his hermitage.

I was now in such a state of nervous resentment that I thought it but prudent to check myself at present from further demonstrations. Bartleby and I were alone. I remembered the tragedy of the unfortunate Adams and the still more unfortunate Colt° in the solitary office of the latter; and how

---

Colt: In a famous murder case in 1841, John Colt used a hatchet to kill Samuel Adams, who owed him money.

poor Colt, being dreadfully incensed by Adams, and imprudently permitting himself to get wildly excited, was at unawares hurried into his fatal act — an act which certainly no man could possibly deplore more than the actor himself. Often it had occurred to me in my ponderings upon the subject that had that altercation taken place in the public street, or at a private residence, it would not have terminated as it did. It was the circumstance of being alone in a solitary office, upstairs, of a building entirely unhallowed by humanizing domestic associations — an uncarpeted office, doubtless, of a dusty haggard sort of appearance — this it must have been which greatly helped to enhance the irritable desperation of the hapless Colt.

165   But when this old Adam of resentment rose in me and tempted me concerning Bartleby, I grappled him and threw him. How? Why, simply by recalling the divine injunction: "A new commandment° give I unto you, that ye love one another." Yes, this it was that saved me. Aside from higher considerations, charity often operates as a vastly wise and prudent principle — a great safeguard to its possessor. Men have committed murder for jealousy's sake, and anger's sake, and hatred's sake, and selfishness' sake, and spiritual pride's sake; but no man that ever I heard of ever committed a diabolical murder for sweet charity's sake. Mere self-interest, then, if no better motive can be enlisted, should, especially with high-tempered men, prompt all beings to charity and philanthropy. At any rate, upon the occasion in question, I strove to drown my exasperated feelings towards the scrivener by benevolently construing his conduct. Poor fellow, poor fellow! thought I, he don't mean anything; and besides, he has seen hard times, and ought to be indulged.

I endeavored also immediately to occupy myself, and at the same time to comfort my despondency. I tried to fancy that in the course of the morning, at such time as might prove agreeable to him, Bartleby of his own free accord would emerge from his hermitage and take up some decided line of march in the direction of the door. But no. Half-past twelve o'clock came; Turkey began to glow in the face, overturn his inkstand, and become generally obstreperous; Nippers abated down into quietude and courtesy; Ginger Nut munched his noon apple; and Bartleby remained standing at his window in one of his profoundest dead-wall reveries. Will it be credited? Ought I to acknowledge it? That afternoon I left the office without saying one further word to him.

Some days now passed, during which at leisure intervals I looked a little into "Edwards on the Will," and "Priestley on Necessity."° Under the circumstances, those books induced a salutary feeling. Gradually I slid into the persuasion that these troubles of mine touching the scrivener had been all predestinated from eternity, and Bartleby was billeted upon me for some

---

commandment: See John 15.12.   "Edwards . . . Necessity": writings by eighteenth-century philosophers who took the position that free will does not exist

mysterious purpose of an all-wise Providence which it was not for a mere mortal like me to fathom. Yes, Bartleby, stay there behind your screen, thought I; I shall persecute you no more; you are harmless and noiseless as any of these old chairs; in short, I never feel so private as when I know you are here. At least I see it, I feel it; I penetrate to the predestinated purpose of my life. I am content. Others may have loftier parts to enact; but my mission in this world, Bartleby, is to furnish you with office-room for such period as you may see fit to remain.

I believe that this wise and blessed frame of mind would have continued with me had it not been for the unsolicited and uncharitable remarks obtruded upon me by my professional friends who visited the rooms. But thus it often is, that the constant friction of illiberal minds wears out at last the best resolves of the more generous. Though to be sure, when I reflected upon it, it was not strange that people entering my office should be struck by the peculiar aspect of the unaccountable Bartleby, and so be tempted to throw out some sinister observations concerning him. Sometimes an attorney having business with me, and calling at my office, and finding no one but the scrivener there, would undertake to obtain some sort of precise information from him touching my whereabouts; but without heeding his idle talk, Bartleby would remain standing immovable in the middle of the room. So after contemplating him in that position for a time, the attorney would depart, no wiser than he came.

Also, when a reference was going on, and the room full of lawyers and witnesses and business was driving fast, some deeply occupied legal gentleman present seeing Bartleby wholly unemployed would request him to run round to his (the legal gentleman's) office and fetch some papers for him. Thereupon, Bartleby would tranquilly decline, and remain idle as before. Then the lawyer would give a great stare and turn to me. And what could I say? At last I was made aware that all through the circle of my professional acquaintance, a whisper of wonder was running round having reference to the strange creature I kept at my office. This worried me very much. And as the idea came upon me of his possibly turning out a long-lived man, and keep occupying my chambers, and denying my authority, and perplexing my visitors, and scandalizing my professional reputation, and casting a general gloom over the premises, keeping soul and body together to the last upon his savings (for doubtless he spent but half a dime a day), and in the end perhaps outliving me, and claiming possession of my office by right of his perpetual occupancy: as all these dark anticipations crowded upon me more and more, and my friends continually intruded their relentless remarks upon the apparition in my room, a great change was wrought in me. I resolved to gather all my faculties together, and forever rid me of this intolerable incubus.

Ere revolving any complicated project, however, adapted to this end, I first simply suggested to Bartleby the propriety of his permanent departure. In a calm and serious tone, I commended the idea to his careful and mature consideration. But having taken three days to meditate upon it, he apprised

170

me that his original determination remained the same, in short, that he still preferred to abide with me.

What shall I do? I now said to myself, buttoning up my coat to the last button. What shall I do? what ought I to do? what does conscience say I *should* do with this man, or rather ghost? Rid myself of him, I must; go, he shall. But how? You will not thrust him, the poor, pale, passive mortal — you will not thrust such a helpless creature out of your door? you will not dishonor yourself by such cruelty? No, I will not, I cannot do that. Rather would I let him live and die here, and then mason up his remains in the wall. What then will you do? For all your coaxing, he will not budge. Bribes he leaves under your own paperweight on your table; in short, it is quite plain that he prefers to cling to you.

Then something severe, something unusual must be done. What! surely you will not have him collared by a constable, and commit his innocent pallor to the common jail? And upon what ground could you procure such a thing to be done? — a vagrant, is he? What! he a vagrant, a wanderer, who refuses to budge? It is because he will *not* be a vagrant, then, that you seek to count him *as* a vagrant. That is too absurd. No visible means of support: there I have him. Wrong again: for indubitably he *does* support himself, and that is the only unanswerable proof that any man can show of his possessing the means so to do. No more then. Since he will not quit me, I must quit him. I will change my offices; I will move elsewhere, and give him fair notice that if I find him on my new premises I will then proceed against him as a common trespasser.

Acting accordingly, next day I thus addressed him: "I find these chambers too far from the City Hall; the air is unwholesome. In a word, I propose to remove my offices next week, and shall no longer require your services. I tell you this now, in order that you may seek another place."

He made no reply, and nothing more was said.

On the appointed day I engaged carts and men, proceeded to my chambers, and having but little furniture, everything was removed in a few hours. Throughout, the scrivener remained standing behind the screen, which I directed to be removed the last thing. It was withdrawn, and being folded up like a huge folio, left him the motionless occupant of a naked room. I stood in the entry watching him a moment, while something from within me upbraided me.

I re-entered, with my hand in my pocket — and — and my heart in my mouth.

"Good-bye, Bartleby; I am going — good-bye, and God some way bless you; and take that," slipping something in his hand. But it dropped upon the floor, and then — strange to say — I tore myself from him whom I had so longed to be rid of.

Established in my new quarters, for a day or two I kept the door locked, and started at every footfall in the passages. When I returned to my rooms after any little absence, I would pause at the threshold for an instant, and attentively listen ere applying my key. But these fears were needless. Bartleby never came nigh me.

I thought all was going well, when a perturbed looking stranger visited me inquiring whether I was the person who had recently occupied rooms at No. — Wall Street.

Full of forebodings, I replied that I was. 180

"Then sir," said the stranger, who proved a lawyer, "you are responsible for the man you left there. He refuses to do any copying; he refuses to do anything; he says he prefers not to; and he refuses to quit the premises."

"I am very sorry, sir," said I, with assumed tranquility, but an inward tremor, "but, really, the man you allude to is nothing to me — he is no relation or apprentice of mine, that you should hold me responsible for him."

"In mercy's name, who is he?"

"I certainly cannot inform you. I know nothing about him. Formerly I employed him as a copyist, but he has done nothing for me now for some time past."

"I shall settle him then — good morning, sir." 185

Several days passed, and I heard nothing more; and though I often felt a charitable prompting to call at the place and see poor Bartleby, yet a certain squeamishness of I know not what withheld me.

All is over with him by this time, thought I at last, when through another week no further intelligence reached me. But coming to my room the day after, I found several persons waiting at my door in a high state of nervous excitement.

"That's the man — here he comes," cried the foremost one, whom I recognized as the lawyer who had previously called upon me alone.

"You must take him away, sir, at once," cried a portly person among them, advancing upon me, and whom I knew to be the landlord of No. — Wall Street. "These gentlemen, my tenants, cannot stand it any longer; Mr. B — " pointing to the lawyer, "has turned him out of his room, and he now persists in haunting the building generally, sitting upon the banisters of the stairs by day, and sleeping in the entry by night. Everybody is concerned; clients are leaving the offices; some fears are entertained of a mob; something you must do, and that without delay."

Aghast at this torrent, I fell back before it, and would fain have locked 190 myself in my new quarters. In vain I persisted that Bartleby was nothing to me — no more than to anyone else. In vain — I was the last person known to have anything to do with him, and they held me to the terrible account. Fearful then of being exposed in the papers (as one person present obscurely threatened), I considered the matter, and at length said that if the lawyer would give me a confidential interview with the scrivener, in his (the lawyer's) own room, I would that afternoon strive my best to rid them of the nuisance they complained of.

Going upstairs to my old haunt, there was Bartleby silently sitting upon the banister at the landing.

"What are you doing here, Bartleby?" said I.

"Sitting upon the banister," he mildly replied.

I motioned him into the lawyer's room, who then left us.

"Bartleby," said I, "are you aware that you are the cause of great tribulation to me, by persisting in occupying the entry after being dismissed from the office?"

No answer.

"Now one of two things must take place. Either you must do something or something must be done to you. Now what sort of business would you like to engage in? Would you like to re-engage in copying for someone?"

"No; I would prefer not to make any change."

"Would you like a clerkship in a dry-goods store?"

"There is too much confinement about that. No, I would not like a clerkship; but I am not particular."

"Too much confinement," I cried, "why you keep yourself confined all the time!"

"I would prefer not to take a clerkship," he rejoined, as if to settle that little item at once.

"How would a bar-tender's business° suit you? There is no trying of the eyesight in that."

"I would not like it at all; though, as I said before, I am not particular."

His unwonted wordiness inspirited me. I returned to the charge.

"Well then, would you like to travel through the country collecting bills for the merchants? That would improve your health."

"No, I would prefer to be doing something else."

"How then would going as a companion to Europe, to entertain some young gentleman with your conversation — how would that suit you?"

"Not at all. It does not strike me that there is anything definite about that. I like to be stationary. But I am not particular."

"Stationary you shall be then," I cried, now losing all patience, and for the first time in all my exasperating connection with him fairly flying into a passion. "If you do not go away from these premises before night, I shall feel bound — indeed I *am* bound — to — to — to quit the premises myself!" I rather absurdly concluded, knowing not with what possible threat to try to frighten his immobility into compliance. Despairing of all further efforts, I was precipitately leaving him, when a final thought occurred to me — one which had not been wholly unindulged before.

"Bartleby," said I, in the kindest tone I could assume under such exciting circumstances, "will you go home with me now — not to my office, but my dwelling — and remain there till we can conclude upon some convenient arrangement for you at our leisure? Come, let us start now, right away."

"No: at present I would prefer not to make any change at all."

I answered nothing, but effectually dodging everyone by the suddenness and rapidity of my flight, rushed from the building, ran up Wall Street to-

---

bar-tender's business: work as an attendant in a courtroom wards Broadway, and jumping into the first omnibus was soon removed from pursuit. As soon as tranquility returned I distinctly perceived that I had now done all that I possibly could, both in respect to the demands of the landlord and his tenants, and with regard to my own desire and sense of duty, to benefit Bartleby and shield him from rude persecution. I now strove to be entirely carefree and quiescent; and my conscience justified me in the attempt though indeed it was not so successful as I could have wished. So fearful was I of being again hunted out by the incensed landlord and his exasperated tenants that, surrendering my business to Nippers, for a few days I drove about the upper part of the town and through the suburbs in my rockaway; crossed over to Jersey City and Hoboken, and paid fugitive visits to Manhattanville and Astoria. In fact I almost lived in my rockaway for the time.

When again I entered my office, lo, a note from the landlord lay upon the desk. I opened it with trembling hands. It informed me that the writer had sent to the police and had Bartleby removed to the Tombs as a vagrant. Moreover, since I knew more about him than anyone else, he wished me to appear at that place and make a suitable statement of the facts. These tidings had a conflicting effect upon me. At first I was indignant, but at last almost approved. The landlord's energetic, summary disposition had led him to adopt a procedure which I do not think I would have decided upon myself; and yet as a last resort, under such peculiar circumstances, it seemed the only plan.

As I afterwards learned, the poor scrivener, when told that he must be conducted to the Tombs, offered not the slightest obstacle, but in his pale unmoving way, silently acquiesced.

Some of the compassionate and curious bystanders joined the party; and headed by one of the constables arm in arm with Bartleby, the silent procession filed its way through all the noise, and heat, and joy of the roaring thoroughfares at noon.

The same day I received the note I went to the Tombs or, to speak more properly, the Halls of Justice. Seeking the right officer, I stated the purpose of my call, and was informed that the individual I described was indeed within. I then assured the functionary that Bartleby was a perfectly honest man, and greatly to be compassionated, however unaccountably eccentric. I narrated all I knew, and closed by suggesting the idea of letting him remain in as indulgent confinement as possible till something less harsh might be done — though indeed I hardly knew what. At all events, if nothing else could be decided upon, the alms-house must receive him. I then begged to have an interview.

Being under no disgraceful charge, and quite serene and harmless in all his ways, they had permitted him freely to wander about the prison, and especially in the inclosed grass-platted yards thereof. And so I found him there, standing all alone in the quietest of the yards, his face towards a high wall, while all around, from the narrow slits of the jail windows, I thought I saw peering out upon him the eyes of murderers and thieves.

"Bartleby!"

220 "I know you," he said, without looking round — "and I want nothing to say to you."

"It was not I that brought you here, Bartleby," said I, keenly pained at his implied suspicion. "And to you, this should not be so vile a place. Nothing reproachful attaches to you by being here. And see, it is not so sad a place as one might think. Look, there is the sky, and here is the grass."

"I know where I am," he replied, but would say nothing more, and so I left him.

As I entered the corridor again, a broad meat-like man in an apron accosted me, and jerking his thumb over his shoulder said — "Is that your friend?"

"Yes."

225 "Does he want to starve? If he does, let him live on the prison fare, that's all."

"Who are you?" asked I, not knowing what to make of such an unofficially speaking person in such a place.

"I am the grub-man. Such gentlemen as have friends here, hire me to provide them with something good to eat."

"Is this so?" said I, turning to the turnkey.

He said it was.

230 "Well, then," said I, slipping some silver into the grub-man's hands (for so they called him), "I want you to give particular attention to my friend there; let him have the best dinner you can get. And you must be as polite to him as possible."

"Introduce me, will you?" said the grub-man, looking at me with an expression which seemed to say he was all impatience for an opportunity to give a specimen of his breeding.

Thinking it would prove of benefit to the scrivener, I acquiesced, and asking the grub-man his name, went up with him to Bartleby.

"Bartleby, this is a friend; you will find him very useful to you."

"Your sarvant, sir, your sarvant," said the grub-man making a low salutation behind his apron. "Hope you find it pleasant here, sir — spacious grounds — cool apartments, sir — hope you'll stay with us some time — try to make it agreeable. What will you have for dinner today?"

235 "I prefer not to dine today," said Bartleby, turning away. "It would disagree with me; I am unused to dinners." So saying he slowly moved to the other side of the enclosure, and took up a position fronting the dead wall.

"How's this?" said the grub-man, addressing me with a stare of astonishment. "He's odd, ain't he?"

"I think he is a little deranged," said I, sadly.

"Deranged? deranged is it? Well now, upon my word, I thought that friend of yourn was a gentleman forger; they are always pale and genteel-like, them forgers. I can't help pity 'em — can't help it, sir. Did you know Monroe Edwards?" he added touchingly, and paused. Then, laying his hand pityingly on my shoulder, sighed, "he died of consumption at Sing-Sing. So you weren't acquainted with Monroe?"

"No, I was never socially acquainted with any forgers. But I cannot stop longer. Look to my friend yonder. You will not lose by it. I will see you again."

Some few days after this, I again obtained admission to the Tombs, and went through the corridors in quest of Bartleby, but without finding him. 240

"I saw him coming from his cell not long ago," said a turnkey, "maybe he's gone to loiter in the yards."

So I went in that direction.

"Are you looking for the silent man?" said another turnkey passing me. "Yonder he lies—sleeping in the yard there. 'Tis not twenty minutes since I saw him lie down."

The yard was entirely quiet. It was not accessible to the common prisoners. The surrounding walls, of amazing thickness, kept off all sound behind them. The Egyptian character of the masonry weighed upon me with its gloom. But a soft imprisoned turf grew under foot. The heart of the eternal pyramids, it seemed, wherein, by some strange magic, through the clefts, grass-seed dropped by birds had sprung.

Strangely huddled at the base of the wall, his knees drawn up, and lying on his side, his head touching the cold stones, I saw the wasted Bartleby. But nothing stirred. I paused; then went close up to him; stooped over, and saw that his dim eyes were open; otherwise he seemed profoundly sleeping. Something prompted me to touch him. I felt his hand, when a tingling shiver ran up my arm and down my spine to my feet. 245

The round face of the grub-man peered upon me now. "His dinner is ready. Won't he dine today, either? Or does he live without dining?"

"Lives without dining," said I, and closed the eyes.

"Eh!—He's asleep, ain't he?"

"With kings and counselors," murmured I.°

There would seem little need for proceeding further in this history. Imagination will readily supply the meager recital of poor Bartleby's interment. But ere parting with the reader, let me say that if this little narrative has sufficiently interested him to awaken curiosity as to who Bartleby was, and what manner of life he led prior to the present narrator's making his acquaintance, I can only reply that in such curiosity I fully share, but am wholly unable to gratify it. Yet here I hardly know whether I should divulge one little item of rumor which came to my ear a few months after the scrivener's decease. Upon what basis it rested, I could never ascertain; and hence how true it is I cannot now tell. But inasmuch as this vague report has not been without a certain strange suggestive interest to me, however sad, it may prove the same with some others; and so I will briefly mention it. The 250

"With . . . counselors": Job 3.14

report was this: that Bartleby had been a subordinate clerk in the Dead Letter Office at Washington, from which he had been suddenly removed by a change in the administration. When I think over this rumor, I cannot adequately express the emotions which seize me. Dead letters! does it not sound like dead men? Conceive a man by nature and misfortune prone to a pallid hopelessness, can any business seem more fitted to heighten it than that of continually handling these dead letters and assorting them for the flames? For by the cart-load they are annually burned. Sometimes from out the folded paper the pale clerk takes a ring — the finger it was meant for, perhaps, moulders in the grave; a bank note sent in swiftest charity — he whom it would relieve, nor eats nor hungers any more; pardon for those who died despairing; hope for those who died unhoping; good tidings for those who died stifled by unrelieved calamities. On errands of life, these letters speed to death.

Ah, Bartleby! Ah, humanity!

Edgar Allan Poe
The Cask of Amontillado

The thousand injuries of Fortunato I had borne as I best could; but when he ventured upon insult, I vowed revenge. You, who so well know the nature of my soul, will not suppose, however, that I gave utterance to a threat. *At length* I would be avenged; this was a point definitively settled — but the very definitiveness with which it was resolved precluded the idea of risk. I must not only punish, but punish with impunity. A wrong is unredressed when retribution overtakes its redresser. It is equally unredressed when the avenger fails to make himself felt as such to him who has done the wrong.

It must be understood, that neither by word nor deed had I given Fortunato cause to doubt my good will. I continued, as was my wont, to smile in his face, and he did not perceive that my smile *now* was at the thought of his immolation.

He had a weak point — this Fortunato — although in other regards he was a man to be respected and even feared. He prided himself on his connoisseurship in wine. Few Italians have the true virtuoso spirit. For the most part their enthusiasm is adopted to suit the time and opportunity — to prac-

THE CASK OF AMONTILLADO   First published in 1846. Edgar Allan Poe (1809–1849) was one of the first modern practitioners and theorists of the short story as a literary form, prescribing as its highest goal the creation of "a certain unique or single effect." His own achievement best matches his theory in his horror tales, of which this is an example. Poe was born in Boston, abandoned at the age of three by his father after the death of his mother, and raised by adoptive parents in Virginia. As a young man he failed in attempts at education at the University of Virginia and at West Point. Difficulty with alcohol combined with nervous sensitivity led to continuing health problems and his early death. "Amontillado" is a dry Spanish sherry wine; "carnival" is the festive season preceding Lent.

tise imposture upon the British and Austrian *millionaires*. In painting and gemmary Fortunato, like his countrymen, was a quack — but in the matter of old wines he was sincere. In this respect I did not differ from him materially: I was skillful in the Italian vintages myself, and bought largely whenever I could.

It was about dusk, one evening during the supreme madness of the carnival season, that I encountered my friend. He accosted me with excessive warmth, for he had been drinking much. The man wore motley. He had on a tight-fitting parti-striped dress, and his head was surmounted by the conical cap and bells. I was so pleased to see him, that I thought I should never have done wringing his hand.

I said to him — "My dear Fortunato, you are luckily met. How remarkably well you are looking today! But I have received a pipe of what passes for Amontillado, and I have my doubts."

"How?" said he. "Amontillado? A pipe? Impossible! And in the middle of the carnival!"

"I have my doubts," I replied; "and I was silly enough to pay the full Amontillado price without consulting you in the matter. You were not to be found, and I was fearful of losing a bargain."

"Amontillado!"

"I have my doubts."

"Amontillado!"

"And I must satisfy them."

"Amontillado!"

"As you are engaged, I am on my way to Luchesi. If anyone has a critical turn, it is he. He will tell me — "

"Luchesi cannot tell Amontillado from Sherry."

"And yet some fools will have it that his taste is a match for your own."

"Come, let us go."

"Whither?"

"To your vaults."

"My friend, no; I will not impose upon your good nature. I perceive you have an engagement. Luchesi — "

"I have no engagement; — come."

"My friend, no. It is not the engagement, but the severe cold with which I perceive you are afflicted. The vaults are insufferably damp. They are encrusted with niter."

"Let us go, nevertheless. The cold is merely nothing. Amontillado! You have been imposed upon. And as for Luchesi, he cannot distinguish Sherry from Amontillado."

Thus speaking, Fortunato possessed himself of my arm. Putting on a mask of black silk, and drawing a *roquelaire*° closely about my person, I suffered him to hurry me to my palazzo.

roquelaire: a knee-length cloak worn in the eighteenth century

There were no attendants at home; they had absconded to make merry in honor of the time. I had told them that I should not return until the morning, and had given them explicit orders not to stir from the house. These orders were sufficient, I well knew, to insure their immediate disappearance, one and all, as soon as my back was turned.

I took from their sconces two flambeaux, and giving one to Fortunato, bowed him through several suites of rooms to the archway that led into the vaults. I passed down a long and winding staircase, requesting him to be cautious as he followed. We came at length to the foot of the descent, and stood together on the damp ground of the catacombs of the Montresors.

The gait of my friend was unsteady, and the bells upon his cap jingled as he strode.

"The pipe," said he.

"It is farther on," said I; "but observe the white web-work which gleams from these cavern walls."

He turned towards me, and looked into my eyes with two filmy orbs that distilled the rheum of intoxication.

"Niter?" he asked, at length.

"Niter," I replied. "How long have you had that cough?"

"Ugh! ugh! ugh! — ugh! ugh! ugh! — ugh! ugh! ugh! — ugh! ugh! ugh! — ugh! ugh! ugh!"

My poor friend found it impossible to reply for many minutes.

"It is nothing," he said, at last.

"Come," I said, with decision, "we will go back; your health is precious. You are rich, respected, admired, beloved; you are happy, as once I was. You are a man to be missed. For me it is no matter. We will go back; you will be ill, and I cannot be responsible. Beside, there is Luchesi — "

"Enough," he said; "the cough is a mere nothing; it will not kill me. I shall not die of a cough."

"True — true," I replied; "and, indeed, I had no intention of alarming you unnecessarily — but you should use all proper caution. A draught of this Medoc will defend us from the damps."

Here I knocked off the neck of a bottle which I drew from a long row of its fellows that lay upon the mold.

"Drink," I said, presenting him the wine.

He raised it to his lips with a leer. He paused and nodded to me familiarly, while his bells jingled.

"I drink," he said, "to the buried that repose around us."

"And I to your long life."

He again took my arm, and we proceeded.

"These vaults," he said, "are extensive."

"The Montresors," I replied, "were a great and numerous family."

"I forget your arms."

"A huge human foot d'or, in a field azure; the foot crushes a serpent rampant whose fangs are imbedded in the heel."

"And the motto?"

"*Nemo me impune lacessit.*"°

"Good!" he said.

The wine sparkled in his eyes and the bells jingled. My own fancy grew warm with the Medoc. We had passed through walls of piled bones, with casks and puncheons intermingling, into the inmost recesses of the catacombs. I paused again, and this time I made bold to seize Fortunato by an arm above the elbow.

"The niter!" I said; "see, it increases. It hangs like moss upon the vaults. We are below the river's bed. The drops of moisture trickle among the bones. Come, we will go back ere it is too late. Your cough — "

"It is nothing," he said; "let us go on. But first, another draught of the Medoc."

I broke and reached him a flacon of De Grâve. He emptied it at a breath. His eyes flashed with a fierce light. He laughed and threw the bottle upwards with a gesticulation I did not understand.

I looked at him in surprise. He repeated the movement — a grotesque one.

"You do not comprehend?" he said.

"Not I," I replied.

"Then you are not of the brotherhood."

"How?"

"You are not of the masons."

"Yes, yes," I said, "yes, yes."

"You? Impossible! A mason?"

"A mason," I replied.

"A sign," he said.

"It is this," I answered, producing a trowel from beneath the folds of my *roquelaire*.

"You jest," he exclaimed, recoiling a few paces. "But let us proceed to the Amontillado."

"Be it so," I said, replacing the tool beneath the cloak, and again offering him my arm. He leaned upon it heavily. We continued our route in search of the Amontillado. We passed through a range of low arches, descended, passed on, and descending again, arrived at a deep crypt, in which the foulness of the air caused our flambeaux rather to glow than flame.

At the most remote end of the crypt there appeared another less spacious. Its walls had been lined with human remains, piled to the vault overhead, in the fashion of the great catacombs of Paris. Three sides of this interior crypt were still ornamented in this manner. From the fourth the bones had been thrown down, and lay promiscuously upon the earth, forming at one point a mound of some size. Within the wall thus exposed by the displacing of the bones, we perceived a still interior recess, in depth about four feet, in width three, in height six or seven. It seemed to have been

"*Nemo . . . lacessit*": No one can provoke me and get away with it.

constructed for no especial use within itself, but formed merely the interval between two of the colossal supports of the roof of the catacombs, and was backed by one of their circumscribing walls of solid granite.

It was in vain that Fortunato, uplifting his dull torch, endeavored to pry into the depth of the recess. Its termination the feeble light did not enable us to see.

"Proceed," I said; "herein is the Amontillado. As for Luchesi — "

"He is an ignoramus," interrupted my friend, as he stepped unsteadily forward, while I followed immediately at his heels. In an instant he had reached the extremity of the niche, and finding his progress arrested by the rock, stood stupidly bewildered. A moment more and I had fettered him to the granite. In its surface were two iron staples, distant from each other about two feet, horizontally. From one of these depended a short chain, from the other a padlock. Throwing the links about his waist, it was but the work of a few seconds to secure it. He was too much astounded to resist. Withdrawing the key I stepped back from the recess.

"Pass your hand," I said, "over the wall; you cannot help feeling the niter. Indeed it is *very* damp. Once more let me *implore* you to return. No? Then I must positively leave you. But I must first render you all the little attentions in my power."

"The Amontillado!" ejaculated my friend, not yet recovered from his astonishment.

"True," I replied; "the Amontillado."

As I said these words, I busied myself among the pile of bones of which I have before spoken. Throwing them aside, I soon uncovered a quantity of building stone and mortar. With these materials and with the aid of my trowel, I began vigorously to wall up the entrance of the niche.

I had scarcely laid the first tier of the masonry when I discovered that the intoxication of Fortunato had in a great measure worn off. The earliest indication I had of this was a low moaning cry from the depth of the recess. It was *not* the cry of a drunken man. There was then a long and obstinate silence. I laid the second tier, and the third, and the fourth; and then I heard the furious vibrations of the chain. The noise lasted for several minutes, during which, that I might harken to it with the more satisfaction, I ceased my labors and sat down upon the bones. When at last the clanking subsided, I resumed the trowel, and finished without interruption the fifth, the sixth, and the seventh tier. The wall was now nearly upon a level with my breast. I again paused, and holding the flambeaux over the masonwork, threw a few feeble rays upon the figure within.

A succession of loud and shrill screams, bursting suddenly from the throat of the chained form, seemed to thrust me violently back. For a brief moment I hesitated — I trembled. Unsheathing my rapier, I began to grope with it about the recess: but the thought of an instant reassured me. I placed my hand upon the solid fabric of the catacombs, and felt satisfied. I reapproached the wall. I replied to the yells of him who clamored. I re-echoed — I aided — I surpassed them in volume and in strength. I did this, and the clamorer grew still.

It was now midnight, and my task was drawing to a close. I had completed the eighth, the ninth, and the tenth tier. I had finished a portion of the last and the eleventh; there remained but a single stone to be fitted and plastered in. I struggled with its weight; I placed it partially in its destined position. But now there came from out the niche a low laugh that erected the hairs upon my head. It was succeeded by a sad voice, which I had difficulty in recognising as that of the noble Fortunato. The voice said —

"Ha! ha! ha! — he! he! — a very good joke indeed — an excellent jest. We will have many a rich laugh about it at the palazzo — he! he! he! — over our wine — he! he! he!"

"The Amontillado!" I said. 80

"He! he! he! — he! he! he! — yes, the Amontillado. But is it not getting late? Will not they be awaiting us at the palazzo, the Lady Fortunato and the rest? Let us be gone."

"Yes," I said, "let us be gone."

"For the love of God, Montresor!"

"Yes," I said, "for the love of God!"

But to these words I harkened in vain for a reply. I grew impatient. I 85 called aloud —

"Fortunato!"

No answer. I called again —

"Fortunato!"

No answer still. I thrust a torch through the remaining aperture and let it fall within. There came forth in return only a jingling of the bells. My heart grew sick — on account of the dampness of the catacombs. I hastened to make an end of my labor. I forced the last stone into its position; I plastered it up. Against the new masonry I re-erected the old rampart of bones. For the half of a century no mortal has disturbed them. *In pace requiescat!°*

Katherine Anne Porter
The Jilting of Granny Weatherall

She flicked her wrist neatly out of Doctor Harry's pudgy careful fingers and pulled the sheet up to her chin. The brat ought to be in knee breeches. Doctoring around the country with spectacles on his nose! "Get along now, take your schoolbooks and go. There's nothing wrong with me."

THE JILTING OF GRANNY WEATHERALL   First published in 1930. Katherine Anne Porter (1890–1980) was born and grew up in Texas, was educated at convent schools in New Orleans, and lived in Chicago, Fort Worth, Mexico, and New York City before writing this story.

In pace requiescat! May he rest in peace!

Doctor Harry spread a warm paw like a cushion on her forehead where the forked green vein danced and made her eyelids twitch. "Now, now, be a good girl, and we'll have you up in no time."

"That's no way to speak to a woman nearly eighty years old just because she's down. I'd have you respect your elders, young man."

"Well, Missy, excuse me." Doctor Harry patted her cheek. "But I've got to warn you, haven't I? You're a marvel, but you must be careful or you're going to be good and sorry."

"Don't tell me what I'm going to be. I'm on my feet now, morally speaking. It's Cornelia. I had to go to bed to get rid of her."

Her bones felt loose, and floated around in her skin, and Doctor Harry floated like a balloon around the foot of the bed. He floated and pulled down his waistcoat and swung his glasses on a cord. "Well, stay where you are, it certainly can't hurt you."

"Get along and doctor your sick," said Granny Weatherall. "Leave a well woman alone. I'll call for you when I want you. . . . Where were you forty years ago when I pulled through milk-leg and double pneumonia? You weren't even born. Don't let Cornelia lead you on," she shouted, because Doctor Harry appeared to float up to the ceiling and out. "I pay my own bills, and I don't throw my money away on nonsense!"

She meant to wave good-by, but it was too much trouble. Her eyes closed of themselves, it was like a dark curtain drawn around the bed. The pillow rose and floated under her, pleasant as a hammock in a light wind. She listened to the leaves rustling outside the window. No, somebody was swishing newspapers: no, Cornelia and Doctor Harry were whispering together. She leaped broad awake, thinking they whispered in her ear.

"She was never like this, *never* like this!" "Well, what can we expect?" "Yes, eighty years old. . . ."

Well, and what if she was? She still had ears. It was like Cornelia to whisper around doors. She always kept things secret in such a public way. She was always being tactful and kind. Cornelia was dutiful; that was the trouble with her. Dutiful and good: "So good and dutiful," said Granny, "that I'd like to spank her." She saw herself spanking Cornelia and making a fine job of it.

"What'd you say, Mother?"

Granny felt her face tying up in hard knots.

"Can't a body think, I'd like to know?"

"I thought you might want something."

"I do. I want a lot of things. First off, go away and don't whisper."

She lay and drowsed, hoping in her sleep that the children would keep out and let her rest a minute. It had been a long day. Not that she was tired. It was always pleasant to snatch a minute now and then. There was always so much to be done, let me see: tomorrow.

Tomorrow was far away and there was nothing to trouble about. Things were finished somehow when the time came; thank God there was always a little margin over for peace: then a person could spread out the plan of life and tuck in the edges orderly. It was good to have everything clean and folded away, with the hair brushes and tonic bottles sitting straight on the white embroidered linen: the day started without fuss and the pantry shelves laid out with rows of jelly glasses and brown jugs and white stone-china jars with blue whirligigs and words painted on them: coffee, tea, sugar, ginger, cinnamon, allspice: and the bronze clock with the lion on top nicely dusted off. The dust that lion could collect in twenty-four hours! The box in the attic with all those letters tied up, well, she'd have to go through that tomorrow. All those letters — George's letters and John's letters and her letters to them both — lying around for the children to find afterwards made her uneasy. Yes, that would be tomorrow's business. No use to let them know how silly she had been once.

While she was rummaging around she found death in her mind and it felt clammy and unfamiliar. She had spent so much time preparing for death there was no need for bringing it up again. Let it take care of itself now. When she was sixty she had felt very old, finished, and went around making farewell trips to see her children and grandchildren, with a secret in her mind: This is the very last of your mother, children! Then she made her will and came down with a long fever. That was all just a notion like a lot of other things, but it was lucky too, for she had once for all got over the idea of dying for a long time. Now she couldn't be worried. She hoped she had better sense now. Her father had lived to be one hundred and two years old and had drunk a noggin of strong hot toddy on his last birthday. He told the reporters it was his daily habit, and he owed his long life to that. He had made quite a scandal and was very pleased about it. She believed she'd just plague Cornelia a little.

"Cornelia! Cornelia!" No footsteps, but a sudden hand on her cheek. "Bless you, where have you been?"

"Here, Mother."   20

"Well, Cornelia, I want a noggin of hot toddy."

"Are you cold, darling?"

"I'm chilly, Cornelia. Lying in bed stops the circulation. I must have told you that a thousand times."

Well, she could just hear Cornelia telling her husband that Mother was getting a little childish and they'd have to humor her. The thing that most annoyed her was that Cornelia thought she was deaf, dumb, and blind. Little hasty glances and tiny gestures tossed around her and over her head saying, "Don't cross her, let her have her way, she's eighty years old," and she sitting there as if she lived in a thin glass cage. Sometimes Granny almost made up her mind to pack up and move back to her own house where nobody could remind her every minute that she was old. Wait, wait, Cornelia, till your own children whisper behind your back!

In her day she had kept a better house and had got more work done. She   25 wasn't too old yet for Lydia to be driving eighty miles for advice when one of the children jumped the track, and Jimmy still dropped in and talked things over: "Now, Mammy, you've a good business head, I want to know what you think of this? . . ." Old. Cornelia couldn't change the furniture around without asking. Little things, little things! They had been so sweet when they were little. Granny wished the old days were back again with the children young and everything to be done over. It had been a hard pull, but not too much for her. When she thought of all the food she had cooked, and all the clothes she had cut and sewed, and all the gardens she had made — well, the children showed it. There they were, made out of her, and they couldn't get away from that. Sometimes she wanted to see John again and point to them and say, Well, I didn't do so badly, did I? But that would have to wait. That was for tomorrow. She used to think of him as a man, but now all the children were older than their father, and he would be a child beside her if she saw him now. It seemed strange and there was something wrong in the idea. Why, he couldn't possibly recognize her. She had fenced in a hundred acres once, digging the post holes herself and clamping the wires with just a negro boy to help. That changed a woman. John would be looking for a young woman with the peaked Spanish comb in her hair and the painted fan. Digging post holes changed a woman. Riding country roads in the winter when women had their babies was another thing: sitting up nights with sick horses and sick negroes and sick children and hardly ever losing one. John, I hardly ever lost one of them! John would see that in a minute, that would be something he could understand, she wouldn't have to explain anything!

It made her feel like rolling up her sleeves and putting the whole place to rights again. No matter if Cornelia was determined to be everywhere at once, there were a great many things left undone on this place. She would start tomorrow and do them. It was good to be strong enough for everything, even if all you made melted and changed and slipped under your hands, so that by the time you finished you almost forgot what you were working for. What was it I set out to do? she asked herself intently, but she could not remember. A fog rose over the valley, she saw it marching across the creek swallowing the trees and moving up the hill like an army of ghosts. Soon it would be at the near edge of the orchard, and then it was time to go in and light the lamps. Come in, children, don't stay out in the night air.

Lighting the lamps had been beautiful. The children huddled up to her and breathed like little calves waiting at the bars in the twilight. Their eyes followed the match and watched the flame rise and settle in a blue curve, then they moved away from her. The lamp was lit, they didn't have to be scared and hang on to mother any more. Never, never, never more. God, for all my life I thank Thee. Without Thee, my God, I could never have done it. Hail, Mary, full of grace.

I want you to pick all the fruit this year and see that nothing is wasted. There's always someone who can use it. Don't let good things rot for want of using. You waste life when you waste good food. Don't let things get lost. It's bitter to lose things. Now, don't let me get to thinking, not when I am tired and taking a little nap before supper. . . .

The pillow rose about her shoulders and pressed against her heart and the memory was being squeezed out of it: oh, push down the pillow, some-body: it would smother her if she tried to hold it. Such a fresh breeze blow-ing and such a green day with no threats in it. But he had not come, just the same. What does a woman do when she has put on the white veil and set out the white cake for a man and he doesn't come? She tried to remember. No, I swear he never harmed me but in that. He never harmed me but in that . . . and what if he did? There was the day, the day, but a whirl of dark smoke rose and covered it, crept up and over into the bright field where everything was planted so carefully in orderly rows. That was hell, she knew hell when she saw it. For sixty years she had prayed against remembering him and against losing her soul in the deep pit of hell, and now the two things were mingled in one and the thought of him was a smoky cloud from hell that moved and crept in her head when she had just got rid of Doctor Harry and was trying to rest a minute. Wounded vanity, Ellen, said a sharp voice in the top of her mind. Don't let your wounded vanity get the upper hand of you. Plenty of girls get jilted. You were jilted, weren't you? Then stand up to it. Her eyelids wavered and let in streamers of blue-gray light like tissue paper over her eyes. She must get up and pull the shades down or she'd never sleep. She was in bed again and the shades were not down. How could that happen? Better turn over, hide from the light, sleeping in the light gave you night-mares. "Mother, how do you feel now?" and a stinging wetness on her fore-head. But I don't like having my face washed in cold water!

Hapsy? George? Lydia? Jimmy? No, Cornelia, and her features were swollen and full of little puddles. "They're coming, darling, they'll all be here soon." Go wash your face, child, you look funny.

Instead of obeying, Cornelia knelt down and put her head on the pillow. She seemed to be talking but there was no sound. "Well, are you tongue-tied? Whose birthday is it? Are you going to give a party?"

Cornelia's mouth moved urgently in strange shapes. "Don't do that, you bother me, daughter."

"Oh, no, Mother. Oh, no. . . ."

Nonsense. It was strange about children. They disputed your every word. "No what, Cornelia?"

"Here's Doctor Harry."

"I won't see that boy again. He just left five minutes ago."

"That was this morning, Mother. It's night now. Here's the nurse."

"This is Doctor Harry, Mrs. Weatherall. I never saw you look so young and happy!"

"Ah, I'll never be young again — but I'd be happy if they'd let me lie in peace and get rested."

She thought she spoke up loudly, but no one answered. A warm weight on her forehead, a warm bracelet on her wrist, and a breeze went on whisper-ing, trying to tell her something. A shuffle of leaves in the everlasting hand of God, He blew on them and they danced and rattled. "Mother, don't mind, we're going to give you a little hypodermic." "Look here, daughter, how do ants get in this bed? I saw sugar ants yesterday." Did you send for Hapsy too?

It was Hapsy she really wanted. She had to go a long way back through a great many rooms to find Hapsy standing with a baby on her arm. She seemed to herself to be Hapsy also, and the baby on Hapsy's arm was Hapsy and himself and herself, all at once, and there was no surprise in the meeting. Then Hapsy melted from within and turned flimsy as gray gauze and the baby was a gauzy shadow, and Hapsy came up close and said, "I thought you'd never come," and looked at her very searchingly and said, "You haven't changed a bit!" They leaned forward to kiss, when Cornelia began whispering from a long way off, "Oh, is there anything you want to tell me? Is there anything I can do for you?"

Yes, she had changed her mind after sixty years and she would like to see George. I want you to find George. Find him and be sure to tell him I forgot him. I want him to know I had my husband just the same and my children and my house like any other woman. A good house too and a good husband that I loved and fine children out of him. Better than I hoped for even. Tell him I was given back everything he took away and more. Oh, no, oh, God, no, there was something else besides the house and the man and the children. Oh, surely they were not all? What was it? Something not given back. . . . Her breath crowded down under her ribs and grew into a monstrous frightening shape with cutting edges; it bored up into her head, and the agony was unbelievable: Yes, John, get the Doctor now, no more talk, my time has come.

When this one was born it should be the last. The last. It should have been born first, for it was the one she had truly wanted. Everything came in good time. Nothing left out, left over. She was strong, in three days she would be as well as ever. Better. A woman needed milk in her to have her full health.

"Mother, do you hear me?"

"I've been telling you — "

"Mother, Father Connolly's here."

"I went to Holy Communion only last week. Tell him I'm not so sinful as all that."

"Father just wants to speak to you."

He could speak as much as he pleased. It was like him to drop in and inquire about her soul as if it were a teething baby, and then stay on for a cup of tea and a round of cards and gossip. He always had a funny story of some sort, usually about an Irishman who made his little mistakes and confessed them, and the point lay in some absurd thing he would blurt out in the confessional showing his struggles between native piety and original sin. Granny felt easy about her soul. Cornelia, where are your manners? Give Father Connolly a chair. She had her secret comfortable understanding with a few favorite saints who cleared a straight road to God for her. All as surely signed and sealed as the papers for the new Forty Acres. Forever . . . heirs and assigns forever. Since the day the wedding cake was not cut, but thrown out and wasted. The whole bottom dropped out of the world, and there she was blind and sweating with nothing under her feet and the walls falling away. His hand had caught her under the breast, she had not fallen, there was the freshly polished floor with the green rug on it, just as before. He had cursed like a sailor's parrot and said, "I'll kill him for you." Don't lay a hand on him, for my sake leave something to God. "Now, Ellen, you must believe what I tell you. . . ."

So there was nothing, nothing to worry about any more, except some- 50
times in the night one of the children screamed in a nightmare, and they both hustled out shaking and hunting for the matches and calling, "There, wait a minute, here we are!" John, get the doctor now, Hapsy's time has come. But there was Hapsy standing by the bed in a white cap. "Cornelia, tell Hapsy to take off her cap. I can't see her plain."

Her eyes opened very wide and the room stood out like a picture she had seen somewhere. Dark colors with the shadows rising towards the ceiling in long angles. The tall black dresser gleamed with nothing on it but John's picture, enlarged from a little one, with John's eyes very black when they should have been blue. You never saw him, so how do you know how he looked? But the man insisted the copy was perfect, it was very rich and handsome. For a picture, yes, but it's not my husband. The table by the bed had a linen cover and a candle and a crucifix. The light was blue from Cornelia's silk lampshades. No sort of light at all, just frippery. You had to live forty years with kerosene lamps to appreciate honest electricity. She felt very strong and she saw Doctor Harry with a rosy nimbus around him.

"You look like a saint, Doctor Harry, and I vow that's as near as you'll ever come to it."

"She's saying something."

"I heard you, Cornelia. What's all this carrying-on?"

"Father Connolly's saying—" 55

Cornelia's voice staggered and bumped like a cart in a bad road. It rounded corners and turned back again and arrived nowhere. Granny stepped up in the cart very lightly and reached for the reins, but a man sat beside her and she knew him by his hands, driving the cart. She did not look in his face, for she knew without seeing, but looked instead down the road where the trees leaned over and bowed to each other and a thousand birds were singing a Mass. She felt like singing too, but she put her hand in the bosom of her dress and pulled out a rosary, and Father Connolly murmured Latin in a very solemn voice and tickled her feet. My God, will you stop that nonsense? I'm a married woman. What if he did run away and leave me to face the priest by myself? I found another a whole world better. I wouldn't have exchanged my husband for anybody except St. Michael himself, and you may tell him that for me with a thank you in the bargain.

Light flashed on her closed eyelids, and a deep roaring shook her. Cornelia, is that lightning? I hear thunder. There's going to be a storm. Close all the windows. Call the children in. . . . "Mother, here we are, all of us." "Is that you, Hapsy?" "Oh, no, I'm Lydia. We drove as fast as we could." Their faces drifted above her, drifted away. The rosary fell out of her hands and Lydia put it back. Jimmy tried to help, their hands fumbled together, and Granny closed two fingers around Jimmy's thumb. Beads wouldn't do, it must be something alive. She was so amazed her thoughts ran round and round. So, my dear Lord, this is my death and I wasn't even thinking about it. My children have come to see me die. But I can't, it's not time. Oh, I always hated surprises. I wanted to give Cornelia the amethyst set — Cornelia, you're to have the amethyst set, but Hapsy's to wear it when she wants, and, Doctor Harry, do shut up. Nobody sent for you. Oh, my dear Lord, do wait a minute. I meant to do something about the Forty Acres, Jimmy doesn't need it and Lydia will later on, with that worthless husband of hers. I meant to finish the altar cloth and send six bottles of wine to Sister Borgia for her dyspepsia. I want to send six bottles of wine to Sister Borgia, Father Connolly, now don't let me forget.

Cornelia's voice made short turns and tilted over and crashed. "Oh, Mother, oh, Mother, oh, Mother. . . ."

"I'm not going, Cornelia. I'm taken by surprise. I can't go."

You'll see Hapsy again. What about her? "I thought you'd never come." Granny made a long journey outward, looking for Hapsy. What if I don't find her? What then? Her heart sank down and down, there was no bottom to death, she couldn't come to the end of it. The blue light from Cornelia's lampshade drew into a tiny point in the center of her brain, it flickered and winked like an eye, quietly it fluttered and dwindled. Granny lay curled down within herself, amazed and watchful, staring at the point of light that was herself; her body was now only a deeper mass of shadow in an endless darkness and this darkness would curl around the light and swallow it up. God, give a sign!

For the second time there was no sign. Again no bridegroom and the priest in the house. She could not remember any other sorrow because this grief wiped them all away. Oh, no, there's nothing more cruel than this — I'll never forgive it. She stretched herself with a deep breath and blew out the light.

Jean Rhys
Pioneers, Oh, Pioneers

As the two girls were walking up yellow-hot Market Street, Irene nudged her sister and said: "Look at her!" They were not far from the market, they could still smell the fish.

PIONEERS, OH, PIONEERS   First published in 1969. Ella Gwendolen Rees Williams (1890–1979), who wrote under the name of Jean Rhys, was born of Welsh descent in Dominica, then part of the British West Indies. She went to England in 1907, and lived there and on the continent. She published several books in the 1920s and '30s, and nothing further until 1966. This story, recalling life in colonial Dominica, is from her last collection of stories.

When Rosalie turned her head the few white women she saw carried parasols. The black women were barefooted, wore gaily striped turbans and highwaisted dresses. It was still the nineteenth century, November 1899.

"There she goes," said Irene.

And there was Mrs. Menzies, riding up to her house on the Morne for a cool weekend.

"Good morning," Rosalie said, but Mrs. Menzies did not answer. She 5 rode past, clip-clop, clip-clop, in her thick, dark riding habit brought from England ten years before, balancing a large dripping parcel wrapped in flannel on her knee.

"It's ice. She wants her drinks cold," said Rosalie.

"Why can't she have it sent up like everybody else? The black people laugh at her. She ought to be ashamed of herself."

"I don't see why," Rosalie said obstinately.

"Oh, you," Irene jeered. "You like crazy people. You like Jimmy Longa and you like old maman Menzies. You liked Ramage, nasty beastly horrible Ramage."

Rosalie said: "You cried about him yesterday." 10

"Yesterday doesn't count. Mother says we were all hysterical yesterday."

By this time they were nearly home so Rosalie said nothing. But she put her tongue out as they went up the steps into the long, cool gallery.

Their father, Dr. Cox, was sitting in an armchair with a three-legged table by his side.

On the table were his pipe, his tin of tobacco and his glasses. Also *The Times* weekly edition, the *Cornhill Magazine*, the *Lancet* and a West Indian newspaper, the *Dominica Herald and Leeward Islands Gazette*.

He was not to be spoken to, as they saw at once though one was only 15 eleven and the other nine.

"Dead as a door nail," he muttered as they went past him into the next room so comfortably full of rocking chairs, a mahogany table, palm leaf fans, a tigerskin rug, family photographs, views of Betws-y-Coed° and a large picture of wounded soldiers in the snow, Napoleon's Retreat from Moscow.

The doctor had noticed his daughters, for he too was thinking about Mr. Ramage. He had liked the man, stuck up for him, laughed off his obvious eccentricities, denied point blank that he was certifiable. All wrong. Ramage, probably a lunatic, was now dead as a door nail. Nothing to be done.

Ramage had first arrived in the island two years before, a handsome man in tropical kit, white suit, red cummerbund, solar topee. After he grew tired of being followed about by an admiring crowd of little Negro boys he stopped wearing the red sash and the solar topee but he clung to his white suits though most of the men wore dark trousers even when the temperature was ninety in the shade.

Betws-y-Coed: town in Wales

Miss Lambton, who had been a fellow passenger from Barbados, reported that he was certainly a gentleman and also a king among men when it came to looks. But he was very unsociable. He ignored all invitations to dances, tennis parties and moonlight picnics. He never went to church and was not to be seen at the club. He seemed to like Dr. Cox, however, and dined with him one evening. And Rosalie, then aged seven, fell in love.

After dinner, though the children were not supposed to talk much when guests were there, and were usually not allowed downstairs at all, she edged up to him and said: "Sing something." (People who came to dinner often sang afterwards, as she well knew.)

"I can't sing," said Ramage.

"Yes you can." Her mother's disapproving expression made her insist the more. "You can. You can."

He laughed and hoisted her on to his knee. With her head against his chest she listened while he rumbled gently: "Baa baa black sheep, have you any wool? Yes sir, yes sir, three bags full."

Then the gun at the fort fired for nine o'clock and the girls, smug in their stiff white dresses, had to say good night nicely and go upstairs to bed.

After a perfunctory rubber of whist with a dummy, Mrs. Cox also departed. Over his whiskey and soda Ramage explained that he'd come to the island with the intention of buying an estate. "Small, and as remote as possible."

"That won't be difficult here."

"So I heard," said Ramage.

"Tried any of the other islands?"

"I went to Barbados first."

"Little England," the doctor said. "Well?"

"I was told that there were several places going along this new Imperial Road you've got here."

"Won't last," Dr. Cox said. "Nothing lasts in this island. Nothing will come of it. You'll see."

Ramage looked puzzled.

"It's all a matter of what you want the place for," the doctor said without explaining himself. "Are you after a good interest on your capital or what?"

"Peace," Ramage said. "Peace, that's what I'm after."

"You'll have to pay for that," the doctor said.

"What's the price?" said Ramage, smiling. He put one leg over the other. His bare ankle was hairy and thin, his hands long and slender for such a big man.

"You'll be very much alone."

"That will suit me," Ramage said.

"And if you're far along the road, you'll have to cut the trees down, burn the stumps and start from scratch."

"Isn't there a half-way house?" Ramage said.

The doctor answered rather vaguely: "You might be able to get hold of one of the older places."

He was thinking of young Errington, of young Kellaway, who had both bought estates along the Imperial Road and worked hard. But they had given up after a year or two, sold their land cheap and gone back to England. They could not stand the loneliness and melancholy of the forest.

A fortnight afterwards Miss Lambton told Mrs. Cox that Mr. Ramage had bought Spanish Castle, the last but one of the older properties. It was beautiful but not prosperous — some said bad luck, others bad management. His nearest neighbor was Mr. Eliot, who owned *Malgré Tout*. Now called Twickenham.

For several months after this Ramage disappeared and one afternoon at croquet Mrs. Cox asked Miss Lambton if she had any news of him.   45

"A strange man," she said, "very reserved."

"Not so reserved as all that," said Miss Lambton. "He got married several weeks ago. He told me that he didn't want it talked about."

"No!" said Mrs. Cox. "Who to?"

Then it all came out. Ramage had married a colored girl who called herself Isla Harrison, though she had no right to the name of Harrison. Her mother was dead and she'd been brought up by her godmother, old Miss Myra, according to local custom. Miss Myra kept a sweet shop in Bay Street and Isla was very well known in the town — too well known.

"He took her to Trinidad," said Miss Lambton mournfully, "and when they came back they were married. They went down to Spanish Castle and I've heard nothing about them since."   50

"It's not as though she was a nice colored girl," everybody said.

So the Ramages were lost to white society. Lost to everyone but Dr. Cox. Spanish Castle estate was in a district which he visited every month, and one afternoon as he was driving past he saw Ramage standing near his letter box which was nailed to a tree visible from the road. He waved. Ramage waved back and beckoned.

While they were drinking punch on the veranda, Mrs. Ramage came in. She was dressed up to the nines, smelt very strongly of cheap scent and talked loudly in an aggressive voice. No, she certainly wasn't a nice colored girl.

The doctor tried — too hard perhaps — for the next time he called at Spanish Castle a door banged loudly inside the house and a grinning boy told him that Mr. Ramage was out.

"And Mrs. Ramage?"   55

"The mistress is not at home."

At the end of the path the doctor looked back and saw her at a window peering at him.

He shook his head, but he never went there again, and the Ramage couple sank out of sight, out of mind.

It was Mr. Eliot, the owner of Twickenham, who started the trouble. He was out with his wife, he related, looking at some young nutmeg trees near the boundary. They had a boy with them who had lighted a fire and put on water for tea. They looked up and saw Ramage coming out from under the trees. He was burnt a deep brown, his hair fell to his shoulders, his beard to his chest. He was wearing sandals and a leather belt, on one side of which hung a cutlass, on the other a large pouch. Nothing else.

60   "If," said Mr. Eliot, "the man had apologized to my wife, if he'd shown the slightest consciousness of the fact that he was stark naked, I would have overlooked the whole thing. God knows one learned to be tolerant in this wretched place. But not a bit of it. He stared hard at her and came out with: 'What an uncomfortable dress — and how ugly!' My wife got very red. Then she said: 'Mr. Ramage, the kettle is just boiling. Will you have some tea?'"

"Good for her," said the doctor. "What did he say to that?"

"Well, he seemed rather confused. He bowed from the waist, exactly as if he had clothes on, and explained that he never drank tea. 'I have a stupid habit of talking to myself. I beg your pardon,' he said, and off he went. We got home and my wife locked herself in the bedroom. When she came out she wouldn't speak to me at first, then she said that he was quite right, I didn't care what she looked like, so now she didn't either. She called me a mean man. A mean man. I won't have it," said Mr. Eliot indignantly. "He's mad, walking about with a cutlass. He's dangerous."

"Oh, I don't think so," said Dr. Cox. "He'd probably left his clothes round the corner and didn't know how to explain. Perhaps we do cover ourselves up too much. The sun can be good for you. The best thing in the world. If you'd seen as I have . . ."

Mr. Eliot interrupted at once. He knew that when the doctor started talking about his unorthodox methods he went on for a long time.

65   "I don't know about all that. But I may as well tell you that I dislike the idea of a naked man with a cutlass wandering about near my place. I dislike it very much indeed. I've got to consider my wife and my daughter. Something ought to be done."

Eliot told his story to everyone who'd listen and the Ramages became the chief topic of conversation.

"It seems," Mrs. Cox told her husband, "that he does wear a pair of trousers as a rule and even an old coat when it rains, but several people have watched him lying in a hammock on the veranda naked. You ought to call there and speak to him. They say," she added, "that the two of them fight like Kilkenny cats. He's making himself very unpopular."

So the next time he visited the district Dr. Cox stopped near Spanish Castle. As he went up the garden path he noticed how unkempt and deserted the place looked. The grass on the lawn had grown very high and the veranda hadn't been swept for days.

The doctor paused uncertainly, then tapped on the sitting-room door, which was open. "Hallo," called Ramage from inside the house, and he appeared, smiling. He was wearing one of his linen suits, clean and pressed, and his hair and beard were trimmed.

70   "You're looking very well," the doctor said.

"Oh, yes, I feel splendid. Sit down and I'll get you a drink."

There seemed to be no one else in the house.

"The servants have all walked out," Ramage explained when he appeared with the punch.

"Good Lord, have they?"

"Yes, but I think I've found an old woman in the village who'll come up and cook."

"And how is Mrs. Ramage?"

At this moment there was a heavy thud on the side of the house, then another, then another.

"What was that?" asked Dr. Cox.

"Somebody throwing stones. They do sometimes."

"Why, in heaven's name?"

"I don't know. Ask them."

Then the doctor repeated Eliot's story, but in spite of himself it came out as trivial, even jocular.

"Yes, I was very sorry about that," Ramage answered casually. "They startled me as much as I startled them. I wasn't expecting to see anyone. It was a bit of bad luck but it won't happen again."

"It was bad luck meeting Eliot," the doctor said.

And that was the end of it. When he got up to go, no advice, no warning had been given.

"You're sure you're all right here?"

"Yes, of course," said Ramage.

"It's all rubbish," the doctor told his wife that evening. "The man's as fit as a fiddle, nothing wrong with him at all."

"Was Mrs. Ramage there?"

"No, thank God. She was out."

"I heard this morning," said Mrs. Cox, "that she disappeared. Hasn't been seen for weeks."

The doctor laughed heartily. "Why can't they leave those two alone? What rubbish!"

"Well," said Mrs. Cox without smiling, "it's odd, isn't it?"

"Rubbish," the doctor said again some days later, for, spurred on by Mr. Eliot, people were talking venomously and he could not stop them. Mrs. Ramage was not at Spanish Castle, she was not in the town. Where was she?

Old Myra was questioned. She said that she had not seen her goddaughter and had not heard from her "since long time." The Inspector of Police had two anonymous letters — the first writer claimed to know "all what happen at Spanish Castle one night"; the other said that witnesses were frightened to come forward and speak against a white man.

The *Gazette* published a fiery article:

> The so-called 'Imperial Road' was meant to attract young Englishmen with capital who would buy and develop properties in the interior. This costly experiment has not been a success, and one of

the last of these gentlemen planters has seen himself as the king of the cannibal islands ever since he landed. We have it, on the best authority, that his very eccentric behavior has been the greatest possible annoyance to his neighbor. Now the whole thing has become much more serious. . . .

It ended: "Black people bear much; must they also bear beastly murder and nothing be done about it?"

"You don't suppose that I believe all these lies, do you?" Dr. Cox told Mr. Eliot, and Mr. Eliot answered: "Then I'll make it my business to find out the truth. That man is a menace, as I said from the first, and he should be dealt with."

"Dear Ramage," Dr. Cox wrote. "I'm sorry to tell you that stupid and harmful rumors are being spread about your wife and yourself. I need hardly say that no one with a grain of sense takes them seriously, but people here are excitable and very ready to believe mischiefmakers, so I strongly advise you to put a stop to the talk at once and to take legal action if necessary."

But the doctor got no answer to this letter, for in the morning news reached the town of a riot at Spanish Castle the night before.

A crowd of young men and boys, and a few women, had gone up to Ramage's house to throw stones. It was a bright moonlight night. He had come on to the veranda and stood there facing them. He was dressed in white and looked very tall, they said, like a zombie. He said something that nobody heard, a man had shouted "white zombie" and thrown a stone which hit him. He went into the house and came out with a shotgun. Then stories differed wildly. He had fired and hit a woman in the front of the crowd. . . . No, he'd hit a little boy at the back. . . . He hadn't fired at all, but had threatened them. It was agreed that in the rush to get away people had been knocked down and hurt, one woman seriously.

It was also rumored that men and boys from the village planned to burn down Spanish Castle house, if possible with Ramage inside. After this there was no more hesitation. The next day a procession walked up the garden path to the house — the Inspector of Police, three policemen and Dr. Cox.

"He must give some explanation of all this," said the Inspector.

The doors and windows were all open, and they found Ramage and the shotgun, but they got no explanation. He had been dead for some hours.

His funeral was an impressive sight. A good many came out of curiosity, a good many because, though his death was said to be "an accident," they felt guilty. For behind the coffin walked Mrs. Ramage, sent for post-haste by old Myra. She'd been staying with relatives in Guadeloupe. When asked why she had left so secretly — she had taken a fishing boat from the other side of the island — she answered sullenly that she didn't want anyone to know her business, and she knew how people talked. No, she'd heard no rumors about her husband, and the *Gazette* — a paper written in English — was not read in Guadeloupe.

"Eh-eh," echoed Myra. "Since when the girl obliged to tell everybody where she go and what she do chapter and verse. . . ."

It was lovely weather, and on their way to the Anglican cemetery many had tears in their eyes.

But already public opinion was turning against Ramage.

"His death was really a blessing in disguise," said one lady. "He was evidently mad, poor man — sitting in the sun with no clothes on — much worse might have happened." 110

"This is All Souls Day," Rosalie thought, standing at her bedroom window before going to sleep. She was wishing that Mr. Ramage could have been buried in the Catholic cemetery, where all day the candles burnt almost invisible in the sunlight. When night came they twinkled like fireflies. The graves were covered with flowers — some real, some red or yellow paper or little gold cut-outs. Sometimes there was a letter weighted by a stone and the black people said that next morning the letters had gone. And where? Who would steal letters on the night of the dead? But the letters had gone.

The Anglican cemetery, which was not very far away, down the hill, was deserted and silent. Protestants believed that when you were dead, you were dead.

If he had a letter . . . she thought.

"My dear darling Mr. Ramage," she wrote, then felt so sad that she began to cry.

Two hours later Mrs. Cox came into the room and found her daughter in bed and asleep; on the table by her side was the unfinished letter. Mrs. Cox read it, frowned, pressed her lips together, then crumpled it up and threw it out of the window. 115

There was a stiff breeze and she watched it bouncing purposefully down the street. As if it knew exactly where it was going.

Leslie Marmon Silko
Private Property

All Pueblo Tribes have stories about such a person — a young child, an orphan. Someone has taken the child and has given it a place by the fire to sleep. The child's clothes are whatever the people no longer want. The child empties the ashes and gathers wood. The child is always quiet, sitting in its place tending the fire. They pay little attention to the child as they complain and tell stories about one another. The child listens although it has nothing

PRIVATE PROPERTY   First published in 1989. Leslie Marmon Silko was born in 1948 in Albuquerque and raised on the Laguna Pueblo Reservation fifty miles away. She earned a B.A. at the University of New Mexico, taught for two years at the Navajo Community College in Arizona, and then spent another two years in Ketchikan, Alaska, writing and doing research on the Eskimo-Aleut culture. She now teaches at the University of Arizona.

to gain or lose in anything they say. The child simply listens. Some years go by and great danger stalks the village — in some versions of the story it is a drought and great famine, other times it is a monster in the form of a giant bear. And when all the others have failed and even the priests doubt the prayers, this child, still wearing old clothes, goes out. The child confronts the danger and the village is saved. Among the Pueblo people the child's reliability as a narrator is believed to be perfect.

Etta works with the wind at her back. Sand and dust roll down the road. She feels scattered drops of rain and sometimes flakes of snow. What they have been saying about her all these years is untrue. They are angry because she left. Old leaves and weed stalks lie in gray drifts at the corners of the old fence. Part of an old newspaper is caught in the tumbleweeds; the wind presses it into brittle yellow flakes. She rakes the debris as high as her belly. They continue with stories about her. Going away has changed her. Living with white people has changed her. Fragments of glass blink like animal eyes. The wind pushes the flames deep into the bones and old manure heaped under the pile of dry weeds. The rake drags out a shriveled work shoe and then the sleeve torn from a child's dress. They burn as dark and thick as hair. The wind pushes her off balance. Flames pour around her and catch the salt bushes. The yard burns bare. The sky is the color of stray smoke. The next morning the wind is gone. The ground is crusted with frost and still the blackened bones smolder.

The horses trot past the house before dawn. The sky and earth are the same color then — dense gray of the night burned down. At the approach of the sun, the east horizon bleeds dark blue. Reyna sits up in her bed suddenly and looks out the window at the horses. She has been dreaming she was stolen by Navajos and was taken away in their wagon. The sound of the horses' hooves outside the window had been the wagon horses of her dreams. The white one trots in the lead, followed by the gray. The little sorrel mare is always last. The gray sneezes at their dust. They are headed for the river. Reyna wants to remember this, and gets up. The sky is milky. Village dogs are barking in the distance. She dresses and finds her black wool cardigan. The dawn air smells like rain but it has been weeks since the last storm. The crickets don't feel the light. The mockingbird is in the pear tree. The bare adobe yard is swept clean. A distance north of the pear tree there is an old wire fence caught on gray cedar posts that lean in different directions. Etta has come back after many years to live in the little stone house.

The sound of the hammer had been Reyna's first warning. She blames herself for leaving the old fence posts and wire. The fence should have been torn down years ago. The old wire had lain half-buried in the sand that had drifted around the posts. Etta was wearing men's gloves that were too large for her. She pulled the strands of wire up and hammered fence staples to hold the wire to the posts. Etta has made the fence the boundary line. She has planted morning glories and hollyhocks all along it. She waters them every morning before it gets hot. Reyna watches her. The morning glories and hollyhocks are all that hold up the fence posts anymore.

Etta is watching Reyna from the kitchen window of the little stone house. She fills the coffee pot without looking at the level of water. Reyna is walking the fence between their yards. She paces the length of the fence as if she can pull the fence down with her walking. They had been married to brothers, but the men died long ago. They don't call each other "sister-in-law" anymore. The fire in the cookstove is cracking like rifle shots. She bought a pickup load of piñon wood from a Navajo. The little house has one room, but the walls are rock and adobe mortar two feet thick. The one who got the big house got the smaller yard. That is how Etta remembers it. Their mother-in-law had been a kind woman. She wanted her sons and daughters-in-law to live happily with each other. She followed the old ways. She believed houses and fields must always be held by the women. There had been no nieces or daughters. The old woman stood by the pear tree with the daughters-in-law and gave them each a house, and the yard to divide. She pointed at the little stone house. She said the one who got the little house got the bigger share of the yard. Etta remembers that.

Cheromiah drives up in his white Ford pick-up. He walks to the gate smiling. He wears his big belly over his Levi's like an apron. Reyna is gathering kindling at the woodpile. The juniper chips are hard and smooth as flint. She rubs her hands together although there is no dust. "They came through this morning before it was even daylight." She points in the direction of the river. "They were going down that way." He frowns, then he smiles. "I've been looking for them all week," he says. The old woman shakes her head. "Well, if you hurry, they might still be there." They are his horses. His father-in-law gave him the white one when it was a colt. Its feet are as big around as pie pans. The gray is the sorrel mare's colt. The horses belong to Cheromiah, but the horses don't know that. "Nobody told them," that's what people say and then they laugh. The white horse leans against corral planks until they give way. It steps over low spots in old stone fences. The gray and little sorrel follow.

"The old lady said to share and love one another. She said we only make use of these things as long as we are here. We don't own them. Nobody owns anything." Juanita nods. She listens to both of her aunts. The two old women are quarreling over a narrow strip of ground between the two houses. The earth is hard-packed. Nothing grows there. Juanita listens to her Aunt Reyna and agrees that her Aunt Etta is wrong. Too many years living in Winslow. Aunt Etta returns and she wants to make the yard "private property" like white people do in Winslow. Juanita visits both of her aunts every day. She visits her Aunt Etta in the afternoon while her Aunt Reyna is resting. Etta and Reyna know their grandniece must visit both her aunts. Juanita has no husband or family to look after. She is the one who looks after the old folks. She is not like her brothers or sister who have wives or a husband. She doesn't forget. She looked after Uncle Joe for ten years until he finally died. He always told her she would have the house because women should have the houses. He didn't have much. Just his wagon horses, the house and a pig. He was the oldest and believed in the old ways. Aunt Reyna was right. If her brother Joe were alive he would talk to Etta. He would remind her that this is the village, not Winslow, Arizona. He would remind Etta how they all must share. Aunt Reyna would have more space for her woodpile then.

Most people die once, but "old man Joe he died twice," that's what people said, and then they laughed. Juanita knew they joked about it, but still she held her head high. She was the only one who even tried to look after the old folks. That November, Uncle Joe had been sick with pneumonia. His house smelled of Vicks and Ben-Gay. She checked on him every morning. He was always up before dawn the way all the old folks were. They greeted the sun and prayed for everybody. He was always up and had a fire in his little pot belly stove to make coffee. But that morning she knocked and there was no answer. Her heart was beating fast because she knew what she would find. The stove was cold. She stood by his bed and watched. He did not move. She touched the hand on top of the blanket and the fingers were as cold as the room. Juanita ran all the way to Aunt Reyna's house with the news. They sent word. The nephews and the clansmen came with picks and shovels. Before they went to dress him for burial, they cooked the big meal always prepared for the gravediggers. Aunt Reyna rolled out the tortillas and cried. Joe had always been so good to her. Joe had always loved her best after their parents died.

Cheromiah came walking by that morning while Juanita was getting more firewood. He was dragging a long rope and leather halter. He asked if she had seen any sign of his horses. She shook her head and then she told him Uncle Joe had passed away that morning. Tears came to her eyes. Cheromiah stood quietly for a moment. "I will miss the old man. He taught me everything I know about horses." Juanita nodded. Her arms were full of juniper wood. She looked away toward the southeast. "I saw your gray horse up in the sand hills the other day." Cheromiah smiled and thanked her. Cheromiah's truck didn't start in cold weather. He didn't feel like walking all the way up to the sand hills that morning. He took the road around the far side of the village to get home. It took him past Uncle Joe's place. The pig was butting its head against the planks of the pen making loud smacking sounds. The wagon horses were eating corn stalks the old man had bundled up after harvest for winter feed. Cheromiah wondered which of the old man's relatives was already looking after the livestock. He heard someone chopping wood on the other side of the house. The old man saw him and waved in the direction of the river. "They were down there last evening grazing in the willows." Cheromiah dropped the halter and rope and gestured with both hands. "Uncle Joe! They told me you died! Everyone thinks you are dead! They already cooked the gravediggers lunch!"

From that time on Uncle Joe didn't get up before dawn like he once did.
But he wouldn't let them tease Juanita about her mistake. Behind her back,
Juanita's cousins and in-laws were saying that she was in such a hurry to
collect her inheritance. They didn't think she should get everything. They
thought all of it should be shared equally. The following spring, Uncle Joe's
wagon horses went down Paguate Hill too fast and the wagon wheel hit a big
rock. He was thrown from the wagon and a sheepherder found him. Uncle
Joe was unconscious for two days and then he died "This time he really *is*
dead, poor thing," people would say and then they'd smile.

The trouble over the pig started on the day of the funeral. Juanita caught
her brother's wife at the pig pen. The wife held a large pail in both hands.
The pail was full of a yellowish liquid. There were bones swimming in it.
Corn tassels floated like hair. She looked Juanita in the eye as she dumped
the lard pail into the trough. The pig switched its tail and made one push
through the liquid with its snout. It looked up at both of them. The snout
kept moving. The pig would not eat. Juanita had already fed the pig scraps
from the gravediggers' plates. She didn't want her brothers' wives feeding
the pig. They would claim, they had fed the pig more than she had. They
would say that whoever fed the pig the most should get the biggest share of
meat. At butchering time they would show up to collect half. "It won't eat
slop," Juanita said, "don't be feeding it slop."

The stories they told about Etta always came back to the same thing.

While the other girls learn cooking and sewing at the Indian School, Etta
works in the greenhouse. In the evenings the teacher sits with her on the
sofa. They repeat the names of the flowers. She teaches Etta the parts of the
flower. On Saturdays while the dormitory matrons take the others to town,
Etta stays with the teacher. Etta kneels beside her in the garden. They press
brown dirt over the gladiola bulbs. The teacher runs a hot bath for her. The
teacher will not let her return to the dormitory until she has cleaned Etta's
fingernails. The other girls tell stories about Etta.

The white gauze curtains are breathing in and out. The hollyhocks bend
around the fence posts and lean over the wire. The buds are tight and press
between the green lips of the sheath. The seed had been saved in a mason jar.
Etta found it in the pantry behind a veil of cobwebs. She planted it the length
of the fence to mark the boundary. She had only been a child the first time,
but she can still remember the colors — reds and yellows swaying above her
head, tiny black ants in the white eyes of pollen. Others were purple and
dark red, almost black as dried blood. She planted the seeds the teacher
had given her. She saved the seeds from the only year the hollyhocks grew.
Etta doesn't eat pork. She is thinking about the row of tamarisk trees she will
plant along the fence so people cannot see her yard or house. She does
not want to spend her retirement with everyone in the village minding her

business the way they always have. Somebody is always fighting over something. The years away taught her differently. She knows better now. The yard is hers. They can't take it just because she had lived away from the village all those years. A person could go away and come back again. The village people don't understand fences. At Indian School she learned fences tell you where you stand. In Winslow, white people built fences around their houses, otherwise something might be lost or stolen. There were rumors about her the whole time she lived in Winslow. The gossip was not true. The teacher had written to her all the years Etta was married. It was a job to go to after her husband died. The teacher was sick and old. Etta went because she loved caring for the flowers. It was only a job, but people like to talk. The teacher was sick for a long time before she died.

15   "What do you want with those things," the clanswoman scolded, "wasting water on something we can't eat." The old woman mumbled to herself all the way across the garden. Etta started crying. She sat on the ground by the hollyhocks she had planted, and held her face. She pressed her fingers into her eyes. The old woman had taken her in. It was the duty of the clan to accept orphans.

Etta tells her she is not coming back from Indian School in the summer. She has a job at school caring for the flowers. She and the clanswoman are cleaning a sheep stomach, rinsing it under the mulberry tree. The intestines are coiled in a white enamel pan. They are bluish gray, the color of the sky before snow. Strands of tallow branch across them like clouds. "You are not much good to me anyway. I took you because no one else wanted to. I have tried to teach you, but the white people at that school have ruined you. You waste good water growing things we cannot eat."

The first time Etta returned from Winslow for a visit, Reyna confided there was gossip going on in the village. Etta could tell by the details that her sister-in-law was embroidering stories about her too. They did not speak to each other after that. People were jealous of her because she had left. They were certain she preferred white people. But Etta spoke only to the teacher. White people did not see her when she walked on the street.

The heat holds the afternoon motionless. The sun does not move. It has parched all color from the sky and left only the fine ash. The street below is empty. Down the long dim hall there are voices in English and, more distantly, the ticking of a clock. The room is white and narrow. The shade is pulled. It pulses heat the texture of pearls. The water in the basin is the color of garnets. Etta waits in a chair beside the bed. The sheets are soaked with her fever. She murmurs the parts of the flowers — she whispers that the bud is swelling open, but that afternoon was long ago.

Ruthie's husband is seeing that other woman in the cornfield. The cornfield belongs to her and to her sister, Juanita. Their mother left it to both of them. In the morning her husband walks to the fields with the hoe on his shoulder. Not long after, the woman appears with a coal bucket filled with stove ashes. The woman follows the path toward the trash pile, but when she gets to the far corner of the cornfield she stops. When she thinks no one is watching she sets the bucket down. She gathers up the skirt of her dress and steps over the fence where the wire sags.

Ruthie would not have suspected anything if she had not noticed the 20 rocks. He was always hauling rocks to build a new shed or corral. But this time there was something about the colors of the sandstone. The reddish pink and orange yellow looked as if they had been taken from the center of the sky as the sun went down. She had never seen such intense color in sandstone. She had always remembered it being shades of pale yellow or peppered white-colors for walls and fences. But these rocks looked as if rain had just fallen on them. She watched her husband. He was unloading the rocks from the old wagon and stacking them carefully next to the woodpile. When he had finished it was dark and she could not see the colors of the sandstone any longer. She thought about how good-looking he was, the kind of man all the other women chase.

Reyna goes with them. She takes her cane but carries it ready in her hand like a rabbit club. Her grandnieces have asked her to go with them. Ruthie's husband is carrying on with another woman. The same one as before. They are going after them together — the two sisters and the old aunt. Ruthie told Juanita about it first. It was their mother's field and now it is theirs. If Juanita had a husband he would work there too. "The worst thing is them doing it in the cornfield. It makes the corn sickly, it makes the beans stop growing. If they want to do it they can go down to the trash and lie in the tin cans and broken glass with the flies," that's what Reyna says.

They surprise them lying together on the sandy ground in the shade of the tall corn plants. Last time they caught them together they reported them to the woman's grandmother, but the old woman didn't seem to care. They told that woman's husband too. But he has a job in Albuquerque, and men don't bother to look after things. It is up to women to take care of everything. He is supposed to be hoeing weeds in their field, but instead he is rolling around on the ground with that woman, killing off all their melons and beans.

Her breasts are long and brown. They bounce against her like potatoes. She runs with her blue dress in her hand. She leaves her shoes. They are next to his hoe. Ruthie stands between Juanita and Aunt Reyna. They gesture with their arms and yell. They are not scolding him. They don't even look at him. They are scolding the rest of the village over husband-stealing and corn that is sickly. Reyna raps on the fence post with her cane. Juanita calls him a pig. Ruthie cries because the beans won't grow. He kneels to lace his work shoes. He kneels for a long time. His fingers move slowly. They are not talking to him. They are talking about the other woman. The red chili stew she makes is runny and pale. They pay no attention to him. He goes back to hoeing weeds. Their voices sift away in the wind. Occasionally he stops to wipe his forehead on his sleeve. He looks up at the sky or over the sand hills. Off in the distance there is a man on foot. He is crossing the big sand dune above the river. He is dragging a rope. The horses are grazing on yellow rice grass at the foot of the dune. They are down wind from him. He inches along, straining to crouch over his own stomach. The big white horse whirls suddenly, holding its tail high. The gray half-circles and joins it, blowing loudly through its nostrils. The little sorrel mare bolts to the top of the next dune before she turns.

Etta awakens and the yard is full of horses. The gray chews a hollyhock. Red petals stream from its mouth. The sorrel mare watches her come out the door. The white horse charges away, rolling his eyes at her nightgown. Etta throws a piece of juniper from the woodpile. The gray horse presses hard against the white one. They tremble in the corner of the fence, strings of blue morning glories trampled under their hooves. Etta yells and the sorrel mare startles, crowding against the gray. They heave forward against the fence, and the posts make slow cracking sounds. The wire whines and squeaks. It gives way suddenly and the white horse stumbles ahead tangled in wire. The sorrel and the gray bolt past, and for an instant the white horse hesitates, shivering at the wire caught around its forelegs and neck. Then the white horse leaps forward, rusty wire and fence posts trailing behind like a broken necklace.

Eudora Welty
A Worn Path

It was December—a bright frozen day in the early morning. Far out in the country there was an old Negro woman with her head tied in a red rag, coming along a path through the pinewoods. Her name was Phoenix Jackson. She was very old and small and she walked slowly in the dark pine shadows, moving a little from side to side in her steps, with the balanced heaviness and lightness of a pendulum in a grandfather clock. She carried a thin, small cane made from an umbrella, and with this she kept tapping the frozen earth in front of her. This made a grave and persistent noise in the still air, that seemed meditative like the chirping of a solitary little bird.

She wore a dark striped dress reaching down to her shoe tops, and an equally long apron of bleached sugar sacks, with a full pocket: all neat and

A WORN PATH   First published in 1941. Eudora Welty was born in 1909 in Jackson, Mississippi, where she was raised and to which she returned after studying at the University of Wisconsin and Columbia University. In the mid-1930s she was employed by the federal Work Projects Administration (WPA) to travel throughout Mississippi writing newspaper copy and taking photographs, a job that enabled her to observe many varieties of rural life in her native state.

tidy, but every time she took a step she might have fallen over her shoelaces, which dragged from her unlaced shoes. She looked straight ahead. Her eyes were blue with age. Her skin had a pattern all its own of numberless branching wrinkles and as though a whole little tree stood in the middle of her forehead, but a golden color ran underneath, and the two knobs of her cheeks were illumined by a yellow burning under the dark. Under the red rag her hair came down on her neck in the frailest of ringlets, still black, and with an odor like copper.

Now and then there was a quivering in the thicket. Old Phoenix said, "Out of my way, all you foxes, owls, beetles, jack rabbits, coons, and wild animals! . . . Keep out from under these feet, little bobwhites. . . . Keep the big wild hogs out of my path. Don't let none of those come running my direction. I got a long way." Under her small black-freckled hand her cane, limber as a buggy whip, would switch at the brush as if to rouse up any hiding things.

On she went. The woods were deep and still. The sun made the pine needles almost too bright to look at, up where the wind rocked. The cones dropped as light as feathers. Down in the hollow was the mourning dove — it was not too late for him.

The path ran up a hill. "Seem like there is chains about my feet, time I get this far," she said, in the voice of argument old people keep to use with themselves. "Something always take a hold of me on this hill — pleads I should stay." 5

After she got to the top she turned and gave a full, severe look behind her where she had come. "Up through pines," she said at length. "Now down through oaks."

Her eyes opened their widest, and she started down gently. But before she got to the bottom of the hill a bush caught her dress.

Her fingers were busy and intent, but her skirts were full and long, so that before she could pull them free in one place they were caught in another. It was not possible to allow the dress to tear. "I in the thorny bush," she said. "Thorns, you doing your appointed work. Never want to let folks pass, no sir. Old eyes thought you was a pretty little *green* bush."

Finally, trembling all over, she stood free, and after a moment dared to stoop for her cane.

"Sun so high!" she cried, leaning back and looking, while the thick tears went over her eyes. "The time getting all gone here." 10

At the foot of this hill was a place where a log was laid across the creek. "Now comes the trial," said Phoenix.

Putting her right foot out, she mounted the log and shut her eyes. Lifting her skirt, leveling her cane fiercely before her, like a festival figure in some parade, she began to march across. Then she opened her eyes and she was safe on the other side.

"I wasn't as old as I thought," she said.

15   But she sat down to rest. She spread her skirts on the bank around her
and folded her hands over her knees. Up above her was a tree in a pearly
cloud of mistletoe. She did not dare to close her eyes, and when a little boy
brought her a plate with a slice of marble-cake on it she spoke to him. "That
would be acceptable," she said. But when she went to take it there was just
her own hand in the air.

So she left that tree, and had to go through a barbed-wire fence. There
she had to creep and crawl, spreading her knees and stretching her fingers
like a baby trying to climb the steps. But she talked loudly to herself: she
could not let her dress be torn now, so late in the day, and she could not pay
for having her arm or her leg sawed off if she got caught fast where she was.

At last she was safe through the fence and risen up out in the clearing.
Big dead trees, like black men with one arm, were standing in the purple
stalks of the withered cotton field. There sat a buzzard.

"Who you watching?"

In the furrow she made her way along.

20   "Glad this not the season for bulls," she said, looking sideways, "and the
good Lord made his snakes to curl up and sleep in the winter. A pleasure I
don't see no two-headed snake coming around that tree, where it come once.
It took a while to get by him, back in the summer."

She passed through the old cotton and went into a field of dead corn. It
whispered and shook and was taller than her head. "Through the maze
now," she said, for there was no path.

Then there was something tall, black, and skinny there, moving before
her.

At first she took it for a man. It could have been a man dancing in the
field. But she stood still and listened, and it did not make a sound. It was as
silent as a ghost.

"Ghost," she said sharply, "who be you the ghost of? For I have heard of
nary death close by."

25   But there was no answer—only the ragged dancing in the wind.

She shut her eyes, reached out her hand, and touched a sleeve. She found
a coat and inside that an emptiness, cold as ice.

"You scarecrow," she said. Her face lighted. "I ought to be shut up for
good," she said with laughter. "My senses is gone. I too old. I the oldest
people I ever know. Dance, old scarecrow," she said, "while I dancing
with you."

She kicked her foot over the furrow, and with mouth drawn down, shook
her head once or twice in a little strutting way. Some husks blew down and
whirled in streamers about her skirts.

Then she went on, parting her way from side to side with the cane,
through the whispering field. At last she came to the end, to a wagon track
where the silver grass blew between the red ruts. The quail were walking
around like pullets, seeming all dainty and unseen.

30   "Walk pretty," she said. "This the easy place. This the easy going."

She followed the track, swaying through the quiet bare fields, through the little strings of trees silver in their dead leaves, past cabins silver from weather, with the doors and windows boarded shut, all like old women under a spell sitting there. "I walking in their sleep," she said, nodding her head vigorously.

In a ravine she went where a spring was silently flowing through a hollow log. Old Phoenix bent and drank. "Sweet-gum makes the water sweet," she said, and drank more. "Nobody know who made this well, for it was here when I was born."

The track crossed a swampy part where the moss hung as white as lace from every limb. "Sleep on, alligators, and blow your bubbles." Then the track went into the road.

Deep, deep the road went down between the high green-colored banks. Overhead the live-oaks met, and it was as dark as a cave.

A black dog with a lolling tongue came up out of the weeds by the ditch. 35 She was meditating, and not ready, and when he came at her she only hit him a little with her cane. Over she went in the ditch, like a little puff of milkweed.

Down there, her senses drifted away. A dream visited her, and she reached her hand up, but nothing reached down and gave her a pull. So she lay there and presently went to talking. "Old woman," she said to herself, "that black dog come up out of the weeds to stall you off, and now there he sitting on his fine tail, smiling at you."

A white man finally came along and found her — a hunter, a young man, with his dog on a chain.

"Well, Granny!" he laughed. "What are you doing there?"

"Lying on my back like a June-bug waiting to be turned over, mister," she said, reaching up her hand.

He lifted her up, gave her a swing in the air, and set her down. "Anything 40 broken, Granny?"

"No sir, them old dead weeds is springy enough," said Phoenix, when she had got her breath. "I thank you for your trouble."

"Where do you live, Granny?" he asked, while the two dogs were growling at each other.

"Away back yonder, sir, behind the ridge. You can't even see it from here."

"On your way home?"

"No sir, going to town." 45

"Why, that's too far! That's as far as I walk when I come out myself, and I get something for my trouble." He patted the stuffed bag he carried, and there hung down a little closed claw. It was one of the bobwhites, with its beak hooked bitterly to show it was dead. "Now you go on home, Granny!"

"I bound to go to town, Mister," said Phoenix. "The time come around."

He gave another laugh, filling the whole landscape. "I know you old colored people! Wouldn't miss going to town to see Santa Claus!"

But something held old Phoenix very still. The deep lines in her face went into a fierce and different radiation. Without warning, she had seen with her own eyes a flashing nickel fall out of the man's pocket onto the ground.

50 "How old are you, Granny?" he was saying.

"There is no telling, mister," she said, "no telling."

Then she gave a little cry and clapped her hands and said, "Git on away from here, dog! Look! Look at that dog!" She laughed as if in admiration. "He ain't scared of nobody. He a big black dog." She whispered, "Sic him!"

"Watch me get rid of that cur," said the man. "Sic him, Pete! Sic him!"

Phoenix heard the dogs fighting, and heard the man running and throwing sticks. She even heard a gunshot. But she was slowly bending forward by that time, further and further forward, the lids stretched down over her eyes, as if she were doing this in her sleep. Her chin was lowered almost to her knees. The yellow palm of her hand came out from the fold of her apron. Her fingers slid down and along the ground under the piece of money with the grace and care they would have in lifting an egg from under a setting hen. Then she slowly straightened up, she stood erect, and the nickel was in her apron pocket. A bird flew by. Her lips moved. "God watching me the whole time. I come to stealing."

55 The man came back, and his own dog panted about them. "Well, I scared him off that time," he said, and then he laughed and lifted his gun and pointed it at Phoenix.

She stood straight and faced him.

"Doesn't the gun scare you?" he said, still pointing it.

"No, sir, I seen plenty go off closer by, in my day, and for less than what I done," she said, holding utterly still.

He smiled, and shouldered the gun. "Well, Granny," he said, "you must be a hundred years old, and scared of nothing. I'd give you a dime if I had any money with me. But you take my advice and stay home, and nothing will happen to you."

60 "I bound to go on my way, mister," said Phoenix. She inclined her head in the red rag. Then they went in different directions, but she could hear the gun shooting again and again over the hill.

She walked on. The shadows hung from the oak trees to the road like curtains. Then she smelled wood-smoke, and smelled the river, and she saw a steeple and the cabins on their steep steps. Dozens of little black children whirled around her. There ahead was Natchez shining. Bells were ringing. She walked on.

In the paved city it was Christmas time. There were red and green electric lights strung and crisscrossed everywhere, and all turned on in the daytime. Old Phoenix would have been lost if she had not distrusted her eyesight and depended on her feet to know where to take her.

She paused quietly on the sidewalk where people were passing by. A lady came along in the crowd, carrying an armful of red-, green-, and silver-

514   A WORN PATH

wrapped presents; she gave off perfume like the red roses in hot summer, and Phoenix stopped her.

"Please, missy, will you lace up my shoe?" She held up her foot.

"What do you want, Grandma?"

"See my shoe," said Phoenix. "Do all right for out in the country, but wouldn't look right to go in a big building."

"Stand still then, Grandma," said the lady. She put her packages down on the sidewalk beside her and laced and tied both shoes tightly.

"Can't lace 'em with a cane," said Phoenix. "Thank you, missy. I doesn't mind asking a nice lady to tie up my shoe, when I gets out on the street."

Moving slowly and from side to side, she went into the big building, and into a tower of steps, where she walked up and around and around until her feet knew to stop.

She entered a door, and there she saw nailed up on the wall the document that had been stamped with the gold seal and framed in the gold frame, which matched the dream that was hung up in her head.

"Here I be," she said. There was a fixed and ceremonial stiffness over her body.

"A charity case, I suppose," said an attendant who sat at the desk before her.

But Phoenix only looked above her head. There was sweat on her face, the wrinkles in her skin shone like a bright net.

"Speak up, Grandma," the woman said. "What's your name? We must have your history, you know. Have you been here before? What seems to be the trouble with you?"

Old Phoenix only gave a twitch to her face as if a fly were bothering her.

"Are you deaf?" cried the attendant.

But then the nurse came in.

"Oh, that's just old Aunt Phoenix," she said. "She doesn't come for herself—she has a little grandson. She makes these trips just as regular as clockwork. She lives away back off the Old Natchez Trace." She bent down. "Well, Aunt Phoenix, why don't you just take a seat? We won't keep you standing after your long trip." She pointed.

The old woman sat down, bolt upright in the chair.

"Now, how is the boy?" asked the nurse.

Old Phoenix did not speak.

"I said, how is the boy?"

But Phoenix only waited and stared straight ahead, her face very solemn and withdrawn into rigidity.

"Is his throat any better?" asked the nurse. "Aunt Phoenix, don't you hear me? Is your grandson's throat any better since the last time you came for the medicine?"

With her hands on her knees, the old woman waited, silent, erect and motionless, just as if she were in armor.

"You mustn't take up our time this way, Aunt Phoenix," the nurse said. "Tell us quickly about your grandson, and get it over. He isn't dead, is he?"

At last there came a flicker and then a flame of comprehension across her face, and she spoke.

"My grandson. It was my memory had left me. There I sat and forgot why I made my long trip."

"Forgot?" The nurse frowned. "After you came so far?"

Then Phoenix was like an old woman begging a dignified forgiveness for waking up frightened in the night. "I never did go to school, I was too old at the Surrender," she said in a soft voice. "I'm an old woman without an education. It was my memory fail me. My little grandson, he is just the same, and I forgot it in the coming."

"Throat never heals, does it?" said the nurse, speaking in a loud, sure voice to old Phoenix. By now she had a card with something written on it, a little list. "Yes. Swallowed lye. When was it? — January — two, three years ago — ?"

Phoenix spoke unasked now. "No, missy, he not dead, he just the same. Every little while his throat begin to close up again, and he not able to swallow. He not get his breath. He not able to help himself. So the time come around, and I go on another trip for the soothing medicine."

"All right. The doctor said as long as you came to get it, you could have it," said the nurse. "But it's an obstinate case."

"My little grandson, he sit up there in the house all wrapped up, waiting by himself," Phoenix went on. "We is the only two left in the world. He suffer and it don't seem to put him back at all. He got a sweet look. He going to last. He wear a little patch quilt and peep out holding his mouth open like a little bird. I remembers so plain now. I not going to forget him again, no, the whole enduring time. I could tell him from all the others in creation."

"All right." The nurse was trying to hush her now. She brought her a bottle of medicine. "Charity," she said, making a check mark in a book.

Old Phoenix held the bottle close to her eyes, and then carefully put it into her pocket.

"I thank you," she said.

"It's Christmas time, Grandma," said the attendant. "Could I give you a few pennies out of my purse?"

"Five pennies is a nickel," said Phoenix stiffly.

"Here's a nickel," said the attendant.

Phoenix rose carefully and held out her hand. She received the nickel and then fished the other nickel out of her pocket and laid it beside the new one. She stared at her palm closely, with her head on one side.

Then she gave a tap with her cane on the floor.

"This is what come to me to do," she said. "I going to the store and buy my child a little windmill they sells, made out of paper. He going to find it hard to believe there such a thing in the world. I'll march myself back where he waiting, holding it straight up in this hand."

She lifted her free hand, gave a little nod, turned around, and walked out of the doctor's office. Then her slow step began on the stairs, going down.

Tobias Wolff
Say Yes

They were doing the dishes, his wife washing while he dried. He'd washed the night before. Unlike most men he knew, he really pitched in on the housework. A few months earlier he'd overheard a friend of his wife's congratulate her on having such a considerate husband, and he thought, *I try.* Helping out with the dishes was a way he had of showing how considerate he was.

They talked about different things and somehow got on the subject of whether white people should marry black people. He said that all things considered, he thought it was a bad idea.

"Why?" she asked.

Sometimes his wife got this look where she pinched her brows together and bit her lower lip and stared down at something. When he saw her like this he knew he should keep his mouth shut, but he never did. Actually it made him talk more. She had that look now.

"Why?" she asked again, and stood there with her hand inside a bowl, not washing it but just holding it above the water.   5

"Listen," he said, "I went to school with blacks and I've worked with blacks and lived on the same street with blacks and we've always gotten along just fine. I don't need you coming along now and implying that I'm a racist."

"I didn't imply anything," she said, and began washing the bowl again, turning it around in her hand as though she were shaping it. "I just don't see what's wrong with a white person marrying a black person, that's all."

"They don't come from the same culture as we do. Listen to them sometime — they even have their own language. That's okay with me. I *like* hearing them talk" — he did; for some reason it always made him feel happy — "but it's different. A person from their culture and a person from our culture could never really *know* each other."

"Like you know me?" his wife asked.

"Yes. Like I know you."   10

"But if they love each other," she said. She was washing faster now, not looking at him.

Oh boy, he thought. He said, "Don't take my word for it. Look at the statistics. Most of those marriages break up."

"Statistics." She was piling dishes on the drainboard at a terrific rate, just swiping at them with the cloth. Many of them were greasy, and there were

SAY YES First published in 1985. Tobias Wolff was born in 1945 in Birmingham, Alabama, and raised in the state of Washington. He dropped out of high school and worked as an apprentice seaman, then joined the U.S. Army Special Forces in 1964. He served as a paratrooper in Vietnam, and was a first lieutenant when he left the army in 1968. He then earned degrees at Oxford University and Stanford, and now teaches at Syracuse, where he lives with his wife and two sons. This story is from his collection titled *Back in the World*, a phrase used by the military in Vietnam to signify a return to civilian life.

flecks of food between the tines of the forks. "All right," she said, "what about foreigners? I suppose you think the same thing about two foreigners getting married."

"Yes," he said, "as a matter of fact I do. How can you understand someone who comes from a completely different background?"

15 "Different," said his wife. "Not the same, like us."

"Yes, different," he snapped, angry with her for resorting to this trick of repeating his words so that they sounded crass, or hypocritical. "These are dirty," he said, and dumped all the silverware back into the sink.

The water had gone flat and grey. She stared down at it, her lips pressed tight together, then plunged her hands under the surface. "Oh!" she cried, and jumped back. She took her right hand by the wrist and held it up. Her thumb was bleeding.

"Ann, don't move," he said. "Stay right there." He ran upstairs to the bathroom and rummaged in the medicine chest for alcohol, cotton, and a Band-Aid. When he came back down she was leaning against the refrigerator with her eyes closed, still holding her hand. He took the hand and dabbed at her thumb with the cotton. The bleeding had stopped. He squeezed it to see how deep the wound was and a single drop of blood welled up, trembling and bright, and fell to the floor. Over the thumb she stared at him accusingly. "It's shallow," he said. "Tomorrow you won't even know it's there." He hoped that she appreciated how quickly he had come to her aid. He'd acted out of concern for her, with no thought of getting anything in return, but now the thought occurred to him that it would be a nice gesture on her part not to start up that conversation again, as he was tired of it. "I'll finish up here," he said. "You go and relax."

"That's okay," she said. "I'll dry."

20 He began to wash the silverware again, giving a lot of attention to the forks.

"So," she said, "you wouldn't have married me if I'd been black."

"For Christ's sake, Ann!"

"Well, that's what you said, didn't you?"

"No, I did not. The whole question is ridiculous. If you had been black we probably wouldn't even have met. You would have had your friends and I would have had mine. The only black girl I ever really knew was my partner in the debating club, and I was already going out with you by then."

25 "But if we had met, and I'd been black?"

"Then you probably would have been going out with a black guy." He picked up the rinsing nozzle and sprayed the silverware. The water was so hot that the metal darkened to pale blue, then turned silver again.

"Let's say I wasn't," she said. "Let's say I am black and unattached and we meet and fall in love."

He glanced over at her. She was watching him and her eyes were bright. "Look," he said, taking a reasonable tone, "this is stupid. If you were black you wouldn't be you." As he said this he realized it was absolutely true.

There was no possible way of arguing with the fact that she would not be herself if she were black. So he said it again: "If you were black you wouldn't be you."

"I know," she said, "but let's just say."

He took a deep breath. He had won the argument but he still felt cor-   30
nered. "Say what?" he asked.

"That I'm black, but still me, and we fall in love. Will you marry me?"

He thought about it.

"Well?" she said, and stepped close to him. Her eyes were even brighter. "Will you marry me?"

"I'm thinking," he said.

"You won't, I can tell. You're going to say no."   35

"Let's not move too fast on this," he said. "There are lots of things to consider. We don't want to do something we would regret for the rest of our lives."

"No more considering. Yes or no."

"Since you put it that way — "

"Yes or no."

"Jesus, Ann. All right. No."   40

She said, "Thank you," and walked from the kitchen into the living room. A moment later he heard her turning the pages of a magazine. He knew that she was too angry to be actually reading it, but she didn't snap through the pages the way he would have done. She turned them slowly, as if she were studying every word. She was demonstrating her indifference to him, and it had the effect he knew she wanted it to have. It hurt him.

He had no choice but to demonstrate his indifference to her. Quietly, thoroughly, he washed the rest of the dishes. Then he dried them and put them away. He wiped the counters and the stove and scoured the linoleum where the drop of blood had fallen. While he was at it, he decided he might as well mop the whole floor. When he was done the kitchen looked new, the way it looked when they were first shown the house, before they had ever lived here.

He picked up the garbage pail and went outside. The night was clear and he could see a few stars to the west, where the lights of the town didn't blur them out. On El Camino the traffic was steady and light, peaceful as a river. He felt ashamed that he had let his wife get him into a fight. In another thirty years or so they would both be dead. What would all that stuff matter then? He thought of the years they had spent together and how close they were and how well they knew each other, and his throat tightened so that he could hardly breathe. His face and neck began to tingle. Warmth flooded his chest. He stood there for a while, enjoying these sensations, then picked up the pail and went out the back gate.

The two mutts from down the street had pulled over the garbage can again. One of them was rolling around on his back and the other had something in her mouth. Growling, she tossed it into the air, leaped up and caught it, growled again and whipped her head from side to side. When they saw him coming they trotted away with short, mincing steps. Normally he would heave rocks at them, but this time he let them go.

45 The house was dark when he came back inside. She was in the bathroom. He stood outside the door and called her name. He heard bottles clinking, but she didn't answer him. "Ann, I'm really sorry," he said. "I'll make it up to you, I promise."

"How?" she asked.

He wasn't expecting this. But from a sound in her voice, a level and definite note that was strange to him, he knew that he had to come up with a right answer. He leaned against the door. "I'll marry you," he whispered.

"We'll see," she said. "Go on to bed. I'll be out in a minute."

He undressed and got under the covers. Finally he heard the bathroom door open and close.

50 "Turn off the light," she said from the hallway.

"What?"

"Turn off the light."

He reached over and pulled the chain on the bedside lamp. The room went dark. "All right," he said. He lay there, but nothing happened. "All right," he said again. Then he heard a movement across the room. He sat up but he couldn't see a thing. The room was silent. His heart pounded the way it had on their first night together, the way it still did when he woke at a noise in the darkness and waited to hear it again — the sound of someone moving through the house, a stranger.

APPENDIX

Writing about Fiction

I. Why Write about Literature? 522

II. For Whom Do You Write? 522

III. Choosing a Topic 524

1. Papers that Focus on a Single Story 524
2. Papers of Comparison and Contrast 526
3. Papers on a Number of Works by a Single Author 527
4. Papers on a Number of Works with Some Feature in Common Other than Authorship 528

IV. Proving Your Point 528

V. Writing the Paper 530

VI. Introducing Quotations (Q1–Q10) 532

VII. Documentation 537

1. Textual Documentation (TD1–TD5) 538
2. Parenthetical Documentation (PD1–PD6) 540

VIII. Grammar, Punctuation, and Usage: Special Problems 542

1. Grammar (G1–G2) 542
2. Punctuation (P1–P2) 543
3. Usage (U1–U2) 544

IX. A Sample Analysis 546

The Function of the Frame Story in "Once Upon a Time"

WRITING ABOUT FICTION

I. Why Write about Literature?

Written assignments in a literature class have two purposes: (1) to give you additional practice in writing clearly and persuasively, and (2) to deepen your understanding of literary works by leading you to read and think about a few works more searchingly than you might otherwise do. But these two purposes are private. To be successful, your paper must have a public purpose as well: it should be written to enlighten others besides yourself. Even if no one else ever reads your paper, you should never treat it as a private note to your instructor. You should write every paper as if it were intended for publication.

II. For Whom Do You Write?

The audience for whom you write will govern both the content and expression of your paper. You need to know something about your readers' backgrounds — national, racial, social, religious — and be able to make intelligent guesses about their knowledge, interests, and previous reading. In presenting Graham Greene's "The Destructors" (page 49), your editors have felt it necessary to provide information (in footnotes) that would not be needed by a British audience; for "The Son from America" (page 99) and "Defender of the Faith" (page 117), footnotes provide definitions and explanations that would not be necessary for an audience familiar with Jewish religious practices. But the most crucial question about an audience is, *Has it read the work you are writing about?* The book reviewer in your Sunday paper generally writes about a newly published book that the audience has not read. A reviewer's purpose is to let readers know something of what the book is about and to give them some notion of whether they will enjoy or profit from reading it. At an opposite extreme, the scholar writing in a specialized scholarly journal can generally assume an audience that *has* read the work, that has a knowledge of previous interpretations of the work, and that is familiar with other works in its period or genre. The scholar's purpose, not infrequently, is to persuade this audience that some new information or some new way of looking at the work appreciably deepens or alters its meaning or significance.

Clearly, essays written for such different audiences and with such different purposes differ considerably in content, organization, and style. Book reviewers reviewing a new novel will include a general idea of its plot while being careful not to reveal the outcome. Scholars will assume that readers already know the plot and will have no compunction about discussing its outcome. Reviewers will try to write interestingly and engagingly about the novel and to persuade readers that they have valid grounds for their opinions of its worth, but their manner will generally be informal. Scholars are more interested in presenting a cogent argument, logically arranged, and solidly based on evidence. They will be more formal, and may use critical terms and refer to related works that would be unfamiliar to nonspecialized readers. In documentation the two types of essays will be quite different. Reviewers' only documentation is normally the identification of the novel's title, author, publisher, and price, at the top of the review. For other information and opinions they hope that a reader will rely on their intelligence, knowledge, and judgment. Scholars, on the other hand, may furnish an elaborate array of citations of other sources of information, allowing the reader to verify the accuracy or basis of any important part of their argument. Scholars expect to be challenged, and they see to it that all parts of their arguments are buttressed.

For whom, then, should *you* write? Unless your instructor stipulates (or you request) a different audience, the best plan is to assume that you are writing for the other members of your class. Pretend that your class publishes a journal of which it also constitutes the readership. Your instructor is the editor and determines editorial policy. If you write on a work that has been assigned for class reading, you assume that your audience is familiar with it. (This kind of paper is generally of the greatest educational value, for it is most open to challenge and class discussion, and places on you a heavier burden of proof.) If you compare an assigned work with one that has not been assigned, you must gauge what portion of your audience is familar with the unassigned work, and proceed accordingly. If the unassigned story were A. Conan Doyle's "The Adventure of the Speckled Band," you would probably not need to explain that "Sherlock Holmes is a detective" and that "Dr. Watson is his friend," for you can assume that *this* audience, through movies, TV, or reading, is familiar with these characters; but you could not assume familiarity with this particular story. You know that, as members of the same class, your readers have certain backgrounds and interests in common and are at comparable levels of education. Anything you know about your audience may be important for how you write your paper and what you put in it.

III. Choosing a Topic

As editor of this imaginary publication, your instructor is responsible for the nature of its contents. Instructors may be very specific in their assignments, or they may be very general, inviting you to submit a paper on any subject within a broadly defined area of interest. They will also have editorial policies concerning length of papers, preparation of manuscripts, and deadlines for submission (all of which should be meticulously heeded). Instructors may further specify whether the paper should be entirely the work of your own critical thinking, or whether it is to be an investigative assignment — that is, one involving research into what other writers have written concerning your subject and the use of their findings, where relevant, to help you reach your own conclusions.

Let us consider four kinds of papers you might write: (1) papers that focus on a single literary work; (2) papers of comparison and contrast; (3) papers on a number of works by a single author; and (4) papers on a number of works having some feature other than authorship in common.

1. Papers that Focus on a Single Story

If your assignment is a specific one (Define the conflicts in "The Child by Tiger." How is the landscape symbolic in "Hills Like White Elephants"? What is the theme of "There Are a Lot of Ways to Die"?), your task is clear-cut. You have only to read the selection carefully (probably more than once), formulate your answer, and support it with corroborating evidence from within the text as cogently and convincingly as possible. In order to convince your readers that your answer is the best one, you will need to examine and account for apparently contrary evidence as well as clearly supportive evidence; otherwise skeptical readers, reluctant to change their minds, might simply refer to "important points" that you have "overlooked."

Specific questions like these, when they are central to the work considered and may be a matter of dispute, make excellent topics for papers. You may discover them for yourself when you disagree with a classmate about the interpretation of a story. The study questions following many of the selections in this anthology frequently suggest topics of this kind.

If your assignment is more general, and if you are given some choice as to what story you wish to write on, it is usually best to choose one you enjoyed, whether or not you entirely understood it. (You are more likely to write a good paper on a selection you liked than on one you disliked, and you should arrive at a fuller understanding of it while thinking through your paper.) You must then decide what kind of paper you will write, and this will be related to the length and kind of selection you have chosen and the amount of space at your disposal. Probably your paper will be either an *explication* or an *analysis*.

An *explication* (literally, an "unfolding") has been defined as "an examination of a work of literature for a knowledge of each part, for the relations of these parts to each other, and for their relations to the whole."* It is a detailed elucidation of a work, sometimes line by line or word by word, which is interested not only in *what* that work means but in *how* it means what it means. It thus considers all relevant aspects of a work — characterization, point of view, theme, setting, style, symbolism, irony, and so forth — and discusses, if not all of these, at least the most important. (There is no such thing as exhausting the meanings and the ways to those meanings in a really rich piece of literature, and the explicator must settle for something less than completeness.) Explication follows from what we sometimes call "close reading" — looking at a piece of writing, as it were, through a magnifying glass.

Clearly, the kinds of literature for which an explication is appropriate are limited. First, the work must be rich enough to repay the kind of close attention demanded. One would not think of explicating "The Ant and the Grasshopper" (unless for purposes of parody), for it has no meanings that need elucidation and no "art" worthy of comment. Second, the work must be short enough to be encompassed in a relatively brief discussion. A thorough explication of "Bartleby the Scrivener" would be much longer than the story itself and would tire the patience of even the most dogged reader. Explications in fact work best with short poems, though explication may be valuable for exceptionally rich or crucial passages taken from a work of fiction, perhaps the final paragraphs of stories like "Defender of the Faith," "Paul's Case," or "Miss Brill." But explication as a critical form should perhaps be separated from explication as a method. Whenever you elucidate even a small part of a literary work by a close examination that relates it to the whole, you are essentially explicating (unfolding). For example, if you point out the double meaning in the title of "The Most Dangerous Game" as it relates to that story's action, you are explicating the title.

The text of this book uses the explicative method occasionally, but has no pure examples of explication. The discussion of "Hills Like White Elephants" (pages 195–99) comes close to being explication, and

*George Arms, "A Note on Explication," *Western Review* 15 (1950): 57.

might be considered so if it had included answers to the study questions and one or two other matters. The General Questions for Analysis and Evaluation on pages 318–20 should be helpful to you in writing an explication of a prose passage. Not all the questions will be applicable to every story, and you need not answer all those that are applicable, but you should start by considering all that apply and then work with those that are central and important for your explication.

An *analysis* (literally a "breaking up" or separation of something into its constituent parts), instead of trying to examine all parts of a work in relation to the whole, selects for examination *one* aspect or element or part that relates to the whole. Clearly, an analysis is a better approach to prose works than is an explication. A literary work may be usefully approached through almost any of its elements — point of view, characterization, plot, setting, symbolism, structure, and the like — so long as you relate this element to the central meaning or the whole. As always, it is important to choose a topic appropriate to the space available. "Characterization in Flannery O'Connor's 'Greenleaf'" is too large a topic to be usefully treated in a few pages, but a character analysis of Mrs. May or of her two sons might fit the space neatly. For an example of an analysis, see "The Function of the Frame Story in 'Once Upon a Time'" (page 546).

2. Papers of Comparison and Contrast

The comparison and contrast of two stories having one or more features in common may be an illuminating exercise, because the similarities highlight the differences, or vice versa, and thus lead to a better understanding not only of both pieces but of literary processes in general. The selections chosen may be similar in plot but different in theme, similar in subject but different in tone, similar in theme but different in literary value, or, conversely, different in plot but similar in theme, different in subject but similar in tone, and so on. In writing such a paper, it is usually best to decide first whether the similarities or the differences are more significant, begin with a brief summary of the less significant, and then concentrate on the more significant.*

---

*Some of the stories in this book have been "paired" to encourage just this kind of study: "The Most Dangerous Game" and "The Child by Tiger" in Chapter 1; "The Storm" and "Once Upon a Time," "The Catbird Seat" and "The Drunkard," "A Christmas Memory" and "The Night Old Santa Claus Came" in Chapter 7; "A Municipal Report" and "A Jury of Her Peers," "Spotted Horses" and "Mule in the Yard" in Chapter 9.

3. Papers on a Number of Works by a Single Author

Most readers, when they discover a story they particularly like, look for other works by the same author. The paper that focuses on a single author rather than a single work is the natural corollary of such an interest. The most common concern in a paper of this type is to identify the characteristics that make this author different from other authors and therefore of particular interest to the writer. What are the author's characteristic subjects, settings, or themes? With what kinds of life does the author characteristically deal? What are the author's preferred literary forms? Is the author's approach ironic, witty, serious, comic, tragic? Is the author's vision directed principally inward or outward? In short, what configuration of patterns makes the author's fingerprints unique? Your paper may consider one or more of these questions.

A more ambitious type of paper on a single author examines the work for signs of development. The attitudes that any person, especially an author, takes towards the world, may change with the passing from adolescence to adulthood to old age. So also may the author's means of expressing attitudes and judgments. Though some writers are remarkably consistent in outlook and expression throughout their careers, others manifest surprising changes. To write a paper on the development of an author's work, you must have accurate information about the dates when works were written, and the works must be read in chronological order. When you have mastered the differences, you may be able to illustrate them through close examination of two or three stories, one for each stage.

When readers become especially interested in the works of a particular author, they may develop a curiosity about that author's life as well. This is a legitimate interest, and, if there is sufficient space and your editor/instructor permits it, you may want to incorporate biographical information into your paper. If so, however, you should heed three caveats. First, your main interest should be in the literature itself: the biographical material should be subordinated to and used in service of your examination of the work. In general, discuss only those aspects of the author's life that bear directly on the work: biography should not be used as "filler." Second, you should be extremely cautious about identifying an event in a work with an event in the life of the author. Almost never are stories exact transcriptions of the writers' personal experiences. Authors fictionalize themselves when they put themselves into imaginative works. If you consider that even in autobiographies (where they intend to give accurate accounts of their lives) writers must select incidents from the vast complexity of their experiences, that the memory of past events may be defective, and that at best writers work from their own points of view—in short, when you realize that even autobiography cannot be an absolutely reliable transcription of historical fact—you should be more fully prepared not to expect such an equation in works whose object is imaginative truth. Third, you must document the sources of your information about the author's life (see pages 537–42).

4. Papers on a Number of Works with Some Feature in Common Other than Authorship

Papers on works by various authors that have some feature in common—subject, form, setting, point of view, and the like—where the purpose is to discover different ways that different works may use or regard that common feature, are often illuminating. Probably the most familiar paper of this type is the one that treats works having a similar thematic concern (love, war, religious belief or doubt, art, adolescence, initiation, maturity, old age, death, parents and children, racial conflict, social injustice). But a paper may also examine particular forms of literature, for example, the short story with an unreliable narrator, stream of consciousness as a narrative technique, direct versus indirect characterization. Topics of this kind may be further limited by time or place or number—four attitudes toward death, nineteenth-century stories about social isolation, racial conflicts in Mississippi and South Africa.

IV. Proving Your Point

In writing about literature, your object generally is to convince your readers that your understanding of a work is valid and important and to lead them to share that understanding. When writing about other subjects, it may be appropriate to persuade your readers through various rhetorical means—through eloquent diction, devices of suspense, analogies, personal anecdotes, and the like. But readers of essays about literature usually look for "proof." They want you to show them *how* the work, or the element you are discussing, does what you claim it does. Like scientists who require proof of the sort that they can duplicate in their own laboratories, readers of criticism want access to the process of inference, analysis, and deduction that has led to your conclusions, so that they may respond as you have done.

To provide this proof is no easy task, for it depends on your own mastery of reading and writing. You must understand what a work means and what its effects are; you must be able to point out precisely how it communicates that meaning and how it achieves those effects; and you must be able to present your experience of it clearly and directly. When you have spent considerable time in coming to understand and respond to a work of literature, it may become so familiar that it seems self-evident to you, and you will need to "back off" sufficiently to be able to put yourself in your readers' position — they may have vague feelings about the work ("I like it" or "It moves me deeply"), without knowing what it is that produced those feelings. It is your job to refine the feelings and define away the vagueness.

Some forms of "proof" rarely do the job. Precision does not result from explaining a metaphor figuratively ("When Lawrence reports that the house whispered 'There must be more money!' the effect is like hearing footsteps in the dark"). Nor can you prove anything about a story by hypothesizing about what it might have been if it did not contain what it does ("If Blackie had stood up to Trevor, Old Misery's house would still be standing" — this is equivalent to saying "If the story is not what it is, it would not be what it is"). Your own personal experiences will rarely help your readers ("The swipe's frustration reminds me of how I felt when I discovered my phone had been out of order for a week"). Even your personal history of coming to understand a story will seldom help, though you present it in more general terms ("The first few paragraphs of 'Hills Like White Elephants' confuse the reader because they do not reveal what the man wants the woman to do"). Just as in formal logic argument by analogy is not regarded as valid, so in critical discourse analogies are usually unconvincing ("Daru's dilemma is like choosing between two kinds of poison"). These strategies all have in common the looseness and vagueness of trying to define something by saying what it is not, or what it is like, rather than dealing with what it *is*.

"Proof" in writing about literature is primarily an exercise in strict definition. Obviously, comparing this kind of proof to that required by science is inexact, since what you are doing is reminding your readers, or perhaps informing them, of feelings that are associated with language, not of the properties of chemical compounds. Furthermore, a scientific proof is incomplete if it does not present every step in a process. If that requirement were placed on literary analysis, a critical essay would be interminable, since more can always be said about any interpretive point. So, rather than attempting to prove every point that you make, you should aim to demonstrate that your *method* of analysis is valid by providing persuasive proof of your major point or points. If you have shown that your handling of a major point is sound, your readers will tend to trust your judgment on lesser matters.

V. Writing the Paper

The general procedures for writing a good paper on literature are much the same as the procedures for writing a good paper on any subject.

1. As soon as possible after receiving the assignment, read carefully and thoughtfully the literary materials on which it is based, mulling over the problem to be solved or — if the assignment is general — a good choice of subject, jotting down notes, and sidelining or underlining important passages with a pencil if the book is your own.* If possible, read the material more than once.

2. Then, rather than proceeding directly to the writing of the paper, put the materials aside for several days and let them steep in your mind. The advantage of this is that your unconscious mind, if you have truly placed the problem in it, will continue to work on the problem while you are engaged in other activities, indeed even while you are asleep. Repeated investigations into the psychology of creativity have shown that great solutions to scientific and artistic problems frequently occur while the scientist or artist is thinking of something else; the answer pops into the mind as if out of nowhere but really out of the hidden mental recesses where it has been quietly incubating. Whether this apparent "miracle" happens to you or not, it is probable that you will have more ideas when you sit down to write after a period of incubation than you will if you try to write your paper immediately after reading the materials.

3. When you are ready to write (allow yourself as long an incubation period as possible, but also allow ample time for writing, looking things up, revising, copying your revision, and correcting your final copy), jot down a list of the ideas you have, select connecting ideas rele-

---

*If you use a library book, make notes of the page or line numbers of such passages so that you can readily find them again.

vant to your problem or to a single acceptable subject, and formulate a thesis statement that will clearly express in one sentence what you wish to say about that subject. Make a rough outline, rearranging your ideas in the order that will best support your thesis. Do they make a coherent case? Have you left out anything necessary to demonstrate your thesis? If so, add it in the proper place. Then begin to write, using your rough outline as a guide. Write this first draft as swiftly as possible, not bothering about sentence structure, grammar, diction, spelling, or verification of sources. Concentrate on putting on paper what is in your head and on your outline without interrupting the flow of thought for any other purpose. If alternative ways of expressing a thought occur to you, put them down for a later decision. Nothing is more unprofitable than staring at a blank sheet of paper, chewing on a pencil — or staring at a blank monitor, hearing the word processor's hum — wondering, "How shall I begin?" Just begin. Get something down on paper. It may look awful, but you can shape and polish it later.

4.   Once you have something on paper, it is much easier to see what should be done with it. The next step is to revise. Does your paper proceed from an introductory paragraph that either defines the problem to be solved or states your thesis, through a series of logically arranged paragraphs that advance toward a solution of the problem or demonstrate your thesis, to a final paragraph that either solves the problem or sums up and restates your thesis but in somewhat different words? If not, analyze the difficulty. Do the paragraphs need reorganization or amplification? Are more examples needed? Does the thesis itself need modification? Make whatever adjustments are necessary for a logical and convincing demonstration. This may require a rewriting of the paper. Or it may call only for a few strike-outs, insertions, and circlings with arrows showing that a sentence or paragraph should be shifted from one place to another.

5.   In your revision (if not earlier), make sure that the stance expressed in your statements and judgments is firm and forthright, not weak and wishy-washy. Don't allow your paper to become a sump of phrases like "it seems to me that," "I think [or feel] that," "this word might suggest," "this sentence could mean," and "in my opinion." Your readers know that the content of your paper expresses your thoughts; you need to warn them only when it expresses someone else's. And don't be weak-kneed in expressing your opinion. Even though you are not 100 percent sure of your rightness, write as if you are presenting a truth. Realizing beforehand that you will need to state your interpretations and

conclusions confidently also should help you to strive for a greater degree of certainty as you read and interpret.

6. Having revised your paper for the logic, coherence, confidence, and completeness of its argument, your next step is to revise it for effectiveness of expression. Do this slowly and carefully. How many words can you cut out without loss of meaning? Are your sentences constructed for maximum force and economy? Are they correctly punctuated? Do the pronouns have clear antecedents? Do the verbs agree with their subjects? Are the tenses consistent? Have you chosen the most exact words and spelled them correctly? Now is the time to use the dictionary, to verify quotations and other references, and to supply whatever documentation is needed. A conscientious writer may put a paper through several revisions.

7. After all is in order, write or type your final copy, being sure to follow the editorial policies of your instructor for the submission of manuscripts.

8. Read over your final copy slowly and carefully, and correct any mistakes (omissions, repetitions, typographical errors) you may have made in copying from your draft. This final step — too often omitted due to haste or fatigue — is extremely important and may make the difference between an *A* or a *C* paper, or between a *C* paper and an *F*. It is easy to make careless mistakes in copying, but your editor should not be counted on to recognize the difference between a copying error and one of ignorance. Moreover, the smallest error may utterly destroy the sense of what you have written: omission of a "not" may make your paper say the exact opposite of what you meant it to say. Few editors require or want you to recopy or retype a whole page of your paper at this stage. It is enough to make neat corrections in ink on the paper itself.

VI. Introducing Quotations

In writing about literature it is often desirable, sometimes imperative, to quote from the work under discussion. Quoted material is needed (a) to provide essential evidence in support of your argument, and (b) to set before your reader any passage that you are going to examine in detail. It will also keep your reader in contact with the text and allow you to use felicitous phrasing from the text to enhance your own presentation. You must, however, be careful not to overquote. If a paper consists of more than 20 percent quotation, it loses the appearance of closely knit argument and seems instead merely a collection of quotations strung together like clothes hung out on a line to dry. Avoid, especially, unnecessary use of long quotations. Readers tend to skip them. Consider carefully whether the quoted material may not be more economically presented by paraphrase or effectively shortened by ellipsis (see Q8 below). Readers faced with a long quotation may reasonably expect you to examine it in some detail; that is, the longer your quotation, the more you should do with it. As with every other aspect of good writing, the amount of quotation one uses is a matter of intelligence and tact and cannot be decreed. Effective use of quotation is an art.

Principles and "Rules"

There is no legislative body that establishes laws governing the formal aspects of quoting, documenting, or any other aspect of writing. The only "rules" are the editorial policies of the publisher to whom you submit your work. There is, however, a national organization — the Modern Language Association of America — that is so influential that its policies for its own publications and its recommendations for others are adopted by most journals of literary criticism and scholarship. The instructions below are in general accord with those stated in the *MLA Handbook for Writers of Research Papers*, 3rd edition, by Joseph Gibaldi and Walter S. Achtert (New York: MLA, 1988). In your course, your instructor will inform you of any editorial policies in effect that differ from those given here or in the *MLA Handbook*. The examples used in this section are all drawn from Hemingway's "Hills Like White Elephants"(page 171).

Q1. If the quotation is short (normally not more than four typed lines of prose), put it in quotation marks and introduce it directly into the text of your essay.

<blockquote>

   The opening paragraph describes a mixed

a scene, "no shade and no trees" on one side

b and "the warm shadow of the building" on

   the other (171).

</blockquote>

Q2.   If the quotation is long (normally more than four typed lines of prose), begin it on a new line (and end it on its own line); double-space it (like the rest of your paper); and indent it twice as far from the left margin (ten spaces) as you do for a new paragraph (five spaces). *Do not enclose it in quotation marks*: since the indentation signals a quotation, the use of quotation marks would be redundant.

```
The objective point of view is momentarily broken

when the girl's perspective is reported:

    Far away, beyond the river, were mountains.

    The shadow of a cloud moved across the field

    of grain, and she saw the river through the

    trees.                                    (173)
```

The two preceding examples illustrate (Q1) the "run-in" quotation, where the quotation is "run in" with the writer's own text, and (Q2) the "set-off" or "block" quotation, which is separated from the writer's text.

Q3.   In general, sentences containing a quotation are punctuated as they would be if there were no quotation. In Q1.a. above, a comma precedes the quoted statement as it would if there were no quotation marks. In Q2, a colon precedes the quoted sentences because of their length. In Q1.b., there is no punctuation at all before the quotation. Do not put punctuation before a quotation unless it is otherwise called for.

Q4.   Your quotation must combine with its introduction to make a grammatically correct sentence. The normal processes of grammer and syntax, like the normal processes of punctuation, are unaffected by quoting. Subjects must agree with their verbs, verbs must be consistent in tense, pronouns must have their normal relation with antecedents.

WRONG	```In the opening description, "the warm shadow of the building"(171).``` (Incomplete sentence)
RIGHT	```In the opening description, "the warm shadow of the building" is contrasted to the tree- less side of the station(171).```

WRONG	The girl says that "'I was being amused'" (172).
	(Incorrect mixture of direct and indirect quotation)
RIGHT	The girl says, "'I was being amused'" (172).

Q5. Your introduction must supply enough context to make the quotation meaningful. Be careful that all pronouns in the quotation have clearly identifiable antecedents.

WRONG	When the beers are put on the table, the girl sees that "they were white in the sun and the country was brown and dry" (171).
	(Were the beers white?)
RIGHT	When the beers are put on the table, the girl notices the hills "white in the sun" (171).

Q6. The words within your quotation marks must be quoted *exactly* from the original.

WRONG When the man says he doesn't "'want her to do it if she feels that way,'" she replies that they "'could have all this,'" looking at the beautiful landscape (173).

Q7. It is permissible to insert or supply words in a quotation *if* you enclose them within brackets. Brackets (parentheses with square corners) are used to indicate *editorial* changes or additions. If parentheses were used, the reader might interpret the enclosed material as *authorial* (as part of the quotation). Since brackets do not appear on some typewriters, you may have to put them in with a pen or pencil. Avoid excessive use of brackets: they have a pedantic air. Find other solutions. Often paraphrase will serve as well as quotation.

VI.

CORRECT	When the man says he doesn't " 'want [her] to do it if [she prefers not to],' " she replies " 'we could have all this' " (173).
BETTER	When the man claims not to be insisting on his preference, her response implies that this conversation is destroying all their hopes (173).

Notice that a word within brackets can either replace a word in the original (as in the substitution of "her" for "you" above) or be added to explain or complete the original (as with "she prefers not to" above). Since a reader understands that brackets signal either substitutions or additions, it is superfluous to include the words for which substitutions have been made.

WRONG   The man says he doesn't " 'want you [her] to do it' " (173).

Your sentences, including bracketed words, must read as if there were no brackets.

Q8.   It is permissible to omit words from quoted material, but *only* if the omission is indicated. Three *spaced* periods are used to indicate the omission (technically they are called "ellipsis marks"). If there are four periods, one is the normal period at the end of a sentence; the other three indicate the ellipsis.

The statement just concluded, if quoted, might be shortened in the following way: "It is permissible to omit words . . . if the omission is indicated. Three *spaced* periods are used to indicate the omission. . . . If there are four periods, one is the normal period at the end of a sentence."

It is usually not necessary to indicate ellipsis at the beginning or ending of a quotation (the very act of quoting implies that something precedes and follows) — unless what you quote is in some way contradicted by its context, as for example with a "not" preceding the material you quote.

Q9.   Single quotation marks are used for quotations within quotations. Thus, if the material you are quoting in a run-in quotation includes a quotation, you should reduce the original double quote marks to single quote marks. (In a block quotation, the quotation marks would remain unchanged.)

```
Looking at the field and river, the girl says,
" 'And we could have all this' " (173).
```

```
When the girl looks at the field and river, she
says:
        "And we could have all this. . . . And we
        could have everything and every day we make it
        more impossible. . . . I said we could have
        everything." (173)
```

Q10.   At the conclusion of a run-in quotation, commas and periods are conventionally placed *within* quotation marks; semicolons and colons are placed outside. (The convention is based on appearance, not on logic.) Question marks and exclamation marks are placed inside if they belong to the quoted sentence, outside if they belong to your sentence. (This is logic.) Special rules apply when the quotation is followed by parenthetical documentation (see PD4, page 541). The following examples are all correct:

```
"The beer's nice and cool," says the man (172).
The man says, "The beer's nice and cool" (172).
"Should we have another drink?" the man asks (172).
How eager is the girl to "have another drink" (172)?
```

VII. Documentation

Documentation is the process of identifying the sources of materials used in your paper. The sources are of two kinds: primary and secondary. *Primary* sources are materials written *by* the author being studied, and may be confined to the single work being discussed. *Secondary* sources are materials by other writers *about* the author or work being discussed, or materials having some bearing on that work. Documentation serves two purposes: (1) it enables your readers to check any material they may think you have misinterpreted; (2) it enables you to make proper acknowledgment of information, ideas, opinions, or phraseology that are not your own.

It is difficult to overemphasize the second of these purposes. The use of someone else's ideas or insights in your own words, since it does not require quotation marks makes an even heavier demand for acknowledgment than quoted material does. Although you need not document matters of common knowledge, your use without acknowledgment of material that is uniquely someone else's is not only dishonest but illegal, and could result in penalties ranging from an *F* on the paper through expulsion from school to a term in jail, depending on the magnitude of the offense.

Documentation may be given in (a) the text of your essay; (b) parentheses placed within the text of your essay; or (c) a list of Works Cited placed at the end of your essay but keyed to parenthetical references within the essay. The three methods are progressively more formal.

Documentation by a list of Works Cited is required when several sources have contributed to an essay—and is necessary in a research paper or term paper for which you have consulted a number of works. If you are assigned such a project in conjunction with studying this book, your instructor will supply you with information about the method to use. The *MLA Handbook for Writers of Research Papers* (mentioned earlier) provides a full account of the appropriate method, in the event that your instructor does not provide you with other information.

In any case, the type of documentation required in your class will be chosen by your instructor, who may wish to have you practice several methods so that you will learn their use.

1. Textual Documentation

Every literary essay contains textual documentation—identifying source material by referring to it in the text of your writing. A title like "The Frame Story in 'Once Upon a Time'" identifies the story that will furnish the main materials in the paper. A sentence beginning "In the second and third paragraphs . . ." locates more specifically the source of what follows. An informally documented essay is one that relies on textual documentation exclusively. Perhaps the majority of articles published in newspapers and periodicals with wide circulation are of this kind. Textual documentation works best for essays written on a single short work, without use of secondary sources, for readers without great scholarly expectations. A first-rate paper might be written on Herman

Melville's "Bartleby the Scrivener" using only textual documentation. The author's name and the title of the story mentioned somewhere near the beginning of the essay, plus a few phrases like "In the opening paragraph" or "When Bartleby answers the lawyer's advertisement for additional scriveners" or "At the story's conclusion" would provide all the documentation needed for this audience. The action of the story is straightforward enough that the reader can easily locate any detail within it. If the essay is intended for our hypothetical journal published by your literature class (all of whose members are using the same anthology and have presumably read the story), its readers can readily locate the story and its events. But textual documentation, although less appropriate, can also be used for more complex subjects, and can even accommodate secondary sources with phrases like "As Yvor Winters points out in his essay on Melville in *In Defense of Reason* . . ."

Principles and "Rules"

TD1. Enclose titles of short stories, articles, and poems (unless they are book-length) in quotation marks; underline titles of plays, magazines, newspapers, and books. Do not underline or put the titles of your own paper in quotation marks. The general principle is that titles of separate publications are underlined; titles of selections or parts of books are put within quotation marks. Short novels, like Melville's *Billy Budd* and James's *Daisy Miller*, though often reprinted as part of an anthology, were published as separate books, and their titles should be underlined. Underlining, in manuscripts, is equivalent to italics in printed matter.

TD2. Capitalize the first word and all important words in titles. Do not capitalize articles, prepositions, and conjunctions except when they begin the title ("A Christmas Memory," "I'm a Fool").

TD3. Never use page numbers in the body of your discussion, for a page is not a constituent part of a story. You may refer in your discussion to paragraphs, chapters, or numbered sections, as appropriate, but use page numbers *only* in parenthetical documentation where a specific edition of the work has been named.

TD4. Spell out numerical references when they precede the unit they refer to; use numbers when they follow the unit (the second chapter, or chapter 2; the fourth paragraph, or paragraph 4). Use the first of these alternative forms sparingly, and only with small numbers. Never write "In the thirty-fourth and thirty-fifth paragraphs . . . ," for to do so is to waste good space and irritate your reader; write "In paragraphs 34–35. . . ."

2. Parenthetical Documentation

Parenthetical documentation makes possible fuller and more precise accreditation without a forbidding apparatus of footnotes or an extensive list of Works Cited. In a complex or lengthy story (or a full-length novel), a phrase like "midway through the action" is insufficient to allow the reader to locate the passage readily. It is always most useful to locate a quotation by referring specifically to events: "When Bartleby turns up at the lawyer's door seeking a job . . ." This kind of textual documentation may then be supplemented by giving a page number, within parentheses, after the passage cited. But the reader needs to know also what book or edition the page number refers to, so this information must be supplied the first time such a citation is made, or preferably the first time the story is mentioned.

Parenthetical documentation is the method most often required for a paper using only the primary source, or, at most, two or three sources — as, for example, most of the writing assigned in an introductory literature course. The information given in parenthetical documentation should enable your reader to turn easily to the exact source of a quotation or a reference. Full publishing details should be given, but parenthetical documentation should supplement textual documentation; that is, information provided in the text of your essay should not be repeated within the parentheses. For the readers of our hypothetical journal, the first reference to a story might look like this:

```
In Ernest Hemingway's "Hills Like White Elephants"
(reprinted in Laurence Perrine and Thomas R. Arp,
Story and Structure, 8th ed. [Fort Worth:
Harcourt, 1993] 171-74), the characters are
sitting . . .
```

In subsequent references, provided no other source intervenes, only the page number need be given.

```
When the girl walks to the end of the platform,
she signals the emotional distance she defines in
her next remark. "'And we could have all this'"
(173).
```

If more than one source is used, each must be identified, if referred to a second time, by an abbreviated version of the main entry, normally the author's last name, for example (Hemingway 173), but in any case the shortest identification that will differentiate it from the other sources. Notice, in the first entry above, that brackets are used for parentheses within parentheses.

Principles and "Rules"

PD1. For the first citation from a book, give the author's name; the title of the selection; the name of the book from which it is taken; the editor (preceded by the abbreviation ed. for "edited by") or the translator (preceded by the abbreviation trans. for "translated by"); the edition (designated by an Arabic number) if there has been more than one; the city of publication (the first one will suffice if there is more than one); the publisher (this may be given in shortened form, dropping all but the first name named); the year of publication or of most recent copyright; and the page number. Do not, however, repeat parenthetically documentation already given textually. The following example correctly combines textual with parenthetical documentation.

```
In "Hills Like White Elephants," Hemingway re-
veals the man's repressed anger when he thinks
about the other people "all waiting reasonably
for the train" (reprinted in Laurence Perrine and
Thomas R. Arp, Story and Structure, 8th ed. [Fort
Worth: Harcourt, 1993] 171).
```

PD2. For your principal primary source, after the first reference, only a page number is required.

PD3. Documentation for run-in quotations always follows the quotation marks. If the quotation ends with a period, move it to the end of the documentation. If it ends with an exclamation point or question mark, leave it, but put a period after the documentation as well.

```
The girl asks, " 'What did she say?' " (174).
" 'That the train is coming in five minutes' "
(174).
```

PD4. With block quotations, parenthetical documentation follows the last mark of punctuation without further punctuation after the parentheses:

> The couple's recent history is suggested by an-
> other detail:
>> He did not say anything but looked at the bags
>> against the wall of the station. There were
>> labels on them from all the hotels where they
>> had spent nights. (174)

PD5.   Avoid cluttering your paper with excessive documentation. When possible, use one note to cover a series of short quotations. (See example, Q1.) Do not document well-known sayings or proverbs that you use for stylistic purposes and that form no part of the substance of your investigation (and of course be wary of including hackneyed commonplaces in your formal writing).

PD6.   It is customary in a formal paper to document all quoted materials. Do not, however, fall victim to the too frequent delusion that *only* quotations need documentation. The first purpose of documentation (see page 537) implies that any major or possibly controversial assertion concerning interpretation may need documentation. If you declare that the turning point in a long story occurs with an apparently minor event, it may be more important for the reader to have a page number for that event than for any quotation from the story. Judgment must be exercised. You cannot and should not provide page numbers for every detail of a story; but neither should you think that you have necessarily done your duty if you merely document all quotations.

VIII. Grammar, Punctuation, and Usage: Special Problems

1. Grammar

G1.   In discussing the action of a literary work, rely primarily on the present tense (even though the work itself uses the past), keeping the past, future, and perfect tenses available for prior or subsequent actions; for example,

> When the girl looks at the rich fecundity of the
> "fields of grain," the "trees along the banks of

```
the Ebro," and the "river through the trees,"
she knows what will be lost should she have the
abortion.
```

G2.   Do not let pronouns refer to nouns in the possessive case. Antecedents of pronouns should always hold a strong grammatical position: a possessive is a mere modifier, like an adjective.

WRONG	In Hemingway's story "Hills Like White Elephants," he writes . . .
	(Antecedent of "he" is in possessive case.)
RIGHT	In his story "Hills Like White Elephants," Hemingway writes . . .

2. Punctuation

P1.   Do not set off restrictive appositives with commas. A "restrictive" appositive is one necessary to the meaning of the sentence; a "nonrestrictive" appositive could be left out without changing the meaning.

WRONG	In his story, "Hills Like White Elephants," Hemingway . . .
	(The title of the story is necessary to the meaning of the statement. As punctuated, the sentence falsely implies that Hemingway wrote only one story.)
RIGHT	In his story "Hills Like White Elephants," Hemingway . . .
RIGHT	In his only story in <u>Story and Structure</u>, "Hills Like White Elephants," Hemingway . . .
	(The adjective "only" identifies the story. The title simply supplies additional information and could be omitted without changing the meaning.)

P2.   Words used simply as words should be either underlined or put in quotation marks; be consistent in using one or the other in an essay.

WRONG	The word describing the countryside is brown.
	(This statement is false; all the words in the story are black.)
RIGHT	The word describing the countryside is "brown."

3. Usage

U1.   Though accepted usage changes with time, and the distinctions between the following pairs of words are fading, many instructors will bless you if you try to preserve them.

convince, persuade   *Convince* pertains to belief (conviction); *persuade* pertains to either action or belief. The following sentences observe the distinction. "In 'Hills Like White Elephants,' the man tries to persuade the woman to have an abortion." "In 'Hills Like White Elephants,' the man tries to convince the woman that she will be happy after the abortion." "She is persuaded to go through with the abortion though she is not convinced that it will make her happy."

disinterested, uninterested   A disinterested judge is one who has no "stake" or personal interest in the outcome of a case and who can therefore judge fairly; an uninterested judge goes to sleep on the bench. A good judge is interested in the case but disinterested in its outcome. An uninterested reader finds reading boring. A disinterested reader? Perhaps one who can enjoy a good book whatever its subject matter.

imply, infer   A writer or speaker implies; a reader or listener infers. An implication is a meaning hinted at but not stated outright. An inference is a conclusion drawn from evidence not complete enough for proof. If you imply that I am a snob, I may infer that you do not like me.

sensuous, sensual   *Sensuous* normally pertains to the finer senses, *sensual* to the appetites. Good poetry is sensuous: it appeals through the imagination to the senses. A voluptuous woman or an attractive man makes a sensual appeal that stirs a desire for possession.

quote, quotation   *Quote* was originally used only as a verb. Today the use of "single quotes" and "double quotes" in reference to quotation marks is almost universally accepted; but, although the use of "quote" for "quotation" is common in informal speech, it is still unacceptable in formal writing. — Note also that quoting is an act performed by the writer about literature, not by the writer of literature.

WRONG	Shakespeare's famous quotation "To be or not to be" . . .
RIGHT	The famous quotation from Shakespeare, "To be or not to be" . . .
RIGHT	Shakespeare's famous line "To be or not to be" . . .
BETTER	Hamlet's famous line "To be or not to be" . . .
BEST	Probably the most-quoted line by Shakespeare is Hamlet's "To be or not to be" . . .

U2.   Other words and phrases to be avoided:

center around   A geometrical impossibility. A story may perhaps center *on* a certain feature, but to make it center *around* that feature is to make the hub surround the wheel.

lifestyle   An over-used neologism, especially inappropriate for use with older literature.

what the author was trying to say was   The implication of this expression is that the author failed to say what he meant, and its use puts you in the patronizing position of implying that you could have done a much better job of it — to which the only proper rejoinder is "If you're so smart, why ain't you famous?"

Others suggested by your instructor:

_____	_____
_____	_____
_____	_____
_____	_____
_____	_____
_____	_____
_____	_____
_____	_____
_____	_____
_____	_____

IX. A Sample Analysis

The Function of the Frame Story in "Once Upon a Time"

Nadine Gordimer's "Once Upon a Time" (reprinted in Laurence Perrine and Thomas R. Arp, Story and Structure, 8th ed. [Fort Worth: Harcourt, 1993] 253–57) is a complex, ironic presentation of the results of fear and hatred. This "children's story," so flat in its tone, characterization, and reporting of events, proceeds by gradual steps to show a family systematically barricading itself behind various

security devices, the last of which has an effect opposite of what was intended in destroying the child
that the parents are trying to protect.

The tale is especially harrowing because of the
tone, which is first hinted at in the title. This is
an easy, casual narration that repeats such standard
phrases as "living happily ever after" (254) and
identifies its characters only by their functions and
relationships, never exploring motivations or revealing the steps of their decision making. The deeper
causes for fear are not defined in the tale. All these
qualities, and others, establish the tone of fairy
tales and other stories for children. In this story,
however, no one lives "happily ever after," for in
attempting to safeguard themselves, they destroy their
lives.

But that tale doesn't begin until the ninth paragraph of Gordimer's story. What precedes it is the
frame story of a writer who has been asked to write a
story for a children's collection, who refuses to contribute, and then is awakened in the night by some
noise that frightens her. Her fear first chillingly
creates a burglar or murderer "moving from room to
room, coming up the passage -- to [her] door" (253).
Then the actual cause of her waking comes to her: deep
down, "three thousand feet below" her house, some
rock face has fallen in the gold mine beneath (254).
She is not in personal danger, then. Yet she cannot
return to sleep, so she tells herself "a bedtime
story" to relax her mind -- and the story is of the
family that grows obsessed with security and protec-

tion, the awful story of the mutilation of the little boy.

The frame story initially seems little more than an introductory explanation of how the tale came to be written, against the writer's will and purpose. Its details are unrelated to the children's tale -- explicitly so, as the writer, despite her knowledge of two recent murders in her neighborhood, and the rational fears that such events arouse, has "no burglar bars, no gun under the pillow" (253), in contrast to the precautions taken in the tale. There is no fairy-tale gold mine in her life, only the knowledge of the mining of the gold a half-mile beneath her. So what does this frame have to do with the tale, other than to place the reader within the literal reality of a writer's time and place, from which the imagination journeys to "once upon a time"? Is it more than an ironic contrast in subject and tone?

For answers, we need to consider the writer's time and place as parallels to those of the tale. Both are located in South Africa, both are in the present (even though the phrase "once upon a time" normally signals a long time ago, in a far off place). The family in the tale, with their burglar bars, walls, alarms, and finally "the razor-bladed coils all round the walls of the house," are like those people in the writer's world who <u>do</u> keep guns under their pillows. Like the real people of the writer's neighborhood, their fears are focused on the black African populace who surround and outnumber them. On the one hand, in the writer's

world, the fears focus on "a casual day laborer . . .
dismissed without pay" who returns to strangle the
watchdogs and knife the man who treated him unfairly
(253); on the other hand, in the children's story, the
fears focus on the hungry, out-of-work, and begging
multitudes who fill and spoil the suburban streets of
the fictitious family's neighborhood. In both worlds,
unfairness, want, and deprivation mark the blacks,
while the whites feel surrounded and threatened
by them.

Why cannot the writer return to sleep, after she
has discovered the innocent cause of her awakening?
Because the comforting natural explanation, which re-
moves her from personal danger, is in fact more horrifying than a murderous prowler. She thinks of

> the Chopi and Tsonga migrant miners who might [be]
> down there, under [her] in the earth at that mo-
> ment. The stope where the [rock] fall was could
> have been disused, dripping water from its rup-
> tured veins; or men might now be interred there
> in the most profound of tombs. (254)

Two possibilities occur to her -- one harmless to
men, the other burial alive, both a consequence of
the wage-slavery of "migrant miners" over whose
heads (literally and figuratively) the white society
lives in "uneasy strain . . . of brick, cement, wood
and glass" (254). If no miner has been harmed by
this rock fall, others have been and will be; and
moreover, being killed in that subterranean world of
"ruptured veins" is not the only harm that the

whites have inflicted on the original inhabitants of
the country they control, nor on their own sensi-
tivities and consciences.

The frame story of "Once Upon a Time," then,
foreshadows the fear, the violence, and the pain of
the children's tale, and points to the ultimate
cause of its terrible sacrifice of a child -- the
systematic maltreatment of one race by another and
the brutality and self-destruction that is its
result.

Comments

This analysis has as its subject an aspect of the story that can be fully
developed in a limited space. It is written for our hypothetical class journal, as indicated by the way in which the writer refrains from giving
detailed summary of the tale enclosed in the frame (since the audience is
known to be familiar with the story), and presents details from the frame
narration as they support the writer's argument. It employs some information about the author that is common knowledge to the class (her
nationality and her contemporaneity having been supplied in the introductory footnote to the story). Notice the way in which quotations are
integrated into the sentence structures and the manner in which the
writer's interpolated words are presented in the extended quotation.

Glossary of Fictional Terms

The definitions in this glossary sometimes repeat and sometimes differ in language from those in the text. Where they differ, the intention is to give a fuller sense of the term's meaning by allowing the reader a double perspective on it. Page numbers refer to discussion in the text, which in most but not all cases is fuller than that in the glossary.

Antagonist   Any force in a story that is in conflict with the *protagonist*. An antagonist may be another person, an aspect of the physical or social environment, or a destructive element in the protagonist's own nature. See *Conflict*. 42–43

Artistic unity   That condition of a successful literary work whereby all its elements work together for the achievement of its central purpose. In an artistically unified work nothing is included that is irrelevant to the central purpose, nothing is omitted that is essential to it, and the parts are arranged in the most effective order for the achievement of that purpose. 47, 239–40, 315–17

Chance   The occurrence of an event that has no apparent cause in antecedent events or in predisposition of character. 47–48

Character   (1) Any of the persons involved in a story (sense 1). (2) The distinguishing moral qualities and personal traits of a *character* (sense 2). 66–70

  Developing (or *dynamic*) *character*   A *character* (sense 1) who during the course of a story undergoes a permanent change in some aspect of *character* (sense 2) or outlook. 70

  Flat character   A *character* (sense 1) whose *character* (sense 2) is summed up in one or two traits. 68–70

  Foil character   A minor character whose situation or actions parallel those of a major character, and thus by contrast sets off or illuminates the major character; most often the contrast is complimentary to the major character.

Round character   A *character* (sense 1) whose *character* (sense 2) is complex and many sided. 68–69

Static character   A character who is the same sort of person at the end of a story as at the beginning. 70

Stock character   A stereotyped character: one whose nature is familiar to us from prototypes in previous fiction. 69–70

Climax   The turning point or high point of a plot. 48

Coincidence   The chance concurrence of two events having a peculiar correspondence between them. 44–48

Commercial fiction   Fiction written to meet the taste of a wide popular audience and relying usually on tested formulas for satisfying such taste. 6

Conflict   A clash of actions, desires, ideas, or goals in the plot of a story. Conflict may exist between the main character and some other person or persons; between the main character and some external force—physical nature, society, or "fate"; or between the main character and some destructive element in his or her own nature. 42–43

Denouement   That portion of a plot that reveals the final outcome of its conflicts or the solution of its mysteries.

Deus ex machina ("god from the machine")   The resolution of a plot by use of a highly improbable chance or coincidence (so named from the practice of some Greek dramatists of having a god descend from heaven at the last possible minute—in the theater by means of a stage machine—to rescue the protagonist from an impossible situation. 47

Developing character   See *Character*.

Dilemma   A situation in which a character must choose between two courses of action, both undesirable. 43–44

Direct presentation of character   That method of characterization in which the author, by exposition or analysis, tells us directly what a character is like, or has someone else in the story do so. 67–68

Dramatic irony   See *Irony*.

Dramatic point of view   See *Point of view*.

Dramatization   The presentation of character or of emotion through the speech or action of characters rather than through exposition, analysis, or description by the author. See *Indirect presentation*. 68, 241–42

Dynamic character   See *Character*.

Editorializing   Writing that departs from the narrative or dramatic mode and instructs the reader how to think or feel about the events of a story or the behavior of a character. 242

Escape literature Literature written purely for entertainment, with little or no attempt to provide insights into the true nature of human life or behavior. 3–8

Falling action That segment of the plot that comes between the climax and the conclusion. 48

Fantasy A kind of fiction that pictures creatures or events beyond the boundaries of known reality. 289–91

First person point of view See *Point of view*.

Flat character See *Character*.

Foil character See *Character*.

Happy ending An ending in which events turn out well for a sympathetic protagonist. 45–46

Indeterminate ending An ending in which the central problem or conflict is left unresolved. 46–47

Indirect presentation of character That method of characterization in which the author shows us a character in action, compelling us to infer what the character is like from what is said or done by the character. 67–68

Interpretive literature Literature that provides valid insights into the nature of human life or behavior. 3–8

Irony A situation, or a use of language, involving some kind of incongruity or discrepancy. 199–201 Three kinds of irony are distinguished in this book.

> *Verbal irony* A figure of speech in which what is said is the opposite of what is meant. 199–200
>
> *Dramatic irony* An incongruity or discrepancy between what a character says or thinks and what the reader knows to be true (or between what a character perceives and what the author intends the reader to perceive). 200
>
> *Irony of situation* A situation in which there is an incongruity between appearance and reality, or between expectation and fulfillment, or between the actual situation and what would seem appropriate. 200–201

Limited omniscient point of view See *Point of view*.

Moral A rule of conduct or maxim for living expressed or implied as the "point" of a literary work. Compare *Theme*. 94

Motivation The incentives or goals that, in combination with the inherent natures of characters, cause them to behave as they do. In poor fiction actions may be unmotivated, insufficiently motivated, or implausibly motivated. 68

Mystery An unusual set of circumstances for which the reader craves an explanation; used to create *suspense*. 43–44

Objective point of view   See *Point of view*.

Omniscient point of view   See *Point of view*.

Plot   The sequence of incidents or events of which a story is composed. 41–49

Plot manipulation   A situation in which an author gives the plot a twist or turn unjustified by preceding action or by the characters involved. 47

Poeticizing   Writing that uses immoderately heightened or distended language to sway the reader's feelings. 242

Point of view   The angle of vision from which a story is told. 142–48 The four basic points of view are as follows:

Omniscient point of view   The author tells the story, using the third person, knowing all and free to tell us anything, including what the characters are thinking or feeling and why they act as they do. 142–44

Limited omniscient point of view   The author tells the story, using the third person, but is limited to a complete knowledge of one character in the story and tells us only what that one character thinks, feels, sees, or hears. 142, 144–45

First person point of view   The story is told by one of its characters, using the first person. 142, 145–46

Objective (or *Dramatic*) *point of view*   The author tells the story, using the third person, but is limited to reporting what the characters say or do; the author does not interpret their behavior or tell us their private thoughts or feelings. 142, 146–47

Protagonist   The central character in a story. 42–43

Quality fiction   Fiction that rejects tested formulas in an attempt to give a fresh interpretation of life. 6

Rising action   That development of plot in a story that precedes and leads up to the climax. 48

Round character   See *Character*.

Sentimentality   Unmerited or contrived tender feeling; that quality in a story that elicits or seeks to elicit tears through an oversimplification or falsification of reality. 241–42

Setting   The context in time and place in which the action of a story occurs.

Static character   See *Character*.

Stock character   See *Character*.

Stream of consciousness   Narrative which presents the private thoughts of a character without commentary or interpretation by the author. 193

Surprise   An unexpected turn in the development of a plot. 45

Surprise ending   A completely unexpected revelation or turn of plot at the conclusion of a story. 45

Suspense   That quality in a story that makes the reader eager to discover what happens next and how it will end. 43–45

Symbol (literary)   Something that means *more* than what it is; an object, person, situation, or action that in addition to its literal meaning suggests other meanings as well. 194–99

Theme   The central idea or unifying generalization implied or stated by a literary work. 92–99

Unhappy ending   An ending that turns out unhappily for a sympathetic protagonist. 45–46

Verbal irony   See *Irony.*

Index of Authors and Titles

Authors' names appear in capitals, titles of stories in italics. Numbers in roman type indicate the page of the selection, and italic numbers indicate discussion of the story.

ADAMS, ALICE
  Fog, 376
ANDERSON, SHERWOOD
  I'm a Fool, 71, 95, 99, 145–47, 200, 315–16
ATWOOD, MARGARET
  Rape Fantasies, 68, 163, 200

Bartleby the Scrivener, 456
BISSOONDATH, NEIL
  There Are a Lot of Ways to Die, 105, 200
Bride Comes to Yellow Sky, The, 407
Bridle, The, 385

CAMUS, ALBERT
  The Guest, 201
CAPOTE, TRUMAN
  A Christmas Memory, 273
CAPPS, BENJAMIN
  The Night Old Santa Claus Came, 282
CARVER, RAYMOND
  The Bridle, 285
Cask of Amontillado, The, 484
Catbird Seat, The, 258, 290, 317
CATHER, WILLA
  Paul's Case, 70, 148
CHEEVER, JOHN
  The Swimmer, 398, 290
CHEKHOV, ANTON
  Gooseberries, 299, 316
Child by Tiger, The, 24, 46, 70, 98, 145, 198–99

Christmas Memory, A, 273
CONNELL, RICHARD
  The Most Dangerous Game, 8, 42, 44, 46, 143, 195, 200, 316
CRANE, STEPHEN
  The Bride Comes to Yellow Sky, 407

Defender of the Faith, 117, 145–46, 199–201, 289
Destructors, The, 49, 67–68, 97, 143, 195, 200
Drunkard, The, 265, 317–18

ERDRICH, LOUISE
  A Wedge of Shade, 416
Everyday Use, 80, 97, 195, 197–99

FAULKNER, WILLIAM
  Mule in the Yard, 363
  Spotted Horses, 349, 145
  Fog, 376
FORD, RICHARD
  Great Falls, 424

GAINES, ERNEST J.
  Just Like a Tree, 175, 195, 316
GLASPELL, SUSAN
  A Jury of Her Peers, 332
Gooseberries, 229, 316
GORDIMER, NADINE
  Once Upon a Time, 253, 317–18
Great Falls, 424

GREENE, GRAHAM
  The Destructors, 49, *67–68*, 97, *143*,
    195, 200
Guest, The, 201

HAWTHORNE, NATHANIEL
  Young Goodman Brown, 303
HEMINGWAY, ERNEST
  Hills Like White Elephants, *146*, 171,
    195–99
Hills Like White Elephants, *146*, 171,
    195–99
HENRY, O.
  A Municipal Report, 320

I'm a Fool, 71, *95*, 99, *145–47*, *200*,
    315–16

JACKSON, SHIRLEY
  The Lottery, *146*, *290*, 436
Jilting of Granny Weatherall, The, 489
JOYCE, JAMES
  Eveline, 443
Jury of Her Peers, A, 332
Just Like a Tree, 175, *195*, *316*

LAWRENCE, D. H.
  The Rocking-Horse Winner, 291
Lottery, The, *146*, *290*, 436

MCDONALD, WALTER
  The Track, 447
MALMAR, MCKNIGHT
  The Storm, 243, *290*, *316–17*
MANSFIELD, KATHERINE
  Miss Brill, 88, *47*, *98*, *144*, *197–200*,
    316
MASON, BOBBIE ANN
  Wish, 450
MELVILLE, HERMAN
  Bartleby the Scrivener, 456
Miss Brill, 88, *47*, *98*, *144*, *197–200*, *316*
Most Dangerous Game, The, 8, *42*, *44*, *46*,
    143, *195*, *200*, *316*
Mule in the Yard, 363
Municipal Report, A, 320
MUNRO, ALICE
  Prue, 64, *144*

Night Old Santa Claus Came, The, 282

O'CONNOR, FLANNERY
  Greenleaf, 212
O'CONNOR, FRANK
  The Drunkard, 265, *317–18*
Once Upon a Time, 253, *317–18*

Paul's Case, 70, 148
Pioneers, Oh, Pioneers, 496
POE, EDGAR ALLAN
  The Cask of Amontillado, 484
PORTER, KATHERINE ANNE
  The Jilting of Granny Weatherall, 489
Private Property, 503
Prue, 64, *144*

Rape Fantasies, 68, 163, *200*
RHYS, JEAN
  Pioneers, Oh, Pioneers, 496
Rocking-Horse Winner, The, 291
ROTH, PHILIP
  Defender of the Faith, 117, *145–46*,
    199–201, 289

SILKO, LESLIE MARMON
  Private Property, 503
SINGER, ISAAC BASHEVIS
  The Son from America, 99, *143*
Son from America, The, 99, *143*
Spotted Horses, *145*, 349
Storm, The, 243, *290*, *316–17*
Swimmer, The, *290*, 398

There Are a Lot of Ways to Die, 105, *200*
THURBER, JAMES
  The Catbird Seat, 258, *290*, 317
Track, The, 447

WALKER, ALICE
  Everyday Use, 80, 97, *195*, *197–99*
Wedge of Shade, A, 416
WELTY, EUDORA
  A Worn Path, 510
Wish, 450
WOLFE, THOMAS
  The Child by Tiger, 24, *46*, 70, *98*,
    145, *198–99*
WOLFF, TOBIAS
  Say Yes, 517
Worn Path, A, 510

Young Goodman Brown, 303